THE COLLECTED
WORKS OF
JEREMY BENTHAM

General Editor
Philip Schofield

PRINCIPLES OF LEGISLATION

'Preparatory Principles' is not a linear text in the conventional sense, but consists of a series of short passages on a variety of topics, whose themes are summarized in marginal headings. The material constitutes a philosophical commonplace book, compiled by Bentham in the mid-1770s, in which he worked out the foundational ideas for his new science of legislation. He then drew on this material when composing such works as *A Fragment on Government* and *An Introduction to the Principles of Morals and Legislation*. Inspired by such figures as John Locke and Claude Adrien Helvétius, Bentham developed an original ontological and epistemological basis for legal terminology, with the aim of replacing the traditional terminology of English law with that of universal jurisprudence. The work which dominates the text, in that Bentham returns to it time and time again in order to offer criticism of it, is William Blackstone's *Commentaries on the Laws of England*. While unorganized and fragmentary, the material in 'Preparatory Principles' constitutes a remarkable record of the evolving ideas of a major legal philosopher at a formative stage of his career.

The Collected Works of Jeremy Bentham

The new critical edition of the works and correspondence of Jeremy Bentham (1748–1832) is being prepared and published under the supervision of the Bentham Committee of University College London. In spite of his importance as jurist, philosopher, and social scientist, and leader of the utilitarian reformers, the only previous edition of his works was a poorly edited and incomplete one brought out within a decade or so of his death. The overall plan and principles of this edition are set out in the General Preface to *The Correspondence of Jeremy Bentham*, vol. 1 (Athlone Press), which was the first volume of the *Collected Works* to be published.

Volumes published by Oxford University Press

Constitutional Code
Volume 1
Edited by F. Rosen and J. H. Burns

Deontology, together with A Table of the Springs of Action and Article on Utilitarianism
Edited by Amnon Goldworth

Chrestomathia
Edited by M. J. Smith and W. H. Burston

First Principles preparatory to Constitutional Code
Edited by Philip Schofield

Securities against Misrule and other Constitutional Writings for Tripoli and Greece
Edited by Philip Schofield

Official Aptitude Maximized; Expense Minimized
Edited by Philip Schofield

Colonies, Commerce, and Constitutional Law: Rid Yourselves of Ultramaria and other writings on Spain and Spanish America
Edited by Philip Schofield

'Legislator of the World': Writings on Codification, Law, and Education
Edited by Philip Schofield and Jonathan Harris

Political Tactics
Edited by Michael James, Cyprian Blamires, and Catherine Pease-Watkin

Rights, Representation, and Reform: Nonsense upon Stilts and other writings on the French Revolution
Edited by Philip Schofield, Catherine Pease-Watkin, and Cyprian Blamires

Writings on the Poor Laws
Volumes 1 & 2
Edited by Michael Quinn

A Comment on the Commentaries and A Fragment on Government
Edited by J. H. Burns and H. L. A. Hart

Of the Limits of the Penal Branch of Jurisprudence
Edited by Philip Schofield

Church-of-Englandism and its Catechism Examined
Edited by James E. Crimmins and Catherine Fuller

On the Liberty of the Press, and Public Discussion and other Legal and Political Writings for Spain and Portugal
Edited by Catherine Pease-Watkin and Philip Schofield

Of Sexual Irregularities, and other writings on Sexual Morality
Edited by Philip Schofield, Catherine Pease-Watkin, and Michael Quinn

The Book of Fallacies
Edited by Philip Schofield

Writings on Political Economy
Volume 1
Edited by Michael Quinn

Correspondence, volumes 6–12: January 1798 to June 1828
Edited by J. R. Dinwiddy, Stephen Conway, Catherine Fuller, and Luke O'Sullivan

PREPARATORY PRINCIPLES

edited by

DOUGLAS G. LONG

and

PHILIP SCHOFIELD

CLARENDON PRESS · OXFORD

OXFORD
UNIVERSITY PRESS

Great Clarendon Street, Oxford, OX2 6DP,
United Kingdom

Oxford University Press is a department of the University of Oxford.
It furthers the University's objective of excellence in research, scholarship,
and education by publishing worldwide. Oxford is a registered trade mark of
Oxford University Press in the UK and in certain other countries

First Edition published in 2016
Impression: 1

Published in the United States of America by Oxford University Press
198 Madison Avenue, New York, NY 10016, United States of America

British Library Cataloguing in Publication Data
Data available

Library of Congress Control Number: 2016934369

ISBN 978-0-19-878290-2

Typeset by Anne Joshua, Oxford

Printed and bound by
Clays Ltd, St Ives plc

PREFACE

The Bentham Committee wishes to thank the the British Academy and University College London for their continuing support of *The Collected Works of Jeremy Bentham*. Professor Long would like to thank the Social Sciences and Humanities Research Council of Canada, the Academic Development Fund of the University of Western Ontario, and the Office of the Dean of the Faculty of Social Science at the University of Western Ontario for financial assistance in support of the preparation of this volume

The initial transcription of the 'Preparatory Principles' manuscripts was undertaken by Professor Long, taking advantage of a bespoke computer program called 'Jeremy' developed by the Social Science Computing Laboratory at the University of Western Ontario. Professor Long is profoundly grateful to the Laboratory Director Douglas G. Link and staff members Les Flodrowski and Steven Rumas for their creativity and indefatigable assistance.

Professor Long would like to thank Katherine Fyfe and Paul Baxter, who provided excellent research assistance under the auspices of the Department of Political Science, University of Western Ontario, and the staff of the Bentham Project, in particular Claire Gobbi in the 1980s and Dr Michael Quinn more recently, who have given constant encouragement and scholarly support of the highest quality. The late Professor John R. Dinwiddy and Professor Frederick Rosen gave essential support as successive General Editors of *The Collected Works of Jeremy Bentham*.

Professor Schofield would like to thank Dr Louise Seaward for her expertise and assiduity in researching and checking much of the annotation in the volume; Mr Philip Baker for administrative assistance; Professor David Ibbetson and Dr Ian Williams for solving a Roman Law query; Mr Benjamin Bourcier and Professor Emmanuelle de Champs for assistance with the French material; and Mr Christopher Riley for solving the Horne query and for other assistance with the annotation, the preparation of the tables of marginal contents, and proofreading. His Bentham Project colleagues Dr Oliver Harris and Dr Michael Quinn have assisted in a variety of ways. Finally, and most importantly, he would like to pay tribute to Professor Douglas Long, without whose commitment, knowledge, and hard work over many years this volume would never have appeared. In essence, Professor Long provided an initial draft of the Editorial Introduction, text, and annotation, and Professor Schofield revised it. Professor Schofield is solely responsible for the indexes.

Thanks are due to University College London Library for permission to publish material from its collection of Bentham Papers. The task of working on Bentham's manuscripts has been greatly facilitated by the digitization of the Bentham Papers being undertaken by Mr Tony Slade and his staff at UCL's Creative Media Services. Grateful acknowledgment is also made to the authors, editors, and translators of standard reference works such as the *Oxford Dictionary of National Biography* and the *Loeb Classical Library*, without whose scholarship the annotation of a volume such as this would hardly be feasible.

The late Professor James H. Burns first suggested this project to Professor Long in 1973, and supported it unwaveringly for the rest of his life. We greatly regret that he did not live to see its completion, but dedicate the volume to his memory.

P.S.
D.G.L.

CONTENTS

SYMBOLS AND ABBREVIATIONS

Symbols

| |	Space left in manuscript.
[to]	Word(s) editorially supplied.
[?]	Reading doubtful
[. . .?]	Word(s) proved illegible.
⟨. . .⟩	Torn manuscript.
⟨so⟩	Conjectural restoration of missing words.

Bowring	*The Works of Jeremy Bentham*, published under the superintendence of . . . John Bowring, 11 vols., Edinburgh, 1843 (initially issued in 22 parts 1838–43).
Comment/ Fragment	*A Comment on the Commentaries and A Fragment on Government*, ed. J.H. Burns and H.L.A. Hart, London, 1977 (*CW*).
CW	This edition of *The Collected Works of Jeremy Bentham*.
Dig.	Digest.
Op. Mag.	Opus Magnum.
'PP'	'Preparatory Principles'.
'PP: Law'	'Preparatory Principles: What a Law is'.
UC	Bentham Papers in the Library of University College London. Roman numerals refer to boxes in which the papers are placed, Arabic to the folios within each box.
MS add.	Text added to the original manuscript reading.
MS alt.	Alternative manuscript reading, usually interlinear or marginal.
MS del.	Word(s) deleted in manuscript.
MS orig.	Original manuscript reading.

EDITORIAL INTRODUCTION

The present volume reproduces three related bodies of manuscripts, under the titles 'Preparatory Principles: Inserenda', 'Preparatory Principles: Introduction', and 'Preparatory Principles: What a Law is', written by Jeremy Bentham in the mid-1770s and dealing generally with the philosophy of law. The vast bulk of the volume is composed of 'Preparatory Principles: Inserenda', while the remaining two pieces are relatively short. The manuscripts are divided into sections, of which around two-thirds for 'Preparatory Principles: Inserenda' and the whole of 'Preparatory Principles: Introduction' and 'Preparatory Principles: What a Law is' have been numbered by Bentham, and which have been editorially denominated as 'paragraphs'.[1] While the two shorter pieces are relatively coherent, there is no continuous argumentative or narrative thread that gives shape to 'Preparatory Principles: Inserenda'. A paragraph or set of paragraphs on one subject-matter is followed by another paragraph or set of paragraphs on a different subject-matter, and so on until an earlier subject-matter is resumed, sometimes being rewritten, sometimes being approached from a different perspective, and sometimes being added to or exemplified. This material does not, therefore, constitute a conventional work: it is rather a philosophical commonplace book in which Bentham attempted to work out the foundational ideas for his new science of legislation. The 'Preparatory Principles' material was central to Bentham's wider jurisprudential endeavours that began in the early 1770s and continued into the 1780s, in which his overarching ambition was to draw up a complete penal code. It was a storehouse of ideas on which he drew while composing a number of related texts. The contents of the present volume constitute a mine of raw materials—working documents on which Bentham drew when executing a series of writing projects, some of which were printed and published in his lifetime, and some of which were not, and including 'A Comment on the Commentaries', *A Fragment on Government*,[2] *An Introduction to the Prin-*

[1] Paragraph numbers have been editorially supplied for the final third of 'PP: Inserenda'. It was Bentham's practice at this time to number each paragraph or group of paragraphs as a convenient means of organizing his text.

[2] Both texts appear in *A Comment on the Commentaries and A Fragment on Government*, ed. J.H. Burns and H.L.A. Hart, Oxford, 1977 (*CW*). 'A Comment on the Commentaries' and *A Fragment on Government*, which was extracted from the former work and published by Bentham in 1776, formed a critique of William Blackstone, *Commentaries on the Laws of England*, 4 vols., Oxford, 1765–9. Sir William Blackstone (1723–80) was first Vinerian

ciples of Morals and Legislation,[1] and 'Of the Limits of the Penal Branch of Jurisprudence'.[2] The ideas worked out in the 'Preparatory Principles' manuscripts, therefore, had a profound and enduring value for Bentham's work not only in the 1770s and 1780s, but for the remainder of his career.

HISTORY OF THE WORKS

'Preparatory Principles: Inserenda' consists of over 600 pages of text.[3] The title is taken from the heading which appears, in the hand of a copyist, on almost all of the component manuscript pages.[4] None of the pages are dated. It seems quite likely that the text was added to over the course of many months, and that the bulk of it was written in and around 1775. The latest date that can be definitely assigned to any part of the text is 2 February 1775, the date of publication of the third edition of Edmund Burke's *Speech on American Taxation, April 19, 1774*, a reference to which appears in a note to paragraph 675.[5] The allusion is to what Bentham took to be Burke's statement that he hated metaphysics. The same allusion

Professor of English Law at Oxford University 1758–66, Justice of Common Pleas 1770, 1770–80 and Justice of King's Bench 1770.

[1] *An Introduction to the Principles of Morals and Legislation*, ed. J.H. Burns and H.L.A. Hart, London, 1970 (*CW*). This work was printed by Bentham in 1780, but not published until 1789, and was originally written as the first part of an introduction to his penal code.

[2] *Of the Limits of the Penal Branch of Jurisprudence*, ed. P. Schofield, Oxford, 2010 (*CW*). This work, which was written in 1780–2 but not printed or published by Bentham himself, was originally intended as a single chapter in continuation of *An Introduction to the Principles of Morals and Legislation*.

[3] UC lxix. 87–8, 91–241, cxl. 21–2. The pages are consecutively numbered 1–614, though there are, in fact, 620 pages: four pages were interpolated and numbered 21*–24* (UC lxix. 95), and three pages were each numbered 609 (lxix. 240). A small number of pages contain no text, including the third page 609, 610, and 612–14. For a comparative list of 'PP: Inserenda' paragraph numbers, folio numbers, and page numbers see the Table of Manuscripts, pp. xxviii–xxxiii below.

[4] Variant main headings are as follows: p. 1 (UC lxix. 86) carries the main heading 'Introd. Preparatory Principles'; pp. 21–6 (lxix. 95–6) 'Preparatory Principles. A Law when compleat'; p. 29 (lxix. 97) 'Preparatory Principles. A Law What'; p. 48 (lxix. 101) 'Preparatory Principles. A law, entirety of'; p. 49 (lxix. 102) 'Preparatory Principles. Law, entirety of'; p. 52 (lxix. 102) 'Preparatory Principles. No Command, no Law'; p. 60 (lxix. 104) 'Preparatory Principles. A Law'; pp. 250–2 (lxix. 151) 'Preparatory Principles. Common Law. Division of it into Customs and Maxims'; and pp. 267–72 (lxix. 155–6) 'Preparatory Principles. Powers in a State'.

In a related fragment at UC lxix. 85, headed 'Prepar. Principles. Legislation) (Taxation. Inserenda', Bentham deals with the question much agitated in relation to the American War of Independence as to whether an act of taxation was an act of legislation. The point is taken up at 'PP: Inserenda', para. 688, pp. 220–1 below.

[5] See p. 217 n. below. The date of publication of the third edition of this speech of Edmund Burke (1729–97), statesman and politician, is given in *The Writings and Speeches of Edmund Burke: Volume II. Party, Parliament, and the American Crisis 1766–1774*, ed. P. Langford and W.B. Todd, Oxford, 1981, p. 406.

appears on two other occasions in the text, the earlier of which is at paragraph 518.[1] Assuming that Bentham had not read this remark until the publication of the third edition of the speech, this dates the bulk of the text to the period after 2 February 1775.[2]

The text is divided into 1313 numbered paragraphs, of which the enumeration up to paragraph 747 is supplied by Bentham, and thereafter editorially.[3] The enumeration of the paragraphs and sequences of paragraphs does not, however, always follow the strict page order, in that Bentham on occasion resumes a discussion, together with the appropriate paragraph enumeration, after a gap of several paragraphs. The order of the text in the present volume follows the enumeration of the paragraphs, rather than the pagination, since this appears to reflect Bentham's intention. Apart from these relatively rare instances, the order in which the text of 'Preparatory Principles: Inserenda' appears in the present volume may be assumed to reflect the chronological order in which the material was written. In addition to the manuscripts that constitute the text of 'Preparatory Principles: Inserenda', there survive three tables of contents, which list the marginal headings on the text sheets, but none of which are complete.[4] Numerous minor

[1] See p. 165 below.

[2] The first edition of the speech had been published on 10 January 1775 (see *Writings and Speeches of Burke: II*, p. 406), and so it would make little practical difference if Bentham had seen the remark immediately on publication of the first edition.

There are, however, two possible indications that the compilation of the text went on into 1776, and perhaps even beyond. There is a possible allusion, at para. 1246, p. 393 below, to Richard Price, *Observations on the Nature of Civil Liberty, the Principles of Government, and the Justice and Policy of the War with America*, published at London on 10 February 1776. The date of the publication of the first edition of this pamphlet by Richard Price (1723–91), philosopher, demographer, and political radical, is given in D.O. Thomas, J. Stephens, and P.A.L. Jones, *A Bibliography of the Works of Richard Price*, Aldershot, 1993, p. 54. Other references to the American controversy may also as well have been written before as after the American Declaration of Independence on 4 July 1776. It seems quite plausible that composition of the 'Inserenda' continued into 1776, but more problematic is a possible allusion at para. 872, p. 268 below, to a comment made by Burke in a speech in the House of Commons on 23 March 1778. It is possible, of course, that Bentham and Burke were both alluding to a view expressed by an earlier writer or speaker.

[3] For further details see pp. xxvii–xxviii below.

[4] Bentham has listed the marginal headings of 'PP: Inserenda', paras. 1–97, 211–664 and corresponding page numbers, in some cases providing brief summaries of main text contents that do not replicate the marginal headings on the text sheets, at UC lxix. 77–80, headed 'Contents of Prep. Princ.' He has listed the marginal headings for 'PP: Inserenda', paras. 367–747 and corresponding page numbers at UC lxix. 83–4. In both these lists, 'PP: Inserenda', para. 393 is noted as 'enter'd P.P.', while a number of marginal headings are marked with a small cross in red ink. Bentham has listed the marginal headings for 'PP: Inserenda', paras. 1–228 at UC lxix. 82, where some of the headings have been crossed through and others cancelled. The exact significance of the annotations on these lists is unclear, though they probably indicate that Bentham had consulted and used the material in other works and projects.

alterations and annotations indicate that Bentham revisited these tables, which he presumably used as a guide to the contents of the main text.

It is impossible to know at what point in the process of drafting 'Preparatory Principles: Inserenda' it was that 'Preparatory Principles: Introduction' and 'Preparatory Principles: What a Law is' were written, though the latter appears to be a redrafting of the former.[1] It is possible that they represent a second, more advanced stage in the process of composition than the 'Inserenda'. The essay presented first, 'Preparatory Principles: Introduction', consists of twelve pages divided into forty-two consecutively numbered paragraphs written on three bifolia.[2] The first page, from which the title is taken, is headed 'Introduction. Preparatory Principles', while the remainder are headed 'Preparatory Principles'. The essay presented second, 'Preparatory Principles: What a Law is', consists of twenty-one pages divided into fifty-three consecutively numbered paragraphs written on six bifolia.[3] Most of the pages carry the full heading.[4] An ancillary body of 'Preparatory Principles' manuscripts headed 'Inserenda Permanent' consists of nine consecutively numbered passages on four pages written on one bifolium,[5] each passage one or two paragraphs in length. In the text of 'Preparatory Principles: What a Law is', Bentham has indicated the specific location where each passage should be inserted, and his instructions have been followed in the present volume.

Since there survive neither rudiments, plans, nor text sheets for any work entitled 'Preparatory Principles', it seems unlikely that Bentham had in mind a work with that title into which 'Preparatory Principles: Inserenda' would eventually be incorporated. At first glance, it might appear that the title 'Preparatory Principles: Introduction' suggests that this material was intended as the draft of an introduction to a work entitled 'Preparatory Principles'. Moreover, in a marginal note in 'Preparatory Principles: Inserenda', in relation to a discussion of the 'Origin of the Ideas Law is

[1] The content of the two pieces is very similar, but the much neater presentation of 'What a Law is' suggests that it is the later version.

[2] UC lxix. 86, 89–90. For a comparative list of 'PP Introduction' paragraph numbers, folio numbers, and page numbers see the Table of Manuscripts, p. xxxiii below.

[3] UC lxix. 70–5. For a comparative list of 'PP: Law' paragraph numbers, folio numbers, and page numbers see the Table of Manuscripts, p. xxxiv below.

[4] The exceptions are pp. 2–5 (UC lxix. 70–1), which carry the marginal sub-heading 'B. I. Ch. I', which may refer to Book I, Chapter 1 of 'A Comment on the Commentaries', where Blackstone's definition of a law is discussed (see *Comment/Fragment* (*CW*), pp. 3–10). Of the three unused pages at UC lxix. 75, pp. 22–3 are blank, while p. 24 has been headed and numbered. For the relationship of the 'PP' materials to 'A Comment on the Commentaries' see pp. xv–xvii below.

[5] UC lxix. 76.

conversant with', Bentham wrote 'BEGINNING *for* PREP. PRINC.'[1] Yet it should be noted the 'Introduction' and the 'Beginning' deal with different subject-matters, and so even these indications, given the difficulty in reconciling the content of the two bodies of material, militate against the view that Bentham ever seriously intended to produce a work with this title. It seems more likely that he viewed the 'Preparatory Principles' material as a possible starting point for a whole range of works and projects, given the foundational character of much of its content. It should also be noted in this context that around one third of the pages of 'Preparatory Principles: Inserenda' have been crossed through, or cancelled, by Bentham: sometimes he crossed through an entire page of text, and sometimes particular paragraphs or shorter passages. This does not mean that he was dissatisfied with this material: cancellation was not deletion. Deleted words and sentences in 'Preparatory Principles' are usually struck through with heavy horizontal strokes.[2] Cancelled passages often state views that Bentham is known to have endorsed consistently. Indeed, the cancellation of passages usually indicates that the relevant material had been used in some way: for instance, that Bentham had consulted it at some point and copied or adapted it for use elsewhere in his writings. Hence, the 'Preparatory Principles: Inserenda' manuscripts are best seen as a storehouse of definitions, explanations, and critical comments, to which Bentham would add as and when some point occurred to him, and on which he would draw when composing his more sustained and coherent texts.

The works to which the 'Preparatory Principles' material is linked most closely, both chronologically and thematically, are 'A Comment on the Commentaries' and its offshoot *A Fragment on Government*. 'A Comment on the Commentaries' has its own inserenda,[3] but at one point in the process of its composition Bentham considered drawing on 'Preparatory Principles: Inserenda', as he noted on a text sheet headed 'Comment on the Comm.^{y} Conduct of the work':

In every Section of the Comment, refer to that part which belongs to it of the Preparatory Principles: and vice versâ, divide the Preparatory Principles into Sections correspondent to the Sections of the Comment.

[1] See 'PP: Inserenda', para. 628, p. 200 n. below.

[2] Bentham often used the term 'Qu.', i.e. 'Quere', in order to indicate his uncertainty in relation to a point. On occasion he was more explicit: see, for instance, his comment below the marginal heading of 'PP: Inserenda' para. 963, p. 294 n. below, '*non placet*', which was to say that he regarded this passage as unsatisfactory.

[3] See *Comment/Fragment* (*CW*), Editorial Introduction, p. xxxvii.

> Go on with the Prep. Principles till there is enough for one Chapter of the Comment. After that Chapter, entitle the next Preparatory Principles resumed, and so *toties quoties*.[1]

In the event Bentham does not seem to have 'conducted' the work in this way, nor did he divide 'Preparatory Principles: Inserenda' according to the sections of 'A Comment on the Commentaries'. Nevertheless, in 'A Comment on the Commentaries' and *A Fragment on Government*, as well as later works such as *An Introduction to the Principles of Morals and Legislation* and 'Of the Limits of the Penal Branch of Jurisprudence', Bentham explicitly pursued themes and expounded ideas which were also discussed in the 'Preparatory Principles' manuscripts. For example, the distinction outlined in 'Preparatory Principles: Inserenda' between law as it is and law as it ought to be appears in *A Fragment on Government*.[2] More specifically, the criticism made in 'Preparatory Principles: Inserenda' that Blackstone, in relation to the desirable qualities in rulers, had turned for an answer to theology, and hence 'to the old orthodox method of explanation, *ignotum per ignotius*', is reiterated in *A Fragment on Government*.[3] In 'Preparatory Principles: Inserenda', Bentham states that, 'The obedience paid to any *particular* Law rests ultimately on . . . a *general habit* of obedience. A habit of executing, upon all occasions and in all points, commands of some one person at least, or body of persons, in the state.'[4] The notion that the habit of obedience was the foundation of political society was taken up in *A Fragment on Government*.[5] The first six chapters of *An Introduction to the Principles of Morals and Legislation* deal with the principle of utility and its basis in human psychology,[6] reflecting themes addressed in 'Preparatory Principles: Inserenda'.[7] In the seventh chapter of *An Introduction to the Principles of Morals and Legislation*, Bentham deals with aspects of human action,[8] again reflecting themes addressed in 'Preparatory Principles: Inserenda'.[9] In *An Introduction to the Principles of Morals and Legislation*,

[1] UC xxviii. 1.

[2] Cf. 'PP: Inserenda', paras. 1023–8, pp. 321–2 below, and *Comment/Fragment* (*CW*), p. 397, and see pp. xxiv–xxv below.

[3] Cf. 'PP: Inserenda', para. 867, p. 266 below, and *Comment/Fragment* (*CW*), p. 450.

[4] 'PP: Inserenda', para. 1088, p. 343 below.

[5] See, for instance, *Comment/Fragment* (*CW*), pp. 429–31 n.

[6] *An Introduction to the Principles of Morals and Legislation* (*CW*), pp. 11–73.

[7] See, for instance, 'PP: Inserenda', paras. 184–5, 383–4, 395, and 500, pp. 88, 130–1, 133, and 161 below respectively.

[8] *An Introduction to the Principles of Morals and Legislation* (*CW*), pp. 74–83.

[9] See, for instance, 'PP: Inserenda', paras. 205–6, 327, 510–14, 923–37, 950, 1077, and 1252–5, pp. 91–2, 119, 163–4, 286–8, 290, 341, and 395 below respectively.

Bentham describes punishment as 'an *artificial* consequence, annexed by political authority to an offensive act, in one instance; in the view of putting a stop to the production of events similar to the obnoxious part of its natural consequences, in other instances.'[1] In 'Preparatory Principles: Inserenda', in similar language, Bentham notes that 'Punishment is pain connected with an act or a forbearance, as an effect is with a cause. . . . Now, whatever it be that is done by Law is but punishment connected with some act or some forbearance.'[2] The link between the 'Preparatory Principles' materials and Bentham's wider jurisprudential writings is strikingly clear in relation to the definition of a law. 'Preparatory Principles: Inserenda', 'Preparatory Principles: Introduction', and 'Preparatory Principles: What a Law is' all deal with this theme, and in particular the question of distinguishing a law from other forms of command or imperation.[3] The investigation of the question 'What is a law', Bentham wrote in 'Preparatory Principles: Inserenda', was one of the subjects that Blackstone had, or should have, attempted to answer in *Commentaries on the Laws of England*, but had failed to do so satisfactorily.[4] It was a question that Bentham took up in 'A Comment on the Commentaries',[5] and again in 'Of the Limits of the Penal Branch of Jurisprudence'.[6] Such connections, of which these are a sample, reflect the fact that 'A Comment on the Commentaries', *A Fragment on Government*, *An Introduction to the Principles of Morals and Legislation*, and 'Of the Limits of the Penal Branch of Jurisprudence' drew on the ideas that had been outlined in the 'Preparatory Principles' material.

Bentham also drew on the 'Preparatory Principles' material for other more inchoate projects in the late 1770s. In a series of text sheets headed 'Crit. Jur. Crim.' (Critical Jurisprudence Criminal),[7] which focus on crimes, offences, and punishments, Bentham proposed to include a 'Chapter called Key' dealing with the 'Exposition of certain fundamental terms of Universal Jurisprudence'.[8] Bentham wrote an 'ordo' for this chapter on a text

[1] *An Introduction to the Principles of Morals and Legislation* (*CW*), p. 157.

[2] 'PP: Inserenda', para. 417, p. 139 below.

[3] See, for instance, 'PP: Inserenda', paras. 3–30 and 141–65, pp. 61–5 and 80–5 below respectively; 'PP: Introduction', paras 17–42, pp. 431–7 below; and 'PP: Law', paras. 25–53, pp. 447–54 below.

[4] 'PP: Inserenda', para. 214, p. 93 below.

[5] See 'A Comment on the Commentaries', I. Of the Nature of Laws in General, in *Comment/Fragment* (*CW*), pp. 3–117.

[6] See *Of the Limits of the Penal Branch of Jurisprudence* (*CW*), pp. 24–41.

[7] See UC lxix. 1–42, cxvii. 1–2, cxl. 1–20, and clix. 262–70.

[8] See UC clix. 269. At UC lxix. 44–51 there are thirty-one consecutively numbered pages of draft material for 'Key', while at lxix. 52–3 there are five consecutively numbered pages

sheet whose original heading had been 'Preparatory Principles'.[1] Beside the first of the twelve headings listed on this sheet, 'Punishment is Pain', Bentham has noted: '1. Right. 2. Power v. p. 373'. This reference is to 'Preparatory Principles: Inserenda', paragraph 913, on page 373, which is headed 'All Power is over persons.'[2] At the side of the sixth heading, 'Commands before State', Bentham has noted: 'v. 462 for the reason.' This reference is to 'Preparatory Principles: Inserenda', paragraph 1078, on page 462, which is headed 'Right &c. from Command or habit of Punishment, before the definition of a Law.'[3] On the same bifolium, Bentham produced a list headed 'Key—Ordo of Heads'. Beside several of these 'Heads' Bentham has written numbers referring to paragraphs of 'Preparatory Principles: Inserenda' where the same subjects are discussed.[4] Furthermore, the first sentence of the first 'Key' text sheet—'The whole system of Jurisprudence displays itself in the coercing of one party for the benefit of another'—repeats verbatim a sentence from 'Preparatory Principles: Inserenda',[5] and the five sheets headed 'Chap. I. Key. What things exist' echo a marginal heading that was, as has already been noted, used in 'Preparatory Principles: Inserenda'.[6]

There were other projects for which Bentham drew on the 'Preparatory Principles: Inserenda' manuscripts. One of these was entitled 'Opus Magnum', often abbreviated to 'Op. Magn.' or 'Op. Mag.', but the nature of it remains obscure. The title, if that is what it is, occurs on about a dozen occasions in the marginal headings to 'Preparatory Principles: Inserenda', always in reference to aspects of crime or punishment.[7] It may, therefore, have referred to the penal code to which Bentham's efforts were being ultimately directed at this time. Possibly related to 'Opus Magnum' was an 'ordo' of headings for a preface to a work identified only as 'O',

headed 'Chap. I. Key. What things exist' and at lxix. 54–6 twelve consecutively numbered pages headed 'Key. Inserenda'.

[1] UC lxix. 43.

[2] See pp. 281–2 below.

[3] See p. 341 below.

[4] After the heading 'What Things exist' Bentham has inserted '512'. 'PP: Inserenda', para. 1168 on p. 512 is headed 'Entities classed', but MS del. is 'What things exist' (see p. 368 & n. below). After the next 'Key' heading, 'Rights and wrongs do not exist', he has inserted '521–4'. At 'PP: Inserenda', para. 1196, on p. 521, Bentham notes that, 'The terms right and wrong are not fit to stand as the names of classes' (see p. 379 below). After the final heading, 'Power, To give a. Development of the figure', he has noted: 'p. 524'. 'PP: Inserenda', para. 1201, on p. 524, carries the marginal heading '"Power" not definable, only expoundable' (see p. 380 below).

[5] See UC lxix. 44 and 'PP: Inserenda', para. 1195, p. 378 below.

[6] i.e. 'PP: Inserenda', para. 1168, on p. 512, at p. 368 n. below.

[7] The first occurrence is at para. 581, p. 188 below, and the last at para. 1015, p. 319 below.

which may have stood for 'Opus'.[1] Bentham devoted a column on one marginal contents sheet to identifying seven paragraphs from 'Preparatory Principles: Inserenda' dealing with 'metaphysical' topics. He presumably intended to draw on these sources in constructing the arguments of 'O'. Another title that appears about a dozen times in the marginal headings of 'Preparatory Principles: Inserenda' is 'Digest', or more commonly its abbreviation 'Dig.', which relates to Bentham's plan to turn the Common Law into statute.[2] At some point in the mid-to-late 1770s or early 1780s, Bentham compiled a list entitled 'PROJECTS, List of. Works projected for the improvement of the Law', and listed thirty-one such projects. 'Of almost all of these', he noted, 'the leading principles are fixed upon. In several of them some progress has been made.'[3] One project in the list is 'An Utopian proposal for a new compact between the Crown and the subject: the subject to give up the right of appeal; and the Crown to consent to some conditions & restrictions to the power of pardoning.' It is followed by a note in Bentham's hand: 'v. P.P.I. 366.'[4] A passage in 'Preparatory Principles: Inserenda', at page 366, carries the marginal heading 'Pardon—proposal for modifying', and a main text which reads in part: 'The subject gives up the right of punishing his injurer when it appears that his punishment is not for the good of the community. The King gives up his power of exempting the injurer from punishment in cases where it appears that it *is* for the good of the community.'[5] Another item in this list, one which was closely linked in subject-matter to 'Preparatory Principles: Inserenda', was 'A Vocabulary of terms of Universal Jurisprudence with their Definitions: the Definitions disposed in an uninterrupted chain, commencing at words importing simple ideas.' This was immediately followed in the list by 'A Vocabulary of terms purely Technical used in English Jurisprudence—viz: 1. Technical Terms; terms appropriated to the Science. 2$^{\text{dly.}}$ Terms expressive of the several classes of things, persons and modes of conduct at large, that are liable to be render'd objects of the Science.'[6] These two items share with the 'Preparatory Principles' materials the theme of the reform of the language of jurisprudence.

This emphasis on the clarity of language remained a constant concern of Bentham, as indicated by the 'Preface' written in 1789

[1] The headings that Bentham drew up for 'O' indicate that it would have been concerned partly with penal law and partly with law in general.

[2] The first occurrence is at para. 305, p. 114 below, and the last at para. 1272, p. 401 below. Cf. 'A Fragment on Government', Ch. V, para. 11, in *Comment/Fragment* (*CW*), p. 499.

[3] UC clxix. 1–2.

[4] See UC clxix. 2.

[5] See 'PP: Inserenda', para. 885, pp. 275–6 below.

[6] See UC clxix. 1.

for the published version of *An Introduction to the Principles of Morals and Legislation*, where he outlined 'the titles of the works by the publication of which his present designs would be completed'. Of the ten titles, the first nine were all concerned with 'Principles of legislation', including substantive, procedural, constitutional, and international law, while the tenth would consist of

> Plan of a body of law, complete in all its branches, considered in respect of its *form*; in other words, in respect of its method and terminology; including a view of the origination and connexion of the ideas expressed by the short list of terms, the exposition of which contains all that can be said with propriety to belong to the head of *universal jurisprudence*.[1]

Bentham's interest in the reform of the language of the law had been a distinctive feature of his thought, if not before, at least from the point at which he discovered his 'genius for legislation' in 1769, and for which, in his reminiscences to his editor and disciple John Bowring,[2] he gave a great deal of credit to Helvétius.[3] His mature recollection of the importance of Helvétius in his intellectual development is confirmed in a letter of 1778 to John Forster.[4] He admitted that he had given up his scheme 'of trying to penetrate into the interior parts of South America' in the hope of using his knowledge of botany and chemistry in order to 'enable me perhaps to be of service to mankind', partly from 'the weakness of my constitution' and 'partly from the instruction I gathered from Helvetius'. He continued:

> From him I got a standard to measure the relative importance of the several pursuits a man might be engaged in: and the result of it was that the way of all others in which a man might be of most service to his fellow creatures was by making improvement in the science that I had been engaged to study by profession. I had indeed gone but a little way in it before I began to take more pleasure in the idea of seeing its imperfections remedied, than in that of converting them to profit: for the defects of the science are you know the patrimony of the profession. That illustrious philosopher (whose principles however I am very far from adopting without distinction) at the same time that he suggested

[1] *An Introduction to the Principles of Morals and Legislation* (*CW*), pp. 5–6.

[2] Sir John Bowring (1792–1872), merchant, radical MP, and diplomat, was responsible for overseeing the publication of *The Works of Jeremy Bentham*, published at Edinburgh, which initially appeared in 22 parts between 1838 and 1843, and was then issued in 11 volumes in 1843.

[3] Bowring, x. 27. Claude Adrien Helvétius (1715–71), French materialist, educational theorist, egalitarian, atheist, and tax farmer, was the author of *De l'esprit*, Paris, 1758.

[4] Bentham described John Forster as 'a sort of atheist parson' who 'had been chaplain to the ambassador at Petersburg' and who had introduced him 'to many Russians': see Bowring, x. 67.

incentives, furnished me with instruments, for making the attempt. From him I learnt to look upon the tendency of any institution or pursuit to promote the happiness of society as the sole test and measure of its merit: and to regard the principle of utility as an oracle which if properly consulted would afford the only true solution that could be given to every question of right and wrong.[1]

Having qualified for the bar in 1769 and embarked on the legal career that his father Jeremiah had planned for him,[2] Bentham had soon turned aside from a professional career to that of remedying the imperfections of the law. In 1772 he sent a 'small specimen' of his work to his father, who, while in general giving his approval, had apparently complained of its 'abstruseness'.[3] Bentham may have had his father's comment in mind when, in 'Preparatory Principles: Inserenda', beside the marginal heading 'Prefatoria. Apology for Abstruseness', he acknowledged that, 'It is painful for a man to turn his thoughts into an entire new channel', but insisted that, 'Discourse on this topic, to be new and just, cannot be otherwise than abstruse.'[4] On 5 October 1774 he wrote to John Lind,[5] who had sent him a manuscript copy of a critique of Blackstone's *Commentaries on the Laws of England* on which he had been working. Bentham's criticism of Lind's efforts seems to have led the latter to give up the enterprise at the same time that it stimulated Bentham to undertake it. Noting that Lind had failed to take 'a commanding view of the field', and that this had led him 'in some places [to] take larger compass than perhaps is necessary', he continued:

Leading ideas, principles, take up many more words in their first disclosure than are sufficient to contain them afterwards. This Locke has seen, has intimated in his preface: and his own work as he acknowledges, and as itself proves, is an example of it.[6] Without Locke I could have known nothing. But I think I could now take Locke's Essay

[1] Bentham to Rev. John Forster, April/May 1778, *Correspondence* (*CW*), ii. 98–9

[2] Jeremiah Bentham (1712–92), lawyer and property speculator, hoped that Jeremy would rise to eminence by following a career in the law.

[3] Bentham to Jeremiah Bentham, 14 October 1772, *The Correspondence of Jeremy Bentham*, vol. i, ed. T.L.S. Sprigge, London, 1968 (*CW*) pp. 154–5.

[4] 'PP: Inserenda', para. 95, p. 75 below.

[5] John Lind (1731–81), political author and unofficial representative in England of the King of Poland, was a close friend of Bentham.

[6] John Locke (1632–1704), philosopher, was author of *An Essay concerning Human Understanding*, which had been first published in 1690. In 'The Epistle to the Reader' (see *An Essay concerning Human Understanding*, ed. P.H. Nidditch, Oxford, 1975, p. 8), Locke noted: 'I will not deny, but possibly it might be reduced to a narrower compass than it is; and that some Parts of it might be contracted: the way it has been writ in, by catches, and many long intervals of Interruption, being apt to cause some Repetitions.'

and write it over again, so as to make it much more precise and apprehensible in half the compass.[1]

In 'Preparatory Principles: Inserenda', Bentham took inspiration from Locke's work on language, but also moved beyond it in developing his own views on the subject. He lauded Locke as 'in a manner the inventor' of 'Metaphysics, modern Metaphysics, genuine Metaphysics'.[2] Bentham had a very specific understanding of the term 'metaphysics':

> The business of Metaphysics is neither more nor less than this, to examine what ideas we have belonging to the terms we use, and whether they are clear or no. Every science . . . has it's Metaphysics: for every Science has it's leading terms, terms that are in constant use in every discourse that is held upon the subject of it, terms used for the making of others to be understood, terms of which, because they are much used, men are apt to suppose that they are thoroughly understood, but which very often, when examined into, turn out to be very far from thoroughly understood.
>
> Every science, then, has it's Metaphysics. . . . Now the metaphysics of this our science Law, consists in ascertaining the meaning, in fixing [the] ideas, belonging to the several terms of universal Jurisprudence, through the medium of which the technical terms of the particular Jurisprudence of any country are endeavoured to be explained.[3]

Bentham argued that establishing an accurate understanding of the relationship between words and the entities that they represented was the first step in the construction of any body of knowledge, including jurisprudence. Yet metaphysics, in this sense, although the '[n]ursing-mother, if not parent, of the whole train of Sciences', was 'disowned and slighted by [her] children!'[4]

Again with a view to explaining the relationship between the clarification of legal terminology and his wider jurisprudential project, in 'Preparatory Principles: Inserenda' Bentham recognized that it might be objected that such a metaphysical work made no apparent contribution to 'that great and only legitimate end of all political speculations, the ascertaining in matters of law the point of expedience or inexpedience'. The 'present' work, however, was 'but a vestibule to a building that is to follow, an introduction of a work that is to come', the object of which would be 'the construction of a standard of right and wrong, and the application of it to the several Laws that still present themselves, and in conse-

[1] Bentham to Lind, 5 October 1774, *Correspondence* (*CW*), i. 205–6.
[2] 'PP: Inserenda', para. 863, p. 265 below.
[3] 'PP: Inserenda', para. 615, pp. 196–7 below.
[4] 'PP: Inserenda', para. 1041, p. 329 below.

quence to the several modes of conduct that are the objects of them'. This 'work . . . to come' was 'the end of all'; it had, he added, 'presented itself to my mind, before the necessity of the present one was even so much as suspected'. He realized, however, that he could not proceed with 'the common stock of words': before commencing his main work, he observed, 'I had a vast load of difficulty to remove. Tools, materials, every thing to make; I had my materials to parcel out and to find names for.'[1]

Bentham described the task in which he was engaged in writing the 'Preparatory Principles' materials as that of the 'Architect', which he contrasted with that of the 'Scavenger'. Locke had acted as a 'Scavenger' in natural philosophy, removing 'that rubbish under which it lay buried, of words that never had a meaning'. Jurisprudence was now in need of an 'Architect', in order 'to build up for it a competent suite of terms and expressions'.[2] That task, it seems, Bentham intended to undertake in 'A Treatise on Universal Law', in which he would give 'an account of such rights, powers, duties and restraints as subsist, or are liable to subsist, in every or any state. In such a treatise, the terms employ'd will be such as, being as well understood in one state as another, are as well calculated to signify the rights, powers, duties and restraints that subsist in one state, as those that subsist in another.'[3] He envisioned a further book, entitled 'An Expository Treatise on Universal Law applied to the State of England', which would consist in 'an exposition of the peculiar Jurisprudence of this state, given in terms of universal Jurisprudence: that is, in short, in terms of common use among all mankind'.[4] Such a work would render English law intelligible to lawyers from other countries, whereas 'A treatise on English Law, written in terms of English Law, is intelligible to none but English Lawyers.'[5] The point was that the new terminology could be used to expound the laws of each and every state in a way that would make sense to lawyers in each and every other state.

Having his new terminology, he would take on the role of architect in building up the structure of law as it ought to be.

[1] 'PP: Inserenda', para. 879, p. 274 below. A similar idea is expressed in *An Introduction to the Principles of Morals and Legislation* (*CW*), p. 215 n.: 'Striving to cut a new road through the wilds of jurisprudence, I find myself continually distressed, for want of tools that are fit to work with. To frame a complete set of new ones is impossible. All that can be done is, to make here and there a new one in cases of absolute necessity, and for the [r]est, to patch up from time to time the imperfections of the old.'

[2] 'PP: Inserenda', para. 921, p. 285 below:

[3] 'PP: Inserenda', para. 410, p. 136 below. A list of other possible titles for what appears to be a work of this kind is given at 'PP: Inserenda', para. 1151, p. 365 below.

[4] 'PP: Inserenda', para. 411, p. 136 below.

[5] 'PP: Inserenda', para. 412, p. 136 below.

After defining jurisprudence as 'the art of knowing what has actually been done in the way of internal Government',[1] he went on to state:

A Science which might be conceived is, the art of knowing what *ought* to [be] done in the way of internal Government.

Now the fact is, no such science as yet existeth. No wonder, therefore, there should be no name for it. No such science as yet exists: for no such book hath as yet appeared as professes to contain a body of any such science, or any regular branch of such a body. And such is the power of names, over the workmanship of the intellect, that scarcely can a science be said to exist, till it has a name.

He considered several possible names for this science: 'the *Art of Legislation*', '*Critical Jurisprudence*', 'the Science of Internal Politics', 'the Science of Legal Politics', and 'the science of Jurisprudential Politics'. 'All these names', he wrote, 'lie open to objections', but the most apposite was 'Critical Jurisprudence'.[2]

Bentham's approval of the term critical jurisprudence in 'Preparatory Principles: Inserenda' is echoed in 'A Comment on the Commentaries', where he used it when rewriting a passage in Blackstone's *Commentaries on the Laws of England*. Where Blackstone had said that God 'has graciously reduced the rule of obedience to this one paternal precept, "that man should pursue his own happiness"', and that 'This is the foundation of what we call ethics, or natural law',[3] Bentham, italicizing his own words, rendered the passage as follows: 'This is the foundation of *what may be* called *Critical Law or Critical Jurisprudence*'.[4] Bentham eventually came to prefer the phrase 'censorial jurisprudence', but it was, in essence, merely a different term for the same enterprise. In *A Fragment on Government*, for instance, he explained the roles of the expositor and the censor by linking them to the study of the law as it is and the law as it ought to be respectively.

That which *is* Law, is, in different countries, widely different: while that which *ought to be*, is in all countries to a great degree the same. The *Expositor*, therefore, is always the citizen of this or that particular country: the *Censor* is, or ought to be the citizen of the world. To the *Expositor* it belongs to show what the *Legislator* and his underworkman the *Judge* have done *already*: to the *Censor* it belongs to suggest what the *Legislator*

[1] 'PP: Inserenda', para. 1023, p. 321 below.
[2] 'PP: Inserenda', para. 1027, pp. 321–2 below.
[3] Blackstone, *Commentaries on the Laws of England*, i. 41.
[4] See *Comment/Fragment* (*CW*), pp. 20, 294.

ought to do *in future*. To the Censor, in short, to *teach* that *science*, which when by change of hands converted into an *art*, the LEGISLATOR *practises*.[1]

The terminology of expository and censorial jurisprudence was reiterated in *An Introduction to the Principles of Morals and Legislation*,[2] but the substance of the idea is present in the 'Preparatory Principles' material.

Despite Bentham's admiration for both Locke and Helvétius, the figure who dominates Bentham's thoughts in 'Preparatory Principles' is Blackstone. There are multiple references and allusions, explicit and implicit, to Blackstone's *Commentaries on the Laws of England*. The close relationship of the 'Preparatory Principles' manuscripts to 'A Comment on the Commentaries' and *A Fragment on Government* has been discussed above, and in many respects 'Preparatory Principles' forms a companion piece to those texts. It is here that Bentham engages with Blackstone's interpretation of English law, working out how his own exposition of legal entities was related to the existing terminology and practice, criticizing the vagueness, inconsistency, and immorality of the Common Law, and pointing the way to its reform. In the same letter to John Forster quoted above, Bentham explained that he had been

working hard, though in a manner underground, and without producing any apparent fruits: for I was working deep. I was engaged in a set of speculations which insensibly led me into the formation of a plan for determining upon fixed principles the best Laws under every head of Jurisprudence. I have now settled my leading principles: I have advanced some way in the execution of my design: and see I think with tolerable clearness through the whole of it: the completion of it will be the business of my life. I keep in view all along the Jurisprudence of all nations: applying the principles however as you may imagine, more particularly to that of my own.[3]

While unorganized and fragmentary, the material in 'Preparatory Principles' was a central part of this process, and constitutes a remarkable record of the developing ideas of a major legal philosopher at a formative stage of his career.

Presentation of the Text

The texts of the works in the present volume have been entirely reconstructed from Bentham's manuscripts. It has been editorial

[1] *Comment/Fragment* (*CW*), pp. 397–8.

[2] See *An Introduction to the Principles of Morals and Legislation* (*CW*), pp. 293–4. The passage also appears in *Of the Limits of the Penal Branch of Jurisprudence* (*CW*), p. 16.

[3] Bentham to Forster, April/May 1778, *Correspondence* (*CW*), ii. 100.

policy to reflect as far as possible the manuscript sources on which the texts in this volume are based, but without sacrifice thereby of clarity and sense. All of the text is written on double sheets of foolscap (bifolia). The sheets are ruled with a wide margin to the left-hand side on the rectos and to the right-hand side on the versos, and with a double line at the top and at the bottom. The main heading 'Preparatory Principles' was almost invariably added in the centre at the top of the page, and, for some of the material, in the centre at the bottom of the page.[1] The margins for 'Preparatory Principles: Inserenda' are invariably headed 'Inserenda'. At this time Bentham was not in the habit of dating his text sheets. He wrote on both the rectos and versos of the text sheets, which he paginated consecutively with Arabic numerals. He divided his text with paragraph numbers using Arabic numerals, which he inserted above the relevant paragraph (to refer to these as paragraph numbers is convenient, if slightly misleading, in that one such number might represent a sequence of several paragraphs, and in some cases several pages). He also often added marginal headings or marginal contents, that is short summaries of the subject-matter of the text, in the margin at the head of the relevant paragraph in the text. These marginal contents are reproduced in the margin of the present volume. Bentham devised a specialized character, mainly in marginal headings, reproduced in the present volume as)(and hence replicating Bentham's handwritten representation of it, to designate a 'distinction or opposition' between the terms in question.[2] Bentham's spelling and capitalization have been retained in most instances, although editorial discretion has been exercised with regard to his punctuation, which is often inconsistent and sparse. Punctuation marks have been adjusted and supplied where clearly indicated by the sense, or required for the sake of clarity, but not in cases where this might involve a dubious interpretation of the meaning. The words and phrases underlined by Bentham for emphasis have been rendered in italics, as have all foreign words and phrases, some of which Bentham underlined and some of which he did not.

The manuscripts contain many additions (either interlinear or marginal), deletions, and emendations which represent Bentham's later corrections to the text. The latest variant has usually been preferred, while original readings have not usually been indicated. Square brackets in the text are reserved for editorially inserted

[1] For variants see p. xii n. above.

[2] For Bentham's explanation and description of the character see 'PP: Inserenda', para. 300, p. 112 below.

words, while Bentham's original is, where appropriate, given in an editorial footnote. Bentham's square brackets are replaced by braces. Round brackets are those supplied by Bentham. Vertical strokes indicate a gap or blank space in the manuscript. Bentham's own footnotes are indicated by superscript letters, and editorial footnotes by superscript numerals, with a separate sequence for each page of text.

There are particular editorial issues which arise from Bentham's use of French. He wrote French with considerable fluency, and had at his command a large vocabulary, almost always equal to the task of expression. Nevertheless, his style is sometimes awkward, betraying the influence of English constructions and vocabulary. He often makes errors of grammar, syntax, and vocabulary, some of which are due to 'anglicisms'. Minor errors of spelling, where there is no question of confusion, have not been corrected; moreover archaisms, such as the spelling 'étoit' for 'était', have been preserved. In some instances, Bentham's spelling is simply inconsistent, for instance using 'fraix' and 'frais', and 'quelcun' and 'quelqu'un' interchangeably, and these inconsistencies have not been adjusted. Some minor slips have been corrected without explanatory footnotes. These include missing or misplaced accents, which have been added or amended to conform with modern usage; grammatical slips relating to number, gender, and agreement, affecting nouns, pronouns, and adjectives; the common misuse of certain grammatical constructions, and the occasional use of the wrong pronoun, the wrong auxiliary verb, and the addition of an extra particle; and the redundant repetition of a word. The insertion of the correct word in square brackets, with an explanatory editorial footnote, marks the rare instances where Bentham uses the wrong tense of a verb, or confuses the use of the subjunctive and the indicative form.

The organization of the text has been ascertained by paying regard, where applicable, to the pagination of the text sheets, the numbering of the paragraphs, and, of course, the sense. The text of 'Preparatory Principles: Inserenda' carries a continuous set of paragraph numbers, with only minor discrepancies, from 1 to 747. These have been retained, albeit with editorial intervention, marked by square brackets, in cases of inconsistency. The paragraph numbers from 748 onwards have been supplied editorially. In the main, Bentham's practice was to insert a paragraph number where he wrote a marginal heading at the start of a paragraph. Hence an editorial paragraph number has been supplied (more mechanically, of course, than Bentham would have done) where there is both a new paragraph and a corresponding marginal heading. For clarity of presentation, the editorially supplied paragraph numbers, that is from 748 to 1313, have not been enclosed in square brackets. The text is divided by short rules, which almost always replicate a line drawn across the page by Bentham himself in order to indicate a change of subject-matter. The editorial principles explained above have also, where appropriate, been applied to the contents of 'Preparatory Principles: Introduction' and 'Preparatory Principles: What a Law is', which have their own sequences of paragraph numbers. For the manuscripts used in this edition, reference should be made to the Table of Manuscripts below.

Table of Manuscripts

Preparatory Principles: Inserenda

Paragraph numbers	*MSS (UC lxix unless otherwise indicated)*	*Page numbers*
1–15	87	1–4
15–29	88	5–8
30–44	91	9–12
45–55	92	13–16
56–66	93	17–20
66–82	94	21–4
83–103	95	21*–4*[1]
103–21[2]	96	25–8
122–37	97	29–32
137–48	98	33–6
149–57	99	37–40
157–65	100	41–4
165–74, 176–80[3]	101	45–8
181–7	102	49–52
188–97	103	53–6
197–210	104	57–60
211–17	105	61–4
218–28	106	65–8

[1] Pages 21*–4* are later insertions. Bentham's usual practice was to add asterisks to the numbers of inserted material.

[2] The numbers for paras. 104 and 115–21 have been editorially supplied.

[3] There is no para. 175.

Paragraph numbers	*MSS (UC lxix unless otherwise indicated)*	*Page numbers*
229–36	107	69–72
237–49	108	73–6
249–59	109	77–80
260–6[1]	110	81–4
267–74	111	85–8
274–82	112	89–92
283–8	113	93–6
289–300	114	97–100
300–6	115	101–4
306–12	116	105–8
313–25	117	109–12
326–39	118	113–16
340–3	119	117–20
343–54	120	121–4
354–64	121	125–8
365–80	122	129–32
380–1	123	133–6
381–9	124	137–40
389–98	125	141–4
399–412	126	145–8
412–17	127	149–52
417–23	cxl. 22	153–6
424–38	128	157–60
439–51	129	161–4
452–60	130	165–8
451, 461–71	131	169–72
471–6	132	173–6
476–83	133	177–80
483–6	134	181–4
485*, 486*, 486–93[2]	135	185–8
493–509[3]	136	189–92

[1] The number for para. 263 has been editorially supplied.
[2] Paragraph numbers 485* and 486* are later insertions.
[3] The same para. is numbered 502 and 503.

Paragraph numbers	*MSS (UC lxix unless otherwise indicated)*	*Page numbers*
510–20	137	193–6
521–30	138	197–200
531	139	201–4
532–4	140	205–8
534–9	141	209–12
540–2	142	213–16
542–7[1]	143	217–20
548–9, 550*, 550, 551–2	144	221–4
545, 552–60, 561/2[2]	145	225–8
561/2, 563–6, 566*	146	229–32
567–73	147	233–6
574–8	148	237–40
579–91	149	241–4
590*, 591*,[3] 592–606	150	245–8
607–11	151	249–52
612–18	152	253–6
618–29	153	257–60
630–9	154	261–4
640–6[4]	155	265–8
645, 646*, 646–52, 652*, 653–6	156	269–72
657–67	157	273–6
667–74[5]	158	277–80
675–84[6]	159	281–4
685–96	160	285–8
697–708	161	289–92
708–12	162	293–6
712–22	163	297–300
723–40	164	301–4
740–5/7,[7] 746	165	305–8

[1] Para. 545 includes text from UC lxix. 145
[2] Bentham has numbered the same paragraph both 561 and 562.
[3] Paras. 590* and 591* are later insertions.
[4] Para. 645 is continued at UC lxix. 156.
[5] Para. 674 is continued at UC lxix. 177.
[6] Para. 675 is continued at UC lxix. 177.
[7] Bentham has numbered the same paragraph both 745 and 747.

Paragraph numbers	*MSS (UC lxix unless otherwise indicated)*	*Page numbers*
748–51,[1] 753[2]	166	309–12
752, 753–7	167	313–16
757–67	168	317–20
768–83	169	321–4
784–95	170	325–8
796–807	171	329–32
807–21	172	333–6
822–30	173	337–40
831–45	174	341–4
846–51, 859–62	175	345–8
851–8, 863	176	349–52
674,[3] 675,[4] 863–70	177	353–6
871–3	178	357–60
873–9[5]	cxl. 21	361–4
880–95	179	365–8
895–912	180	369–72
913–20	181	373–6
921–33	182	377–80
933–44,[6] 947–50	183	381–4
950–2,[7] 953–4	184	385–8
952, 955–63	185	389–92
963–8	186	393–6
968–72,[8] 974–5	187	397–400
972–3, 976–8	188	401–4
978–84	189	405–8
984–90	190	409–12
990–1000	191	413–16

[1] Paragraph numbers from para. 748 have been editorially supplied: for further details see the Editorial Introduction, pp. xxvii–xxviii above.
Para. 750 is continued at UC lxix. 168.
[2] Para. 753 is continued at UC lxix. 167.
[3] Para. 674 is continued from UC lxix. 158.
[4] Para. 675 is continued from UC lxix. 159.
[5] Para. 876 is continued at UC lxix. 204.
[6] Para. 945 is at UC lxix. 208 and para. 946 at lxix. 195.
[7] Para. 952 is continued at UC lxix. 185.
[8] Para. 972 is continued, and para. 973 appears, at UC lxix. 188.

Paragraph numbers	*MSS (UC lxix unless otherwise indicated)*	*Page numbers*
1000–6	192	417–20
1006–12	193	421–4
1012,[1] 1013	194	425–8
946, 1014–27	195	429–32
1012,[2] 1030–4	196	433–6
1027–9, 1034–6	197	437–40
1037–9,[3] 1040–1	198	441–4
1039, 1041–5	199	445–8
1045–50	200	449–52
1051–62	201	453–6
1063–73	202	457–60
1073–86	203	461–4
876,[4] 1087–93[5]	204	465–8
1094–1104	205	469–72
1105–9	206	473–6
1093,[6] 1109–14	207	477–80
945, 1115–19	208	481–4
1119–24, 1178–81,[7] 1187[8]	209	485–8
1125–31	210	489–92
1131–40	211	493–6
1141–7	212	497–500
1147–50	213	501–4
1150–5	214	505–8
1155–68	215	509–12
1168–78[9]	216	513–16
1182–5	230	569–72
1185–6, 1187–9[10]	231	573–6

[1] Para. 1012 is continued at UC lxix. 196.
[2] Para. 1012 is continued from UC lxix. 194.
[3] Para. 1038 is continued at UC lxix. 199.
[4] Para. 876 is continued from UC cxl. 21.
[5] Para. 1093 is continued at UC lxix. 207.
[6] Para. 1093 is continued from UC lxix. 204.
[7] Para 1178 is continued from UC lxix. 216.
[8] Para. 1187 is continued at UC lxix. 231.
[9] Para. 1178 is continued, and paras. 1179–80 appear, at UC lxix. 209.
[10] Para. 1187 is continued from UC lxix. 209.

Paragraph numbers	*MSS (UC lxix unless otherwise indicated)*	*Page numbers*
1190–4	217	517–20
1195–1201	218	521–4
1202–14	219	525–8
1214–23	220	529–32
1223–35	221	533–6
1236–40	222	537–40
1240	223	541–4
1240–4	224	545–8
1244–8	225	549–52
1248–57	226	553–6
1258–65	227	557–60
1265–8	228	561–4
1268–75	229	565–8
1276–80	232	577–80
1280–4	233	581–4
1284–96	234	585–8
1296–1300	235	589–92
1301–3	236	593–6
1303–16	237	597–600
1316–18	238	601–4
1318–19	239	605–8
1320–2	240	609–10[1]
1323	241	611–14

Preparatory Principles: Introduction

Paragraph numbers	*MSS (UC lxix)*	*Page numbers*
1–18	86	1–4
18–27	89	5–8
27–42	90	9–12

[1] The first three pages of this bifolium are each numbered 609.

Preparatory Principles: What a Law is

Paragraph numbers	*MSS (UC lxix)*	*Page numbers*
1–7,[1] 9–16	70	1–4
17–21, 22,[2] 23–7[3]	71	5–8
28–32[4]	72	9–12
32–9[5]	73	13–16
39–51	74	17–20
52–3	75	21–4

[1] Para. 8 appears at UC lxix. 76

[2] Paras. 21 and 22 are both continued at UC lxix. 76.

[3] Bentham's note to para. 26 is continued at UC lxix. 72.

[4] Bentham's note to para. 30 is continued at UC lxix. 73, while his note to para. 32 appears at lxix. 76.

[5] Bentham's note to para. 38 is continued at UC lxix. 74.

PREPARATORY PRINCIPLES: INSERENDA

MARGINAL CONTENTS

[1] Where a paragraph lacks a marginal heading, an indication of its subject matter has been editorially supplied.

---

[1] Bentham has given two paragraphs the number 110.

[1] Bentham has given two paragraphs the number 139.
[2] Bentham has given two paragraphs the number 157.

[1] Bentham has given two paragraphs the number 165.
[2] There is no para. 175.

[1] Bentham has given two paragraphs the number 193.

---

[1] Bentham has numbered the same paragraph both 372 and 373.

[1] Bentham has indicated that para. 461 should follow para. 451.

[1] Bentham has numbered the same paragraph both 502 and 503.

---

[1] Bentham has numbered this paragraph both 561 and 562.

[1] Bentham has indicated that para. 605 should precede para. 602.
[2] The marginal heading has been abandoned.

---

[1] Bentham has given two paragraphs the number 669.

[1] Bentham has numbered this paragraph both 745 and 747.

[2] Paragraph numbers have been editorially supplied from para. 748 onwards. For further details see the Editorial Introduction, pp. xxvii–xxviii above.

INSERENDA

1. That motion, without which some other thing, it is supposed, could[1] not be, is stiled *a cause*: that motion which, without a cause, it is supposed, could not be, is stiled an *effect*. Cause. Effect. Instrument ⲭ Work.

2.[2] There are 4 articles of consideration, without all of which together, no thing or portion of matter that is the object of an action, could, it has been supposed, exist, to each of which, therefore, has been given the name of cause; they are the *Final cause*, or end:[a] the *Material cause*, or *matter* of which the thing is made:[b] the *Formal cause*, or *form* in which it appears:[c] the *efficient cause*, or the person or thing that has acted upon it to make it what it is.[d] 4 sorts of Causes.[3]

3. A Law is an Act of State.[4] State.[5]

A number of persons accustomed or agreed to act in all things as a certain person or persons shall command, is called a State.

4. The articles with which it is proper to compare the idea of a Law, in order to settle whether it should be understood to be distinct from, or include them, are: 1st. A Command by a private person. 2dly. A Sentence. 3dly. Certain Acts of the supreme Legislative power, less than Laws. *Distinguenda.*

5. Every Law must be an Act of the supreme power in a state or of a power deriving it's authority from that power: that is every Law must be an act of the person or persons who are already in use to give commands to the whole State, or else of some person or persons whom the former are in use to permitt to give such commands for the whole state or for a certain division of it. Law, Source of— An Act of State.

[a] i:e: the Idea that is the instrument, the motive to the man's action.

[b] The work[6] consider'd with respect to it's matter.

[c] The [work][7] consider'd with respect to it's form.

N.B. It is absurd to speak of the work as being the cause of itself.

[d] The instrument or Author.

---

[1] MS alt. 'can'.

[2] In the text, Bentham has noted at this point: 'v. p. 133–138.' See para. 381, pp. 128–30 below. The cross-reference, like many others in the text, is to the page numbers of the manuscripts: for further details see the Editorial Introduction, pp. xii–xiv above.

[3] Bentham recounts the theory of causation put forward by Aristotle (384–322 BC), the celebrated Greek philosopher, in *Physics*, II. iii.

[4] MS orig. 'the State'.

[5] In the margin, Bentham has noted at this point: 'v. Prep. Princ. p. 7.' See 'PP: Introduction', para. 26, p. 434 below.

[6] MS del. 'instrument'.

[7] MS del. 'instrument'.

But it does not follow that every act of the supreme power is a Law.

Resolution of Opinion.

[6.] A resolution of Judgment is not itself a Law: tho' it may be the foundation of a Law: it may be the cause of a Law, as in an individual a resolution of judgment is the cause of an act of the Will: it is an act of the judicial faculty affirming the probability of some benefit to be attained, the prospect of which constitutes a motive.

Sentence is not a Law.

7. The Supreme Legislative body may pass sentences as it may do any thing else: but this does not make a Sentence be a Law.

Direction not a Law. Law must be compulsory.

8. Any man can command any man: but it belongs to the Supreme Power only to furnish motives that shall be *compulsive* upon every man.

Therefore, a naked Command, tho' issued by the Legislature, does not come properly under the notion of the Law.[1]

That command, therefore, only is a Law, which, being issued by the Supreme power, has belonging to it a motive of the same power's providing.

Law compleat.

9. A Law is compleat which contains a compleat designation of the sort of act it wills to be done or not done, together with a compleat assignment also of those other acts, consequences of the first act, in which consists the motive.

Volition Original)(Modifying. Statutes.

10. The immediate object of a Volition to be communicated may either be some act to be done by a person other than the party *willing*, or an expression of the volition of the party willing that has already been communicated.

Statute original)(modifying.

11. In like manner, the immediate object of a Statute may be some act to be done by a person or persons other than the Statute-makers as such, or some Statute that has already been enacted.

Statute.

12. By a Statute, I mean any instrument containing the expression of any command or commands, or parts of a command or commands, of the Supreme power in a state, whereof the object, immediate or ultimate, is the act of some party or parties other than the Legislature itself as such.

Law.

13. By a Law, I mean such an expression of the Will of that supreme power, [as] contains a compleat designation of some point of conduct to be done or not done, as also of the motive to it.

Law compleat.

A Law is compleat in it's substance when &c.

Law when authentic.

14. A Law is *authentic* in it's original, when it is the Will of the accustomed Lawgiver or Lawgivers, expressed with the accustomed formalities.

[1] In the margin, Bentham has noted at this point: 'V. p. | |. *Aliter*.' Bentham may have had in mind para. 146, p. 82 below

15. The use of those formalities (that is of such as have any) is, first, to make it sure that the commands in the Law are in fact what were meant to be given by accustomed parties, 2[d] that they have had proper opportunities to form the opinions by which those Commands have been determined, 3[dly] to make it apparent that they are so to those who are to obey them. Formalities—Use of.

A Law is either Temporary by Nature, or Temporary by establishment.

16. It is temporary by nature, when the act or acts it commands cannot, in the nature of them, be performed but during a certain time: this is the case where either the agent, or the subject, or the object of the act in question are *individual*.[a] Law Temporary by Nature.

17. A Law is temporary by establishment, when there is nothing in the nature of the act to prevent the Law's being perpetual: but, by an express provision annext to the Law, it is made temporary. Temporary by Establishment.

18. We have seen what are acts of a Legislator: which of them are Laws: and which more or less than Laws. Let us now see what the acts are of a Judge. Acts Judicial.

19. A Sentence is a command concerning some individual act or train of actions to be done by some individual person or persons *at the instance* of some other individual person or persons, on account of some individual *past* act or train of actions. Sentence.

20. The ground of a Sentence is either a Law or somewhat else. On Statute, or Common Law.

A Sentence, again, is either Definitive or Interlocutory.

21. A Definitive Sentence corresponds to a Law of the Substantive kind: an Interlocutory, to a Law of the Adjective kind. Definitive or Interlocutory.

Suppose the apparatus of Adjective Laws belonging to a Substantive Law to be a compleat one: tho' perhaps as yet there is no such thing—then, *ut supra*. A Definitive | |

22. The apparatus of Adjective Laws annexed to a Substantive Law is a compleat one, when all the powers necessary to carry the Substantive Law into execution are expressly given, and all the limitations to those powers expressly specified. Adjective Apparatus when compleat.

23. The idea of a Legislator and a Judge are thus distinct: but nothing hinders their being united in the same person: in fact, they are in many instances thus united: sometimes in the individual only by accidental concurrence: sometimes in the species by permanent establishment, in the way of Office. Judges Legislators— by Accident— by Office.

[a] As for a certain person to pay money, or for any persons to pay a certain sum of money, or for any persons to pay any money, to a certain person.

By Accident. **24.** Under our constitution, a Judge of the superior Courts[1] may be a Legislator of the Upper House of the supreme body of Legislators;[2] tho' he is not so of course.

By Office. **25.** But he is a Legislator of course, and, by virtue of his office of Judge, to many purposes.

Rules and Orders. **26.** He makes General permanent Laws concerning many parts of the apparatus of procedure or System of Adjective Laws—these are called Rules and orders of the Court which makes them.

Recognizances. **27.** He makes also Privilegia, *assessing* penalties where not *assessed* by Statute—these are called Recognizances. But N.B. they are Contracts with the Conizee, for he has his option to go to Pris⟨on;⟩ also they are imposed sometimes at the instance of an individual.[3]

Recognizance. **28.** A Recognizance answers the double purpose of a Monitory Proclamation, and a Penal Law.

Judges can not make Substantive Laws. Scroggs. **29.** The Power of Judge of our Superior Courts extends not in any instance that I know of to the making a Substantive Law: Ld. Ch. Justice Scroggs, in the tyrannical time of Charles 2d,[4] made a Substantive Law concerning Libels:[5] he was universally understood to have exceeded his jurisdiction: and so it was resolved by the House of Commons. They resolved that he had been guilty of usurping Legislative power: meaning a power that, in the matter in question, the supreme Legislative body alone were in use to exercise:[6] not that he had no power to make his Laws in any matter whatsoever: for, in the matters above mentioned, those

[1] i.e. the Courts of Chancery, King's Bench, Common Pleas, and Exchequer.

[2] i.e. the House of Lords.

[3] For an account of the recognizance, and the relationship between cognizor and cognizee, see William Blackstone, *Commentaries on the Laws of England*, 4 vols., Oxford, 1765–9, ii. 341–2. Sir William Blackstone (1723–80) was first Vinerian Professor of English Law at the University of Oxford 1758–66, Justice of Common Pleas 1770, 1770–80 and Justice of King's Bench 1770.

[4] Charles II (1630–85), King of England, Scotland, and Ireland from 1660.

[5] Bentham has indicated that a footnote should be inserted at this point, but no corresponding text has been located.

[6] Sir William Scroggs (*c.* 1623–83), Justice of Common Pleas 1676–8, Chief Justice of King's Bench 1678–81, had sought to impose stricter controls on the press in a series of rulings in 1679–80, and in particular by declaring that the Crown possessed the power to prohibit the printing and publishing of unlicensed newspapers and pamphlets. On 23 December 1680 the House of Commons adopted resolutions condemning the actions of Scroggs and three other judges as 'illegal and arbitrary', accusing them of 'thereby usurping to themselves Legislative Power', and calling for the impeachment of Scroggs for 'High Treason, and other Great Crimes and Misdemeanors' (see *Commons Journals* (1667–87) ix. 688–90). On 7 January 1681 articles of impeachment were thereupon brought against Scroggs, who, together with the three other judges, was accused of 'an open Invasion upon the Right of the Subject, and an encroaching and assuming to themselves a Legislative Power and Authority' (see *Lords Journals* (1675–81) xiii. 738–9). Scroggs's impeachment was eventually aborted when Charles II dissolved the Oxford Parliament on 28 March 1681.

whose place he filled, had been as much used to make them, as the Parliament itself.

30. Subordinate Legislation is exercised either 1st by express appointment of the supreme [legislative body], or 2dly without express appointment.[1]

Subordinate Legislation—By Appointment—By Sufferance.

31. It is the characteristic of the Judicial sanction not to act but when set in motion *ab extra*.[a]

Judges moved *ab extra*.

33. The inconvenience of a Judge's being party, as in contempts, is mitigated, or rather remedied, by *Appeal*.

Appeal in Contempts.

34. The Supreme Court of Appeal, being one of the 3 branches of the Supreme power, cannot be regularly appealed from: the only check to them, in the exercise of Judicial power, is in the other two co-ordinate branches.[2]

Appeal from the Lords.

The Appeal in this case is to the people: the people, as it were, Judges, the other two branches, as it were, Appellants.

35. It were an advantage in this one respect, if the branch of the supreme Legislative that exercises supreme judicative power, were that branch, which the supreme executive can dissolve.

Supreme Judicature dissolvable.

36. Something shall be done *by* you, says the Directory part of a Substantive Law: or if not, something, says the vindicatory part of it, shall be done *to* you—and this thing and that thing, say the Directory parts of so many Adjective Laws, shall be done by this person or that person to the end that it may be known whether the first thing has been done *by* you, or the second thing is to be done *to* you: if the latter is the case, then such an one shall do it to you.

Laws Substantive ⨯ Adjective—distinction.

37. Here is a plain distinction: and one that, on many occasions, it is requisite to bring into view. I would call the subjects of it by any name that should be thought proper. I would call Laws of the 1st sort Substantive, as they may be conceived by themselves, and Laws of the 2d sort Adjective, as these cannot: or Laws of the 1st sort *Prime* Laws, and Laws of the 2d sort *Secondary*: Laws of the 1st sort *Radical*, Laws of the 2d sort *Subservient*: or Laws of the 1st sort Principal, and Laws of the 2d sort Subsidiary, Mediatory, or Instrumental: Laws of the 1st sort Laws *in pays*, Laws concerning acts *in pays*, Laws of the 2d sort Laws *in foro*, Laws concerning acts *in foro*: Laws of the 1st sort *Prime*, Laws of the 2d sort Laws of

D°—various names for.

[a] **32. Note.** But observe *Contempts* and Prosecutions order'd for Perjury. They are set in motion *ab extra*, and they act in obedience to an act of Parliament, and Contempts are new causes in which they (if not the Crown) are Parties.[3]

[1] MS orig. 'By Sufferance.'

[2] i.e. the Crown and the House of Commons.

[3] For an account of contempts in the Common Law courts see Blackstone, *Commentaries on the Laws of England*, iv. 280–5, and for perjury see ibid. 136–8.

Procedure. I would call them by any of these names. It is the distinction that is of concernment (for it will be of use) and not the name. That name of all these is the best, that is most apt to excite an idea of the thing.

Legislature Supreme: *Divisum imperium.*[1]

38. Parts of a state that have been accustomed to submitt to the Will of the supreme power in it in all things in time past, must be understood as being [willing] to submitt to it in future. But nothing hinders men from engaging by express contract [to] submitt to one body as the supreme power in some thing, and to another body as the supreme power in another. So that the particulars in which they submitt to the first, can clearly be distinguished by description from the particulars in which they submitt to the second. The period of resistance, in which the subjection shall be dissolved, which in one case is left at large, is in the other ascertained.

Purpose of a Definition.

39. The *purpose* for which a word is defined, is to distinguish the idea belonging to it, from such different ideas as it might be in danger of being confounded with. This *purpose* is an *useful* purpose when[2]

40. The ideas which that properly belonging [to] the word Law are in danger of being confounded with are those of 1st a Simple command 2dly an incomplete command: [3dly] an aggregate of compleat, or of incomplete, commands, or of compleat with incompleat ones.

Domestic Powers.

41. Domestic Powers are powers exercised over fixed individuals certain.

Civil[3] Powers.

42. Civil Powers are powers exercised over a fluctuating body of uncertain individuals.

Civil Powers there are none over *persons* but what are *fiduciary*.

43. The Powers called [Civil] are created by the State: but Domestic Powers are so too: i:e: as far, but no farther, as not constituted by the Sanctions, Physical, Moral and Religious: no mark of distinction, therefore, between these two sorts of powers is to be taken from their origin.

Powers Civil X Domestic.

The Relations called civil are what are constituted by the Powers called Civil. The Powers stiled Civil are what are given by the state. Civil Powers have nothing to stand opposed to but Physical. Whatever power we speak of, not meaning a barely physical power, is a Civil one. {Salvo for Moral and Religious.} The

[1] i.e. 'divided jurisdiction'.

[2] The passage has been abandoned at this point.

[3] MS alt. 'Political'.

Relations stiled Natural are also constituted by the Powers called Civil. For they are constituted by Powers given by the State.

Power is created by Punishment.

44. The essence of Power over intelligent objects consists in the punishment impending over those who oppose it's exercise. Where there is such punishment, power is created by it: where there is no such punishment, no power is created.

Relations Domestic and Natural, *quot*?[2]

45. Relations Domestic there are [five]:[1] $1^{st.}$ That of Husband and Wife. $2^{d.}$ That of Parent and Child. $3^{dly.}$ That of Guardian and Ward. $4^{thly.}$ That of Master and Servant. 5. That of Tutor and Pupil.[3] Of these, the two first are termed Natural.[4]

In Relat:^{s} *Natural* the Powers are *Civil*.

46. It cannot, indeed, be said in strictness that the Relations themselves are created by the force of Law, by the power of the State: but the only occasions the Law can have of considering them result from power created by the state. The only occasion the Law can have to consider these relations, is that of the powers incident to those relations: and those powers are created by the State.

In Matrimony.

47. A Man and Woman copulate: in this the State, indeed, has no part: but this does not render them Husband and Wife. It does not give to either any of those powers which alone make the relation an object of notice.

In Paternity.

48. A Child is born of a Man and Woman. This, indeed, denominates the Man and Woman Parents, Father and Mother to the Child: and the Child, Son or Daughter to those the Parents. But this does not give to the Parents those *powers*, or to the child those rights, which make the relation the object of notice.

In Guardianship.

49. A relation or other friend may intermeddle in the management of the person or property of an orphan: but this does not make the intermeddler Guardian: nor the Orphan, Ward.

In Herility.

50. One man may do an act to promote the pleasure of another: but this does not make the 1st man Servant, nor the 2^{d} Master.[5]

Powers Matrimonial.

51. What makes the Man and Woman Husband and Wife is *powers* given by Law, in consequence of the contract of their Marriage. Powers given to the Wife over the possessions of the Husband. Powers given to the Husband over the possessions and person of the Wife. 'Tis punishment creates those powers.

[1] MS 'four'.

[2] i.e. 'how many?'

[3] See Blackstone, *Commentaries on the Laws of England*, i. 410, where the 'three great relations in private life' are listed as those of master and servant, husband and wife, and parent and child, with the latter giving rise to 'a fourth relation' of guardian and ward.

[4] According to Blackstone, the relation of husband and wife is 'founded in nature, but modified by civil society' (ibid.), while that of parent and child is 'the most universal relation in nature' (ibid. 434).

[5] In the text, Bentham has noted at this point: 'In Tutorship v. p. 66.' See para. 221, p. 95 below.

The Husband *may* (within certain bounds) deal as he pleases with the possessions of the Wife. He is not punishable for so dealing with them.[1] Any other person is: any other person is punishable for opposing him in so dealing. No person is punishable for assisting him in so dealing: any person is punishable for opposing those who assist him in so dealing.

Power)(Right.

52. The idea annexed to the word *Power* is larger than that annexed to the word Right. Wherever a man has a Power, he thereby has a Right. But it is not true (according to the common import of the two words), that wherever a man has a Right, he has a Power.

53. The difference lies in this: We say a Power to do; We say a Right to *get done*. What a man has a power to do, he *may* do, in the first instance, in his own person, without waiting for the licence of any other: {by his own physical agency: the act *may* be done by the person empowered himself, immediately as it is when pronounced for by his own *volition*.} What a man has only a *right* to *have done*, either *may* not be done by him at all, or at any rate not unless pronounced for by the will of some third person (for instance a Judge) to whose will the Law refers it.

Power Legal, how created.

Power, Legal Power to do an act, is conferred by the amotion of punishment from the doer {of the act in question}, and the transference of it on opposers.

What does the Law when it gives a man a Power? It leaves him free to do an act: and it punishes others who shall oppose him in it.

Power)(Right.

54. We say a man has *a power* to *do* a thing: we say a man has a *right* to *have* it *done*. Whatever a man has a *power* to do, he has a *right* to do: here *power* and *right* mean the same thing: they may be indiscriminately employ'd. But it is not true, that whatever a man has a right to *have* done, he has *power* to do: we might say, indeed, in this case, that he has *power* to *have* it *done*: but the phrase is not a common one.

Power)(Right: Example.

55. Any man has *power* to arrest a delinquent caught in an act of Robbery.[2] For he is not punishable for so doing, [while] any man is punishable for opposing him in so doing. One may equally say he has a *right* to do it. The one word does as well in this place as the other.

[1] For a husband's rights in relation to his wife's property see Blackstone, *Commentaries on the Laws of England*, ii. 433–6.

[2] According to ibid., iv. 289–90, private persons were obliged, 'on pain of fine and imprisonment', to arrest the perpetrator of a felony committed in their presence.

56. The same man, we say, has a right to money as a reward for arresting the delinquent, so he be convicted.[1] But the word *power* has no place here. It would be *ungrammatical* to say he has power *to* the reward: it would be loose and obscure to say, he has power *over* it. Power ⅹ Right.

57. But let us take another example, where the accompanying words and grammatical form of the sentences is in both cases the same.

58. A reward is offer'd by the Law to any man who shall apprehend a Robber (so that he be convicted). A certain man does apprehend a Robber: and the Robber is convicted. We say the apprehender has a *right* to the reward. We say not that he has a *Power.*

59. Let us observe, now, how the difference stands between the two cases in respect of punishment. A man has *power* to take his own goods: he may take them by force, if necessary, without consent of the robber from whom he takes them: he may take them himself of his own movement, let others do as they will.[2] He is not punishable if he do so. Any man is punishable that opposes him. The Law permits a man to take his own goods from a Robber, consenting or not consenting. We say he has a *power* to do so. We say also that he has a *right.*

60. Is this the case with the reward? no. He may take it, indeed: that is, peaceably, if given him by consent of a person appointed by Law to give it him, the Sheriff for instance, and not otherwise: for so taking it, he is not punishable: the Sheriff is punishable if he withold it.[3] The apprehender has a right to take it. At the same time, he may not take it by force, without consent of the Sheriff: he has not a *power* to take it, in this last sense of the word {power} and the word 'take': for he is punishable if he thus take it: and others are not punishable if they oppose him.

---

61. There is a well known division of rights among Jurists into perfect and imperfect.[4] Rights perfect ⅹ imperfect.

[1] For the rewards provided by statute for the apprehension and prosecution to conviction of various felons, including highwaymen, burglars, and housebreakers, see ibid. 291–2.

[2] According to ibid., iii. 4–5, by the 'natural right of recaption', the owner of stolen personal property was permitted to take back possession of it without recourse to the ordinary process of law, 'so it be not in a riotous manner, or attended with a breach of the peace'.

[3] The Apprehension of Highwaymen Act of 1692 (4 Wil. & Mar., c. 8, §2) required sheriffs to pay a reward of £40 to the apprehender of any person convicted of highway robbery. If the reward was not paid within a month of conviction, the sheriff became liable for twice the amount.

[4] See, for instance, Samuel Pufendorf, *De Officio Hominis et Civis Juxta Legem Naturalem,*

A right they call perfect where there is punishment appointed by Law for the violation of it: imperfect where there is none. Right imperfect created by the Moral or Religious Sanctions only, incapable of being created by the Political. Perfect such as are *capable* of being created by the Political. What is it, then, that in their conceptions constitutes the *right* in this latter case?[1] The supposed authority of the moral or religious Sanction.

Rights imperfect better not called Rights.

62. It were better not to use the word '*right*' (I mean '*a right*', the substantive) in this latter case; since it makes confusion, and is apt to give birth to false inferences in practise. Observance of a *perfect* right is matter of *Justice*, matter of *legal* obligation: observance of an *imperfect* right is matter of obligation merely moral.

Power and it's conjugates refer to Punishment.

63. The Substantives *Power*, *Right*, *Title*, *Duty*, *Obligation*, with their conjugates, whether Participles, Verbs, or Adjectives, also the Verbs *may* and *can*, which are quasi-conjugates to some of them, refer to punishment, and to Law, real or fictitious, by which punishment is appointed. By punishment they may be explained, and by nothing else.

Wherever these words occur, take away the idea of punishment, and you leave nothing.

{Right} Adj.)({*A* Right} Subst.

Right the Adjective imports only approbation of the speaker.

64. The same word used adjectively or substantively has two very different meanings: I *have a right* to have such a thing done for me: It *is right* such a thing should be done for me. In the latter phrase, the word {*right*} denotes nothing more than mere opinion: in the former, it refers to a matter of fact; the establishment of punishment by Law, for him who by Law ought to do for me the thing in question, and does not. It is right a child, unless in case of enormously undutiful misbehaviour, should have maintenance left him by a parent at the parent's decease in preference to a stranger: but I have not a right to it. I am unable to get my living: I have a right to sustenance from my parents: they are punishable if, being able, they do not give it me, but I have no *power* to take it: I am punishable if I do.

Law when compleat.

65. Rule whereby to know if a Law is compleat.

Consider the act Commanded by the Law: consider the punish-

London, 1673, Bk. I, Ch. IX, §4, pp. 84–5; Francis Hutcheson, *A Short Introduction to Moral Philosophy, in three books; containing the Elements of Ethicks and the Law of Nature*, Glasgow, 1747, pp. 122–3; and John Taylor, *Elements of the Civil Law*, 3rd edn., London, 1769, p. 88.

[1] i.e. in the case of the imperfect right. Bentham is referring back to the first sentence in the paragraph.

ment appointed for non-performance of that act. If there be any case in which it is to be supposed that he who made the Law would not wish to have the command observed, or not that punishment inflicted (i.e. in case of the command's not being observed), the Law is not to be conceived as a compleat one, till a proposition be annexed to the Law expressive of that exception: that is, till a proposition expressive of that case be conceived as annexed in limitation of the principal proposition that commands.

66. Therefore, a large volume, or many large volumes, may be written, promulgated authoritatively by the supreme power, on matter of Law, without containing a single entire thing of that sort which is properly signified by the term Law: it may consist entirely of propositions limitative, and of propositions limiting those propositions; having but one common principal proposition to which they all belong, and that not expressed but understood. This may in particular be the case with the Jurisprudence of Contracts. Whole Books may consist of Fragments. Law compleat, a—may not be found in a whole Book.

---

67. A particular command given to a Wife, a Child, a Ward, a Servant, to a stranger by a stranger uncommissioned by the supreme power, is not a Law, because the motive to it is not derived from the volition of the state, the punishment is not applied by the Executive-Judicial power of the State. What Commands are not Laws.[1]

---

68. We all know but too well what pain is. It is a simple idea. It is felt: it is not to be defined. Pain.

69. Punishment is Pain inflicted *for* an act done. Punishment.

70. Punishment is said to be inflicted *for* an act, a man is said to be punished *for* an act, when, that act done, the punishment is suffer'd: when, that act or some other act punished in like manner not done, the punishment is not suffer'd: in other words, when the idea of the act done that is to be punished, is, in the mind of him who inflicts or who appoints the punishment, a cause of the act of punishing. Punishment *for* an act.

71. We all know, it is to be hoped, what *Pleasure* is: it is to be felt: it is not to be defined. Pleasure.

72. Reward is to Pleasure, what Punishment is to Pain. Reward.

---

73. A limitative proposition, when detached from the proposition Proviso.

[1] In the margin, Bentham has noted at this point: 'p. 35.' See para. 145, p. 81 below.

or propositions which it limits, is termed, in our Statute Book, a Proviso.

A Law)(a Statute: Fish.

74. A Law and a Statute agree in this: the matter of them is the same. For all this, what men speak of when they say *a Statute*, is not the same thing altogether as what we have been describing under the name of *Law*. A Statute has generally either more or less of that matter than what serves to make either an entire Law or any number of entire Laws. By accident, the matter in a Statute may be as much as amounts to one or more entire Laws, neither more nor less; but it would be difficult, I believe, to find an instance of it. In general, a Statute consists of fragments.

Non bene junctarum discordia semina rerum.[1]

A Law)(A Statute: Fish.

75. Mr Bergman[2] of Upsala in Sweden, if his word were to be taken, by certain tricks he plaid with the spawn of fishes, produced a whimsical race of beings. He got, every now and then, two heads joined together, or two tails joined together, instead of a head and a tail: all alive and lusty. Mr Bergman doubtless said the thing that is not. It is much easier to find ten such story-tellers than one such Fish. However, existing or not existing, they may serve as alike by way of Emblem. Mr | |'s Fish are to common Fish, what a Statute is to a Law.

Law)(Edict. Law (Matter) Durability.

76. 5th[3] Susceptibility of Duration—Durability.

1.[4] It must be issued by Government.

Let us see what is Government.

State Commands if not executive are repealative *pro tanto* of Laws.

77. Commands that are backed by the force of the Political Sanction, if not *orders* in execution of some General Law, are *exceptions* to some General Law.

Exception—or Regulation—is Repeal *pro tanto*.

78. To take an exception to a General Law is, *pro tanto*, to repeal it. To repeal a Law is a Power equal to that of enacting it.

[1] i.e. ‘a rough, unordered mass of things’, Ovid’s description of primordial chaos in *Metamorphoses*, I. 9.

[2] In the text, Bentham has noted after Bergman’s name ‘Qu.’, indicating that he was unsure whether the account of the fish came from Torbern Olof Bergman (1735–84), Swedish chemist and mineralogist, Professor of Chemistry at the University of Uppsala. Bentham was later involved in the translation of Bergman’s work that appeared as *An Essay on the Usefulness of Chemistry and its Application to the Various Occasions of Life* (first published in German in 1779), London, 1783 (see Bentham to Samuel Bentham, 3–11 January 1780, *The Correspondence of Jeremy Bentham*, vol. ii, ed. T.L.S. Sprigge, London, 1968 (*CW*), p. 377 & n.) No account by Bergman of the experiment described by Bentham has been traced.

[3] It is unclear why this is listed as the fifth point.

[4] Bentham does not list any further points.

79. Hence it appears that a Command, tho' particular, from persons in authority, in order not to run counter to a General Law, must be issued in execution of some General Law: must be issued under it: must be issued in virtue of it's prescription: must be a command to an individual or individuals of some of those *sorts* of acts for which there is a Law commanding them: viz. either a Law *real*, or a Law fictitious.

Regulation Exceptive. Exception is Repeal *pro tanto.*

---

80. A Volition for which there is no other Sanction than a Premiary one, such a volition, tho' expressed by Government, is not a Law. It is not a Law: because it is not a Command. It is not a Command: because the party willing does not stand in the station of a superior in respect of the party whose act is the object of the wish; it does not stand in the station of a superior to him because he can be in no certainty of attaining what he wishes.

Law X Invitation.

---

81. Parents, Husbands, &c., tho' their commands are invested with a Sanction from the state, are not understood as being a branch of Government.

Law X Domestic Command.

82. A Command, tho' Authoritative, is not a Law issued by persons having power to command, if the personal object of that power is assignable: viz. some particular individual or individuals who can at any time be numerically described.

Law regards *Sorts* of Actions.

---

83. The parts of a Law, that is the parts that do or may go to the making up of a compleat Law, are of 4 sorts.

Parts of a Law.

84. First, a Principal Regulation.[1] A command to do some thing or not to do it under a penalty, pointing out a mode of conduct as the object of volition.

Secondly, Propositions Definitional or Definitive,[3] including Definition, Distinction, Enumeration, &c.

Thirdly, Propositions Limitative or Restrictive.

Fourthly, Propositions conditioning.

4 Sorts of Propositions: 1. Regulation[2] Principal. 2. Regulation Conditionalizing. 3. Regulation Exceptive to either. 4. Regulation Expository to any of the three.

85. To the creation of all the different sorts of Property in the Kingdom, there goes, properly speaking, but one Law. The directory part—the principal proposition announcing the command—is throughout one and the same. The Armature, or that part which predicts so much punishment as is necessary for the

Exemplified in A Law of Property.

[1] MS orig. 'Proposition'.

[2] MS orig. 'proposition' in each occurrence of 'Regulation' in this marginal heading. Bentham presents the propositions in a different order in the text.

[3] MS orig. 'Expository'.

purpose of creating the right, is also throughout one and the same.

Directory Part.

86. The Principal Proposition of the Directory part commands persons in general to abstain from such acts in general as tend to hinder a man from doing what he pleases with an Immoveable thing that is his own.

Comminatory, Threatening Part.[a]

87. The Principal Proposition of the Sanctional part declares what in general shall be the punishment for the person who does what he has been thus commanded not to do.

—in a Law of Property: Expository Part.

88. An Expository[1] part enumerates the various acts or events by any of which an immoveable article may become a man's own. It enumerates the different *Titles* to such property.

—Is various according to the various *Titles*.

89. The Descriptions given by this Definitional part vary, one sees, with every different species of Title. So much of the Jurisprudence on the head of Property as enumerates and states the nature of the different sorts of Titles consists, therefore, of a number [of] Definitional propositions.

—How compleatable into a Law.

90. These, in order to be compleated, any of them, into Laws are to be conceived as being tacked to a Directory proposition and a Sanctional of the purport that has been mentioned.

Exceptive Part or Limitative or Restrictive. Number and [. . .?] of the Tenant.[?]

91. The *Power* is limited, that is the Mass of acts which the Proprietary is permitted to do, and other men are commanded not to hinder him from doing, is limited: 1st in respect of the persons that are thus prohibited from doing the like acts. 2. The time in and during which the doing of those acts is permitted.

None of these parts of itself a Law.

92. It is not a Proposition on any of these topics that can constitute a Law: for by none of them, nor all of them together, is there any Will expressed.

A Law compleat concern[g] Property difficult to assign.

93. The idea of a Law is much easier collected from a regulation of Police than from an article of Jurisprudence concerning a sort of property. Why? because the object of a Law of Police is some *principal* act, that of a Law of Property, Circumstances.

[a] 'Tis the name that *Ovid* gives it: *Nec verba mina[n]tia fixo aere legebantur,* speaking of the Golden Age.[2]

---

[1] MS orig. 'Definitional or Explanatory'.

[2] See Ovid, *Metamorphoses*, i. 89–92:

> *Aurea prima sata est aetas, quae vindice nullo,*
> *sponte sua, sine lege fidem rectumque colebat.*
> *Poena metusque aberant, nec verba minantia fixo*
> *aere legebantur . . . .*

i.e. 'Golden was that first age, which, with no one to compel, without a law, of its own will, kept faith and did the right. There was no fear of punishment, no threatening words were to be read on brazen tablets'.

94. Besides those Powers over an article of property with which the Law invests a man as Proprietary, it communicates to him a portion of Legislative power whereby he is enabled to invest other persons with the whole, or a portion, of the same powers. —in a Law of Conveyancing.

---

95. It is painful for a man to turn his thoughts into an entire new channel. Prefatoria. Apology for Abstruseness.[1]

For the terms of a discourse to be familiar to the ear is one thing: for it to be understood or to be intelligible is a very different one. A discourse containing words in it meant to convey complex ideas is never made intelligible, till the simple ideas involved in those complex ones are made assignable. This Locke has said.[2] Whatever else of his saying has been controverted; this never has been controverted; and, I suppose, never will be.

Abstruse is the opposite to familiar. Discourse on this topic, to be new and just, cannot be otherwise than abstruse. A discourse that calls men to a task so painful as that of searching into the recesses of their thoughts, and trying whether they have clear ideas annexed to the terms they use, cannot but be irksome.

---

96. The description of a compleat Law varies according to the different articles it may have for it's subject matter.

We will endeavour to shew what it takes to make it compleat in each case. For this purpose, the whole Law must pass under review.

97. The Ends of the Law are either to secure men's persons against pain: or against the loss of such instruments of pleasure as they have: or to put them in a way of acquiring more. This it aims at by means of two operations, those of Power and Restraint. Ends[3] of Law.

98. Correspondent to these several ends, it has various functions. Different Functions of Law.

99. 1st. It restrains acts of persons upon persons. 1. Law restrains Personal Mischief.

100. 2. It gives to persons power over, or in other words gives them right to, *things*—the instruments of pleasure: by restraining acts of other persons upon those things. 2. Gives Right to Things.

101. 3. It adopts and sanctions Contracts, that is it gives powers, or rather rights, to persons to compel other persons to 3. Adopts Contracts.

[1] MS orig. 'obscurity'.

[2] John Locke (1632–1704), philosopher, had argued that complex ideas consisted of combinations of simple ideas in *An Essay concerning Human Understanding* (first published in 1689), ed. P.H. Nidditch, Oxford, 1975, Bk. II, Ch. XXII, pp. 288–95.

[3] The words '(*pene generalissima*)' follow at this point, but their meaning is obscure.

improve such instruments of pleasure as they have undertaken to improve, or in other ways to do such acts, subservient to the pleasure of the parties empowered, as the parties bound have undertaken to do.

4. Adopts Conveyances. **102.** 4. It adopts and sanctions Dispositions of the instruments of pleasure, to have effect in the life time of the disposers.

5. Adopts Wills. **103.** 5. It adopts and sanctions Dispositions of the same instruments, to have effect not till after the death of the disposers.

6. Establishes Successions. **104.** 6. It disposes of instruments of pleasure left undisposed of at the death of the Proprietary.

7. Gives Domestic Powers *beneficial*. **105.** 7. It confers and limits powers to persons over persons to do such acts upon the party bound as are subservient to the pleasure of the party empower'd. Conjugal, Parental, Tutelary, Herile Powers.

8. Gives Domestic Powers upon Trust. **106.** 8. It gives and limits powers upon *Trust*. Powers to be employ'd to purposes other than that of subserviency to the pleasure of the Party empower'd.

Prefatoria. Perspicuity necessary. **107.** This is one of the first and most indispensable tasks of one who writes a work of the institutional kind,[1] to give a clear notion what sort of a thing that is of which he is discoursing.

Power Beneficial. **108.** The end it proposes for the power to be applied to is either the *benefit* of the party himself who is empower'd, or of some other.[2]

Power to his own use X Power fiduciary. **109.** In the first case, the Power may be said to be a Power Beneficial, or *to his own use*:[a] in the second, a Power fiduciary, or *upon Trust*.

Powers on Trust. **110.** In Powers upon Trust, there are concerned two parties. The party empower'd, The Trustee: and the party for whose benefitt the other is empower'd, called, in the Elliptical Language of our Jurisprudence, the *Cestuy que Trust*, more fully *Cestuy al benefit de qui le Trust est crée*. In English, 'He for whose benefit the Trust is created.'

110.[3] 9thly. It gives *Public* or *Constitutional* Powers.

1. It creates Offices holden in severalty. 2. It creates Offices holden in conjunction. 3. It gives to Officers Rights to Things: viz:

[a] Autochrestic.

[1] MS orig. 'a book of institutes'.

[2] In the margin, Bentham has noted at this point: 'v. N. Def. 25, 26.' The cross-reference is obscure: paras. 108–10 themselves appear on pp. 25–6 of the manuscript.

[3] Bentham has given two paragraphs the number 110.

Instruments of Security. 4. It gives to Officers *Rights* to *Money*, the common pledge and substitute of Instruments as well of security as of pleasure. 5. It gives Powers Military. 6. It gives Powers Forensic. These are: 7. Powers to inflict punishment personally. 8. Powers to direct the infliction of Punishment. 9thly. Powers to stop the infliction of Punishment. 10thly. Powers of Arrest. 11thly. Powers of Seizure. 12. Powers of Search (Powers occasional and *extra-ordinary* over things). 13. Rights *Consiliary*. Rights of being heard in giving Opinion concerning the exercise of any of the above-mentioned Rights or Powers.

Incorporeal Hereditaments.[1]

111. An Advowson is a right of *Conveying*, not of enjoying, an Office, viz: Ecclesiastical.[a] The Glebe, Tithes, and Dues form together the Premium[2] annexed to that Office. Advowsons.

112. Tithes are Taxes imposed for the purpose of raising such Premium.[3] Tithes.

113. Common is a Right of the beneficial kind to a thing, an article of property: viz: to a thing which, to other purposes, is another man's. It is created by taking off, from the party empower'd, the penalty with respect to such acts to the exercise of which the right extends. Common.

114. Way, is another Right of the Private Beneficial kind. Way.

[115.] Offices give Powers of the Public or Constitutional kind upon Trust. The Profits annexed to them consist of Taxes. They form a Premiary Sanction to enforce the acceptance of the Office. The Right to take them is a Right of the *Private beneficial* kind. Office.

[116.] Dignities, mere naked Dignities without Official Power or Profit, are Draughts drawn by those who have the disposal of the Political Sanction upon the managers for a portion of the Moral Præmiary Sanction. A Dignity conveys no right, except it be to the using the *signs* of the dignity: and this is of the Private Beneficial kind. Dignities.

[117.] Franchises sporting are Rights of the Private beneficial kind. They are Interests *in*, or *partial* rights to, Property immoveable. Franchises, sporting.

[a] The Right of performing Divine Service &c. is a Power upon Trust.

---

[1] For Blackstone's discussion of this topic, which Bentham is following here, see *Commentaries on the Laws of England*, ii. 20–43.

[2] MS orig. 'Premiary Sanction'.

[3] Bentham has marked the following passage, which appears in the text at this point, for deletion: 'The Right to them is a Right originally of the Public kind. Qu.'

Franchises of derelicts.

[**118.** Franchises of Waifs, Strays and Wrecks, &c., are Rights of succession to Things Derelict. Premiums to a Public Office, viz: the Royal, transferred to private hands.

Franchises Official.

[**119.** Other Franchises than these are Offices.

Corodies.

[**120.** Corodies (the Right of presenting to) are Rights of Conveying a Right to unliquidated Articles of Property.

το κοινον[1] in the 3 Sorts.

[**121.** Observe what these three sorts of things have in common to make them be called by the same name, Franchises.[2]

Law different from a Resolution. 1st of Opinion. A resolution of Opinion tho' of the power that makes Laws.

122. Those whose Commands are Laws conceive a Resolution of Opinion and record, that is give it a permanent expression. But this does not make it a Law. For this is an expression of an act of the Judgment, but it is an act of the Will of which a Law is an expression.

2[d] | | of Will)(of Opinion.

123. There are two sorts of acts of the supreme power in this country, or of a part of it, the expression of which goes by the name of a Resolution—one is an act of the Judgment. It may be termed a Resolution of Opinion. The other is an act of the Will: it may be termed a Resolution of Volition.

A Resolution of *Volition* is an act of Volition which, for it's object, has no other act than an act of the party himself who resolves.

An act of the *Judgment* is one thing: an act of the Will is another. Nothing but an act of the Will can be a *Law*. To an act merely of the Judgment, the term a *Law* has never been applied.

A Resolution of Opinion in a Legislator may govern an act of Volition: it may be the cause of it. So is it in a private person: but it is not on that account itself an act of Volition. It is not on that account a Law. For it is not a *Command*.

Prefatoria.

124. Neither Rights nor Powers are created but by *Command*, enforced by *Punishment*. It is the signification of the Command, coupled with the signification of the Punishment, that composes the Law.

Corodies.

125. Corodies (the thing presented to) are rights to certain unliquidated articles of Property: viz: so much of the eatables and drinkables to be met with in a certain place, as are requisite to the sustenance of the Coroder.

Annuity.

An Annuity is a Right to Money to be paid at stated intervals.

Rent charge and Rent-seck.

126. A Rent charge, or Rent-seck, is a Right to a certain sum of money, or mass of articles of moveable property, the payment of

[1] i.e. 'the common element'.

[2] This paragraph appears to consist in Bentham's instruction to himself.

which is annexed as a condition to the Right to the article of immoveable property on account of which the Rent is made payable, and out of which it is said to issue.

127. A Rent-Service is a private beneficial right of persons over persons: a right of having certain acts done to the benefit of the party entitled, the doing of which is annexed as a condition to the Right to the article of immoveable property out of which the Rent issues. Rent-Service.

128. By the Laws that create Tithes,[1] Commons, Ways and Sporting Franchises, are created a sort of limited and limiting *Parasitical* engrafted rights, carved out from more extensive Rights of immoveable property. They may have one and the same individual substance for their subject matter as other Rights, and one of them as another. Rights with a Common Subject. Rights engrafted.

---

129. ☛ Shew all along the *material substance*, that is the *subject-matter* of the Law in these several cases. —Physical. Memorandum. Subject-matter of.

---

130. The *Expository*[2] matter annex'd to the Law adopting contracts consists of Propositions declaring: 1st what act, or assemblage of acts, in the several cases that may be put, creates a contract: 2dly when a contract, having been made, shall be understood to be fulfilled. It is in the cases where it is not fulfilled, that the punishment applied by the Law attaches. Law of Compacts. Expository matter.

131. The *Limitative* or *exceptional* matter consists of propositions declaring what Contracts shall be invalid. Exceptive matter.

132. Foreign *Conditional* matter it has none: each Promise is a condition of the other. Conditionalizing matter.

---

133. Laws creating Estates in Fee Simple do two things. Laws creating Fee Simple.

1st. To the Holder himself they give: 1st the power of using *durante vitâ*; 2dly the power of Alienation *durante vitâ*; 3dly *post obitum*, by Will. 2dly. To others—in respect of their relation to him: viz: his Heirs, they establish the same right in succession. Subject always to Dower, unless barred.

134. Laws creating *Qualified*, or in other words *Base Fees*, give all the aforesaid powers, but liable to be defeated, all of them together, by a *condition*. Fees Qualified.

135. Laws creating Fees conditional at Common Law give the first power alone absolutely: viz: the power of using to the Holder: Fees Conditional.

[1] Bentham has marked the word 'Tithes' for deletion.

[2] MS orig. 'explanatory or *Definitional* or Definitive'.

together with the other before-mention'd powers upon a condition: viz: that of the Holder's having an Heir of his body.

Power &c. Definition of. Prefatoria.

136. One definition of the word Power and it's Relatives must serve once for all: for it were endless to substitute at every turn the Definition for the thing defined. But we must carry with us all along the idea of punishment, and of the manner in which it is applied to create the *power*, whatever it is, otherwise no determinate idea will be annext to it.

Fees Tail.

137. A Law that created Fee Tail would, as it stands at present, give to the instant holder the 1st power, the power of using. $2^{dly.}$ To others of a more limited description, in virtue of their relation to him, the like power in succession. $3^{dly.}$ In default of those persons, the Reversion, in Fee Simple, to the Donor or his Heirs. 4. In default of them, to the King.[1]

Subjects of Property.

138. The several Subjects, or (to use another word) Articles of Property are the several sorts of Substances, the physical bodies that surround us: Animals, those even of our own species, not excluded.

Differentiation, according to their use. Instruments of Pleasure. —Security.

139. The value these are, any of them, of to us is either 1st as instruments of pleasure: 2dly as instruments of security.

139.[2] An instrument of security is either an instrument of defence, or of offence; or both in one.

Things {Valuable {Posses. Not Posses. Not val.

Things, considered with respect to their subserviency to Man's use, are either Articles of Value, or not of Value. Articles of Value are either Articles of Property, or not of Property.

Money.

140. Money is the common pledge, substitute and measure of the several instruments whether of pleasure or of security. He who has money in a certain quantity may, generally speaking, have any of them in exchange. He who has any of them may have money in exchange. How this comes to be the case is matter of consideration for a work of another sort: it is sufficient for the purpose of the present, that the fact is so.

Article of Com. Law, not a Law.

141. 'Stealing is punished with hanging.' The proposition in our Jurisprudence, as an universal one, is not true:[3] but to cut

[1] In the text, Bentham has noted at this point: 'Establishes Succession in this wise.'

[2] Bentham has given two paragraphs the number 139.

[3] The general rule was that all persons convicted of grand larceny, the theft of property to

matters short, we will suppose it so. This is not a Law, nor any part of one.

Of such articles consists the Common Law. In the infancy of our Jurisprudence, the Saxon Laws being, either by oblivion or by express repeal, superseded, and no others substituted in the room of them, there was no such thing as any Command to men not to steal: but if a man stole, an order went out to another man to go and hang him.

A maxim of Common Law is collected, indeed, from Commands: but from what Commands? from Commands to whom adressed? [From][1] commands adressed, not to those whose acts the Maxim, when framed, is supposed to govern, but to some other persons.

---

142. A Command is a Rule of action.[2] It may be so. What do we get by this? The term command itself is a plain expression. It suggests directly and without ambiguity a known idea, and that a simple one. The phrase '*A Rule of Action*' is a metaphorical expression: the best that can be said of it is that it may serve to suggest indirectly and figuratively the same simple idea that is directly and familiarly expressed by the term *command*. Command a '*Rule of Action*'.

143. An order of a Judge or Executive Officer is not a Law because not capable of being ***permanent***, not extending to persons in Succession. Judicial Order.[3]

144. Rules of a Voluntary Society, an Assembly of diversion, The Society of Arts, a Club, not Laws (tho' permanent, as extending to persons in succession), because they have not any part of the Political sanction to enforce them. Voluntary Society.

145. Domestic Orders have the Political sanction to enforce them: for if a Son resist a Father during a certain period, a Pupil his Tutor, a Wife her Husband, a Ward his Guardian, a Servant his Master, the Law will inflict punishment for such resistance.[5] Domestic Orders.[4]

a value greater than 12d., were to be hanged, but in some instances offenders were entitled to benefit of clergy, while juries might undervalue the goods stolen: see Blackstone, *Commentaries on the Laws of England*, iv. 238–9.

[1] MS 'To'.

[2] Cf. Blackstone, *Commentaries on the Laws of England*, i. 38: 'Law, in it's most general and comprehensive sense, signifies a rule of action; and is applied indiscriminately to all kinds of action, whether animate, or inaminate, rational or irrational.'

[3] In the margin, Bentham has noted at this point: 'Princ.[s] p. 11. Inserenda p. 41.' The former cross-reference is to 'PP: Introduction', para. 35, p. 436 below, where Bentham intended to insert paras. 143–4. The latter cross-reference is to para. 160, p. 85 below, which Bentham may have intended to follow paras. 143–4.

[4] In the margin, Bentham has noted at this point: 'v. 21.' See para. 67, p. 71 above.

[5] For the power of the master to correct his servant, and the husband to correct his wife,

Private Laws.[1]

146. A particular act of the Legislature made to dispense with the Law, tho' the dispensation be transient in it's nature as not extending to persons in succession, is still a Law, for it is *pro tanto* a repeal of Laws that are permanent in their nature. These are those to which the appellation of Private Acts should be confined. The others now called Private might be stiled Local or Particular (in respect of person) Acts. So is a Law made to impose a new obligation for this is virtually a dispensation, a repeal *pro tanto* of the Laws which protected him before in resisting such obligation.

Prefat.—Definitions justified.

147. The idea suggested by the term act is an idea easily and immediately resolvable into it's component simple ones. An act is motion or the stoppage of it. The idea of motion or the stoppage of it is a simple idea: the Motion is always the motion of some substance that moves. That substance, whatever it be, if it make itself perceived to us, it is by means of the particular modifications it presents to us of figure, colour and impenetrability: of all which modifications, the ideas we have are simple ones.

The idea of pain is also a simple one.

The idea of association between two events, the action and the punishment for it, this idea, such as it is, is, I suppose, a simple one.

Proceeding in this way, we lose not sight of simple ideas for a moment: we take not a single step without having hold of a chain of definitions terminating ultimately in an assemblage of simple ideas as in it's last link. Beyond this, the power of words can never reach.

Law, a)(Statute.

148. I cannot say that a Statute is not a Law: for if I did, usage would contradict me. But this I say: that it does not correspond to the idea I would wish to have exclusively annext to the word Law.

What be mean[t] when we say a Statute has that appellation, a known and fixed appellation, by which it stands distinguished from every thing else? I could wish that[2]

1. Resolution of opinion not a Law. Example.

149. 'Resolved that General Warrants are illegal.'[3] This is not a Law: tho' it was an act of one branch out of three of which the

servants, and children, see Blackstone, *Commentaries on the Laws of England*, i. 416, 432–3, 440.

[1] In the margin, Bentham has noted at this point: 'If a Command wanted the volition of the Legislative body to warrant it, it was because acts of that same body were to be controuled by it.'

[2] The passage has been abandoned at this point.

[3] The question of the legality of general warrants had been raised following the arrest in 1763 of John Wilkes (1725–97), MP for Aylesbury 1757–64 and Middlesex 1768–9, 1774–90, for seditious libel, which culminated in his expulsion from the House of Commons on 19 January 1764. Although the House of Commons passed a motion in favour of the legality of general warrants on 17 February 1764, their use was effectively ended by decisions made by William Murray (1705–93), first Baron and first Earl of Mansfield, Chief Justice of King's Bench 1756–88 on 18 June 1764 and 8 November 1765.

supreme power, the Legislature, in this country is composed. It would not have been tho' it had been an act of all the three. For it would have been but a Resolution of Opinion.

150. 'Resolved that this House will on Friday resolve itself into a Committee to consider of the legality of General Warrants.' This was not a Law. It was, indeed, a Volition, but whose was the act to which it was directed? It was the act of no other than the assembly itself by which the volition was conceived. 2. Resolution of Volition not a Law. Example.

151. 'Lewis, my people shall be at peace with thine.' This is not a Law. For it is but a Resolution expressed to do those acts, to issue those commands, which shall make the people of him who speaks at peace with those of Lewis, who is spoken to. 3. A Promise not a Law. Example.

152. 'Lewis, my people shall be at peace with thine, upon condition that thy people be at peace with mine.' 4. Nor a *Compact* a Law. Example.

'George, my people shall be at peace with thine, upon condition that thy people be at peace with mine.' Still this is not a Law: for it is but a pair of Promises: and it is not a thousand pair of promises that can constitute a Command.

153. 'All men within the Manor of Dale carry their corn to John Trot's Mill': the successive assemblage of spontaneous acts hereby spoken [of] is not a Law. For to be one of many who, for a length of time, have, without commanding, carried their corn to John Trot's Mill is one thing: to command them to carry it there is another. 5. Nor a Custom. Example.

154. 'Parents in general maintain their children. What causes them so to do is an instinctive affection implanted in their breasts.' The idea, such as it is, of this instinctive affection is not a Law: nor yet the words expressing it a Law. For a succession of sentiments of love or any other passion, or the idea of such a succession, is one thing: but a Command is another and a very different one. 6. Nor an imaginary *Cause* of Uniformity among *Actions*.

155. All bodies near the earth have a tendency to move towards it's center. The cause of this is Attraction of Gravity. The Sap ascends between the solid parts of vegetables. The cause of this is Attraction of Cohesion. 'Attraction of Gravity' and 'Attraction of Cohesion' are not Laws. For a Law is a Command. But neither is the vague idea of an unknown cause of an assemblage of visible effects, nor the phrase used to denote it, any thing like a Command. Not knowing, nor being able to shew, the Cause of all these motions and their uniformity, we find a name for it to mark it by, in case it ever should be known; and, in the mean time, to express what we are in quest of. 7. Nor an imaginary cause of Uniformity among *phænomena*.

156. Parents feed their young. It is their Custom, but this custom is not a Law. 'It is of advantage to a community that Parents should feed their young.' The custom, in Parents, of maintaining 8. Nor a Dictate of Utility.

their children is an useful one. In saying this, I have made no Law: I give a reason, I alledge a fact. I vouch experience, I allege the existence of certain pains and pleasures which men have felt in themselves or observed in others. This is to give a reason for an article of conduct. Every other pretended reason is but empty declamation. This I say. This is my opinion. I do suppose that it is true: I do suppose that nobody will dispute it. But [it] is never the nearer being a Law. For to say that it would be useful for people to do thus or thus is one thing: but to command them to do so is another.

Laws Spurious adopted by Montesquieu.

NOTE. 157.[1] The 5th, 6th, 7th and 8th of these articles stand jumbled together under the common name of Law by Montesquieu throughout his work:[2] in the first book of it in particular. Nothing can be more brilliant than the style of that whole book: nothing can be less intelligible.[3] In this he copied others, beginning with the ancients: and others have copied him: and most others continue still to copy him: which is the reason that most others, when they use the word Law, know not what it is they mean. Nor will men ever know exactly what it is they mean by it, till, as it were, with a common consent, they can persuade themselves to purge it of these it's heterogeneous senses.

A Point of History.

A point of History is not a Law. For a point of History is any sort of act whatever, considered as past, and at an end. But a Law is the expression of a Command.

A Passage of History.

A passage of History is but a set of signs serving to communicate the belief of the Historian concerning a point of History.

Supreme Power in Government.

157.[4] The supreme power in a state is *that person*, or *those persons acting in a body*, whose commands touching any matter all the rest of the persons in the state are in the habit of observing or enforcing, himself or themselves being commanded by none.

Body, to act in a.

158. A number of persons are said to *act in a body* when the wills of the greater number of them assembled together are taken for a command, those of the lesser number going for nothing.

[1] Bentham has added the words 'NOTES to pp. 9, 10, and 11' at the head of the page on which para 157 is written. See 'PP: What a Law is', pp. 448–9 n., 449–50 n. below.

[2] Charles Louis de Secondat, Baron de la Brède et de Montesquieu (1689–1755), French political philosopher and social commentator, was author of *De l'esprit des loix*, 2 vols., Geneva, 1748, translated into English by Thomas Nugent (*c.* 1700–72) as *The Spirit of Laws*, 2 vols., London, 1750.

[3] MS del. 'That book may be considered a master-piece of brilliant confusion.'

[4] Bentham has given two paragraphs the number 157.

159. A Law is said to be *enforced* when punishment is inflicted on any for disobeying it. Enforced.

---

160. A command which is temporary by it's own nature, and not merely by express appointment, it is not usual to term a Law. Such a Command is either stiled a Command simply, or more frequently an Order: tho' 'Order' is sometimes applied also to persisting Laws. Order.[1]

161. Coming from the King, it is stiled a Proclamation: tho' Proclamations there are which have the character of permanent persisting Laws. Proclamation.

162. Coming from a Judge in his own name, or in the name of the King when fictitiously spoken of as acting in a Judicial Capacity, it is sometimes stiled a *Writ*. Writ.

163. That Command is temporary by nature, whereof the act that [is] commanded, the person that is the object, the thing that is the subject, are numerically assignable. Command; in what case temporary by Nature.

164.[2] A Command, to be a Law, must be such as, by possibility, may subsist and have effect for ever, at least for a term to which no numerical limit can be assigned. Law)(Command temporary.

Writ is the name given to those Precedents of Commands that began to be in use at the first establishment of Procedure: those that have been devised of modern times have been stiled Rules or Orders. Writ.

165. Enumerate them. Receipt to the Sheriff, Warrant of a Justice, Writ, Rule, Order. Judiciary Commands—Synonyma.

165.[3] The Expository matter of a Law fixes the import of the command: this it does by shewing at large what objects are the objects of it, out of those concerning which, it is supposed, a doubt could arise whether they were objects of it or not. Definitive or Expository matter.

166. The Limitative matter narrows the description of the command: this it does by declaring that such an object is not the object of it, out of those concerning which, it is supposed, would be deemed objects of the Law, were it not for such restriction. Limitative or Restrictive matter is one species of Expository—as also is Exceptive.

167. Conditional matter is either conditional to the act commanded, or conditional to the punishment. Conditional.

[1] In the margin, Bentham has noted at this point: 'v. 34, 35.' See paras. 143–4, p. 81 above, to which Bentham may have intended this paragraph to form a continuation.

[2] In the text, Bentham has noted at this point: '☛ Mem. Look at some Precedents of Writs. &c.'

[3] Bentham has given two paragraphs the number 165.

Expository matter.

168. It does something towards ascertaining the number and identity of the species or individuals meant to be included in the general terms employ'd, which might or might not, it is supposed, be understood to be included under them.

Exceptive.

169. It discards some species or some individuals meant to be excluded out of the import of the general terms employ'd, and which, it is supposed, would be understood to be included were it not for such express exclusion.

Conditional matter.

170. The Conditional matter pronounces under what condition the Command shall, and under what it shall not, have it's effects. A Condition is[1]

Law of Security.

171. The General Law in behalf of Personal Security is that no man shall *do* any thing to—that is exert any act on the person of—any other man against that other's *will*: that is make the person of another man the object of any act of his.

Law of Liberty.

172. The General Law in behalf of Personal Liberty is that no man shall do any act whereby the motion of any other man's person may be prevented or impeded.

Laws of Property.

173. To these two Laws, one or other, or both, the Laws constitutive of Property form so many exceptions.

Laws Constitutional.

174. So also do the Laws constitutive of Constitutional Powers. Laws giving Constitutional Rights are exceptions to and defences against Laws constitutive of Constitutional Powers.

'A Law' shall express a *Single* Command.

176.[2] There will, every now and then, be occasion to speak of a Command without speaking of the punishment by which it is enforced If the member of the assumed discourse that is expressive of the command, and the other member expressive of the punishment, were to be spoken of as together constituting but one Law, some other appellation must be found to express the first of these members by itself. Now there is no such appellation comprized in a single word.

This will save words &c.

177. The appellation, such as it is, that has been used for this purpose (tho' as the topic has been little scrutinized, even this appellation has been but little used) is a phrase consisting of many words. '*The directory part of a Law*' is the appellation I am speaking of.

The objections to this are: 1st that it consists of so many words. 2dly that it draws the attention to the old, obscure and indefensible division of which it has passed as a member. The division, I mean, of a Law into 4 parts: viz: this for one: the declaratory, the remedial

[1] The passage has been abandoned at this point.

[2] There is no para. 175.

and the sanctional for the others.[1] 3[dly] that it is not peculiar to that one of the two members it is applied to. For, as one member directs somebody to do a thing, so the other member may be understood to direct somebody else to do another thing: viz: punish him [who][2] omitts to do the first.

'Law' to express a Single Command.

This appellation, therefore, is inconvenient: and, unless it be the word *Law* itself, I am acquainted with no other.

178. To use the word Law in this confined sense, is not to introduce a new usage: it is not to give it a new import which it never had before. It is often used when the simple original command is all that is meant to be offer'd to consideration. It is even oftener used to bring the command alone into consideration than to bring the punishment along with it.

And is frequently so used.

179. The Sanctional part, in as much as it is directed to the same party to whom the original command is directed, may more properly be stiled a *Promise* or a Threat.

Comminatory Part[3]—in what respect a Promise.

180. In this case, a Law that has a Sanction to it, in order to be distinguished from one that has none, may be stiled a Law *armed*: the other, a Law *unarmed*.

Law *armed*.

181. The Sanction, separated from the Law, may be stiled it's *armature*.

Armature of a Law

182. The Discourse that is adressed to one set of persons in form of a Promise is the armature of one Law, adressed to another set of persons, is itself a Law.

—becomes itself another Law.

---

183. **Note { }.**[4] It is the nature of a command, when backed by punishment, to produce uniformity among actions. Men love to know the causes of things. To this they have interest to spur them: and when they do not know them, to talk as if they did. {To this they have vanity to prompt them.} Seeing uniformity any where else, they must there also have a cause for it: and this cause must be a Law. And this imaginary sort of Law, this phantasm of the brain that had no archetype in actual existence, in order that it

Law of Nature—Origin of the expression.

[1] According to Blackstone, *Commentaries on the Laws of England*, i. 53–4, 'every law may be said to consist of several parts: one, *declaratory*; whereby the rights to be observed, and the wrongs to be eschewed, are clearly defined and laid down: another, *directory*; whereby the subject is instructed and enjoined to observe those rights, and to abstain from the commission of those wrongs: third, *remedial*; whereby a method is pointed out to recover a man's private rights, or redress his private wrongs: to which may be added a fourth, usually termed the *sanction*, or *vindicatory* branch of the law; whereby it is signified what evil or penalty shall be incurred by such as commit any public wrongs, and transgress or neglect their duty.'

[2] MS 'to'.

[3] MS orig. 'Sanction'.

[4] Bentham has added 'from p. 39', indicating that this passage is a continuation from para. 156, pp. 83–4 above.

might pass the better, was to be cover'd up under one denomination with the genuine. This confusion soon rooted itself in men's language: it is visible in the earliest writings that are left us: it is abundant in the works of Plato,[1] the grand original mint of moral unintelligibles.

NOTE. Imaginary Cause of Uniformity among Phænomena not a Law.

NOTE { }. 184. When a man disapproves of a mode of conduct consider'd independently of any actual system of Jurisprudence, he says there is a Law of Nature against it. If he knows why he disapproves of it, this Law of Nature is a dictate of Utility. If he can't tell why he disapproves of it, but yet will disapprove, and will have others disapprove of it: he begins talking of a Rule of Right, a Fitness of things, a Moral Sense, or some other imaginary standard which, howsoever varied in the description, is neither more nor less all the while than his own opinion in disguise.

Imaginary Cause of Uniformity among Phænomena not a Law.

185. NOTE continued. These pretended sacred, inviolable, irrepealable Laws of Nature are an invention devised by men's impatience in concert with their indolence. When a man is very angry with a usage he sees prevail, or a Law he sees established, when he is very angry, I say, but cannot express why, This usage, or this Law, he says, is against a Law of Nature. He says not that it is inconsistent with the happiness of the community: for that would call upon him to shew how: which is more, perhaps, than he is able. He says not that it is contrary to a dictate of utility: for a dictate of utility, it would be seen, is no more than his opinion of what is useful, and other men may have an opinion as well as he. But he says it is against a Law of Nature: and, a Law of Nature being a sacred thing, which multitudes have concurred in magnifying, it is but crying out profanation; this gives him a pretence to indulge his spleen, and to run out into invectives.

Imaginary Cause of uniformity among Phænomena not a Law. Law, an entire; difficult to pick out.

NOTE { }. 186. Such is the manner in which Lawyers, as well theoretical as practical, have disposed their speculations . . . . . . that to pick out matter to compose an entire Law, we must often hunt through almost every division of their system.

Difficulty of expressing the Spurious Senses of the word Law.

NOTE { }. 187. I hope, in what I have said of these 4 articles,[2] I shall be understood: but I am not certain. To give a clear and precise notion of a non-entity is no easy matter. What has been said

[1] Plato (c. 429–347 BC), the celebrated Athenian philosopher.

[2] i.e. the four articles 'jumbled together' by Montesquieu in *Spirit of the Laws*: see 'PP: Law', para. 28 n., pp. 448–9 n. below.

is all that can at present be allotted to them: this is not a place to enter into discussions.

---

188. The reason why Reward and not Punishment is [attached][1] to some sorts of actions as a motive to produce them is, that Punishment for not doing an act can be of no use where there is no *power* to do the act: and in acts that depend upon the exertion of extraordinary talents, of rare powers of the mind, there is no knowing before hand whether it is the case with the party or no. Reward when preferable.

It is in every man's power to *forbear*: it is not in every man's power to *act* in every case.

Apply reward, and the pleasure expended is but a trifle: nor is that trifle expended unless the benefit wished for is attained.

Apply punishment, the quantity of pleasure expended, or, what is equivalent, of pain produced, is indefinitely great; and it is expended at all events; whether the benefit be attained or no.

189. The discovery of the Longitude may serve for an example. This has long been the wish of most of the Governments in Europe. To accomplish it, they have offer'd rewards for the discovery.[2] Example—Longitude.

190. This is one way of going to work, and in this way their wishes have been successful. There was another way: and that was, to send for all the Mathematicians and philosophers of that class that were to be met with, and say to them, You must find it out by a time certain, or be hanged. The method I am speaking of is not so purely imaginary as might be supposed: it is precisely the method Nebuchadnezzar.

[1] MS 'affected' appears to be a slip.

[2] Since the second half of the sixteenth century various European states had offered rewards for a solution to the problem of the measurement of longitude, a key to improved navigation. In Great Britain, for instance, the Longitude Act of 1714 (12 Ann., c. 15) established the Board of Longitude and offered a reward of up to £20,000 for a successful scheme. The English horologist John Harrison (bap. 1693, d. 1776) invested forty years of his professional life in developing a portable sea clock. Although in 1749 Harrison had been awarded the Copley Gold Medal for his experimental work in watch-making, and his sea clocks had been successfully employed in voyages to the West Indies in 1761 and 1764, the Board of Longitude withheld half of the reward promised by the Longitude Act on the ground that Harrison's method had not been sufficiently demonstrated. In 1773, however, following the intervention of George III (1738–1820), King of Great Britain and Ireland from 1760, an Act of Parliament (13 Geo. III, c. 77) provided for the payment of the balance. Bentham reported that his brother Samuel (1757–1831), mechanical engineer and naval architect, had around 1776–7 'projected an improvement in Time-pieces with a view to the Longitude', but had abandoned his work due to the opposition of Thomas Hornsby (1733–1810), Savilian Professor of Astronomy at the University of Oxford from 1763 and a member of the Board of Longitude. See Bentham to John Forster, April/May 1778, *Correspondence* (*CW*), ii. 112–13.

taken, if we may believe the Scriptures, by Nebuchadnezzar with his Magicians, men of a profession that once made a figure but is now fallen into disrepute, to get his dreams found out.[1] For getting dreams found out, it may be as good a way as another; but for the Longitude, the absurdity of it is such as strikes every one at first sight. Being, then, absurd, the point is to know why it is so.

His conduct why absurd.

191. It were easy to say that it is cruel, inequitable, unjust, contrary to natural Justice, and so forth: and this is what men are in use to say upon like occasions: but this is but to stave off the difficulty, and not to solve it.

Reward whether a stronger motive doubtful.

192. It is much to be doubted, whether this way of reward is such as would promise to be more efficacious than this punishing way. What a man had ability [to] do, he certainly would be as ready to do to save his life as to get money by it. It is not certain that the hope of good is more efficacious than the dread of evil in producing new abilities. The spur that poverty is to authors is a known phænomenon. It is that, for instance, which made Dryden what he was:[2] it is the removal of that which has stopped so many from being what they might have been.

It is the best Œconomy.

193. It could not be certain before hand that the Longitude was at all discoverable, and if not, whatever mischief there was done in the way of punishment would be all of it to no purpose.

Reward best Œconomy.

193.[3] To give reward is to give the instrument of Pleasure. Instruments of pleasure given to me must have been taken from someone else. To take from any one Instruments of Pleasure is Pain to him.

Reward where preferable and why. Evidence for Punishment difficultly obtainable.

194. Another reason why Punishment will sometimes not answer the purpose is the difficulty of getting Evidence in many cases. Before Punishment [is] to be inflicted, it must be made appear, it must be proved, that the act commanded to be done, has not been done. When the proofs, the facts calculated to evince this persuasion, depend upon the party whose act is wished for[4]

Punishment makes certain mischief for uncertain Gain.

195. 1st. One reason, then, is the not knowing whether any thing is to be done by Punishment.

[1] For the story of the dream of Nebuchadnezzar II (b. *c.* 634 BC, d. *c.* 562 BC), King of Babylon from *c.* 605 BC, and his threat to kill 'the magicians, and the astrologers, and the sorcerers, and the Chaldeans' see Daniel 2: 1–13.

[2] For the poverty of John Dryden (1631–1700), poet, playwright, and critic, see, for instance, Samuel Johnson, *Prefaces, Biographical and Critical, to the Works of the English Poets*, 10 vols., London, 1779–81, iii. 156–7, 233.

[3] Bentham has given two paragraphs the number 193.

[4] The sentence appears to have been abandoned at this point

196. 2[nd.] No expense is incurred unless the gain accrues. In Reward, gain is inseparable from expenditure.

---

197. Where Reward only, and not Punishment, is offer'd as a MOTIVE, the wish expressed, is not, in common acceptation, understood to be a *command*: one should rather call it an *invitation*. A command is understood to be backed by a motive, that is *compulsory*: and of the two sorts of motives, Punishment and Reward (that is Pain and Pleasure), it is Punishment only that is understood to be *compulsory*. Law)(Invitation.

198. The Motive of Punishment is said to be compulsory, and not that of Reward; because it is the first only, which, in the kinds and quantities in which it is ordinarily in men's disposal, is at any uniform certainty of producing the action wished for. If the sources of pleasure were as inexhaustible as those of pain, and as frequently employ'd, the epithet compulsory would no more belong to Punishment than to Reward.

---

199. The matter a Law is composed of must be such as serves either 1st to characterize the article of conduct that is commanded, or else 2[dly] the conditions upon which it is to be observed.[1] Law—Matter of.

200. Hence, to understand aright any point of Law, any proposition that occurrs in a book of Jurisprudence, the following is the course that is to be taken.[2] Point of Law, a, how to be referred to it's Station in the System.

201. It is to be consider'd 1st whether it be *actual* Law of which it is an article, or fictitious. Actual or Fictitious.

202. If Actual, then 2[dly] whether the purport of it be to characterize 1st the object of command: or 2[dly] some conditions upon which the command takes place. Actual {Act itself. Conditions.

203. If to characterize the object of the command, then whether it be in the way 1st of Definition or 2[dly] of Modification, and if of Modification, then whether 1st of Exception[3] or 2[dly] of Enlargement. Definitive or Modificative {Restrictive or Enlarging.[4]

204. The subject of Definition or Modification is either 1st the bare act itself stripped of all circumstances, or 2[dly] any one of the circumstances attending it. Bare act itself or a circumstance.

205. The bare act itself is some motion, the object of the external senses: or some thought, the object of internal sentiment. Bare act, what.

[1] In the text, Bentham has noted at this point: 'See p. 12, Prep. Princ. "Condition."' See 'PP: Introduction', para. 42, p. 437 below.

[2] In the text, Bentham has noted at this point: 'v. "*Parsing*" in Ms 4[to.]' The quarto manuscript has not been identified, but for a discussion of parsing see para. 878, p. 274 below.

[3] MS orig. 'Restriction'.

[4] For the correct form of layout of the marginal see p. 9 above.

The idea that is suggested by either of these to one who considers them is a *simple* idea.

Act of the Mind, how manifested.

206. No act can be the object of a Law but in virtue of the impressions it makes on the external senses of any one who considers it, because all our ideas are received through the senses: an act of the mind can become perceived no otherwise than by some phænomena of the body that serve as signs of it. 'Tis only through the intervention[1] of these phænomena that it can be known whether any act of the mind have, according as may have been commanded, been done or not done. To command that of which there is no knowing whether it have been done or no, is to no purpose.

For Matter Conditional find the Act commanded.

207. The article of Jurisprudence in question may be of such a nature as to serve to characterize the conditions upon which the command takes place. In this case, in order to understand the article aright, a further enquiry must be made: and that is, what is the *command* with which the article in question stands connected as a condition.

208. The idea of command is that which all Laws and parts of Laws[2] have belonging to them in common. To shew, in the case of any given article, how it applies itself to that article, is the only way of making the relation it bears to any other given article perspicuously understood.

A Law—Entirety of.

209. A Law is *entire* when it has all it's parts. A Law has all it's parts when it has all that matter which is necessary to it's being what it is.

What are those parts?—what is that matter? This we can understand no otherwise than by considering what it is that is the general purport of a Law; the purport which all Laws as such have belonging to them in common.

Purport common to all Laws.

210. A Command can be only either to do a thing or not to do it. [These are] the two general purports one or other of which every law must have that has any. All the matter, therefore, that a Law can have, or can be conceived to have, belonging to it must be such as contributes, in some way or other, to express this purport.

The Command or invitation describes *the article of conduct*. The Threat or Promise presents the motive.

Act ⅩCircumstances.

211 The Laws stiled Civil concerning Property, and the Laws stiled Criminal, differ not in the principal act itself that is the object of them, but only in the *circumstances* attending it.

[1] MS orig. 'intermediation'.

[2] MS alt. 'every thing that goes by the name of Law'.

212. The Laws that give property thereby confer rights, and, what is the same thing, protect them: protect men in the enjoyment of them: protect them against invasion: protect them against acts of invasion. Laws Penal ☓ Civil chiefly in the Circumstances.

[To] protect them against acts of invasion, they threaten punishment on any who shall commit those acts. Now those acts, whether threaten'd with a lighter punishment by the Laws called Civil or with a heavier by the Laws called Penal, the acts themselves, I say, are the same: the physical motions they consist in are the same: they differ only by circumstances: by concomitant phænomena. Few are the sorts of acts that are punished criminally in all circumstances.[1]

---

213. 'Tis a task easy enough to explain our Author's[2] errors: but that, of itself, would give but little satisfaction in comparison of substituting some truths that can be depended upon in their room. An unpleasing vacuity is left unless we build as we demolish. Prefat. *Diruens ædifico.*[3]

The attempt to do this is the business of the present book.

The enterprize is arduous: it leads us into a path alike intricate and untrodden, in which success is glorious, and even to stumble is no disgrace.

214. What is here proposed is to find an answer to the following questions: Questions which the nature of our Author's undertaking led him to find an answer for: and to which, that is to such of them as he has thought of answering, his answers have proved so confused, so lame, so erroneous, or defective, as will be seen hereafter. Answer'd or not answer'd, answer'd well or ill by him, by me, by any one, they are questions of the most fundamental and cardinal importance: upon a clear solution of which depend[s] all the certainty we can have of the accuracy of our speculations on any topic of the science that is before us.[4] Subject proposed.

These Questions are 1st. What is a Law?[5]

[1] In the text, Bentham has noted at this point: 'Example.' Bentham refers to two such acts at para. 290, p. 110 below.

[2] i.e. Blackstone's.

[3] i.e. 'Demolishing, I build.'

[4] MS orig. 'Jurisprudence'.

[5] In the text, Bentham has noted at this point: '&c. v. Table of Contents.' Bentham's reference is perhaps to the following material headed 'Preparatory Principles. Table of Contents' at UC lxix. 69:

'A Law, what.

'1. Command and it's Relatives.
'2. A Law, a Command.
'3. No Command, no Law. Eight spurious Laws that are not Commands.
'4. Of Commands, what are not Laws.
'5. Three Articles in which a Law may differ from other Commands.

Prefat. Method employ'd the Analytic.

215. The method I have proceeded in is that of Analysis. This is not the most satisfactory: it wants the Synthetic as a key to it. It serves to announce the truths that are discover'd, but it does not mark out the path that led to the discovery. It takes up generals, and breaks them down into particulars. But it was at particulars that the investigation began. It was from consideration of particulars that those general notions that are advanced were, by means of abstraction, derived in the last place, tho' here presented first.

Not the Synthetic, why.

216. Attended as the Synthetic would have been with these advantages, the analytic is the only one that could here have been pursued. It is the only one that the requisite proportion to that which constitutes the principal business of the work would admitt of. The Synthetic, it is easy to perceive, would be by much the most particular and diffuse.

Laws Optional.

217. There are instances in which it is indifferent, or nearly so, to the Legislature whether the Command be observed or the punishment submitted to, where the subject has the choice given him of two commands. This is the case when the end of the command is *accumulation* and the penalty pecuniary: it may happen that the quantum of the penalty in a given instance bears such a proportion to that of the wealth to be acquired to the state by the party's observing the Law in that instance, that it may be indifferent to the rest of the State (the party himself out of the question) whether the conduct prescribed be observed or the penalty paid. In this case, it may well happen not only that it may be indifferent to the party whether he incur the penalty or no, but that, even after paying the penalty, he may be a gainer: the payment which, if the sum were larger, would be a penalty is in this proportion of it, to the detriment and profit of disobedience (*detriment* to the rest of the State, *profit* to the party in question),

'6. *Private* Commands that are not Laws.
'7. *Public* Commands that are not Laws.
'8. Points of Doctrine, inferences from Commands.
'9. Maxims, *extensive* Points of Doctrine.
'A Law. Parts of.
'1. Point of Individuation. *Entirety* of a Law—what constitutes it.
'2. Laws confined to denote a *single* Command (with it's appenditious matter), not *two* Commands
'3. Forms of a Law. Different manner in which a Law may be expressed.
'4. Laws Directory)(Sanctional.
'5. Laws Substantive)(Adjective.
'6. Laws Absolute)(Relative.'

part of the object of the primary Command. The Command is not *simple*, but *disjunctive*: not peremptory,[1] but *optional*.

---

218. As to it's Source, a Law is such a Command as is an act of *State*: an act of Government. Source.

A state is &c. State.

219. As to it's matter, a Law is such a sort of Command whereof the objects are a *sort* of, or sorts of, actions, not *individual* actions. Matter.

---

220. {Note.} To say that a thing ought not to be done because there is a Law of Nature against it's being done, what does it amount to? an obscure and roundabout way of saying one of two things: 'It ought not to be done, because it would be mischievous or dangerous to the community:' or else 2dly, 'It ought not to be done, because I say it ought not. Without having any reason to give, I pronounce it ought not.' The grand mischief of this expression is that most commonly, when examined into, the only meaning which it is found to cover is the latter. There are two sorts of people who find their account in making use of it. Some, hoodwinked by Superstition, who tremble to take up the standard of utility, and those who are ready, perhaps, to take it up, but know not how to go about it. Law of Nature.

---

221. Schoolmaster's *General Standing* Rules—are they or are they not Laws? Matter and Source. Pædagogic Rules, whether Laws.

They have a Civil Sanction by Delegation from the Parent.

The Power, as to the person, is entirely fiduciary.

The Commands concern sorts of acts.

They are *Temporary* by *Nature*, determining with the Schoolmaster's life.

Yet they may be *adopted* in *Succession*.

Qu. University Statutes. These are spoken of as Laws, because[2]

---

222. A Parent, we say, has *powers* over the Child, meaning over the person of the Child. Power ⅹ Right between Parent and Child.

The Child, we say, has rights against the Parent: namely rights to have a portion of the Parent's Property allotted him.

We do not say he has *Powers over* the Parent.

---

[1] 'Peremptory' has been bracketed by Bentham for deletion.

[2] The passage has been abandoned at this point.

Power Physical, Idea of.

223. The expression Power (Physical) is relative to Opinion.[1] If you are of opinion that, were you to conceive the volition, the physical effect would follow, you think you have a *power* to produce it. If *I* think that, were you to conceive the volition, the physical effect would follow, I think you [have][2] power to produce it.

Powers and Rights, Source of.

224. From General state Commands *armed* result *Powers* and *Rights*. From Commands armed, or from Uniformity of Punishment.

Prefatoria. A Law, what.

225. The word 'Law', 'a Law', is in the mouth of every man. None can be more familiar. It were to be expected, at least it were to be wished, that the idea belonging to it were precise. There is scarce any, perhaps, that is less so.

Law, distribution of. Order of precedence. Laws regulating private Interests to come first.

226. In delineating a Map of the Law, the most simple method of proceeding is to begin with a draught of such powers as are beneficial and have no reference to the complex idea of a body politic.

It is true the very act of issuing Law, on the topic first consider'd, whatever that be, as on any other, is the act of a body politic. But in this stage of the enquiry, all that is complex and intricate in the consideration of such a body may be laid out of the case.

All that the case requires to be supposed, and conceived, is, in one man or set of men, a habit of commanding, in the rest, a habit of obeying. This is the only postulatum that is demanded. A truer or more simple one cannot be conceived.

Class:[n.] Those regulating Public Interests not intelligible but through the other.

227. From Laws regulating *Private* interests, by establishing Private *powers*, *duties* and *restraints*, we advance to the notion of Laws regulating *Public* interests, by establishing *Public powers*, *duties* and *restraints*.

This is the natural order of intellection: for the latter class are no otherwise to be understood than by their similitude to the former. Many writers, indeed, begin with the latter: they take the latter to explain first: but this they can do no farther than the former are already understood: and in proceeding thus they are obliged to take up with the gross conceptions that men have of them from habit without instruction.

What a man is most conversant with and best understands is what sort of an interest he has in that which [is][3] called his own. It

[1] MS orig. 'dependent on *Belief*'.

[2] MS 'has'. Bentham failed to amend this word when amending the remainder of the sentence.

[3] MS 'the goods that are'.

is proposed to explain to him the interest that Corporate bodies and persons in public Trust have in the goods under their charge: how is this to be done? By comparing the sort of interest with which he is supposed unacquainted, and with which he is to be made acquainted, with that which he is acquainted with already. The idea of private powers over things is simple—the limitations to them are few. That of public powers is more complex—the limitations to them are many.

228. The Author of the *Commentaries*. 'Tis with exceptions he begins: after them come the General Rules to which they are exceptions. Confusedness of the current methods.

What distinguishes an Alien from a native is the former being debarred from acquiring some of those powers to which the latter is admitted.[1]

One thing [that] distinguishes the Clergy from the Laity is the method whereby they acquire the Title to certain things in which, in virtue of their Clerical character, they have power.[2]

229. A Law that gives *Powers*, issues to the party *empower'd*, Permission: to every one else, Command: that is a Command to forbear, a Prohibition. The description of the acts they are commanded to forbear, is a description of the Power. Law, a, empowering, what it does.

---

230. The reason of the ill success men have met with in defining many a moral or metaphysical term is their adhering implicitly to the old method *per genus et differentiam*, when the term in question had, perhaps, no superior genus to which it could be referred. All they had left for it was their taking a word explicitly synonymous to the word pretended to be defined, by which they did not at all better themselves: or obscurely synonymous, by which they stood worse off than before. Such has been, and must ever be, the fate of those who go about to define in the regular way such words as Power, Possession, Property, &c. in Morals: Ratio, Part, Multiple, &c. in Mathematics. In words like these, if you find the Definition beginning, 'Such a thing (the Definand) is a', or 'such a thing is the', You may be sure the Definition will prove unprofitable.[3] The words expressive of genera of the highest order are, in comparison of those expressive of subordinate Genera, few. Hence the method *per Genus et differentiam* is the common method. It is always the first that occurrs. It is often the only Prefat. Definitions, current, why unsuccessful.

[1] For the rights of aliens see Blackstone, *Commentaries on the Laws of England*, i. 359–62.
[2] For the method of appointment and the rights and duties of the clergy see ibid. 364–82.
[3] MS orig. 'fallacious and uninstructive'.

one that occurrs. In the instances in question, the word to be defined is itself expressive of a highest genus: it has no higher. This is what expositors do not consider: but, proceeding in the *routine* they have been accustomed to, they torment themselves at any rate to find one. The consequence is they either take up such a definition as is useless, or give up altogether the task of finding one, as being either unnecessary or impracticable. 'Tis by this means that so many words, of a sort that want it most, have either no definition at all, or such an one as is worse than none.

SECT. | | Divine Law. Prefat. Truths in which mankind are thus deeply interested.

231. Weak reasoners in Morals, by a kind of instinct, take shelter behind the altar. Yet not even this shall save him. Mankind is too deeply interested in the display of those truths which he would bury there, and in the exposure of those errors which he would shelter under it, to make it pardonable to desist from the pursuit. The Sanctuary is, in it's own nature, common ground, unless where fenced about by Intolerance, which it can never be but by the help of Usurpation. Yet will not the holiness of the place be profaned by any other hand than his own. 'Tis his own hand shall pierce him, we shall see. On his own head must be his blood. As in many other places, so in this. There needs no foreign arguments to set against his doctrines: to expound is to expose them: to *confront* them is to *confute*.

A Statute.

232. A Statute, *one* Statute, is so much of the expressed Will of the Legislator, as is stamped for such by one act of Authentication.

Law Original X Alterative.[1]

233. A Law may be compleat in itself, or compleatable by relation.

A Command may be *original*: or *relative*, serving to modify former commands.

A Law Adjective is *intelligible*, but unoperative, without a Law Substantive. A Law Alterative is not only unoperative without a Law Original, but *unintelligible*.[2]

A Law, Definition.

234. A Law (original), if a command, is a *Command* of the *State* concerning the acts of a sort of persons not individually assignable, appointing what shall be done or not done on any subject, and upon what conditions.

—If a Permission[3]

[1] MS orig. 'Modificative'.
[2] In the text, Bentham has noted at this point: 'Qu.'
[3] The sentence has been abandoned at this point.

235. An Article of Common Law is a general rule deduced (at hazard by the persons it concerns) from State Commands to particular persons individually assignable, or from the avow'd opinions upon which such particular commands have been declared to be grounded, or from an uniformity observ'd in the application of punishment to particular actions fashioned, by abstraction of the indifferent circumstances, into sorts of actions.[1] Those circumstances are indifferent which do not appear to have weighed in the judgment which determined the command that, in the instance in question, appointed punishment.

An Article of Common Law, Definition of.

236. These particular Commands are either primary commands to observe a mode of conduct, or Commands to punish for not observing it, or to oblige to do it by physical compulsion.[2]

Article of Common Law—defined. Commands primary ✕ Secondary.

237. The *reasons* are the expressions of such acts of the understanding as have or are declared or appear to have contributed to determine that sort of act of the Will of which the command in question is.

Article of Common Law. *Reasons*: what.

238. 'Defendant, yield up the house that is demanded of thee.' This is a primary judicial command.

Command Primary. Example.

239. 'Sheriff, remove that Defendant out of the House that has been demanded of him, and let none but the Plaintiff enter.'

This is a judicial secondary command of the physically compulsive kind.

Command Secondary: physically compulsive. Example.

240. 'Sheriff, bear away to prison the Defendant that withstood thee, when thou shouldst have removed him out of the House that was demanded of him.'

This is a particular judicial secondary command of the penal or mentally compulsive kind.

Command Secondary. Mentally[3] compulsive.

241. As to it's Source, a Law is a State Command issued by persons invested with such Powers as are exercised by persons standing, with respect to the parties commanded, in relations any other than domestic.

Law—Source.

---

242. That which can be understood by itself should be treated of before that which is not to be understood but by reference to the former: which necessar[il]y involves such a mention of the former as, if it depends upon gross and popular conceptions, must necessarily be inaccurate and confused.

Order of precedence in a didactic view.

---

[1] This sentence has been heavily emended by Bentham, and its reconstruction is conjectural.

[2] In the text, Bentham has noted at this point: 'v. 78.' See para. 251, p. 101 below.

[3] MS orig. 'Morally'.

Prefat.

243. As to the accuracy of these speculations, I must confess, I am far from having succeeded to the extent of my desires. All I trust on with any degree of confidence is that something will be found done here towards paving the way for the more satisfactory speculations of others, or of myself in a more advanced state of my researches.

That much of what is here offered is new, I can be certain: whether, as far as it goes, it be satisfactory, let others judge.

Laws {Restraint. Powers.

244. A Law, be the purport of it what it will, has this in common with other Laws. They either impose primary Restraints, or confer Powers or impose secondary restraints limitative of those Powers. One or other of these things they do, as being Prohibitions.

The Law that commands not to do an act, imposes a restraint. The Law that commands others not to [oppose][1] him in doing such or such an act, confers a Power.

Power)(Right. Right)(Power.

If the subject matter of his action be a *thing*, it gives him a *Power* as over that thing: a *Right* as against other persons.

Power over Persons.

If a person, it gives him a Power over that person.

Duty.

If a Law commands a man to do an act, it imposes on him *a duty*.

Command: Right, Power, Interest.

245. To command every person but one to forbear using a thing, is to give that one a *right* to that thing: in other words, is to give him *power* over it: is to give him an interest in it. The extent of this interest, power or right, whichever name it is called by, is as the number of such sorts of uses which men at large are commanded to forbear putting it to, the party empowered being left free. To command all persons to forbear opposing A in acting after a given manner upon B, is to give to A power over B: if this given manner be any manner whatsoever, then B is put upon the footing of a thing: we speak of a RIGHT to S: of an *interest* in S.

Right to 'a *person*' generally)(Right to Services.

246. If the manners in question be not any manners whatsoever, but certain assignable manners only, the way, then, is not to speak of M as having a *right to* S, or an *interest* in S, but only a *right to* S's services, an *interest in* S's services. Meaning certain particular services correspondent to the particular manners in which M is permitted to make use [of] S.

Services { passive. active.

247. Services are either passive or active. Active consist in some kind of motion; passive in quiescence or submission. Example. My Master bids me walk; I walk for him: my services are active. I stand for him to rest himself on my shoulder. My

[1] MS 'impose'.

service is of the passive kind. It consists in forbearance. I forbear to withdraw myself from his elbow.

Submission without Service.

248. There is, however, a case where we speak of M as having a power over S: tho' it is not usual to speak of him as having a right to, or an *interest in*, any services of S. Because not beneficial: but fiduciary only. This is the case with powers that are given for the sake of carrying Judiciary powers into execution.

Power ✕ Simple Permission.

249. There are two degrees or cases of Power over persons. Power given by permission simply, and Power created by Command. The first, indeed, is not properly to be spoken of as Power: it is only the *amotion of restraint*. It is not created by Command, but by the revocation *pro tanto* of a Command. The truth is, it is not Power, but Liberty; naked Liberty. No legal power is given to the party: but only he is left to his physical power: the legal restraint there was to his physical power is taken away.

Legislative Powers not peculiar to Parliament.

250. With respect to our own Government, it is commonly said that neither of the two Houses has of itself Legislative power, that the King alone has not Legislative power: that Courts of Justice have not Legislative Power.

By this nothing more is meant, or if any thing more is meant, nothing more is true, than that there are bounds more or less narrow to the Legislative powers of those different bodies, whereas to those of the whole body of the Parliament there are none. For if the Commands those bodies are allowed, either by usage or by express commission, [to issue] are not Laws, I know not how it can ever be ascertained what are.

Manifestation explicit ✕ implicit of a Wish.[1]

251. There are two ways in which a wish may be made manifest; it may be manifested *explicitly* or *implicitly*: *explicitly*, by *words* directed to the party whose act is the object of the wish: *implicitly*, by *words* directed to some *other* party, or by *actions*. Actions by which the wish of a person in power is manifested are acts of punishment, acts inflicting pain. The words are commands to some other to inflict it.

Power and Restraint go together.

252. Power and Restraint are established in conjunction. They are, as the Logicians phrase it, *Simul cognitione*.[2] What is called Power with respect to one, is Restraint with respect to another. It is by one person's being restrained that another is empower'd.

[1] In the margin, Bentham has noted at this point: 'continued from p. 72, N° 236.' See para. 236, p. 99 above.

[2] i.e. 'encountered' or 'learned simultaneously'.

Whose act is it that is the object of a command creating power? not that of the party empower'd: but that of the party restrained.

Prohibition, by Restraints makes Powers.

253. The Law does two things. The force of the Law is manifested in two ways: by imposing *duties*, and by imposing *restraints*.

Command makes Duties.[1]

In imposing *restraints*, it takes the name of a *Pro*[*hi*]*bition*: in imposing duties, it retains the name of a *Command*.

254. 'Tis by imposing *Restraints* that it creates *Powers*.

Permission original operates nothing.

255. To permitt is not among the primary offices of Law: for by permitting, no other situation of things is brought about than would subsist without any Law at all about the matter. Simply to permitt would be to restore men in that behalf to their natural, to their pristine, liberty. Permission supposes previous restraint: for what is permission? It is the removal of restraint. It is nothing more.

Command = Duties. Prohibition = Restraints.

256. The two Primary or Radical operations of Law are Command and Prohibition. By Command, it imposes duties: by Prohibition, it imposes Restraints.

Command = Action. Prohibition = Forbearance.

257. The mode of conduct that is the object of a Command is *Action*: that is some sort of Motion: of a Prohibition, *Forbearance*: that is the negative of Motion, Rest.

Punishment all in all.

258. The instrument the Law has to work with, in creating as well Duties as Restraints, is *Punishment*: or to speak as free as possible from figure, when it imposes duties, it punishes or threatens punishment: when it imposes restraints, it punishes or threatens punishment. 'Tis by punishment that it does both: 'tis by punishment alone that it can do either. Punishment is pain. Of pain, the idea is a simple one.

Prefat. Method observed. Simple ideas the ground.

259. To the words Pain, Pleasure, Volition, Motion, Rest,[2] the ideas that are annexed are simple ones. These nobody defines, or if any one defines, nobody makes clearer by defining. They need not be defined, they can not. For to define a word is to point out, in some way or other the simple ideas that go to the composing of the more complex idea of which usage has made that word the sign. But of these, each is the sign of one simple idea, and no more.

With these words, therefore, we set out, supposing the meaning of them understood. 'Tis by their relation to these, that we shall endeavour to make those others understood, which we shall find

[1] In the margin, Bentham has noted at this point: 'Qu. Rights?'

[2] In the margin, Bentham has noted at this point: 'insert here the whole list when it is compleated.' The words 'Wish, Demand, Resolution', originally in this list, have been bracketed by Bentham for deletion.

occasion to explain. These are the Capital we have to trade with. These, to speak with the Algebraists, are our known quantities, our *a*'s, *b*'s and *c*'s. 'Tis by reference to these that we are to elicit the import of the *x*'s, *y*'s and *z*'s, whose import there is occasion to make known.

---

260. A Command is individual, which has an individual mode of conduct for it's object. Command, an individual.

261. The amplitude of a Power over a thing is as the number of uses persons other than the party empower'd are restrained from making of the thing in question, he being left free. Power, *amplitude* of.

262. The amplitude of protection is as the magnitude of the Punishment wherewith the restraints that constitute that power are backed. Power, Protection for, amplitude of.

[263.] There are 4 ways in which a man's power may be narrow'd: [1$^{\text{stly.}}$] By Powers given, or 2dly by permission left to be exercised by others in concurrence. 3$^{\text{dly.}}$ By Restraints imposed on him and them alike. 4$^{\text{thly.}}$ By conditions annexed to the establishment of the Power. Power, ways in which it may be limited.

---

264. Herein lies the difference between Power *Legislative* and *Executive*. Power *Legislative* has for it's object *sorts* of actions: Power *Executive*, individual actions. Power Legislative ⪤ Executive.

The persons to whose office it belongs to exercise *Legislative* Power most frequently may sometimes exercise *Executive*. In like manner, those to whom it belongs most frequently to exercise Executive Power, may sometimes exercise Legislative. But this does not alter the nature of the two Powers, nor make one the same as the other. It is not the difference of the person exercising it that constitutes the difference of the Power. The King, by exercising Legislative power, that is by laying down Rules to govern sorts of actions, does not make it Executive: does not reduce those sorts of actions to individual actions. To the King is acknowledged to belong the supreme executive power: if, then, by exercising any other power, that is Legislative Power, he could turn it into Executive, to the King would belong the whole power of the Government.

Supreme Legislative Power is distinguishable from Subordinate Legislative Power no otherwise than by the sort of Persons who are respectively in use to exercise them. Legislative Power, as well subordinate as supreme, is distinguished from Executive Power by the nature of the Powers themselves. Power Legislative Supreme ⪤ Subordinate.

Powers Legislative and Powers Executive are distinguishable in themselves. Powers Legislative subordinate and supreme are distinguishable no otherwise than in respect of the persons who exercise them respectively.

Powers Executive Public—Division of.

265. Powers Executive are either 1st. Military, or 2d. Fiscal, or 3dly. Judiciary.

Military are either Maritime or Terrestrial: they concern either the Sea or Land Force. In Powers Judicial consists the Force that is to secure men against invasion from within.

Fiscal Powers are Public fiduciary powers concerning the Receipt and Expenditure of Public Wealth.

Public Wealth consists either in instruments of Security or of Pleasure.

Instruments of Pleasure that are articles of Public Wealth are bestowed upon Public Officers and Servants in the way of Reward for services real or supposed.

Judges—Measure of their Judgments.

266. Persons in Judicial capacities act either according to a superior Command, or according to a Pattern—a co-ordinate Command.

In judging on Statute Law, they judge according to a Superior Command: in judging on Common Law, they judge according to co-ordinate Commands which they take as Patterns.

Prefat. Method in Defining. Definitions in a Chain.

267. Of the several abstract terms I shall have occasion to employ, the import will be fixed by a chain of Definitions, beginning at words expressive of simple ideas, and continued on as far as there is occasion, so as to take in every word in which there can be any obscurity or ambiguity.[1]

Judges why so called.

268. The Acts of Judges, of persons invested with what is called the Judicial character, possessed of what are called Judicial Offices, tho' volitions, acts of the willing faculty, are called by a name which refers to the Judicial faculty.

The acts of Judges are commands: commands are volitions. But these volitions are governed by judgments, acts of the understanding: the judgment formed, the command[2] follows of course. 'Tis in forming the judgment that all the pains and difficulty consists. It is in determining whether stealing in general, for example, is made

[1] In the text, Bentham has added at this point: 'gradually unfold'.
[2] MS orig. 'order'.

punishable by hanging; and whether the act I.S. is charged with is an act of stealing, and whether I.S. has done the act he has been charged with; 'tis in this that lies all the difficulty: these determined in the affirmative, the order to hang him follows as of course.

Their name is taken from that part of their employment which is most striking, and which makes a greater figure in them than in any others tho' exercising the same operations.

269. To the whole Mass together we give the name of Common Law: but take any part of it from the rest, we know not what name to give it: to what genus to refer it: we know not how to point out in it the characterizing properties of Law.[1]

Common Law. Articles of it non-descript.

We know in general, at least we recognize it, I suppose, when we are told of it, that the office of Law is to Command: that this that is called Common Law must, therefore, display itself, somehow or other, in commands. But to pick out any proposition, or any other larger division, and to understand how it contributes to the composition of a Command, this is what appears not to have been ever so much as thought of.

270. To illustrate this matter, let [us] apply what has been here said to what goes by the name of the Divine Law: it may give rise to a train of interesting speculation. It will lead us to a very remarkable circumstance attending that body of precepts. It is this. There is scarce such a thing any where as an entire Law to be met with. In the precepts that have been most celebrated, something or other is always wanting to compleat them, in order to entitle them, even according to the notions of those who utter'd them, to universal obedience. Something expository or exceptive or conditional to be added.

Divine Law. Articles of incompleat.

I say Expository, for exposition is a matter not of mere *abundans cautela*:[2] not of grace, but of necessity, so long as the general command is not sufficiently explicit to enable the party commanded to call up in mind with certainty the idea of the mode of conduct which is the object of it.

271. 'Thou shalt not steal,'[3] is not merely a concise Law, but an imperfect one; seeing that what sort of act is to be denominated stealing and what not, is that concerning which the subject, without some more explicit designation, has nothing to inform him.[4]

Instance—'thou shalt not steal.'

[1] In the margin, Bentham has noted at this point: 'This whole branch of Science is in the Catalogue of non-descripts.'

[2] From the legal maxim '*abundans cautela non nocet*', i.e. 'an abundance of caution does no harm'.

[3] Exodus 20: 15.

[4] In the margin, Bentham has noted at this point: 'Sir Matthew Hale owns himself unable to give a Definition of Stealing.' Sir Matthew Hale (1609–76), Chief Baron of the Exchequer 1660–71, Chief Justice of King's Bench 1671–6, had written in *Historia*

It is in vain to say that the exposition is included in the text. Words, to be of use, must serve for signs to our ideas, must serve to excite precise ideas in the minds of those that hear them. A text that will not serve to call up precise and distinct ideas, such a text, in the instances where it fails of doing so, will not serve for any thing. A principal proposition, without the exceptive matter that belongs to it, is a false representation of the Will of the Legislator: without the definitive matter, it is not, indeed, a false one: but neither is it a true one: it is none at all. In the instances in which it will not serve to point out those acts which are the object of the volition, it is [not] any representation at all of the Legislator's Will.

2[d] Instance. 'Do as you would be done by.'

272. 'Whatsoever thou wouldst that men should do unto thee, do thou even so unto them.'[1] This last, before it can be taken for a precept that could possibly have been meant to be obey'd, stands in need of exceptive matter to be subjoined to it: and much exceptive matter. I will not undertake to say how much: but what follows may serve as a specimen. It cannot be practised towards a criminal by a Judge. The Judge, if he were in the criminal's place, would wish to be acquitted. But he is not on this account to acquit the criminal. Thus to act throughout the world would be, at one stroke, to destroy the whole fabric of the Laws, and lay Society in ruins.

Entirety—difficult to compass.

273. To frame, on any given topic, a Law that shall be intire, is one of the most trying exertions of sagacity that can be assigned: but this is what should be always aimed at. And this Idea of the intirety of a Law, it is hoped, may serve in some degree for a direction.

'Do as you would be done by,' corrected.

274. 'In whatever thou dost, consult the happiness of other men: that is of such a part of mankind whose happiness is liable to be affected by the mode of conduct thou art about to enter on.' This alteration, made in the rule, will answer the purpose of the exceptive matter that is requisite: and thus corrected, it may serve as a *maxim*, if not particular enough for a *Law*. What a man would have done to him, what treatment given to him, is such treatment, upon all occasions, as shall tend to make him as happy as possible. To compleat it into a Law, or rather to break it down

Placitorum Coronæ. The History of the Pleas of the Crown, ed. Sollom Emlyn, 2 vols., London, 1736, i. 509, that, 'in cases of larciny the variety of circumstances is so great, and the complications thereof so mingled, that it is impossible to prescribe all the circumstances evidencing a felonious intent, or the contrary, but the same must be left to the due and attentive consideration of the judge and jury, wherein the best rule is *in dubiis* rather to incline to acquittal than conviction'.

[1] Matthew 7: 12.

into a body of Laws, a large assortment of Definitional matter must be provided.

---

275. Power Supreme is that which hath for it's objects all or any persons, all or any things, and upon all or any occasions. Power Supreme.

276. The Constitution is the System or Distribution[1] of Public Powers in a State. Constitution, what.

---

277. In our own Constitution, it is the King, or rather different persons appointed by the King, that are invested with a share of power, the chief part of which comes under the denomination of what is called Executive. It happens, that these persons, and in some measure the King himself, are directed and controuled in their operations by the supreme Legislative Power. Having this state of things perpetually before our eyes, we are apt to form a notion, as if Power of the Executive kind was of it's own nature subordinate to the Legislative. But this is a mistake. It is as easy to form an idea of a Power Legislative, and a Power merely Executive exerting a supremacy over that, as what we are most accustomed to see actually exemplified, a Power Executive acting under the direction of a Legislature. All Power Executive not essentially Subordinate to all Legislative.

278. The amplitude of the Power a person has depends upon the number of acts he can make the objects of his commands. It gains nothing by setting them down in writing, and gathering them into sorts. In many Mahometan Countries there are no Laws, or next to none, but the power of the Sovereign[2] is not the less on that account. He appoints his Ministers, who, in their several departments, carry on the business of Government for the most part by particular Commands. Indeed, if we take into our idea of Executive power it's executing, on particular objects, such general commands as are already issued by the Legislator, if that subordination be taken into the essence of those [general commands], then indeed is the Executive inferior and ministerial to the Legislative. But if all we annex to the notion of executive power is the habit of issuing commands concerning individual actions only, in this last view it is no more necessarily inferior to the Legislative than the Legislative is to that. Amplitude of a Power. All Power executive not essentially Subordinate to all Legislative.

279. One thing, indeed, must be confessed, that ultimately some Power of the executive kind must be undermost. Some Power to apply the general provisions of Legislature to particular objects, there must always be. But some is.

[1] MS orig. 'Assemblage'. [2] MS orig. 'Emperor'.

But some is a necessary employment.

280. The persons that execute the Commands of the Legislature, where there is one, must necessarily be employ'd in issuing particular commands. But we suppose no Legislature, no man or body of men in the habit of issuing general commands, commands concerning sorts of actions. The business of Government may be carried on in this way, as in the other. It actually is carried on thus in many States. It is carried on, therefore, solely by particular commands.

Commands of the *Supreme* Power may be all *particular.*

281. A body in a state is in the habit of issuing particular commands. If these particular commands are confined to a conformity with the general commands, issued by another body, then is the second [superior][1] to the first. But we will suppose it not thus confined. We take away the Legislative body: then is this body *supreme*: and yet it exercises itself in commands which are of the nature of those issued by the power we are used to call executive.

Law (Substance))(Particular Commands Supreme.

Permanency.

282. Permanency is a characteristic belonging to general Commands: because, while individuals perish, *sorts* continue.

By permanency is here meant not actual endurance, but the capacity to endure. A general command, a command concerning sorts of actions, in a word a Law, may be limited in it's duration: but if not limited, nothing hinders (in ordinary cases) but that it may endure for ever. Actions of the sort it specifies may be performing by different persons to the end of time.

Power Executive. Commands issued by the Executive Power, when Subordinate to Legislative, and when equal.

283. The Executive Power issues Commands concerning individual actions. If these Commands are no other than Commands of a sort issued or permitted to be issued by another Power, the Legislative, the Executive has another Power to which it is subordinate, namely that Legislative Power. If not, an Executive, as well as any Legislative, may be the Supreme Power in the State.

'Power' æquivocal to the *person* and the *relation.*

284. The term Power, by a figure very frequent in discourse, is transferred to the persons exercising it: as Property is to the thing in which it is exercised. This is an equivocality too inveterate to be corrected, nor is there any need it should: it breeds no confusion. Nobody is [in] any danger of mistaking a fictitious moral entity for a real person or a real thing. I shall, therefore, use the term, without scruple, indiscriminately in the two senses.

Government. Legislature. Administration.

285. The words *Government*, *Legislature*, *Administration*, and many others, have the like double signification.

[1] MS 'inferior' contradicts the evident sense of the passage.

286. It may happen that the Supreme Power in a State issues no general Commands: no Commands concerning sorts of actions, makes in short no Laws: then is it not a Legislature: it's functions, in this case, answer (except as to the being subject to the controul of a superior Power) to the functions of the Power we are in use to stile the Executive.

Power Supreme)(Legislature.

This is nearly the case in many absolute Governments, for example in the Empire of Morocco.

It is as easy to conceive a Legislative Power acting in subordination under the controul of an Executive (or rather of a Power not Legislative), as an Executive under the Controul of a Legislative. Only a Legislative can never be the lowest in a chain of Public Powers. It must always have an Executive to carry, in the several particular instances that occur, it's general commands into effect.

287. The Power whose function it is to *execute* a set of general Commands, must have those Commands in contemplation. The particular Commands in the issuing of which such execution consists, or the general command executed,[1] do not originate in the breast of the executive Power: they are handed down from the Legislative.

Legislation Supreme)(Subordinate)(Power Executive.

But the general commands of a Legislature, however subordinate, however low it stand in a chain of Public Powers, do originate in the breast of that Legislature: they are *there* conceived: they are *their* commands, and never were the commands of any other.

A subordinate Power in a State issues general commands. Take away all Powers that are superordinate, these Commands, without dispute, are Laws. The *Supreme* Power in a state issues *particular* Commands: these Commands never can be *Laws*, because they are *particular*. They are concerning *individual* actions, not *sorts* of actions.

There are three conceivable Powers in a state that are perfectly distinguishable from each other; and that in practise do often require to be distinguished. The Power that issues Commands concerning sorts of actions, without any Power above it to make null those Commands; the Power that issues Commands concerning sorts of actions, with a power above it that may make null those commands; and the Power that issues Commands not concerning sorts of actions, but individual actions only. Call the two first of these both Legislative, the one supreme, the other subordinate, and the third executive, you have three names whereby to distinguish the three Powers: call the second and last by the

[1] Bentham has noted at this point: 'Qu. which.'

same name executive, and you make confusion. Executive you *oppose* to Legislative. What is Executive, you say, is not Legislative. If by Legislative you mean that power which issues commands concerning sorts of actions, and by Executive you mean, as by the supposition, one sort of power that does issue commands concerning sorts of actions; in saying that what is Executive power is *not* Legislative, you contradict yourself. If by Legislative Power you do *not* mean the power that issues Commands concerning *sorts* of actions, what is it, then, that you *do* mean?

Expressed—Synonyms to.

288. Synonymous to 'expressed', as applied to Commands, are 'uttered', 'issued', 'deliver'd', 'published', 'manifested', 'presented', 'signified'.

Conditions in a Law.

289. The Condition in a Law may be annext to either [1st] the Command, or 2d the Threat.

Bare acts few forbidden.

290. Few, very few indeed, are the sorts of acts simply and unconditionally, that is universally, commanded or forbidden. I can think of none commanded. I can think of but two forbidden: Unnatural Coition, and Cruelties.[1] Indeed, even here, it is manifest the act[2] can not be said to be simply forbidden, unless under the idea of the act be included that of the object on which it is exerted.

Crimes unnatural.

Cruelties.

Indeed, such acts inflicting pain in such sort as is never inflicted by public authority in the way of punishment, or on private occasions in the way of defence, are other instances of acts universally prohibited.

'Act' includes the Object.

291. Under the idea of the act, even consider'd in a physical light only, come these two at least: 1st that of the motion in which it consists, and 2dly that of the object on which it is exerted. Unless this was the case, you could not speak of an act of killing, an act of

[1] MS orig. 'but one forbidden. It is the sort of act commonly called the Crime against nature.' According to Blackstone, *Commentaries on the Laws of England*, iv. 215–16, the infliction of the death penalty on those found guilty of 'the infamous *crime against nature*, committed either with man or beast' was 'an universal, not merely a provincial, precept'. In relation to cruelties, Bentham may have had in mind Blackstone's discussion of self-defence at ibid. iii. 3–4, where he states that the law 'considers that the future process of law is by no means an adequate remedy for injuries accompanied with force; since it is impossible to say, to what wanton lengths of rapine or cruelty outrages of this sort might be carried, unless it were permitted a man immediately to oppose one violence with another. Self-defence therefore, as it is justly called the primary law of nature, so it is not, neither can it be in fact, taken away by the law of society.'

[2] i.e. 'the crime against nature'.

maiming. For the motion being supposed the same, killing can take place with respect to such bodies only, it is plain, as are possessed of life. 'Tis from the nature of the object, therefore, that the act is apt to take it's name.

---

292. A Parent has Powers over the Child: a Parent has rights against the Child. A Child has rights against the Parent: but a Child has no Powers over the Parent. Powers)(Rights. Parent and Child.

There are cases where the two words Power and Right can be used indiscriminately: there are others where they can not.

293. For a Command to be a Law, the Command itself, as well as the armature, must originate with Government. The Commands of persons invested with Domestic powers have their armature from Government: but the Commands themselves do not originate with Government.[1] Laws)(Domestic Commands.

294. Powers beneficial over persons, Rights to the services of a person, are in many States (ought to be in all states) limited by the consideration of sensibility. When this is the case, we do not say Right *to* the person generally, which would mean to all his services without regard to such limitation, but right to his services, meaning such services only as are consistent with it. Rights to Person's Services)(Rights to Things.

In things, being either such as are not indued with sensibility, or whose sensibility is not regarded, we speak of a right to them. We speak of a right to things, meaning, with respect to things animate, a right to all such services as they are capable of performing (saving the restrictions imposed for the sake of strangers), or, to use the most general expression, a right to put them to all such uses (under the above restriction) as they are capable of being put to.

---

295. Words that do not stand for simple ideas, or substances which are determinate assemblages of simple ideas, are to be understood only by reference to words that do. Prefat. Beginn^g·

Many Moral terms, as Power, Right, &c., have no genus better known than themselves, to which, by being referred, they can be made known. For they have no superior genus: they do not belong to any genus.

I hear speak of a *Cacalianthemum*: I want to know the meaning of it. I enquire and am told it is a plant. This helps me somewhat. Of a plant, I have an idea, such as it is, which, indeed, is loose enough, but which perpetual use has made familiar to me, an idea collected

[1] In the text, Bentham has noted at this point: 'v. p. 100 infra.' See para. 299, p. 112 below.

by abstraction from individuals with which I have been made acquainted by my senses.

Motive. Sanction.

296. A Motive of the Law's providing is termed a Sanction.

A Sanction is the term given to such a Motive as is produced by operation of Law in the design to give birth to some mode of Conduct commanded by the Law.

Instruments of Security internal.

297. Instruments of Security against Internal Mischief are $1^{st.}$ Instruments of Confinement—Prisons. $2^{dly.}$ Instruments of Punishment—Scourges, &c. $3^{dly.}$ Instruments of Offence and Defence—Arms of any kind—are the same as against [external],[1] with the addition of Instruments of mere punishment which are not in use against external enemies.

Pleasure of Relief.

298. Opposed to Pain positive is—Pain of *Privation*: to Pleasure positive, is Pleasure of *Relief* (*d'adoucissement*).

Domestic Commands = Compacts.

299. 'Tis in regard to Domestic Commands as in regard to such Compacts as are sanctioned by the Law. The Volition in the first case is a Command: in the second case, a Promise. [The Volition] is not of the Law's own production, but only of it's adoption: the armature is of it's own production.[2]

Prefat. Advertisement.

300. Advertisement to the Reader.

When a Character consisting of two Semicircles placed back to back thus)(is placed between two words or phrases, it is used as a mark of distinction or opposition, and shews that the two words or phrases between which it stands are set in opposition to each other. It is used for this purpose in many Dictionaries. It is here adopted for Brevity sake in the marginal contents which the shorter they are, the better they answer their purpose. Thus Law)(Domestic Order is put instead of Difference betwixt a Law and a Domestic Order.

Com. Law *in genere* unexplained.

301. On Statute Law something has been attempted, either by our Author, or else (it matters not which) by those whom he has copied.[3] Of an *integrant* part of it, some notion has been conceived, such as we shall see. Of such integrant part, the constituent parts

[1] MS 'internal' may be a slip. The syntax is, however, confused.
[2] In the text, Bentham has noted at this point: 'v. p. 98 supra.' See para 293, p. 111 above.
[3] 'either . . . copied' has been bracketed by Bentham for deletion.

have in like manner been assigned, and names bestowed on them.[1] A Partition, such as it is, has been made of the whole: and a nomenclature attributed to the parts of it.[2] Even this ill-considered and unskilful culture is more than has as yet been ever bestow'd upon the trackless expanse of Common Law. It remains to this day, as the Naturalist Dillenius said of the Family of the mosses, a perfect chaos, the opprobrium of the Science.[3] The System of Mosses might wait some time for a hand to methodize it, and the world be no great sufferer by the delay. But what is it's situation under the Chaos of Common Law, of that System which is the rule and measure of men's actions, on which dependeth so large a portion of their felicity?

302. Of an integrant part of Statute Law, a general delineation has been given. We come now to Common Law. Statute Law is *real* Law. Common Law is *fictitious*. How, then, shall it be delineated? How? but after the model of that according to the similitude of which it is feigned.

Comm. Law, to be analysed upon the Model of the Statute.

[1] Bentham perhaps had in mind Blackstone's division of statutes into those that were either general (public) or special (private), and into those that were either declaratory of the Common Law or remedied defects in it, with the latter being again divided into enlarging and restraining statutes: see *Commentaries on the Laws of England*, i. 85–7.

[2] In *Commentaries on the Laws of England*, Blackstone divided his subject matter into four Books entitled 'Of the Rights of Persons', 'Of the Rights of Things', 'Of Private Wrongs', and 'Of Public Wrongs'.

[3] Johann Jakob Dillenius (1687–1747), German botanist, first Sherardian Professor of Botany at the University of Oxford 1734–47, was author of *Historia Muscorum generibus xx. absoluta*, Oxford, 1740, which appeared in English translation as *Historia Muscorum: A General History of Land and Water, &c. Mosses and Corals. Containing All the Known Species, Exhibited by about 1000 Figures, on 85 large Royal 4to Copper Plates, drawn and engraved in the best Manner from the Originals*, London, 1763. Bentham may, however, have had in mind a passage from William Hudson, 'An Account of a Work, intituled, Jacobi Christiani Schaeffer icones et descriptio Fungorum quorundam singularium et memorabilium; simul Fungorum Bavariæ icones nativis coloribus expressæ editioni jam paratæ propediem evulgandæ, denunciantur', in *Philosophical Transactions, giving some Account of the Present Undertakings, Studies, and Labours, of the Ingenious, in many Considerable Parts of the World. Vol. LII. Part II. For the Year 1762*, London, 1763, pp. 495–506 at 505: 'Micheli [Pier Antonio Micheli (1679–1737), Italian botanist] and Dillenius were the first botanists that examined this order of plants [fungi], with any degree of accuracy; and though their observations are very considerable, and have been of great service to preceding botanists, yet Linnæus, who mentions them with applause, says, Philosophia Botanica, p. 241. that the order of Fungi, to the reproach of botany, still remains a chaos, as we are ignorant what is a species, and what a variety.' The reference is to the Swedish botanist Carl Linnaeus (1707–78), who, in *Philosophia Botanica*, Stockholm, 1751, p. 241, had stated: 'FUNGORUM ordo in opprobium artis etiamnum Chaos est, nescientibus Botanicis in his, quid Species, quid Varietas fit.' The passage was translated in James Lee, *An Introduction to Botany. Containing An Explanation of the Theory of that Science, and an Interpretation of its Technical Terms. Extracted From the Works of Dr. Linnæus, and calculated to assist such as may be desirous of studying that Author's Method and Improvements*, London, 1760, p. 235, as follows: 'The whole Order of the *Fungi*, to the Scandal of the Science, is still a Chaos, the Botanists not being yet able in these to decide with Certainty what is a Species, and what a Variety.'

Comm. Law. Elements real) (Body fictitious.

303. Of Common Law, the Elements are real. They are the work of authority: they are Public Commands—Commands concerning individual actions. The body composed of them—commands concerning sorts of actions—is fictitious. It is not the work of authority. The Body consists of (or at least contains in it) a system of *inductions* from those elements, which inductions are unauthoritative, made by every man for himself and for such others as choose to take him for their guide. In as far as the Domain of Common Law extend, even these days may be said of this Country, and indeed of any country, with some little variation what was said of old of Israel. There is no Law in it.[1] But every man guesseth at it, according to what seemeth true in his own eyes.

Comm. Law. Assertive matter *not* fictitious.[2]

304. The *principal* matter, the Commanding, of the Common Law is, I have said, *fictitious*. It is not so altogether with the *appenditious* matter. This *appenditious* assertive matter is, we may observe, an expression of some act, not of the will, as is the principal, but of the judgment. Tho' the act of the Will, the Command, must have been particular, since it is an individual case always that calls it forth, yet the act of the judgment which has served to determine it may be expressed in general terms; and, as such, may stand as a proposition fit to be tacked on as appenditious matter to a general Command: to a general command, a command concerning actions of that *sort* of which the particular command in question is.

The Model of such an Analysis is the Model for a Digest.

305. To resolve the Mass of Common Law into articles that might stand for it's integrant parts of Real, Statute Law, and to dispose these integrant into parts that might stand for their constituent, to do this through the several topics over which it is extended, to do this is the task of him to whom, if to any one, the grand work of a Digest shall be committed. This done, that arduous and mighty enterprize is atchieved. If these rules be just, that work, conducted to it's best advantage, will be throughout but an exemplification of these rules.

All matter of Law imports Volition expressed by words or Action.

[305.*] Every proposition in Law, is either itself a Command, or supposes a Command. It supposes a Command, for the effect of it can never be clearly explained or understood, but by means of it's

[1] An echo of II Chronicles 15: 3.

[2] In the margin, Bentham has noted at this point: 'Qu.? Since general propositions of judges have no *coercive* force on their Successors: such as Particular Commands have over their subordinate Officers. There is no Punishment for a succeeding Judge, simply for not conforming to a rule laid down by a preceding Judge, as there is for a Ministerial Officer for not conforming to a single Command of a Judge.

'It is true that a single instance of conformity in a Judge may go along with other instances to serve as evidence of Corruption: but &c.'

relation to a Command. It is by means of that relation alone that it can be made out to be an Article of Law; of which '*to command*' is the essential characteristic.[1] A man finds no bottom, till he comes to understand some discernable act or assemblage of acts which the Law has made it his interest to do or to abstain from.

---

306. From that which is another's,[2] let every man abstain, on pain of forfeiting so much money's worth as shall serve for restitution, compensation, and costs of suit, or on default thereof, imprisonment. 'Tis the mandatory part that expresses the restraint by which the Powers that a man has over the thing that is called his own are constituted. To the Expository part belongs the doctrine concerning Titles: it shews the several sorts of means by one or other of which it is that that which is called a man's property must have become so. It answers the question, what is a man's property?: that which has come to him by some one or other of the several means that are called Titles. To the Definitional part belongs also the Doctrine concerning Tenures: it shews the several conditions upon which that which is called his property is made [so]. By specifying the conditions annexed to the subject in question by these Tenures, it shews several of the ways by which that which has been a given person's property may cease to be so: viz: upon breach of any of these Conditions, and proper steps taken by the other parties interested in consequence.

Law creative of Property. Parts of.

---

307. In this, as in every other Science, the Definitions that are given should be disposed into a chain. An insulated, unconnected, incomplete assemblage answers very little purpose. If I might be allowed an Allegory, I would say, they prevent not the import of the several terms from being still tossed in the ocean of uncertainty. Here and there one may, by accident, be brought somewhat nearer shore, but very seldom is any one brought to land: nor, if it be, does it bring the others with it. To moor them fast in the Road of Precision,[3] there is but one method: it is to bring the first of them to an anchor upon the *Terra firma* of simple ideas: and with that first, in a chain of unbroken continuity, to connect the whole groupe of those that follow.

Prefat. Chain of Definitions. Allegory.

This is the way, and the only way, of putting together that compage over which, as over a bridge, a man may, with security

[1] This sentence has been marked by Bentham for deletion.
[2] Above this phrase, Bentham has written: 'Mandatory Part.'
[3] MS orig. 'certainty'.

and care and expedition, range over the depths of Science till he arrive at the regions of discovery.

Prefat. Current Definitions are *Repetends* or *Circulates*. Ex.g. 'Title'.

308. 'A Title' to Things real, our Author informs us, is 'the means whereby a man cometh to the just possession of his Property.'[1] Thus much concerning Title. What is 'Possession', or what is 'Property', we are left to understand as we are able. Yet [to] do this clearly and satisfactor[il]y is quite as difficult to understand as what Title is.

Those who have undertaken to give Definitions of Legal terms seem to have had no higher ambition, nor any other aim, than this: to contrive their definitions so as not to contain any thing that should be demonstrably false: to fit them to convey any instructive truth, is what they have either not cared to go about, or not known how.

Ex.g. Estate.

'*Estates* in Lands, Tenements and Hereditaments, are such *Interest* as the Tenant hath therein.'[a] What we gain by this, is, instead of the word Estate, putting the word Interest. We should have learnt precisely as much by being told that 'Estate' applied to Lands, Tenements and Hereditaments meant the same as 'Interest'. This may be very true. But what are we the wiser for it? The idea men formed upon hearing the word Estate, would, it was apprehended, be apt not to be a very clear one: hence it was thought proper to give it a definition: this definition consists in putting another into the room of it—the word interest—of which the difficulty of forming a clear idea is much the same.

Physical Possession.

309. A thing may be said to be *possessed*, in the physical sense of the word possession, when there neither is, nor is believed by the possessor to be, any physical impediment to it's being used.

Or—Physical Possession of a thing is the absence, both real and supposed, of every physical impediment to it's being used.

Or—Possession (in a physical sense) is the Physical Power to use.

[a] *Anal*. p. 38.[2]

[1] See Blackstone, *Commentaries on the Laws of England*, ii. 195: 'A title is thus defined by sir Edward Coke, *titulus est justa causa possidendi id quod nostrum est*; or, it is the means whereby the owner of lands hath the just possession of his property'. The reference is to Edward Coke, *The First Part of the Institutes of the Lawes of England. Or, A Commentarie upon Litteton, not the name of a Lawyer onely, but of the Law it selfe* (known as *Coke on Littleton*) London, 1628, fo. 345v. This work of Sir Edward Coke (1552–1634) was itself an extended commentary on a work on tenures by Sir Thomas Littleton (d. 1481), Justice of Common Pleas 1466–81, which had been first published in 1481 or 1482.

[2] See William Blackstone, *An Analysis of the Laws of England*, Oxford, 1756, p. 38. There are some minor inaccuracies in the rendering of the passage; Blackstone, moreover, has 'Man' rather than 'Tenant'.

310. Possession, in a legal sense, stands distinguished from Non-possession, on the one hand, and from Property on the other. Legal Possession.

311. Legal Possession depends upon Protection. Legal Possession. Protection.

Where a Man is not legally possessed of a thing, he is not protected in the use of it: he is *restrained* from using it.

Where a man is legally possessed of a thing but has not the property of it, protection takes one course. Possession without Property.

Where a man has the property of a thing but not the Possession of it, Protection takes another course. Property without Possession.

Where a man has both property and possession, Protection takes a third course. Property with Possession.

312. Lawyers, in treating of Possession of Property, of Right of Possession, of Right of Property, proceed under a great mistake. They begin with supposing fixed ideas to be originally attendant on those expressions: namely the ideas of certain relations: they then go on with stating certain dispositions of Law as consequences of that relation, supposing it already to be understood. Whereas no idea at all can be formed of it, but what is collected from those consequences. Error concerning these words. Falsely assumed by Lawyers as understood.

313. In the whole compass of Jurisprudence, there is nothing more unsettled than the import of these expressions, nothing more difficult to settle. I will attempt it. Possession &c. Difficulty of defining.

---

314. That thing or object of possession is an *article* of *value* that can contribute to a man's Happiness. Article of Value: Valuable objects of Possession analysed according to their uses.

315. There are two ways in which a thing may contribute to a man's Happiness: one is, by adding to the stock of Happiness he has by means of other things. In this case, it is an Instrument of Pleasure. Instrument of Pleasure.

316. The other is, by serving to prevent the stock of Happiness he has by means of other things from being diminished. In this case, it is an instrument of Security. Instrument of Security.

317. Danger of losing Happiness arises: $1^{st.}$ From events at large: or $2^{dly.}$ From Actions. Security against $1^{st.}$ Calamity. $2^{d.}$ Mischief.

Unhappiness from events is stiled Calamity. Unhappiness from actions is stiled Mischief. Hence we have instruments of security 1st against Calamity, 2dly against Mischief.

318. Instruments of Security against Mischief are either $1^{st.}$ Instruments of Defence, or $2^{dly.}$ Instruments of Offence. Instruments of Defence.

Men, in their attempts to do such acts as are causes of pain, may be restrained by means which affect them either 1st as they are mere Physical agents; or 2dly as they are thinking agents.

As physical agents, they may be restrained by physical impulse, or physical *vis inertiæ*.

Substances serving to restrain them, by physical impulse or physical *vis inertiæ*, are instruments of defence.

Offence.

319. As sensitive and thinking agents, men may be restrained by the expectation of pain.

Necessary to producing the expectation of pain is the power of actually producing pain.

To produce Death is always to produce Pain.

Instruments serving to produce pain or Death are instruments of offence

Their uses interconvertible.

320. It is manifest, the same thing which serves as an instrument of *defence*, may serve as an instrument of *offence*, and *vice versâ*: but if it be such as is most frequently used for the purpose of defence, it is stiled an instrument of defence; if of offence, an instrument of offence.

An instrument is named according to which of the two uses above it is most usual for it to be put to.

Calamity.

321. Calamity is Unhappiness in which man is not consider'd as an instrument. Calamity is unhappiness arising from *events*.

Mischief.

322. Mischief is Unhappiness in which man is an instrument. Mischief is Unhappiness arising from the volition of man.[1]

Mischief { Pain or Danger.

323. Unhappiness is either *certain* or in Contingency. Unhappiness *certain* may be spoken of simply under the name of Pain.

Danger.

Danger is unhappiness consider'd as contingent.

Hence Mischief is either Pain or Danger.

Cause)(Instrument.

324. A Cause is an instrument in action.

An instrument is a Substance; a Cause, a Mode of that substance.

The word Cause is in general promiscuously bestow'd on the substance and the mode: but as we have another name full as expressive for the *Substance*, for precision's sake, it is better to confine it to the mode.

Ex.g. Barometer.

325. It is said indifferently, '*the Air* is the cause of the rising of the Quicksilver in the Barometer,' and, 'the *pressure of the Air* is the cause of the rising of the Quicksilver in the Barometer.' Here, the Air is the *Substance* acting as an *instrument* on the Quicksilver; I would call it, therefore, the instrument. The pressure of the Air is the mode, viz: a motion, of that Substance. This mode has no other name, that I can think of, to express it's relation to the effect: to this, therefore, let us confine the name of *Cause*.

[1] MS orig. 'men's *actions*.'

There is the more reason for narrowing the import of the word cause to signify a mode, in as much as it's correlative term *effect* is, in many if not in all cases, applied indisputably [to] a mode, and nothing else. It is so here in this example before us: what is it that is the effect of the pressure of the Air? it is not the Quicksilver itself, the Substance: it is the *mode* of it, the motion the quicksilver has when we say it rises.

---

326. Of incidental Military Commands (not being Laws), the duration of the sort of acts commanded is limited, in the nature of them, at the utmost to the term of the continuance of the *War*, if not of the *Campaign*.[1]

Law (Substance) ⲭ Commands Military incidental ⲭ Permanent.

327. When an act is individual, the act itself (viz: the species of motion), the agent and the subject are individually assignable at the time of issuing the command: assignable, that is, either simply or in the disjunctive.[2]

Act Sortal ⲭ Individual.

328. The agent may be assignable either by a standing description or an incidental description: 'Go and apprehend John Thomas:' or 'Go and apprehend any man you see in arms at such a place.'

Agent's description permanent ⲭ incidental.

---

329. Simple ideas are the *ne plus ultra* of expository investigation: the mind neither can go deeper in it's researches, nor has occasion. He who cannot understand a word when the explanation of it is rightly conducted upon that plan, can never.

Prefat. Simple Ideas the *Ne plus ultra*.

---

330. Between the subject and the Legislative Power when exerting itself in Laws of the *Substantive* kind, no Executive Power[3] interposes to point out and ascertain the individual agent, act and object: the subject, in order to [pay] his obedience, is left to find out those individual articles of himself by the general description. 'Tis in the execution of Laws of the Adjective [kind] that the party that is to *obey*, to *execute* (for here obedience is called *execution*), that is the Ministerial officer of Justice, waits the direction, the particular command, of another, that is the Magisterial officer of Justice, the Judge, in order to have the individual act, agent and object ascertained.

Law ⲭ Particular Commands.—In Adjective Laws, Particular Commands interposed between Law and acts of obedience.

[1] In the text, Bentham has noted at this point: '☛ But they are Laws: only Subordinate. They concern *sorts* of acts. They are not perhaps written.'

[2] MS orig. 'alternative'.

[3] In the margin, Bentham has noted at this point: 'The Executive Power is that in whose hands any Fiduciary Power is deposited, other than Legislative.'

The Law says, whoso hath stolen, let the Sheriff hang him: not this or that individual man in particular, but any man that hath stolen. What is it that the Sheriff does in consequence? He does not, of his own accord, take and hang the individual John Thomas who *he* thinks is of the *sort* of persons that have stolen; but he waits and hears the *opinion* of the Judge, telling him that John Thomas is the person who has stolen, and, what comes in consequence of such opinion, the Command of the Judge telling him that John Thomas is the person he is to hang.

King—his *Procuratorial* Powers.

331. The King, in foreign concerns, is invested with a *Procuratorial* character. He is Agent for the State. He makes Treaties. He makes Peace and War.

Peace and War signification complex.

332. Of Peace and War, the sounds are familiar to our ears; but the meaning is so complex, as not to be made accurately intelligible without intricate discussions.

King—his Judiciary Powers.

333. In Judicial Concerns, his Power is confined to the nomination of the persons who are really empower'd to exercise that sort of Power. This Power is immediately over persons.

King—his Fiscal Powers.

334. Fiscal Powers over Money concern Fabrication, Receipt, Transport, Lodgment and Expenditure.

Fiscal Powers over other Articles of Wealth concern Fabrication, Receipt, Lodgment, Transport, Consumption and Reparation.

In Fiscal concerns, except as to his Peculium, his Power is confined to the nomination of persons empower'd.

These Powers are immediately over Things.

Law—matter of. *Adjective* part indistinctly conditional to that of *Substantive*.

335. In Procedure, the legal propositions descriptive of the steps necessary to be taken in order to convict for an offence form so many conditions to the command appointing the Punishment for that offence—Conditional not to the Command, but to the armature.

King—his Military Powers.

336. Military Powers are Powers immediately over *Persons*, and such *Things* as are implements of War. They are Powers of issuing Commands from which there is no Appeal. They are limited in point of Place, to the Scene of War: and in point of Time, to the Time of War. They are not limited as to the nature of the acts.

King—his Legislative Powers in certain Commercial matters.

337. The Commercial Power of settling Weights and Measures has a reference to Litiscontestation: it is a Power of ascertaining what, in case of legal debate, shall be received as *evidence* of the quantity of the Subject-matter in debate.

---

338. *Circumstances* are phænomena naturally connected with the *act*: *Conditions* are phænomena artificially and arbitrarily connected with it. Circumstances ⨯ Conditions.

339. Phænomena is the most extensive denomination for the objects of our senses, our appetites and intellection: it includes Modes and Substances. It includes[1] Phænomena.

340. The Common Law consists either 1st of Particular Commands, or 2dly of General assertive Propositions, assumed as the ground of those Commands, or 3dly of Precedents, viz: of Procedure of the Parties.[2] These General Assertive propositions are reducible to one of the 3 classes of assertive propositions that are fit to make parts of an actual Law. Common Law.

He who would come to a right understanding of the effect of them, must be able to assign that General command to which, as appenditious propositions, they are fit to stand annexed.

The Particular Commands are coercive: the immediate objects of them are men at large.

The General Propositions are Propositions modificative of a fictitious General Command: this General Command, being fictitious, neither with any such modification nor without it, is not compulsory: it's objects are persons standing upon a level with those who framed it, Judges: the persons to whom it belongs to issue such particular Commands. The Common Law respects either Substantive matter or Adjective. In Adjective, it respects either parties or officers or other strangers. The Adjective matter, as far as regards the parties and their cause, consists, as has been said, entirely of conditions annexed to the punishment or absolution of the Defendant. As far as it regards the conduct of officers, it consists of mandatory matter prohibiting (under penalties) the various species of misconduct that it may come in their way to practise.[3]

---

341. The whole train of Adjective Laws is dispensed with in Domestic Government and in a great degree in Despotic Government, which comes nearest in it's simplicity to the domestic. The Cadi, without form or process, takes cognizance of a complaint, and, without the delays of pleading or the intervention of official Laws Substantive ⨯ Adjective. Adjective '*carent*'[4] in Domestic and Despotic Governments.

[1] Bentham has abandoned the passage, but noted at this point: 'v. Appearances.' See paras. 366 and 628, pp. 126 and 200–1 below, respectively.

[2] In the text, Bentham has noted at this point: 'v. p. 125.' See paras. 356–7, p. 125 below.

[3] In the text, Bentham has noted at this point: 'v. Sheets marked "Misdemesnors of Magistrates" for the species of misconduct.' See the brouillons headed 'Misdemeanours of Officers. Magistrates' at UC lxx. 210–12.

[4] i.e. 'lacking' or 'absent'.

functions, issues his definitive command upon the spot. Laws Substantive have each a different end of their own. Laws Adjective, the regulations of Procedure, have but one general end which is common to them all, the ascertaining whether a man has or has not embraced the mode of conduct alleged against him, being a mode of conduct prohibited by some General Law, actual or fictitious: whether he has or has not incurred that punishment which, if he has, it is the business of a particular command to cause to be inflicted on him.

No restraints upon the Option between Punishing and not punishing: no conditions to conviction.

Law (parts). Object expressed in a Single word.

342. A Law, then, is a Command.—If the object of the Command is an act characterizable by a single word, then a Command and nothing more. One single proposition would be sufficient to express it: an *imperative* proposition.

'Steal.'

343. 'Steal not,' may be conceived as an example of such a proposition: of such a Law: or, to bring the idea at once to it's maximum of simplicity, '*steal.*' Here the act which is the object of the command is expressed by a single word: and the *Command*, the Volition, the act of the speaker's mind that is directed to that object, is expressed also by the same word: the word being that sort of word which Grammarians call a Verb, and that verb in what is called the imperative mode of it: a form or *mode* fitted of itself without additament to express Command. This Command is general, for the act which is the object of it is not confined to an individual by any particular limitations. It is not said, 'steal this thing, or from this man, or at this time, or in this place, or (more generally) in these circumstances:' but without limitation, 'any thing, from any man, at any time, in any place, where you are able, steal.'[1]

'Steal not.'

This Command is positive: the mode of conduct which is the object of it, is action. The proposition expressing the command and the mode of conduct, is mandatory. Add the word '*not*' to the word 'steal', and the command is *negative*: the mode of conduct which is the object of it, is *forbearance*: the proposition expressing the command and the mode of conduct, is *prohibitive*. The command is still a *general* one, for the mode of conduct which is the object of it is not confined to an *individual* by any *particular* limitations. It is not said 'steal not this thing, or from this man, or at

[1] In the margin, Bentham has noted at this point: 'Qu. As to conditions and matter Definitional.'

this time, or in this place, or (more generally) in these circumstances,' but without limitation, '*any* thing, from *any man*, at *any* time, in *any* place, in any circumstances, *steal not*.'[1]

344. Good Will is the desire of contributing to the happiness of the person who is the object of it. Good Will.

345. Wealth is the general fund of pleasures. Wealth has from the first been said to be possessed. For the several articles of it are true and proper objects of Possession. At length, what is called Reputation, was observed to be also a fund of pleasures. Hence this also was, by a Metaphor, called a possession. Hence this also was said to be possessed. Reputation an Object of Possession.

A man is said to have a good reputation, to be in good reputation, when he is the object of the esteem of such persons as are acquainted with him. Reputation, def.

---

346. By the word Cause is meant some times the action of an Instrument: some times the instrument itself, without considering it's action. I would wish to confine the word to the former idea: since the latter idea has this other word 'instrument' to denote it. 'Cause' æquivocal.

---

347. Regulation is a term that may be applied indifferently to any portion, great or small, of the matter of a Law; whether it be of the *substantial* kind, or of the *modificative*, or of both together. *Regulation* in Stat. ⵋ *Rule* [in] Comm. Law.

348. By the Principal [or] Primary or Substantial or Imperative part of a Law may be meant that portion of the matter of it by which the Command, the Volition, is signified. Imperative Part.

349. The other portion may be termed the Appenditious or Demonstrative or Assertive. Demonstrative or Assertive Part.

350. A Maxim is an unauthoritative discourse, containing the opinion of some person whose maxim it is, concerning the agreement or coincidence of a number of regulations, real or fictitious, in any point of view. Maxim.

A Maxim of Statute Law is of regulations real: a Maxim of Common Law, of fictitious.

When I say, of Rules, this or that is a Maxim of Law, I mean one of two things: either that [it] is a Maxim of my own framing, which I now communicate and deliver as a truth: or that it is a Maxim which, framed by some one else, has been generally known, and generally assented to. I give it as a maxim that I *make*, or a maxim that I *cite*.

---

[1] In the text, Bentham has noted at this point: 'v. p. 124, N° 351.' See para. 351, p. 124 below.

Law—*bulk* and *Structure* of *a*—depends not upon the acts in question but on the Language they are described in.

351. What appendicious matter a Law shall have depends in great measure upon the turn of the language. 'Tis upon the richness of the language in that behalf that it depends whether a single word shall be sufficient to design the act with all the conditions and limitations that are thought proper to be annexed to it, or whether there must be many. A command to do no murder, were the conditions that are to be annexed to the act of killing in order to bring it under the idea of murder sufficiently settled and notorious, might serve, in our language, to express a Law which could not, in any other language, be expressed without the addition of much appenditious matter. Whether a Command shall be signified in two Laws or in one, whether a Law shall contain much appenditious matter, or but little, depends not so much upon the nature of the acts themselves that are the objects of it, as upon the number of ideas the language happens to have collected under one expression.[1]

Comm. Law, not *unwritten*, but *not Law*.

352. The common account given of Common Law is that it is a Law, only not written: just the reverse of this is the truth. It is a something written; but that something is not Law. Written it is, or how have we come by it?

Comm. Law. It's Elements are Ephemera.

353. Common Law, as matter of Law, of authoritative Command, expires with the particular transactions that are the objects of the particular Commands of which it consists. When a Sheriff has apprehended a man as he was commanded, there is an end of so much Law, if it is to be called Law, as that command amounted to.

King—what he does when he proclaims War.

354. The making of War by the King involves in it the exercise of two Powers: 1st. Power Dispensatorial, in putting the instruments of Offence and Defence that are at his disposal to their use: 2dly. Power Legislative, in suspending the Code of Peace, and reviving the Code of War. To raise an army is to subject a number of persons (the Soldiers of that army) to a new System of Government. The Laws protective of Liberty, the Laws of Judicial Procedure, are suspended as to them: viz: as against their Commanders.

---

[1] In the text, Bentham has noted at this point: 'v. p. 118. N° 342 an Example.' The cross-reference should perhaps be to para. 343 (not 342), pp. 122–3 above.

355. To understand a proposition in a Law Book, we should be able to say whether it is a Command or not a Command: if not a Command, what *is* the Command that it belongs to? Is it of the real kind, or the fictitious? If real, what is it? if fictitious, what may it be conceived to be?

Prefat. Law—how to *parse*.

---

356. Precedents (i:e: of forms of Allegation and defence) are matters of Adjective Law, conditional to the armature of a Substantive Law. The punishment for such an act, says the Law, shall not be inflicted on the Def[t] unless the allegations of the Plff be conformable to these Precedents.

Comm. Law. Precedents.

357. Neither shall it, unless the steps of Process taken by the Plff be conformable to these Precedents of Steps of Procedure.

Descriptions of Steps of Procedure.

358. Every step added as a condition to the execution of a Law, that is not necessary to the ascertainment of the truths in dispute, or to the guarding against some collateral abuse, is an impediment to Justice: because the more these conditions are multiplied, the more difficult is the complying with them all.

Procedure. Forms not necessary, are mischievous.

359.[1] The questions in a Suit are either: 1[st.] Whether the Law, if real, has so and so commanded: if fictitious, is to be conceived as having so and so commanded; or 2[d] are such or such the conditions to the command, or conditions to the armature?

Parsing. Questions in a Suit how referable to a Law—as here analysed.

As to the fact alleged—was it done? this is matter of fact. If the question is concerning a Command, was it such an act as is opposite to the act commanded? if concerning the conditions to the command, is it out of the conditions? In either of these cases, Punishment is to take place: or if concerning conditions to the armature, is it out of these conditions? if so, then no Punishment denounced by the armature is to take place. Has the Adjective Matter conditional to the armature been observed? if so, not otherwise, the Punishment of the armature is to take place. All this is matter of Law.

360. The Rules of Evidence are Rules expressive of *one* set of the Conditions *on* which the transgressor of the Law in question shall undergo the threat of it. Transgressor or not transgressor, he is not to undergo the threat of it, unless the fact of transgression be made appear by such or such signs.

Rules of Evidence conditions to the threat.

361. The business, therefore, of the Rules concerning the competency of Evidence is to ascertain in what cases phænomena

—concern[g] competency.

[1] In the text, Bentham has noted at this point: 'Obscure. ☛'

that might be apt to be taken, were it not for such rules, as signs of the fact in question by those who are to judge of it, shall not be offer'd to their consideration.

Procedure—conditions to the threat.

362. In the complicated System of regular Procedure, it is surprising the number of hands the matter passes through, the number of incidents that must concur, of operations that must be performed, before the threat of a Law can be carried into execution. All these incidents form so many conditions to the comminatory part of the Law.

Division of Judiciary Functions = manufacturing processes.

363. The contrast between the Domestic[1] and the Political Jurisdiction compared to that between the Woollen manufacture and the Indians weaving Hammocks. *Ideopsia*[2] of the Domestic Judge, one cause of simplicity. *Heteropsia* of the political. *Autochiria*)(*Heterochiria. Autodogmatia*)(*Heterodogmatia.*[3]

Aspects)(incidents.

364. Sensible objects suggest ideas either by their quiescent aspects, in a state of rest: or by their motions, when in motion. This distinction is made in conformity to popular conception: for in strict truth, no idea is ever excited by a sensible object, but by means of motion. The difference is that, when the object itself that is said to excite the idea is said to be at *rest*, the motion is not of that body, but of the rays of light that issue from it, if a visible body, or the odorous particles of it, if an odorous substance. Accordingly, with respect to bodies not odorous, persons destitute of sight have no other method of acquiring ideas of them but by motion: that is of those substances with respect to their own bodies; or of their own bodies with respect to those substances.

Author)(Cause.

365. An intelligent being, when spoken of as a first-moving instrument in the production of any phænomenon, is stiled it's *Author.*

Phænomenon = Appearance.

366. N.B. Instead of the word *Phænomenon*, every where may be used the word *Appearance.*

Sanction.

367. A Sanction is Pain or Pleasure proceeding from an

[1] MS orig. 'Parental'.

[2] 'MS orig. '*Autopsia*'.

[3] With the exception of 'heteropsia' (a medical term for different vision in each eye), all these terms appear to have been coined by Bentham from ancient Greek. In each pair of terms, the term applied to domestic power or household production begins with 'auto' or 'ideo', meaning 'one's own', while the term applied to political power begins with 'hetero', meaning 'various'. In 'autopsia' and 'heteropsia', the contrast is between seeing with one's own eye, or from one's own point of view, and seeing with a variety of eyes, or from various points of view. In 'autochiria' and 'heterochiria', the contrast is between production or rule by one's own hand and production or rule by the interaction of a variety of hands. In 'autodogmatia' and 'heterodogmatia', the contrast is between production or rule on the basis of one's own ideas alone and production or rule on the basis of a variety of ideas.

intelligent being in consequence of his approbation or disapprobation of a mode of conduct in the party *pained* or *pleased*.

When it is Pain, it is stiled Punishment: when Pleasure, it is stiled Reward.

It is the expectation of a Sanction that forms what may [be] stiled a determinative: which, if the tendency of it be to determine to *action*, is a motive: if to forbearance, it may be stiled a restrictive. Determinative. Motive. Restrictive.

368. When we speak of Pain as present or certain, we call it Pain: when we speak of it as *contingent*, let us call it Danger. Mischief may serve as a neutral expression, capable of standing indifferently or conjunctively for the other two. 'Tis in this sense we speak of the mischief of a Law: or the mischief a Law was designed to remedy. Pain)(Danger)(Mischief.

369. What is it the pretended Law of Nations is composed of? Compacts. That makes one half of it. Compacts between the supreme power in one nation and in another. A branch of the Municipal Law of each nation. That makes the other half of it. So much of the Law of the nation in question as concerns the intercourse of the people of it with the people of another nation. Law of Nations.

370. There is no such thing as an offence against the Laws of Nations: for there is no such thing as a Law of Nations.

371. There is no such thing as an offence against the Law of Nature: because there is no such thing as any Law of Nature. *Law of Nature.*

372. 373.[1] There is such a thing as an usage of Nations: for wherever a certain number of acts resemble one another in any assignable point of view, there may be said to be an usage. That usage may be departed from. But such a departure is not an offence. Usage between Nations.

374. Expectation may be generated by such an usage. This, if an expectation of things interesting to the parties expecting, is a pleasure: defeated by a departure from that usage, it may turn into a pain of disappointment.

375. This is all the matter of Law contained in the pretended Law of Nations: if by Law we mean acts internal: acts tho' externally expressed: acts of Will. Take external acts into the notion of it, and, besides these, it contains Usage.

376. Usage, then, among nations is the matter from whence the Common Law of Nations is abstracted: as Usage in a nation is the matter from whence the Common Law of a nation is abstracted. Treaties are the Statute Law of Nations.

377. Usage between Nations may be: 1st as between the Law of Nations.

[1] Bentham has numbered this paragraph both 372 and 373.

representatives of one nation and the representatives of another: 2d between the representatives of one nation and the subjects of another: 3dly between the subjects of one nation and the subjects of another: 4thly between the supreme power of one nation and the subjects of another: 5thly between the supreme power of one nation and the supreme power of another.

378. The representatives of a nation to another nation must be the Delegates either of the supreme power of the nation whose representatives they are, or of the Delegates of that supreme power.

379. In G. Britain, the Representatives of the nation to other nations are Delegates not immediately of the supreme power, but of it's delegate, the King.

Law of or Usage between Nations.

380. The King alone, it is plain, cannot be the supreme power to the purpose of making War and Peace, no more than to any other: since he can be bound by an act of the supreme power to make or not to make either. He is, therefore, only the standing delegate of the supreme power, with liberty to appoint others under him.

Harris's four Causes.

381. The elegant and mysterious author of *Hermes*[1] makes no distinction between the Cause and the instrument: between the effect, and the work. But he makes four sorts of causes: '*the* four sorts of causes', as he calls them: referring to a list which, having been settled there is no saying how many hundred years ago by the Greek Metaphysicians,[2] is the exact list, both in specie and number, against all the world: as all the world knows, that is to say, the very few followers of those Greek Metaphysicians:[3] before whom, the Lockes and Newtons[4] and Bacons[5] and whatever else has born name for science in the world, is but as dross.

The effect he instances to exemplify his four sorts of causes upon is, the sounding of a Trumpet. Now, of this sounding, says he, there are four causes. 1st. The Material Cause: the Metal of the Trumpet. 2. The Formal cause: the Shape of the Trumpet. 3. The Efficient cause: the man who blows the Trumpet. 4thly. The Final Cause: the idea of the train of effects this effect is to have; viz: of the raising of the courage of those that hear the sounding of the trumpet. His

[1] James Harris (1709–80), politician and grammarian, MP for Christchurch 1761–80, Comptroller to the Queen 1774–80, was author of *Hermes: or, a Philosophical Inquiry Concerning Language and Universal Grammar*, London, 1751.

[2] For the four sorts of causes identified by Aristotle see para. 2, p. 61 & n. above.

[3] The remainder of the sentence has been marked by Bentham for deletion.

[4] Sir Isaac Newton (1642–1727), philosopher and scientist.

[5] Francis Bacon (1561–1626), first Baron of Verulam and first Viscount St Alban, Lord Chancellor 1618–21.

words are: 'As to causal conjunctions, there is no one of the four species of causes, which they are not capable of denoting. For example: the Material cause—The Trumpet sounds, because 'tis made of Metal. The Formal—The Trumpet sounds, because 'tis long and hollow. The Efficient—The trumpet sounds, because an artist blows it. The Final—the Trumpet sounds, that it may raise our courage.'[1]

Now, before the effect has it's groupe of causes assigned it, it were not amiss first to settle, what it is we mean by that effect itself. Whether it be: 1. the idea of the sound of the Trumpet in the minds of those that hear it: or 2dly the supposed vibrations of the auditory nerve producing that idea: or 3dly the vibrations in the air producing the corresponding vibrations in the auditory nerve: or 4^thly^ the vibration in the metal producing the corresponding vibrations in the air. I suppose the latter: and it is, therefore, that, to denote the effect in question, I have used the words 'the *sounding* of the Trumpet'. For the author I am speaking of, only hints at the effect, without giving it a name. Had I used, instead of the participle '*sounding*', the substantive '*sound*', and said 'the *sound* of the trumpet', the word would have been capable indifferently of the three first-mentioned significations: and, by that means, there would have been three different things, either of which would have been liable to have been taken for the effect in question. This being the case, to speak of the instrument itself being the cause (whatever epithet the word cause have tacked to it), of it's being the cause, I say, of it's own vibrations, that is of it's own motion: the substance itself, a cause of the mode of that same substance, is a mode of speech that alike seems unusual, useless and confused. The matter of the trumpet is not any thing that exists of itself, distinct from the trumpet or distinct from any thing: no more than is the form. But the Trumpet (take it matter and form together) is one existing thing, one existing substance: capable of being consider'd with respect to it's matter, or with respect to it's form. And as the whole trumpet taken together cannot properly be spoken of as a cause of the effect in question, no more can either of these imaginary parts of it. If this be just, here, then, is an end of two out of these four causes: the Material and the Formal. To proceed to the efficient. The Vibration of the Air that was in the man's lungs and mouth, I should say (and I believe any one else would be ready to say too), is the cause; viz: the immediate cause of the particular vibration, i:e: of the sounding of the trumpet: that

[1] Harris, *Hermes*, p. 248. There are some minor inaccuracies in the rendering of the passage.

air itself others might be apt also to call the cause: but I, for distinction's sake, would call it the instrument of the same effect: viz: the immediate instrument. The motion given to the man's lungs and mouth, I would call a cause once removed: the lungs and mouth themselves, instruments of the first remove. And thus far we have nothing but material instruments, and the motions of them, material causes.

Instrument immediate.

Final Cause.

To come, lastly, to what is stiled the Final cause. This is an immaterial one. The act of volition by which the particular motions of the man's lungs and mouth were produced, I would stile the immediate immaterial cause. The idea of the pleasure he expected from the seeing the men's courage raised, and which pleasure was the motive to that volition, I would call an instrument remote, viz: an instrument of the first remove, among these immaterial instruments: the action of that idea upon the mind, the cause once removed among these immaterial causes: the idea of the courage to be raised in the men's breasts, or perhaps, rather, of that complicated train of events denoted by the term *victory* that might result from the raising of the men's courage, this idea, or this assemblage of ideas, being the instruments of that same pleasure, might be stiled an instrument of the 2[d] remove among immaterial instruments of the effect in question. It must, however, be acknowleged that, when we come to objects immaterial, the distinction between cause and instrument, if at all maintainable, becomes very obscure. Here, however, we have the Final Cause, which is always an idea, and supposes a being endow'd with ideas as forming one link of the chain of circumstances productive of the event in question. Such a being, with respect to the event, we stile it's author. Suppose the event produced without any such being, and there is an end of any Final Cause. As suppose, it was not the breath from any man's lungs and mouth, but the wind, that produced the sounding of the trumpet.

Cause immediate immaterial.

Instrument of the first remove.

Cause once removed.

Instrument (immaterial) of the 2[d] remove.

Author.

However, be it as it may in regard to operations of the mind, in speaking of those of matter, by keeping to this distinction between cause and instrument, one copious and unintermitting spring of confusion will be dried up.

A Sentence, what.

382. A Sentence is a command to a party to submitt to punishment, or to another to administer punishment to him, on account of the transgression of some Law, real or fictitious.

Utility.

383. Utility is the property of an action to encrease Happiness. Happiness is no otherwise encreased than by averting pains or increasing pleasures.

384. Perniciousness is the property in an action to encrease Unhappiness: Unhappiness is no otherwise encreased than by averting pleasures or encreasing pains. Perniciousness.

385. It is not on every occasion easy to determine which of these very different things this non-entity is designed to represent: thus much, however, it is to be hoped, is clear, that, to speak justly, there is no such thing as any Law of Nature. Consequently, there is no such thing as any offence against the Law of Nature. Nor can any Law be contrary to it. For nothing has no contraries. Law of Nature—Nothingness of.

386. It is much to be doubted, however, whether any thing that can be said will be sufficient to prevail on some men to throw away this rattle: or to wean men from an instrument at once so soothing to their indolence, and flattering to their pride, a sort of conjuring-stick, by which any man that pleases may turn himself into a Legislator: and opposition to his notions, into an act of rebellion. Law of Nature—Obstinate attachment to.

387. In these days, when a man does not like a Law of the State, he falls to work immediately, and makes a Law of nature against it, which declares it void. For every man has the sceptre of Nature in his own keeping. The Law that grieves him then becomes illegal. For inexpedient will not serve him. Inexpedient is too cold a term. —Subserviency to impatient tempers.

388. As good a way to the full as this is the old sober method of Grotius and Puffendorf,[1] who, without talking either of a sense or of an understanding, without form or ceremony, without justification or apology, without troubling themselves about privilege or patent, but with all the composure and self-satisfaction imaginable, make as many Laws of Nature, at a minute's warning, as they have occasion for. To investigate the quality of an act through all it's train of penal and pleasurable consequences is matter of nice and laborious enquiry. To make Laws of Nature is quite another affair. With such ready journeymen as Reason, Right Reason, Nature of things, Fitness of Things, Justice, Natural Justice, Equity, Natural Equity, and others equally dextrous and obsequious, their associates, nothing is more easy. 'Tis a way of acquiring the title of a Legislator at a small expence, and of exercising the functions of one with no other labour than that of the hand. Grotius and Puffendorf, &c.

389. A plain proof that this expression is not a matter of indifference, and that somthing more is meant by it than a mere figure of speech, an ornamented and rhetorical cover for delivering an opinion, is this. No man so extravagant as to pretend to treat every Law that he does not like as void without distinction. At the same time, to speak of a Law as being void for being contrary to a Law of Nature, Mischief of. Not reconcileable to Utility.

[1] Hugo Grotius (1583–1645), Dutch jurist, and Samuel Pufendorf (1632–94), German jurist, were leading exponents of natural law.

pretended Law of Nature is common. They mean, therefore, something more by a Law's being contrary to a Law of Nature, than merely it's being contrary to their notion of what is fitting. What it is that distinguishes a Law from the number of those that are simply bad, and makes it so bad as to be void, is what no one has yet, I believe, undertaken to ascertain. Amidst all the magnificent things that have been utter'd of these celestial gorgons,[1] which petrify into nullity every human Law that dares to strike against them, no one has ever yet, I believe, undertaken to give a list of them, or even of such marks whereby to make them known.

Law of Nature—Mischief of. Not reconcileable to 'Utility'. Destroys proportion.

390 Another thing proper to be consider'd by the advocates for a Law of Nature, is: whether the reason for considering a Law of the State as being void rises with it's mischievousness: whether it's mischievousness is the measure of it's opposition to the Law of Nature, and consequently of it's nullity. If not, then it comes to what I have been saying, that repugnance in a Law of the State to a Law of Nature means a property in a Law of the State distinct from mischievousness. If it is, then this odd consequence will follow. Between nullity and validity there is no medium: either a Law, be it ever so bad, is null, or else 'tis valid. There is, then, a certain degree of mischievousness at which it changes colour[2] all on a sudden and becomes void: at the same time that every degree short of that has no effect upon it at all. This puts to the rout every idea of measure and proportion.

Law of Nature. A tool to party rage.

391. To argue with men against it who, in the paroxysm [of] party rage, snatch it up to brandish it in the teeth of their antagonists, is to argue with the winds: but if the inanity and ill effects of it are such as have been alleged, one might at least hope to see it no longer admitted into grave and systematical treatises of Jurisprudence.

'Law of Nature' to be proscribed.

392. I can not help concluding, upon the whole, that till the Law of Nature is erased from the Vocabulary of Jurisprudence, and banished to the land of second intentions, and quiddities and quodditites and substantial forms, it will be in vain to expect precision or perspicuity among the first principles of the science.

Reason an affair of Pain and Pleasure.

393.[3] A Reason, if it is any thing, for or against a point of conduct is the allegation of certain pains or pleasures to ensue from it. It is not necessary that it should name them: tho' perhaps it

[1] MS orig. 'Laws of Nature'; MS alt. 'tremendous Gorgons'.
[2] MS orig. 'turns round'; MS alt. 2 '[. . . ?] round'.
[3] In the text, Bentham has noted at this point: 'Enter'd.' The meaning is unclear.

were always better. But it must point to them at least. To have any pretence to the name of reason, or any claim upon the attention, if not openly announce them, it must at least give some distant intimation of them. The word reason, to mean any thing, applied to mere physical events and appearances, is synonymous to cause: applied to moral actions, it is still synonymous to cause, by being synonymous to motive. And what is motive ever, but pain and pleasure? This seems to be the true test of what is genuine in reasons; but if it be, how many of those strings of phrases, by Lawyers called reasons, shall abide it? As wax melteth, says the Psalmist, before the sun,[1] at the presence of these genuine ones, they will melt away.

Let us conclude from hence, that the only firm foundations that Law can have must be a set of accurate speculations concerning pain and pleasure.

---

394. Disputes would be much shorter, and men would be much wiser, if those who find fault with a Law, or with any other act, instead of saying it is contrary to the Law of Nature, Natural Justice forbids it, Justice forbids it, Right Reason forbids it, and so forth without end, would smooth their countenances, lay down their pens, sink gently back into their chairs, and say, 'I have a very bad opinion of it, but I can't tell why.'

Law of Nature—shews distress of argument.

---

395. Principle is the unfashioned rudiment of a Maxim. Examples. Principle of association amongst ideas. Principle of Utility.

Principle, a—what.

---

396. Definition, that sole and sovereign specific against the maladies of confusion and debate, which he {Locke} had discernment to prescribe, but wanted resolution and perseverance to apply.[2]

Prefat. Method of defining.

397. To understand with precision what a Law is, the first step to be taken is to know what it is not, of all that variety of things, one after another, in their order, that have on different occasions been confounded with it. These are &c.[3] To do this, we must take an ample range. We must mount aloft in the prædicamental Scale. We

Prefat. Necessity of going deep.

[1] Psalm 68: 2.

[2] See Locke, *Essay concerning Human Understanding*, Bk. III, Ch. III, § 10, pp. 412–13; Ch. IV, §§ 4–10, pp. 421–4; and Ch. XI, §§ 24–7, pp. 520–4.

[3] For terms with which 'law' might be 'confounded' see paras. 149–56, pp. 82–4 above; 'PP: Introduction', para. 22, p. 433 below; and 'PP: Law', paras. 25–39, pp. 447–52 below.

must find a Genus Paramount that shall include the term in question, together with all the various terms that are to be distinguished from it. The once famous Tree of Porphyrius[1] is but a dwarf to that it will be necessary for us to climb.

Contracts. Matter conditionalizing to.

398. The Contract is not to be performed: the party is not to be punished for not performing it: *if* it be of any of those sorts which the Law excepts against it—if &c.—IF *it has been performed already.* The foresight of the Law fills up the gap left by the narrow sightedness of the parties.

Till the several exigencies of the several cases can be all comprehended and provided for, the general key to the decision is—What would the expectation be of an impartial person? For exigencies resulting from a primary contract, it does, as it were, make new Contracts supplemental.

Promise of the Law. Immunities. Reward, in what respect an act peculiar to Law.

399. The Law, by way of rewards, may grant immunities: i:e: permission to forbear fulfilling duties imposed by itself: on this account, therefore, in the affair of rewarding, it is not on the footing of a common person.

Exemption = Permission. Duty. Restraint.

400. Exemption is either from Duty or restraint. Exemption from duty is permission to forbear. Exemption from restraint is permission to act.

Law of Nature. Right)(A Right. Pseudo-conjugates.

401. The adjective {right}, and substantive {*a right*}, {*the right*}, tho' conjugates in appearance, are far from being so in signification. They may be termed false or PSEUDO-CONJUGATES. The true conjugate to {right} the substantive is a quasi-conjugate—{lawful}. The true conjugate to {right} the adjective is also a quasi-conjugate, {*expediency*}. The supreme power *has a right* to do any thing whatsoever. There are many things which a man may properly [say] it *is not right* that it should do: because here the word *right* (it is here an adjective) stands for nothing but the speaker's opinion[2] applied to the conduct in question: which, if it be grounded on the principle of utility, points to matters of fact as grounds for it, and demands attention: it is, then, his vote with reasons, a rational judgment: if it be not grounded upon the principle of utility, but upon the chimerical support of the pretended Law of Nature, [it] deserves no attention any otherwise than as conveying his single voice. It is a naked vote, a vote without reasons, an irrational

[1] The so-called Porphyrian tree, illustrating the method of division *per genus et differentiam* in relation to existence, was regarded as having its origin in the *Isagoge* of Porphyry (234–*c.* 305), Greek scholar and philosopher, and was subsequently widely copied and adapted in scholastic textbooks on logic.

[2] MS orig. 'approbation or disapprobation'.

judgment—an opinion taken up without foundation: resting either upon authority, that is the opinion of other men, or upon mere caprice.

402. The great mischief of the expression is that, by furnishing men with the semblance of a reason ready made, it prevents them from looking after a real one. I consider all these fictitious moral entities as so many chimæras, prowling about the confines [of][1] the mount of science, and blocking up all approaches to the summit.

Law of Nature. Mischief of the expression—what. It stops enquiry.

---

403. What is it that a man does by making a conveyance of Property? He invests the alienee with those powers over the subject which he, the alienor, had before. A Conveyance differs from a Contract. A Conveyance does what is to be done, in present. A Contract promises to do something in future.

Conveyance ⟩⟨ Contract.

404. A naked promise, *Nudum Pactum*, is that which hath neither conveyance nor compact to match with it on the other side: that is which hath no valuable consideration. For either of these is termed a valuable consideration.

Nudum Pactum.

405. The Law has a determinate set of Powers which go to the composing of the several species of Interests in the several species of property. When any one is invested with any such set, it only waits for a sign, usually from him, but sometimes from some one else, to transfer the same set of properties, or perhaps a determinate parcel carved out of it, to some other possessor. He who executes a conveyance, makes a Will, or dies without one, gives that sign.

Conveyance ⟩⟨ Contract.

406. To give a man power to do an act (I mean a physical act in contradistinction to a Symbolical act) is to appoint punishment for any one who, by physical resistance, shall oppose him in it.

Power how given.

407. Acts may be divided into Physical and Symbolical. Physical acts are acts external. Symbolical acts are acts external, no otherwise interesting [than as] indicative of acts of the mind.

Acts Symbolical ⟩⟨ Physical.

408. Possession in a legal sense, without the right of Possession, is (notwithstanding the contradiction the words may seem to import), is, I say, the right of having any one punished who does any thing to hinder the possessor from acts of using, till divested of it by course of Law.

Possession Legal.

A Thief has possession of the moveables he has stolen in the physical sense: he has not the right of possession over them, nor has he even *possession* in the legal sense.

[1] MS 'to'.

A Carrier is in possession of my goods *as against* every body but me: i:e: he has a right of having any one punished, but me, who meddles with them without his consent. He is in possession of them against me, on any other terms than those of my paying him his hire; he is to such a degree in possession of them against me, that if I take them in a thieve's manner, I am liable to be punished as for theft.

Law Natural)(Universal.

409. Natural Law is a contradiction in terms. A treatise of Natural Law is as much as to say an account of such Laws as subsist in a state of things where there are none.

Treatise expository on Universal Law, what.

410. ‘A Treatise on Universal Law’ is an expression that has a real meaning capable of being explained. It is calculated to signify a treatise giving an account of such rights, powers, duties and restraints as subsist, or are liable to subsist, in every or any state. In such a treatise, the terms employ'd will be such as, being as well understood in one state as another, are as well calculated to signify the rights, powers, duties and restraints that subsist in one state, as those that subsist in another.

Treatise expository on English Law in terms of Universal Law—

411. An Expository Treatise on Universal Law applied to the State of England will be an exposition of such rights, powers, duties and restraints as subsist in the State of England, but given in such terms as would serve equally well to expound the system of rights, powers, duties and restraints that subsist in any other state. It is an exposition of the peculiar Jurisprudence of this state, given in terms of universal Jurisprudence:[1] that is, in short, in terms of common use among all mankind.

would be of universal use.

412. These terms will be a common measure, a common standard of interpretation, for the several technical terms, as they are called, in the several systems of Jurisprudence of particular states. A treatise on English Law, written in terms of English Law, is intelligible to none but English Lawyers. A Treatise on English Law written in terms of Universal Law will be as intelligible to French Lawyers as to English, and [to][2] French and English *Laics* as to either.

—of universal Law could be given only in patches unless applied to some particular Law.

413. An expository treatise of Universal Jurisprudence, to be an exposition of matters of fact actually subsisting, cannot but be applied to some state in particular: and the state it is most natural for a man to apply it to, is that state of which he is himself a member. I say to some state in particular: for as applied to all states

[1] The remainder of the sentence has been marked by Bentham for deletion.
[2] MS ‘of’.

in general, it would be nothing. Some assignable rights there may be, some powers, some duties, some restraints, that subsist alike in all states. But in point of number they would be few: and in point of order, nothing could be more lacerated, more disconnected, more maimed, than a system made up of propositions representing them, if it were to represent them only. So broken, in short, would be the thread of connection between the parts of such a universal system, that, unless the gaps were filled up by materials taken from some particular system, it would probably be utterly unintelligible and useless.

Grotius, &c., their object unsettled.

414. Grotius and Puffendorf, and Heineccius[1] and Vattel,[2] Burlamaqui[3] and the many others who have hitherto professed to give treatises on Natural Law, or on Universal Law, or on Public Law, on Civil Law, on Political Law, not having settled with themselves which of these several objects they had in view, have written large books that have contained every thing and nothing.[4] Here they tell us what men have done or do or would do in an ungoverned state;[5] next, of something men ought to do, as they are pleased to say, without telling us why or wherefore; then, of something men actually do in all governed states: then, of something men do in the governed state in which the writer lives; then, of something they ought to do in all states; then, of something they ought to do in that particular state. No notice, perhaps, given all this while, or but seldom given, of the transition from one of these very different objects to another. Thus confused, thus illusive[6] and unsatisfactory have been most, if not all, of those pyeballed performances with which this department of science has hitherto been peopled: entirely for want of a distinct view of their respective objects.[a]

Bracton, &c. their object unsettled.

[a] NOTE. **415.** Of the antient writers on Jurisprudence in this country, Bracton, who wrote in the time of Hen. 3[d],[7] and the Author of the treatise

[1] Johann Gottlieb Heinecke or Heineccius (1681–1741), German philosopher and jurist.

[2] Emer de Vattel (1714–67), Swiss jurist, philosopher, and diplomat.

[3] Jean-Jacques Burlamaqui (1694–1748), Swiss legal and political philosopher.

[4] Bentham may have had the following 'large books' in mind: Hugo Grotius, *De Iure Belli ac Pacis Libri Tres. In quibus ius naturæ & Gentium: item iuris publici præcipua explicantur*, Paris, 1625; Samuel Pufendorf, *Elementorum Jurisprudentiæ Universalis Libri II*, The Hague, 1660, *De Jure Naturae et Gentium Libri Octo*, London, 1672, and *De Officio Hominis et Civis Juxta Legem Naturalem Libri Duo*, London, 1673; Gottlieb Heineccius, *Elementa Ivris Natvrae et Gentivm, commoda avditoribvs methodo adornata*, Halle, 1738; Emer de Vattel, *Le droit des gens. Ou principes de la loi naturelle, appliqués à la conduite & aux affaires des nations & des souverains*, 2 vols., London, 1758; and Jean-Jacques Burlamaqui, *Principes du droit naturel*, Geneva, 1747.

[5] MS orig. 'the state of nature'.

[6] MS orig. 'fallacious'.

[7] The legal treatise first published as *De Legibus & consuetudinibus Angliæ Libri*, London, 1569, traditionally attributed to Henry of Bratton or Bracton (d. 1268), Justice of King's

I cite not any examples: the discussions which that would lead me into would fill a volume: nor would I have it thought that the censure here made is applicable in equal degree to all the authors that have been mentioned. I throw it out that it may be kept occasionally in mind, and serve as a clue to unravel much of the difficulty that is apt to occurr on reading them.

Treatise Expository on English Law in terms of Universal Law would be of universal use.

416. An expository treatise on universal jurisprudence applied to the Law of England, or in other words, an expository treatise on the Laws of England written in terms of universal jurisprudence, couched in untechnical universal language,[1] at the same time that

stiled Fleta who wrote about the time of Edw. 2d,[2] are liable to the same censure. Glanville, who wrote so early as the time of Hen: 2d, is free from it.[3] He confines himself to telling us, what was actually, on the topics he treats of, the usage of the English Law. Bracton and Fleta, there is no knowing what to make of. Sometimes it is what the English Law does, sometimes it is what so much of the Roman Law as is admitted in England does, sometimes it is what Roman Law at large does, sometimes it is what he thinks the one or the other ought to do. The half-crazy author of the *Mirrour*, idolized by Sir Edw. Coke, hawls in Religion to encrease the jumble. In the same breath in which he tells us that Treason is a mortal offence, he tells us that Fornication is so too.[4]

In the short essay of Glanville, the military Chief Justice, there is a spirit of method and precision, which one might in vain look for even in modern times.

Bench 1247–57 (and hence commonly known as *Bracton*), was written during the reign of Henry III (1207–72), King of England from 1216.

[1] The phrase 'couched . . . language' has been marked by Bentham for deletion.

[2] The anonymous treatise first published as *Fleta seu commentarius juris anglicani*, London, 1647 was probably written in the final decade of the thirteenth century, during the reign of Edward I (1239–1307), King of England from 1272, rather than his successor Edward II (1284–1327), King of England from 1307.

[3] The treatise first published as *Tractatus de legibus et consuetudinibus regni angliæ*, London, [155-?], traditionally attributed to Ranulf de Glanville (d. 1190), Justiciar of England 1180–9, was written during the reign of Henry II (1133–89), King of England from 1154.

[4] See W.H., *The Booke Called, The Mirrour of Justices: Made by Andrew Horne. With the Book, called, The Diversity of Courts, And Their Jurisdictions. Both translated out of the old French into the English Tongue*, London, 1646, a translation into English by William Hughes (1587/8–*c.* 1663) of a manuscript in law-French often attributed to Andrew Horn or Horne (*c.* 1275–1328). Bentham may have had in mind the following passage, headed 'Of the Offence of Majesty', at p. 16: 'The Crime of Majesty is an horrible offence done against the King; and that is either against the King of Heaven, or an earthly King.

'Against the King of Heaven in three manners. *Heresie, Venery, Sodomy.*

'Against the earthly King in 3. manners.

'1 By those who kill the King, or compasse so to doe.

'2 By those who dis-inherite the King of his Realm, by bringing in an Army, or compasse so to doe.

'3 By those Adulterours who ravish the Kings Wife, the Kings lawfull eldest Daughter before she be married, being in the Kings custody; or the Nurse, or the Kings Ant, heire to the King.'

In the preface headed 'Deo, Patriæ, Tibi' to *The Ninth Part of the Reports of Sir Edward Coke Kt. Chief Justice of the Common Pleas* (first published in Latin in 1613), London, 1727, the work is described as 'a very ancient and learned Treatise of the Laws and Usages of this Kingdom'.

it is a key to the Laws of England, is a Key to the Laws of any other country. It were a business comparatively of small difficulty, to adapt it to the jurisprudence of any other country. To the Laws of England, it is a key ready fitted to the lock. To the Laws of France, it is a key ready to be fitted into the lock, by any Artist who can enter, with a tolerable degree of facility, into the views of him that made it. A work written on this plan, even upon the Laws of our Island, would bear translation[1] into the languages of the continent. Sr W. Blackstone's *Commentaries*, that collection of technical terms technically explained, will never be translated.[2]

417. The idea of an act of the mind is a simple one. The idea of an act of the body is an assemblage of determinate assignable simple ones. The idea of a forbearance is, in like manner, simple. The idea of pain is a simple one. Punishment is pain connected with an act or a forbearance, as an effect is with a cause. The idea of such a connection is a simple one. Now, whatever it be that is done by Law is but punishment connected with some act or some forbearance. Whatever is deliver'd concerning the Law is but an account of the several cases in which punishment is or is not made the effect of action or forbearance.

Provisions of every particular Law expoundable in universal terms. Punishment.

To appoint punishment for an act, is to impose a restraint. To appoint punishment for a forbearance, is to impose a duty. To be one in whose favour punishment is appointed for an act or for a forbearance, is to enjoy a right, is to enjoy a power. Now, of all these several terms, there is no one but what is in common use. There is nothing strange or formidable in their appearance. A word or two was all that was wanting to make the sense of them as familiar to men's conceptions as the sound of them is already to men's ears.

Punishment—action—forbearance—restraint—duty—right—power.

---

418. I PROMISE to deliver you £100 tomorrow, in consideration of your promising to deliver me £105 tomorrow twelvemonth.

Consideration. Condition.

I give you to understand that I have RESOLVED to deliver you £100 tomorrow: but it is upon this CONDITION I have resolved to do so, that you have RESOLVED to deliver me £105 tomorrow twelvemonth.

Under the notion of a condition are included two events: whereof one at least must be the effect of an action, and that a voluntary one.

Condition, a—what.

A Condition is either precedent or subsequent to the act.

[1] The remainder of the sentence has been marked by Bentham for deletion.

[2] Blackstone's *Commentaries on the Laws of England* was translated into a number of languages, including French, Italian, and German, the earliest being *Commentaires sur les loix angloises, de M. Blackstone, traduits de l'anglois par M. D. G***. Sur la quatrieme édition d'Oxford*, 6 vols., Brussels, 1774–6. The translator was August Pierre Damiens de Gomicourt.

Condition precedent.

418.* A Condition is an event such that, if it happen or not happen a certain other event is to happen or not happen accordingly.

I deliver you £100 upon this condition, that you promise to deliver me £105 tomorrow twelvemonth. There, your delivering me 105£ is the condition annex'd to my act of delivering you £100. That act of mine may be called the principal act. This principal act is present: the act of your delivering me £105 tomorrow twelvemonth is yet to come. The condition here, then, is subsequent to the principal act.

Example.

I promise to deliver you £105 tomorrow twelvemonth upon this condition, that you deliver me £100 tomorrow. Here, the act of my delivering you £105 tomorrow twelvemonth is the principal act: the act of your delivering me £100 tomorrow is the [condition].[1] The condition is here precedent. From this exemplification, it appears that the meaning of the word condition in the two cases of a condition precedent and a condition subsequent is materially different. In the case of a condition precedent, there are, as has been said before, two events, and two events only, between which a connection of existence is appointed. If the condition have not been done at the time when the principal act comes to be done, the principal act is not to be done at all. Here the future existence, the ever-happening, if one may so say, of the principal act is made to depend upon the past existence, the *having-happen'd*, of the condition.

Condition Subsequent.

But when the condition is subsequent, how stands the matter then? that the existence of the principal act is made to depend upon the *having-happen'd*, of the condition? no. For, by the supposition, the condition is not to happen till afterwards. What, then, is it, the existence of which is made to depend upon the to-be-past existence, upon the *having-happen'd*, of the condition? It is some *third event*, such as, upon my not paying the 105£ tomorrow twelvemonth, that of my being made to go to Prison, or suffering such other punishment as the Law shall have appointed for breach of promise. The expression Condition Subsequent is contradictory. It is pardonable in no other light than consider'd as *elliptical*. The fact is, a condition subsequent is not a condition to taking of the estate, but a condition to the retaining. The Estate is pure till the time for the performing or happening of the condition comes.

Condition = Forfeiture.

419. A Condition subsequent annext to an Estate, not-performed, works Forfeiture.

[1] MS 'principal act'.

420. A Condition where the Heir takes the benefit of Non-performance, is stiled by Lawyers a Condition, in contradistinction to a Limitation. A Condition where a substituted taker takes the benefit of Non-performance, is stiled by them a Limitation, in contradistinction to a Condition. Condition ✕ Limitation.

---

421. No Definition can be a good one, unless it either come home to simple ideas, or fit into an uninterrupted chain of other Definitions of which the first link *does*. Prelude. Definition—what a good one.

---

422. The idea belonging to the word Conveyance as applied to an estate, i:e: a right to or in an estate, is a simple one. It is as simple as that belonging to Motion. Motion is the change of place. Conveyance is a change of person.[1] Conveyance, a Simple Idea.

423. To charge an Estate in favour of a person, is to annex a condition to the party's enjoyment of it at whose expence the charge, viz: to pay a certain sum of money, is made. On non-performance of which condition, the rule of Law is, that the estate shall be *sold*, and the sum charged paid to the INCUMBRANCER out of the purchase-money, i:e: in case of a Mortgage, or in case of a Rent charge.[2] To *charge* an Estate.

---

424. TO SELL is TO CONVEY for money. To sell.

---

425. A man is said to convey an estate, when he purposely exhibits a sign of his will that the Law should convey the right to it. A Man how said to convey.

---

426. *Definitio est enumeratio notarum nec plurium, nec paucorum quàm quœ ad rem definitam agnoscendam, et ab aliis discernendam sufficiunt.* Wolf. *Logit.* 153. in Sauvag. *Nosologia*, Prolegom, p. 23. Edit. Amst. 1763 8vo.[3] *Definitio.* Sauv.

---

[1] In the text, Bentham has noted at this point: 'Qu?'

[2] In the text, Bentham has noted at this point: 'Qu. if not to the Annuitant.'

[3] i.e. 'A definition is an enumeration of neither more nor less than those signs which are sufficient to understand [or recognize] the thing defined, and to distinguish it from other things.' See Francisco Boissier de Sauvages (1706–67), *Nosologia Methodica Sistens Morborum Classes, Genera et Species, Juxtà Sydenhami mentem & Botanicorum ordinem*, 5 vols., Amsterdam, 1763, i. 23, citing Christian Wolff, *Philosophia Rationalis sive Logica, Methodo Scientifica Pertractata et ad Usum Scientarum atque Vitœ Aptata*, Frankfurt and Leipzig, 1728, §153, p. 190, which appeared in English translation as *Logic, or Rational Thoughts on the Powers of the Human Understanding; with their Use and Application in the Knowledge and Search of Truth*, London, 1770, where the relevant passage appears at p. 41.

Phænomenon. Sauv.

427. *Phænomenon est omne id, quod in sensus incurrit, vel inde quàm proximè deducitur.* Boerhaave Instit. 875 in Sauv. *Nosologia*, Prolegom, p. 130. Edit. Ams. 1763 8vo.[1]

Principle. Sauv. *Conditiones.*

428. *Etiamnum, usu ita volente, solent, sub communi nomine, confund tùm* causæ *efficientes, quæ mortum re verâ faciunt, tùm causæ seu ut meliùs dicamus* conditiones *sine quibus, quæ præsentes quidem morbum non producunt, sed absentes, ne produceretur, impedirent.* ib. 75.[2]

Principia sunt tùm conditiones, tùm occasiones, tùm circumstantiæ, nec non materia, instrumentum, finis, et prophasis. ib. 75.[3]

Action, a. Sauv.

429. *Mutatio statûs, cujus ratio sufficiens continetur in subjecto, cujus status mutatur, vocatur actio*: {Ontol. 713} ib. 73.[4]

Comment. Synonyms in the Author.[6]

430. For this malady, this *oratorico-poetical pruritus*,[5] if I did not think it so inveterate in him as to be incurable, there is an intelligent French Physician[7] I would call in to administer a corrective prescription. But our Author, and with good reasons, would turn his back upon the prescription. Our Author knows better than to part with a habit, on which the chief title he has to applause is grounded; and which is his best certificate of recommendation to the multitude of those who labour under the like infirmity. Our Author, who loves Latin as well as Poetry, may find very good reasons expressed in both. What would the substance of his work be divested of these gaudy decorations? '*Si fuerim sanus*',

[1] i.e. 'A phenomenon is every thing which strikes the senses, either immediately or derived as closely as possible therefrom.' There are some minor inaccuracies in Bentham's rendering of the passage. See Sauvages, *Nosologia Methodica*, i. 130, citing *Institutiones Medicae In usus annuae Exercitationis Domesticos Digestae ab Hermano Boerhaave. Editio altera primâ longê auctior* (first published in 1708), Leiden, 1713, §875, p. 345.

[2] i.e. 'Even now, and by willing use, sometimes *efficient causes*—which really are causes of deaths—sometimes causes, or, let us speak better, necessary *conditions*—which when present indeed do not produce illness, but when absent prevent it, so that it will not be produced—are accustomed to be confused, under a common name.' See Sauvages, *Nosologia Methodica*, i. 74–5.

[3] i.e. 'Principles are sometimes conditions, sometimes occasions, sometimes circumstances, and not immaterial, an instrument, an end, or a prognosis.' See ibid., i. 75.

[4] i.e. 'A change of state whose sufficient reason is contained within the subject whose state is changed, is called an action.' See ibid., i. 72–3, citing Christian Wolff, *Philosophia Prima sive Ontologia, Methodo Scientifica Pertractata, qua Omnis Cognitionis Humanæ Principia Continentur*, Frankfurt and Leipzig, 1736, pp. 536–7.

[5] i.e. 'itch'.

[6] i.e. Blackstone.

[7] i.e. Sauvages, as Bentham goes on to explain.

he might say, *'coccina quid facient?'*[1] *'Pol me occidistis amici, Cui demptus per vim mentis gratissimus error.'*[2]

The prescription I will nevertheless transcribe; it may serve as a preservative to such young patients, in whom the infirmity has not yet got to such a height as to have made it their interest not to accept a cure.

Sauvages, *Nosologia*, Prolegom: p. [52].[3] N° 99. Edit. Amst. 1763. 8vo.

Poetis et Oratoribus.[4]

Thus far the intelligent Physician. From whose Prolegomena to his *Method of Diseases* there is more, perhaps, instruction to be derived, relative to the Metaphysical part of the Law, by one who would study the Law in a critical view, than in all the *'fors'*, *'therefores'* and *'becauses'* in our Author's *Commentaries.*

---

431. Parts of a Law are the several distinguishable kinds of Matter. [1.] A Command. 2. A Threat. 3. A Condition to the Command. 4. A Condition to the Threat. Parts of a Law.

---

432. What are the parts that are in a Law? this question answered, the question what is one Law, how much of the Parts of a Law.

[1] See Martial, *Epigrammata*, II. 16: *si fuerit sanus, coccina quid facient?*, i.e. 'If he gets well, what will be the use of his scarlet coverlets?' Bentham's version amends the passage from the third to the first person.

[2] See Horace, *Epistulae*, II. 138–40:

. . . pol, me occidistis, amici,
non servastis, ait cui sic extorta voluptas
et demptus poer vim mentis gratissimus error.

i.e. 'truly, friends, you have killed, not saved me, by taking away my mind's favourite delusion.'

[3] MS '53'.

[4] Sauvages, *Nosologia Methodica*, i. 52: 'Poetis & oratoribus suas ideas synonimis & homonimis exprimere solemne est, illis enim non vera loqui, sed auri potiùs quàm menti jucunda proferre animus est; sed in scientiâ gravi & seriâ æquivocas voces adhibere prorsus inconsultum est, & ex illâ pravâ consuetudine fluunt illlæ indecoræ scholasticorum tricæ & disputationes, quæ Geometris & Sapientibus nauseam movent, in quibus scilicet de verbis continuò luditur, quoniam cum voces æquivocæ inconsideratè vel consultò adhibeantur, tutum est respondenti, vel præsidi in distinctionibus repetitis perfugium, unde argumenta eluduntur, & disputatio philosophica in rixam muliebrem vel puerilem altercationem degenerat', i.e. 'It is the custom for Poets and Orators to express their ideas by synonyms and homonyms, for to them the aim is not to speak truths, but to offer things pleasing to the ear rather than to the mind. But in weighty and grave sciences to employ ambiguous terms is absolutely ill-advised, and from that crooked habit flow those unbecoming trumperies and reasonings of the scholastics, which provoke nausea in Geometricians and wise men; because when once ambiguous expressions are employed, either designedly or without thought, it is prudent for the person replying to seek refuge or remedy in repeated distinctions, whence arguments are parodied, and philosophical reasoning degenerates into a womanly quarrel or a childish argument.'

matter Laws are made of goes to the making of *one* Law, is also answered.

A Law Compleat.

433. A Law is compleat, when all the Conditions &c. *intended*, are *expressed*.

Action involuntary.

434. An Action *involuntary* is an action performed without the concurrence of the Will. In common speech, it is usual also to speak of an action as being involuntary where it is the result of Volition but of a Volition the motive to which is Pain.

Action reluctantly performed or reluctant.

435. An Action *reluctant*, an action *unwillingly* performed, is such an action the motive to which is the difference between two evils, two portions of pain: between the pain of which the action is thought to be the cause, and the pain of which it is meant to be the preventive.

Action willingly performed.

436. An action willingly performed, is an action to which the motive is a good—a portion of pleasure.

Action Spontaneous.

Things not Laws tho' they are Commands. Introduction.

437. Thus far, we have travelled with tolerable certainty and satisfaction. It appears pretty plainly that, if the term Law has been, by accident, applied to any of the *x* sorts of things above enumerated, it has been improperly and unwarrantably applied.[1] The usage has run with sufficient constancy in one channel to characterize a departure from it with impropriety.[2]

Now, however, we are at Sea again. Our Compass varies: and if we would steer clear of ambiguity, we must construct one for ourselves.

Some sorts of Commands there are to which, tho' the term Law has not been commonly applied to them, it will be necessary to extend it, as whatever one may have occasion to say of those to which it is most indisputably due, there will be equal occasion to say of *them*. Such are acts of subordinate Legislation, when exercised by Officers the principal part of whose duty, in respect of frequency, is of another kind than Legislation—I mean the King, and certain Judges.

---

[1] See para. 397, p. 133 & n. above.

[2] In the text, Bentham has noted at this point: 'Sauv. p. 44. N°. 85. p. 45. N°. 86. 87.' The reference is to Sauvages, *Nosologia Methodica*, i. 44–6, where criteria for the differentiation of species and genera are discussed.

438. A Law, to be a Law, must be a Command. 'Tis Command in general that constitutes it's general essence. 'Tis in Command, as above limited, that is contained it's specific essence. A Command, one command, would be sufficient to constitute a Law, one Law. Nevertheless, certain adjuncts there are, that are indeed accidental to it by nature, but without one or other of which it is in no instance, perhaps, found in practise. It might easily be framed without them consistently with it's nature; but it can never be, perhaps, consistently with it's answering it's design. Parts of a Law.

439. [1st.] A Law is a Command.

2d. Issuing from Government.

440. By this it stands distinguished from Domestic orders. Domestic orders take a Sanction from the State, but do not themselves issue from the State. Law X Domestic Commands.

3dly. Concerning sorts of actions: actions of sorts of persons: viz: objects susceptible of indefinite continuance.

Law is that which is made by Legislation.

441. A Law ought to be that kind of performance that is the product of Legislation. Law and Legislation, being conjugates in sound, ought to be kept conjugates in sense. Legislation is the act of making Laws. Laws are those things which are made by Legislation. A Command given to an individual comes not up to our idea of a Law. Executory Commands.

This is all it has to distinguish it from occasional Commands issued by Officers to individuals under their authority: such as, when they are Commands of Judicial Officers, are stiled Rules of Court, Orders of Court, Warrants, Writs.

442. 1st. Regulations of a voluntary Society; when the Sanction is limited to the privation of the advantages afforded from the Society. These neither issue themselves from the State, nor take a Sanction from the state. Of these Societies, the Commands are subject to *no* limitation with respect to the modal or real objects of them. They are limited only with respect to the personal objects and the armature. They are limited with respect to the personal objects by being limited with respect to the armature. The armature consists in being deprived of the advantages derived from the association. Now these advantages are what are perceptible by the persons associated, and those only. Here except Mony societies—over these the State will hold a controll.[1] Law X Regulations of a Voluntary Society.

[1] Money clubs, in which some portion of the accumulated assets of the club was divided among the members each year, emerged in eighteenth-century England, along with various kinds of benefit clubs formed in hopes of securing financial assistance for respectable lower

Instrument ⁐ Circumjacent Bodies. Cause ⁐ Circumstances.

443. No body, no particle of matter, stands alone. Bodies which are contiguous to an instrument of which the motion is a cause, but which are at rest, or whose motion, if they move, does not influence the motion of the instrument, may be stiled circumjacent bodies. Their aspects and situations may be stiled circumstances.

Obligation—Essay on.

444. A discourse of 76 8vo pages has been written on the import of this single term Obligation.[1] I have written page after page myself upon the same subject, which have gone into the fire. So long as we have not as yet acquired a clear conception of our subject, there is no end to what we write. 'Tis this makes Law voluminous. Error is infinity, where truth is but a point.

Quasi-Conjugates.

445. '*Fero*', say the Grammarians, *makes 'tuli'*—*Τρέχω* makes *δραμοῦμα* . Just as well might it be said, and in the same sense, that 'bound' *makes* 'obligation'. Grammar is as yet but an imperfect Science. These adjuncts to one and the same radical idea that are expressed by the terms -us, -i, -o, -um, -e; by the terminations -us, -a, -um; by the terminations -ευς, -εε, -εις; by the terminations -o, -as, -at &c.; by the terminations -o, -abam, -avi, &c.; by the terminations -o, -a, -em, -are; by the terminations -atus, -aturus, -andus; all these have their distinctive names. For those which are indicated by the terminations -atio, -amentum, -ator, -antia, names are yet to seek. Much would the science owe to that philosopher who should find them.

Conjugates.

446. Conjugates are words that are yoked together—{Con} is {together} and {jugatus} is {yoked}. How, then, are they yoked together? By the identity of some of the letters which compose them. These letters, which are the same in all of them, form what is called the *radical* part of the several words: those which vary, form what is called the *servile*.

class individuals, such as skilled artisans, in time of need. The financial activities of such clubs were later regulated by the Friendly Societies Act of 1793 (33 Geo. III, c. 54), largely to ensure that they would not constitute a burden on state resources already strained by the rising cost of poor relief. See P. Clark, *British Clubs and Societies 1580–1800: The Origins of an Associational World*, Oxford, 2000, pp. 362–72.

[1] In a letter to John Lind of 5 October 1774 (see *The Correspondence of Jeremy Bentham*, vol. i, ed. T.L.S. Sprigge, London, 1968 (*CW*), p. 206), Bentham mentions 'the short treatise on Obligation for which Payne gave a hundred Pound'. The 'short treatise' in question may have been that published by the bookseller Thomas Payne (1716x18–99) in *A Summary of the Roman Law, taken from Dr. Taylor's Elements of the Civil Law. To which is prefixed a Dissertation on Obligation*, London, 1772, pp. i–lxx, and which, in John Nichols, *Literary Anecdotes of the Eighteenth Century*, 9 vols., London, 1812–16, v. 394 n., is attributed to William Ellis. Bentham frequented Payne's shop in Castle Street near Mews Gate, and Payne would later publish *An Introduction to the Principles of Morals and Legislation* in 1789.

447. Conjugates in sound and in sense. Conjugates simply. Conjugates in sound but not in sense, Pseudo-conjugates. Conjugates in sense but not in sound, Quasi-Conjugates. Conjugates Pseudo- and Quasi-.

---

448. 'Tis in it's formalities that a Law which is a regular one differs from such an apparent Law as, tho' it may have every other property of a Law, is, on account of it's wanting these formalities, irregular and therefore void. Formalities.

449. The effect of a Condition is to narrow the extent of it: to lessen the number of the individuals comprized under the general term expressing the act that is the object of the command. It's difference from an exception consists in this. Condition, it's effect on a Law.

450. The effect of an Exception to a Law is also to narrow the extent of it. The difference between a Condition and an exception lies in this—an exception lessens the number of individual objects under all circumstances, without referring to contingency . . . . . Condition ⫘ Exception to a Law—effect of.

---

451. In the chain of events, that immense and complicated chain, of which the prime link, say the Mithologists, is hung upon the hand of Jupiter[1]—in this vast plexus, two sorts of events may be distinguished. The one sort hung, as it were, upon the rest by actions of us mortals, by actions that are in our power, events that are in our power. The other sort pushed forward and germinating, as it were, out of the rest by a secret force uninfluenced by any force of our's. In regard to a link of the first sort, it depends upon us, whether at all, and if at all, at what time, at what conjuncture, it shall be suspended. The party who is to hang it on this link, the party whose conduct is in question, may be directed to hang it on at sight of some other appointed as *a signal*. This link, then, which he is to hang on or not, this mode of conduct which he is to observe or not, according to the determination of his will, must be in his own power. The link, the event appointed for a signal, may be either in his power or may not. Condition—Introd. Chain of events.

461.[2] The effect of the signal may be to produce or to prevent an event, an event may be produced or prevented by an action of Condition creative ⫘ accelerative ⫘ retardant.

[1] See Francis Bacon, *The Advancement of Learning* (first published in 1605), ed. M. Kiernan, Oxford, 2000 (*The Oxford Francis Bacon: Vol. IV*), p. 9: 'when a man passeth on further, and seeth the dependance of causes, and the workes of prouidence; then according to the allegorie of the Poets, he will easily beleeue that the highest Linke of Natures chaine must needes be tyed to the foote of *Iupiters* chaire', and p. 79, where Bacon writes of 'that excellent and Diuine fable of the Golden Chayne: *That men and Gods were not able to draw Iupiter down to the Earth, but contrariwise, Iupiter was able to draw them up to Heaven*', an allusion to Homer, *Iliad*, viii. 19–26.

[2] Bentham has indicated that para. 461 should follow at this point.

our's without which it would not have been produced at all. Or the effect of the signal may be barely to accelerate or retard an event, an event may be barely accelerated or retarded by an action of our's without which it would have been produced, but either sooner or not so soon.

A Law when contrary to another.[1]

452. From this Analysis, if accurately performed, we shall now, for the first time, be able to ascertain when it is, that [an] act is an offence against a Law, and when it is that a given Law is contrary to another.

453. A Subordinate Law is not contrary to a Superior Law, by being contrary to either of the three Fundamental Laws.[2] For no Laws at all can be made, but what are contrary to them. Yes, it would be, if *these* were *written* ones. Unwritten Law admitts of Local Customs growing up against it. If these three Laws were written they would abolish all Law that was unwritten.

Laws Contrari*ent* X Contrari*ant.*

454. Contrariety is reciprocal. No Law can be contrary to another, but that other is also contrary to *that*. As no line can be parallel to another, but that other must also be parallel to that. Of a pair of contraries, as of a pair of parallels, either one is capable of being taken for the standard to which the other is applied. That which is made the standard, the conception[3] figures to itself under the image of something that is at rest, while the other is applied to, that is moved towards it, for the purpose of comparing them. But, as it is but one of them that is the standard at a time, they are, for that time, distinguishable from each other by appellations that shall mark which of them is, and which is not, at the time in question, taken for the standard. Let that, therefore, which is made the standard for the time being be termed the *contrariate*, or that to which some other is contrary, and that other, the *contrarient*, or that which is spoken of as being contrary to some other.

Law contrarient to a Law *mandatory.*

455. The description of a Law CONTRARIENT varies according to the nature of the Law CONTRARIATE.

If the Law CONTRARIATE be a Law that commands an act to be done, a Law CONTRARIENT to it is a Law that either permitts that act not to be done, or commands it not to be done. When it permitts it not to be done, it may be said to be SIMPLY CONTRARIENT, and the contrariety there is betwixt them may be called a contrariety of the

[1] In the margin, Bentham has noted at this point: 'See 329 where this is settled.' See para. 796, pp. 249–50 below.

[2] i.e. the fundamental laws of liberty, security, and property: see paras. 171–3, p. 86 above, and para. 558, p. 180 below. 'Fundamental' has been marked by Bentham for deletion.

[3] MS orig. 'imagination'.

inferior order, or the LESSER CONTRARIETY. When it commands the act not to be done, it may be said to be DOUBLY CONTRARIENT, and the contrariety there is betwixt them may be stiled a contrariety of the superior order, or the GREATER CONTRARIETY.

456. If the Law CONTRARIATE be a Law that commands an act not to be done, a Law CONTRARIENT to it is a Law that either permitts it to be done, or commands it to be done. Law contrarient to a Law *prohibitive*.

456.* A Law contrariant to a Law permissive is one that either commands or prohibits to be done the act that was permitted.[1] Law contrariant to a Law permissive.

457. Permission is a declaration of the Legislator that he has no Will at all about the matter. It presupposes a Command. It revokes that Command; and restores things to the same state they would have been in if no Command had ever issued. Law Permissive.

458. A point, this, which one should imagine merited to be settled. When the supreme Legislature or the Deputy of the Supreme Legislature creates subordinate Legislatures, when it founds Colonies abroad, or Corporations at home, it provides that their Laws shall not be contrary to it's own. Not contrary? what, in no sense? then no Laws can they ever make at all. In what sense, then? This is what no one as yet knows, or no one at least hath set himself down as yet to tell us. And yet it were worth the while. But a Lawyer of that fry which wallows in the slime of technical jurisprudence, a Lawyer who begins with breeding doubts that he may end with stifling them but never thinks of anticipating them, who hopes to stifle on the Bench the doubts he engender'd at the Bar but never thought at either of intercepting, such a Lawyer does not lift up his head above the eddy of official routine, tho' it were to put the stamp of eternity upon the peace of empires. A Law when *contrary* to another—importance of the question. Lawyers. Indolence and Interestedness the causes of their Ignorance.

But there is that in indolence and rapacity that may account for any thing. It is easy to copy, it is difficult to define. If it is profitable to sell opinions, it is profitable to breed the doubts that call for them. Precedent puts a varnish upon every defect. Nor can a man be expected to pry with any very anxious eye into a flaw of which the profit is to himself and the reproach goes to his departed predecessors.

---

459. A Warrant is a particular order conferring on an individual powers at the expence of the rights created by one or other of the three fundamental Laws of Liberty, Security and Property. Warrant, a dispensation of one of the 3 Fundamental Laws.

A warrant of Arrest is that sort of Warrant that is opposed to the Law of Liberty.

[1] In the text, Bentham has noted at this point: 'Next see how it is in regard to Conditions.'

Warrants of Execution for Death, Whipping, &c., are of that sort which stand opposed to the Law of Security.

Warrants of Search and Seizure are those that stand opposed to the Law of Property.

Power—a fictitious quality.

460. Power, then, as attributed to the person empower'd is an imaginary quality attributed to him whereby he is enabled to do certain things by the removal of resistance that otherwise might oppose his physical powers. Give a man a new physical power, the sphere of his activity is enlarged: give him a legal power, the sphere of his activity is enlarged: in the first case by the encrease of force: in the other, by the removal of resistance: viz: of that resistance that might otherwise arise from the activity or *vis inertiæ* of the persons who are made the objects of restraint.

Condition to a Resolution.

462.[1] A condition to a RESOLUTION necessarily supposes only two events besides the act of resolving.—1st. The event taken for a signal: 2dly. The action or forbearance of the RESOLVING party upon the appearance of that signal.

Condition to a Command.

462.* A condition to a Command, Requisition or Petition (we will take only a Command) necessarily supposes three events over and above the act of commanding. 1st the event given for a signal. 2dly the action or forbearance of the party whose obedience is in question. 3dly the Punishment appointed in consequence (on condition, as we may say) of disobedience.

An Event contingent.

463. An event is spoken of as contingent either as consider'd on it's own account or on account of some other on which it depends. An event that depends upon another event that is contingent, is said to depend upon a *contingency*.

Events certain ⩙ contingent.

464. Of events in prospect, some we are disposed to rely upon as certain, others to be in doubt about as contingent.

Certainty is relative to opinion.

465. The same event that is certain to one man, shall be contingent to another.

The action of a man may appear certain to the man himself, and only contingent to another: and this is the more common case: as a man generally does know, and is generally thought to know, better what he shall do himself, than others do.

But in some cases it shall happen that an action of a man which appears contingent only to himself shall appear certain to a bystander. And the bystander may be right, if he has been more used to examine into the motives of that man's conduct, than the

[1] For para. 461 see pp. 147–8 above.

man himself has. The words certainty and contingence are expressive not so much of the constitution of the events themselves, as of the constitution of the minds of us who think of them. Of our disposition to expect their happening or not happening. This disposition depends upon our experience: experience either original or communicated by report, experience of events of a sort like that in question having happen'd before in circumstances of a sort like that of the circumstances of the event in question.

Condition to an Estate.

466. Let us examine the meaning of the word Condition in the following phrases:

In Possession.

1st. The Condition upon which I hold my estate.

In Expectancy under a Devise.

2d. The Condition upon which my estate was left me.

Covenant in a Conveyance)(Condition.

467. The effect of a *Covenant* in a Deed conveying an estate to me is, I am to do the act covenanted for, or pay damages.

Condition)(Limitation.

468. The effect of a *Condition* in a Deed conveying an estate to me is, I am to do the act prescribed, the act conditioned for, or lose the Estate: viz: to the Conveyor or his Heirs.

Limitation)(Condition.

469. The effect of a *Limitation* in a Deed conveying an Estate to me is, I am to do the act prescribed, the act conditioned for, or lose the Estate: viz: to some third person to whom the conveyor in this case is said to limit it.

Condition)(Limitation.

470. In treating of a Covenant, a question made by Lawyers is, what is to be deemed a breach of it? In treating also of a Condition, a question made by Lawyers is, what is to be deemed a breach of it?

In treating of a *Limitation,* was it a question ever made by Lawyers, what shall be a breach of a Limitation? No—never. The impropriety of the expression strikes one at first sight.

Condition)(Limitation.

471. At the same time, a question made and much agitated by Lawyers is, 'what shall be a Condition and what a Limitation?'[1]

A condition is a thing that can be broken—this is clear beyond a dispute. Now, a Limitation is a thing very like a condition: so like that it is sometimes one of the hardest things imaginable to know the difference. A Limitation, then, a thing that can not be broken? Somwhat very strange in this: that, of things so like as scarce to be distinguished, one should be so tough, while the other is so brittle.

The truth of the matter is, not that a Limitation is less brittle than a Condition, but that the conceptions of Lawyers have been so muddy, and their Sculls so hard.

[1] See, for instance, Blackstone, *Commentaries on the Laws of England*, ii. 155: 'A distinction is . . . made between a *condition in deed* and a *limitation*, which Littleton denominates also a *condition in law*.' Blackstone cites '§380. I Inst. 234', i.e. Coke, *First Part of the Institutes of the Lawes of England*, fo. 234v.

The question, in proper terms, never was, or could have been, what shall be a Condition and what a Limitation, but what shall be a Condition with a Limitation annexed to it, and what a Condition without a Limitation annext to it? or to state the question in a more commodious form, 'In what cases shall a condition be deemed to have a Limitation annexed to it, and in what not?'

A Condition Subsequent in a Will.

A Condition, or to speak more properly, a clause prescribing a condition to an Estate, is a clause appointing an event upon which that estate shall pass away from me.

A Limitation in a Will.

A Limitation is a clause appointing the person who is to take the Estate when it passes away from me, upon the happening of that event. A Limitation is a disposal of an Estate, to take effect upon the breach of a Condition.

The Question, then, whether a thing is a Condition or a Limitation is a question whether a thing is an event upon which the Estate is to pass away from me, or a clause appointing the person who is to take the Estate when it passes away from me upon the happening of that event: or, making every allowance, it is a question whether a thing is a *clause prescribing an event* upon which an Estate is to pass away from me, or a clause appointing the person who is to take the estate when it passes away from me upon the happening of that event.

Covenant)(Condition)(Limitation.

472. In a Covenant, the person to receive the damages upon the breach of it, is the person to take advantage, as the phrase is, of the breach of it. In an instrument of conveyance which tacks a Condition to the conveyance of an estate, the person who is to take the estate upon the breach of the condition is the person to take advantage of the breach.

Condition)(Limitation.

When *no* person *is* deemed to be appointed by the disponer to take advantage of the breach of a Condition, the Law appoints the disponer or his Heirs to take advantage of it as of course. And then the clause in question is stiled simply a Condition.

Limitation)(Condition.

Where *some* person *is* deemed to be appointed by the disponer to take advantage of the breach of a Condition, the clause in question is then stiled a Limitation.

Nothing, therefore, can be more confused than the expression of those who have made it a question whether a thing shall be a Condition or a Limitation; since in both cases there is a Condition: *only* in the first, without a Limitation; in the second, with one.

Right—It's Synonyms and Conjugates.

473. Right {the Adjective} Synonymous [with] 1st lawful, viz: according to the Law of Nature. 2. Expedient, according to the principle of utility. Abstract—Lawfulness—expedience. N.B. In one sense it has no synonyms at least—lawful is not synonymous to it. That is, the sense it has in this phrase: It is right that, &c.

474. We want to know whether a mode of conduct is *right* or no—positive Law out of the question. How, then, to proceed? To enquire whether God is pleased, it should be observed, is to go just so much out of our way to no purpose. Put this second question, and in order to answer it, the first thing you have to do is to come back again to the first. Is God pleased with it? No, if it be wrong. Yes, if it be right.

Law of Nature. Idea of God—no foundation of Morals.

In Morals, therefore, it is plain that this idea of God can be of no use in framing of the precepts: the only use it can be of (good or bad) is when we are enquiring after a Sanction.

475. What it is that has made Moralists so fond of bringing God upon the stage is not difficult to perceive. Not knowing how to bring men's judgments to his opinion, he has tried to make their passions of his party, and has gone to work upon their fears. Unable to convince, his aim has been to silence: unable to reason them into assent, he has tried to frighten them into submission. I have been speaking hitherto of his proceedings with others: but the same nearly, perhaps, might be said of his dealings with himself. A mode of conduct, suppose, is disapproved of by the generality. The reason has been, it is of a nature to be hurtful to the generality. I[1] see that it is disapproved of: but [I do][2] not see the reason. [I see][3] that it is disapproved of: I disapprove of it myself. 'Well then,' say I to myself, 'it is wrong.' 'Very well, wrong it is then,' say you, 'but why?' I do not know. But I am a Moralist, and I ought to know: and I am writing a treatise on Morality, and something must be said about it. How, then, to manage? bring in God. Say it is a mode of conduct that God disapproves of: that it is odious to God: that God hates it. That God will punish him that's guilty of it. 'O then,' say you, 'now you come to talk of God, I see if that's the case I must take care of myself. If he hates it, I must hate it too: if I don't, he may punish me. God hate it? why yes, it will be strange if he does not. Don't I see how every body disapproves of it? Don't I see how every body hates it? Don't I see how wrong it is? Out of question, the best way is to be on the safe side: I'll e'en hate it, then, to make sure.' This, then, is the use the idea of God is of in a treatise of morality, without affording the shadow of a reason. This is the reason why weak moralists are generally so pious.

Disturbs men's judgments.

Idea of God—cannot be a foundation of Morals—introduced to awe.

[1] MS. orig. 'Our Moralist'. [2] MS 'he does'. [3] MS 'He sees'.

Idea of God—leads to ipse-dixit arguments, founded on the Moral Sense &c.[1]

476. If you press me further, and ask me why God hates it, you are rather troublesome: however, for this time, my answer is, because he is good, or because he is just, or for some such reason. If you press me further still, and ask me, why God, allowing him to be good, or just, or what I please, hates it? it is all over with me. I have now nothing left to say, but that it's wrong again: and there am I just where I was at first. If this won't satisfy you, I must go another way to work. I will say that I have an *understanding*: and my *understanding* is the immediate source of the ideas of right and wrong, which are simple ones: and if I think the thing is wrong, and there is no judgment in the case, my understanding says so: and if my understanding says it is wrong, wrong it is, and God help you if you think otherwise. Or else I have a particular kind of sense, which tells me any thing about morality I want to know. The name of it is the Moral Sense. It is called a Sense, least you should think it can be mistaken: which is what I would not have you suppose. Now I, having this Sense, can not be mistaken. And I say the thing is wrong: and so, then, wrong it is.

Understanding.

Moral Sense.

Law of Nature.

If you still continue at a loss, if God leaves you w[h]ere he found you, and neither my *sense* nor my *understanding* will go down with you, then let me see what God and I can do together. I say it is wrong, and God and I being perfectly of a mind about all these matters, God says so too: and his saying so, tho' nobody ever pretended to have heard him, is a Law of Nature. And so he hates it and will punish it: and, therefore, as a friend, I would advise you to hate it too.

Now then, as I have got a sense or an understanding, which I please, and which is a pattern for all other senses or understandings, if your's does not agree with it, you are in this present world a fool, or 'a hypocrite' and 'a villain', according as I am in a humour: and in the next, in the next I say, I am sorry it happens so, God is a just and merciful God, but between friends, not to mince the matter, you are damned.

In this harangue, tho' in a nutshell, is contained the full and true substance of the discourses of all those moralists who, prejudiced against the principle of utility for want of understanding the proper method of applying it, have strained after another: which other, in the region of intelligibles, is no where to be found.

Contract ⅹ Compact ⅹ Covenant.

477. Contract is the term generally employ'd in commercial transactions concerning moveables: especially where the public is

[1] MS alt. 'gives rise to overbearingness.'

a party. Thus we hear of Army and Navy Contracts, Contracts for Stores, Provisions, Cloathing for those services: Cases in which, for any thing there is in the original and general import of the three terms to hinder it, the words Compact and Covenant, if particular usage warranted it, might be just as well employ'd.

---

478. Such is the dependence among moral terms, that, of any of them singly, a definition can not be given that shall be fit to stand the test of time.

They must be all struck upon a Common Center.

Prefat. Definitions—connexion they must have.

---

479. A Condition is put in contradistinction to 1st a Limitation. 2dly a Covenant. 3dly a Qualifying or explicatory Proviso. 4. a Trust. A Grant to one, to the *intent* he shall do so and so, is not a Condition, but a Trust. Dy. 138 in Jac. Dict.[1] A Trust accepted, has the effect of a Compact as to compelling performance, tho' not as to damages.

Condition ⲭ Limitation ⲭ Covenant ⲭ Proviso ⲭ Trust.

---

480. By the word Condition, 3 different things are signified. 1st. An event made dependent on another event. 2dly. The dependence there is between those two events. 3dly. The discourse serving to express the act of volition by which that dependence is established.

Condition—3 Conjugate Senses.

---

481. Expectation is belief of an event to come.

Expectation.

482. The idea of an event expected to come has the same degree of vivacity as the idea of the same event expected not to come. This is sufficient to prove that Belief is not what Mr Hume[2] supposes it to be, a bare degree of vivacity superadded to the idea of the event believed.[3] I may have a very faint idea of your person: and yet believe strongly that you exist. I may have a very vivid idea of your person: and yet believe strongly that you do not exist, or believe very weakly that you do exist. Yes, but I can not have a lively one, without believing that you have existed.

A Belief is an act of the judgment.

Belief not a bare vivacity—what it is.

---

[1] See Giles Jacob, *A New Law-Dictionary*, London, 1729, s.v. 'Condition', citing James Dyer, *Cy ensuont ascuns nouel cases*, London, 1585, fo. 138.

[2] David Hume (1711–76), Scottish philosopher and historian.

[3] See David Hume *A Treatise of Human Nature* (first published in 1739–40), ed. D.F. Norton and M.J. Norton, 2 vols., Oxford, 2007 (*The Clarendon Edition of the Works of David Hume*), i. 67: 'So that as belief does nothing but vary the manner, in which we conceive any object, it can only bestow on our ideas an additional force and vivacity.'

Condition.

483. How one act is made dependent on another.

How a dependence is established between two acts.

One event merely physical can not be made (that is cannot, *by men*, be made) to depend on another prior event purely physical.

One event merely physical can not be made to depend on a prior human act: for an event dependent on such an act is not an event merely physical.

A Condition is an event, on which a RELATION is made dependent.

But what is a *Relation* when resolved into Events? The Relation in question, with respect to an Estate, is that of Proprietorship, either total or partial.

Proprietorship.

Proprietorship consists in being not restrained from acts of using, while other people are.

Condition—Controlling events—[11][2] sorts of.

That which the Relation is dependent on may be either: 1st. A single event physical. 2dly. A single moral event, a human act.[1] 3. An assemblage of physical events simultaneous. 4. An assemblage of moral events simultaneous. 5. A mixt assemblage of physical and moral events simultaneous. 6. An assemblage of physical events in succession. 7. An assemblage of moral events in succession. 8. A mixt assemblage of physical and moral events in succession. 9. An assemblage of physical events in simultaneity and succession. 10. An assemblage of moral events both in simultaneity and succession. 11. A mixt assemblage of events both physical and moral, both in simultaneity and succession.

Condition—it's 3 Senses.

484. We speak 1st of the *Non-performance* of a Condition. Here, what is meant by the word Condition is the *act*, viz: the act *made to depend*. 2dly. We speak of the *Breach* of a Condition. Here, what is meant by the word Condition is the discourse constituting the rule which serves to create the dependence: to announce the disposition of things by which the dependence is created.[3]

Controlling Event usually complex.[4]

485. It scarce ever happens that the *signal* is a single event or act: but it often happens that it consists of an assemblage of events appearing under a form of singleness. This is the case, when it is a single proposition that serves to express them. For instance, the *act*, as it is called, of a man's going from London to York. The act of

[1] The words 'a human act' have been marked by Bentham for deletion.

[2] MS '12'

[3] Bentham does not go on to describe the third sense, but see para. 480, p. 155 above.

[4] MS del. 'A signal is usually an assemblage of Events, not one only.'

his performing the journey. This act includes necessarily an innumerable multitude of acts of the same person in succession: it includes an innumerable multitude of motions, to every one of which the name of act may be attributed.

---

486. A Vocabulary is a necessary accompaniment *to*, or rather ingredient *in*, a Digest of the Law. That Digest and this vocabulary once composed, the Law will cease to be a Science. The only questions debated in Courts of Justice would be questions of Fact. Counsellors or Attornies there would be none. Those two races would expire and yield their place to Orators and Agents. Orators, to whom men would resort for defect of eloquence: and Agents, to whom they would resort for defect of leisure. Mystery, that scare-crow to weakness, and screen to knavery, Mystery, with his parent Fiction, would be driven into everlasting exile. Prefat. Definitions—Vocabulary of.

The business of fixing the import of words by means of Definitions is not to be looked upon as an hopeless one, on account of the little success of the attempts that have been made hitherto. The fault lies not in the science itself, but in the manner in which it has been treated. There is but one way in which it can possibly succeed: in this it never has been attempted yet. It is not possible to fix the import of words properly by an assemblage of unconnected Definitions. It is not possible that a body of Definitions not connected can be just. It is not possible to explain the import of every term by the common form of Definition *per genus et differentiam*. It is not possible to trace the dependence of the import of every word by itself immediately up to simple ideas. Many are the terms, in the Definitions of which must be employ'd other terms, that neither are themselves expressive of simple ideas, nor can in the same proposition be traced up to such as are. Should be in a chain.

An Indian Philosopher, being asked what it was supported the Earth? replied, an Elephant: and what the Elephant? replied, a Tortoise. And what the Tortoise? That was more than he had ever thought about.[1] Our Jurists have not the acumen even of this Indian. 'Tis seldom that they advance beyond the Elephant. Ask them what such a term means? it means a certain something, which something it never enters into their conceptions to give a further definition of, tho' the need it has of one is just the same as that which it was brought to define. The only thing they think of doing in a definition, is the putting of a word or an assemblage of

[1] This idea is referred to by Locke in *Essay concerning Human Understanding*, Bk. II, Ch. XIII, §19, p. 175 and Ch. XXIII, §2, p. 296, where it is attributed to 'an *Indian* Philosopher'.

words one meets with oftener, in the room of a word one meets with not so often, when, at the same time, the former is just as far from having clear ideas annext to it, as the latter. With Lawyers, who never look beyond the words, so the sound of a word be familiar to our ears, it is the same thing as if the sense of it were familiar to our understandings.

Condition—*cognata* to.

485. 1. Signal. 2. Act controlled, clogged, conditionalized. 3. Connecting motive.

Pleasure of Acquisition.

486. A Pleasure of Acquirement is a Pleasure of Possession at it's commencement.

A Pleasure of Possession may, at it's commencement, be stiled a Pleasure of acquisition.

Condition to a Law.

487. A Condition to a Law, that is when ARMED, is either 1st. A Condition to the Command, or 2dly a Condition to the Threat. A Condition to the Command of a Law is a dependence created between that Command and some event or assemblage of appearances as a signal.

Objects real ⅹ personal ⅹ modal.

488. The sort of act is one thing: the sort of agent is another. Two acts may be of the same sort: when the agents are different sorts of persons. In two acts that are of different sorts, the agent may be one and the same.

The sort of motion is one thing: the sort of body moving is another. Two motions may be of the same sort, when the bodies moving are different sorts of bodies.

In two motions that are of different sorts, the body moving may have been one and the same. The same individual portion of space may have been moved over by a drop of water and a pebble, but a drop of water and a pebble are bodies of different sorts. The same individual pebble, in moving over a portion of space, may have described at one time a right-lined surface, at another time a parabolic but a right-lined surface and a parabolic are figures of different sorts.

Relative to a Command, the act which is the object of it, may be stiled the modal object. The *person* whose act it is, the personal object. The *thing*, if any, on which that person's act is exerted, the real object. That *person* or that *thing*, either of them, consider'd as opposed to the modal object, the material object.

With regard to a Command, therefore, who the personal objects of it, who the modal objects, and who the real objects, are so many distinct articles of consideration.

The personal object, then, real object and modal object of a command, suppose, are given: and it is simple, without condition. Add now a condition. A signal is now given: that is an event or situation of things on which depends the direction of the Command, to any one, or any two, or all three, of the sorts of objects mentioned.

A Material object and a modal object, every command, as such, must have belonging to it. A real object besides, many commands have belonging to them.

489. The Command itself is susceptible of but two *qualities*,[1] as the term is, i:e: of propositions, among Logicians: a *positive* and a *negative*. These are qualities not of the command, but of the action.

Command, positive X negative.

The command in itself is simple and undiversifiable: it is the expression of an emotion: of an emotion of pain or pleasure felt at the contemplation of an idea: of pain on the idea of an action as performed; or, what comes to the same thing, of pleasure at the idea of it's being not performed: or else of pain at the idea of it's being not performed, of pleasure at that of it's being performed: the only varieties, therefore, which the thing expressed by the command itself, viz: the emotion of the mind admitts of, are accidental and inessential. All the varieties of it that are constant and essential, in short that immense assemblage of varieties that constitute the different sorts of Laws, to say nothing of commands that are not Laws, are to be sought for in the description of the mode of conduct that is the object of command. I wish that the window were open'd: I communicate that wish to my servant: in so doing, I do as much as command him to open it. Now, whether it was the pain I felt from the present heat, or the pleasure I expected from the coolness that would ensue, that produced or that constituted (I know not well which to say, nor is it material) my wish, in effect it makes no difference: my command is in either case the same: the act that is the object of it is the same: it is the opening of the window.

490. As to any one or more of these articles, therefore, the Command may undergo a change: while, as to the rest, it may remain the same: preserving a sort of identity, more or less entirely, so long as any of them remains the same. Time and Place are Articles of consideration respecting the modal object of

A Command—of what varieties susceptible.

[1] MS alt. 'varieties'.

the Command, which are not commonly understood to affect the genus of the Command.

A Command, therefore, may be changed: by rendering either modal, personal or real object of it particular: being before universal; or universal, having been before particular: or of one species or genus, being before of another species or genus: or including, having before excluded, or excluding, having before included, any single individual.

Condition, to a Command, destructive or modificative.

491. A Condition to a Command is either a Condition to it's total existence: or to it's species. In other words, on the signal given may depend either whether there shall be any command at all relative to that matter: or only whether there shall be a Command of such a sort, or of such another sort. A condition in the first case may be stiled a condition *destructive*: in the latter, a condition *modificative*.

It is the same with a condition to a threat.

—destructive.

A Condition *destructive* destroys the act clogged[1] upon appearance of the signal, destroys it, I say, and does no more.

—modificative.

A condition modificative, at the same time that it destroys one act conditionalized,[2] sets up another.[3]

REGULATIONS divided according to their SOURCE.

492. REGULATIONS[4]—with respect to their SOURCE—may be divided in the first place into 1st. AUTOGRAPHIC and 2dly. ADSCITITIOUS.

REGULATIONS AUTOGRAPHIC.

493. By the term AUTOGRAPHIC[a] may be stiled such REGULATIONS as are made by the SUPREME POWER.[5]

REGULATIONS ADSCITITIOUS.[6]

By the term ADSCITITIOUS may be stiled such Laws as have been made by any person or any body other than that invested with the supreme power.

A Regulation autographic.

494. A REGULATION AUTOGRAPHIC is an expression of such a VOLITION or assemblage of VOLITIONS as have been issued expressly and immediately by the supreme power as having originated in their own breast.

[a] *Αυτογραφικος*, from *αυτος*, one's self, and *γραφω*, to write, enact Laws. The word autograph is already in the language. Applied to a writing, it signifies the original in contradistinction to a Copy.

[1] MS orig. 'conditioned for'.
[2] MS alt. 'clogged' has been marked by Bentham for deletion.
[3] In the text, Bentham has noted at this point: 'Give an example. Qu. of all this, one mode, one motion, must be destroy'd, before another mode can be set up at the same time, &c.'
[4] MS orig. 'Laws'.
[5] MS orig. 'that body itself which stands invested with the *supreme power*.'
[6] MS alt. 'adsentitious'.

A REGULATION ADSCITITIOUS.

495. A REGULATION ADSCITITIOUS is an expression of such a volition or assemblage of volitions as, without issuing expressly and immediately from the supreme power, has been tacitly adopted by them, and had the same force given to it, as if it had originated with them.

Regulations adscititious.

496. REGULATIONS ADSCITITIOUS may again be divided into NATIVE and IMPORTED.

REGULATIONS NATIVE.

497. By native, I mean such adscititious regulations as have originally issued from a subordinate Legislature of the state in question.

REGULATIONS IMPORTED.

498. By IMPORTED, I mean such ADSCITITIOUS REGULATIONS as have originally issued from a Legislature, whether SUPREME or SUBORDINATE, not of the STATE in question, but of some other STATE.

REGULATIONS REAL)(FICTITIOUS, &c.

499. Regulations adscititious, whether native or imported, that is all regulations but such as are autographic, may be either 1st of the real kind: or 2dly of the fictitious, imaginary, or conjectural, inferential kind.

Principle, a—what.

500. A Principle is to a proposition expressive of a Maxim, what the words '*Quia emptores*', for example, are to the Statute which they entitle.[1] Examples—Principle of Utility in Morals—Principle of Superposition in Mathematics—Principle of Attraction in Physics.

Condition of the 1st &c. Order.

501. Condition to a Command—a Condition of the first order—Condition to a Condition, a Condition of the 2^{d} order, and so on.

'Comment.'[a] Four Sanctions.

502. 503.[2] There are [four][3] distinct sources from which men are accustomed to expect Pain and Pleasure. Three issue from the earth, a [fourth] from Heaven. Of those that issue from the earth, the first is that which arises not from the will of any being we discern, but from the concatenation of such events, wherein volition is not instrumental. This may be called the Physical

[a] I. Comm. 42.[4]

---

[1] The Statute of Westminster III of 1290 (18 Edw. I, c. 1) came to be known by its opening phrase *quia emptores*.

[2] Bentham has numbered this paragraph both 502 and 503.

[3] Bentham's addition of the physical sanction was an afterthought that rendered his original enumeration of the sanctions inconsistent. The enumeration has, therefore, been amended editorially.

[4] At *Commentaries on the Laws of England*, i. 42, Blackstone claims that 'all human laws' rest on the 'two foundations' of 'the law of nature and the law of revelation'. The relationship of the reference to the text at this point is unclear.

Sanction. [The second] is that which is derived from the conduct of a particular person or assemblage of persons acting under command from Government. This is sometimes called, at least it may be called, the Political Sanction. The [third] is derived from the will of uncertain individuals, acting spontaneously without command. This is sometimes called, at least it may be called, the Moral Sanction. That which is supposed to be derived from the will of an invisible being, author of our own existence and that of the phænomena we see: and capable, we suppose, upon the determination of his will, of being author of whatever other phænomena we can imagine, is sometimes called, at least it may be called, the Religious Sanction. Of these [last] three Sanctions, it is Law that indicates the 1st; Morality, or Ethics as it is called, the 2d; Theology, the third. The accrual of the two first in past instances is matter of experience: that of the 3d in past cases is matter of inference. That of all three in instances yet to come is alike matter of inference.

Obligation. **504.** Obligation is the action of a motive. A motive is an idea. An idea of Pain or Pleasure. Obligation signifies the act obliged to, the act which is the object of the obligation. Obligations *ex contractu*, &c.

Conscience. **505.** By Conscience is meant the faculty of judgment, upon the occasion of it's pronouncing that an action is of that sort, which is apt to be follow'd by pain or pleasure from either of the two Sanctions, the Moral or the Religious: or else it is a judgment that the individual action in question will be follow'd by such Pain or Pleasure: in other words, it is the expectation of Pain or Pleasure as about to ensue from one or other of those sources.

Forum Conscientiæ. **506.** The phrase '*forum conscientiæ*' is plainly metaphorical. '*Forum*' is a Court of Justice. When we speak, therefore, of the *Forum Conscientiæ*, we take the faculty of conscience and suppose it to be a person. We suppose it to be a Judge sitting in his court, and decreeing that the person in whose mind all this is supposed to pass shall experience a certain allottment of Pain or Pleasure accruing from one or other of these sources.

Comment &c. Obligation *in Foro Conscientiæ.* **507.** When we speak of an obligation *in foro conscientiæ*, we mean the idea of Pain or Pleasure as about to accrue from one or other of them in consequence of the action in question, according to the decree of this imaginary judge.

To say, then, that a human Law annexing punishment, i:e: pain, to an action does not superadd any fresh obligation to abstain from it, what does this mean? Just thus much and no more, viz: that the issuing of [pain] from one of these three sources, is not the same thing with the issuing of it from either of the other two: or in one word, that one of these 3 sources is not the same with another that is different from it. That a stroke expected [from] A is not a stroke expected from B.

---

508. We want a middle term to characterize indifferently a Law in this strict sense of it, or any distinct, intelligible portion of the substance of a Law. A Regulation ⪤ Law.

Let the term for this purpose be, a Regulation.

509. We want a term to express any such body of discourse which serves to [characterize] that assemblage of personal, real and modal objects of a State command, without need of any further exception to be made to either class of objects, for bringing it within what it is reasonable to suppose would be the volition of persons actuated by the motives, and enlightened by the views, of those whose volition is in question. A Law ⪤ a Regulation.

---

510. Circumstances affecting the description of the *personal* object. Circumstances to the 3 objects.

Circumstances affecting the description of the *real* object.

Circumstances [affecting the description of the] *modal* object.

511. The words {*action*}, {*act*}, are used in two very different senses, the one an extensive sense, the other a confined one. To the latter I shall appropriate the terms {act}, {simple act}: to the former, the terms {action}, {complex action}. The idea I annex to the term {act} is a simple one. In this sense it denotes nothing more than a mode of motion, except that the body moving is the body or a part of the body of a person of the human species. The motion a man's hand makes, for example, in giving a blow. By the term action, I mean a simple act consider'd as it is, complicated with an indefinite variety of circumstances: i:e: with all those circumstances upon the presence or absence of which depends the influence the act has on the happiness of the agent and the rest of the community. Act ⪤ Action.

512. The Circumstances *of an act*, the circumstances in an action, may be distinguished into *moral* and *physical*. Circumstances moral ⪤ physical.

By moral or mental circumstances, I mean acts of some one's mind. As the intention, the desire, I may have of giving pain to the person I strike, when I give a blow. Circumstances moral or mental.

513. By physical circumstances, I mean any such material objects or physical qualities of those objects as are supposed to contribute to give the act the influence just mentioned. Circumstances Physical.

Moral influence of the action may result from physical circumstances.

Circumstances of the first description only I call moral: circumstances of every other description, physical: but circumstances barely physical, circumstances that are not themselves moral, concur equally together with such as are moral, to produce the moral influence of the action.

Circumstances mental how discernible.

Circumstances of the moral kind, being acts of the mind, acts secret and internal, are not discernible directly: they are discernible no otherwise than by means of such physical circumstances as serve for signs of them. Thus the affection of the mind called anger is not discernible of itself, but by means of the change of aspect, that is, for example, by change of colour by means of the motion of the blood, and by the motions of the various muscles of the face.

Signs (of acts internal) natural X conventional.

514. Signs of acts of the mind may be distinguished into 1st. Natural 2d. Conventional: i:e: words.

Condition to a Law Permissive—Taxation.

515. When a tax is laid upon any commodity, the use of that commodity is prohibited, unless the tax be paid: it is permitted *on condition* the tax be paid. What is in this case the *signal*? what the *act conditionalized*? There is always a something taxed: that something is expressed by a name denoting it either to be a substance or an action. If a substance, by it is meant the possession of that substance. For taxation is a condition to a mode of conduct permitted.

Condition to a Permission: i.e. Taxation.

In order to answer this, we are to consider, that permission imports precedent prohibition. We must, therefore, for a moment consider that mode of conduct with respect to the article taxed, as being absolutely prohibited. A command, then, is given to certain persons to pursue a certain course of conduct that is requisite to bring the offender (that is the person who so uses the object) to punishment. That course of conduct is in this case the course of conduct commanded. Any act that serves to denominate a man the user of the commodity may be consider'd as the *signal* upon which the course of conduct above mentioned is to be pursued. The act of payment of the duty is then *a contrarient* signal on appearance of which the course of conduct leading to punishment is countermanded; and a prohibition set up against it instead.

Command penal, signal to a.

516. The signal to a command of the penal kind is an act of disobedience to some command, penal or otherwise.

Law (the) is never neutral—where it restrains not, it protects.

517. In a regular government, the Law is never neutral. If it does not prohibit a mode of conduct, it protects a man in it. That is, it punishes those who by physical force, or other forbidden means, obstruct or endeavour to obstruct him in it.

---

518. Those who affect to despise the sure tho' painful track of definition, who stigmatize it with the epithet metaphysical, as if accuracy were a thing to be shunned, choose rather to chatter like parrots than to discourse like men. I hate Metaphysics, said Burke.[1] So *Cacus* hated day-light.[2]

Prefat. Definition—Apologetica, Metaphysic.

---

519. A large part of the Common Law is composed of Rules of Interpretation—Rules for the interpretation of Deeds. Matter expository of those expressions of will which the Law adopts into itself.[3] These Rules have been made as they have been wanted: as the instruments to be interpreted have come under litigation.

Common Law of Contracts has grown up by degrees.

520. One question under Contracts is, whether this or that transaction shall be deemed to amount to such or such a contract. The Rule for determining this question points to a matter of fact—Consider whether the transaction in question is of the nature of those that have been found to excite the expectation which the contract in question, if clearly enter'd into, is of a nature to excite. Of such matters of fact, are not occasional judges, for instance a Jury, as good judges, as those that are so by profession?

Rules for Silent Contracts.[4]

---

521. A Command has 3 objects—$1^{st.}$ The active object,[5] 2. the passive,[6] and 3dly the act.

Command—3 objects of a—passive, active, and act.

522. The act is either $1^{st.}$ The simple act, presenting a simple idea, or $2^{dly.}$ The action, viz: the simple act combined with circumstances.

Act simple)(complex action.

523. Circumstances are either 1st moral, or, to use another word, metaphysical, or 2dly physical. Physical circumstances are either $1^{st.}$ Quiescent appearances, or $2^{dly.}$ Events. In other words, either Substances in a certain situation, or Substances in motion.

Circumstances physical)(moral. Physical, Appearances)(Events.

N.B. Existence becomes known to us no otherwise than by motion.

The Agent and patient may be the same: when different, the patient may be either a person or a thing.

[1] For this remark of Edmund Burke (1729–97), statesman and politician, see p. 217 below.

[2] In classical mythology, Cacus was a cave-dwelling monster slain by Hercules: see Virgil, *Aeneid*, VIII. 184–305.

[3] This sentence, originally positioned at the end of the paragraph, has been editorially inserted at this point.

[4] MS del. 'Rules for determining by what signs such or such a Contract or Conveyance shall be understood to be expressed.'

[5] MS orig. 'agent'.

[6] MS orig. 'patient'.

Act—instrument of an.

524. When the raising of a sensation in a personal patient is the end of an action, [and] any intermediate series of patients, whether real or personal, however long, is passed over, then the patient in whom the sensation is meant to be excited is spoken of as the sole patient: the intermediate series of patients are spoken of as instruments. Thus, when one man beats another with a stick: the striker is the agent: the striker, by the powers of his mind, contracts certain muscles of his hand: that contraction gives motion to the stick, which becomes the immediate patient of the act: the stick, by the motion communicated to it by the hand, becoming an agent, now acts upon the person stricken: who is the 2d or more remote of the two patients in the action. But the end in contemplation of the striker being the production of pain in the person stricken, that, and not any motion to be given to the stick, being the event of which the idea formed the motive in the striker's mind, it is the person stricken that alone is spoken of under the character of the patient, of the material object of the act, the stick being consider'd but as the instrument.

The series will be diversified if, instead of the stick, we suppose a person pushed against him in whom it is meant to excite pain. It will not only be diversified but greatly lengthen'd if we suppose the instrument, as in the former case, a person; and that person served, as a French consul was once served, by one of the tyrants of Morocco.[1]

Command punitory.

525. From the Mass of Commands at large, a particular class may be distinguished under the name of penal, or punitory.

By a Penal or punitory command, I mean a Command, whereof the modal object is a mode of conduct whereof the end is to excite pain in some person. For instance, a command to an Officer of Justice to whip, to hang, to behead, a criminal.

Object active X passive.

526. Among the 3 objects of a Command, the agent may be stiled the active object; the patient, the passive object.

Commands none unconditional.

527. There are few simple acts, or perhaps none at all, that are either absolutely commanded or absolutely forbidden. Every thing is dependent upon circumstances. A Command unconditional is that of which the modal object is a naked act. A [Command][2] conditional, an act under particular circumstances. The same act is commanded under one set of circumstances, that is permitted only or forbidden under another. An act that, under one set of circumstances, is forbidden under a certain penalty, is, under another set of circumstances, forbidden under a higher.

[1] The incident to which Bentham alludes has not been identified.
[2] MS | |.

Suppose a simple act the constant effect of which is known to be the killing of the person who is the passive object of it. That act, under every regular system of Laws, would be prohibited under the highest penalty under a certain set of circumstances, under penalties of different magnitude under so many other sets of circumstances; it would be permitted without being commanded under another, it would be again commanded under penalties more or less severe under other sets of circumstances.

528. The objects of a Law are either direct or collateral. The direct are three—the active object of the act; the passive object of the act; and the act itself. The collateral are circumstances of the act. Under the description of objects of a Law, may be comprized a variety of articles. These may, in the first place, be distinguished into direct objects of a Law, and collateral objects of a Law.

Command—objects of a—are Direct Ӿ Collateral.

---

529. What a man stipulates for in a Contract, is something pleasurable: when it is promised him by the other party, he expects it. He has, therefore, a Pleasure of Expectation. This Pleasure, if in due time it be not improved and consummated into a Pleasure of Possession or Enjoyment, turns into a Pain of Disappointment.

False Decision—Mischief of a.

---

530. 'Tis seldom that a single circumstance constitutes a controlling event:[1] it is generally a numerous assemblage of circumstances that constitutes a *signal*: or rather there are (to every condition) a numerous assemblage of concurrent *signals*.

Conditions—A controlling event[2] usually an assemblage.

---

531. That the idea of God is of no use as to the pointing out the modes of conduct proper to be pursued. That all the use it can be of is to furnish a motive to the pursuing of such a mode of conduct as, from other considerations, shall have been previously determined to be a proper one. It is impossible, therefore, that Theology can throw any light upon either Morality or Jurisprudence. To maintain that there is a command from God to such or such an effect, and at the same time to allow that no signs of it can be produce[d], is to make no difference between expression and non-expression: between signs and no signs: between speaking and non-speaking: between writing and non-writing. It is not from any speculations concerning God that any assistance can be derived towards determining what, in point of MORALITY, *is*, or, in point of LEGISLA-

Idea of God useless in Jurisprudence.

[1] MS orig. '*signal*'.

[2] MS orig. 'signal'.

TION, *ought* to be *made*, our duty to our neighbour. The idea of God may give us motives, but it can not give us direction. It may give us a spur, but it can not give us reins. The less we have to do with it, therefore, on such occasions, the better. It can not instruct us: it can only serve to disturb, to fascinate, to terrify, to confound us. This piety, therefore, with which books on these subjects are apt to be interlarded by their authors, from the same motives as the panegyrics they bestow on their earthly patrons, is as impertinent as those panegyrics and as foreign to the purpose. But it is not only useless: it is mischievous: as calculated to give a predominance to the sentiments of those who introduce it, which no man's sentiments are entitled to, over those of another. I have not any more right to turn my opinions into Commands of God, than another man: nor any other man than I. It is an artifice which the despotism and overbearingness that, in a greater or less proportion, enters into the composition of every man's temper accounts for, and may excuse, but can not justify.[1] I may give them a better chance for being submitted to, true or false, but I do not bring them awhit nearer to being true by thus falsifying their character.

The piety of the pen may be very good in it's season and in it's place: in | | and in Devotions for every day in the week. But, when this is not the case, it is a merit, in point of probity so suspicious, in point of utility so trivial, and in point of facility so mechanical, that it may very well be spared. In point of utility, a book of Cookery might as well be interlarded with ejaculations, as a book of Jurisprudence with theological speculations. It might, indeed, better: for the devotions in a book of Cookery would only be useless. In a book of Jurisprudence, it can certainly do no good, and it is a thousand to one but, for the reasons that have been given, it does mischief.

In attempting to deduce moral duties or political regulations from the consideration of a Deity, we turn about in a circle: but we advance not a single jot.

Law of Property. Regulations concerning Title—what they do.

532. The several regulations concerning Title are regulations which serve to describe the Owner: i:e: the person who, under the general Law of property, shall, in respect of the several subject-matters of property therein distinguished, upon the different events therein specified, and as far as concerns the several sorts of acts of ownership specified, be the party favoured by the Law: the party excepted from the restraint which it is the Law's business to impose: the party left at liberty while others are restrained.

---

[1] This sentence has been marked by Bentham for deletion.

533. *Events*, that is bodies in motion, impress certain sensible images on the mind. *Situations*, that is the same bodies at rest, impress also certain sensible images on the mind. These images, in either case, are bundles of simple ideas, determinate and assignable.

Law—modal objects of, are 1st. Events; 2. Situations.

533.* The Events, I say, are bodies in motion. The situations, I say, are bodies at rest. This may seem an impropriety: and so it is with respect to the custom of discourse: but with respect to real existence, to the nature of the things discoursed of, it is not.[1] In discourse, the motion may be separated from the body moving: but in the nature of things, they are inseparable. The body that moves, and the motion that it makes, may be spoken of, and for many purposes they must necessarily be spoken of, as two things: but in fact they are but one thing. The one thing that exists is the body itself that makes the motion. In like manner, to constitute a situation, there must be at least two bodies. In discourse, the situation may be separated from the bodies situated: but in the nature of things, they are inseparable. The bodies situated, and the situation that each of them is in in respect of the other, may be spoken of, and for many purposes they must necessarily be spoken of, as four things: but in fact they are but two things. What exists is, the two bodies themselves that are so situated.

No Ideas purely abstract.

The motion may be spoken of, but it not only does not exist, but it can not so much as be conceived without a body moving: it cannot be separated from it so much as in idea. I can have no idea, for example, of a motion in a right line, without having the idea, an idea very indeterminate and confused indeed, but still an idea, of some body or other, that at some time or other I have seen moving in such a line. A round dot of a pen, for example, if I have been upon Geometry, or a star, such as it appears to us, if I have been upon Astronomy, or a Billiard Ball, if I have been at Billiards. What these objects have to offer to the senses besides the motion is a certain colour and figure: which colour and figure together make up the visible idea of their substance. Now, of a substance, I must have the idea, at the time that I have that of motion, or I have none at all. I may think as little as I please of the colour and figure of the body I represent to myself as moving: I may dwell on these two modes: I may bend my attention towards them as little as I please: I

[1] In the margin, Bentham has made the following addition, which may belong here: 'Our words make mention of them as if they were abstract, but in fact they are not. Our words make mention only of one idea. But the idea which that word is designed to bring up alone, brings others with it unavoidably. Although those others be placed in so obscure a light, as that they are scarcely perceptible.'

may withdraw my attention from them altogether. As to the particular colour or figure, I may take any that happens at the instant to lie next at hand in the storehouse of my memory. But some colour, and some figure, I must take, or no idea of motion have I at all.

It will here be asked, what becomes of abstract ideas all this while. I answer, that to speak strictly there are, I take it, no such things. Abstract terms there are, but abstract ideas there are none. Terms there are put to signify one of these modes without the other, terms used to dispose the mind to point it's attention to one of them without pointing it to any other: but ideas of any one of them without an idea of the other, it is not, I conceive, in the power of terms, or of any thing else, to raise up in the mind. They subsist not there, nor are capable of subsisting separately: they subsist only in composition. They may be compared in this respect to the *phlogiston* of the chymists; which bears a great part in the composition of a great part of the number of bodies that we see, which may be driven about from one body to another, but which has never been sensible any where by itself.[1] They may be compared to the particles *con-*, *dis-*, and *re-* of the grammarians, which in Latin enter into the composition and modify the signification of so many words, without being words or possessing any signification of themselves.

Imaginary existences no proof of abstract ideas.

534. What becomes, then, it will be said, of sphinxes and chimæras, of Golden mountains, and the multiform objects we see in sleep? These, it is true, we know, have no existence in reality: but will it be said that they are not even imagined? that they have not so much as an existence in the mind? I answer, by no means; in the mind, doubtless they have existence: that is in the mind they do appear. To the mind, ideas corresponding to these names are often present.

But how it will be said, can they be present if no such things as abstract ideas are admitted? I answer thus.

We can not, it is true (I am speaking of such of us as possess the sense of seeing), we cannot have the idea of a colour without associating with it the idea of some figure; nor, perhaps, of a figure, without associating with it the idea of some colour. But we can take a colour we have seen, and associate with it the idea of a figure we have never seen associated with that colour, provided we have

[1] According to the theory elaborated by the chemist and physician Georg Ernst Stahl (1659–1734), drawing in part upon the ideas of Johann Joachim Becher (1635–82), phlogiston was the element released from burning matter into the air during the process of combustion. Although forming part of all combustible substances, phlogiston was not thought to exist in a pure state, and hence was not directly observable.

seen it associated with some other colour. We may in like manner take a figure we have seen, and associate with it the idea of a colour we have never seen associated with that figure, provided we have seen it associated with some other figure: and thus form ideas of imaginary substances at pleasure; such as in fact we do form. A Diamond Billiard Ball is what I have never seen: but I have seen a Diamond, and I have seen a Billiard Ball. A Diamond Billiard Ball is, therefore, what I can imagine. Though I never have had the substance of a Diamond Billiard Ball before my eyes, I can have, I now have, the idea of it in my mind. I can take the colour of the Diamond, and associate with it the figure of the Billiard Ball: or I can begin with the figure of the Billiard Ball, and associate to it the colour of the Diamond.

---

535. Note. I say nothing here of the perception of bulk: it enters not necessarily into the composition of an idea. To those who judge by the eye, no single impression can suggest the idea of any determinate bulk. To determine the bulk of an object is an operation which, tho' perpetual practise has render'd it familiar, is in fact an affair of very complex calculation. It is managed by comparing the appearance of the object in question with that of other objects of which the bulk has been made known by feeling.

Bulk no necessary ingredient in the idea of a Substance.

536. Note. I say as little of impenetrability: it is the power of exciting a certain feeling: which, by a multitude of objects that are seen, is never excited: which objects notwithstanding have indisputably an idea in the mind. Such, for example, are the celestial bodies.[1]

Nor Impenetrability.

---

537. The word *condition* seems to indicate that the *signal* is an *event* in the power of the person affected by the condition: as when we say, 'upon condition of his doing so or so:' otherwise—we say, 'upon such or such an *event*.'

Condition—seems to suppose the influencing event to be an act.[2]

---

538. The effect of every Law is to give power.[3]
Power is either over persons or over things.
Power over persons is created by &c.
Power over things is created by &c.

---

[1] In the text, Bentham has noted at this point: 'Qu. Since all seeing men can feel; tho' all blind men cannot see.'
[2] MS del. '—refers rather to an *act* than to an *event*.'
[3] In the text, Bentham has noted at this point: 'Qu.'

Ingredients in a blind man's idea of a Substance.

539. As a seeing man's idea of a substance is made up of a visible figure, and a peculiar colour within the limits of that figure: so a blind man's idea of the same substance is made up of a tangible figure and a peculiar feeling within the limits of that figure.

Law, it's Spurious Senses—History of.

540. Rise of the derivative and improper senses of the term Law out of the original and proper one. Relation of the sense of the word Law as used to denote an unknown and imaginary cause of uniformity of action in involuntary agents,[1] or in voluntary[2] objects in those motions which are not the result of volition, to that in which it is employ'd to denote a known and real cause of action in voluntary agents as such. In what manner, by what process, the [former][3] was deduced out of the [latter].[4] Why the impropriety of applying the word Law to denote an unreal cause of motion in involuntary agents, as if known, is innocent, while in respect of voluntary agents it is pernicious. Why the misapplication is mischievous—in one case more, in another less, in another not at all.

Law, Original Sense of.

The term Law, that is the correspondent terms to it in the original languages, was invented, it should seem, to denote a General Command of Public Government. Such sort of Command was observed to produce a certain degree of uniformity among the human acts that were the objects of it.[5] Hence it came to be consider'd as a cause of uniformity among such acts. Such acts were referred to the Law enjoining them as to their cause. Looking forward from the Law, men observed an uniformity produced by it: and looking backwards from an assemblage of uniform actions, saw them resulting [from] a Law.

It soon became convenient for various purposes, in respect of such assemblages of actions amongst which an uniformity was observed or wished for, although no certain cause of it was assignable, and although in particular it had not any Law, in the proper sense of the word, for it's cause, to speak of such uniformity as if it had a cause: to suppose a cause for it, and for such supposed cause to find a name. The plea for this extension was, that if there

[1] MS orig. 'unsentient objects'.
[2] MS orig. 'sentient'.
[3] MS 'latter'.
[4] MS 'former'.
[5] In the margin, Bentham has noted at this point: '*Ανακες Βασιλεες*, were before *Νομοι* [i.e. 'Imperial Commands were before Laws']. Law of the Jews: Consult Goguet.' See Antoine Yves Goguet and Alexandre Conrad Fugère, *De l'origine des loix, des arts, et des sciences; et de leurs progrès chez les anciens peuples*, 3 vols., Paris, 1758, ii 8–9 for a brief discussion of the laws of the Hebrews.

had been a Law about the matter, things would, it is supposed, have been in the state in which they were in fact observed to be.

541. The first, because the slightest and most natural, extension of the word Law, seems to have been from a general command of Public government to a supposed cause of uniformity of conduct produced in fact by a conformity amongst particular commands, also of public government: in a word, from an article of Statute, to an article of Common Law. When the assemblage of propositions expressive of General Commands of Public Government, commands concerning a whole class of objects, came to be enumerated, it was natural to insert among them, and to mention on the same occasions and in the same views, an assemblage of propositions expressive of what had been the particular commands of persons bearing a part in public government relative to such particular objects as could be formed into a class. When the corrupting of another man's wife, for instance, was an act constantly follow'd in past instances, when detected, by a certain punishment, in consequence of a particular command of a person of one certain description to a person of another certain description; when the observation of such uniformity of punishment in past instances of commission had begot an uniformity of forbearance in subsequent instances of temptation, an uniform disposition in citizens at large to expect such punishment, and in judges to order it to be inflicted, it became as material to persons of all descriptions to be informed of such uniformity of punishment, though grown up without law, as if it had been created by Law. It was a concise and expeditious way of intimating the past existence of such uniformity and generating the expectation of it in future, to speak of it as if it had resulted from a Law: to make mention in a single word of *a Law*, as the supposed and fictitious cause of the disposition of things in question, instead of taking a multitude of words to express that disposition of things itself. Nor could any prejudice result from this fiction with respect to popular and ordinary purposes. Only with respect to such persons as might have occasion to consider the subject accurately and systematically, it laid them under difficulties, by applying to a fictitious entity a name before that peculiar to an object really existing, and thereby putting them upon the scent of an object, which, when searched after, was not to be found. Hence followed an obscurity in our ideas as well of the thing which had thus been made to usurp the name of another, as of the other whose name it had usurped. This other was left unprovided with any name that could serve to distinguish it from the former: and as to the former, by it's being

First extension of the term Law from an article of Statute Law, to an article of Common Law.

made to signify now something, and now nothing, it became difficult to say what it signified.

Second extension of it from an article of municipal Law, to a supposed Moral Law of Nature, *prescribing* what *ought* to happen.

542. Subsequent to that already mentioned in point of time, and wider in point of distance from the original signification, seems to have been the import given by men to the word Law, in speaking of a Law of nature, as a something by which men's conduct is to be governed, though no general command of public Government, nor indeed the command of any person at all.

The only thing which the idea annext to this word Law in this case had in common with those annext to it in the former was that of being a cause of uniformity. The only thing in the two cases that was common was uniformity among motions, those motions the motions of voluntary agents, and voluntary themselves. The particulars in which this case differ'd from the two former were considerable. In the first case there was a general command productive of uniformity; and it was this general command that the term in question was applied to signify. In the second case, there was an assemblage of particular commands productive of an expectation which was itself productive of uniformity like to that issuing from a general command: and it was a general command supposed suited to the case that the term was in that second case applied to signify. In this third case, there was no such thing as any assignable command at all; there was indeed a certain degree of uniformity in contemplation, but that uniformity rather the object of wish than of observation.

Third extension of it, from . . . . to a quite different thing under the name of a Law [of] Nature, asserting what in certain cases, it is supposed, *does* happen.

543. The Third and last extension of it was from a proposition real or supposed, of a nature to become a cause real or supposed, of motions voluntary, to a proposition asserting the existence of uniformity among motions involuntary.

It now signified not any cause, any written instrument, at all real or supposed. It signified not any act of the will, or any symbol of any act of the will, real or supposed. It signified a mere assertive proposition formed by the understanding: and expressive of a matter of fact concerning a class of objects. The derivative meaning being drawn out thus wide from the original one, is in no danger of being confounded with it. It is plainly not identical with the original, but only analogous to it, and that very remotely: so remotely, that there is scarce any proposition applicable to the object signified by the word in it's original meaning, that a man would think of applying to it in this derivative one. If he did, it would be said of him, not that he asserted what was false, but that he talked nonsense. Suppose a man were to get up and maintain a Law of the State to be void, on pretence of it's being contrary to one of Sir Isaac Newton's Laws of Nature:[1] what should we say of such a man? that he was mistaken? no: but that he did not know what he said. It would be an extravagance greater than even our Author[2] could ever have thought of uttering. I have said that the term Law in this last sense of it does not so much as express a cause of any thing: does not express any thing that is or is supposed to be a cause. This is very true; howsoever, from the inaccurate application it is common [to] see made of it, one might suppose otherwise.[3] It signifies no more than a *reason*, a consideration serving to induce the *mind* to believe the existence of a fact mentioned as it's effect. Not any thing that operates upon the object consider'd, but upon the mind by which it is consider'd.

Main Instrument, Main Cause)(Concurrent Instruments, Causes, and situations.

---

544. In attempting to deduce moral duties from the consideration of the Deity, we twist about in a circle: but we do not advance a single inch. Theology of no use in Morality or Jurisprudence.

---

545. The general command constitutive of ***property*** is to this effect. Law, the, constitutive of Property.

Meddle not with that {substance}[4] which is another's {property}[5] as far as, and so long as, it is another's.

The threats with which the command is backed are various, according to the differences in the modal objects, active and passive objects, and the several circumstances of each.

The several heads of regulations relative to this command are those which settle: Law,—the general, of Property—Heads of matter expository to.

1st. What it is for a thing to be a person's property.

2. For what length of time the several thing[s] or assemblage[s] of things may be a person's property. Duration of the Estate when of certain continuance.

3. Upon what events the thing in question may begin and when

[1] Newton's three laws of motion (he did not refer to them as laws of nature, though they were often referred to as 'Newton's laws of nature') were first described in *Philosophiae Naturalis Principia Mathematica*, London, 1687, which appeared in English translation as *The Mathematical Principles of Natural Philosophy*, trans. Andrew Motte, 2 vols., London, 1729.

[2] i.e. Blackstone.

[3] The remainder of the paragraph has been marked by Bentham for deletion.

[4] Above this word, Bentham has noted '*subaudito*', i.e. implied or understood.

[5] Above this word, Bentham has again noted '*subaudito*'.

cease to be that person's property. Duration of the Estate when of continuance uncertain.

4. Sets of circumstances one or other of which a man must stand in to have property in a thing. Herein of the different species of Title.

5. How many persons may be deemed to stand in each set of circumstances at a time. Herein of the Number of the Owners.

How the several species of Property are created.

6. Ceasing to be one person's property, by what means it may become another's. Herein of Conveyance.

7. Upon what concomitant conditions it is continued a person's property. Herein of Tenures.

8. The several species of Property; their characteristic differences whence taken.

9. From what species persons of what descriptions are debarred and for what time. Who are capable, and who not capable, of being owners of the different species of Property.

Commercial Laws.

546. What acts a man is prohibited [from] exercising upon what is his own property, or that of another who consents to them.

Taxing Laws.

547. What acts a man is permitted to exercise on his own property no otherwise than upon condition to pay taxes: i:e: to pay a certain quantity of money or money's worth to the Government.

Command—unity of a—by what constituted. Point of Individuation.

548. The unity or plurality of a Command depends, we may observe upon the unity or the plurality of the sentence or sentences in which it is expressed. It does not depend upon the individuality of the object, either modal, active or passive: for if it did, there could be no such thing as a general command. It does not depend any more on the unity of the sort of either class of objects: for the number of sorts into which an assemblage of individuals of any kind may be distributed, has no other limit than the number of the differences observable in the number of those individuals. When, therefore, we speak of the unity of a general command, it is plain that, by the term command, we mean not the assemblage of ideas that is in the mind of the person commanding, but the assemblage of words he makes use of to express it.

A Command is the expression of a wish; namely when it is the wish of a superior. Separating, therefore, from the consideration of a wish the three sorts of objects of it with their circumstances, all that remains is the wish itself: that is the mixed and fluctuating sensation composed of pleasure in the expectation of the attainment of the object, and pain in the expectation of the non-attainment of it. Now, there is no system of events with their circumstances so complicated, that this feeling may not be annext to, as well as to any single simple one: only the more it is extensive, the more transient the contemplation, the more indistinct and vague the ideas of those objects must necessarily be. I wish that all mankind would maintain such conduct as would make them happy. This wish is but a single wish. Yet does it include as many wishes as, were they turned into Laws, would equal, and much more than equal, the whole number of the Laws that, were it in my power, I should see good to make for the government of the species. The above particulars consider'd, we shall be acquitted of self-contradiction, if we should have occasion to speak of the same form of words, at one time as constituting a single command, at another as capable of being resolved into a number of forms of speech each of itself alike entitled to the same appellation of a command. The same collection of persons, things, acts and circumstances that may be indicated as the objects of a wish, by one form of speech constituting a command, may be indicated by an indefinite multitude of forms of speech, each of itself entitled to the appellation of a command, but all together no more than equivalent to the first. Thus much, however, is certain—that, be the objects of it more or less extensive, to constitute it an entire one, all the CONDITIONS DISTINCTIVE to it must be expressed.

Writ of Execution—what.

549. A judicial Writ of Execution is a command to an individual Officer, as the active object, to perform such an act or train of acts upon the party losing or his property, as the passive object, as when performed shall be in execution of the threat which constitutes the armature of the principal command in question. This act, if the pain be a pain of privation, is an act of conveyance.[1]

Judgment on a claim of property—Universal description of.

550.* In all causes relative to title to property, the solution of the question in dispute is contained in a proposition declaring what?—that the party having right is the individual personal object marked out by some person having the right of investment in respect of the real object in question as that individual object for the time being who is of the sort of personal objects favoured by the general Law of Property. This account will hold good with respect to any claim of property that can be proposed.

King, his 4 capacities.

550. The powers belonging to the King in this country belong to him in 4 capacities. 1$^{st.}$ His Conjunctly-Legislative. 2$^{dly.}$ His

[1] On writs of execution see Blackstone, *Commentaries on the Laws of England*, iii. 412–25.

Separately-Legislative. 3dly. His Procuratorial. 4^thly. Dispensatorial or Proprietary. In his *Conjunctly-Legislative* capacity, he acts along *with* the supreme body, as *part* of it. In his *separately-Legislative* capacity, he acts apart from the Supreme body, as *under* it. In his *procuratorial capacity*, he acts apart again from the supreme body, as *for* it. In his *dispensatorial* or *Proprietary*, he acts apart again from the supreme body, as under it again. He either appoints the use of the property of the State, or the conveyance.

In his *procuratorial* capacity, he either promises to repeal or actively repeals a certain set of regulations of the supreme body, and promises to set up or sets up others in favour of certain persons with whom he is contracting.

In his Dispensatorial capacity, he either exercises the powers of issuing commands, particular or general, concerning a limited class of passive objects: viz: such as constitute the property of the State: or the acts of a limited class of active objects: viz: the servants of the State (Judiciary excepted), or of appointing the persons who shall issue them.

Compact ⵋ Contract ⵋ Conveyance.

551. A *Compact* is *de futuro*. A Contract is either *de futuro* or *de præsento*.

A Contract includes Conveyance.

A Conveyance is either of a whole passive object: i:e: of all the powers that can be exercised over that subject: or of powers: i:e: certain limited powers in particular.

Power Legislative ⵋ Judiciary.

552. The supreme Government absorbs and includes every subordinate act of power whatever it be: Judicial, therefore, among the rest.

Supreme *Legislation* is the business of Supreme Government carried on in the gross.

Supreme Legislation, therefore, includes the exercise of Judicial power.

The difference between Legislative power and Judicial does not consist in that the first is concerned in issuing Commands only concerning sorts of actions; the latter only concerning individual actions. For a Command to a single person to do an act which he was before free to do or not do, may be such as shall be presently recognized to belong not to the Judiciary, but only to the Legislative power.

Of a Judiciary Command, however, one of the 3 classes of objects at least must be individual:[1] as in an Injunction in

[1] In the text, Bentham has noted at this point 'Qu.'; and in the margin: 'Qu?'

Chancery. The active object must be either one or more determinate persons, or at least an assemblage of persons so cemented in a body as to constitute *one party*. As a Parish, a Borough, a County, a Judicial Court.

But the characteristic difference between Legislative and Judicial authority seems to consist in this. Judicial authority, to remain such, can act no otherwise than under the Laws, real or fictitious, that are subsisting. It is reserved to Legislative authority to act even against such Laws.

When a Judge issues a command, it must be on the ground of an act already done, contrary to some pre-existing Law, supposed at least, if not real: inconsistent with some supposed pre-existing obligation. Again, the Judge, as such, can act in no other case than at the instigation, at the request, of some party, and that a party in a precise and determinable manner concerned in, the party favoured by, the act in question. The Legislator can act of his own mere motion without the instance or request of any one.

Law Statute = *Authoritative*: Law Common = *Conjectural*.

---

553. By the naked act I mean the bare motion and nothing else. The motion *abstracted* from the person moving, and the body acted on. Act naked—semicomplex.

By the semicomplex act, I mean the naked act, when, to the consideration of it, is superadded that of the active and passive object, but without that of any circumstances. Semicomplex.

---

554. The modal objects of the General Law of property are all acts whatsoever on the passive objects in question, and under all circumstances whatsoever, except those of consent by the proprietor, general or specific, tacit or express; command or permission by persons invested by public powers over private property; and circumstances of necessity. Law, general, of Property—Modal objects of, what.

555. The modal objects of the general Law of Personal Security are all acts whatsoever on the person in question as the passive object of them, and under all circumstances whatsoever, with the same exceptions as before. D° of Law of Personal Security.

556. The modal objects of the general Law of Liberty are all acts whatsoever on all passive objects whatsoever, whereby the loco-motive faculty of any person is obstructed, under the same circumstances. D° of Law of Personal Liberty.

Prefat. Every thing to be reduced to the settled Nomenclature.

557. When a stock of Nomenclature has been laid in large enough to express all we have to say upon the subject, in order to avail ourselves of it, and take the benefit of that clearness and precision which it is calculated to spread over the whole discourse, it will be necessary to reduce every thing we have occasion to observe originally as from ourselves, or to introduce the mention of, whether in the way of argument or example, from others—to reduce it, I say, to a conformity with the scale thus fixed, to translate it into the language thus, as it were, invented.

General Law concerning Property, what it leaves for the matter of other Laws of which *things* are the passive objects. Moral field of Dominion it leaves untouched.

558. Thus large a division of the body of the Law is comprized under a single command; the purport of which is to prohibit all persons whatsoever, one or a certain number only excepted, to abstain from almost all acts whatsoever exercisable on all [passive][1] objects whatsoever. What are the acts, therefore, exercisable upon articles of property as their correspondent passive objects that are left for any other commands to work upon? The answer is, those acts and those only, in respect to each person, and those passive objects, which, in that person's favour, are excepted out of the general prohibition.

Where there is Law, there is Command: to understand this of *Stat.* Law.

559. If every Law is a Command, then is Command traceable in every thing that bears the name of Law. Under Statute Law, men are governed by the expectation of Punishment announced by Law.

How the case is in *Common* Law.

Under Common Law, as it is called, men are governed by like expectation resulting from usage without Law.

Omnipotence of Parliament, how limited.

560. The only thing that gives the sovereign body the power it possesses is the habit of submission. The only thing that can limit the same power is the same habit of submission. Now, certainly in a body of people with arms in their hands, the habit of submission has never extended to commands the obedience to which they concurred in believing would be prejudicial to them. In these cases I would not say that by Law such and such commands can not be issued: but that in such and such cases it is still less dangerous to the community, that the Law should be withstood, than that it should be obey'd.

Notion of a legal limitation to Parliamentary power, how dangerous.

561. 562.[2] The drift of this medium of argument is easily explained, and it is fit it should be understood. It is to beget an antipathy against, and a disposition to oppose, the obnoxious

[1] MS 'active'.

[2] Bentham has numbered this paragraph both 561 and 562.

measures beyond what the tendency of them, as it is thought likely to appear to the people in general, will warrant. The measure, though mischievous perhaps, is not mischievous to such a degree, or does not so plainly appear to be so, as to induce the body of those who disapprove it, to rise up to oppose it by force of arms. But persuade them that there are such things as Laws of Nature, that Laws of the State, if contrary to any such Laws of Nature, ought to be so opposed, that the State-Law in question is contrary to some of these Laws of Nature, which will [be] no hard matter to do if they disapprove it, then, according to the argument, if they are sway'd by it, they ought to rise up to rebel against the Law. Or persuade them that the command in question is beyond the original power of the supreme body to issue, tho' without saying any thing about Laws of Nature, it comes to the same thing. The Legislators, tho' supreme, are *pro tanto* usurpers, and as such ought to be opposed. In this last case, we are to understand there is a regulation issued which, though it wear the guise of Law, is, however, no Law at all. In the first, a Law is made which, consider'd by itself, might be very good Law, but which, the instant it offers to lift up it's head, is demolished by a superior. Thus much I thought it of use to say, not for the sake of casting a censure on those who have embraced this or that side of this or that particular question, but with respect to political questions in general, to bring them to a fair and speedy issue, to cut off uninstructive and irritating argumentation, and, with regard to a measure really inexpedient, such as I myself would deem so, to prevent people's being trepanned by technical subtleties into a repugnance to it beyond what the real tendency of it will warrant.

Original Compact and total dissolution of Government by a single violation of it. Mischief of this notion.

563. Mischievousness and futility[?] of Locke's doctrine that, by a violation of the original compact, the constitution is dissolved.[1]

It is a common and, in general at least, if not universally, a just notion that by one party's not performing his part of a compact (this, however, must be confined to a simple uncompounded compact), the other party is set at liberty, and the whole compact is dissolved.

Thence extended to entire systems of Law.

Ground of this proposition in point of utility.

[1] See John Locke, *Two Treatises of Government* (first published in 1690), ed. P. Laslett, Cambridge, 1960, Ch. XIX, pp. 406–28.

That it does not extend so much as to all compacts—to none that are very complex.

Much less to the whole body of Laws in a nation.

Argument that might be brought *e contra* from this logic, viz: that past Laws are continued in force only by the inexplicit volition of present Legislators.

Law of Property, what relates to Title is definitional matter to.

564. Persons who have come by the legal possession of a subject in the several different ways in which a man may come by it, may be taken for persons of so many different descriptions. The doctrine, therefore, concerning title is so much Definitional matter to the General Law of Property.

Commands *themselves* indivisible.

565. Commands can be classed no otherwise than from the acts that are the objects of them. The volition itself is a thing simple, uniform, and incapable of division. It is nothing but a certain feeling of the mind; annexed to the modes of conduct, when in contemplation, that are the objects of it.

Law of Property but one, and why.

566. The Law constitutive of Property is certainly but one. The command in which it would stand expressed is but one. Why but one? because the acts that are the modal objects of it are comprehendible in a single description. What are these acts? Acts of this particular sort, of that sort, and of another? No: but all acts of what sort soever. All acts whatsoever. The Law makes a thing my property: how? by commanding all persons but one, or those who have my leave, to abstain from exercising upon it all acts whatsoever.

A Law, when compleat.

566.* A Law is given, where volition affirmative or negative is signified to be annext to one mode of conduct: when that mode of conduct, to which a volition affirmative or negative is so declared to be annext, is compleatly described, a Law, one entire compleat Law and no more, is expressed.

Of a mode of conduct, as of any thing else, the description is performed in words. Whether a description of the mode of conduct that is the object of the Law in question be dispatched in a single sentence, or whether it take up a whole volume, depends upon the amplitude of the terms which the language employs, and which are adopted.

---

567. Copy Right is the exclusive right of making for sale an assemblage of marks of the same significance upon one material substrature, as what have been made before upon another. The way to create it is to punish all persons but the invested party, if ever they make for sale an assemblage of marks of the same significance.

Copy-right defined—how created.

To create a right in me to an individual Volume, every person must be debarred from exerting any act upon that book, it being not his, but mine. To create a Copy right, a person must be debarred from exerting an act with instruments of his own upon a thing which is his own.

568. Selling, the act of Sale, is not an *act* exerted upon the object sold. That object is not the *passive object* of the *act*. The *act* has no *passive object*. It is an act or assemblage of acts *intransitive*. An *act* or assemblage of *acts external*, indeed, but which become attended with the effects they are attended with, no otherwise than by being understood to be acts significative of other *acts* that are *internal*, *acts*, to wit, *of the mind*.

Selling, what—it requires not a material object[1] for the thing sold.

569. There are those who have declared themselves unable to form a notion of property, without a material object to it: and here, say they, is no material object. I understand what property in a book is, because the book is what I can see and handle: but I understand not what property in the copy of a book is, because the copy of a book in this sense is what I can not touch or handle.

Whence it came to be thought an object incapable of possession.

This seems to come of a false idea entertained by them of possession. Possession they conceive to be a kind of manual operation exerted upon a thing, a book for instance, like touching and handling. Touching, handling, must have a material object. Possession, therefore, must have a material object. Somthing solid there must be to touch, to handle. Something solid, therefore, there must be to possess. A material substance there must be, say they, to be the passive object of the act in the exercising of which the property consists. This notion takes it's rise from the grammatical structure of the language. *Possedere*, 'to possess', is a verb active. Of verbs active, it is the nature, they have been taught to believe, to denote an action whereof the substance denoted by the noun substantive which the verb is said to govern is the object. To Possess, then, denotes necessarily some sort of action performed upon the thing possessed. This, however, is a mistaken notion. Possession physical is but the absence of restraint. To possess a thing physically is, not to be restrained from using it: from exerting any acts upon it, as a passive subject, one has a mind [to do]. To

[1] MS alt. 'subject' is inconsistent with the main text.

possess a thing legally is not to be restrained from using it, other persons being at the same time restrained from using it by fear of punishment appointed by Law.

Now, certainly, where there is possession, somthing solid, somthing tangible, there must be in the case. Somthing that is capable of being the passive object of those acts, in the liberty of exercising which possession consists, and which other persons are restrained from exercising. So, therefore, in the right to a copy, somthing solid and tangible there must be in the case. Somthing that is capable of being the passive object of those acts, in the liberty of exercising which possession consists, and which other persons are at the same time restrained from exercising. There must be paper, for instance, or somthing equivalent, and printer's types or somthing equivalent. The difference between legal possession of these materials and legal possession of a copy right is, that to create the 1st, all persons but the possessor must be restrained from using them, they being thereby understood to be constituted his own. To create the other, it is the possessor himself of the materials that must be restrained from making use of them in a certain manner, they being understood all the while, as to every other purpose, to remain his own.

Command produces not obedience of itself. It is Expectation of Punishment that produces it.

570. What produces obedience to a Law is the expectation of punishment for disobedience. When action or forbearance is produced by a Law, it is no otherwise than by the expectation of pain which the Law excites. It is not difficult, therefore, to understand how the same expectation should produce the same action or forbearance even without a Law. Command a child to forbear reaching out at the window, if he has found punishment has been usually the consequence of disobedience, he will forbear. But, without saying any thing to him in the way of command, punish him whenever he goes to reach out at the window, he will in like manner also forbear. He will forbear in this case reaching out at the window, just as he will forbear meddling with the flame of the candle, when his hands have been two or three times slightly pained by it.

Command not essential to Common Law.

571. There is no mode of conduct, therefore, producible by Command, but what is equally producible without Command. Hence it is easy to understand, how the same effect that is produced by Statute Law, that is by Command, may be produced by Common Law, that is by a course of punishings without

Command. Not that in the operations of Common Law no such thing as Command enters actually into the affair, but it does not enter into it essentially. In a numerous and complicated society, the same person who is Judge, cannot always be executioner. He issues his Command to another person who is executioner, and it is by means of that command in point of fact that the punishment is inflicted, the pain produced. But the same effect would equally have been produced, if, instead of commanding another, he had inflicted it himself.

---

572. When, in a body of men, a habit has been formed of submission to the punishments and obedience to the commands of persons of a certain description among them, there is formed a State.

A State, when formed.

---

573. A Judgment on a claim of property is an assertive proposition declaring that the claimant or party claimed against, one or other of them, is in some one or other of those various sets of circumstances which constitute the party circumstanced owner of the subject claimed as against the other party.

A Judgment on a claim of property, what.

---

574. Nothing can be more erroneous than the notion that liberty is in general favoured by the multiplicity of the Laws: when spoken of them in the Lump.

'The more Laws, the more Liberty'[1] not true.

Political Liberty, that is, more properly speaking, political security, is indeed in some degree in proportion to the multiplicity of the Laws.

Of Laws of the constitutional class, indeed, to a certain length it is true. On these depends the power of the governors and the security of the governed. On the one hand, they confer powers, public fiduciary powers: on the other hand, they prescribe limits to those powers.

Now, the regulations narrowing the description of the modes of acting authorised must occupy a certain space: as far as the space necessary for that purpose extends, so far is the bulk and multiplicity of Law favourable to Liberty. It certainly takes up less room to say, deal with these men, or with these things, as you think proper, than deal with them in such or such a particular mode, and no other. A Turkish Bacha is undoubtedly sooner instructed than a

[1] This exact phrase has not been traced, though Bentham may have had in mind the notion expressed by Locke, *Two Treatises of Government*, Bk. II. Ch. VI, §57, p. 306: '*the end of Law* is not to abolish or restrain, but *to preserve and enlarge Freedom*'.

Governor of Jamaica or an English Lord Chief Justice of the King's Bench at Westminster.

But under every other title, the more Laws, the less Liberty. Let us consider the Laws of Property. The Law gives a man an estate, a simple unlimited, unconditional power of enjoying it. It may annex conditions to his enjoyment of it. Some few, perhaps, are necessary. But of others not necessary, an infinity may be conceived. A great number utterly unnecessary, burthensome to the proprietor in a much greater proportion than they are profitable to any one else, detestable offspring of the Feudal Anarchy, actually infest the Laws of almost every nation in Europe. Of these the number is capable of being yet further augmented *in infinitum*. For as every event, physical as well as moral, is capable of being turned into a condition, the magazine of conditions is plainly inexhaustible. The more of them there are established, the more room they will take to specify. The more regulations will be necessary to express them. The more various and the more voluminous will the whole assemblage of regulations of which the Law is composed be render'd. Let us particularise a little. Tenure by Knight's Service was formerly one of the tenures by which, in this country, landed property was holden. This Tenure was composed of a multiplicity of conditions annexed to the enjoyment of the property in question: conditions, the greatest part of them, useless, capricious, burthensome or oppressive. In the reign of Ch. 2^{d}, this Tenure was taken away;[1] consequently these conditions, consequently the regulations, actual or fictitious, which served to specify them, were cut off. The total mass of Law was, therefore, lessen'd in that proportion. Was this diminution unfavourable to the liberty of the subject?

We have two modes of Tenure still remaining, Copyholds and Freeholds. Would the liberty of the subject be the less were all Copyholds converted into Freeholds?

Are Taxing Laws productive of Liberty? Is it the Liberty of the subject that is promoted by the Laws of Excise and Customs? Far be it from me to reprobate the necessary means of supplying the exigencies of the state. But did ever any one think that the liberty of the subject was promoted by the multiplicity of these?

In France, where they have so much less liberty than we have, they have much more Law. It is the Characteristic of Law to produce restraint. Liberty is the absence of restraint. How should Law, then, produce Liberty? How should the quantity of Liberty be in proportion to the quantity of Law?

[1] Tenure by knight's service was abolished by the Military Tenures Abolition Act of 1660 (12 Car. II, c. 24).

A certain quantity of Law under the head of Constitutional is certain[ly] necessary to promote Political security. But that [that] quantity approaches in any degree to the whole mass of Law we see actually in force, there is no imaginable reason to conclude.

---

575. A Condition precedent is where a power is made not to commence until a certain event have happen'd. Condition precedent.

A Condition subsequent is where a power is made first to commence and then, upon a certain event's happening, thereupon to cease. —subsequent.

---

576. The great want of definitions is not for terms of municipal Jurisprudence; but for terms of universal Jurisprudence: words which are in every man's mouth, tho' perhaps in scarce any man's understanding. Books, indeed, there are in which expressions composed of terms of the 1st sort are reduced to expressions composed of terms of the 2d. But there they leave us. Prefat. Definitions most wanted for terms of Universal Jurisprudence.

Not to produce in us a persuasion of our understanding words which before we did not suppose ourselves to understand: but to make us really understand words which before we supposed ourselves to understand, while in reality we did not.

---

577. From a habit of punishing in men of a certain description, joined to a habit of submission in the rest, from such a habit, whether internal and spontaneous, or originating from external command, we get the notion of a legal right. Legal Right—Origin of the idea.

578. We hear also of a certain natural right—but this supposes a Law of Nature. Now, there is no such thing as a Law of Nature. For those who speak of a Law of Nature, tell us they mean the Law that prevails in a State of Nature.[1] But for a State of Nature it is impossible to find any other meaning, than that state an assemblage of men may be supposed to be in when there is no such thing as Law. When there is no habit of punishing established in any of them, accompanied by a habit of submission in the rest. Natural Right—no such thing as.

---

579. Problem—to shew how a clause expressive of a condition annexed to a Command is convertible into, and in what light it is capable of being viewed as constituting, a command. Condition, how convertible into a Command.

---

[1] See, for instance, Locke, *Two Treatises of Government*, Bk. II, Ch. II, §6, p. 271: 'The *State of Nature* has a Law of nature to govern it, which obliges every one'; and Montesquieu, *Spirit of Laws*, Bk. I, §2, i. 5: 'In order to have a perfect knowledge of these laws [i.e. laws of religion, laws of morality, and political and civil laws], we must consider man before the establishment of society: the laws received in such a state would be those of nature.'

Prefac[e]. Definitions. Resolution into Simple Ideas.

580. Having got thus far, we neither are able, nor have any reason for wishing to be able, to go farther: there is no farther for us to go. For having gone thus far, we understand what is before us. In the strictest and fullest sense of the word, we understand.

Opus magnum.[1] Punishment.

581. The rules proper to limit Punishment on the side of defect are these:

1st. The Penalty should not be less than what is suffic[ient] to overbalance the profit of the offence.

2dly. In offences merely public, the penalty, as far as it is pecuniary, should not be less than what is sufficient to afford an adequate inducement to the Informer.

What is thus sufficient will depend, amongst other things, upon the expensiveness of the mode of Procedure in which it is made recoverable.

In this, as in all other cases, in the æstimate of the value of the Profit and cost are to be taken into consideration the 5[2] dimensions of Pain and Pleasure.[3]

Op. magn. Project. Offences Accessory. Obnoxious ⅹ Odious.

582. Project. To compleat the train of misdeeds *obnoxious by relation* incident to each misdeed *obnoxious per se*.

Obnoxious to the Legislator or Politician ⅹ *odious* to men in general.

A Law ⅹ A Regulation.

583. By a Law I mean a Command: an entire command and no more: some one single command, including under the notion of command, the expression not only of the act of volition, but of the sort of act that is the modal, the sort of person that is the active, and the sort of person or of thing that is the passive, object of it: also of the whole assemblage of propositions serving to express the conditions on which it is willed and intended to take place: together with such propositions as serve to fix the import of any of the terms employ'd about expressing it: also such proposition or propositions as serve to express the threat which serves to arm it.

[1] The work or project to which the phrase 'Opus magnum' and its abbreviations 'Op. magn.' and 'Op. Mag.' relates remains obscure. For further details see the Editorial Introduction, p. xviii above.

[2] MS alt. '7' has been marked by Bentham for deletion.

[3] The five '*elements or dimensions of value* in a pleasure or a pain' identified in *An Introduction to the Principles of Morals and Legislation*, ed. J.H. Burns and H.L.A. Hart, London, 1970 (*CW*), Ch. IV, paras. 2–7, pp. 38–9 are intensity, duration, certainty, propinquity, and extent. Two further elements, purity and fecundity, are said 'scarcely to be deemed properties of the pleasure or the pain itself'.

By a regulation I mean any constituent part of a Law forming a logical proposition, or a grammatical sentence; any entire *proposition* (in the logical sense of the word *proposition*) serving to express any of the particulars abovementioned. A Regulation) (A Law.

By a clause, I would mean no member of a Law but what was less than a regulation. As a regulation, therefore, is [an] assemblage of words equal to a grammatical Sentence, a clause is a portion of speech less than a sentence: in short, I would mean by it in Law, precisely what is meant by it in Grammar. A Clause, what.

---

584. They talked, it is true, of Definitions: they gave what they meant for definitions: but they understood not the fundamental nature and true use of a Definition. They understood not, that a Definition is but a progress made towards the resolution of the complex idea signified by the word defined into it's component simple ones. For they knew not what simple ideas [were].[1] Prefat. Definition ill-understood by the Antients.

---

585. An Offence is a mode of conduct forbidden by the Law. An offence, therefore, supposes a Law; nor does the word intimate any other quality of the mode of conduct, than barely this, it's being prohibited by Law. It intimates not whether the mode of conduct be mischievous, innocent, or meritorious; nor whether the Law forbidding it be (in consequence) expedient or inexpedient. An Offence.

Conjugatæ to the word '*Offence*' are the words '*Offender*', to 'offend'. A Pseudo-conjugate is the word 'offensive'. Quasi-Conjugates are unlawful, unlawfulness; illegal, illegality; delinquent, delinquency. Synonymous is transgression. Synonymous to offender is transgressor, delinquent.[2]

586. By a Crime was originally meant an offence supposed to be mischievous in a high degree: from thence by rhetorical extension, it was made to signify any mode of conduct supposed to be highly mischievous, whether an offence or no: or in short any mode of conduct supposed to be highly odious, whether on theaccount of it's supposed mischievousness, or any other. Conjugates to the word Crime, are the words Criminal, Criminality. A Crime.

587. By a Sin we mean a mode of conduct contrary to the Will, or rather, to speak more accurately, to the wish of God. It is to a A Sin.

[1] MS 'where'. In the text, Bentham has noted at this point, '☛ continued at p. 248', i.e. para. 606, p. 193 below, where Bentham has noted '☛ continued from 584'.

[2] In the margin, Bentham has noted at this point: 'To disobey, Disobedient, Disobedience: these rather to "*Command*".'

law of God, real or fictitious, what an offence is to a Law of man. A Sin, therefore, supposes a Law of God, real or fictitious: nor does it intimate any other quality of the mode of conduct, than barely this, it's being prohibited by Law. It intimates not (*ex vi termini*)[1] whether the mode of conduct be mischievous, innocent or beneficial; nor whether the Law supposed to forbid it be (in consequence) expedient or inexpedient. Conjugates to the word Sin, are the words Sinful, Sinfulness.

A Misdeed.

588. The term Misdeed I would wish to have used to signify generally any mode of conduct supposed to be mischievous, or of a mischievous tendency. It should not either suppose or exclude a Law: nor should it intimate any other quality in the mode of conduct it is applied to, than barely this, that it is mischievous at least in tendency. It should not intimate whether it were an Offence, a Crime or a Sin. Nor should it be confined to intimate a mode of conduct of the sort of those that are of mischievous tendency every where and at all times, but it should comprehend all such as are supposed to be so in the state in question at the time in question.

It's train of Relatives.

Quasi-conjugate to Misdeed should be: Expressive of the Agent, Misdoer. Synonymous to Misdoer, Evil-doer almost obsolete. Expressive of the Verbal Attributive, none but Poly-epic,[2] To do amiss. Synonymous to to do amiss, to do evil.

An Immorality.

589. By an immorality we either mean such a misdeed as to be so at all times and in all places, to appear obviously to be so, or else such an act as, though not itself a misdeed, serves to evidence a disposition likely to be productive of misdeeds of a certain description; acts that shall be mischievous to the society by being mischievous either to others or to the agent himself.

A Vice.

590. A Vice is a habit of committing, or disposition to commit, immoralities of a certain description.

A Meanness.

591. A Meanness is any article of conduct, whether a misdeed or no, that is punished by the Moral Sanction with contempt.

A Condition defined.

590.* A Condition is an expression of a Volition, whereby one event is made to depend upon another event in such manner that if the last mentioned event shall have taken place, then the former shall take place, in as far as the volition in question has power to produce it: that is, that if the last mentioned event takes place, then there is that probability, whatever it may be, for the other event's taking place, which there is of the volition in question taking effect.

[1] i.e. 'on the strength of the words'.

[2] MS orig. 'by circumlocution only'.

591.* Of the two events thus related, that upon which the other thus depends may be stiled the Antecedent: that which is itself thus dependent, the Consequent. Event Antecedent ⅹ Consequent.

592. This being the nature of a Condition, it is plain that the *consequent* event must always be an action, or an event in the production of which some action has concurred. For it is only over actions, or other events in as far as they are the effects of actions, that Will has influence. The Consequent must be an action.

593. The Antecedent may be chosen indiscriminately either from the magazine of events which happen without will, or of actions or their effects in the production of which Will is concerned. The Antecedent need not.

594. That a Condition being an expression of Volition, as well as a Law is an expression of Volition, A Condition is not a thing different from a Law. A Condition = A Law.

595. That a Condition annexed to a Law, is one concomitant Law *pro tanto* repealing another. Condition annex'd to a Law.

596. That a Condition is a clause establishing an exception to the circumstances of the main act as described by the Law. A Conditionalizing clause, what.

597. And that what may be peculiarly stiled an exceptive clause is a clause establishing an exception to the main act itself as described by the Law; that is taking some species out of the genus signified by the term standing for that act.[a] An Exceptive clause.

598. Of the infinite Magazine of events, those events and situations are taken for *Circumstances* of an action, which are seen to influence such effects of it as mankind are interested in upon themselves or such things as they are interested in. Circumstances of an Action.

599. Such things, such situations and such events mankind may be said to be interested in, as tend to encrease or diminish their Happiness or Unhappiness. To be 'interested in', what?

600. Events distinguish into Simple and Complex. Simple answering to simple Acts. Complex answering to trains of conduct. The unity, the point of individuation, of an event is determined by the extent of denomination. A Battle is spoken of as one event. A stroke is spoken of as one event. The motion of a single muscular fibre may be spoken of as one event. There are no other limits than what are given by the name. Events Simple ⅹ Complex.

601. Whether a regulation shall, in the mode of expressing it, wear the form of a command, or only of a proposition serving [to] Command explicit ⅹ implicit or inexplicit.

[a] So may a clause expressive of a condition have an exceptive clause tacked to it: and an exceptive clause to the act may have a condition tacked to it: and one exceptive clause may have another tacked to it: and one conditionalizing clause may have another conditionalizing clause tacked to it: and so on indefinitely.

conditionalize, except, or define a command, depends upon this: whether there has been any proposition importing a command, to which that in question can apply. If not, to have any force it must be conceived as itself importing a command. For a Command concerned in every thing that bears the name of a Law, some how or other there must be. The essential point is to intimate the connection there is established between the obnoxious act in question and punishment. Whether this is done by a sentence in a form imperative, or by a sentence in a form not imperative, makes no difference.

Command indirectly expressed.

605.[1] That character of volition, that mandatory character (if one may be allow'd the expression) which is so essential to every thing that belongs to Law, is oftentimes so masked, that without a very attentive examination it may escape our notice.

Volition—Command. Indirect ways of expressing them.

602. Indirect ways of intimating a command, by means of the words a right, lawful, good, valid, or such others as in the nature of them suppose a command.

By this means, an assertive proposition coming from authority, i:e: being the assertion of persons in use to command, has the effect of a volitional one. The reason is, it is assertive of their volition.

Volitional propositions are at bottom assertive.

603. The difference, therefore, between an assertive proposition and a volitional one, is a difference that goes no deeper than the expression. It is a grammatical difference only, and not a logical or metaphysical one.

Understand the above under this limitation, that any volitional proposition is indeed convertible without a change of the idea into an assertive proposition. But it is not every assertive proposition that is convertible into a volitional one. It is plain that none other is, but what is intimative of a volition. Where there is no volition in the case, no proposition in the volitional form can be used. Any volition is expressible as well by a proposition in the assertive form, as by one in the volitional. The Imperative mode, which is a form used for expressing one sort of volition, viz: a command, was invented not of necessity, but for brevity. Steal not: my will is that thou steal not: of both these expressions the import is the same: both imply volition: both imply a command. The first is a volitional proposition: the latter is an assertive.

Harris's division of propositions superficial—why.

604. Mr Harris divides propositions into | | and | | as if the difference of the idea follow'd that of the phrase.[2] His Logic and his

[1] Bentham has indicated that para. 605 should serve as an introduction to para. 602.

[2] For Harris's statement that all sentences are either assertive or volitional see para. 712, p. 227 below.

Grammar being the Logic and the Grammar of the antients, having no foundation in Metaphysics, being made up of words and being founded but upon words, descending not to the solid platform of ideas, taking that for simple in the idea, which is simple in the expression, taking those things as different in idea, which are distinguished in expression, has the strength which that fabric may be supposed to have which should be founded upon air.

606.[1] Very plain it is they were strangers to the true nature and application of a Definition. For of Definition, if rightly and steadily applied, the necessary effect was the scorification of almost every thing that in their days went by the name of Science. A great part of their Ethics, all their metaphysics, all their physics.[2] Their Geometry alone would at all stand the test, nor even that without considerably changing colour. Of Euclid's propositions, the truth is indubitable, but his Definitions are as much as need be unsubstantial and confused.[3]

Prefat. Definition ill understood by the Antients.

---

607. In treating this subject, we have the misfortune to labour under a very distressing want of words; having disengaged a number of ideas from the chaos in which they lay involved, we must, therefore, either create a new stock of words to clothe them in, or leave the subject in the state of confusion in which we have found it.

Condition &c. Apolog. for new words.

---

608. Of the Common Law, one knows not what account to give. What is it that it consists of? Is it the particular acts of command, the particular acts of punishment, themselves? But these in their nature are evanescent—in point of fact they are vanished, past and gone. They do not now exist: it is not of them that a system now existent can be composed.

Common Law—what it consists of.
1st. Not articles of imperative conduct.

609. Is it, then, an assemblage of the respective ideas of those acts? Of *these*, the existence may, it is true, be permanent: but what are they? where is it they exist? where are they to be found? They are, the idea that *you* have formed of the act in question, the idea that *I* have formed of it, the idea that *Titius* has formed of it. These

2d. Not of ideas of Articles of Conduct.

[1] In the text, Bentham has noted at this point: '☛ continued from 584': see p. 189 above. For para. 605 see p. 192 above.
[2] MS orig. 'natural philosophy'.
[3] Euclid (fl. 300 BC), Greek mathematician, who taught in Alexandria during the reign of Ptolemy I Soter (323–285 BC), was the author of the celebrated *Elements*, which remained a standard textbook for mathematics for 2,000 years.

ideas exist, the 1st in your mind, the 2d in mine, the third in that of Titius. There they are to be found. But are these three ideas of one and the same description? Perhaps they are; perhaps not. But if they are, how shall it be known but by means of words by which they may be expressed? But what words have they belonging to them? None. By whose words shall they be expressed?[1] By your's? no, not rather than by *Titius's* or mine. By mine? no, not rather than by your's or *Titius's*. By Titius's? no, not rather than by your's or mine.

But grant it were by Titius's. What, then, would follow? That we should have a System of Law? that we should have a set of rules by which to regulate our conduct? by no means. The ideas, dress them in the words of Titius, still are but particular. They are but the ideas of individual articles of conduct. To draw any inference from the individual article of conduct of another man to our own, we must make out a sort from it: we must then see whether our's be of that sort. For such an article of conduct, Sempronius once was punished: shall I, therefore, be punished for the article of conduct, I have it in contemplation to practise? To answer that, I must see whether mine is of the sort that his was. To do this, from the idea of his individual act I must, in the first place, draw off to myself the idea of a sort: and then see whether mine be of that sort. Of his I must first take, as it were, a *draught*: and then see whether this draught, agreeing with his, agrees also with mine.

To enter, then, into the composition of a system of Law, we must have not ideas of individual articles of conduct, but ideas of sorts of articles of conduct: General ideas taken off from these particular ones: and for clothing these general ideas, words. But who shall take them off? Titius? Whose shall be those words? Titius's? Then would Titius be a Legislator. But Legislator, by the supposition, there is none.

3dly. Not of any certain assemblage of words.

610. If neither of the two above mentioned, what other stuff, then, shall we find of which we can say that the System of Common Law is made? Is it the words given to the acts of authority by those whose acts they were? It is not of necessity, that there should be *any* words. He who determines the punishment, may be the same person who inflicts it. He who is Judge may also be Executioner. It is often so in young political societies. Thus it still is in the

Government capable of being carried on without words.

[1] The three manuscript pages comprizing the text from this point to the end of para. 611 (i.e. the second, third, and fourth pages of UC lxix. 151) are headed 'Common Law. Division of it into Customs and Maxims', which appears as the title of 'A Comment on the Commentaries', II. 4, in *A Comment on the Commentaries and A Fragment on Government*, ed. J.H. Burns and H.L.A. Hart, London, 1977 (*CW*), pp. 180–91.

domestic every where. In this case, there being no one to speak to, there is nothing spoken. The act of power in question consist[s] not in command but action. Words belonging to it, there are none.[1] Even thus may be formed ideas of certain modes of conduct to be observed as if commanded, of certain others to be abstained from as forbidden. Even thus may be formed the idea of a System of Common Law.

But suppose it otherwise. Suppose the act of authority in every instance to be a command, and that command to have it's expression: to be signified by words which are the words of him whose command it is. These words, however, may not have been preserved. If preserved, they still are but | |. They do not necessarily express the mode of conduct punished. They express the person who is the object [of] the mode of punishment, but not necessarily the cause. 'Lictor, bear Sempronius to prison.' This expresses not the cause for which Sempronius is sent to prison. But this cause, if expressed, is still some mode of conduct particular to Sempronius. The expression of it marks not necessarily any other. Caius, deliberating upon a mode of conduct, is in doubt whether his be of the same sort. It is not the Judgment passed on Sempronius that informs him. Caius must conjecture for himself. There are no words issuing from authority intended equally to express the one mode of conduct and the other: the mode that has existed, and the mode that may exist in future. Are there any such words? Then are they the words of a Legislator. It is not, then, an affair of Common Law, but of Statute. From this loose and general view of what is called Common Law, it is manifest how difficult it is to say what it is it consists of. It exists not in any certain form of words: the acts it is founded on are acts of authority: but the words in which they are expressed are your's, are mine, are any one's.

611. Considering it, then, as a collection of words, what shall we say of it? and as a collection of words we must consider it, or not at all, since it is words only that, in treating of it, we can refer to.[3] 4. But of[2]

---

612. One of the occupations of the Common Law concerning Contracts is the compleating of imperfect contracts. Example—the Law of Contracts.

[1] In the text, Bentham has noted at this point: 'To be governed by Statute Law, belongs only to men. By Common Law it is, that even Beasts are governed. A mode of Government that is fit only for Beasts, and for them only because incapable of a better.'

[2] The marginal heading has been abandoned.

[3] In the margin, Bentham has noted at this point: '☛ continued under the undermost title.' The cross reference has not been identified.

Hiring of a House or Lodgings. Supplying of stipulations unthought of, to the act of conveyance thought of and performed.

Conveyance)(Compact.

613. A Conveyance is not to be reckoned among compacts. It is essentially different from a compact. A compact, many compacts, may indeed be joined with it, but still a conveyance is one thing, a compact is another.

If it were a Compact, then it would be a promise in the conveyer to abstain from the land (we will say) convey'd; a compact of this sort would be equivalent to a conveyance. But this is not the case. This promise, being the promise of the conveyer only, would not be binding upon other men: it would not oblige them to cease to treat the thing conveyed as being the property of the conveyer, or treat it from thenceforward as being the property of the conveyee.

'Upon Condition.' The expression traced up to it's Source.

614. Conditions may *mount* upon conditions.

The difficulty we find in finding a clear idea for the words 'condition', 'upon condition', is not to be wonder'd at. The phrase is elliptical: and when you have filled up the Ellipsis, you find a metaphor. Now, therefore, to understand the meaning of it, we must first fill up the Ellipsis, and then apply the metaphor. *Dare* is to give, to propose a thing for consideration. The inseparable particle *con* in composition imports concomitancy, connection. *Conditio* is, therefore, the proposing or establishing one thing in concomitancy or connection with another.

Prefat. Apology for Metaphysics.

615. The business of Metaphysics is neither more nor less than this, to examine what ideas we have belonging to the terms we use, and whether they are clear or no. Every science, therefore, M[r] D'Alembert[1] justly observes, has it's Metaphysics:[2] for every Science has it's leading terms, terms that are in constant use in every discourse that is held upon the subject of it, terms used for the making of others to be understood, terms of which, because they are much used, men are apt to suppose that they are thoroughly understood, but which very often, when examined into, turn out to be very far from thoroughly understood.

[1] Jean le Rond D'Alembert (1717–83), French philosopher, mathematician, and physicist.

[2] See D'Alembert, *Mélanges de littérature, d'histoire et de philosophie*, 5 vols., Amsterdam, 1767, v. 255: 'A proprement parler, il n'y a point de science qui n'ait sa *Métaphysique*, si on entend par ce mot les principes généraux sur lesquels une science est appuyée, & qui sont comme le germe des vérités de détail qu'elle renferme & qu'elle expose; principes d'où il faut partir pour découvrir de nouvelles vérités, ou auxquels il est nécessaire de remonter pour mettre au creuset les vérités qu'on croit découvrir.'

Every science, then, has it's Metaphysics, this,[1] then, among the rest. Now the metaphysics of this our science Law, consists in ascertaining the meaning, in fixing [the] ideas, belonging to the several terms of universal Jurisprudence, through the medium of which the technical terms of the particular Jurisprudence of any country are endeavoured to be explained. These terms of universal Jurisprudence are no other than what are in universal use.

'I hate Metaphysics.' Orator Burke.[2]

Metaphysics—Atheism—good Souls.

'Vantage-ground' of History trodden—of Metaphysics yet untrodden.[3]

Hume censurable not for having enter'd into Metaphysics, but for having lost his way.

---

616. Upon condition that Titius dies without issue, I give you the Manor of Dale. To Titius, I give my House in Dale during his life: to you I give it upon his death, upon condition that you first pay ten Pound to his representatives. What do I mean by this? It is as if I had said: 'The accruing of the right I give you to my House is an event I make *dependent* on the happening of an antecedent event, which event, on account of that dependence of the consequent upon it, I call a condition. I give you a right to my House, to my House in Dale, commencing at his death, but depending upon the condition of your first paying ten Pounds to his representatives.'

'Upon Condition.' The use of the expression exemplify'd, and traced up to it's source.

In some such way may we fill up the Ellipsis. The sentence now compleated, let us endeavour to find out and to apply the Metaphor which it imports.

In setting up a right, I have erected a sort of fabric. This fabric,

[1] MS orig. 'Jurisprudence'.

[2] For Burke's remark see p. 217 n. below.

[3] See Henry St. John, Lord Viscount Bolingbroke, *Letters on the Study and Use of History*, 2 vols., London, 1752, i. 186: 'there have been lawyers that were orators, philosophers, historians: there have been BACONS and CLARENDONS [i.e. Edward Hyde (1609–74), first Earl of Clarendon, politician and historian] . . . . There will be none such any more, till in some better age, true ambition or the love of fame prevails over avarice: and till men find leisure and encouragement to prepare themselves for the exercise of this profession [i.e. law], by climbing up the *vantage ground*, so my lord BACON calls it, of science; instead of groveling all their lives below, in a mean but gainful application to all the little arts of chicane. Till this happen, the profession of the law will scarce deserve to be ranked among the learned professions: and whenever it happens, one of the vantage grounds, to which men must climb, is metaphysical, and the other historical knowledge.' For Bacon's use of the expression 'vantage ground' see 'Of Truth' (first published in 1625), in *The Essayes or Counsels, Civill and Morall*, ed. M. Kiernan, Oxford, 1985 (*The Oxford Francis Bacon: Vol. XV*), p. 8, where it appears as a translation of a phrase from Lucretius, *De rerum natura*, II. 8.

like every other fabric, must have a foundation. Now, the foundation I have given it is that event spoken of under the name of antecedent. Upon this event the fabric depends; or to speak more properly, that is more consistently with the metaphor, more consistently with the nature of a building, rests.

Condition.

617. However, we will say ***depends***; since that is the term most usually employ'd.[a] Now it is plain, if the foundation fails, if the foundation at any given period does not subsist, the superstructure, that is the fabric depending upon it, fails likewise. The fabric likewise subsists no longer. Now this is what I mean should be the case between the right and the event I have connected with it in the character of a condition. The right, I mean, should depend upon that condition. If the condition fails, I would have the right fail also.

'Signal', why adopted.

619. *Signal*', another Metaphor: why both the others departed from and this adopted.[1]

Ease, a quality of discourse. Short Sentences.

620. The great secret of *easy* writing is, the breaking down of the matter of our discourse and thereby providing frequent breathing-places for the attention.

Ease is a term originally and properly expressive of a condition of the reader: and from thence transferred to that quality in the

'Depend', why applied to a Condition. Jupiter's Chain.

[a] **618.** It is easy to see why the idea of *dependence* is not so consonant to the Metaphor, as the idea of *resting*. Depend comes from the Latin *dependeo*. *Dependeo* is to hang down. What hangs down, hangs from something. It is connected for certain with something that is above it; whether connected or not with any thing that is below. Now a building does not hang down: it is not connected with any thing above it. It stands: it rests solely on the foundation.

The occasion of the word depend's having been employ'd upon occasions like these, I take to be this. The universal assemblage of events, according to a well-known allegory of the Heathen Mythology, is woven into an immense chain, the top link of which is holden in the hand of Jupiter:[2] from this top link, all the rest may be said to hang down. And thus, I take it, the words '*pendeo*', '*dependeo*', came to be used by the Romans whenever they had to signify a connection between events. The Metaphor in this case, we see, is taken not from a building, but from a chain. However, this latter, it was found, taken from a chain, would not, on all occasions, answer the purpose. 'Tis on this account, in the formation of the language on this subject, the former was adopted. However, as the first formers of a language are not apt to be very nice in their disquisitions, and the inaccuracy of *mixing* metaphors is an inaccuracy we are very apt to fall into, it happen'd, that a word belonging to one metaphor was engrafted into the other.

---

[1] In the text, Bentham has noted at this point: 'But Qu. whether to adopt it at all? and whether "*influencing circumstance*" may not answer the purpose as well. Now *infl^{g} circ:* will chime in with dependence.'

[2] See p. 14[illegible] n. above.

discourse which has a tendency to place or keep him in that condition. As *heat*, to the fire.

---

621. There are a thousand conditions annext to every Law; that is, there are a thousand events must take place, or to change the phrase, a thousand situations things must be in, before the threat of it can take effect. Among these events are the successes of the several measures to be taken by the Ptff previous to judgment. Conditions annexed to every Law are numerous.

622. 4 Senses of the word Liberty (3 in Jurisprudence). 1st as opposed to Restraint in general, physical or legal. 2d. As opposed to Legal restraint. 3dly as opposed to Physical restraint produced by Imprisonment. 4th. Used improperly for Political security. Liberty, it's 3 or 4 Senses.

623. Possession is *liberty* to use. Physical possession is physical liberty to use. Legal possession is Legal liberty to use, accompanied with legal power, determinable, however, upon condition of disproval of legal right. Possession.

---

624. The expression a Free government, a Free constitution, originates from the improper sense of the word liberty, where it is used for security against those in authority. The proper expression would be, a popular government, a popular constitution. Every government being necessarily all-powerful can be no otherwise than free; that is unrestrained by any restraint that can be called legal. Yes, but in another sense a Government may be said to be free, as providing for the freedom, i:e: security, of the governed. A Government may be said to be more or less free, as more or less care is taken in it of the security[1] of the people. 'Free Government.' 'Free Constitution.' The expressions improper. Metonymical.

---

625. An Innkeeper, as such, can not be a Bankrupt. II. Blackst. 476.[2] Alehouse-keepers.

Divine Law—Interest—Usury. II. Bl. 455.[3] Divine Law.

[1] MS orig. 'political liberty'.

[2] According to Blackstone, *Commentaries on the Laws of England*, ii. 476, only persons making their living principally by both buying and selling could qualify to be a bankrupt, but an innkeeper could not, 'for his gain or livelyhood does not arise from buying and selling in the way of merchandize, but greatly from the use of his rooms and furniture, his attendance, and the like: and though he may buy corn and victuals, to sell again at a profit, yet that no more makes him a trader, than a schoolmaster or other person is, that keeps a boarding house, and makes considerable gains by buying and selling what he spends in the house, and such a one is clearly not within the statutes'.

[3] In relation to the lending of money, Blackstone, ibid. 455–7, distinguishes between 'a moderate and exorbitant profit; to the former of which we usually give the name of interest, to the latter the truly odious appellation of usury: the former is necessary in every civil state, if it were but to exclude the latter, which ought never to be tolerated in any well-regulated society'.

Custom, for example Title by Custom. II. Bl.[1]

Interpretation of Statutes by the Judge.

626. Admitt latitude of interpretation, not where the punishment in question is only of the ordinary kind; which, if it does not fall on one party, must upon the other. But use it where the punishment is of the extraordinary kind: in so far as is necessary to save the accused from incurring the punishment where it is not necessary he should for the answering the intentions of the regulation.

Prefat. Logic X Metaphysics.

627. In the more extensive sense of the word Logic, Logic and Metaphysics are the same.[2]

But the sense in which the word Logic is most apt to be taken, is that in which it stands for the art of making a partial application of Metaphysics to the purpose of disputation. It was indeed cultivated in no other view than as the art of disputation. Whatsoever was deliver'd under that head was composed in the view of being either directly or mediately subservient to the purpose of disputation.

Logic, then, in the state in which Locke found it, was so much of Metaphysics as was subservient to the purpose of disputation.[3] What they meant at that time by Metaphysics, was so much of their Logic as was applied to subjects of a theological nature. The subject of it was the pretended Natural History of God, of the Soul of man, and other spirits.[4] It was the Natural History of Souls apart from Bodies. It was the Natural History of Chimæras.[5]

Origin of the Ideas Law is conversant with.[6]

628. The ideas we have are *all* ultimately derived from substances; that is, from the *several natural bodies that surround us. The origin of our ideas relative to Law can, therefore,* be sought for in no other source. These bodies are either in motion, or at rest. The impression that a body at rest excites in us, may be stiled a

[1] See ibid. 422–9, dealing with the acquisition of personal property by custom, and in particular heriots, mortuaries, and heir-looms.

[2] Cf. Robert Sanderson, *Logicæ Artis Compendium* (first published in 1615), 11th edn., Oxford, 1741, i. 43: 'neque sit ea tractatio propriè *Logica*, sed potius *Metaphysica*'; i.e. 'and this work ought not to be thought properly logical but rather metaphysical'. As an undergraduate at Oxford, Bentham had used this edition of the work as his textbook on logic.

[3] For Locke's criticism of scholastic disputation see *Essay concerning Human Understanding*, Bk. III, Ch. X, §§6–8, pp. 493–5.

[4] MS orig. 'other imaginary spirits'.

[5] Cf. Locke, *Essay concerning Human Understanding*, Bk. IV, Ch. VIII, §9, p. 615: 'a Man may find an infinite number of Propositions, Reasonings, and Conclusions, in Books of Metaphysicks, School-Divinity, and some sort of natural Philosophy; and after all, know as little of GOD, *Spirits*, or *Bodies*, as he did before he set out'.

[6] In the margin, Bentham has noted above this heading: '☛ BEGINNING *for* PREP. PRINC.'

quiescent appearance, or simply an *appearance*. The impression that a body [in motion][1] excites in us may be stiled a *moving appearance*, or in one word, *an Event*. Appearances, as well moving as quiescent, may be stiled by one common term phænomenon, which in truth is nothing but Greek for an appearance.[2] Philosophers have naturalized it among us: and I use it, having occasion to employ the English word in the more confined signification above mentioned.

An Appearance, what.

An Event, what.

A Phænomenon, what.

629. In vain should we endeavour to fix the point of individuation in[3] any single thing to which we are in use to fasten the appellation of an event. Fixed point of individuation, it has none.[a] How much motion we mean to speak of, when we use the word event, *how much*, I say, whether as to the quantity of the substance moving or number of distinct parts in it, or the quantity of the space it moves through, it is impossible by any general description to determine. 'How much' does any one ask? the answer is any quantity, be it more or less, that you can mark out by a particular description. A simple event is the motion of one body, or one part of a body. But as parts of bodies are divisible *ad infinitum*, so are events multipliable and divisible *ad infinitum*. A Battle is spoken of as one event. A stroke is spoken of as one event. The motion of a single muscular fibre is spoken of as one event. The revolution of Saturn round the Sun is one event. The passage of a ray of light from Sirius to our eyes is an event. It's passage from the exterior to the interior surface of the eye of a mite is an event.

What makes one Event not ascertainable.

---

630. 'Office'—what. Burn. Oaths. III. 233, from Burr. 999.[4] Office.

631. Refuse, to, what. Burn. Oaths. III. 229.[5] To refuse.

---

[a] The point of individuation of each particular event is determinable no otherwise than by the name given to that event.

☛ Point of Individ.[n] in an *act*, how determined.

---

[1] MS 'at rest' contradicts the evident sense of the passage.

[2] In the margin, Bentham has noted at this point: '☛ But remember *Situations*.'

[3] The remainder of the sentence has been marked by Bentham for deletion.

[4] See Richard Burn, *The Justice of the Peace and Parish Officer*, 12th edn., 4 vols., London, 1772, iii. 233, s.v. 'Oaths', citing *R. v Turkey-Company* (1760), in James Burrow, *Reports of Cases adjudged in the Court of King's Bench Since the Time of Lord Mansfield's Coming to preside in it*, 5 vols., London, 1766–80, ii. 999–1005, where it was decided that membership of a chartered company, in this case the Turkey or Levant Company of London, could not be considered an 'office or place of profit in the government'.

[5] See Burn, *Justice of the Peace and Parish Officer*, iii. 229, s.v. 'Oaths', dealing with the oaths administered by magistrates to those suspected of Catholic or Jacobite sympathies, and the grounds on which a person refusing those oaths might be 'adjudged a popish recusant convict'.

Definition Ӿ Enumeration.

632. Definition is only a make-shift for enumeration: it is only used either because the particulars to be enumerated are not all known, or if known, are too numerous to mention. When such particulars, therefore, are all known and come within a moderate compass, Enumeration is always to be preferred.

Mischief Ӿ Malignity Ӿ Odiousness.

633. Mischief may denote what is actually produced by a given crime.

Mischievousness or Malignity, the *tendency* of it to produce mischief.

Odiousness, the tendency of it to produce hatred in him who thinks of it.

Two ways of producing Obedience. 1st. Silent. 2d. Enuntiative, i:e: by a Habit of Punishment.

634. One is by actual Punishment: the other is by words causing punishment to be expected.

Words of command have no other influence than as significative of will: and acts may be significative of will as well as words.

Volition is a sentiment of pain or pleasure annext to the idea of that event which we term the object of the volition.

N.B. In the case of an act of the party himself [of] whose volition we are speaking, and that an act in his power, where there is any degree of pleasure, the act follows instantaneously, upon the principle of Association. See Locke's *Essay* | | and Hartley on *Man*.[1]

A Command is the expression of a Volition &c.

Now the intent of a Command is to produce the mode of conduct in question.

A mode of conduct is producible no otherwise than by motives.

A motive is the expectation of Pain or Pleasure.

Now, the expectation of Pain or Pleasure may be generated either: 1st. From Commands backed, as all Commands are, with threats implicit or expressed; or 2d. From observation of like Pain or Pleasure resulting to the agent in question in consequence of the mode of conduct in question.[a]

If, amongst a number of men, when, as any one killed another, he himself were killed on that account (no matter how), this, after

[a] We have mentioned Commands first as generative of such expectation, as being the simplest of the two in it's conception; but strictly speaking, the other is the only true and original source of it, as we shall see presently.

---

[1] See Locke, *Essay concerning Human Understanding*, Bk. II, Ch. XXXIII, pp. 394–401, and David Hartley, *Observations on Man, his Frame, his Duty, and his Expectations*, 2 vols., London, 1749.

a certain number of instances, to those to whom it should have been known, would, as to the preventing of future instances of killing, have the effect of a command: of a command not to kill. Every such act of consequential killing, may be termed an act of Punishment. When acts of Punishment had gone to a certain number, they would be taken notice of as having grown into a habit; into a habit of Punishment. A habit of Punishment, then, applied to a mode of conduct, may have the effect of a command: that is of a command not to practise that mode. And it was a habit of Punishment following such a mode of conduct, upon it's having been made the object of some such command, that could alone have at first formed the original connection between command and the expectation of Pain or Pleasure.

Obedience, therefore, may be produced in either of two ways. 1st. By a habit of Punishment: 2dly. By Command, when understood to be backed by Punishment, in case of disobedience.

635. The misfortunes of using a habit of Punishment without command to produce obedience are: 1st. That there is so much Pain wasted as there is produced before the habit of Punishment is seen to be formed; 2dly. That all that while obedience is not obtained. On the other hand, issue a command, and if the expectation of the pain with which it is supposed to be backed be strong enough, obedience is obtained *gratis*, and at once.

Disadvantages of the Silent.

636. Understanding now the two different ways in which obedience may be produced, we understand what it is that makes the difference between what is called Common or Unwritten, and Statute or Written, Law. Common Law contains the History of those cases in which, to certain modes of conduct, Punishment has without warning been applied, from whence men are left to form, as well as they can, their own conclusions to what cases it is likely to be applied in future. Statute Law is a collection of commands to perform or not to perform in future the modes of conduct therein specified: declaring in most instances that punishment shall thenceforward be applied in case of disobedience: that is where the mode of conduct commanded having been action, forbearance shall have been that which has been pursued: or where forbearance, action.

Hence is to be taken the distinctive characters of Common and Statute Law.

---

637. Principles. List of, for examples to explain the word by. 1st. That of Association in Metaphysics. 2d. That of the Moral Sense, and that of Utility, in Morals. 3d. That of Superposition in Geometry.

'Principle', list of examples.

Punishment—how it has the effect of Command.

638. N.B. Single acts of Punishment annext to so many articles of conduct will have the effect of Commands not to pursue articles of conduct of that sort when issuing from persons who either are in a habit of punishing, or stand in the place of those who have been. It is rather Command has the effect of a Punishment, than Punishment of Command. For Punishment must have come first, before Command could have been efficacious.

Volition, whether any thing but a sentiment of Pain or Pleasure.

639. It may be asked how the case stands where the event which is the object of volition actually takes place in consequence of the Volition, as is the case with such events as are acts of our own, and in our own power to perform. Is there nothing here in the mind besides the idea of the event that is the object of volition; and the sentiment of pain or pleasure occasioned by the view of it? Is there not what we call a volition, something distinct from such a pain or pleasure? Is it the pain or pleasure that produces the action immediately without the intervention of any other operation of the mind? These questions, I must confess, I know not how to answer to my satisfaction. But be the answer which side it may, it makes no difference to the present purpose. Either the sentiment of pain or pleasure, which ever it be, the instant it has got the ascendant over the sentiment, if any, that is opposed to it, produces the action immediately in virtue of the principle of Association, or else it first produces the volition, and then the volition produces the action.

Prefat. Vantage grounds. Metaphysics.

640. The more difficult vantage ground of metaphysic lore is yet unclimbed. It is virgin soil: new are the honours that will be that man's due who shall give it a vigorous and manly culture, pierce into it's hidden treasures, and render it prolific of instruction.[1]

Prefat. Metaphysics. Apology for.

641. Now, the metaphysics which obscures our conceptions is worthless: but is it so with that which makes them clear? Is it mischief, is it not benefit, to understand what it is we mean? Now, when Metaphysics is what it ought to be, it is that which we owe to Metaphysics.

To be skilled in Metaphysics is neither to hold for Atheism nor for Theism.[2] It is not to profess [to] know what belongs to God, or what belongs to Angels: nor to profess to know that there are neither God nor Angels. It is not to hold the Soul to be mortal, nor to hold it to be immortal; to hold the existence of matter, or the

[1] In the margin, Bentham has noted at this point: 'mixed metaphor'.

[2] In the text, Bentham has noted at this point: 'Metaphysics is neither infidelity nor credulity.'

non-existence. But it is this: in talking, whether of God or of Angels, or of the immortality of the Soul or of it's mortality, or of the existence of matter or of it's non-existence, or of any other subject, to know, and to be able to make others know, what it is we mean. To explain all the words we use, as there is occasion, by marking out their relation to some other words expressive of determinate collections of simple ideas, or of simple ideas themselves.

To observe the situation of our minds on the occasion of the several phænomena of Nature, and how the words we employ are qualified to express it.

In a word, it is the science of Definitions; and wheresoever there are words to be defined, wheresoever there is any thing to be made known by means of words, *there* is place for Metaphysics.

Of all things, to be a Metaphysician is not to give one's own opinion or pretended opinion the name of Sense, or Moral Sense, or Common Sense, or of any thing else, in order to brand with the name of Villains or Madmen all who do not embrace it's dictates.

To such Metaphysics, all who have an abuse to palliate, a sinister point to gain, an imposture to defend, all those by whom words are abused that men may be deluded, all Bigots and listed partizans, all Sophists and Rhetoricians, all who, by weakness of apprehension, are incapacitated from close reasoning, or who by indolence are averse to it, or who by obstinacy are afraid of it, will be mortal foes. They love darkness better than light, because their mind's eye is weak, or because their deeds are evil. They hate the light, and tremble as they hate.

On these obscure and much litigated questions, to be an adversary to this side or to that side may be to be mistaken; but to be an adversary to free enquiry is to be an enemy to mankind.

---

642. In all that vast variety of regulations concerning property, the description of the mode of conduct remains for the most part unchanged: the efficacy of the regulation is spent in the description of the *circumstances*.

Act X Circumstances, in a Regulation of Property.

---

643. When a General regulation commands any thing concerning a sort of things or a sort of persons, and the appointment of the individual things or persons that are to be deemed of that sort rests with any man, that man and the Legislator act in conjunction. The individual thing or person that is the object of the regulation is not known but by the act of the man, whom we may term the Executive

Powers Legislative and Investitive. Mutual Co-operation.

Magistrate. Problem—to assign the respective limits and specify [the] difference between the Legislative and Executive powers. How far the Executive is *bound* by the Legislative, and how far the Legislative is determined by the Executive.

Take an instance from official duties.

The Officer, by being appointed such by the Executive power, is subject to a certain set of duties. But to what duties? No others than those which are presented to Officers of that denomination by the Legislative power. On the other hand, persons of that description are subject by the Legislative power to a certain set of duties. But what persons? No other than those that are appointed by the Executive Power.

The Legislative Power, then, as such of itself reaches no man. Even the Supreme Legislative power in a state of itself can not reach the lowest criminal. Much less, then, can it reach the Supreme Executive. It can only direct, and point out, sorts of persons as objects for punishment. It cannot punish any person. It cannot punish, therefore, the Supreme Executive Power. All that it can do is to point him out as a proper object to be punished by any one at large. The supreme Legislative must make use of the hand of any one that offers to punish the supreme Executive in case of his disobedience: in the manner that it makes use of his hand to punish disobedience in any one else.

Power Legislative and Executive—Co-operation of—A case supposed.

644. Suppose the King out of the question. Suppose the House of Commons the Supreme Legislative Body. Suppose the House of Lords in all cases, as it is in most, the supreme executive. Now, suppose the House of Lords to disobey a regulation of the House of Commons. What course could the House of Commons take to enforce its mandates? It could do but one of two things. It must either go itself in person, and judge the House of Lords, and appoint Punishment if it found them guilty, and in that case it would itself become the supreme executive power: or[1]

Powers in a State. Confusion in the current notions.

645. It is said the supreme Legislative Power is superior to the supreme Executive. How is this to be understood? At the same time, it is certain that every act of power that is performed is performed not by the Legislative, but by the Executive. How are these propositions to be reconciled?

'What is Legislative power?' 'It is what Parliament exercises.' 'What is Executive Power?' 'It is what the King exercises.' 'What is Judicial Power?' 'It is that share of Executive power which Judges

[1] The passage has been abandoned at this point.

exercise.' Hitherto, we have seen no better than these answers to these questions.

At the same [time], it is certain that each of these three bodies has exercised and does exercise, and that without dispute, those which are commonly spoken of as being the peculiar functions of the other two. The Legislature exercises the executive function in many instances, as well judiciary as dispensatorial. The King makes Laws. And Judges too make Laws.

Powers in a State. Prefat.

646. To describe accurately the limits between the Legislative and Executive Powers is a task the most novel and the most arduous. If I accomplish it, I am sure I shall have done a great thing. Whether I have or no belongs to others to determine.

Executive Power, 3 branches of.

Executive Power [is] either Power over persons or over things.

Power Judiciary is it's Power over Persons.

Power Dispensatorial is it's Power over Things.

By it's Power Investitive, it co-operates with Legislative.

Powers Executive, 3 branches of. Investitive, Dispensatorial, and Judicial.

646.* That the King is not the supreme executive power in general.

That the supreme Judiciary power is above every other sort of executive power: and all supreme Judiciary power, the King is excluded from exercising himself.[1]

In some few cases, he has the power of appointing *pro re natâ, pro hac vice*,[2] those who shall exercise it: that is those who, in that behalf, shall exercise it in the last resort. I am speaking of the power of appointing the Court of Delegates.[3]

In crimes of the higher class (supposing Impeachment not to hold), a Jury are the supreme Judges of fact; since no one can take it out of their hands. Yet the King, by his power of pardoning, can frustrate the acts of all other persons in authority; and, as it were, wrest the supremacy out of their hands.[4]

[1] Cf. Blackstone, *Commentaries on the Laws of England*, i. 257–8: 'It is probable, and almost certain, that in very early times, before our constitution arrived at it's full perfection, our kings in person often heard and determined causes between party and party. But at present, by the long and uniform usage of many ages, our kings have delegated their whole judicial power to the judges of their several courts; which are the grand depositary of the fundamental laws of the kingdom, and have gained a known and stated jurisdiction, regulated by certain and established rules, which the crown itself cannot now alter but by act of parliament.'

[2] i.e. 'as required, for this occasion only'.

[3] The Court of Delegates was the final court of appeal in ecclesiastical causes. Established by the Submission of the Clergy Act of 1533 (25 Hen. VIII, c. 19), the members of the Court were appointed by the Crown on a case by case basis. See Blackstone, *Commentaries on the Laws of England*, iii. 66–7.

[4] On the Crown's power of pardon see ibid., iv. 389–95.

The Earl of Argyle was Hereditary Justitiary of Scotland.[a] Therefore, not displaceable by the King. His power was vast and excessive. But was it absolute? no. What prevented it's being [so]? The subsistence of a Parliament. And by what means could Parliament prevent it? By no other than assuming itself the executive power.

Power Military.

647 The Military power being a branch of the Kingly, and the King sole being the only executive Magistrate, I could not persuade myself of a long time to see that a General could as such exercise legislative power.

Reciprocal Judicability.

648. Reciprocal judicability, no contradiction nor absurdity, therefore none in the King's being punishable. It actually obtains in numberless instances—the moral field of Jurisdiction being different. The necessity of an accuser keeps the two Jurisdictions from running foul.

Prejudices adverse. Prefat. To Powers.

649. If we define legislation to be the power of appointing the fate of persons in sorts for actions in sorts, we are unwilling to see that Judges and the King have this power, because that puts them upon a level with the Legislature.

Prefat. These discoveries make little shew.

650. I am apt to think the person who should content himself with representing the naked truth on these subjects, without confronting it with and exposing the opposite errors, would scarce find any one to acknowledge he had done any thing. Those who agreed with him would say it was no more than we all knew before: others would say that it was false, heterodox and unsupportable. Those who should have brought themselves to apprehend these truths and to assent to them would not know the acquisition they had made: the extent, importance, and value of their knowlege would be unknown to them: for want of knowing how different they are from the current notions, and to what a degree the current notions are different from the truth.

Prefat. Prejudices adverse.

651. These prejudices for months, even for years, served as bugbears to frighten me from embracing, though within arm's length of it all the while, what I now take to be the truth. I take it to

[a] Dalrymple.[1]

---

[1] See John Dalrymple, *An Essay towards a General History of Feudal Property in Great Britain*, London, 1757, p. 282: 'at last by one grant, the king in a manner surrendered the sword of justice out of his hands, by making the office of the justiciarius of Scotland, an office of inheritance in the family of Argyle'.

be the truth: because embracing it now, it seems to me that I see clearly: and it never seemed to me so until now.

---

652. That Parliament has acted as the executive power oftentimes in this country, and that without dispute, that it is, therefore, an executive power: and as it is supreme, it is, therefore, the supreme executive. Parliament Supreme executive.

Consequently, the King alone is not the supreme executive. Not the King.

652.* Why the body of Executioners (or, for simplicity's sake, supposing there to be but one), why the Executioner is not the supreme executive power. Sole Jatch Ketch,[1] why not Supreme.

---

653. If I explain these matters clearly, I may be a means of giving perpetuity to the constitution of my country. I may stifle in embryo, or rather intercept, the conception of all manner of political disputes, prevent civil wars, fix the peace of empires, and save the lives of Millions. For[2] Prefat. Utility of these Speculations.

654. It is ignorance and misanthropy under the mask of penetration to maintain that, in political disputes, all men take the wrong side with their eyes open, that men never engage in rebellion but . . . . . . nor in an attempt to stretch authority too far but . . . . In Political quarrels *bonâ fides* frequent.

That the leaders in unwarrantable political enterprizes have for the most part, and in most instances, been knaves, is what I am far from being persuaded of. But if the leaders have been knaves, their followers are always for the most part dupes.

It is an error the more insinuating and seducing as it passes under the name of knowlege, to compliment men's understandings at the expence of their hearts.

Nor is it by any means sure that when men have changed their conduct, they have not changed their principles.

The Historian or Political critic who represents a man as acting upon the principles he avows to act upon has made no discovery: to manifest his sagacity, he must find other principles that he acted from that he disavows. Ostentation of Sagacity.

---

655. The Supreme Military power includes in it Legislative, Executive, Judicial, Dispensatorial, Place-appointing = Investitive. Power Military.[3]

[1] John or Jack Ketch (d. 1686), public executioner, was the common hangman of London in the late 1660s and 1670s. His name came to stand for the common hangman in general.

[2] The paragraph has been abandoned at this point.

[3] In the margin, Bentham has noted at this point: 'The function of a General in time of War.'

It is limited only by three things: Time,[1] subsequent responsibility, and amoveability. From all necessity, it is absolute and despotic while it continues.

Order: that all Centinels fire at all persons who do not return the parole; that they remove all things &c. they see in such a place or any where. These are acts of Legislation.

The King has a subordinate legislative power.

656. To admitt of the least scantling of legislative power in the Judges, much more in the King alone, would be a sin, would be a Treason against the Constitution.

Nevertheless, I attribute to him no more than what he has been all along in use to exercise with as little dispute as any other power that he exercises, when I attribute to him a legislative power.

The ideas of Legislation and supremacy, of execution and subordinacy, have, in the conceptions of some persons, acquired so intimate a connection, that they have no notion of a person's possessing Legislative power of himself without being supreme; nor of exercising executive power without being subordinate.

Subordination between governing bodies—different ways in which it may subsist.

657. One governing body in a state may be superior to another governing body in two ways. Superiority and inferiority may subsist in either of two ways. The commands of the inferior may be liable to be nullified by contradictory commands of the superior. This is one way. The commands of the inferior remaining good notwithstanding any contradictory commands of the superior, the inferior may be liable to punishment for having issued them; this is another way.

An instance of this difference we meet with in the Law respecting the licensing of Public Houses. The Body of Justices of Peace within a certain District are the inferior governing body. The Court of King's Bench is the superior. The share of government committed to the inferior body in this behalf is that part of the executive power that may be termed the Investitive; the appointing the *individuals* who are to come within the sort of persons marked out by the Legislature under the denomination of Publicans. By the King's Bench, a man can not be invested or disinvested with that character. But the Justices may, for such appointment or rejection, be punished.[2]

[1] MS add. 'Persons' would make a fourth limitation.

[2] By the provisions of the Unlawful Games Act of 1729 (2 Geo. II, c. 28) and the Alehouses Act of 1753 (26 Geo. II, c. 31), Justices of the Peace were empowered to issue licences to inns and alehouses retailing alcohol. In *R. v Young and Pitts* (1757), an information was filed against two Justices of the Peace for refusing to grant such a licence, whereupon Chief Justice Mansfield ruled that it was 'certain' that the Court of King's Bench 'has no power or

The Judges of the Ecclesiastical Courts are subordinate to the King's Bench in both those ways.[1]

658. The greatest subordinate power of which we have any instance is that possessed by a Dictator among the Romans. While it subsisted, it was supreme. It was limited only in respect of time. The term of his Dictature subsisting, no man could vacate his acts: no man could punish him. After it was expired, he might be punished. Instance Roman Dictator.

---

659. The King possesses not the least atom of Judiciary Power. For he cannot punish, or order the punishment of, any man on any occasion. He cannot touch the hair of any man's head more than any other master of a family. The contents of his own privy purse excepted, he cannot, by any mandate of his own, command one penny of the Revenue. Powers in a State. Power of the King.

Legislative Power he possesses for three purposes. That of making War or peace. That of making Treaties. That of granting Charters.[2]

His power of Pardoning comes under the denomination of his *Investitive*, or rather Disinvestitive, power. By this power he may invalidate the Laws over which it extends by piece-meal.

Powers Judicial do not belong to him: but he possesses Investitive power with respect to the persons of those to whom they do belong. However, he possesses not the Divestitive.[3]

In some very few and not very important instances, He is in use to exercise this power only *pro hâc vice*:[4] which approaches in it's consequences to his exercising the *Divestitive* power.

His possessing unconditionally the *Divestitive* power along with the Investitive with respect to many beneficial Political characters

claim, to review the reasons of justices of the peace, upon which they form their judgments in granting licences, by way of appeal from their judgments, or over-ruling the discretion intrusted to them. But if it clearly appears, that the justices have been partially, maliciously, or corruptly influenced in the exercise of this discretion, and have consequently abused the trust reposed in them; they are liable to prosecution by indictment or information; or even possibly by action, if the malice be very gross and injurious.' See Burn, *Justice of the Peace and Parish Officer*, i. 25–7.

[1] See [Matthew Hale], *The History and Analysis of the Common Law of England*, London, 1713, pp. 27–32, 42–4.

[2] See Blackstone, *Commentaries on the Laws of England*, i. 249–50, discussing the king's prerogative to make treaties and to make war and peace, and ii. 346–8 for the king's right to make grants in the form of charters.

[3] By the terms of the Act of Settlement of 1701 (12 & 13 Wil. III, c. 2), judges were to be appointed no longer *durante bene placito*, that is at pleasure, but *quamdiu bene se gesserint*, that is during good behavior, and could only be removed on the address of both Houses of Parliament. See Blackstone, *Commentaries on the Laws of England*, i. 258.

[4] i.e. 'for this occasion only'.

gives him the autocratic power of punishment to the extent of that portion of pain which is producible by the privation of the benefit attached to those characters.

Prefat. Formal Language.

660.[1] The truth of things is universally masked from our eyes by forms of words. Nothing is as it is said to be. Every thing is full of latent meanings. Thanks to the blindness of some, and the sycophantical respects of others, every thing in constitutional Law is confusion, uncertainty and contradiction. Sometimes we are to understand a thing in the manner it is said, sometimes in a manner directly opposite. We know not where we are. This veil a few may have strength of discernment to pierce through: but the greater part remain entangled in it to the end.

Powers {In-/De-} vestitive. {Conditional. / Unconditional or Absolute.

661. Powers Investitive and Devestitive may be either 1st. Conditional, or 2dly. Unconditional or absolute, at pleasure.

Privileges X Exemptions.

662. Privileges are 1st of a positive nature, viz: Peculiar benefits; 2dly of a negative nature: exemptions.

Exemptions suppose burthen laid on a generality; out of which generality the class or party privileged is excepted.

He is exempted who is not subjected to a burthen to which others are, and he, if it were not for the privilege, would be, subjected.

He is privileged who possesses a positive benefit which others do not, and he, if it were not for the privilege, would not, possess.

Repugnant X contrary.

663 Upon the idea annext to the word repugnant as prædicated of one set of Laws in respect to another depends the authority of the adscititious Ecclesiastical Law which is binding throughout England. Upon the same idea depends the authority of the British Legislature over many of the Colonies.[2]

---

[1] In the text, Bentham has noted at this point: 'v. 664.' See para. 664, p. 213 below.

[2] The Submission of the Clergy Act of 1533 (25 Hen. VIII, c. 19) stipulated that the existing body of canon law would remain in force pending a review by thirty-two persons taken half from the clergy and half from members of the Houses of Lords and Commons, provided such canon law 'be not contrarient or repugnant to the Laws, Statutes and Customs of this Realm'. The measure to establish the commission of thirty-two persons was re-enacted by 27 Hen. VIII, c. 15, but no commission was ever appointed. The Plantation Trade Act of 1696 (7 & 8 Wil. III, c. 22) declared that colonial 'Laws, By-laws, Usages or Customs' relating to plantations 'which are in any wise repugnant' to existing or subsequent Parliamentary legislation relating to the colonial plantations would be 'illegal, null and void, to all Intents and Purposes whatsoever'.

664.[1] Those who read the Constitutional Law in the account of it given in the *Commentaries*,[2] see it as through a glass, darkly: a glass deeply tinged with the prejudices or ignorances or interests of men of the profession. I would wish to see it face to face.[3] Preface—Formal Language.

---

665. By the investitive power, or the power of investment, I mean the power of investing persons or things with the character of some class, i:e: causing the person or thing in question to be of some class of persons or things that is expressed by the general terms made use of in the Law. Investitive Power, what.

---

666. Proceeding step by step, he is led on gradually and, as it were, insensibly from acquisition to acquisition: he is at no particular period more sensible of the progress he has made than at the next preceding, till at last he turns round, and beholds his journey finished: then it is that he finds himself at the summit of that mountain, when he has scarce perceived himself to have advanced, from whence he may behold the crowd beleag[uer]ing, wondering, toiling and rolling over one another in the mazes of perplexity. Preface. Progress insensible.

---

667. The expectation of Pain or Pleasure supposed to be connected with a mode of conduct as it's consequence is termed it's Sanction. A Sanction, what.

This Sanction takes one or other of three different names according to the source from which it proceeds: it may accord-ing[ly] be distinguished into the moral, the political, and the Religious. 3 Kinds of it.

The Moral Sanction is pain or pleasure, uncertain in quantity or quality, expected to result from the will of persons numerous and uncertain: viz: members of society in general, as it may happen. The Moral.

The Political Sanction is pain or pleasure, limited usually in quantity and quality, expected to result from the Will of persons few and certain; viz: political superiors. Particular persons in whom powers Legislative or Judicial are placed. The Political.

The Religious Sanction is pain or pleasure expected to result from the positive will of the Deity. The Religious.

[1] In the text, Bentham has noted at this point: 'v. 660.' See para. 660, p. 212 above.
[2] Blackstone discusses aspects of constitutional law at many points, though Bentham may have had in mind the passage at *Commentaries on the Laws of England*, i. 47–53, which he subjected to detailed criticism in *A Fragment on Government*.
[3] An echo of I Corinthians 13: 12.

The Physical. What might be called the Physical Sanction is pain or pleasure resulting from mere events, in which either will has no part, or, if any will, the will of a being not consider'd as being endowed with reason. Thus the pain of burning is the Physical Sanction which is the consequence of the act of handling red hot coals: the pain of being stung, of the act of handling wasps. The pain of being bitten, of the act of handling Vipers, and so forth.

Constitution. **668.** The Regulations and usages serving to distribute the powers of persons in the Government, or to ascertain the description of the persons who are to have the right of choosing of persons to be in the Government, or the collection of those powers and those rights themselves, [is] the Constitution.

Government *popular.* In proportion as the number of persons in the Government is great with respect to the numbers of the persons in the State, and the powers that are lodged in great bodies of the Government great in proportion to the powers lodged in small bodies, the Government is popular.

Government *free.* In a Government to some degree popular, in proportion as the subjects are able [to] know before hand the extent of the several powers exercised over them, as the extent of the several powers of persons in the Government is fixed, so the condition of the people is free, or rather secure: and thence improperly, by a metonymy, the Government is said to be free.

In proportion as the interest [of] persons in the Government approaches to being the same with the interest of the subjects, the Constitution is well-regulated.

Governors—their interest when the same as that of Subjects. It is the interest of persons in Government to consult the interest of the subjects, when the same persons are alternately Governors and subjects.

The right of voting in the Election of a Governor does not take a person out of the condition of a subject.

Common Law and Stat. Origin of. Brief Idea. A State. Acts of Government. Statute Laws. Rules of Common Law. When a man or body of men (but to save words I will suppose only a single man), when a man, I say, has got, no matter how, an established superiority, so that, whatever commands he were to issue, it is clear he would be obey'd, hence, were there even none before, cometh a state. His particular commands are acts of Government. His general Commands are Statute Laws. His acts of violence, acts of punishment. From his violences, and his particular commands, men learn to form to themselves ideas of sorts of actions favoured or obnoxious: of sorts of actions which by that means become, as it were, commanded or prohibited; and the description given by any man of these sorts of actions in his own words is what forms Common Law.

If our Adventurer robs with a few associates, and is hanged, he is a Highwayman. If with many and he is beheaded, he is a Rebel. If with more, or with better fortune, and he is crowned, he is a King. He is a King *de facto* and *de Jure*, so men cry out to one another aloud in public. He is a King *de facto* but not *de Jure*, say they one to another in whispers and in private; those, I mean, who are pleased with him: for with them who are not pleased with him, he is an Usurper.

A Highwayman.
A Rebel.
A King
—*de facto*.
—*de Jure*.
An Usurper.

What, then, is it that makes a State? It is the habit of command in the few, or we will say the one, coupled with the habit of submission in the many. Are those habits formed, he is become a lawful Sovereign. Is it as yet unformed? He is an Usurper.

A State—what makes it. Habit.

The persons in use to be commanded by him, taken individually, his subjects. The portion of country which they are in use to occupy, the Geographical or Local field of his Dominion. The aggregate body of those who are born within that country, the Nation. The aggregate body of those, whether born within the Geographical field of his dominion, or only residing in it for the time being, The People. The number of his People, the personal field of his dominion. He and those co-ordinate or subordinate to him in Dominion, the Government. The Government and Subjects taken together, the State. The aggregate collection of the actions, positive or negative, of his subjects, the moral field of his Dominion.

A Subject
Dominion—Geographical or local field of.
The Nation.
The People
The Government.
The State.
Dominion—moral field of.

---

669. Correspondent to the Dominion of the Monarch, is the Jurisdiction of the Judge.

Dominion = Jurisdiction.

669.[1] An orderly, unbroken, well-compacted chain of definitions is the only sure ladder whereby a man can place himself on the heights of science.

Prefat. Chain of Def.^{s} a Ladder to Science.

---

670. Conditions to a Command, are either 1st concomitant to the mode of conduct commanded, viz: circumstances of the action; or 2^{d} subsequent, viz: transactions of Procedure.

A Law.
Conditions in a—
{ Concomitant to.
{ Subsequent.[2]

---

[1] Bentham has given two paragraphs the number 669.
[2] For the correct form of layout of the marginal see p. 29.

Prefat. Definitions. Progress insensible.

671. He will fancy himself to have been doing nothing, and he will find himself to have done every thing. He will fancy his work yet to begin, and he will find it done.

Prefat. Defin:^s. Difficulty of the operation. Apologet.

672. Proportioned to it's ease to the reader, is it's difficulty to the writer. Proportioned to the facility with which the work is survey'd by the reader, is the difficulty the writer must have surmounted in executing it. As the application of those terms extends itself throughout the whole science, 'tis no less than the whole science that he must travel over to assure himself of the truth of any one of them.

If to compose such a work a man must be a metaphysician, it follows not that a man must be a metaphysician to read it.

A man must be a taylor to make a coat: but it is not necessary that he should be a taylor to put it on.

No objection to the use of it.

The most knowing are not too knowing to compose a Dictionary: but, if well composed, the most uninstructed are not too uninstructed to consult it.

Power. Legislation. Executive. Autocratic.

673. Subordinate Executive power shews less than subordinate Legislative, because the party empower'd in a regular constitution like ours, if he has any thing above him, has laws above him.

But a Basha in Turkey, though he never think of making a Law, is not less absolute than if he made a thousand. A Basha, though he be but the Basha of some petty Town, though he have but a single tail,[1] exercises no new powers within that Town by exercising acts of Legislation. He only does more work of the same kind in less time.

We can conceive a supreme power in a state without conceiving a Law in it.

Subordination of powers, how produced, [4][4] ways.

674. Subordination among powers is produced [4][2] ways. [1st.][3] By a condition to the application of punishment to the common inferior. [2^cly.] By the application of punishment to the subordinate superior. 3^cly. By the application of punishment to the instruments of the subordinate superior, where, to be physically capable of exercising the act of power, he must have instruments. 4^thly. Qu. Whether by the Right of Investment.[5]

[1] The rank of a Basha or Pasha was indicated by the number of horse-tails attached to his personal standard.

[2] MS '3'. [3] MS | |. [4] MS '3'.

[5] In the text, Bentham has noted: 'Answered p. 356.' The cross-reference is to the following paragraph.

And this makes a 4th way in which subordination may be produced, viz: by the common subject's being left exposed to the uncontrolled commands of both powers: only the punishment to which he is exposed from the superior is greater than that to which he is exposed from the inferior.

Subordination. 4th case of.

---

675. I doubt not but that a man warm on the popular side reading this will be very ready to say 'I hate Metaphysics':[a] hereafter I shall have men of the ruling party hating Metaphysics. If I can expect no better than alternately to incur the displeasure of all parties that divide the state, I am sorry for it: it is not out of any spleen I have to any. Many persons I respect of both, or rather, for I know not how many of them there are, of all: and not the less for respecting those of the opposite. If respect mean partiality, Science is no respecter of persons: Science is not of any party.

Prefat. Metaphys. ☛ Occasional.

Whenever any man of either, through artifice or through passion, should seek, by sophistry and the abuse of words, to carry a point at the expence of truth, I hope he will ever find in genuine metaphysics that sharpness that shall cut the throat of his designs.

That most consummate, most enchanting rhetorician, the most enchanting writer, perhaps, the world ever has yet seen,[1] is apt to give himself but too much reason for hating Metaphysics.

They will be driven from their fastnesses . . . . .

---

676. A Consent to a thing's being done is tantamount to a promise neither to impede it's being done, nor to endeavour to make any one suffer on account of it's being done.

Consent tantamount to a Promise.

---

677. If I signify my will to be that such an act be done, and no more, I signify my will to be that the act be done under whatever circumstances. Such a volition may be stiled *pure*: the expression of it is a pure wish without any *conditionalizing clause.*

Volition pure ⨯ modified.

---

[a] Burke's *Speech on American Taxation. April 19. 1775.* p. 89. 3d Edition.[2]

[1] i.e. Burke.

[2] In the House of Commons on 19 April 1774, addressing the question of Parliament's power to tax the North American colonies, Burke stated: 'I am not here going into the distinctions of rights, nor attempting to mark their boundaries. I do not enter into these metaphysical distinctions; I hate the very sound of them.' See *Speech of Edmund Burke, Esq. on American Taxation, April 19, 1774*, 3rd edn., London, 1775, p. 89, reproduced in *The Writings and Speeches of Edmund Burke: Volume II. Party, Parliament, and the American Crisis 1766–1774*, ed. P. Langford and W.B. Todd, Oxford, 1981, pp. 406–63 at 458.

Two methods of carrying on the business of Government. Silent and Enuntiative.

678. There are two ways, therefore, of intimating a mode of conduct to be obnoxious. The one is by Command: the other is by Punishment without [command], at least without any command of which the person whose conduct it is that is in question is the object.

The first may be stiled the direct, or enuntiative.

Enuntiative, direct and ante-ambulant)(Silent, indirect, and *Ex-post-facto*.

In the first, a discourse is made on the part of the superior, addressed to all persons of that sort whose conduct it is that is in question, capable of [practising][1] the mode of conduct which it is his purpose to signify to be obnoxious. In the second, no such discourse is holden. With respect to them, all that is acted is acted in dumb shew. In the first, what is proposed, on occasion of any such mode of conduct, to be done, is convey'd to their apprehension by the *direct* and most *proper* means. In the second, the means that serve to convey it to them are indirect and oblique; they are left to catch an intimation of it as they can. The first, therefore, may be stiled the *enuntiative*, or *direct* method; the second, the *silent*, *indirect*. The first may take effect *before* any individual article of conduct has ever existed which it means to render obnoxious. The second cannot take effect or display itself but *in consequence* of the existence of some such article. In the first, the superior *gives warning* before he *strikes*. In the second, he must *strike* in order to *warn*. The first may, therefore, with respect to the mode of conduct in question, be stiled the *ante-ambulant*, *præcursory*, or *præmonitory* method: the 2d, the *subsequent*, *pedissequal* or *ex-post-facto* method.

Comment. Censure on *Ex-post-facto* Law repugnant to his panegyric on Comm. Law.

679. Our Author censures *ex-post-facto* law, because others have declaimed against it before him.[2] He idolizes Common Law for the like reason: and sees not that his censure cuts the throat of his panegyric. He magnifies Common Law at the expence of Statute: and sees not that whatever is done in the way of Common Law is done *ex necessitate rei* by *ex-post-facto* acts of power.

The Enuntiative method, how far it supposes past instances of Punishment.

680. True it is, that punishment in past instances is necessary to the efficacy of a Command. But, to the efficacy of a Command, all the punishment that is necessary is acts of punishment in sufficient number to beget the idea of an act of punishment, exercised by persons of the description of the superior over persons of the description of the inferiors, on account of *any*

[1] MS 'liable to practise'.

[2] Blackstone, *Commentaries on the Laws of England*, i. 46, refers to punishment inflicted for the contravention of *ex post facto* laws as 'cruel and unjust', and cites Cicero, *De domo sua ad pontifices oratio*, XVII. 43.

mode of conduct whatsoever. But to the signifying in the silent way any given mode of conduct to be obnoxious, some person must necessarily have been punished on account of *the particular mode of conduct that is in question*. In the *silent method*, therefore, as many persons must have undergone punishment, as many persons must have been put to pain, as there are distinguishable modes of conduct render'd *obnoxious*.

---

681. A Judge, as such, not only cannot issue commands to sorts of persons, but, of individuals, he can issue commands to such only as are called before him by other individuals.

A Judge)(Legislator. A Judge)(Commander.

But observe a Judge having power to convict on view. There antecedent transgression is necessary to give him Jurisdiction.

---

682. We may conceive the power of Governing without the power of making Laws. We may conceive the power of Executing Laws without the power of making them. We may conceive the power of making them without the power of executing them. We may conceive the power of Governing unlimited by either superordinate Legislature or superordinate Government. We may conceive the power of Governing with either superordinate Legislature or superordinate Government without the other.[1]

Powers in a State Enumerated.

---

683. A Governor has to choose the personal objects of his command or punishment from among all those who are within the several fields of his dominion. In a despotic Government his Legislation is limited by time.[2]

A Governor)(Judge.

---

684. **Note.** The word 'field', in this sense of it, I borrow from Opticians. The field of a Telescope is so much of the Sky as can be seen through it. Were the optician to make reprisals on the Lawyer, so much of the sky, he might say, as it *commands*.

Field of Dominion or Jurisdiction, taken from Optics.

---

685. Consent 1st upon *cognizance*. 2$^{dly.}$ Upon Trust.
Consent revocable or not.
Dissent upon cognizance supersedes consent upon Trust.
Consent is *concomitant* to proposal)(Assent is *subsequent*.

---

[1] The syntax here is obscure, but Bentham may simply be distinguishing between government either with or without a legislature.

[2] In the text, Bentham has noted at this point: 'Qu.'

Election—no power but a Right only.

[685.*] Election.—It is a right: but it gives him no governing power. It only gives him influence.

Power Investitive. Appointment X Election.

686. The Right of investiture with respect to Offices, when in the hands of one or a few, is called the power of Appointment: when in the hands of many, more usually it is called the power, or rather right, of Election: the many are called Electors.

Representation.

In common speech, Electors are said to be *represented* by the party or parties elected. So might the appointer, by the party or parties appointed.

Consent, every man's to a Law, how far necessary.

687. In the British State, the supreme power is distributed between two bodies and one single person, or sometimes, in his stead, a third body. These three are commonly stiled by a common name, *branches*. The supreme power is distributed, then, between three branches.

Of these three branches, one is composed of persons that are elected. This branch is stiled the House of Commons. The electors are numerous, and, for the greater part, do not rise above the class of subjects. From hence occasion has been taken to advance two propositions.

The one is, that, under the British Constitution, no man can be bound to any Law but by his own consent. A second is, that no man can be taxed, i:e: be bound by a Tax, who is not represented.

Taxation a branch of Legislation. Ld Chatham.

688. The second was universally looked upon as included in the 1st, till about —— years ago.

It was in the year 1764, in that part of Great Britain called England, in the City of Westminster, in a chamber called the House of Lords, about —— o'clock in the morning, that it was discover'd that to impose a tax is not to make a Law.

The debate was whether the Legislature should tax a certain body of people. A great person was against it. He wished to be understood to think the Legislature had no right. That great person, therefore, got up and made this argument:

I admit that we have a right to make Laws for that people in all cases whatsoever. But to lay a tax is not to make a Law. Therefore, from our having a right to make Laws for them in all cases whatsoever, it follows not that we have a right to tax them.[1]

[1] In the debate on the repeal of the Stamp Act of 14 January 1766 (not 1764) in the House of Commons (not Lords), William Pitt the Elder (1708–78) (who would not be ennobled as first Earl of Chatham until later in 1766), Secretary of State for the Southern Department 1756–7, 1757–61, leader of the administration as Lord Privy Seal 1766–8, had stated his 'Opinion that this Kingdom has no Right to lay a Tax on the C--l--n--s; at the same time I assert the Authority of this Kingdom over the C--l--n--s to be Sovereign and Supreme in every Circumstance of Government and Legislation whatsoever': see *The Speech of Mr.*

If that great person, at that time, had got up and with a firm tone and commanding gesture said, 'Ton d'apamibonos polufloisboio thalasses,'[a] therefore we have no right to tax these people, it would have been, with a large number of other very respectable persons, an unanswerable argument: and the said respectable persons would have gone away perfectly convinced that they had no right to tax those people, because 'Ton d'apamibomenos polufloisboio thalasses.'

To those who see it upon paper at the distance of | | years after it was invented, this proposition appears to have two meanings. The one is, that a command to pay money is not a command: the other is, that a command to pay money is not the same sort of command as a command to do a different thing.

In the first sense, it will not be true till two contradictory propositions are both true. In the latter sense, it may be very true, but he that has heard it is not much the wiser.

If this be the case, the second of the above pair of propositions may be looked upon as comprehended in the first.[1]

[a] v. Fielding's *Joseph Andrews*[2]—I mean not to make any application of the meaning this assemblage of words might be supposed to have when translated—I give it as an instance of an assemblage of words without a meaning.

P------ And several others, In a certain august Assembly, On a late important Debate: With an Introduction of the Matters preceding it, London, 1766, p. 8.

[1] The following fragment on this theme, headed 'Inserenda. [MS del. 'Introd.'] Prepar. Principles. Legislation ⟩⟨ Taxation', is at UC lxix. 85:

'There are those who that . . . .

'This is, in other words, to say, that a command to pay money is not a command.

'Taxation, in as far as performed by the House of Commons, is not an act of legislation, that is ⟨not⟩ a command. What then? it is but a gift. Why? because in the form of words serving to express a comma⟨nd⟩ to this purpose, the word give is used.

'If I say to you, I give you this money, holding out a purse of money, it is certain⟨ly⟩ a gift: but if I say to you, I give you that money, ⟨pointing⟩ to a purse of money of Titius, if this is not a command ⟨to⟩ Titius to yield up the money, it is nothing.

'Two Highwaymen, A. and B., stop a man to rob him. Says A. to B., take that man's purse. I give it you. A. ⟨is⟩ tried for it. Alas, says he, this was not a robbery, 'twa⟨s a⟩ gift. What should we say to such a plea?

'A command to pay money, is a thing so . . . that, in the description of it, it may be effectually distinguis⟨hed⟩ from a command to do any thing else. A body of men may, therefore, promise to obey the command⟨s⟩ of another body to do every thi⟨ng⟩ else, without promising to obey commands to pay money. This must be, by promising ⟨to⟩ obey commands to every other purpose, in general, this one particular excepted. The question is, have they thus promised?

'Taxation and legislation are inseparable? How this to be und⟨erstood?⟩ That taxation is inseparable from the rest of Legislation? it is not true ⟨. . .⟩'

'The power of commanding ⟨to⟩ do any thing, and the power ⟨of⟩ commanding to do this one ⟨so⟩rt of thing, pay money ⟨. . .⟩ that the act of paying ⟨. . .⟩.'

[2] Bentham's rendering of nonsense words spoken by the Doctor in Henry Fielding, *The History of the Adventures of Joseph Andrews, and his Friend Mr. Abraham Adams*, 2 vols., London, 1742, i. 86. There are some minor inaccuracies in the rendering of the passage.

Consent. Consent single, or *sole*.

689. To understand whether it be true that no man can be bound by a Law, but by his own consent, it will be necessary to understand rightly what it is we mean by the word consent.

Consent is used in many more senses [than][1] one. Let us endeavour to recollect them.

In the original and proper sense of the word, a person is said *to consent* to an act's being done, when he has a right of himself to prevent it's being done, and upon it's being proposed to him whether it shall be done or no, he says, I consent it shall, or intentionally uses words or signs equivalent.[2] This consent of a person standing singly, I would call a consent single, or consent sole. If I were to speak in Latin, borrowing a word from the Greek, I would call it *consensus autocurialis*.

Consensus autocurialis.

Consent *corporate.*

690. A person is said, in another sense, to consent to an act's being done, when, being one of a body which has a right to prevent it's being done, and it being proposed to the body whether it shall be done or no, the majority of that body says, I consent it shall, or intentionally uses words or signs equivalent. In this case, any member of that body may, in a derivative and improper sense of the word, be said to have given his consent. The word consent, in this sense of it, may be stiled a corporate consent.

Dissent.

691. Contrary to consent is dissent.

Option.

692. An indifferent common term, signifying either consent or dissent, is *option*.

Vote.

693. To make an option with others in a body, is to *vote*. To give one's suffrage.

Expression Monoepic ⚹ Polyepic.

694. Synonymous expressions. Monoepic ⚹ Polyepic.

It[3] is plain that a consent corporate may be a very different thing from a consent sole. A man's sole option, may be contrary to his corporate option. A man may have given his consent sole to an act to which [he has not given] his consent corporate.

To give.

695. To give a thing is to *consent* that it may be taken.

Consent corporate how different from sole.

696. It is manifest that to give a consent sole and to give a consent corporate are so far from being the same thing, that they may be opposite. A man's consent corporate may have gone to an act to which no one is further than himself from giving a consent

[1] MS 'on'.

[2] In the margin, Bentham has noted at this point: 'note Metaphysical'. No such note has been identified.

[3] The discussion is resumed from para. 693.

sole. A man's consent corporate may have gone to an act to which his consent sole went not, either because he neither consented nor dissented, made no option, gave no vote at all, or because, making his option, he made the opposite one, he dissented.

697. Again, Consent may either be upon cognizance or upon Trust. And Consent upon cognizance may again be either General or specific. And this may be said as well of Consent corporate as sole.

Consent upon: { Cognizance. Trust. Cognizance: { General. Particular.

---

698. Representation, spoken of as we have been accustomed to hear it spoken of, may be distinguished into two kinds. 1st. That which is not representation; 2dly that which is. The 1st is called virtual representation. The 2d, in contradistinction to the former, may be termed actual. It is plain that, admitting the definition of representation above given, this which has been called virtual representation can have nothing to do with representation. For either a man has a vote for the election of a Member, or he has not. If he has, he is actually represented. If he has not, he is not represented at all. If representation has any thing to do with election, then if any one man who has no vote to give in the election of an Officer can be said to be represented by that Officer, any man whatever may. The King of France, or the Grand Signior, may be said to be virtually represented by a City Member.

Representation: actual and virtual; real and spurious.

[698.*] Form of Government)(Constitution—Constitution takes in Rights of Election.

Why it is usual to say *power* of *appointing*, and *right* of *electing*.

Power of appointing. *Right* of electing.

[698.]** Virtual representation is the condition of those persons who are looked upon as bearing such a relation, either to Superiors or Electors, as that they ought to be subject in the same manner as if they were actually represented.

Actually represented or no? a simple question of fact. Virtually represented or no? A very complex question of opinion.

Representation *virtual*.

---

699. The words defined are all so many given quantities, and possessing which, the Jurist finds himself rich in means for the solution of any problem in his science.

Prefat. Definition, Utility of.

---

700. Edicts *durante vitâ aut officio*[1] of the Governor. As of the Prætor in Old Rome.

Edict)(Statute.

[1] i.e. 'during life and in virtue of one's office'.

Statutes perpetual.

Taxation a branch of Legislation. Arg. *contra*.

701. 'A Law and a Tax are different things. For a Law is a Command. But a Tax, under our Constitution, is a Gift. And a Command and a Gift are different things without dispute.

'A Tax is a Gift: for a Tax cannot be laid on a man without his consent, given by his Representatives. And every man is represented, either actually or else virtually, which comes to the same thing'.

What should have made men a little suspicious of the force of this argument against Taxation, is that it might be urged with equal force against Legislation.

Those who lay taxes are the same as those who make Laws. No man, it is said, can be bound by a Tax without consent. But, so it has been said, no man can be bound by a Law without his own consent.[1] You admitt the right with respect to Laws; you deny it with respect to taxes, though the consent that is given is the same to one as to the other.

Prefat. Metaphysics. Apol. for.

702. The complexion of these arguments, it will be acknowledged, is sufficiently Metaphysical. But to free myself from the pressure of them, I do not find it necessary to profess to hate Metaphysics.[2] They are Metaphysics, but they are false Metaphysics. That which is true in Metaphysics is nothing disparaged by the futility of that which is false. On the contrary, it shines with redoubled lustre by contrast. That which is false in Metaphysics, when tried, as in a Test, by that which is true, runs away into dross. To hate the true on account of the false is as reasonable as it would be to hate the whole science of Chymistry, because men have talked nonsense when they have talked of making Gold.

Conjugates not to be enumerated.

703. Conjugates there will be no occasion to enumerate. Words that have the same grammatical root, that are so resembling each other in sound as to have their radical letters the same, men will of course suppose to be connected in signification, in the manner that words so resembling each other in sound usually are. The collection of conjugates belonging to any root may be had from the common dictionaries.

---

[1] See, for instance, Locke, *Two Treatises of Government*, Bk II, Ch. VIII, §95, p. 330: 'Men being . . . by Nature, all free, equal and independent, no one can be put out of this Estate, and subjected to the Political Power of another, without his own *Consent*.'

[2] An allusion to Burke: see p. 217 n. above.

704. Objects are said to be *related*, when they are so *conditioned* that the mind, on whatever account, is determined to pass from the consideration of one of them to that of the other. The condition such things are in is termed, relation. Relation defined.

704.* Condition is mode of existence. Things are said to be in a certain condition, when they exist in a certain mode. Condition (of things) defined.

705. Objects are said to be *related*, whereof the ideas are said to be *associated.* Relation = Association.

---

706. A cluster of conjugates, associated by a certain principle, form that artificial whole we call a verb. Another cluster of conjugates (of the same root perhaps), associated by a principle somewhat different, form what we call a noun. Conjugates—A Verb. A Noun.

707. The signification of any one word derived from a root being given, any other word derived from the same root is given in like manner. In other words, any one conjugate of a root being given in signification, all the other conjugates of the same root are given in signification by their relation to that one. So it is for the most part. This, therefore, may be laid down as the general rule. If it be otherwise in any instance, that instance it will be proper to produce in the character of an exception. Conjugates: one given, all are given.

708. Of all that will be found here concerning Conjugates, the hint is taken from Saunderson. 'Conjugates', says that abstruse and cloudy writer, in the twenty-second chapter of the 3d book of his Logic, 'are those things which, on account of affinity of signification, are conjoined by affinity of words: as Just, Justice, Justly.'[1] Conjugates—Saunderson.

He had, in the 6th Chapter of his 1st Book, said something like this of what he calls Denominatives, a name he gives to words that seem, by his account of them, to be a species of conjugates:[2] though no sort of intimation does he give of any relation that what he has said under the one of these heads bears to what he has said under the other. Looking no further than words, and of words to those only which belong to the Latin language, the view he gives of the subject is so narrow and confused, that it would be lost labour to dwell on it. The reader who has curiosity may turn to the two chapters I have mentioned.

Of the two words, *Denominatives* and *Conjugates*, I prefer the latter, amongst other reasons, on account of it's being already familiar by the use that is made of it in Grammar. Amongst Grammarians, to *conjugate* a verb is to enumerate such of the Conjugates, why preferred to Denominatives. 'To conjugate' in Grammar.

[1] See Sanderson, *Logicæ Artis Compendium*, pp. 145–6.
[2] See ibid., pp. 14–15.

conjugates (in the large sense in which I here use the word), such of the conjugates, I say, belonging to a given root, as compose that assemblage to which Grammarians have given the name of Verb.[1]

Common Law—what it is composed of. Not the commands explicit or implicit of a Judge.

709. The act of a Judge possesses no binding force beyond the individual article of conduct which called it forth. True it is, he declares the individual article of conduct to be of such a sort; and this a sort he pronounces, perhaps, to be obnoxious or otherwise: but his declaration carries with it no binding force with respect to any article of that sort except the individual article before him. Were it the Legislature who declared the article in question to be of such a sort, and that sort obnoxious, such declaration *would* have a binding force: it would be tantamount to a command. It would be tantamount to a prohibition of the article in question.

The words used by one Judge are not the necessary measure of Decision to a succeeding Judge.

710. Had such a declaration on the part of any given Judge such a binding force over articles of conduct other than that immediately in question, then to have any binding force it must be binding upon the next Judge before whom an article of conduct of the same sort comes in question. For a general regulation can have no efficacy over individuals, unless by an individual command it be brought home in every case to the individual person whose conduct is in question. The prior Judge, then, must stand as Legislator, with respect to whom the subsequent Judge acts in subserviency as executive Magistrate. But this, between Judges of equal rank succeeding one another [in] the same Court, is not the case. They are all equal. What power any given Judge has, this has his successor. The power of each extends over the present individual article of conduct that is before him, and no other.

Accordingly, it is not reckoned disobedience in a Judge to depart from the decision of his predecessor.[2]

A Verb defective.

711.[3] Among the particular species of conjugates which compose a verb, when any member of the assemblage is wanting, the verb is said to be defective: thus the verb *fero* in Latin is defective, wanting, amongst others, that class of conjugates that compose the perfect tense of the indicative mode. In order to supply the place of that member, some word must, therefore, be borrow'd from some other root: namely a word that occupies the correspondent place in some other groupe of conjugates: accordingly the word *tuli*, with

[1] The discussion is continued at para. 711 below.
[2] This sentence appears before para. 709, but seems more appropriately placed here.
[3] The discussion is resumed from para. 708 above.

it's six conjugates that compose that tense, is borrowed for the purpose. *Tuli* we may suppose to have been taken from a Verb formerly in use, of which the Present Indicative was *Tulo*: unless *Tollo* should be consider'd as being that verb, only spelt a little differently. *Fero* and *Tuli*, then, are *quasi-conjugates*. *Fero* is I bear. *Tollo* is I lift, or take up. If *Tuli* is looked upon as not capable of signifying I have lifted, I have taken up, but only I have born, then *Tollo* and *Tuli* are pseudo-conjugates.

Quasi-conjugates.

Pseudo-conjugates.

Volitional Sentences distinguished *verbally* only from Assertive. Harris.

712. I was long perplexed by a distinction of Mr Harris's which, it now seems to me, is a mistaken one. 'Every sentence,' observes that elegant Philologist,[a] 'is either a sentence of assertion, or a sentence of volition.' From this we are to conclude, according to the well-known law of Division,[b] that a sentence of volition is not a sentence of assertion: and that, as by a sentence of assertion nothing is willed, so by a sentence of volition nothing is asserted. But this is not the case. *To will* is not the business of one sentence any more than another: it is not the business of any sentence. To will is an act internal; to utter a sentence is an act external. To assert the existence of a volition may be the business of one sentence as well as another. A sentence asserting the existence of a volition, he would, I suppose, acknowledge to be an instance of what he means by a sentence of volition: now a sentence asserting the existence of a volition is surely a sentence of assertion.

'No but,' says Mr Harris, 'if we assert, then it is a sentence which respects the powers of perception. For what indeed,' says he, 'is *to assert*, but to publish some *perception*, either of the senses or the intellect?'[1] I answer . . . to publish some volition. What the difference is, in this place, between assertion and publication, and why the existence of a volition can not be as well asserted as published, just as the existence of a perception may as well be published as asserted, is what I can not understand. That we will a thing is as much a matter of fact as that we perceive. All this fine-spun confusion comes from reading Ammonius, instead of attending to what passes in one's own mind.

[a] *Hermes* B. 1. Ch. 2d. p. 17. Ed. 1st, after an antiquated grammarian whose name was Ammonius.[2]

[b] Let the condivident members be distinct and opposite.[3]

---

[1] Harris, *Hermes*, p. 16. The initial 'No but' has been added by Bentham, and there are some minor inaccuracies in the rendering of the passage.

[2] Harris, *Hermes*, p. 17 & n., citing the work of the Neoplatonist Ammonius Hermiae (440–*c*. 520), *On Aristotle's On Interpretation*. There are some minor inaccuracies in the rendering of the passage.

[3] Bentham's rendering of the maxim '*Membra condividentia sint contradistincta & opposita*', which appears in Sanderson, *Logicæ Artis Compendium*, p. 47.

But suppose Mr Harris, it will be said, sees reason to use the word assertion in a sense somewhat different from, and more confined than, that it has been in use to bear, why not let him? I answer, for this reason. Suppose he had said, Every sentence is a sentence assertive either of perception, or of volition. This, in the large meaning he has given the word perception, would be unquestionable: why, then, not let himself express it as he has done? I answer, for this reason. By sentence, it is plain, he means not the general import that is in the mind, but the particular form of words employ'd to publish it. Now there is a particular class of words, namely such as compose what is called the imperative mode of every verb, that are peculiarly adapted to express volition, and which indeed express nothing else. By a sentence of volition, then, a man would naturally suppose him to mean (and for aught I know he may have meant) a sentence of which the verb was in that mode, in exclusion of every other kind of sentence. If, then, the appellation sentence of volition be confined to sentences of this sort, in this case, that every sentence is a sentence assertive of perception or a sentence assertive of volition is not true. It is true that sentences of this sort never can assert any thing but a volition, never can assert a perception: but other sentences there are that may serve to assert a volition besides these. 'Shut the door,' I say. Here I have spoken a sentence of volition. I have asserted the existence of a volition. But I express precisely the same thing if I say, 'My will is that you shut the door.' In the sentence 'Shut the door' there is a verb in the imperative mood: the verb shut. In the sentence 'My will is that you shut the door' there is none. This is unquestionably assertive, and yet my will is expressed not a whit less perfectly in the latter than in the former.

The truth is, the *imperative* mode is one mode invented for shortness sake for the purpose of expressing *will*: but there are infinity of other modes of expressing it not less frequently employ'd, nor less effectual. By other modes volition may be expressed in all cases: but it is not in all cases that it can be expressed by this. So far is the imperative mode from being exclusively appropriated to volition, that there are cases where volition can not be properly expressed by it. Such are those where it is a superior whose act is the object of the volition. In using the imperative mode, you are universally understood to announce yourself as the superior to the party you address, unless he be a person (as the deity) whose elevation is too confessed to leave room for the least thought of his being, by any possibility, in any respect your inferior.[1] This mode is stiled by the antients not the volitional, but the imperative. For petition or request, they had another mode, the subjunctive, *des veniam*:[2] which, as it seems, is but an ellipsis for *rogo* (i:e: *volo ego qui tibi par sum vel potius qui in hac parte saltem inferior*) *ut des veniam*.[3]

Volition how exprest. 1st. By external action:

713. Acts of Will, that is internal acts, may be imperfectly expressed by external actions.

viz: by an act of punishment.

714. A volition, the object of which is forbearance of an action, may be expressed by an external act of punishment, punishing the agent who performs the action. Thus it is that the will of a master may be expressed, though imperfectly, even to a dog or other animal insensible to the significance of regular discourse. Thus it is that the will of a parent is oftentimes expressed to infant children. Thus alone it is that the will of one man could, in many instances, be expressed to another not understanding the same language.

2d. By signs, generally written.

715. But in societies in the least degree civilized, in political states, an act of the will of a political superior is generally expressed by words: these words, where the art of writing is general, are in many cases written.

An act of punishment—what.

716. An act of punishment is an act producing pain in the object punished.

By an act of punishment, the act of the party *willing*.

717. The most simple way in which pain is produced is when the act of punishment is the act of the same person of whose will the pain of the party to be punished is the object. This is the way in which it most commonly is produced in the first of the above three instances, and very frequently in the second.

[1] In the text, Bentham has noted at this point: 'We have an interrogative mode in English, as much as an imperative. *Shall* denotes the futurity of the action when the action is that of a person other than the speaker, and when the prime cause of it is the volition of the speaker.'

[2] i.e. 'grant me an indulgence'. Above this phrase, Bentham has written the iussive subjunctive '*Exeas*', i.e. 'Go out.' He does not, however, go on to employ this term in filling the ellipsis in question.

[3] i.e. 'I ask (i.e. I will, I who am equal to you or rather, at least in this respect, inferior) that you should grant me an indulgence.'

The following fragments, referring to Harris, appear in the text at this point:

'In whom all that is good, which is the style and method, is his own, and all that is bad, that is almost all the *materials*, is the best of the trash of the antients, which, by an unhappy prejudice, he set himself to collect and brood over, instead of setting himself to observe, | | preferring the worm-eaten page of philology, to the ever fresh and suc[c]ulent page of nature.

'By what he has done in that acute and elegant performance under such disadvantage, one may judge what, had his pursuits taken a happier direction, he might have done.'

By words or signs commanding another to be the punisher.

718. But in societies in the least degree civilized, it is not thus that punishment is produced by a political superior. By words he expresses his will in that behalf to a second person, that second, perhaps, to a third, and so on indefinitely. In this case, the act of punishment is not the act of him with whom the will to punish originated.

Mode of conduct obnoxious.

719. By the obnoxious mode of conduct, I mean the mode of conduct in the inferior which the superior wishes not to be observed.

Controlling Circumstances to a Law, 3 ranks of:

720 Circumstances controlling the effect of the mandate of the Law, are:

1. Formalities of the Law.

1st. Circumstances precedent to the publication of the Law itself, viz: Formalities of enactment; Circumstances relative to enactment; Circumstances controlling the authenticity of the Law. These must be precedent to any article of conduct of the species made an offence.

2. Circumstances of the Mode of Conduct prescribed.

2d. Circumstances relative to the mode of conduct commanded or prohibited. Circumstances controlling the description of the objects of the Law. These may either be 1st precedent to the article of conduct of the species constituted an offence, [or] 2d Subsequent.

3. Circumstances of Procedure.

3dly. Circumstances relative to the execution of the Law. Circumstances relative to prosecution. Circumstances controlling the execution of the Law. These must, of course, be subsequent to any article of conduct of the species constituted an offence.

Circumstances influencing.

721. Circumstances of an event, consider'd in a moral view, are any other events whatsoever influencing the effect of it with regard to the production of pain or pleasure.

Source of the Expression 'Circumstances'.

722. The image which gave occasion to the word circumstances is this. All the events in the world that have been, or are, or may be, are conceived to be ranged, as it were, in the figure of a circle, or rather of a sphere. Of this sphere, the event in question, with respect to which others are to be termed circumstances, is supposed to be seated in the center. The whole assemblage of other events are standing round it: *circumsto* is to stand round. But what are the events usually spoken of under the name of circumstances of another? are they all events whatsoever without distinction? Not so, but such, and such only, as are supposed to influence the effects of the event in question.

---

723. Power is Power when in exercise, and submitted to. Right is Power whether in exercise or no, and whether submitted to or no. Right is Power in futurity. We say Power over an Estate in possession. We say right to an estate in expectancy. A right of Reversion. A Remainder is a right. Power is *active*. Right is defensive—so we say Right, not Power, of Security.

Power)(Right. Right)(Power.

The word Power is not used where, to the lawfulness of the act of power, the concurrence of another person is necessary. The word we use then is Right.[1]

State: Æra of it's formation.

724. A State depending for it's formation on habit: no one can ascertain the precise Æra of it's formation; except when formed by express compact.

State = Political.

725. *Quasi-conjugate* to 'State' is 'Political'.

Definition)(Distinction.

726. What is called a Definition, is a portion of discourse calculated to distinguish a word or expression from all others in general.

Distinction)(Definition.

727. What is called a Distinction, is a portion of discourse calculated to distinguish the import of a word or expression from that of some one other in particular.[2]

Punishment why more efficacious than Reward.

728. The expectation of pain acts with more force on a man than that of pleasure. Amongst other reasons for this: that if a man does not receive the pleasure offer'd, he may receive some other; but if he receive pain, while that lasts, he is scarcely susceptible of any pleasure. Any cause of pleasure applied to him while in pain, produces but very imperfectly it's effect.

A Regulation may be a whole Sentence or a part.

729. Whether a Regulation shall occupy a whole Grammatical sentence, or only a clause in a sentence, is a matter entirely of accident. It affects not at all the Import of the Law, but only the expression. In either manner may a regulation of any given import be expressed.

Regulation Conditionalizing)(Exceptive. Exceptive)(Conditionalizing.

730. Whether a Regulation shall be Conditionalizing or Exceptive, depends upon the *amplitude* of the term whereby the article of the conduct that is the object of the *Principal* regulation is characterized.

---

[1] In the text, Bentham has noted at this point: 'v. p. 16, 17, 18.' See paras. 54–60, pp. 68–9 above.

[2] In the text, Bentham has noted at this point: 'v. p. 406.' See paras. 981–2, p. 302 below.

Power of Investment Public ⲭ Private.

731. The King and other Magistrates possess the investitive power with respect to Offices giving public powers over persons and public things. Private proprietors possess it with regard to owners of the several articles of property the possession of which constitutes private powers over things. With regard to *open* occupations, any party at pleasure possesses it for himself. With regard to *Appropriate* occupations, third persons of various descriptions.

To Occupations —open. —appropriate.

Occupations open.

732. Occupations are either 1st open—2dly appropriate. Almost all occupations not Offices were originally appropriate. An occupation may be said to be open, when any man is left at liberty by Law to exercise it.

Occupations appropriate.

733. An occupation may be said to be appropriate, when such persons alone are left at liberty [to exercise it] as are endued of certain particular qualifications.

Occupations appropriate. Test—Investor.

734. In the case of an *occupation appropriate*, it may be that a man is obliged, before he exercise it, to submitt his qualifications to a certain test; it may be that he is not. In the 1st case, he who administers the ultimate test, is the party possessed of the investitive power: as the Bishop with respect to the Clerical occupation.[1] In the latter case, the Judge to whom it belongs to try a man for exercising the occupation against Law, is the party possessed of the investitive power in the first instance.[2]

Power ⲭ Right. Right ⲭ Power.

735. An *Officer* has a right to a fee: we do not say power: because the concurrence, the consent, of the party solvable is necessary to the Officer's taking it. He cannot take it by force. We say power over the money when he has got it.

Tests final ⲭ Mediate = intervening = interlocutory.

736. There may be Tests upon Tests. Tests are either ultimate or mediate.

Prefat. Qualifications for the enterprize.

737. A man must possess a *copia verborum*: he must be fully possest of the riches of the language: a qualification which belongs to him in common with the Poet: only they occupy different quarters of the language.

[1] Ordination was subject to the approval of an examining bishop, who was 'not obliged to give any reason for his refusal' of a candidate: see Richard Burn, *Ecclesiastical Law*, 2 vols., London, 1763, ii. 106–13.

[2] Bentham perhaps had in mind the Artificers and Apprentices Act of 1562 (5 Eliz. I, c. 4), which restricted the practice of various trades to persons who had completed a seven-year apprenticeship, specified the classes of persons who could take apprentices and who could be apprenticed, and authorized Justices of the Peace to enforce the provisions of the Act.

He must be acquainted with what are called the learned languages: those roots of our vernacular language, which though in one sense dead, yet have life enough in them to furnish it with a continual encrease:[1] that from them he may *import* expressions where native ones are wanting.

He will also be the better qualified for this task, the more he is acquainted with the various sciences: at least with the import of the terms of them: by a free and extensive commerce of terms with the rest, there is no science but may be considerably enriched.

[737.*] Law Statute = actual)(Common = *inferential*. Law inferential = customary.

---

738. In an *act*, the principle of individuation is easier to fix than in an event.[2] The agent is one man. On the *plus* side, the side of encrease, therefore, the quantity of the event is limited to the motion of that one man. It remains to limit it on the *minus* side, the side of diminution. Now, on this side, it should seem that, for the purposes of Law, it might be limited to signify so much of the motion of the one man in question as is supposed to contribute to the production of the effect in question. *Act*—Point of Individuation.

739. The same limits that would determine the individuality of an act consider'd in a legal view, would not circumscribe the individuality of it consider'd in another view, or consider'd simply as an event. A Blow is given, which occasions death. The party who gave the blow is prosecuted at Law; and occasion arises to make mention of the *act*. What is meant by it in this case? As much of the motion of the man's whole body as is supposed to have contributed to the death, which is the effect in question. A Physiologist, considering the same blow, might find occasion to divide it into as many different acts as there were muscles set in motion, or distinguishable fibres in those muscles. Still, however, all that this principle will do for us is to ascertain the quantity of motion resulting from one single exertion of the will. It will ascertain what we mean by the act in the instance mentioned, when the effect is produced by a single blow. But suppose many blows to have concurred to the production of the effect: what is it we mean by the act in this case? One blow alone, or all of them together? The answer is, either: neither in exclusion of the other. We may mean all of them together, when we speak of the act of killing. We may mean one only, when we speak of the act of giving such or such a blow. *Act*. Principle of Individuation. Instance—in a wound.

[1] The phrase 'those roots . . . encrease' has been marked by Bentham for deletion.

[2] The final four words in the sentence have been marked by Bentham for deletion.

Not ascertainable by any general rule.

740. What follows from this? This, I think: that with respect to the thing signified by the word 'act', as with respect to every thing else, we ought, indeed, to keep an eye to the principle of individuation, as being that without which no clear idea of the object can be attained; but that, if not impossible, it is to the last degree difficult to lay down any general rule that shall serve to ascertain it. All we have to do, is to take warning concerning it, as a point that is to be attended to, and to observe to ascertain it in every particular instance where it is material to the end we have in view.

Exposition—modes of.

741. The different ways in which exposition may be performed are [x]. It may be performed by Definition; by specific enumeration; by Distinction; by Individualization; by Synonymation; by Paraphrasis. These operations may, any of them, properly enough be [referred to] under the name of exposition. Of all of them, examples may be met with in the Statute-Book. Of Expository regulations there will accordingly be [x] sorts. 1. Definitional, 2. Enumerative, 3. Distinctive, 4. Individualizing, 5. Synonymating, 6. Paraphrastic. 7. Divisional.

Individualization what.

742. A proposition may be said to be *individualizing* when the purport of it is to ascertain, with respect to any such mass of matter as is contained under one denomination, the limits between that and all other matter of the same species: a rule given for ascertaining the extent and boundaries of any given individual of the species in question; so as to distinguish an entire individual 1st from[1]

Power X Right. Power to receive.

743. It is a common phrase to say, I give such an one power to receive:[2] but then, in such a case, the consent of the payee is supposed.[3]

Where a man has a power over a thing, he has a right to oppose by force any one who attempts to meddle with it against his consent, or to prevent his meddling with it. A power to punish the man, so it be *propriâ manu*,[4] in the first instance.

---

[1] The passage has been abandoned at this point. In the margin, Bentham has noted: 'instance—what shall be one *House*; a very nice question in many respects.' For a discussion of the individualization of a house see paras. 983–4, pp. 302–4 below.

[2] In the text, Bentham has noted at this point: 'Power of Attorney.'

[3] In the text, Bentham has noted at this point: 'Power of Appointment in a Conveyance.'

[4] i.e. 'with his own hand'.

744. Of persons who could entertain any such conceptions of the science, thus much is plain, that they saw not their way through it: which being the case, they were persuaded it had no bottom, because they could see none.

Law—inutility of Lectures.

The way in which a Master can be of use to a student in any art or science, is either that of doctrine or discipline. In the way of doctrine, by exhibiting, where there are any to exhibit, those phænomena which constitute the subject matter of the science: or even, where there are none, by being ready to obviate such unforeseen and occasional difficulties as may chance to present themselves. In the way of discipline, by overseeing the [pupils],[1] and observing that he does actually take that instruction which the books that are extant present him with.

But Law, unless it be in the way of solving occasional difficulties or of superintendency, it is as preposterous to think of teaching it by lectures as it would Natural History by books.

---

745. 747.[2] The two auxiliary particles, shall and will, have this between them; they both serve to announce futurity. They have also this in common; they both serve, in certain cases, to announce the futurity of the event as the consequence of volition. But the import of them has this difference: Shall imports volition when prefixed to the second and third persons only: it imports it not when applied to the first. 'I or we shall be beaten' does not announce the beating as about to be the consequence of my will. 'Thou shalt', 'you shall', or 'he, she or they shall be beaten' does. Attributed to the second and third persons, it announces the event in question, the beating, to be the consequence of the volition of the first. Active or Passive voice makes no difference.

Shall and Will.[3]

On the contrary, with respect to the particle *will*, it is only when connected with the 1st person, that it is universally significative of volition: applied to either the second or the third person, it is sometimes significative of volition, sometimes not. It may be used indifferently either in the design of intimating the existence of volition, or without such design. 'I, we, will beat you.' 'I, we, will be beaten.' This can not do otherwise than intimate volition, the volition of one who speaks, to be the cause of the event I am speaking of. 'Thou wilt, you will beat him.' 'Thou wilt, you will be

Will—the Particle, it's different Senses. Examples.

[1] MS 'pupils'.

[2] Bentham has numbered this paragraph both 745 and 747.

[3] In the margin, Bentham has noted at this point: 'See Wallis' *Grammar*.' See John Wallis, *Grammatica Linguæ Anglicanæ. Cui præfigitur, De Loquela, sive Sonorum Formatione, Tractatus Grammatico–Physicus*, Oxford, 1653, pp. 93–5, where the signification of 'will' and 'shall' when used as auxiliary verbs is discussed.

beaten: 'he, she, they will beat him;' 'he, she, they will be beaten.' These expressions, at any rate, do all of them intimate the futurity of the event of beating or being beaten: but whether that event is expected to be the consequence of the volition of the party by the agency of whom or to whom it is about to happen, is not expressed. It may be understood to be meant to be represented as the consequence of such volition, or it may not. Whether in any given case it is so meant is to be collected, in speaking, from the context and tone of voice, in writing, from the context only and no otherwise.

'You will beat him.' For your Master has resolved *you shall*.[1] You will beat him: because you yourself have resolved to do it. In the first of these two phrases, the event is not spoken of as the result of the volition of the party whose action is announced as about to take place: but of the volition of another person: or it might be of no person at all.

When the object the action of which is in question, is a being unsusceptible of volition, there the case is clear: volition can not be supposed to be intimated at all.

It shall be beaten—[2]

Shall constitutes a Mood, and is Imperative.

746. The particle *shall*, therefore, besides a tense, not only constitutes what may properly be stiled an imperative mood, but a mood that is much more energetically imperative than that which goes commonly by that name.[3] It intimates the volition of the speaker to be so peremptory and determinate, so necessarily productive of it's effect, that the act of the person *spoken to* or spoken of can do no otherwise than ensue from it. It is not only wished that it may ensue, but it is taken for granted that it will.

In impersonals, *it* shall: *it* will.

In these two particles is allowed to reside a great portion of the energy, and no small share of the difficulty, of our language.

Classification.

748.[4] Technical words will admitt of no other than a technical arrangement. The natural arrangement of the component parts of the system of Jurisprudence is that which distributes them according to the different relations they severally bear to the one

[1] In the margin, Bentham has noted at this point: '☛ Nota.' No relevant note has been identified.

[2] The sentence has been abandoned at this point.

[3] In the margin, Bentham has noted at this point: 'It is only the future time that imperation can respect. 'Tis only in time future that any individual among sorts of things that are the objects of imperation can exist.'

[4] Paragraph numbers from this point on have been editorially supplied. For further details see the Editorial Introduction, pp. xxvii–xxviii above.

common end, Happiness. This end being in universal seeking, the name of it is in universal use. Of every division of Jurisprudence, however narrow or however extensive, thus much [may] be said, that it is distinguishable into an intimation of an act of volition, and of the mode of conduct that is the object of that volition.[1] The act of volition admitts of no variety: it is in all cases simple, indivisible, one and the same. The varieties, therefore, that an article of Law admitts of, are all referable to the description of the mode of conduct that is the object of it. For the prime divisions, therefore, of a natural System of Jurisprudence, for as many as can be thus distinguished, the proper title is always some expression which shall serve to characterise the relation of the mode of conduct comprehended by them to the common end. A division marked out upon this principle will have for it's title some mode of felicity or infelicity which it is the nature of the mode of conduct in question to destroy or to produce. Now, with compartments marked out upon such [a] principle, compartments such as are delineated and characterized by the technical terms in use can never, for any continuance, coincide. When these technical compartments were framed, it was without any attention paid to, or prospect of, the end. Modes of conduct were made obligatory without any thought of their conformity to it: other modes made penal without any thought of their disconformity. The hand of power was stretched over the modifications of men's conduct, either without respect to any end at all, or with respect to a different one. The main and almost only end men had in view in administering what was called Justice, was the advancement of what was called piety and what was called loyalty. What was not done to the honour of God was done to the profit of the King. The King was every thing: the people nothing. The great men of the realm, his chief and only regarded subjects, his tenants, companions and rivals took care of themselves by other methods than come under the denomination of the administration of Justice. In the great, their offensive and defensive operations were performed by public legislation: in the detail, by private violence. Judges were the King's creatures: the breath of his nostrils:[2] the organs of his will. The King was the central point from whence every thing emaned, and towards which every thing gravitated in return.

[1] In the margin, Bentham has noted at this point: 'The contents of a Division are determined by the extent of the terms by which it is named. Where these terms are technical, the whole System must be unnatural, and uninstructive, as those terms themselves are.'

[2] An echo of Job 4: 9.

Punishment. End. False classification the result of principles adverse to utility.

749 Was justice to be done in matters of private property? It was that the King's repose might not be disturbed by the clamours of the injured.[1] Was a man to be punished for base coinage? It was because the King's image had been profaned, or his rights usurped. The King had a monopoly in that sort of forgery, and would bear no concurrents.[2]

Felony.

750. Without any end at all. The punishment of a crime, because the same with that of another in certain respects, was to be the same in all. For the latter, it had been thought fit that a man should be put to death by hanging: his possessions engulphed in those of the King. His Wife and Children reduced to beggary. His very posterity gored through his sides by being [incapacitated][3] from taking a succession from a common Ancestor. Society in general wounded through his sides by being deprived of the chance it might have of receiving [the] benefit of his testimony. This complicated punishment, of which the ingredients are not all even yet enumerated, was called Felony. Was it thought fit that, for any other offence ever so remote in it's nature from this, a man should be put to death? This second man's possessions were to be swept into the same gulph: this second man's wife and children were to be exposed to the same misery: through this second man's sides were his posterity and society at large in like manner to be wounded. For where a man had been punished by hanging, his punishment had been called Felony. Therefore, Felony was the name for the punishment of him who was punished by hanging. And these were parts of the punishment called Felony. In short, when a man had done any thing for which it was thought fit to punish him with hanging, it saved time to say he had done Felony. And so offences for which a man was to be punished by hanging were called Felonies.[4] The essential qualities of the crime described by the nature of the Punishment annext to it by accidental apparitions. And thus a Class of modes of conduct

[1] The phrase *ne amplius inde clamorem audiamus*, i.e. that we no longer hear complaint thereof', appeared in original writs of the *praecipe* type: see Blackstone, *Commentaries on the Laws of England*, iii. 274 and Appendix I, p.i.

[2] Bentham perhaps had in mind ibid., iv. 89–90: 'Clipping or defacing the genuine coin was not hitherto included in these statutes [i.e. respecting treasons relative to the coin]; though an offence equally pernicious to trade, and an equal insult upon the prerogative, as well as personal affront to the sovereign; whose very image ought to be had in reverence by all loyal subjects.'

[3] MS 'incapicated'.

[4] According to Blackstone, *Commentaries on the Laws of England*, iv. 97, 98, although 'capital punishment does by no means enter into the true idea and definition of felony', yet 'The idea of felony is indeed so generally connected with that of capital punishment, that we find it hard to separate them; and to this usage the interpretations of the law do now conform.'

was formed, having nothing in their description common, nor in that of their natural effects, but having this given to them in common, that they were punished by the same punishment. A thick mist was thus thrown over the nature of these offences (thus unnaturally associated) by this detestable appellation, more detestable than many of the crimes which it was made to characterise, and, if possible, than the mode of punishment it announced: pregnant with all the mischief of that mode of punishment, because tending to perpetuate it by screening it from our eyes.

Now, then, what sort of instruction can be expected from that arrangement in which the word Felony must mark out, and stand at the head of, a compartment?

---

751. There is one class of men who are interested by Profession and by engagement against every advancement that shall be made in [the] moral department of science, as Quacks are interested against the progress of genuine physic. *These* men have a nostrum of their own, which, because the patent for it is theirs, they persist in throwing in, notwithstanding every experience of the inefficacy of it to salutary purposes, and the natural and unavoidable efficacy of it to baneful ones. These men, I say, have a perpetual and indefeasible interest in the depression of moral science: were it possible that it should be a secret to them, I would perish rather than make it public. But they know it but too well; nor are they backward, on any occasion, to turn their knowlege into practise. I tell it, therefore, that, of the rest of mankind, such as without warning might be not aware of it, may take heed and guard against the workings of an interest inimical to their own.

Religionists interested against the advancement of morality.

752. No signal progress can be made in [the] moral department of science, but at the expence of the credit of their nostrum. When their nostrum was at the [height][1] of it's repute, when it was the sole antidote depended on for the cure of every moral ailment, morality was at it's lowest ebb: and as morality improves, their nostrum in proportion sinks into neglect.

Relig. Sanction: manners worse in proportion as it has been stronger.

---

753. In the infancy of our history, it was a sort of theocracy that we were governed by: and the felicity of society was what might be expected under such a state. The religious sanction was resorted to upon every occasion: the political sanction was feeble to the last degree of debility: the moral was, in a manner, swallow'd up in the religious. The very names of honour, virtue, probity, reputation,

Religious Sanction—it's evil influence on ancient Law.

[1] MS 'heigth'.

Roman names for Roman sentiments, were unknown; as much as that of a ship is to Bohemians.[1] Force and chance were every thing. If one man did an injury to another, the injurer and injured were to fight it out. Justice maintained a strict neutrality. All that a Judge had to do was to see fair play. Applause and triumph were for the successful villain: scorn and infamy were for the hapless sufferer. If a man was lucky enough to poison the father, his punishment consisted in the having a fair and equal chance given him of ripping open the belly of the son. If he succeeded there too, God saw him and sanctified his ways. This was one way in which God was made to judge.[2] Another way, one might almost have said *the* other way, was this. If you had done a man an injury, you were asked whether you would swear you had not done it: if you would, God, who had sat an unconcerned spectator of the baneful act, was to avenge with present perdition the empty words. If he failed of doing this, you were innocent.[3] This was another way in which God was made to judge. A miracle carried with it nothing extraordinary to men scarce more acquainted than the beasts are with the ordinary course of nature; and with whom, if all they saw was truth, half what they heard, and all they read, was lies. Monks were their daily and, in a manner, their sole intelligencers. Monks were to them what newspapers are to us. As we hear of accidental deaths or fortunate escapes, so did they of signs, providences and prodigies. What thieves and robbers are to us, hobgoblins and devils were to them. If they heard thunder in the clouds, they

[1] In the margin, Bentham has noted at this point: 'See Michaelis. / Mosheim. } Qu.' According to Johann David Michaelis, *De l'influence des opinions sur le langage, et du langage sur les opinions. Dissertation qui a remporté le prix de l'Académie Royale des Sciences & belles lettres de Prusse, en 1759*, Bremen, 1762, p. 77, 'la langue Bohémienne [i.e. Czech] . . . manque absolument de termes pour la marine'. The corrupt state of morality under the pagan religion is the theme of John Lawrence Mosheim, *An Ecclesiastical History, Antient and Modern, from the Birth of Christ to the beginning of the present century: in which The Rise, Progress, and Variations of Church Power are considered In their Connexion with the State of Learning and Philosophy, and the Political History of Europe during that Period*, trans. Archibald Maclaine, 2 vols., London, 1765, i. 1–12.

[2] According to Blackstone, *Commentaries on the Laws of England*, iv. 340, trial by battle, which was introduced into England after the Norman Conquest and formally abolished in 1819, was, like the other ordeals, 'another species of presumptuous appeals to providence, under an expectation that heaven would unquestionably give the victory to the innocent or injured party'.

[3] Wager of law or compurgation, formally abolished in 1833, was a mode of trial available in a limited number of actions where the dispute concerned some private transaction such as the payment of a debt, whereby a defendant could establish his or her innocence by swearing an oath, along with a certain number of other persons, known as compurgators, who would swear that they believed the defendant's oath to be made in good faith. For Blackstone's account of wager of law see ibid., iii. 341–8.

imagined dæmons grumbling in them; if they picked up a stone, it was a thunderbolt: the extraordinary they saw was an unceasing confirmation of the impossible they heard of. Not knowing what was conformable to the course of nature, they knew not what was contrary to it. As all men *were* sinners, and all men *are* exposed to suffer, they never wanted extraordinary providences while they saw calamities. If the impious suffer'd in the body, it was the present punishment of his impiety: if he prosper'd, it was to make the punishment that was to come more bitter: if punishment on the body never came, but the body went on prospering to it's end, tenfold vengeance was to be wreaked upon the soul; and least this should be doubted of, devils were seen, upon occasion, to fly away with it.

---

754. The discourse of our ancestors was altogether of sins and not at all of immoralities. At present, we hear altogether of immoralities and not at all of sins. The grounds for expecting the religious sanction are universally looked upon as so weak, that men are ashamed to use any expressions from which it might be thought they were influenced by the expectation of it. When I mention this, I mention a plain matter of fact, which, however unwelcome it may be to many ears, they are in the highest degree interested to be made aware of, and not at all the less interested because it is unwelcome. As the decay of piety is visible, while that of morality is not so, at least not visible, piety might be suspected as not being of that importance to good morals which it is their interest it should be thought to be.

Relig. Sanction—it's influence weak.

755. To prevent this, the fire of their artillery against the character of the age is at all events to be kept up. Because there are immoralities committed in it, it is immoral: and least the list of these should not be ample enough, it is swelled with the catalogue of our enjoyments. Luxury is the word cherished in this view, as that which, by the convenient ambiguity of it's import, will envelop, under one common covering of infamy, that by which we are made happy and that by which we are made miserable.[1]

The force of it, why levelled against innocent enjoyments—Luxury.

Luxury is the use of Riches: Riches are the very cause and effect and evidence of corruption. The very touch of them is enough to

[1] In the text, Bentham has interposed the following passage at this point:

'This is their stronghold: their strong castle of offence and defence.

'In this war, they have a perpetual and numerous company of auxiliaries; the ignorant, the envious, the malevolent, the disappointed, the splenetic, and the unhappy.

'Nor are his advances any where so conspicuous as those he makes in the character of the whining and lamenting moralist: a phalanx of passions and prejudices then combat on his side.'

damn a man at pleasure. If he gets them, it is covetousness: if he keeps them, it is avarice: if he spends them, it is luxury: if he gives them, it is ostentation. The thunders of the Gospel are hurled at them with tremendous . . . . . . which is then only silent, when, at the same time that Religion is proved the foundation of good morals, the strong-box of the clergy is to be proved the corner-stone of Religion.[1]

Faith defined.

756. Faith may be defined a belief conceived without apparently sufficient grounds, through the influence of fear.

The faith which is the child either of hope or fear, is not a steady perception[2] of the truth of the propositions pretended to be believed: but a determined resolution not to heed any considerations to the contrary. In effect, however, faith and belief will sometimes be much the same: since, in the former case, if the proposition be not strictly speaking believed, yet the result may be, in this case as in the other, to act as if it were.

Religious Sanction. It's strength at the highest in barbarous ages.

757.[3] Perhaps for many centuries, through the whole expanse of ecclesiastical dominion, there was no such person as a steady unbeliever. It is thinking too highly of their understanding, and too badly of their heart, to suppose that even the most crafty and most interested blowers of the bubble were in the secret of it's inanity. There is not a greater error, though it be so natural and so common an one, than to suppose that pious fraud of necessity imports a conviction of the badness of the cause for which it is set-a-going. The impostures of which a man was himself the author, he knew, indeed, to be impostures: but similar impostures framed by his predecessors he credited as truths. And the impostures which he framed, he set-a-going only to give what he thought the due weight to those he credited.

To believe that all those who act in a manner in which it were to be wished, for the sake of others, they did not act, are designing knaves, is an error the more seducing in that it bears upon the face of it the print of perspicacity.

The dupe and the impostor (at least the enthusiast and the impostor) are much nearer allied, are much oftener to be met with in the same person, than people are apt in general to imagine.

---

[1] The discussion is continued at para. 757 below.
[2] MS orig. 'persuasion'.
[3] The discussion is resumed from para. 755 above.

758. An interest which is strong in ***magnitude*** has many a great advantage over one that is strong only in extent, that is in the number of those that are partakers of it.

An Interest strong in magnitude ⪤ in extent.

A great interest is felt when, perhaps, a little interest is scarce seen. Those among whom a great interest is shared, being few, may form themselves into a body and learn to act in concert: if they are already embodied, their power is still more formidable.

A strong interest has more weight in politics than an extensive one.

If the stronger interest, taking extent into consideration, were universally prevalent, every thing would be as it should be: there could be no bad government; men would every where be as happy as good government could make them.

---

759. The word Possession is used by Lawyers in three senses very different, very distinguishable, which yet never are distinguished.

Possession—3 Senses of.

760. The one is that which it may bear without respect to Law. This is that in which it may be stiled *Physical.*

Possession Physical.

761. A second is that in which it has respect to Law in general; to legal obligation in general. This is the sense in which it ranks among the terms of universal Jurisprudence. This sense of it I would stile the *legal.*

Possession Legal.

762. A third is that in which it has a confined respect to English Jurisprudence: in which the right that it expresses is limited by conditions annexed to it by English Jurisprudence. This sense of the word I would call the *technical.*

Possession Technical.

763. Legal Possession may be distinguished into total and partial.

Possession total.
————partial.

By total, I mean the possession of all the uses indiscriminately that can be made of the thing possessed. By partial, I mean of some certain use or uses only.

An Estate, an Income, may consist in [1st] the total legal possession of a moveable: 2^{d} the [partial][1] possession of a moveable: 3dly the total possession of an immoveable: 4^{thly} the partial possession of an immoveable: 5^{thly} a succession of services of the same single person, or of single persons of the same sort in succession.

764. Under the name of services may be comprehended acts of *payment.* Services, then, may be distinguished into Services personal: and these into active and passive. Services energetic[2] are either 1st of body, Corporeal, or bodily services; 2^{d} of mind, mental services; 3dly Mixt.

Services personal.
—concessional.
—Payments.
—active.
—passive.
—corporeal.
—mental.
—mixt.

Corporal services must have a material subject: that is there

[1] MS 'total' appears to be a slip.   [2] i.e. active services.

must be a substance which is the material object of the assemblage of physical acts in which they consist.

Possession Sole. Possession in Society.
Possession in commonalty. Possession in confederacy = conjunction. Possession indiscriminate)(conjunct.

765. Occupancy sole)(Possession in Society.

Possession in Society is either 1st in commonalty, or 2dly in confederacy. Possession in commonalty is that of Jointenants, Coparcenars, and Tenants in Common by the English Law.[1] Possession in confederacy is that which persons that are members of a corporation have of a thing that is the property of the corporation.

Services passive. *Droit de prœlibation.*

766. Instances of corporal services of the passive kind considerable enough to make a figure separately and to acquire a name, instances of such services, I say, resulting from relations other than natural, are not very common. One instance, however, we have of a service of this kind which is pretty remarkable. By custom, in a few places in England and in Scotland, and indeed other parts of Europe, the wife of a Tenant was under an obligation to submitt to the embraces of the Lord on the wedding night.[2]

Profit. How drawn out of Offices.
Fees of Office—Perquisites.

767. A Profit is drawn out of Offices in this manner. A monopoly is given to the Officer of services either naturally or legally beneficial: and then the rendering of other services to the Officer is made the condition to his rendering these. These services beneficial, of which the benefit is to the Officer, are usually services of payment. Whether they are services of payment, or in general services of concession, if due of legal right, they are termed *Fees of Office*; if not due of legal right, but yielded only in virtue of a custom not legalized, they are termed Perquisites.

Service beneficial, by institution.

768. The benefit of a service may be said to be legally or artificially beneficial when the performance of it is render'd as a condition annext to the perception of some special benefit conferred by Law. As the sealing of a patent, the passing an account, the giving a certificate, &c.

---

[1] On possession in commonalty see Blackstone, *Commentaries on the Laws of England*, ii. 180–94.

[2] Bentham may have derived his account of the custom of *jus primae noctis*, also known as *droit de seigneur* and *droit de cuissage*, from the article by François Marie Arouet, known as Voltaire (1694–1778), entitled 'Cuissage ou culage, droit de prélibation, de marquette, &c.', in *Questions sur l'encyclopédie, distribuées en forme de dictionnaire. Par des amateurs*, 9 vols., Geneva, 1770–2, iv. 195–8, which suggested that the right had its origin in Scotland. According to Blackstone, *Commentaries on the Laws of England*, ii. 83, while the practice never existed in England, it did so in Scotland, under the name of 'mercheta' or 'marcheta', until abolished by Malcolm III (d. 1093), King of Scots from 1058.

769. Partial possession is naturally capable of being as various as the ways in which a man may make use of a thing are various. Possession partial. Modes of, naturally infinite.

In a word, legal possession of a thing consists in nothing but in the being at liberty to exercise such acts upon a thing as other men are not left at liberty to exercise upon it. Now these acts, it is evident, are as many as are capable of a separate description. The possible modes of partial possession are, therefore, infinite. What we shall have to speak of are those established and recognized by Law.

---

770. By a service may be meant any such act whereby one man contributes to the pleasure of another. The party so contributing may be termed the party serving: the other, the party served. The ideas belonging to these expressions might, if that tyrannical and capricious organ the ear would admit of it, be more commodiously expressed by the terms *servor* and *servee*. 'A Service.' Defined. Party *serving*. —served. Servor and Servee.

Instruments of enjoyment or preservation, are either things or persons. Persons are so in virtue of the *services* they render.

771. An Income is a successive accession of certain allotments of articles of wealth, things valuable. An Income.

Under the general name Fortune is comprized as well an income as the æstimated value of it in a mass of wealth to be paid down at once. A Fortune.

What wealth, therefore, may consist of is, 1st *powers over* things, 2dly *Rights to* Services.

772. A Volition is either 1st. Pure: or 2dly. Conditional (or upon Condition). It is said to be *pure*, when it is annext to the article of conduct which is the modal object of it under all circumstances whatsoever. It is said to be *conditional*, when it is annext to it only *in certain circumstances*, or when it is annext to it in all circumstances, certain particular ones excepted. In either of these cases it is said to [be] entertained *upon condition*; that is, upon condition these circumstances subsist. Volition pure—Volition Conditional.

773. A condition to a volition is an exception to the circumstances of the mode of conduct which is the object of the volition, as what is commonly called an exception is to the mode of conduct itself. Whether the Volition shall be deemed pure or conditional, depends often upon the name under which the objects of volition make their appearance in the mind. Condition to a Volition.

---

774. In that branch of Metaphysics which may be termed Classification, the business is to find such a term, as in many Rule of Classification. Find a common divisor.

processes of Arithmetic to find such a number, as shall serve as a *common divisor* to other quantities.

A Condition running with the Estate.

775. A Condition running with an estate, is a controuling circumstance annext to the enjoyment of it, as well while in the hands of the immediate conveyee, as in those of any subsequent one.

A Condition precedent.

776. A Condition precedent is an investitive circumstance made necessary to the *commencement* of the estate.

A Condition subsequent.

777. A Condition subsequent is a divestitive circumstance annext to the *continuance* of it.

Effect of it as a Regulation of itself.

778. When the controlling circumstance on which the continuance of the estate is made to depend is an article of conduct of the possessor, an obligation is laid on him to observe that conduct, proportionate in force to the value of the estate. A regulation is made whereof the modal object is the article of conduct in question: a regulation armed with a penalty which consists in being deprived of the estate in question.

A Condition to an Estate may be an armature to a Private Law.

779. Where the condition to a volition serving to confer a benefit is a mode of conduct of the party meant to be benefitted, the making the loss of the benefit the effect of the non-observance of the mode of conduct creates an obligation on the party meant to be benefitted to observe it; an obligation the force of which is as the value of the benefit.

What an obligation so constituted has to distinguish it from other obligations, is, therefore, that it supposes the existence of a benefit issuing from the same *source* that it does itself.

Laws creating property)(Laws restraining use: i:e: particular uses by the person unrestrained as to the generality.

780. Laws concerning things are either Laws creating property in the several sorts of things, or Laws restraining the use of them.

781. There are two ways in which the use of a thing may be restrained: by Prohibition absolute: by Permission not but upon condition.

Restraint absolute)(conditional = permission = on condition.

Party favoured by a restraint on a proprietor may be 1st. An Individual. 2d. The Neighbourhood. 3dly. The Nation.

782. The account on which the use of a thing is restrained may be either 1st. Personal, 2d. Vicinary,[1] 3d. National.

All the possible ways in which the Law can regard the use of a thing are, it is plain, summed up in these two; the binding him to make that use of it: and the binding him not to make it.

[1] MS orig. 'local'.

783. A Law, Regulation, then, or Rule giving a man the property of a thing must be a regulation or rule binding others not to make use of it, he, with respect to all uses but certain particular specified ones, being left free—a party thus circumstanced is called the proprietor of the thing in question.

A Proprietor. An Owner.

784. A man is said to have a right to do an act when, he himself being left at liberty, others are bound not to oppose him. It is the same thing if we say he is entitled to do it.

Right, a man has a.

785. It is said to be a man's duty to do an act, when at the same time that others are restrained from opposing his doing it, he is not left at liberty whether he will do it or no, but is bound to do it.

Duty, it is a man's.

---

786. To one or other of the three first Sanctions the words that follow, bound, restrained, &c., must, if they have any meaning, be referable.[1] That to which they are here all along to be consider'd as referring, unless otherwise expressed, is the Political.

Legal Terms must all refer to one or other Sanction.

---

787. Those who have been attempting to give a Definition of the word right, have been filling a barrel without a bottom.

Of the word right, no definition is to be given. The way to enable us to form an idea upon the mention of it is to bring it with others into a sentence: and then expound that sentence by such another sentence as contains in it words that *are* capable of being defined.

Right—cannot be expounded but by Paraphrasis.

---

788. A word, to be defined by itself, must suggest an idea by itself. The only words that suggest ideas of themselves, are those significative of Substances or Modes, of masses of matter, or modes of motion or situation of that matter.

Definable words.

---

789. Punishment is pain; not any pain whatsoever: but such pain as is inflicted in consequence of volition, in consideration of some mode of conduct of some person, usually the person by whom the pain is suffer'd.

Punishment.

790. Concerned, therefore, in every law that is creative of property, there are two parties. The *proprietor*, who, being left at liberty to reap a set of pleasures while others are debarred from it, may be stiled the *party favoured*, or the *party in whose favour* the law is established: and those others who, being bound to abstain from those pleasures, may be stiled the parties burthen'd, at whose

Party favoured. —coerced.

[1] The four sanctions are listed, albeit in different orders, at paras. 502/3 and 667, pp. 161–2 and 213–14 above, respectively.

Party against whom = *adversus quem.*

expence the Law is established. The parties thus bound are said to be parties against whom the proprietor has a right, against whom he is proprietor. When a man is said to have a right simply, without saying against whom, it is supposed that he has a right against mankind in general.

Co-proprietors.

791. Where there are several persons proprietors against the rest of mankind, but not as against one another, between such persons as to those uses with respect to which they are proprietors, the Law does nothing. There is no Law at all about the matter. Persons thus circumstanced are stiled *Co-proprietors.*

The uses which a man is at liberty to make of a thing or not to make of a thing which is his property are indefinite.

Words undefinable.

792. Words that can not be defined are: 1st. Substantives improper. 2d. All Attributives. 3rdly. All Definitives. 4thly. All Connectives. [5thly.][1] Of Substantives, only certain classes.

The Substantives that are capable of being defined are such only as are significant of themselves. Mr Harris has made this the general characteristic of a Substantive, that it is significant of itself.[2] But of substantives that are not, in truth, significant of themselves, but only by fiction, there is a large class. Such are all those terms, though substantives in point of Grammatical form, which, in universal Jurisprudence, are made use of to express the course taken by punishment in it's application to the several modes of conduct that are made objects of it.[3]

Gratitude—Virtue—Disposition.

It is true that, of these words said to be undefinable, there are many that may stand in subalternation to others: but then such a subalternation, to what length soever it may extend, always ends in some word that is not significant of itself. Thus, we may say of Gratitude that it is a virtue: and of virtue, that it is a disposition. But what idea does the word disposition give us? None.

Substantives undefinable.

793. Words, then, that are undefinable are: 1st. Words that have no superior genus. 2dly. Words of a System the *summum genus* of which is a word not significant of itself.

A term to be capable of being defined, must signify a thing capable of attributes. A word, to signify a thing capable of attributes, must be significant of itself.

[1] MS '4thly.'

[2] See Harris, *Hermes*, p. 37: 'Substantives are *all those principal Words, which are significant of Substances, considered as Substances.*'

[3] In the text, Bentham has noted at this point: 'v. 328.' See para. 795, p. 249 below.

794. The word right is one of those words which, tho' in the grammatical form of substantives, are not, as proper substantives are, significant of themselves, any more than a preposition is significant of itself. The word right, a right, has, it is true, the grammatical form [of] a substantive: and Substantives, in general, are such as denote substances: if not real concrete substances, at least fictitious abstract ones. But the word right, of itself, does not denote a substance, real or fictitious: of itself it does not denote any thing. 'Right, a.'

The word right, tho' a substantive, is not significant of itself, any more than a preposition is significant of itself. The word right is not significant of itself, any more than the word {'for'} is significant of itself. Who is there that ever supposed it possible to define 'for'? No man. As little is it possible to define 'a right'. To give an idea of the use that the word {'for'} is of in the expression of our ideas, we must produce an example of a sentence in which it bears a part. The same method, and no other, must be taken in explaining the word a right. Now, the word right not signifying any thing that is capable of attributes, what signification can those adjectives have that are subjoined to it in the form of attributes? None, till the meaning of it has been explained, as above, by *paraphrase*. 'For.' Paraphrase.

---

795. Of the whole business of Law, thus much may be said in general. [It] consists in nothing more than in setting forth the connection that there is established between punishment and the several modes of conduct that are the objects of Law. Punishment all in all.

---

796. A motion must be [1^{stly}] in some time. It must be 2dly in some place. 3$^{dly.}$ If an action, it must be of some person. 4$^{thly.}$ It must be exerted on some person or some thing. 5$^{thly.}$ It must be in some direction. 6$^{thly.}$ It must be in some *circumstances*. The object moving must be surrounded with some other objects, all of them either moving or at rest. The distinguishable parts of these objects must be at some certain distances from each other, and from those of the moving body in question. Laws repugnant.

A Law, therefore, to be repugnant to another must be identical with it in respect 1st of the Time, sc. of the conduct which is the object of the Law, not of the *passing* of the Law. It must have the same Temporal or Chronological field of Dominion. 2$^{dly.}$ In respect of Place. It must have the same Local or Geographical or Territorial field. 3$^{dly.}$ In respect of personal agent: it must have the same personal field. 4$^{thly.}$ In respect of mode of conduct. It must have the same moral field. 5thly. In respect of passive object: it must concern the same thing or patient. It must have the same real field. In the same place, at the same time, by persons of the same sort, it must will the same act to be done, under the same circumstances in which it's antagonist wills it not to be done; or not to be done, in the same circumstances in which the antagonist wills it to be done. In every other respect they must be identical. In this alone they must be opposite: the modal object of the one must be action, while that of the other is forbearance: or forbearance, while that of the other is action. In other words, the modal object of the one must be feasance, while that of the other is non-feasance; motion, while that of the other is rest. It may be said that the modal object of the one may be motion one way, while that of the other is motion another way. But it is not this that will make them opposite. If one Law commands motion one way, another, to be opposite to it, must command rest that same way; the commanding of motion another way is, then, a third and distinct command from that which was antagonistical to the first. Suppose the motion to be performable both ways (as it may be where the two Laws differ in respect of time) and there is no repugnancy between them.

Antagonist.

Laws different X repugnant.

797. The Laws of France are *different* from those of England. But they are not repugnant: owing to the want of co-incidence in point [of] place: they have not the same local field.

Conveyance absolute.

798. A Conveyance is either absolute: or conditional; upon Condition. Estates according[ly] are held either absolutely or upon condition. They are Estates absolute, or Estates upon condition.

Conveyance conditional.

799. A Conveyance absolute is a command to persons in general, the conveyee excepted, to abstain from using the estate in question (convey'd) in all circumstances, at least without any being specified by the conveyor as circumstances in which he does not command them so to do.

Conveyance upon condition subsequent.

800. A Conveyance upon condition subsequent is two commands: the 1st to persons in general (the conveyee excepted) to abstain from using the estate, not in all circumstances whatsoever: but in all some one circumstance only excepted; the second a command to persons in general, this circumstance subsisting, still to abstain as before; but not the abovementioned conveyee now excepted, but some one else. This circumstance may be stiled the *devesting* circumstance.

Devesting circumstance.

---

801. Technical Possession is legal Possession liable to be vacated by the demonstration of the existence of some prior entitling circumstance to that by which he was invested. Possession Technical.

802. A Right of Possession in the technical sense, i:e: without actual Technical Possession or right of property, is that which a man has who is supposed to be able to demonstrate the subsistence of some entitling circumstance in his favour prior to and exclusive of that by which the party actually in possession became entitled, but which might be render'd ineffective by the demonstration of the existence of some investing incident prior to and exclusive of the former. Right of Possession technical.

---

803. An investing or devesting clause in a conveyance is the appointment of an investing or devesting incident. Investing circumstance) (incident.

---

804. There are two situations which the term to be defined may occupy in the definition: it may precede the rest of the Definition, or it may follow it. In the first case, the form of the Definition may be said to be direct; in the latter, *inverse*. Definition direct. —inverse.

For Definitions of the Paraphrastic kind, the inverse form will often be found the most commodious.

---

805. With respect to occupations, or in general to classes, that are *open*, the investitive power at least, if not the divestitive, belongs to every man for himself. Investment in *open* classes.

---

806. A Conveyance upon a condition precedent is no conveyance till the investing incident subsists. From that period, if there be no devesting incident appointed, it is a conveyance absolute. Conveyance upon Condition Subsequent. Investing Circumstance.

The circumstance may be either: 1$^{st.}$ An event out of man's power, an event purely physical: 2$^{dly.}$ An event within power, an article of human conduct; or situation of things brought about by human conduct. The conduct in question (we will suppose it, for the convenience of discourse, to be an act rather than a forbearance) is an act either of the conveyor himself: 2dly of the Conveyee: or 3dly of some third person.

It is plain that if the thing has an owner, the same event that is the investing circumstance with respect to one man, is the devesting circumstance with respect to another.

Condition—various senses of. Condition = a Law. Condition = an Action.

807. The sense of the word Condition is perpetually shifting in the mouths of Lawyers. At one time they consider it as a Law. 'Tis in this sense they speak of the breach of it when they speak of it as being a thing that may be broken: at another time they look upon it as being the action that is the object of the Law. 'Tis in this sense they speak of it as being *performed* or not performed.

Current Language, how confused.

808. From this, amongst so many other instances, one sees how unfit the current language among lawyers is in it's present state to give any tolerably clear conception of the things it seems designed to signify. How much it stands in want of reformation. It requires to be cleared, and to be enriched. To be cleared of terms equivocal and obscure: to be enriched with terms univocal and precise.

Condition—various senses of.

809. When consider'd as signifying a Law, sometimes it is consider'd as a Law simply without regard to any *armature*: thus it is with it, when spoken of simply as a thing that may be broken. Sometimes it is consider'd as a Law characterized by it's armature: thus it is with it when spoken of as a thing that is to be distinguished from a Limitation or a Covenant. From a Covenant, as being armed not with foreign damages, but with a forfeiture of the thing convey'd. From a Limitation, in that the benefit of the penalty denounced by the armature is appointed to go not to a succedaneous particular conveyee, but to the conveyor himself or his natural Representative.

The great difficulty is to determine in what light to consider it when it has the proposition 'upon' before it, in the phrase 'upon condition'. That is as we say in English. 'Under Condition', said the Latins; 'a condition que' [in] modern French; '*Επι τουτω εφ ω τε*', said the Greeks; 'con conditione che', say the Italians; 'a condiciòn que', say the Spaniards.

A Conveyance.

810. To have a clear idea of a conveyance, we must conceive of it in this manner: a conveyance is an individual command of the investitive kind, issued by a private person with an armature borrow'd from the government, appointing the conveyee to be the party favoured under the general Law of appropriation, as far as concerns that one of the real objects [of] the Law which is the thing that is convey'd, in the room of the conveyor. Repealing, therefore, that Law as against the [conveyee];[1] and establishing it as against the conveyor.

[1] MS 'conveyor' contradicts the evident sense of the passage.

811. Power and Right, when beneficial, are given to one man as against others by their being restrained while he is left at liberty. The person thus left at liberty may, as against those who are so restrained, be said to be favoured, the party favoured: they may be said to be coerced, the parties coerced. Power and Right.

Power over persons or over things that are in the *general* possession of other men, accompanied with duty, is where certain persons, the persons coerced, are restrained from opposing certain actions, but the agent is not left at liberty whether he will perform them or no: but is constrained to perform them. This is the case of Powers *fiduciary*, certain circumstances being supposed subsisting.

812. Possession, whether total or partial, may be distinguished into Ordinary and Extraordinary or occasional. Extraordinary is that which a man may have of a thing which ordinarily is another's. Possession extra-ordinary.

---

813. Favour is pleasure resulting to the party favoured from the spontaneous will of the party favouring. Favour.

---

814. Not having any accurate ideas, they have not any accurate language to express them: the language they have is miserably inapposite and inadequate. This may be seen particularly in their terms relative to Conveyancing, the terms Condition, Limitation, &c. Their learning on these heads is a heap of confusion so much worse than a Babel as that, so far from understanding his Brother, no man can understand himself.[1] One can scarce hope better of a science which has scarce any to cultivate it but mercenaries, whose interest it is to keep it at a distance from perfection. But let us not despair: even these dank and squalid regions, the all-vivifying light of philosophy may at length pervade. Prefat. Law Language inadequate.

---

815. We are apt to be more angry at vice the more it seems to be the result of meditation. It seems then to have sunk the deeper in a man's character. 'Tis this consideration, as it should seem, that has kindled the indignation of well disposed but melancholy men against ingenious frauds; and made them look upon modern times as more fertile in vitious desires, because more inventive in the means of satisfying them. Encrease of Vice. Vulgar error.

---

[1] For the building of the Tower of Babel, and God's confounding the language of 'the children of men' so 'that they may not understand one another's speech', see Genesis 11: 1–9.

Possession—extraordinary investing circumstances.

816. Extraordinary Possession a man may be entitled to on two accounts. $1^{st.}$ That of the Execution [of] Public Justice. 2dly that of Necessity. This Necessity may be either Public or Private.

Opposition. Hindrance. Impediment. Prevention.

817. What *opposition* one man may lawfully give to another man's using that which is another man's own consistently with the propriety of that thing, and what not, may be learnt from the doctrine of Actions on the case.[1]

Opposition &c. direct)(indirect.

818. Opposition is either 1st direct, or physical: or 2^{d} indirect or . . . . . . With respect to *direct* opposition, there is least difficulty.

Law compleat = Command compleat.

819. If it be proper to consider a Law as a species of command, the principle of individuation for a Law will be the same with that for a Command. A Law will be compleat, in the same case in which a Command will be compleat. To try whether any Law given for a compleat one be so, the way will be to suppose it simply a command, and there see whether it be compleat.

Point of Individuation.

820. The point of individuation is easily determined. $1^{st.}$ In such bodies as are organized. $2^{dly.}$ In such others as are works of art: so they be not very complex, as Chairs and Tables.[2]

Aspects)(Situations.

821. By aspects I would mean the visible appearances that things exhibit by means of their situations.

Prefat. New words. Apol.

822. To understand so as to be able to throw new lights upon the subject, one must have clear ideas: but to communicate those ideas, one must have new words to cloath them in. 'Tis this is the only possible way of presenting any of these ideas single: for the words of the current stock are, many of them, stuffed and crammed with three or four ideas stuck in them at once.

Punishment. Object of Personal)(Real.

823. The person by whom the punishment is intended to be suffer'd, may be stiled, in general, the object of Punishment.

[1] For Blackstone's account of the action of trespass on the case, which, he notes, 'is an universal remedy, given for all personal wrongs and injuries without force', see *Commentaries on the Laws of England*, iii. 122–3.

[2] In the text Bentham has noted at this point: 'Qu. of Houses and Ships. i:e: at any given moment.' On the individuation of a house see paras. 983–4, pp. 302–4 below.

But when the punishment consists in a pain of Privation, it consists in the taking away from him, in the depriving him of, some *thing*, either real or fictitious, that, being an object of Possession, was in *his* possession: the thing so taken away may, in this case, be stiled the *real* object of Punishment. In this case, then, the person who is the object of the punishment, to distinguish him from the thing by the loss of which he is punished, may be stiled the personal object. But when the phrase 'object of Punishment' is used without any epithet to the word object, there it may be taken to denote the personal object alone.

---

824. What is it, then, we mean when we say, '*a Condition*'? Is it either of two events that are supposed to be *dependent* the one upon the other? Or is it the *dependance* there is between them? Or is [it] the *Volition* creating that *dependance*? Or is it the assemblage of words or other signs made use of to manifest that volition?

Condition. 4 Senses proposed.

That the third of these senses is not only *one* sense of the word, but the primary one of all the senses it may have been used in, appears from the etymology of it.[1]

It signifies, therefore, an act: an act of the mind: an act of volition. An act of volition the object of which is the non-happening of an event the effect of will, i:e: an action in a certain situation of things, which (i:e: which action) by another act of volition had been willed or had been about to be willed to happen.

---

825. When two events are supposed or intended to be made by means of volition, the one of them dependent upon the other, the expression of the volition creating that dependance is called a condition. This is the original and primary sense of the word Condition.

Condition—primary Sense of.[2]

---

826. Events *in our power* are either: 1st. Acts. [or] 2dly. Physical Events brought about by means of actions: Motions of physical bodies produced by motions of the human body.

Events in our power. 1st. Acts; 2d effects of Acts. viz: either events or situations.

---

827. Dependance is either *immediate*; or intermediate. Of two simple events, the second is said to depend immediately upon the first when the first is looked upon as the cause, or necessarily-preceding circumstance, of the second.

Dependance.

---

[1] In the text, Bentham has noted at this point: 'For this see p. | |.' See, for instance, paras. 614, 616–18, pp. 196, 197–8 above, respectively.

[2] In the margin, Bentham has noted at this point: 'in form.'

Circumstances of an act—analysed.

828. A simple event, at the same time that it depends upon another simple event, i:e: the motion of one body, as it's cause, depends upon situations of other surrounding bodies as it's necessarily preceding circumstances.

These necessarily preceding circumstances are: 1st. The situation of the parts of the agent with respect to each other. 2d. Situation of the agent with respect to circumjacent bodies. 3dly. Situation of the parts of the patient with respect to each other. 4. Situation of the patient with respect to surrounding bodies. 5th. Situation of the agent with respect to the patient.

Events, being motions, are *transitory*: situations, being portions of matter at rest, are *persisting*.

Ex. Wound from a Sword.

829. You have wounded me in the arm with a dagger. Let us see here in this instance what is *cause*, what *effect*: what is active instrument, what is passive instrument: what is consequential situation of the parts of the passive instrument: what is situation of the parts of the active instrument with respect to each other.

Main Instrument—Concurrent Instrument.

830. The *immediate active instrument* is your sword: the immediate *passive object* is my arm. The *effect* is the opening of the wound, the motions made by the parts of my arm where the wound is at the time the sword enter'd. The consequential situation of the passive object is the wound itself—the situation the parts persist in, with respect to each other, after the effect.

The *active instrument of the 1st remove* is your arm that wielded it. The *first pre-disponent* cause, the motion of my arm. This, we see, and the immediate are both corporeal instruments, and the causes both corporeal causes. The instrument of the 2d remove is your mind. The pre-disponent cause is the act, the volition of your mind. This is a mental, moral, intellectual instrument; this a mental, moral, intellectual cause.

The pre-disponent situation of the bodies themselves: viz. the immediate instrument and the passive object, with respect to each other, is that of their being within such a distance as they were of one another; viz: within arm's length. If they had been much further asunder, there might have been no wound at all; the instrument and the object might not have come in contact: if nearer, the wound might not have been so deep.

The situation of the parts of the immediate active instrument with respect to one another is what composes it's figure. If it had been broad and round instead of sharp at the end, it might not have enter'd. If it had been less sharp, it might not have penetrated so deep. If sharper, it might have penetrated deeper. So, of degree of hardness and toughness in the sword. Qualities occult and occasionally display'd. Degree of softness and brittleness in my arm.[1]

The situation of circumjacent bodies with respect to the active instrument and passive object was this. There was Air all round every part of us except our feet; consequently between us. Under each of us was the earth. Had there been no air to resist the stroke, the wound would have been deeper. Had we been out of the sphere of the earth's attraction, the wound might have been less deep. The blow would have lost so much of the force of it as depended upon the velocity which the sword acquired by it's descent.

---

831. Call consequential situations, quiescent effects. Since constant use has bestow'd on them the name of effects.

Consequential Situations = Quiescent effects.

---

832. In events depending upon the chymical properties of the active instrument or passive object, or physiological properties of the latter when a living body, all we can see is the active instrument, and (whether motional or quiescent) some very remote effects of the 1st immediate cause, that is the first application of the active instrument to a part of the passive object.

Occult operations.

---

833. As the modes whereby substances make themselves perceptible to the senses are reducible to motions and situations; hence the perceptible effects produced in any body by the motion of any other body may be distinguished into motional and quiescent.

Effects Motional)(Quiescent.

---

834. As, in order to accommodate the import of our terms to common usage, we have divided effects into motional and quiescent, so as to take in situations—so may we divide them still further into motional, quiescent and substantial, so as to take in bodies themselves: in this case, the motional and the quiescent may be both comprized under the name of modal, and conformably Causes may be distinguished into Substantial and Modal, that is motional: for mere situations produce no effect. Bodies at rest produce no effect upon other bodies.

Effects: { Substantial or Corporeal. / Modal or Incorporeal. { Motional. / Quiescent.

Causes: { Substantial or Corporeal. / Modal or Incorporeal.

---

[1] In the margin, Bentham has noted at this point: 'N.B. what the event depends on is not the general quality itself, which is but a fictitious entity: but the individual exertion of that quality in the case in question; which is a real *fact*.'

Circumstances of an act analysed. Qualities.

835. Necessary qualities of the active instrument, passive object and influencing circumjacent bodies, to be number'd among the necessary influencing circumstances, necessary to the production of an effect. N.B. There is no such object existing, at any given moment, in external nature as a quality: in any man's mind, as a disposition. A disposition is a mere fiction of the mind. All that there is real is some act of the mind or of the body in question, which may be termed an exertion of the quality or disposition in question.

Forbearances—distinguished by *circumstances* alone.

836. Among actions, one is in itself distinguishable from another as a motion in one direction is distinguishable from a motion in another direction. But among Forbearances, all that any one can have to distinguish it from any other is the circumstances it stands in. For rest is uniform. A body at rest during any one portion of time exhibits not in itself any appearance different from what the same body exhibits during any other portion of time.

Circumstances influencing.

837. The terms circumjacent body, circumstance, denote not, it is plain, any peculiar and permanent character in the object they represent. They belong alike to one body and to another. Every *body*, it is plain, is a circumjacent body with respect to every other body; every event is a circumstance to every other event. The thread that links them together may, for aught we know, be the same for all. Every one may influence every other. If the fly that two minutes ago was perched upon the left hand page of the paper I am writing on had perched upon the right hand page, the Turkish empire might have been to have a different sovereign this day 500 years from him it will have. But how many events or situations so ever may really contribute to influence any given event, it is but a few, in comparison, that we can *observe* to influence it. So many, then, how many or how few soever they may be, as we do observe may be stiled, with respect to the event in question, *influencing* circumstances. So many bodies, of which they are the motions or the situations, may be stiled *influencing circumjacent bodies*, or simply *influencing bodies*.

Bodies influencing.

Circumstances of an act analysed. Circumstances uninfluencing. Bodies uninfluencing.

838. Such Events and Situations as we can not observe to influence the event in question, whose influence, if any, on the event in question is imperceptible, may be stiled, with respect to it, uninfluencing circumstances. Such bodies whereof they are the events and situations, uninfluencing bodies.

---

839. To appoint is an act of the mind. To appoint to an office is to take that person for an individual of that sort of persons that are the objects of such volitions as constitute the duties, restraints, rights and powers of persons invested with that office. It is to point the general volitions of the Law to individual objects.

To appoint.

---

840. To the Legislative power it belongs to mark out sorts of things, acts and persons as the objects of it's volitions. To the Executive power it belongs to mark out all along the individuals that shall be deemed to be respectively of those sorts.

Power Legislative ⅹ Power Executive or Investitive.

---

841. Specific characters are either transient or permanent. *Transient* as that of offender in such a mode. Permanent as that of occupier of such an *office*.

Characters (political) (appointed to) Transitory ⅹ Permanent.

---

842. 'Tis only by Will acting on Will that conditions can be created. Concerned, therefore, in the creation of every condition to an act of transitive Volition there must be two wills: one which may be stiled the controlling; the other, the controlled.

Will controlling. Will controlled.

---

843. Instruments operating are those of which the motion is a cause. Instruments concurrent are those of which the situation is an influencing circumstance.

Instrument operating ⅹ concurrent.

---

844. A Volition whereof the object is a mode of conduct of a party other than the party himself who wills may be stiled a transitive volition. A volition whereof the object is a mode of conduct of the party himself who wills, an *intransitive* volition.

Volition transitive.

Volition intransitive.

---

845. An act of investiture bears no appearance of an act creating an obligation. For all that, it supposes a Command. Were it not for a Command, it would be nothing. It is the aggregating of an individual object to a class, which is the object of a command. An appointment to an office does not appear upon the face of it to be a command, but were it not for command, or what is equivalent, obligation, what would the appointment amount to? nothing. The Office entitles the person invested with it to certain Fees. How? by imposing on certain persons an obligation to pay those fees. It is not the act of appointment that can create any general obligation; but what it does is to render the party

Investiture—how allied to Obligation.

—in the instance of Property in an Office.

—of Property in a Material Subject.

appointed the individual object (in this case the object favoured) of a general obligation that has already been created. It is not my conveying you my estate that creates any general obligation. But what it does [is] to render you the sole one, for the time being, of the class of persons that are the objects of that benefit which the general Law of appropriation creates by imposing a general obligation on all persons (some one or more individuals in the case of every article of property excepted) to abstain from all uses in general of all articles of property in general.

Law of Appropriation—Titles how constituted. Characterizing circumstances to a class appropriate.

846. There is no other way for the Law to create a sort of persons as the *favoured objects* of the general Law of property than by determining upon what conditions precedent any person may become a proprietor of the sort of interest in question in any individual of the sort of subjects in question. The enumeration of these several sorts of conditions is the enumeration of the several sorts of Titles.

Laws mandatory, permissive, [prohibitive][1]—changes that may be rung on them.

847. Laws mandatory, prohibitive, and permissive may be, any one of them, an exception to any other. A Nest, as it were, of Laws one within another may be conceived, composed of these Laws succeeding one another in any order; except that a Law simply permissive can never be the outermost.

Of the class of objects of a Law prohibitory, the description may be narrow'd either by a Law mandatory or a Law permissive. Let us conceive, and state the effect of, a nest of these Laws succeeding one another in the several orders of which they are susceptible.

Prefat. Law Language—untechnicalized, will be intelligible to all nations.

848. By banishing as many as we can spare of the terms peculiar to our own local Jurisprudence, and giving a clear and steady exposition of such as we are obliged to retain in terms of universal jurisprudence, an easy and profitable intercourse may be kept up between the Jurists of the several nations, and an Englishman might read a comment upon his own laws in the languages of Spain or Sweden.

Partition in doubtful cases proposed.

849. When the *fact* on which a decision on a claim of property depends is doubtful, let the Jury, with concurrence of the Judge, have the power of dividing the subject in litigation between the claimants as in Stanwix's case.[1] Otherwise, where the doubt is

[1] MS 'prohibited'.

[2] John Stanwix (bap. 1693, d. 1766), army officer and politician, was drowned with his wife and daughter when their ship sank in the Irish Sea, probably on 29 October 1766, giving

concerning the *Law*. Where the *indicia* apply not more strongly to one of two oppositely-intitling incidents than another.

---

850. The controversy concerning the difference between matter of *Law* and matter of *Fact* is, in it's own nature, easily decidable. The question concerning the fact is, whether such a physical act was done, be it external or internal, by such a person, and under such circumstances. The question concerning the Law is, whether the above act, under the above circumstances, is of the sort of acts render'd penal by the Law in persons of that sort, under circumstances of that sort. These two questions are, in their own nature, as distinct as any two that can be imagined. The cause of their being confounded is to be sought for in the structure of the language. For certain modes of conduct, among those most obnoxious to the Law, certain terms have been devised; into the import of these terms are taken the ideas not only of the simple act, and of the circumstances that, when it is obnoxious, naturally are concomitant to it, but of this further circumstance of it's being punishable by Law. Hence, we see that, under our complex idea annext to the term used commonly to express the fact, is included the idea of the Law. This will appear manifest upon taking an example of any term of this sort, of which there are many. Law) (Fact.

851. Let us take theft for an example. He that says a theft has been committed is understood to have said not merely that such an act has been done, and under such circumstances, but that [that] act is of the number of those that are punished in such a manner by the Law. He that has said that such a man is guilty of theft, has said that the man has done an act of such a sort as, under the circumstances in which it was done, is punished by the Law as theft is punished. Would we wish, then, to separate the question of Theft.

rise to a suit in the Court of Chancery. At the commencement of proceedings, the *Middlesex Journal or Chronicle of Liberty*, 12 March 1772, described it as 'one of the most extraordinary cause[s] . . . that perhaps ever came before a Chancellor'. The deceased wife was Stanwix's second wife; the daughter was by his first wife. According to a settlement governing the second marriage, whichever of the three survived the others would inherit the estate. Various arguments were advanced by counsel as to why one or other of the three would have outlived the others, for instance Stanwix would have been on deck, while the ladies would have been below deck, or Stanwix was elderly while the daughter was youthful. Rather than pronounce judgment, 'The Chancellor recommended it to the parties to compromise the matter, or if they persisted in their separate claims, declared he would call in the assistance of some of the Judges.' To ascertain the question of fact, the case was transferred to the Court of King's Bench, where on 7 July 1773 the jury, acting on 'principles laid down by Lord Mansfield', found in favour of the plaintiff, Stanwix's nephew Thomas Conner. See the *London Chronicle*, 6–8 July 1773.

fact from the question of Law, and propose to a Judge or set of Judges the one without the other? We must lay aside altogether the word theft: and in denominating the transaction of which we would be answer'd whether it passed or no, we must take such terms, and such only, as shall give us the idea of the sort of transaction in itself, without intimating whether it is or is not among the sorts of transactions that are made punishable by Law. We must settle with ourselves which, among the various acts performed by the party at[?] the time in question, is the act which, done under such circumstances, is of the number of those acts which, either by usage or by express Law, have been made punishable in the manner theft is.[1] We must describe the act we suppose to have been thus committed: we must describe those circumstances, taking care that none of the words used in the description of either act or circumstances convey any intimation of the manner in which it is regarded by the Law: we must then ask whether the act so described was, under the circumstances so described, done or not done. The answer to our question so worded will be an answer to the question of fact separate from the question of Law. Given by a Jury, it will be a special verdict.

General Verdict

852. A General Verdict is a form of words pronounced by a Jury by which they declare it as their opinion that the Def:[t] has done an act of some such sort as is among those that are punishable by Law; for that is the meaning of the word Guilty.

Special Verdict.

853. A Special Verdict is a form of words by which they declare it as their opinion that the Def:[t] has done simply such and such acts, and those under such and such circumstances, the description of which does not import whether they are or not, any of them, of any such sort as is among those that are punishable by Law.

A General Verdict *finds* the *Law*.

854. From what has been said a conclusion follows, which to me appears inevitable: viz: that whenever a Jury gives a verdict of Guilty, it answers to and determines the question of Law: and in short, which is but the same thing in other words, that in all cases where a general verdict of guilty is returned, the question of Law is, and has uniformly been deemed to be, within the province of the Jury.[2]

[1] In the text, Bentham has inserted the marginal heading 'Mode of Conduct: 2 ways of making it penal. 1. Enuntiative. 2[d.] Silent', together with the following passage at this point: 'Conformable to the two different sorts of Law, an act is made punishable in either of two ways: 1[st.] By a Law prohibiting the sort of act itself: 2. By an usage of punishing individual acts of that sort.'

[2] The following paragraph, which belongs here, has been crossed through by Bentham, presumably because he regarded it as superseded by the continuation of the text: 'In giving, then, a verdict of Guilty, they pronounce two things: 1st that the accused has done the act

855. There are two other points upon which I know not whether we are to say the Jury give their judgment or not:[1] these are 1st that the complex act done by the Def[t] is of that sort of act which he is charged to have done in the written instrument of accusation: 2[dly] that the act which he is there charged to have done is of a sort that is punishable by Law. Upon second thoughts, I think it is clear they must. For it is allow'd on all hands, that unless the act done by him is of that sort with which he is charged, it is allow'd, I say, that be it ever so plainly demonstrated that he has done an act of a sort that is punishable by Law, he is not in that instance punishable; he ought to be acquitted.

A Gen. Verd. finds 1st the fact as charged.[2]

856. The 2[d], too, it must, I think, be taken for granted they have decided upon: for if the contrary be not alleged before the Judge, punishment of course follows from the verdict. What occasioned me to doubt is this, that neither of these questions are directly propounded to them. The Advocates on both sides apply their arguments usually to the idea of the fact at large, taking it, as it were, for granted that the description given of the fact in the accusation is what it ought to be to warrant the punishment expected from the Law; and, therefore, that if proved to have done the act signified by the complex term they give to it in the course of the debate, he is prov'd to have done the act he is charged with.[3]

—2[dly] the *Criminality* of the fact as charged.

857. This, then, is taken for granted upon a Verdict of Guilty being returned: nor is the decision in this point liable to be controverted (unless it be in the case of a new Trial). But whether the act as charged in the Indictment is punishable, is a question with respect to which an appeal is open from the Jury to the Judge. The mode of making this appeal is called a Motion in Arrest of Judgment.[4]

Motion in Arrest of Judgment, what.

(taking into the description of the act the description of the influencing circumstances), the complex act which, in the instrument of accusation, he is alleged to have done: 2[dly] that the act which he is there alleged to have done is of some sort of acts that is punishable by Law. This being the case, the first of these judgments remains at all events (unless in case of a new trial) unimpeachable. The 2[d] is subject to the revision of the Judge.'

[1] In the margin, Bentham has noted at this point: 'This difficulty need not occur in Stat. Law. Except w[h]ere the evidence comes short of the fact, and an inference is necessary which they mean to leave to the Judge. If there can be any room for a special verdict upon a prosecution on a Statute, it is because the Statute either has made use of some term of Univ. Jurispr.: or has made use of a word to describe a sort such that they know not whether the thing in question be of that sort or no.'

[2] In the margin, Bentham has noted at this point: 'Verdict purely special is free from all terms not only of technical but of universal Jurisprudence—it states the nake[d] act.'

[3] In the margin, Bentham has noted at this point: 'brings it within any precise known mode of delinquency'.

[4] For motions for a new trial and motions in arrest of judgment, which were available after

—How to make it unnecessary.

858. To save both these questions, the terms of the charge ought to be the very same with those of the Statute. The form of it might be settled by the Legislator; and the several allegations necessary to bring the act within the description of it given by the Law might be proposed in the form of questions to the Jury.

Expectation which is the measure of Justice is not that of parties but of Bystanders.

859. The expectation to be regarded in decisions concerning claims of property is not so much the expectation of the parties as that of the bystanders. The expectation of the party in the wrong, nay tho' ever so manifestly in the wrong, may be as strong as that of the party in the right: with respect to them, therefore, as much mischief and as much good is done by deciding wrong (let what will be supposed wrong) as by deciding right.

Comm. Divine Law.

860. Consistently with our idea of his benevolence, we can not suppose that there are any sins that are not misdeeds: consistently with our idea of his power and his wisdom, we cannot suppose that, if there were, he would need any help of our's to punish them.

The thing convey'd not the object of the Act of Conveyance. Nor the person of the conveyee.

861. It is plain that no act purely mental can work any immediate change upon any material object; directly, it is only on mind that mind can operate.[1] To the direct influence of mind, it's own body and that alone is subject. The act of Conveyance is an act of the mind. Accordingly, by Conveyance, it is plain, no change is effected in the substance, the article of property whatever it be, that is convey'd. It is not properly speaking that [which] is an object of the act of the mind, the act of conveyance. The object on which an act of conveyance exerts itself must, therefore, be mind. It is the minds of all persons, the conveyee excepted; and it acts upon them by a command of the executive kind, issued in conformity to the State authority, and armed by the state sanction. It is a command to all persons in general to abstain from those external acts of ownership exercisable on that object, in the liberty of exercising which, others being restrained, it is that ownership consists.

---

the verdict but before judgment, see Blackstone, *Commentaries on the Laws of England*, iii. 387–95, and for the more specific point that 'the case laid in the declaration is not sufficient in point of law to found an action upon' see ibid. 393–4.

[1] In the margin, Bentham has noted at this point: 'Illustrate by *Spells* and *Fascination*.'

862. Instance where the Legislative power itself can reach individuals by description, though not by name. An individual may be ascertained by description taken from a natural relation. Heir to the former owner—next of kin. By the institution of some investing circumstances, which can not be found in more than one individual or one assignable assemblage of individuals, at a time.

Investitive power—how exercisable on *future* objects by a Legislature.

---

863. They who hate Metaphysics,[1] hate the only principles by which alone any controverted points in Law can be clearly solved.

Prefat. Metaphysics.

When reason is against a man, a man will be against reason.[2]

If pressed, they will tell us, perhaps, that by Metaphysics here they mean false Metaphysics. But what is it that a man has said who tells us he hates false Metaphysics? Nothing. For who is there that hates not what is false in science in proportion as he loves what's true? The fatigue of attention that is requisite in well conducted metaphysical disquisitions is what no man loves, or can be expected to love: but every man ought to love, and every intelligent and honest man does love, the clearness and certainty that are the fruits of them.

Metaphysics, modern Metaphysics, genuine Metaphysics, of which Locke was in a manner the inventor, is that science which teacheth the signification of words, and [the] origination of the ideas which they signify: which it does by no other means than this, the shewing how to distinguish, upon occasion, the idea annext to any one word from the idea annext to any other, and shewing how all the ideas we have that are complex, arise from, and are made up of, simple ones.[3]

Thus it is that, as an illustrious philosopher has observed, every science has it's metaphysics:[4] there is no science that has not a set of terms that are more peculiarly it's own, standing for ideas that are more peculiarly it's own: words of which the signification, and ideas of which the origination, is to be sought for from metaphysics: from a branch of metaphysics, which, in consideration of the science to which it is applied, may be termed the metaphysics

[1] Perhaps an allusion to Burke's avowed hatred of metaphysics, for which see p. 217 n. above.

[2] See Thomas Hobbes, 'The Epistle Dedicatory' (first published in *Humane Nature* in 1650), in *The Elements of Law Natural and Politic*, ed. J.C.A. Gaskin, Oxford, 1994, p. 19, referring to 'dogmatical', as opposed to 'mathematical, learning': 'as oft as reason is against a man, so oft will a man be against reason'.

[3] For Locke on simple and complex ideas see p. 75 n. above, and on distinguishing different ideas by different words see Locke, *Essay concerning Human Understanding*, Bk. II, Ch. XXIX, §6, pp. 364–5.

[4] This view is attributed to D'Alembert in para. 615, p. 196 above.

of that science. Natural Philosophy has it's metaphysics. Medicine has it's metaphysics. Grammar has it's metaphysics. It were needless to particularize, since there is no science of the whole circle but what has. Legislation, as much as any, has it's metaphysics and in the improvement of this, as of those, experience and metaphysics must go hand in hand

---

Prefat. American dispute turns on words.

864. A great part of the merits of the American controversy,[1] as far as concerns the matter of right, centers on the signification of the words Give, grant, consent, representation, taxation, legislation, constitution.

Prefat. Egot.

865. That, in this first attempt, I shall in all points touched upon have succeeded to the satisfaction of the public is much more than I can presume: certainly I have not in my own.

The Preface is that part of a work in which a man is indulged without scruple in the liberty of saying something of himself: which he may equally do whether he does or does not affix to it his name.

Comm. Divine Law.

866. On a question of Law or political expediency,[2] the subject of Religion can never be introduced but to distract us.

Comm. Forms of Government.

867. Our Author, caught by old-womanly and vulgar . . . . . . runs away from the consideration of the permanent political character of the class, to that of the accidental personal qualifications of the individual. Asking himself what ought to be that disposition, he betakes himself to his old friend theology for a solution: and, according to the old orthodox method of explanation, *ignotum per ignotius*, he answers with great fluency, *the most godlike*. They ought, he says here, to be so and so: and in another place, without knowing any more of them than what their titles tell him, he is happy enough to find they are so.[3]

---

[1] i.e. the question of the political relationship between Britain and her North American colonies.

[2] The phrase 'or political expediency' has been marked by Bentham for deletion.

[3] See Blackstone, *Commentaries on the Laws of England*, i. 48: 'In general, all mankind will agree that government should be reposed in such persons, in whom those qualities are most likely to be found, the perfection of which are among the attributes of him who is emphatically stiled the supreme being; the three grand requisites, I mean, of wisdom, of goodness, and of power: wisdom, to discern the real interest of the community; goodness, to endeavour always to pursue that real interest; and strength, or power, to carry this

868. A man who possesses the investitive and divestitive power, or even the divestitive power alone uncontrolled, with respect to any office that is beneficial to the officer, has the power of issuing any commands whatever to that officer: which commands may, with respect to the personal, real, and modal objects of them, as well be general as individual: they may, therefore, as well be Laws as not Laws. What gives them less force than other Laws, and occasions them not to be spoken of in general under that name, is the feebleness of their armature: their armature being limited to the pain of deprivation. Powers *investitive* and *divestitive*, how far the conjunction of them in the same person constitutes Power autocratic.

Thus it is, for example, that the American provinces are each of them in some degree subject to a Governor without the government's being in any degree despotic, although the office of the Governor lies at the absolute power of the King. The powers of the Governor are controlled by other powers that are local: at the same time that his duties, as against the King that appoints him, are unlimited. By acting contrary to the will of the King, whether he act contrary or not to the will of the entire supreme power, he may be punished by losing his place. But if, in acting conformable to the will of the King, he act contrary to the will of the supreme power, he may, by sentence of the settled interpreters of it's will in that behalf, the Judges within whose jurisdiction the cause is, be made to suffer other punishments that shall exceed that indefinitely.

---

869. For the purpose of defining theft, taking must be defined. Qu. is it the exercising any physical act *upon* the thing taken as the passive object? But then it must be under circumstances indicative of an act of mind indicating a resolution to take possession: i:e: to be at liberty to exercise any physical acts whatsoever indiscriminately, besides the act in question. Of a series of acts of using, the first that is done with that intention, may be said to be the act of taking.[1] Taking.

870. After the act of taking, the forbearing to do any act to change the situation of the thing may, as well as subsequent acts of using, be a mode of conduct coming under the denomination of keeping. Keeping.

---

knowledge and intention into action.' In relation to the British Constitution, Blackstone goes on (ibid. 50–2) to attribute the three qualities to Lords, Commons, and King respectively. Bentham discusses these passages in detail in 'A Fragment on Government', Chs. II–III, in *Comment/Fragment* (*CW*), pp. 449–73.

[1] In the margin, Bentham has noted at this point: 'Taking with an intent to keep, consume, or alien is necessary to Theft.'

Intention.

871. Intention is a term we apply to a volition when directed to an event that appears to be of a nature to be producible by the action of the party, whether supposed to be absolutely in his power or no. An intention is a fainter resolution. I intend, I even resolve, to pull the trigger of the gun I have in my hand. I intend, my intention is, to hit a Hare I see squatting in the bush. I have a Gun in my hand. I level it at her and fire: but it is too much to say I resolve it.

Intention ⲭ Resolution. Example.

Op. Mag. Hard Labour. Punishm. Death Succedanea—defended.

872. It is not of a principle of Oeconomy we take away men's lives.[1]

To take away men's lives out of a principle of oeconomy; to kill them because we care not to be at the expence to keep them is carrying our notions of oeconomy, it must be acknowledged, to a length somewhat extraordinary. We were not this frugal by those enemies of the state whom the chance of war had thrown into our hands; them, when left to perish by their sovereign, we fed and cloathed and thought it not a burthen.[2] Nevertheless, the horrid proverb among assassins, 'Stone dead has no fellow,'[3] has had

[1] In a debate in the House of Commons on 23 March 1778 regarding the continuation of the Criminal Law Act of 1776 (16 Geo. III, c. 43), authorizing the punishment of hard labour for those who would otherwise have been transported, Burke 'observed, that he feared the time would come when we should put prisoners and felons to death on the principle of œconomy': see *Parliamentary History* (1777–8) xix. 970. This speech seems, however, to post-date the composition of the text by two to three years: for further details see the Editorial Introduction, p. xiii n. above.

[2] The Kings of France had habitually paid an allowance, known as the 'Royal Bounty', for distribution among French prisoners of war in Britain for the purchase of clothes. In September 1759 the Office for Sick and Injured Seamen, which was responsible for the management of French prisoners in Britain, requested additional funds from the Admiralty, 'particularly, as their King having withdrawn the Allowance formerly made them which enabled them to purchase Cloaths &c, vast numbers of those poor People are now in all Our prisons becoming almost naked, which may very reasonably be expected to encrease the number of sick': see Commissioners for taking Care of Sick and Wounded Seamen, and for the Care and Treatment of Prisoners of War to the Admiralty, 29 September 1759, cited by E. Charters, 'The Administration of War and French Prisoners of War in Britain, 1756–1763', in *Civilians and War in Europe, 1618–1815*, ed. E. Charters, E. Rosenhaft, and H. Smith, Liverpool, 2012, pp. 87–99 at 96–7). In response to the deteriorating condition of the prisoners in the face of the oncoming winter, several voluntary subscriptions were established to raise money for the purchase of clothing for the prisoners. By July 1760 the largest of these, established at the Crown and Anchor in the Strand in December 1759, had raised £4,139 7s. 11d.: see *Proceedings of the Committee appointed to manage the contributions begun at London Dec. XVIII MDCCLVIIII for cloathing French Prisoners of War*, London, 1760, Appendix No. III. General Account. The generosity of the public was praised by [Oliver Goldsmith], *The Citizen of the World; or Letters from a Chinese Philosopher, Residing in London, to his Friends in the East*, 2 vols., London, 1762, i. 87–9.

[3] According to Edward Hyde, Earl of Clarendon, *The History of the Rebellion and Civil Wars in England Begun in the Year 1641*, 3 vols., Oxford, 1702, i. 191, 'Stone Dead hath no Fellow' was the response of Robert Devereux (1591–1646), third Earl of Essex, Lord Chamberlain 1641–2, Captain-General of the Parliamentary Army 1642–5, to arguments for

such weight with some men, that objections have been raised to every plan that has been proposed for keeping them alive.

It pains me to think to what a degree some of them are frivolous because[1]

Against employing them in any public works, the roads for instance, it has been said, that it would drive honest men from engaging in the like works, as thinking [it] disgraceful to engage in an employment that was the lot of criminals.

Against a supposition thus improbable in itself, we have the testimony [of] experience. It is punishment long established and well known for men to be confined, on account of petty delinquencies, for short times, in workhouses; in which they are employ'd in various kinds of labour.[2] Are these kinds of labour become disreputable? Do men decline to engage in them? It is what I believe has been never heard of.

Almost from the very first planting of America, it has been a punishment to transport men there by force.[3] Has this deterred men from going there of their own accord? The affirmative is what the 3 millions of men with which that country has, in the space of 150 years, been peopled, most of them of British extraction, surely do not testify.[4]

clemency towards Thomas Wentworth (1593–1641), first Earl of Strafford, favourite minister of Charles I (1600–49), King of England, Scotland, and Ireland from 1625. Strafford was executed on 12 May 1641 following a Bill of Attainder voted by the House of Commons.

[1] The sentence has been abandoned at this point.

[2] Punishment of this sort was laid down for various categories of petty offenders, for instance, in the Vagrant Act of 1744 (17 Geo. II, c. 5).

[3] On 24 March 1617 the Privy Council issued an open warrant empowering any six Councillors, including two of the Lord Chancellor or Lord Keeper of the Great Seal, Lord Treasurer, and Lord Privy Seal, and one principal Secretary, to 'Reprive and stay from execution suche persons as now stand Convicted of any Robbery or felony (willfull murther, Rape, witchcraft or Burglary only excepted) who for strength of body or other abilities shall be thought fitt to be employed in . . . Services beyond the Seaes', and certified as such by the judges by whom they had been tried and convicted, and to determine the location and duration of such employment: see *Acts of the Privy Council. Colonial Series*, ed. W.L. Grant and J. Munro, 6 vols., Hereford, 1908–12, i. 11–12. This measure effectively initiated the practice of transportation, which was at first employed only intermittently, generating small numbers of transportees, until the Transportation Act of 1717 (4 Geo. I, c. 11). Thereafter, transportation to the American colonies became the standard punishment for offences against property until the commencement of the American War of Independence in 1776.

[4] Contemporary estimates put the population of the American colonies at about 3m. On 16 March 1775, for instance, Richard Glover (1712–85), author and politician, speaking at the bar of the House of Commons in his capacity of agent for the West India Merchants and Planters of London, estimated the population of the 'associated provinces' of America as between $2\frac{1}{2}$ and 3m. (*Parliamentary History* (1774–7) xviii. 461, 474), while on 3 November 1775 Temple Simon Luttrell (1738?–1803), MP for Milborne Port, spoke of Americans as 'three millions of people, three thousand miles distant' (ibid. 1037).

The disgrace lies in the *motive*, not in the *operation*.

873. It has been said, that honest men, the honest poor, wherever a party of criminals should be thus employ'd, would complain of the work's being taken out of their hands.

This is, in itself, as improbable, and as much contradicted by experience, as the other. Who has ever heard that the honest poor have thought themselves injured by the labour, such as it is, that is done in workhouses? What ground for supposing a notion so extravagant could get into their heads?

Possible it is, that they in whose hands the appointment of the work[1] should be vested, might, were they to take great pains, and make a point of distressing the labouring people in any district, in some measure perhaps effect their purpose: they might go to a quarter of the country where the poor were in want of employment, they might take in hand some road that was already begun, and for the working upon which a number of men were already engaged; they might dismiss these men and set criminals to do the work.

This is possible. But are there any reasons to think it probable? what quarrel can any set of men of high rank in the state [have] with the labouring class of the people? Particular scatter'd individuals may be obnoxious. The governing part of a particular district may be obnoxious. The rulers of a corporation may be obnoxious. A body of Electors may be obnoxious: but by what means can the labouring poor have it in their power to become obnoxious, who have no power, no interest, no vote, nothing by the bestowal of which they can oblige, or by the refusal disoblige; who, by the exertion of their natural strength, are of benefit to all, and by their want of all political strength cannot stand in the way of the interests of any?

Another thing that has been said is, that this is Slavery, that Slavery cannot be endured in England, that Englishmen are so irreconcileable to the very idea of it, that nothing of that sort would be endured.[2]

In the first place, it does not appear that Englishmen are so very irreconcileable to the idea of slavery, but that, when they cross the water, they not only can bear to see men in that condition, but are ready themselves to hold them in it in perfect tranquillity, and without scruple.[3] And who are these men? Men perfectly guiltless; men to whom nothing of criminality is so much [as] imputed.

[1] MS orig. 'disposal of the Criminals'.

[2] See, for instance, Locke, *Two Treatises of Government*, Bk. I, Ch. I, § 1, p. 141: 'Slavery is so vile and miserable an Estate of Man, and so directly opposite to the generous Temper and Courage of our Nation; that 'tis hardly to be conceived, that an *Englishman*, much less a *Gentleman*, should plead for't.'

[3] In the case of *Smith v. Browne and Cooper* (1701), for instance, Sir John Holt (1642–

But let it be so; and doubtless so it is, and happy that it is so, the thought of slavery is, to an Englishman, very odious. That innocent, honest men of his own colour, his own condition, his own country, be reduced to that unhappy state is what Englishmen in general, we may well suppose, could not think of without the utmost horror. But must it needs be so with respect to criminals, to felons, whose lives must otherwise have paid the forfeit, and to whom slavery itself, even real slavery, would be reputed an indulgence?

Meantime, if Englishmen will not bear hard labour[1] to be used as a punishment, how is it that they bear whipping, a punishment infinitely more galling to honour, more severe to sense? how is it they bear the stocks, the pillory, punishments infinitely more disgraceful? How is it they bear, and that with such a degree of frequency, so much tranquillity, and so much to the satisfaction of these objectors, even death itself? How is it, in short, they bear any punishment at all? An argument that applies against all kinds of punishment is good, we may be certain, against none.

Punishment is irksome, who doubts it? were it not, it would not answer it's design.

After all is said that can be said, it is not a man's chusing to call it slavery that can make what is here proposed any thing else than what it is, a punishment long established in, and perfectly familiar to, this country, which men see and are exposed to feel, and suffer to be exercised among them, without an objection and without a murmur. Be it slavery, or any thing else, it is what we are accustomed to: and if it is not slavery, it is not prolonging the term, and regulating the object, of the labour, that will make it so.

But established as it is already, that we may not suffer it without reason to be branded with this odious name: let us see what really is slavery.

874. Domestic Slavery is the state of him who is bound to conform to the uncontrouled will of a private individual; who is bound to do any thing, to suffer any thing. Such for some time was Slavery, what.

1710), Chief Justice of King's Bench from 1689, averred that 'as soon as a negro comes into England, he becomes free: one may be a villein in England, but not a slave', but went on to assert that laws elsewhere that validated chattel slavery were legitimate. In the case before him, 'the sale was in Virginia, and, by the laws of that country, negroes are saleable; for the laws of England do not extend to Virginia; being a conquered country, their law is what the king pleases'. See William Salkeld, *Reports of Cases Adjudg'd in the Court of King's Bench; with Some Special Cases in the Courts of Chancery, Common Pleas and Exchequer, from the First Year of K. William and Q. Mary, to the Tenth Year of Queen Anne,* 2 vols., London, 1717, ii. 666.

[1] MS orig. 'obligation to work'.

the state of the Villain in this country:[1] such is now the state of Negroes in America: life only being excepted. Need this, then, ought it, would it, be the condition of the criminal? Does any man propose it should? Nothing like it. The hours of work, the quality, quantity and object of work, would be fixed by Law. Certain and sufficient times of rest and refreshment would be allow'd. To execute these regulations, certain persons must, then as now, doubtless be employ'd. To these persons, large and to some degree discretionary power must unavoidably be committed. But would there be no check to the exercise of this discretion? Who can think it? Inspectors, disinterested inspectors might, ought, would certainly be appointed: whose ears would be ever open to complaints of grievances, and who would [be] tempted by no interest to connive at them and furnished with power to redress them.

Comm. Prefat. Summary of his principal demerits.

875. Accuse him of entering heartily in that conspiracy against the peace and happiness of mankind, which Lawyers of all ages have been but too forward to engage in.—Of cherishing Mystery, that parent, and nursing mother, of fraud in Law as in Religion.—Of a degree of intolerance, which even Bishops would be ashamed of.—Of an insidious and cover'd enmity to the liberty of the Press, manifested in adulation and an idolatrous and ridiculous display of the fancied attributes of the first Magistrate.—Of a blind and undiscriminating propensity to fall prostrate at the shrine of power. On these and so many other accounts, we seem warranted to give to this book the title that with so much injustice was given to the liberal and the virtuous, the corrupter of youth:[2] of that 'long and illustrious train of noble and ingenuous youth,' by which our Author has now for these twenty years been accustomed to see his lessons follow'd . . .[3]

Merits.

876. He it is who first of all his tribe . . .
diversified it with historical information;
filled up their abrupt ellipses;

[1] On the medieval status of villeins, and the amelioration of their position over time into copyholders, see Blackstone, *Commentaries on the Laws of England*, ii. 92–6.

[2] An allusion to Socrates, who was put to death for '*corrupting the young men*' of Athens: see Xenophon, *Memorabilia*, I. 1.

[3] The word 'follow'd' has been marked by Bentham for deletion.

Blackstone, *Commentaries on the Laws of England*, i. 37, refers to 'the long and illustrious train of noble and ingenuous youth' as the persons whom Charles Viner (bap. 1678, d. 1756), legal writer, intended should benefit from the establishment of the Vinerian Professorship at the University of Oxford, to which Blackstone had been appointed in 1756, though he had begun lecturing on the Common Law in 1753.

adorned it with the charms of harmony;
banished their uncouth phrases.
Merits, those, not mean: but not[1]
An useful repertory in matters of fact: but a very unsafe guide in matters of opinion.

Though the terms are often obscure and equivocal, the construction is remarkably clear and unembarassed.

---

877. I could have wished to have subjoined particular examples for the illustration of every general position: the whole work would by this means have unquestionably been render'd much clearer, the utility of it much more general. The positions themselves thus brought to the test of experiment could not but have gained in point of accuracy very considerably. But the bulk of it would have been encreased to a very great degree; and in no less a degree the time and labour. I cared not to throw in the first instance so huge a load upon the press: nor to hazard on an ambiguous experiment the labour of more years. If there be any thing at all worth notice in it, any industrious and | | students who might be disposed to perform that operation for themselves will undoubtedly find in it their account: the instruction which each person will reap in proving the operation, even where the work itself is false, will richly reward the trouble. Prefat. Apology for Non-exemplification.

Had I proceeded from the statement of the example to the formation of the general position, had I described the path marked out by my mind in it's progress through the field of particulars to the elevated ground of general | |, marked it's various turnings and windings, marked the several objects it saw necessary to leave to the right and left, what has here been despatched in the space of little more than | | hundred pages, might have taken up, for aught I know, as many thousands.[2]

My endeavour has been to give that clearness and precision to the general position, that there shall be at least no *necessity* for the example. For, of an example, there is always the less need, the clearer and more precise the rule. I have a book before me, the work of an elegant modern writer, whom, on so invidious an account, I will not name, because his execution is sometimes happy, and his designs are always meritorious; I have a book, I say,

[1] The sentence has been abandoned at this point.

[2] In the text, Bentham has noted at this point: 'Harris. *Essay on Obligation.* Keymes's *Elements of Criticism.*' The references are to Harris, *Hermes*; possibly *Dissertation on Obligation* attributed to William Ellis (see p. 146 & n. above); and [Henry Home, Lord Kames], *Elements of Criticism*, 3 vols., London and Edinburgh, 1762.

before me, teeming with examples, 5 or 6 perhaps to a rule, and which are the more necessary in that the rules would of themselves absolutely convey no idea.

Prefat. Parsing.

878. To refer any individual object that happens to present itself, in the field of Jurisprudence, to the classes marked out by the several denominations here struck out.

This, in short, is no other than that very useful exercise so long established and so much in vogue in the science of Grammar, called Parsing; in which any word, as it occurs, is referred to the grammatical division it belongs to, first beginning with the part of speech, the *genus generalissimum* of the System, answering to the Class in Natural History, thence descending through the several sub-divisions of Verb, voice, Number, Person, gender, or such others as a word of that part of speech admitts of.

Prefat. This work but Introductory.

879. What cannot escape observation is, that in all these speculations nothing is in appearance done towards the despatching of that great and only legitimate end of all political speculations, the ascertaining in matters of law the point of expedience or inexpedience.

The truth is, the present is but a vestibule to a building that is to follow, an introduction of a work that is to come; which has for it's object no other than that important point which has been mentioned. A work the business of which is the construction of a standard of right and wrong, and the application of it to the several Laws that shall present themselves, and in consequence to the several modes of conduct that are the objects of them.

This was the end of all; this was that which presented itself to my mind, before the necessity of the present one was even so much as suspected. But I had not travelled far in this pursuit before I found that, in proceeding with the common stock of words, I was unable so much as to name that branch of the Law, or of man's conduct, that was the subject of my disquisitions. Here, then, I was obliged to make a pause: to undertake a new and different work, in order to put myself in a condition to undertake what seemed then to me a work still more difficult, but which now, I trust, will be much less so. Before I enter'd upon the main work, I had a vast load of difficulty to remove. Tools, materials, every thing to make; I had my materials to parcel out and to find names for.

---

880. Compact simple—the object of which is a single act, or article of conduct. Compact Simple.

881. Compact complex—the object of which is a course of conduct. [Compact][1] Complex.

---

882. Acts of ownership are either 1st. Use; or 2dly. Conveyance.[2] Ownership {Use. Conveyance.[3]

An act of conveyance, how it respects Law.—Answ.—by being an act of investment.

---

883. Less than death would not be sufficient; more than death would not be endured. Op. Mag. Punishment, Disproportion of.

Less than death would not be sufficient: it has been found not to be sufficient: and therefore it is that death has been appointed: that not yet done, sufficient has not as yet been done: that done, all has been done that can be done.

884. It may seem matter of just wonder, that while the power of executing the Laws is so nicely ballanced, so divided and subdivided, so fenced in on all sides by conditions and modifications, the reasons of every instance of it's exertion so sifted and discussed, the facts that are the grounds of them placed in so broad a day-light, the power of stopping their operation has been abandoned to vague undefinable discretion.[4] Uncertainty, *Pardon* a Cause of. *Sedative* power.

885. Making the Judges independent of the Successor a great thing: it was a sacrifice of a branch of the social affections that stands the next to selfish. Op. Mag. Pardon—proposal for modifying.

It is only in the reign of an excellent prince that such a project could be proposed with any the least prospect of success.[5]

It required such an earnest as that abovementioned.

Equity is *now* circumscribed by settled rules. Why, therefore, should not the power of pardoning?

That power in any other hands should yield to the benefit of the community, but that power in the hands of the Crown should not, a monstrous position.

[1] MS 'Promise'.

[2] In the text, Bentham has noted at this point: 'v. King. 223.' See para. 550, pp. 177–8 above.

[3] For the correct form of layout of the marginal see p. 40.

[4] For the king's power to pardon see Blackstone, *Commentaries on the Laws of England*, iv. 389–95.

[5] The continuance of judges in office following the death of the reigning monarch had been secured by the Commissions and Salaries of Judges Act of 1760 (1 Geo. III, c. 23), a measure which had, according to Blackstone, *Commentaries on the Laws of England*, i. 258, been 'enacted at the earnest recommendation of the king himself [i.e. George III] from the throne'.

Power of pardon in *state* crimes to be reserved as at present:[1] it might possibly be as well that this should submitt to the same modifications: *possibly*: but the necessity of that is not so apparent: there may be many reasons given why *that* should continue on it's present footing which can not be given why this should; and the occasions on which that comes to be exerted are very rare; the occasions on which this comes to be exerted are perpetual.

The Parliament having given up their privilege:[2] a precedent: something remains to be done by the Crown to equal that.—A glorious contest!

This not obnoxious to the invidious constructions: viz: a desire in the Minister to make them more dependent. This would fix the character of the King beyond all possibility of cavil.

The subject gives up the right of punishing his injurer when it appears that his punishment is not for the good of the community. The King gives up his power of exempting the injurer from punishment in cases where it appears that it *is* for the good of the community.

Persons to be examined *vivâ voce* upon oath and in public as to the grounds of application. But the rules of Evidence to be looser. Right of opposing to be given. Examination to be taken down in writing, and sent, with the Judge's opinion, to the King.

Sanction Moral, ought to be the standing substitute to the Political.

886. That no man living should be without *some* check. That mere objects or subordinate Governors should have the political Sanction. Supreme Governors the Moral.

The means of applying the moral Sanction to Governors is notoriety of the grounds of acts of power. That power should be bestow'd any where without any motive to guide the application of it to the purposes of utility is a foul spot in politics. That which opens the door to the influence of the moral Sanction is publicity of debate.

Nomenclature, *quantum prodest*.[3]

887. By having found distinct and apposite names for the various objects of Jurisprudence, we shall find a greater facility in determining their qualities than can easily be imagined.

---

[1] According to ibid., iv. 392–3, the king's pardon could not be pleaded so as to stop or impede an impeachment.

[2] The Parliamentary Privilege Act of 1770 (10 Geo. III, c. 50) provided that no court action against any member of either House would 'at any time be impeached, stayed, or delayed by or under colour or pretence of any privilege of Parliament', though it continued the protection of Members against arrest or imprisonment as a result of such proceedings.

[3] i.e. 'how useful'.

888. *Objects* of the Command they are all;[1] under that name they have all been spoken of. This term, then, marks the common relation there is between them; the three epithets subjoined to it mark that character of each which constitutes it's difference from the other two. Command—3 Objects of a.[2]

---

889. Of the three sets of Conditions to a Law,[3] it is the 2[d] only that attach[es] upon a Command at large. The 1st and 3[d] attach upon a Law as it is such. An Ordinary Command has no formalities in the issuing of it: it has no formalities attending the execution of the tacit threat which forms it's armature. Conditions to a Law, 3 Sets of. What belong to a Law as Such.

890. *Observance* of the Law is what is properly the execution of the Law itself. What is commonly called Execution is execution of the threat which constitutes it's political armature. Observance X Execution.

---

891. Language would fail me were I to attempt to express the sense of what we owe to those Lords who concurred in the order for throwing open the doors of the house to strangers. This is one of those acts of Government, which I can never think of without thanking God that I was born in this age.[4] The Privilege Act is another.[5] The Controverted Election Act is a third.[6] Op. Mag. Pardon—proposal for modifying.

---

892. Patents instances of Legislative power exercised by the Crown. Qu. whether among his Prerogatives as reckoned up by Blackstone.[7] King Patents.

---

[1] For the 'modal', 'personal', and 'real' objects of a law see, for instance, para. 488, pp. 158–9 above.

[2] In the margin, Bentham has noted above this heading: 'Catalogue of Prepositions and causal adverbs "why" &c.'

[3] See para. 720, p. 230 above.

[4] On 15 December 1774 the House of Lords resolved that 'the doors should be opened to the members of the House of Commons, the sons and brothers of peers, peers of Ireland and Scotland, and to so many of the public at large as should be introduced by English peers, each peer to have the privilege of introducing one person': see *Parliamentary History* (1774–7) xviii. 47–8.

[5] See p. 276 n. above.

[6] The Parliamentary Elections Act of 1770 (10 Geo. III, c. 16) made perpetual by the Parliamentary Elections Act of 1774 (14 Geo. III, c. 15), provided that controverted elections to the House of Commons should be adjudicated by a Select Committee of thirteen Members chosen by lot, rather than by a Committee of the whole House, as had been the previous practice.

[7] Bentham presumably had in mind not letters patent (discussed at Blackstone, *Commentaries on the Laws of England*, ii. 346–8), but patents in the sense of an exclusive right to the benefits of an invention, which Blackstone implies were the grant of the king (see ibid., iv. 159).

Prefat. So much of the Language fixed.

893. So much of the language as was thus settled would be fixed for ever. This would be indeed *exigere monumentum ære perennius*.[1] So much, at least, of the language would be exempt from those vicissitudes to which language in general is thought, but I believe erroneously, to be still subject.

Law Common)(Statute.

894. From Statute Law, a man learns to believe that to such or such a mode of conduct punishment will be annext, because he has been told by authority that it shall be. From Common Law, a man learns to believe that to such or such a mode of conduct punishment will be annext, because he thinks he sees it has been.

Lit. Prop.

895. It is amusing enough to observe the shifts which the sages of the Law have been reduced to for want of a clear notion of the nature of Property. A question is started whether Copy right be a species of Property. One learned Judge, taking for granted it will bear squeezing, catches at it, looks in his hands and, finding nothing, can not persuade himself there is any such thing. Another learned Judge, not having patience to unravel the scruples of the former concerning this aerial being, cuts the Gordian knot, calls in Woolaston, stamps existence upon it without more ado by force of the 'great Law of Nature', right reason and truth: that is, in plain English, vows that it is, because it is.[2] In a word, we see Serjeant Skipwith corrected by Justice Schardelow.[3]

---

[1] i.e. 'I have finished a monument more lasting than bronze': see Horace, *Odes*, III. xxx. 1.

[2] Bentham is referring to judicial opinions in *Millar v. Taylor* (1769). The case, in which Blackstone acted as counsel for the plaintiff, turned upon the questions of whether the Common Law provided authors with a property right in their work, and, if so, whether or not this right had been superseded by the Copyright Act of 1709 (8 Ann., c. 19). The existence of such a right was disputed by Sir Joseph Yates (1722–70), Justice of King's Bench 1764–70, Justice of Common Pleas 1770, who expressed scepticism as to whether possession could be demonstrated 'or any Act of Occupancy . . . be asserted, on mere *intellectual Ideas*'. Sir Richard Aston (1717–78), Justice of King's Bench 1765–78, argued that literary property was established in Common Law, on the grounds of '*right Reason*' and '*the great Law of Nature*', and citing William Wollaston, *The Religion of Nature Delineated*, London, 1722. See *The Question concerning Literary Property, determined by the Court of King's Bench On 20th April, 1769, in the cause between Andrew Millar and Robert Taylor: with the Separate Opinions of the four Judges; And the Reasons given by Each, in Support of his Opinion*, ed. James Burrow, London, 1773, pp. 42, 66.

[3] In the text, Bentham has noted at this point: 'v. Blackst. *Anal. Disc. on the Study of the Law*. p. 47. Note.' According to Blackstone, *Analysis of the Laws of England*, p. xlvii n., when Sir William Skipwith (*c.* 1320–90×98), Serjeant-at-Law from 1344, Chief Baron of the Exchequer from 1361, encountered certain Latin terms used in the Civil and Canon Law, he declared the words to be nonsense, whereupon Sir John Shardlow or Shardelowe (d. 1344), Serjeant-at-Law from 1318, Justice of Common Pleas from 1332, informed him that, 'Ceo n'est que un restitution en lour ley, pur que a ceo n'avomus regard', i.e. 'this is merely a

896. The party favoured in the Law of Copy-right is the party who has first made a set of visible marks that are the signs of the audible signs in question; I mean either that party himself, or such other person as, by an act of conveyance, he has put into his place.

Copy right—Object inexhibitable.

897. The object not to be published in this case is not the ideas but the sounds—the spoken language; primary signs of those ideas. Translation into another language may by possibility be so made, at least if the discourse translated be a very short one, as to suggest precisely the same ideas as the original. Yet to publish the translation, I suppose, *would* not, certainly *need* not, be consider'd as an invasion of the Copy-right to the work. Why? because here the primary audible signs suggested by the secondary visible signs in question are different.

Signs primary of Ideas. Sounds spoken. Signs secondary. Translation.

898. Yet to publish a Copy of the same work in short hand, I suppose, would: especially were the use of short hand to become general. Why? because here the primary audible signs suggested by the secondary visible signs in question are the same.

Short-hand Copy.

---

899. Difference between an universal character and an universal language.

Lit. Prop.

---

900. Rule.

No ground of decision ought ever to be suffer'd to be made use of in argument against a party, which men in general, and therefore the party, had no opportunity of being apprised of.[1]

Dig. Com. Law—Rule against dormant Reports, &c.

---

901. To rehearse a book by heart is no invasion, I suppose, of the Copy right.—Why? because here is no selling of any secondary visible signs at all. Consequently, no Copy at all taken. To write it out with a pen and sell the writing, I suppose, *is*: although the forms of the secondary visible signs are greatly different from those of the pattern. Why? Because the secondary visible signs are signs of the same audible ones as those are that are in the pattern.

Rehearsal *vivâ voce*.

Pattern.

restitution in their law, therefore we disregard it'. The story is repeated in *Commentaries on the Laws of England*, i. 22 n.

[1] In the text, Bentham has noted at this point: 'v. an instance in Case of Lit. Prop. p. 121. Salk. M. Rep. of a case argued in 1709. In Ld M.'s possession.' See *The Question concerning Literary Property*, p. 121, where Chief Justice Mansfield cited a copy in his personal possession of '*Salkeld*'s Manuscript Report' of *Company of Stationers v. Partridge* (1709), noting that 'I do not know whether it is got into Print.' The case, reported as *Company of Stationers v.* ——, had been printed in [Robert Lucas], *Cases in Law and Equity, Chiefly during the Time the late Earl of Macclesfield presided in the Courts of King's-Bench and Chancery*, London, 1736, pp. 105–7. For the *Reports* compiled by William Salkeld (1671–1715), Serjeant-at-Law and law reporter, see p. 271 n. above.

First printing of a Speech.

902. To take down a speech and publish it is no invasion, I suppose, of any Copy Right. Why? Because the pattern is of the making of him who takes down the speech. It is he that has first made secondary visible signs that are the signs of those primary audible ones of which the speech consisted.

Digest or Abridgment.

903 To publish a Digest or Abridgment, variant to a certain degree from the pattern, is not, I suppose, an invasion of Copy-right. Why? Because, for the discourse in question to be a copy, the visible signs in the alleged copy must be in the same order with those in the pattern. I say to a certain degree: for what shall be the precise degree in each particular case is what no one general description is capable of expressing.

Compilation.

904. A Compilation from several pattern Books is no invasion of the Copy-right to any one: provided no part of a certain ratio, in respect of quantity, to the remainder be thus copied. But what shall be deemed that certain ratio in each particular case is what no one general description is capable of expressing.

Jury of Authors.

905. The tribunal for determining the particular question in every case should be a Special Jury of Authors. Their names are to be had from the Books of the Stationers Company.[1] The Number recusable by each party might be greater than in common.

Digest. Monopoly of dormant Reports.

906. Of all Monopolies, the most oppressive, though the least complained of, is the Monopoly of the grounds of Justice. Were it proposed by Parliamentary authority to print dormant Reports, and any man possessed of any such Report should refuse to bring it in, such a man would be a monopolizer. Such a monopolizer would be a Caligula.[2]

King. Self-sufficient = Separate Legislative Power ⟗ Conjunct.

907. The King's subordination, therefore, consists not in that he possesses no self-sufficient legislative authority, but in as much as, in respect of that which he has, he is subordinate.

Lit. Prop. How to give an idea of.

908. Suppose you were about to *create* Copy-right, or right to a corporeal article of Property: you being, we are to understand, a Magistrate invested with full authority so to do. How would you do

[1] Under the Copyright Act of 1709 (8 Ann., c. 19), the Company of Stationers was required to keep a register in which 'the Title to the Copy' of all published books was, for a specified fee, to be recorded.

[2] Gaius, better known as Caligula (12–41), Roman Emperor from 37, published laws relating to new taxes in very small writing, and hung them on tablets posted at a great height: see Suetonius, *De vita Caesarum*, IV. xli; Dio Cassius, *Roman History*, LIX. xxviii. 11; and Blackstone, *Commentaries on the Laws of England*, i. 46.

it? The making answer to this question is the only means by which an accurate idea of the nature of those species of property is to be convey'd.

---

909. Defalcations from the utility of the Religious Sanction. 1st. Circumstances enervating it's influence. 2d. Misapplications of it. Op. Mag. Sanction—force of application of.

Of Sanction[s], one is in it's nature less useful than another, either if less powerful, whether well or ill applied, or if, whether more or less powerful, it be ill applied;[1] i:e: applied to the producing of modes of conduct not productive of pleasure, or preventative of pain.

---

910. These signs may, in reference to those abovementioned, be called secondary. Signs primary)(Secondary.

---

911. Hieroglyphics were an attempt to express ideas by secondary signs immediately without the intervention of the primary. But this attempt succeeded so ill, that Hieroglyphical writing is become proverbial for it's obscurity. Copy Right. Hieroglyphics.

---

912. In both cases, the right which the Law gives a man is the right of having other persons punished. Copy-Right.

In both cases, a material substance is concerned; in the one as much as in the other. In both cases, a material substance is the passive object of the act made penal by the Law.

The case of one man's being restrained for the benefit of another from a particular use of an article of property in other respects his own is nothing new. Examples of it are abundant. All powers given upon trust. All restraints laid on Trade. All partial rights of property. Tho' in partial rights of property, a power over the thing in question is given to the partial proprietor. From the instances of a translation and a rehearsal, we may be convinced that it is not ideas that are the objects of literary property; or ever were claimed as such.

---

913. In strict propriety of speech, the original, and indeed only, power that it is in the nature of Law to create is power over persons: when instead of the word 'persons' we put the word 'things', and say, power over things, the word power changes it's All Power is over persons.

[1] The remainder of the sentence has been marked by Bentham for deletion.

signification. It imports not the same relation to things, that it did to persons. What is Power over persons? It is the Right of having persons punished on certain accounts. What, then, is Power over things? Is *this* the right of having *things* punished? This cannot be, it is plain. What, then? Why, nothing more than still to have persons punished, but on this particular *account*, their meddling with things.

Circumstances of an act analysed. Qualities secondary. How far to be taken into account amongst the circumstances on which an effect depends.

914. An effect is said to depend upon secondary *qualities* in the active instrument or influencing circumjacent bodies. But what is *quality*, meaning secondary quality, in a body? Whence come we to say that it has such or such a quality? It is only from having observed bodies that, by means of their primary qualities, appear to us of the same sort to have been concerned as active instruments more or less remote in producing such and such effects in other bodies, that is causing those other bodies to present to our senses such and such primary qualities.

N.B. The qualities by which Bodies make themselves perceptible to the sense of feeling are the only ones that are *constant* and invariable. Those by which Bodies make themselves perceptible to the sight are *occasional* only and *variable*.

Prefat. One of the two sources of litigation sealed by Metaphysics.

915. All Questions of Law are no more than questions concerning the import of words. Questions the solution of which depends upon skill in Metaphysics. As that master science, therefore, advances to it's perfection, this source of litigation will be contracted. Even already we see questions of Law growing every day more rare. Time may come when it shall be sealed up altogether; and when litigation shall be reduced entirely to questions of fact. Towards sealing up this only remaining fountain of forensic strife, unhappily the power of Metaphysics can do but little. Lawyers need never, therefore, despair. At the end of ever so many myriads of centuries, work for them will not be wanting, so long as that be true in sober sadness which David said in his wrath, 'All men are lyars.'[1] Ere the arrival, however, of this comparatively happy period, Lawyers will have changed their function, if not their name. No longer Lawyers, they will then be Orators. The *Advocatus* will remain, when the *Legister* is no more.

Conditions to Conditions.

916. Among events or groupes of events made influencing

[1] Psalm 116: 11.

circumstances by force of conditionalizing expressions of volition, one may be destructive of another; a third of the 2^d; and so on, in a series of alternate destruction, to any length. The appearance of a second signal may be appointed to countermand the first: of a third to countermand the second; and so on. The controul applied to a disposition by a first condition may be taken off by a second condition to that first: set up again by a third condition to that second; and so on.

Opposition destructive of Proprietorship.

917. The opposition which persons in general are debarred from giving to uses made by a proprietor of his property is, $1^{st.}$ Physical acts producing physical restraint. $2^{d.}$ Threats of physical violence producing mental restraint. $3^{dly.}$ Any endeavour to dispose other persons to administer like opposition. 4. Any physical act exercised upon the passive object in question, rendering it unfit for any use of the proprietor. Though this is itself an act of proprietorship, as well as an opposition to the proprietorship of another.

Command—expression of it not confined to sentences in the imperative form.

918. There is no sentence that is not assertive. A sentence expressing volition is as much assertive as any other. A sentence importing interrogation is a sentence importing volition. 'What is your name?' 'My name is Thomas.' The former of these sentences is as much assertive as the latter. 'What is your name?' is as much as 'Tell me what is your name.' 'Tell me what is your name' is as much as 'My will is, that you tell me what is your name.' Every interrogative sentence is resolvable into a volitional, and every volitional one into an assertive: Volitional sentences differing from other sentences only in this, that what is asserted by the former is always an act of Volition.

In man, says Mr Harris, there are two distinct faculties: Perception and Volition.[1]—Be it so. A declaration that I exercise an act of the faculty of Volition is just as much an assertion, as that it is an act of that of perception that I exercise.

Preface. Helvétius. Locke.

919. To that branch of the Science which concerns the substance, that which concerns the form is instrumental: 'tis this

[1] See Harris, *Hermes*, p. 15: 'Now the POWERS OF THE SOUL (over and above the meer nutritive) may be included all of them in those of PERCEPTION and those of VOLITION. By the Powers of PERCEPTION, I mean the *Senses* and the *Intellect*; by the Powers of VOLITION, I mean in an extended sense, not only the *Will*, but the several *Passions* and *Appetites*; in short, *all that moves to Action, whether rational or irrational.*'

last mentioned, therefore, that must be despatched the first. The determining of the acts proper to be done by Legislators; and the determining and marshalling the words that are the signs of them.[1]

Prefat. Disrepute of Metaphysics. Judges quoted.

920. Drenched in obscurity—

'I have avoided a large field which exercised the ingenuity of the Bar. Metaphysical reasoning is too subtile.' *Case Lit. Prop.* J. Willes Arg.^{t} p. 39.[2]

'It has been ingeniously, metaphysically, and subtilly argued on the part of the Defendant, that there is a want of property in the thing itself, wherein the Pltf supposes himself to be injured; and consequently, if there is no Property or Right, there is no Injury or Privation of Right.' *Case of Lit. Prop.* J. Aston's Arg.^{t} p. 41.[3] See Ld Mansf^{d} Arg. p. 114.[4]

Whatever is said amiss, or supposed to be said amiss, in matter of Law, is charged upon Metaphysics. If a Lawyer, in his argument, talks without a meaning, it is charged upon Metaphysics. When a man finds it difficult to apprehend his adversary, and therefore difficult to confute him, he turns upon his heel, and with a pish cries out Metaphysics'.

The labour of straining to find a meaning in a set of words in which, because there is no meaning, no meaning is to be found, is a labour that can not fail of being attended with uneasiness. An uneasiness thus produced, like any other, naturally seeks a vent.

It is [easier][5] to feel that there is an error somewhere, than to see where it is it lies. It is [easier][6] to perceive that the ideas belonging to the words employ'd are confounded with something, than to see always what that something is.

---

[1] Cf. 'A Comment on the Commentaries', in *Comment/Fragment* (*CW*), p. 347: 'Nothing has been, nothing will be, nothing ever can be done on the subject of law that deserves the name of Science, till that universal precept of Locke, enforced, exemplified and particularly applied to the moral branch of science by Helvetius, be steadily pursued, "Define your words".' While Claude Adrien Helvétius (1715–71), French fermier-général and philosopher, does not appear to have used the exact words attributed to him here, Bentham may have had in mind his chapter on the abuse of words in *De l'esprit*, Paris, 1758, pp. 31–41.

[2] From the argument of Edward Willes (bap. 1723, d. 1787), Solicitor General 1766–8, Justice of Kings Bench 1768–87, in *Question concerning Literary Property*, p. 39. There are some minor inaccuracies in the rendering of this and the following passage.

[3] From the argument of Aston in ibid., p. 41.

[4] Mansfield referred to 'the Metaphysical Subtilties from the Nature of the Thing' in discussing whether the Common Law granted ownership of copy to an author before publication, if it did not do so after publication: see ibid., p. 114.

[5] MS 'easy'.

[6] MS 'easy'.

921. It is marvellous to what a degree this hapless science is in disgrace. With some, it stands for Atheism. With others, for whatsoever is unintelligible. Yes, so it is that whatever is unintelligible is laid to the account of that science, which, when taught and practised as it ought to be and might be, is neither more nor less than the art of making one's self understood. Now, what certainly is liable to happen is, that in endeavouring to make what he says more intelligible than before, a man may make it worse. But is this the fault of the science itself? No, but of the manner in which it happens to be practised. An operation in Surgery miscarries. Follows it that Surgery is an useless, a pernicious art? No, surely; but that the practitioner was in that instance unskilful or unfortunate. Prefat. Metaphysics. Apology For.

As doth Jurisprudence still, so did Natural Philosophy once, want the aid of the Metaphysician. Natural Philosophy, when Locke came to it's assistance, saw itself half smother'd, the avenues to it blocked up by a heavy congeries of obscure and useless nomenclature. To this hour would the Orthodox Academics have been disputing about quiddities *a parte rei*, about real essences, and substantial forms in earnest, as they are *pro formâ*,[1] had not the heterodox and apostate Locke stept in and snatched those baubles out of their hands. Locke spake, and those airy phantoms were swept into the ocean of oblivion.[2]

For opposite purposes, Natural Philosophy wanted, at the time of Locke, and Jurisprudence wants still, the aid of the Metaphysician. Natural Philosophy wanted a Scavenger: Jurisprudence wants an Architect. Natural [Philosophy],[3] a Scavenger to clear it of that rubbish under which it lay buried, of words that never had a meaning: and this exploit was atchieved by Locke. Jurisprudence, an Architect to build up for it a competent suite of terms and expressions, to lodge separately those meanings which as yet are either absolutely without a mansion, or else huddled up by half-dozens together in the obscure and ambiguous abodes which the current Nomenclature affords; to say nothing of such terms as, though they have perhaps no more than one idea to inhabit them, require a certain light to be struck out in them before they will place that one inhabitant in any clear and conspicuous point of view. For this work it is, that Jurisprudence wants an Architect: and this Architect, whoever he be that shall undertake it

[1] In the margin, Bentham has noted at this point: 'Note stating the case.' No such note has been identified.

[2] For Locke's criticism of Scholasticism see p. 200 n. above.

[3] MS 'Philosopher'.

with success, or rather these Architects, for scarce can the powers of any single man be equal to any enterprize so mighty, must work according to the rules laid down by Locke.

Comm. Signal of Resistance.

922. A settled disposition to inflict upon the state worse evils than would be the probable consequences of rebellion.[1]

Circumstances of an act analysed.

923. What we have occasion to speak of as Events, are brought about often by occult powers of bodies. Where we see not the operation of the Cause.

It is not so in Actions. By an action, if external, we always mean an event that is visible: a visible motion of man's body directed to a certain end. We not only see a change in the appearance of circumjacent bodies as the consequence of the action when at an end. But we may see the action itself while it is carrying on. All actions that are in the power of the Will are, as it were, Muscular.[2] Actions, i e: Single Motions depending upon occult Chymical and Physiological powers, are not, any further than the mechanical actions introductory to them are. A man may choose whether he will put his hand to his mouth to put a piece of bread into it. He may choose whether he will swallow it. But when it is once swallowed, he cannot by any motion communicated immediately by the Will to any absorbent vessels, prevent or accelerate digestion.

Dependance.

924. An event that is to come after is supposed to depend upon an event that is to go before when the antecedent is supposed to be among the circumstances necessary to the production of the consequent: in other words, when it is conceived that, if the antecedent does not take place, neither will the consequent take place.

Consent.

925. Consent to an act is an assertion, that the idea of the act as done or about to be done (whichever is the case) is pleasurable (gives pleasure) to the party consenting. 'I Consent' is an expression of volition, whereof the object is an act of a person other than the party consenting; but of a volition which did not originate in his mind. It is the union of a subsequent volition with another person's precedent volition having the same set of objects.

Consent given by one man, implies previous *proposal* by another.

---

[1] Cf. 'A Fragment on Government', Ch. IV, in *Comment/Fragment* (*CW*), pp. 474–92.
[2] MS orig. 'Mechanical'.

926. An immense assemblage of circumstances are disposed of together by the different modifications of time and place. Place, limiting the groupe of circumstances co-existent to the act: Time, the train of circumstances subsisting in succession. Circumstances of an act analysed. Circumstances of Time and Place.

927. *Quis, Quid, Ubi, Quando, Cur, Quomodo, Quibus auxiliis.* Circumstances.

928. To the question *Quis*, answers the personal active object: *Quid*, the real passive object: *Ubi*, the Place: *Quando*, the Time. *Quis, Quid* &c. *Quis. Quid.*

929. To the Question *Quando*, tell me as many of the imaginable circumstances as are excluded from being objects of the volition in question by the limitation of the Time. *Quando.*

930. To the Question *Ubi*, answer so many of the circumstances as are excluded from being objects of the volition in question by the designation of the Place. *Ubi.*

931. To put the question *Quis*, is as much as to say, name or describe to me the personal active object. *Quis.*

932. To put the question *Quid*, is as much as to say, tell me the real passive object. This passive object, it is plain, may as well be personal as real; it may as well be a person as a thing. Either this consideration did not occur to the framer of the verse,[1] or if it did, has no question properly adapted. *Quid.*

933. To the bare act or situation itself, no Question seems to be applied. The reason is, we may suppose, that this is designed as an arrangement of what are circumstances only with respect to the bare act or situation: consequently, this of which the articles in question are given as circumstances has no place among a set of articles which are given as so many circumstances of, and therefore distinct from, this. To find an expression already in use for a question adapted to this article of consideration would not, I believe, be easy. Principle act or Situation—no question to.

The word *Quid*, it is true, is as fit to be applied to the *bare act* or *situation* as to the *passive object*. But it cannot, without confusion, be understood to be meant to be applied to both.

934. To put the question *Cur*, is as much as to say, tell me that Pain or Pleasure, that Painful or Pleasurable consideration in the mind of the active object which determined him to that act, or forbearance, which is the modal object. *Cur.*

935. To put the question *Quomodo*, refers to the concurrent physical events and physical situations. *Quomodo.*

[1] Perhaps a reference to the verse which appeared in Thomas Wilson, *The Art of Rhetoric* (first published in 1553), ed. P.E. Medine, University Park, PA, 1994, p. 60:

Who, what, and where, by what helpe, and by whose:
Why, how, and when, doe many things disclose.

Quibus Auxiliis. **936.** To put the Question *Quibus auxiliis*, is as much as to say, tell me the concurrent acts and voluntary situations.

Situation Voluntary ✕ Physical. **937.** A situation of the parts of a voluntary agent (with respect to one another, or any other bodies), such a situation, when brought about by the volition of the agent, may be stiled a Voluntary situation.

Evidence. **938.** Evidence is either direct, or presumptive.

—direct. **939.** A man is said to give direct evidence of an act, or situation, or discourse, when he asserts that the individual act, situation or discourse in question did come within the cognizance of his senses, that the individual act in question not only has happen'd, but that, when it did happen, it made an impression on his senses.[1] That he saw such a blow given by such a person to such another person. That he saw such or such persons sitting in a room together at the same time. That he heard such words spoken. That he saw such and such money put into the hand of such a person by such a person: or that, being blind, he felt it. That he saw or felt the body or bodies in question undergoing such a motion, or resting in such a situation: or that he heard such and such words. Such situation, motion or words being supposed to be the very objects of enquiry.

Evidence presumptive. **940.** A man is said to give, not direct evidence of an event, situation or discourse, but presumptive only, when he asserts, not that [the] act &c. did come within the cognizance of his senses, but some other so connected with it as that the existence of the act &c. not deposed to may reasonably, it is supposed, be inferred from that of the act deposed to. The act in this case deposed to may, with respect to the act not deposed to, be either precedent, concomitant, or subsequent. The act deposed to in this case is, in the ordinary technical language of lawyers, said to be *evidence* of the act not deposed to.

One act Evidence of another act.

The poverty of language, or the inaccuracy of the conceptions of men of Law, has occasioned strange confusion in the use of this word Evidence.

Evidence—assertor, assertion, thing asserted. **941.** The person asserting is said to be Evidence, an Evidence. The discourse by which he asserts is said to be Evidence. The act, situation or discourse which he asserts to have existed, not being that which is the very object of enquiry, is said to be evidence of that which is . . .

Evidence written. **942.** Among evidentiary modes of situations, that which makes

[1] In the text Bentham has noted at this point: 'v. 437.' See para. 1036, p. 325 below.

the greatest figure, and is most frequently apt to come in question, is that which, subsisting between certain particles of matter and other particles of the same or a different sort of matter, forms, in the most extensive sense of the word, writing.

Witness—Testimony—

943. This confusion was nothing less than necessary. For Evidence, as applied to the person, we have the word, Witness: as applied to the discourse, Testimony.

Indicium.

944. For the import, indeed, which it bears as applied to the event or situation deposed to, we have no word in current use. A word, however, that might be made to answer this purpose is the Latin Word, *Indicium*. Such an act, we may [say], or such a situation, is an *indicium* of that act or situation which is the direct object of enquiry. The word is every now and then used for this purpose, especially in the Plural Number.[1]

Evidence. 3 Senses of.

945. The Evidence which the Evidence gave was conclusive Evidence of the Marriage.

The Testimony which the Witness gave was a conclusive *indicium* of the Marriage.

Evidence. *Indicia* real)(symbolical.

946. *Indicia* may be distinguished into Real and Symbolical.

By real may be understood appearances of a body actually exhibited as one that bore on it the marks of it's having been a circumjacent body influenced by the act in question.—As appearance of the bloody cloaths or weapons, produced in a trial for murder. So the subject in dispute in a question of Real Property, when *viewed* by the Jury.

Or *Indicia* deposed to)(produced.

Indicia (whether deposed or produced) substantial[2])(modal.

Indicium written. Authenticity of. Verity of.

947. A piece of writing produced as an *indicium* is most commonly of such a nature as to signify an assertion. In this case, the two questions most open to debate are: 1st. Whether this apparent assertion is the assertion of him whose assertion it purports upon the face of it to be: the other, whether, supposing it to be his, the assertion contained in it be true: whether the events or situations which it asserts to have taken place, did actually take place as asserted. The first of these questions is that which concerns the authenticity of the piece of writing; the 2d that which concerns it's verity, or veracity.

Indicium, cogency of.

948. A third question is, supposing it both authentic and true, concerning the [cogency][3] of the presumption[4] which it affords.

If the assertion which it contains is an assertion of the existence of the act or situation that is the direct object of enquiry, then the

[1] i.e. *indicia*.
[2] MS orig. 'corporeal'.
[3] MS 'cogent'.
[4] MS orig. del. '*indicium*'; MS alt. 1 'indication'.

business of the *indicium* is despatched under the two first questions, concerning it's authenticity and veracity.

If the existence of such an assertion, written by such a person, be all that is the direct object of the enquiry, then the business is despatched under the question of authenticity alone.

Bare Act ⁐ Proximate Situation.

949. The notion of the Bare act is apt to be confounded with that of the situation it is immediately productive of.

Circumstances of an act analysed. Circumstances—Qualities and Powers excluded—why.

950. Strictly speaking, it is not proper to speak of any event or situation as depending upon any secondary qualities, or powers, of the active or passive bodies themselves, or bodies circumjacent. Such qualities, therefore, and powers are not to be number'd among the influencing circumstances belonging to the act or situation spoken of. It is not such a quality or power itself that is among the circumstances concurring to the production of any individual act or situation, but some individual instance of the exertion of such a quality or power: that is some supposable motion or situation among parts too minute for the motions or situations of them to be separately perceptible to our senses.

Thus it is that, notwithstanding secondary qualities and powers, all physical circumstances cognizable by our senses are reduced to motions or situations of circumjacent bodies.

Qualities and Powers, nothing real.

951. The Quality or Power is not any thing the existence of which we have a perception by our senses. All it signifies is a disposition we attribute to the object in question to be instrumental in producing in us such or such ideas, or in things such and such perceptible situations, the result of motions and situations that are unperceptible. A fancied disposition, attributed to it by our imagination, from our having been accustomed to perceive ideas or situations of such or such a sort produced by the instrumentality of the bodies in which we suppose those qualities and powers to inhere.

To rank such qualities and powers amongst objects the existence of which makes itself perceivable to the senses would be a manifest impropriety, and productive of a good deal of confusion.

Law ⁐ Fact.

952. So true it is that it is the Question of Law that the Jury determine as well as of Fact when they give a General Verdict, that if they do not, nobody does; and the question is not at all determined: for before no one else is it brought into debate. As to thus much, therefore, judgment is given without the cause ever being heard.

Were the Jury to be totally ousted from the cognizance of the question of Law, what, it may be said, would be left for them to do, more than barely to report the words of the testimony that may have been given? There would be this: to draw inferences from *indicia* deposed to.

But even this has been made matter of Law: so much has the Jurisdiction of the Judge encroached upon that of the Jury. The greatest part of the books we have that are written upon the subject of Evidence[1] is taken up with a detail of cases of this sort, where Judges have assumed to themselves the province of drawing these inferences, of determining whether the *indicium* in question ought to be deemed conclusive of the principal fact. 'Tis by means of this encroachment only that we have the History of these cases handed down to us: for whatever is submitted to the Jury is understood to be particular, and not proper or not necessary to be drawn into example. Attempts these, many if not most of them, to subject that under general rules which is not susceptible of rules; and much to the impediment of the ends of Justice. Under a secret notion, but too often ill-founded, of bringing out a general utility, by means of the certainty that would result in that behalf from the establishment of some such general rule as it is in the nature of Judiciary decisions (I mean decisions of Judges in contradistinction to those of Juries) to give birth to, the particular utility resulting from the giving satisfaction to the bystanders,[2] in the manner of deciding the pretensions of the particular parties litigant, has been made a most frequent sacrifice.

---

953. Other works might be found, not much less open, perhaps, to the shafts of criticism of which I neither have taken, nor purpose to take, notice. One reason is, because they appeared to me to be written with more sincerity and openness. Another reason is, because they are not, like this, in possession of giving Law to men's opinions.

Comm. Prefat. Why this attacked and not others.

That this book is to a very great degree in possession of setting the Law to men's opinions, one cannot doubt. To their opinions, I mean not merely as to what *is* Law, (that were a small matter) but as to what ought to be. The opinion which it seems to be the

[1] See, for instance, William Nelson, *The Law of Evidence: wherein All the Cases that have yet been printed in any of our Law Books or Tryals, and that in any wise relate to Points of Evidence, are collected and methodically digested under their proper Heads: with Necessary Tables to the Whole*, London, 1717; [John Strange], *A Collection of Select Cases Relating to Evidence,* London, 1754; and Geoffrey Gilbert, *The Law of Evidence*, London, 1754.

[2] MS orig. 'public'.

constant and almost universal scope of the work to inculcate is that that ought ever to be, which *is*.

The influence of the opinion[s] and turns of thought that are interwoven in it cannot but be to a great degree extensive. The natural effect of this influence appear'd to me to produce an epidemic debility in the moral department of men's intellects. A state of listless and abject quietism . . . . . .

Fact { Act. Situation.

954. Fact may be taken for a Common Term, significative as well of event or act as of situation: and like Act, it may be distinguished into simple, or bare, and complex.

Encroachment of Law upon Fact is made *bonâ fide*.

955. In the formation of this erroneous habit, if such it may be deemed, there seems to have been much more of want of discernment than of want of probity. I see not that it is fairly to be attributed to the love of power, or any wish to extend their own Jurisdiction at the expence of that which they have understood to belong properly to [the] Jury. I attribute it to nothing more than to that propensity which is natural to the profession, to subject every thing to rule. For we find the disposition manifesting itself alike in Judges the most popular as the least popular in their affections, and not more in causes of a constitutional nature, than in causes of a nature ever so remote from constitutional.

Where the mischief does not lie.

956. The grand mischief of this lies not in the transference of the question from the Jury to the Judge. Where Juries, conscious of the difficulty of unravelling an intricate question, wish or are content to transfer the task to more experienced hands, it is well: since whether they will do so or no is at their option.

Where the mischief does lie. 1st. In judging by Rule.

957. The grand mischiefs are these. In the first place, the preventing the apparently true conclusion from being drawn, under the notion of it's running counter to some fancied rule, which they suppose ought to be consider'd as established. This disappoints the party, who, if the real truth of the case were known, would have had the decision in his favour. It disappoints the bystanders, who, forming in their own minds a conclusion opposite to that which this rule prescribes to be done, go away possessed with the opinion that, in the instance in question, the end of Justice has not been attained. Hence, from the recurrence of many such particular instances, they are apt, as they see those instances more and more frequent, to be more and more fixed in a persuasion that in general, according to the common course of Procedure, the ends of Justice are in more and more danger of not being attained: thence, in short, to tremble more and more for what may be their own fate, should they, tho' with right on their side, be involved in litigation.

958. In the next place; this decision, being reported and made known to Judges in general, tends to confirm the imaginary rule in question, and by it's example give birth to more and more of these sorts of rules which, when applied to particular instances, are much oftener the occasion of conclusions unconformable to the truth of things than of such as are conformable. Were the Judge to put himself entirely in the place of the Jury, turn a deaf ear to all quotations of precedents, and merely from the particular *indicia* before him set himself to infer the existence or non-existence of the fact, and were his decision no longer to be remember'd than it would be were it the decision of the Jury, nor made any other use of than it would were it the decision of the Jury, it might in general be full as well in his hands, as in their's. To a method of proceeding the reverse of this are owing those mischiefs that must have been so often and so severely felt; and of which the *indicia* are extant in so many of those cases that are to be met with under the head of evidence. —2dly. In giving birth to new Rules.

---

959. All these rules, it ought to be well remember'd (tho' I am persuaded that it is what many a Lawyer, perhaps many a Judge, has never so much as dreamt of), it ought, I say, to be well remember'd that they are good for nothing but in proportion as the conclusion which they prescribe is apt to be the true one. Rules concerning the force of *Indicia*, the end they ought to have.

---

960. Power over things is a Right to have persons punished for meddling with things. Power over Things.

---

961. Power over persons is a Right to have persons punished for not doing certain acts at command of the party empower'd, or for not submitting to bear certain acts of his: among which acts may be acts of punishment. Power over Persons.

---

962. A man has a right to have others punished, when he is under those circumstances which those are under at whose request or on whose behalf others are accustomed to be punished. Right to have men punished.

Circumstances of an act analysed. Time and Place.[1]

963. The idea of Place is diversified, that is ideas of different places are obtained, no otherwise than by means of the ideas of bodies exhibiting certain motions or situations. Were there but one particle of matter in the world, whether at rest or in motion, there would be no such thing as Place. When a Law limits itself in respect of Place, it establishes as a condition to the command or prohibition that it imports, that, of the bodies circumjacent to those which are the material objects of it, some be in such motions, others in such situations, as those bodies are in that occupy the place in question.

So, likewise, the idea of Time is diversified, that is ideas of different times are obtained, no otherwise than by the means of the ideas of bodies in certain motions or situations compared with the ideas in our mind. Were there ever so many sentient beings in the world but only one particle of matter, whether at rest or in motion, to furnish them with Ideas, there would be no such thing as Time any more than place. Were one of those sentient beings transferred on a sudden into such a state of things as that in the world we live in, he could have no memory of any periods of time or distinctions of place subsisting during his former existence. I have supposed one particle only of matter: but that one either at rest or even in motion. But suppose as many particles as there are now, and suppose them, from the first as well as the last, always at rest, even in this case there would be no such thing as time neither no more than Place. It is a conceit, I think, of Plato's, that, after a certain period of I know not how many thousand years, the measure of events would be full, and that, immediately from thence, the same scenes would begin to be acted over again, and so *toties quoties* through as many periods as will fill up eternity.[2] We are now, at the present instant, in the first of these periods. Supposing that the next instant we are in the corresponding instant of the second; at the next of the third; and so continually: annihilating the interval between the correspondent instants of ever so many periods . . . .

Suppose all the sentient beings in the world occupied during the whole period of their existence with but one idea a-piece, there would be no such thing as Time.

When a Law limits itself in respect of Time, it establishes as a condition to the command or prohibition which it imports, that, of the bodies circumjacent to those which are the material objects of it, some be in such motions, others in such situations, as those

[1] In the margin, Bentham has noted at this point '*non placet*', i.e. 'It does not please [me].'

[2] Bentham presumably had in mind the story told by Er, in Plato's *Republic*, x. 614–21, of the cycle of birth and death, which occurs every thousand years for each individual soul.

bodies are in which occupy the place in question during the time in question.

The ideas we have of Time and Place are no otherwise explicable than by reference to the identity or diversity of bodies circumjacent to those in question, and of the motions and situations of such circumjacent bodies.

---

964. Since all legal power is properly speaking Power over persons or Right as against persons, i:e: right to have Power over persons exercised by others; and Power over persons is liberty to exercise certain acts upon persons as the passive objects of those acts, or others productive mediately or immediately of bodily pain in persons, how is it that the name of Power is applicable to what is called the Devestitive power? The truth is, this is properly speaking but a Right. It is the right of taking a person out of a favoured class, and throwing him into the mass of the people at large; that is of such who, if they attempt to meddle with those things in the possession whereof consists the benefit of the class, meet with punishment from the hands of persons in power, in consequence of this declaration of the Will of the divestor.

Power Devestitive respecting beneficial classes, not a power over persons but a Right.[1]

---

965. All that the Legislative Power as such can do is to mark out, by competent denominations or descriptions, so many classes of persons, some the objects of it's coërcion, others of it's favour: to fill up these classes, by appointing the persons who are to compose them, belongs to some branch or other of that Power which is called Executive.

Powers Legislative and Investitive—connection of.

The Legislative Power as such says not ever, Let this or that Individual person be punished: but let such a class (describing it) of persons be punished. What individuals shall be deemed to be of that class, and consequently shall have punishment inflicted on them, belongs to the Power called Executive.

Of the two powers, Legislative and Executive, take away either, and all efficacy is at the same time taken from the other. Take away Executive Power, and the Legislative, if it open it's lips, opens them to no purpose. It composes classes of individuals, but those classes are empty, for want of the Executive Power to fill them up. It declares that persons known by such and such marks shall be so and so dealt with, or be at liberty so and so to deal with others: but for want of the Executive power to set those marks, there are no persons who have those marks upon them.

[1] In the margin, Bentham has noted at this point: 'Qu.'

On the other hand, take away the Legislative Power, and the Executive doth not so much as open it's lips. It fills up no classes with individuals; for there are no classes to fill up. It sets not any marks upon individuals, because there are no marks appointed to set upon them. It declares not that any individuals, on account of their being of such or such classes, shall be so or so dealt with, or be so and so at liberty to deal with others; because no such classes do subsist.

As these two Powers, each dependent on the other, are perfectly distinguishable from each other, so are either of them equally distinguishable from that which, in a state, is independent, and which alone can properly be called supreme.

Power Despotical.

966. The supreme power, it is manifest, can be constituted no otherwise than by the Union of these two. For this strictly supreme power, we want as yet a name. Despotic would serve to express it exactly, did it convey this idea and no other. The misfortune is this: the word Despotic, besides the principal idea which it is here our purpose to give a name to, has got annext to it, as an accessory idea, that of a disapprobation entertained by the party speaking, of the sort of power which is the object of the principal idea. It is used scarce any otherwise than, as the phrase is, [in] a bad sense. Were I, therefore, to apply this expression to the idea of the power I have in view although it were barely to speak of it as subsisting, it would be thought I meant to stigmatize it as mischievous. Were I to speak of it as that which not only does subsist but must subsist, I should then run a risk of being stigmatized myself, as being an advocate for that which is mischievous. 'Out upon him,' would cry the multitude of warm hearts and weak heads, 'out upon him, there goes an advocate for despotism.'

Power Magisterial.

967. I will use, therefore, the word Magisterial, which originally is but a translation of the other, but which is not like that become obnoxious. I will use it, notwithstanding the other senses it has got annext to it, since they are so easily distinguishable from this, that it will be easily seen whether it is in this that it is used on any occasion or in any of them. To make sure, however, I will still guard it with the epithet supreme.[1]

Powers Legislative and Executive.

968. It is the separation of the Powers Executive and Legislative that is the grand preservative against partiality in Government, that abuse which is stiled emphatically, and in a bad sense, Respect

[1] This sentence has been marked by Bentham for deletion.

of persons. The Legislative alone can not respect persons, because it knows not the persons that shall be it's objects. The Executive is restrained in a great degree from respect of persons, by the obligation to confine itself in it's choice to such persons as have those marks upon them that are set by the Legislative. For, if to the Executive it belongs to set certain marks itself, yet can not it do so, but on pretence at least that the individuals on which it sets them bear already certain other marks pointed out by the Legislative.

Use of separating them.

---

969. Supreme Magisterial power in the same hands every where with the supreme Legislative—why. While it exerts itself, it sets itself in the place [of][1] the supreme Executive.

Autocratic Power rarely exerted.

In a well-modelled Government, therefore, like our's, the supreme Magisterial Power exerts itself but rarely. Not frequently to confer benefit: and very rarely to inflict punishment. If for the latter purpose, it is only in a time of danger, at a crisis, as an *ultimum remedium.*

---

970. Legal classes of persons are either Permanent or Transient.

Classes permanent ⟗ transient—how far objects of favour and of coercion.

They are either objects of the Law purely of it's favour, of it's coercion, or both.

Classes of persons that are objects purely of the Law's coercion are transient: they are composed of the several classes of delinquents.

Classes that are objects purely of it's favour are very few, and those narrow. They are classes of mere dignity, without power and without duty.

I know not whether to speak of classes of proprietors as objects purely of the Law's favour, subject as they are to Taxes; since their subjection to taxes is separable from their proprietorship in idea: but, besides this, they are objects of it's coercion in as far as their rights in their respective properties are limited.

Classes which are the objects partly of favour and partly of coercion are those which are the most numerous: only of these, in some, coercion may be seen to predominate, in others, favour.

Mostly favoured—Masters of Hired Servants, Masters of Apprentices, Guardians, Schoolmasters, Persons in Public Office of Profit or Power.

Mostly coerced—Hired Servants, Apprentices, Wards, Scholars.

[1] MS orig. 'above'.

Equally coerced and favour'd on each other's account—Husbands, Wives—*sed Quære*—Joint proprietors, Joint-Traders, Occasional Contract-makers.

Coerced and favoured on the public account—the several classes of persons engaged in Trades or occupations *enclosed*.[1]

Favour cannot be without Coercion.

971. Whatever influences the operations of the Law have upon the conditions of persons are all reducible to the heads of favour and coercion. Coercion, it may administer to any one purely, without administering to any one, by the same operation, favour. Favour it cannot administer to any one, but by means of coercion administer'd to others. Coercion administer'd on account of delinquency is punishment.

Prefat. Law-Premiums—interest *contra*.[2]

972. For improvements suggested in Chemistry, in Clockmaking, in Navigation, in short in a great multitude of those arts which extend the physical powers we have over physical bodies, for all sorts of discoveries tending to the perfection of the physical branch of Science, Premiums have been offer'd by public authority, and Bounties given.[3] For improvements in the art of Legislation, no Premium was ever offer'd, nor bounty given. I mean in this country, nor in any country perhaps, except in the dominions and under the reign of that pattern for absolute Sovereigns, Catherine of Russia.[4] What is the reason? Is it that the art of Legislation is of less importance than the arts of Chemistry, of Navigation or of Clockmaking? By no means. Is it because it is less difficult? Nor so neither. It is because large and liberal minds, in persons entrusted with the business of Government, minds superior to jealousy, to indolence, to political timidity and the whole tribe of selfish interests,[5] are so rare.

No Statesman makes pretensions to Skill in Chemistry, in Navigation, or in Clockmaking; none at least looks to make any personal profit by the exercise of those arts; or flatters himself with being able at pleasure and by his sole strength to turn them to the purposes of his interest. Improvements in those arts neither make themselves an enemy of his jealousy by any lustre they may reflect upon the inventors, nor of his indolence by any trouble they give

[1] In the text, Bentham has noted at this point: 'Trace the application of the Rights of Investment and Devestment with respect to each.'

[2] MS del. 'Cp. Mag. Premiums—why never given for Law Essays.'

[3] On the offering of premiums for the discovery of a method of precisely determining longitude at sea see p. 89 n. above.

[4] Catherine II (1729–96), Empress of Russia from 1762.

[5] The phrase 'and the whole tribe of selfish interests' has been marked by Bentham for deletion.

him in carrying them into execution; nor of his timidity, by the danger of their being censured and opposed.

In Legislation it is otherwise . . . .

He dreads the appearance of a project, the honour of which, if popular, he fears would be the lot of the proposer, while the odium and fatigue and danger of carrying it into execution would be peculiarly his own. To remain neuter is to be a Cypher, and to submitt on that behalf to a suspension of his power. To oppose it may make him unpopular with some; to forward it, with others. To oppose it, or to forward it, will equally give him trouble.

Government in vulgar hands amounts to nothing more than the management of parties, the repelling and providing against the attacks of enemies; the confirming the attachment and encreasing the number of his friends and co-adjutors by a prudent administration of douceurs: the applying occasional cures or palliatives to the occasional diseases of the body politic in as far as, by the uneasiness they raise, they threaten to give him trouble. For these ends, he is of his own force sufficient, or if he is not, it is not by projectors that he can be assisted. To these ends, projects of public and lasting benefit do scarcely, to his conception, contribute any thing. Will they enable him to bring over such an opponent? to satisfy the cravings of such a co-adjutor? Will they calm any of his anxieties; will they rid him of any of his fears? Will they put money into his purse? Will they enable him to substract more moments from those duties of office which are least seasoned with the sweets of gain or power?

While no miseries are felt but what men are accustomed to witness or to suffer[1]

973. Perhaps the annals of History offer not an example at once so much to the consolation of subjects, and to the reproach of sovereigns, as that of Catherine offering premiums for political writings, herself already among the most illustrious of politicians and of writers.[2] Premiums, the subjects of which are the best chosen, the most important, of the greatest utility, and that of a sort the least personal to the sovereign.[3] Cath. of Russia.

[1] The sentence has been abandoned at this point.

[2] Bentham may have had in mind the *Nakaz* or 'Instruction' written by Catherine II to guide the legislative commission she convened in 1767 in order to reform Russian law.

[3] Bentham may have had in mind Catherine II's establishment in 1768 of a Society for the Translation of Foreign Books, with a grant of 5,000 roubles per annum, which led to the translation into Russian of a number of political and legal works, including Montesquieu's *De l'esprit des loix* and Blackstone's *Commentaries on the Laws of England*: see I. de Madariaga, *Catherine the Great: A Short History*, New Haven and London, 1990, p. 95, and S. Dixon, *Catherine the Great*, London, 2009, p. 199.

Invading their province, and taking the business out of their hands . . . . .

Op. Mag. Tax. Lenitive circumstances.

974. A Tax is slightly felt, 1st. By coming at the same time with, and being taken out of, an unexpected benefit. As a Tax on distant Successions and Legacies to remote Relations. 2dly. By being taken out of a large Mass or Capital. As would be a Tax on Conveyances.

Op. Mag. Laws anti-expectational: remedy, postponement.

975. Laws mischievous by thwarting Expectation to be cured by postponing the æra of their commencement till there has been time for expectation to bring itself to a conformity. But Laws in general are mere temporary expedients, nor does any man think of making them for the sole benefit of Posterity. Such a postponing would take away all the odium of the measure; since if the æra were distant enough, it might be plain that the proposer could have no view of personal benefit to himself.

In Com. Law, the very signs not settled.

976. It is true that the same ideas may not present themselves to all men's minds upon the appearance of the same signs: and on that account even Statute Law is to a certain degree liable to misapprehension. Upon the construction even of Statute Law differences will arise. But still there is a common Standard which all men acknowlege, and all men are ready to resort to. Every one understands and is ready to acknowledge that the legitimate import of those signs, whatever that be, contains a true account of the several modes of conduct that, under the penalties thereby intimated, are to be abstained from or observed. If two portions of Statute Law prescribe opposite modes of conduct, it makes no difficulty. It is universally agreed that the latest is to be deferred to.

Common Law not only has this infirmity, as one necessary to every thing that bears the name of Law, but has another that is peculiar to itself. In this, as in Statute Law, the modes of conduct which it renders penal can be characterized no otherwise than by the current signs; of which signs the import is as liable to be mistaken as those which make up the Statute Law. But a misfortune peculiar to Common Law is that the signs themselves are not established. No person can settle with himself, much less can any two persons settle with one another, what book [it is] that[1] contains that standard, that collection of signs, relative to so much as any single mode of conduct, that all men shall abide by.

[1] MS 'another, what collection it is, what book that'. The presentation of the text at this point is conjectural.

In short, in Statute Law the signs are settled; all the difference there can be is about the import of those signs. In Common Law, not so much as the signs are settled.

---

977. In Common Law, men, before they can determine with themselves whether the mode of conduct they propose to pursue be penal or no, have the following tasks to accomplish.

Comm. Law—Difficulties peculiar to.

First they have to make to themselves, out of accounts of the treatment given to individual articles of conduct, an idea of a general mode of conduct, such whereof that in question shall be an individual.

2dly they have to determine whether the treatment given by Judges to the individual mode of conduct pitched upon was legal: that is conformable to the treatment given by preceding Judges to similar modes of conduct.

3dly they have to determine whether the account given of that treatment was just: that is whether the Judges in question did really give that treatment to the individual article of conduct taken for a pattern that the account states them to have done, and that for the reasons which they are stated to have avow'd.

In short, they have to determine $1^{st.}$ Whether the case assumed be in point; or perhaps, of ten different cases that may be equally apt to be assumed, which is most in point. $2^{dly.}$ To take one only for example, whether that one was Law. $3^{dly.}$ Whether the Report given of it be accurate.

. . . In which of a number of proposed cases is contained the essence of that in question . . . .

---

978. How this proposal for so many new coined terms and expressions will be relished by the generality of thinking persons is more than I can foresee. Many, I am persuaded, had rather sit down and submitt still to the disease, with all it's inconveniences, than be at the trouble of the remedy.

Prefat. New-coined words.

To persons of that disposition, so long as they continue in it, I have nothing more to offer. All my wish is to find myself, by the suffrages of more zealous and more scrutinizing readers,[1] warranted to say to them, if at any time, by accident, they should find it worth their while to be able to annex clear ideas relative to the subjects about which these words are conversant, there they are for them.

---

[1] The phrase 'by the suffrages . . . readers' has been marked by Bentham for deletion.

Consent upon Cognizance.

979. No consent to the validity of an instrument containing an expression of Will can be upon cognizance till the contents of it have been read or heard by the party whose consent is in question.

Power Executive = Investitive.

980. Of Executive power (i:e: investitive), some is in Public hands. Such is—Power of Appointment to Offices and Judiciary Power, and Appropriate Occupations[1] and Civil Relations. Some in Private hands—such as that of appointing to Proprietorship of the different articles of Property.

Judge's appointing a man to be one of a class of Criminals, one thing. This is a Decision, and is an act of investment. His command to punish the person so invested is another thing. This is a Command, a Warrant, Order, Writ, &c.

Execution *mediate*)(*Ultimate*. Judicial Investment is Ultimate. Appointment to classes favoured or mixed by respect is Mediate.

Division.

981. Division, when simple, is the enumeration of the next species of a genus without the *differentia*.[2]

Distinction.

982. A Distinction is the giving the *Differentia* between two terms without naming for them any common genus.

Individualization. An Individualizing Proposition, what.

983. The business of Individualization is a business that occurs incessantly in that branch of the Law that concerns Property: none is there more important nor more difficult. Among the several articles of Property—passive objects, therefore, of the Law of Property—none are there that make so conspicuous a figure as Houses. The House I occupy, for the time I have in it, is my own. But what is it that is my house? Of a mass of matter occupying a certain space, for example, of 50 foot square, within which unquestionably this thing that is my house is to be found, how much is it, and what, that is neither more nor less than my house? The making answer to this question is the performing that which, with respect to my House, may be called the business of Individualization. Any Proposition serving to express that answer, or a part of it, may properly be stiled an individualizing proposition. Now then, the business of individualization with respect to houses has, on a great many occasions, been made the subject of legal debate, but is far from being as yet any thing like settled.

Individualization—Instance, of a House.

984. This House I hire for a term: but as I must restore it entire at the end of my term, whatever has at any time been part of it, at

[1] For 'Appropriate Occupations' see paras. 731–4, p. 232 above.

[2] In the text Bentham has noted at this point: 'v. p. 301.' See paras. 726–7, p. 231 above.

least whatever was part of it at the moment I hired it, I must not carry away with me. To know, then, what I must not carry away with me, is to know what, to this purpose, is my house. It may be Law, that whatever was part of the House at the time I hired it, that part I must not only not take away by any act of mine, but if gone without any act of mine, I must supply the loss of it. In legal terms, as I may be restrained from voluntary waste, so may I from permissive. The description of what is Waste, as applied to Houses, depends upon, in part, and includes in it, the individualization of a House. The truth is, that under our Law, the individualization of a house varies, or may vary, according as it is come in question between Landlord and Tenant, between the Heir of a Deceased owner and the Executor or Administrator, between Thief and Prosecutor, between one party charged what is called the Land Tax and another party taxed on account of something within the same portion of space, between Defendant in a suit and Sheriff's Officer; in short, between many other pairs of disputants, perhaps, that might be mentioned.

These differences there are two ways of adjusting. One is, by declaring that the idea, that is that y[e] complex idea to be annexed to the term House, shall be composed of a different assortment of less complex ideas as it's ingredients in these different cases: the other is, to declare that the radical idea of a House shall be the same in all of them, shall in short to all purposes be one and the same, and that other terms shall be employ'd to express those different masses of matter which are meant to be taken for the passive objects of the Law in the different sets of circumstances by which these different cases are distinguished. Of these methods, the first, if practicable, is the more simple, the more consonant to common apprehension, the more accurate, in short the more serviceable, and on these accounts the more philosophical. The latter is, on the opposite accounts, the more Lawyer-like, the more of a piece to what has been hitherto the usage among Lawyers. According to the first, a House is always one and the same thing; according to the latter, it is at one time one thing, at another time, another. This tickles the Lawyer's imagination with the idea of the marvellous; and his pride with the idea of power. That a thing should be a house, and not a house, that, by a kind of legal legerdemain, it should undergo one knows not how many metamorphoses, and that he, by the acumen of his wit, should be the metamorphoser; that, by a puff from his mouth or a dash of his pen, he should change the essences of things, and be able to lead a house a dance, as

Angels did that of our Lady of Loretto,[1] is that sort of conceit of the acceptableness of which the whole Law bears testimony.

Classification. Felony.

985. The Classical name of a mode of conduct that is made penal should convey an intimation of the motive the Law has for making it so.

Writers proceeding in a technical method are forced to take technical terms to set at the head of their compartments. The matter with which those compartments are filled is determined accordingly by the extent that has been given to those terms. Hence it is that matters ever so heterogeneous to each other will often be crowded together in one and the same compartment. One single circumstance that chance has for a time render'd common to modes of action, which other permanent circumstances have render'd as dissimilar as any can be, shall, by thus forcing them into the same compartment and ranking them under the same name, beget an opinion of their similarity. The single circumstance that accident has render'd common to a multitude of acts, their having been, by positive appointment of the law, made to have the effect of bringing death and other penalties on the agent, has made them all to have been thrust under the same name of Felony. While in those circumstances on which depend those constant and natural effects to which they owe their mischievous quality they are so dissimilar, many of them, that scarce any can be more so.

Prefat. Metaphysics: compartment of Law, how far it includes that of the other Sciences.

986. The species of substances that are capable of being the passive objects themselves, or circumjacent to those that are the passive objects, of the Law, the modes of motion or situation that are capable of being the modal objects themselves, or circumstances of those that are the modal objects of the Law, are neither fewer nor other than the species of substances and of modes that are or may be the objects of all the other sciences—than, in short, whatever species of substances or of modes are to be found in nature. The exposition, therefore, which, for the purposes of this science, any one of them may require, may be the exposition that

[1] According to Roman Catholic tradition, the Holy House, or *Santa Casa*, a site of pilgrimage in the Italian town of Loreto, was the birthplace and home of Mary, mother of Jesus, having been carried there from Nazareth by angels at the end of the thirteenth century. Roman Catholics accordingly give Mary the epithet 'Our Lady of Loreto'. See, for instance, D. Jeffereys, *A Journal from London to Rome, by way of Paris, Lyons, Turin, Florence, &c. and from Rome back to London, By Way of Loretto, Venice, Milan, Strasbourg, &c.*, London, 1742, pp. 70–2.

may be required and is given of it for the purposes of any other science as well as for any purpose of common life.

Properly speaking, then, within the Metaphysics of the Law must be included the Metaphysics of all the other sciences.

987. If the Law declares that the Money that is made shall be of a certain fineness, to the Lawyer as well as the Metallurgist it belongs to be assured when it is that Money is of a certain fineness. If the Law requires that Houses should be built in no other than certain proportions, to the Lawyer as well as the Architect it belongs to be assured when it is that Houses are built in those proportions. If the Law requires that, for spirits of a certain strength, there be paid a certain duty, to the Lawyer as well to the Chymist it belongs to be assured what are spirits, and when it is that spirits are of that strength. If the Law requires that noisome substances, i:e: substances that render the circumambient Air less fit for respiration, shall not be manufactured in certain situations, to the Lawyer as well as to the Pathologist it belongs to be assured that certain substances in manufacturing are noisome. If the Law requires that just Scales be employ'd, to the Lawyer as well as to the Mechanician it belongs to be assured when it is that Scales are just. If the Law requires that just measures be employ'd, to the Lawyer as well as to the Gauger it belongs to be assured that measures also are just. If the Law, for the benefit of Trade, requires that certain persons shall not sail within a certain Latitude, to the Lawyer as well as to the Astronomer it belongs to be assured, when it is that men have sail'd within a certain latitude. If the Law, for the benefit of Navigation, and thence of Trade, requires that, if it be possible, the Longitude be discover'd, to the Lawyer as well as to the Astronomer it belongs to be assured where it is that the Longitude can be said to have been discover'd. If the Law requires that mortal wounds be not given, to the Lawyer as well as to the Surgeon it belongs to be assured when it is that wounds are mortal.

Metallurgy.

Architecture.

Chymistry.

Pathology.

Mechanics.

Mathematics.

Astronomy or Navigation.

Surgery.

I could go on and exemplify this observation throughout every science that has been distinguished by a name: but the instances that have been given will, I apprehend, be quite sufficient.

---

988. If the Law has been so unhappy as to require that doctrines against the Trinity shall not be published, to the Lawyer as well as to the Theologian it belongs to be assured, or rather to fill his ears with a certain jargon under the notion of being

Theology.

assured,[1] what doctrines are Anti-Trinitarian.[2] If the Law requires that Witchcraft be not practised, to the Lawyer as well as to the Necromancer it belongs to be assured what practises are acts of Witchcraft.[3]

Necromancy.

Gibberish.

989. If the Law requires that men should believe Kish-copthu-raphorizon to be true, to the Lawyer as well as to the Gibberician it belongs to be assured what is Kish-copthu-raphorizon.

Botany.

990. If the Law requires that, for the security of the land against inundations, the plant called Star or Bent shall not be rooted up,[4] to the Lawyer as well as to the Botanist it belongs to be assured what is the plant that is called Star or Bent.

Metaphysics: what *proper* to Law.

All the words that belong exclusively to Law are those that intimate the annexation of pain to those modes of action above exemplified or any other in consequence of the Will of Men in Power. The mode of conduct not by itself, but as attended by this circumstance, viz: that of it's having pain connected with it by those means.

That department, therefore, of the Metaphysics of Law that is most peculiarly it's own is that which contains the Exposition of those terms.

Stat. Law—a proposition of.

992. Every sentence is either a whole Law or some part or parts of a Law, which serves either to intimate a connection between pain and any mode of conduct formed by the Volition of him who intimates it that is the Lawgiver, or is subservient to the exposition of any such *sort* of conduct between which and pain such a connection is thus established: the speaker being of the number of those by whom the state is in use to suffer such connection to be formed.

Comm. Law—a proposition of.

993. A sentence which serves to intimate a connection that would or would not, as the case is (in the opinion of the speaker),

[1] The phrase 'or rather . . . assured' has been marked by Bentham for deletion.

[2] Dissemination of Anti-Trinitarian beliefs 'by Writing, Printing, Teaching, or advised Speaking' was prohibited by the Blasphemy Act of 1698 (9 & 10 Wil. III, c. 32).

[3] Blackstone begins his discussion of the offence of '*witchcraft, conjuration, inchantment, or sorcery*' at *Commentaries on the Laws of England*, iv. 60–1, by stating that it 'is a crime of which one knows not well what account to give'.

[4] The Starr and Bent Act of 1741 (15 Geo. II, c. 33) imposed a fine of twenty shillings or commitment to a House of Correction for three months for pulling up starr or bent without permission of the landowner.

upon occasion be formed between pain and a sort of conduct, judging from individual articles of conduct supposed of the same sort, between which and pain a connection has, it is supposed, been established by the Volition of a person or persons of that class by whose volition the state is in use to permitt such connection to be formed between pain and individual articles of conduct, a sentence serving to intimate such a connection, or to describe the sort of conduct in question, is what may be termed an Article of Common Law.

994. An Article of Statute Law is either perfectly authentic or utterly inauthentic: it's authenticity admitts of no degrees. Either it is the expression of the Will [of] some competent Legislator or it is not. Because it is certain that, if it be the expression of his will, it will be conformed to by the Judge: and that, if not, it will not be conformed to by the Judge.

Statut. Law—authenticity of a proposition of.

---

995. Of an Article of Common Law, the authenticity does admitt of degrees. It may be more or less authentic. Because, granting it to be the discourse of him whose discourse it purports to be, it is not a matter of certainty, but a chance, whether it will be conformed to by the Judge. This chance is greater or less in proportion to the reputation of him whose discourse it is.

Comm. Law—authenticity of a proposition of.

---

996. A Law is a Command. To the purpose of expressing command, a particular form of speech has been appropriated. This form of speech, consider'd as comprized in a single word, is a Verb in that mode which is stiled the mode of command, that is the mode imperative. Consider'd as subsisting in a sentence, it is such a sentence of which a verb in the imperative mode enters into the composition. Every sentence that contains in it any thing of the nature of a command is of this sort. If a sentence be not of this sort, it contains not in it any thing that is of the nature of a Command.

Stat. Law, proposition of. Form Volitional not essential to it.

If a sentence, then, have not in it a verb in the imperative mood, how is it that it can be a Law, or can enter into the composition of a Law?

---

997. A person possessed of Copy-Right by Authorship is one who, by his own act, is become of that class of persons in whose favour other persons in general are debarred from a particular use of their own property.[1]

Lit. Prop. Copy-owner by Authorship. Debar.

[1] The Copyright Act of 1709 (8 Ann., c. 19) established a statutory copyright for authors and publishers lasting twenty-one years for books already in print, and fourteen years for

Copy-owner by Purchase.

998. A person possessed of Copy-Right by purchase is one who, by an act of the Author or of the Law on occasion of some act or situation of the Author's, has been appointed one of that class of persons.

The profits of the Trade of Bookselling arise from one or other of these two sources. First from the sale of Books of their own publication. 2dly. From the Sale of Books published by others.

Arguments—pro. Stated.

999. I. Because it is consonant to original utility.

II. Because were it originally indifferent, it is now consonant to utility resulting from expectation.

1. That it would be maintained was from the first expected: viz: from the consideration of a supposed moral obligation resulting from the original utility of it's being maintained. 2. It is now expected—on two accounts: 1st on that just mentioned. 2dly. From it's having been for a considerable length of time actually and constantly maintained. For it has been the Custom of Judges to maintain it.

Lit. Prop.

1000. No man is indifferent to money absolutely.

A man may be willing to give up money for the honour of giving it up.

But that motive does not subsist where he never has had it in his power to receive the money. Is there any man alive, in his right senses, who will lay his hand upon his heart, and say, that the knowing it to be in his power to receive a hundred Pound, without making any man a sufferer, without any disgrace to himself, without his violating any duty of Religion, would be no pleasure to him; would not act on him in any degree as a motive to stimulate him to action? If there be, I demand of him, as a proof of his sincerity, to give me a hundred Pound, or to shew how it is that he can have any unwillingness to part with the hundred Pound he has, being utterly indifferent to the hundred Pound he might have.

new books. A long campaign ensued by London booksellers to establish a Common Law right to literary property, culminating in the case of *Millar v. Taylor* (1766–9). On 20 April 1769 the Court of King's Bench gave judgment in that case, to the effect that there was a perpetual Common Law right to literary property. See Burrow, *Reports of Cases adjudged in the Court of King's Bench, Since the Death of Lord Raymond*, iv. 2308–408. In February 1774, however, in the case of *Donaldson v. Beckett*, the House of Lords, after hearing the opinions of the twelve Common Law judges, reversed the decision in *Millar v. Taylor*, holding that authors had an exclusive Common Law right to the first publication for perpetuity, but that this right was annulled once the work had been published: see ibid., iv. 2408–17.

It has been intimated that among literary men, at least among men of honour, pecuniary reward is no incentive to action.[1]

Are the foreign Academies of this opinion when they give their premiums?[2]

Are the Society of Arts of this opinion?[3]

Is the Legislature of this opinion when it annexes Salary to Office?

Are there no men of honour among Merchants?

Are there no men of honour among Judges who accept their Salaries?

Are there no men of honour among Judges who, having retired, and no longer receiving Salaries, accept Pensions?

An illustrious Lawyer, whom no one doubts to be a man of honour, retiring from the high post he occupied, accepts a Pension. Was it for services of the class of literary services that it was granted him, or for services of any other, and what, class, or for no services at all? Before it was granted to him, was he totally indifferent to the acceptance of it: was it without any concurrence of his will that he accepted it, and that he now continues to accept the payments due upon it?

Is the case so, that a man, immediately upon writing a book, be it on one subject or another, let it contain his own sentiments or another's, totally change[s] his nature, becomes totally insensible to pleasure and pain, and to the means of procuring the one, and guarding against the other?

[1] In the House of Lords on 22 February 1774, following the rendering of judgment in the case of *Donaldson v. Beckett*, Charles Pratt (1714–94), first Baron and first Earl Camden, Chief Justice of Common Pleas 1761–6, Lord Chancellor 1766–70, asserted that the claim of a perpetual right to literary property was not supported by 'the positive laws of the land', 'public principles of sound policy', or 'good sense'. 'Glory', he continued, 'is the reward of science, and those who deserve it, scorn all meaner views: I speak not of the scribblers for bread, who teaze the press with their wretched productions; fourteen years is too long a privilege for their perishable trash. It was not for gain, that Bacon, Newton, Milton, Locke, instructed and delighted the world; it would be unworthy such men to traffic with a dirty bookseller for so much a sheet of a letter press. When the bookseller offered Milton five pounds for his Paradise Lost, he did not reject it, and commit his poem to the flames, nor did he accept the miserable pittance as the reward of his labour; he knew that the real price of his work was immortality, and that posterity would pay it.' See *Parliamentary History* (1771–4) xvii. 1000. For the contract of John Milton (1608–74), poet and polemicist, with his bookseller, whereby he sold his copy of *Paradise Lost* for an initial payment of £5, see Iohn Toland, *The Life of Milton; Containing, besides the history of his works, several extraordinary characters of men, and books, sects, parties, and opinions: with Amyntor; Or a defense of Milton's life* (first published in 1699), London, 1761, p. 121 n.

[2] The French Academy, for instance, had awarded annual prizes for eloquence and poetry since 1671.

[3] The Society for the Encouragement of Arts, Manufactures and Commerce, founded in 1754 on the initiative of William Shipley (bap. 1715, d. 1803), set out to support and stimulate the liberal arts and sciences by offering cash prizes, and from 1756 medals, for the successful completion of a range of scientific and technical challenges.

Is what distinguishes the sordid from the liberal, that either of them is indifferent to money? No: but that while one prefers money to fame, the other prefers fame to money.[1]

In general, the less taken a man is with the thoughts of gaining money, the more taken he is with the thought of having it in his power to refuse it.

A man's refusing money that is offer'd him is no proof of his indifference to it. It proves not that [his] love of money is absolutely weak; but only that it is weak in comparison of his love of fame. There are men who would see a | | reward in their judgments worth the pains of no .... pursuit, on the offer of money which they were before determined not to receive.

Indifference absolute)(comparative—absolute impossible.

It is far from being yet proved that a man, the instant he publishes a book, ceases to love his wife and children.

Many a book of merit it may not be prudent, nor safe even, to avow. In this case, where is the fame the love of which is to swallow up that of money?

Comm. Law—'does so and so': how to be explained.

1001. When we find it said, therefore, that the Common Law does so and so, all that we can understand by the expression is, that the writings of some Lawyer give us reason to think that a man would be punished or fail of being punished in such a case.

Prefat. Metaph.

1002. Metaphysics general)(particular.—Particular is so to each respective science; and respects the terms of that science.

General Metaphysics includes as well the several branches of particular Metaphysics, as that remaining field of phraseology which lies in common to men of science and the vulgar.

Prefat. Metaphysics. Bolingbroke.

1003. When Bolingbroke[2] spoke of Metaphysics as presiding over Law,[3] he spoke in the way of prophecy and not of history.[4] For of any such connection, no traces were in his time visible. No such connection is established even yet: unless this feeble attempt should be thought in some degree to have done it. This avowal

[1] In the text, Bentham has noted at this point: 'suppose him an ideal monster, such as the earth ne'er saw'

[2] Henry St John (1678–1751), styled first Viscount Bolingbroke, politician, diplomatist, and author.

[3] See p. 197 n. above.

[4] In the text, Bentham has noted '1' above the word 'history', and '2' above the word 'prophecy', perhaps indicating that the phrase should read 'in the way not of history [but] of prophecy'.

was a sacrifice for which we are particularly indebted to his candour; for in few instances more than that of his own eloquent works is the want of metaphysical knowlege more strikingly display'd. In him, the Orator had swallow'd up the Metaphysician.

1004. A Title to be met with in most of the Abridgments is Condition.[1] What can be more confounding, more perplexing to the apprehension than such a Title? How to catch at the Ariadnean thread[2] by which the mind is to conduct itself to the discovery which is to present [to] it the several objects with which a compartment thus entitled is filled?

'Condition'—contents of such a Title in Law, general idea of.

Thus much is certain, that Condition, being a Title of Law, what the propositions contained under such a Title must have in common amongst them all, is the exhibiting a connection established by appointment of Law between pain or pleasure and certain modes of conduct.

Examining into the contents of those compartments thus entitled, we find the condition intimated by the Title to be a Condition annext to that kind of Private Executive Regulation which is entitled a Conveyance. The contents, therefore, of this Title all come under the General Law of Appropriation. The modes of conduct with which pain is intimated to be connected by the propositions included in this compartment are, therefore, any of those which are the modal objects of the General Law of Appropriation.

1005. Our mind, so long as it is bent to the consideration of any one of these vague and abstract terms, is kept hovering, as it were, upon the wing, in a state of effort and anxiety: nor does it ever feel itself at rest upon a firm footing till it gets a perception of the relation there is between these terms and some one or other of the terms by which some object of sense, some external substance, motion, situation, or some internal feeling, is wont to be denoted.

DIG. Prefat. Abstract terms (such as Condition, &c.): inconvenience of taking for Titles or Heads.

1006. Algebra of Law as yet in use is incommodious. A. and B. are bad personal appellations. The occasional name employ'd to signify a person, bearing a relation to a certain title of Law, should

Algebra of Law. Denomination of fictitious persons.

[1] See, for instance, Matthew Bacon, *A New Abridgment of the Law*, vol. i, London, 1736, pp. 395–438, and Charles Viner, *A General Abridgment of Law and Equity Alphabetically digested under proper Titles with Notes and References to the Whole*, 23 vols., London, 1742–57, v. 41–344.

[2] In Greek mythology, Ariadne, daughter of King Minos, provided the thread which guided Theseus through the Labyrinth at Crete.

Literal cognomental vague: cognomental characteristic.

at least be characteristic of *person* in general. Thus far the John Nokes and Thomas Styles answer'd their intention. Whether it was from the idea of ridicule that Plays or Poems or other engines of wit had connected with these fictitious but useful personages, or the superior expedition of the literal mode of denomination, poor John Nokes and Thomas Stiles have been almost universally discarded[1] To supply the place of these, a new set of personages have been introduced by the Author of the *Commentaries*; whose Antique and Roman appellations, it was supposed, would defend them against the force of that ridicule under which their aboriginal predecessors had sank. These were the Gaii, the Titii, the Xavii, the Sempronii.[2] This intention the contrivance seems effectually to have answer'd: but not, I believe, without an attendant inconvenience. From a recollection of past experience, I am apt to think there is a certain terror inspired by these extraneous visitants that is rather unfavourable than otherwise to the purpose of apprehension. To the difficulties of the Common Law, they are apt to add a certain confused idea of the difficulties belonging to that System of Jurisprudence in which they took their birth.[3]

Exposition—place of the exponend.

1007. In an expository proposition, where the signification given to the exponend is in common use, and the business is only to fix it, there the name of the exponend may come first. Where the signification is new, much more where the name itself is new, it were better it should follow. The exposition serves then to usher it in.

Comm. Divine Law.[4]

1008. Inspired writers not *constantly* inspired, allow'd. If they themselves recommend any mode of conduct contrary to utility, or represent God as enjoining it, they are in that particular to be deemed uninspired.

[1] The generic names 'John-a-Nokes' and 'John-a-Styles' or 'Tom o' Styles' were the names of fictitious persons used in legal writing from at least the sixteenth century: see, for instance, Christopher St German, *The Secunde dyaloge in Englysshe bytwene a doctour of dyuynytye and a student in the lawes of Englande*, London, 1530, Ch. IX, fo. 24; and Hale, *Historia Placitorum Coronæ*, ii. 244. By the eighteenth century, the terms had passed into more general and often frivolous usage: see, for instance, 'The humble Petition of John-a-Nokes and John-a-Styles', *The Spectator*, 6 August 1714; Matthew Prior, 'Alma: or, the progress of the mind', in *Poems on Several Occasions*, London, 1718, p. 377; and John Dryden and Nathaniel Lee, *The Duke of Guise. A Tragedy*, London, 1735, p. 337.

[2] See, for instance, Blackstone, *Commentaries on the Laws of England*, ii. 460–1, where the fictitious characters Titius, Sempronius, and Gaius appear.

[3] In the text, Bentham has noted at this point: 'Initials of official names by Burn. J.P.' Burn explains his use of abbreviations such as '*A.O.*' for 'offender' and '*J.P.*' for 'Justice of the Peace' at *Justice of the Peace and Parish Officer*, i. p. xxiii.

[4] For Blackstone on the divine law see *Commentaries on the Laws of England*, i. 41–2.

Those reports of sense which teach us in what proportion pain or pleasure are the consequences of any action are more to be depended upon [than][1] any reports of history which are supposed to teach us to believe it was forbidden or enjoined.

The enactment of any such Law, a signal of resistance.

If, after all, we are bound to believe there are such Laws, they should give us a precise Catalogue of such Laws; without knowing which, no Government upon earth is safe in moving a finger.

These Laws, either it is easy to know them; or it is not. If it is, I call upon him to produce a Catalogue. If not, then must every Legislator be a profound Divine. None but profound Divines are fit to be Legislators. Not Montesquieu, Beccaria,[2] Helvétius, but Patrick,[3] Lowth,[4] Whitby,[5] Vitringa,[6] &c. should be the furniture of the Statesman's Library.

1009. It is not, I doubt, by any one man that such a Dictionary can be brought to it's perfection. No man has a clear idea annext to any abstract term, untill he is able to mark out it's relation to some of those terms to which simple ideas or determinate assemblages of them stand annext. This is more than any man has [done][7] as yet. There is no man living, therefore, or that ever lived, who could be said thoroughly to understand every term of Law. No man will ever have it in his power to say so, till a compleat Vocabulary shall be formed of Moral terms.

Prefat. Clear ideas how rare.

1010. Seeing the minds of witnesses through a paper[8] is seeing through a glass darkly: how much better were it to see them face to face.[9] How much easier is it for a man to tell a lie with his hand, than with his tongue? with his tongue, than with his looks?

Evidence—Oral better than written.

[1] MS 'that'.

[2] Cesare Beccaria, Marchese de Beccaria-Bonesana (1738–94), was author of the influential work on penal theory *Dei delitti e delle pene*, first published in 1764.

[3] Simon Patrick (1626–1707), Bishop of Chichester 1689–91 and Ely 1691–1707, was a prolific author on religious topics, best known for his devotional works.

[4] Robert Lowth (1710–87), Biblical critic, Professor of Poetry at the University of Oxford 1741–51, Bishop of St David's 1766, Oxford 1766–77, and London 1777–87, was noted for his *Praelectiones De Sacra Poesi Hebrœorum*, Oxford, 1753, and his immensely popular *A Short Introduction to English Grammar: with critical notes*, London, 1762.

[5] Daniel Whitby (1637/8–1726), clergyman and author, was well-known for his *A Paraphrase and Commentary on the New Testament*, 2 vols., London, 1703, but published nearly fifty works in total.

[6] Campegius Vitringa (1659–1722), Dutch Protestant theologian and Hebraicist, was noted for his *Anacrisis Apocalypsios Joannis Apostoli*, Franeker, 1705, and *Commentarius in Librum Prophetiarum Jesaiœ*, 2 vols., Leeuwarden, 1714–20.

[7] MS 'been'.

[8] MS orig. 'the medium of written depositions'.

[9] I Corinthians 13: 12.

If any one doubts this, let him say whether, if he had occasion to draw a confession out of his Wife, his Child or his servant, would he choose to see them and examine them face to face, or send them to a distance, and give them 6 weeks' time to consult Lawyers and to frame an answer.

This is one, and that not the least, of the abuses of that useful art, writing.

Evidences of side[s] adverse should always be confronted.

Evidences of a side, most carefully kept separate. During the time of examination, they should be constantly under guard.

These precautions are in practise shamefully neglected.

Prefat. Metaph.[s] of Cause and Effect the common concern of all Science.

1011. The relation of cause and effect is within the department of every thing that bears the name of science. Every science is interested in the improvement of this capital branch of metaphysics. Every science is in a situation to be benefitted by stocking it with a competent apparatus of Nomenclature. The Lawyer, the Physician the Natural Philosopher are in this way in a situation of affording to each other mutual assistance.

Law ☓ Fact.

1012. Where the complex idea annext to the current name of any mode of conduct includes in it the idea of it's being the object of Law, there a verdict of guilty or not guilty, that is a proposition asserting an opinion that it has happen'd or not happen'd, necessarily involves in it an opinion concerning the matter of Law: viz: that it is a mode of conduct which the Law prohibits or does not prohibit.

By the supposition, the name of the act, i:e: according to the idea annext to it by general usage, includes in it the idea of the relation born to it by the Law. If, then, the Jury annex to that name the same idea that is commonly annext to it, they can do no otherwise than to declare, by a verdict of guilty, that the mode of conduct in question is contrary to some Law.

The very word involves in it the idea of an operation of the Law. It does so necessarily in the mind of every man who ever used it; unless he used it with a determination of using it in a sense different from that given to it by every body else. Strip it of this and you strip it of half it's import. By it are signified uniformly and universally two things. 1[st.] That some individual act has been done or forborn 2[dly.] That that act or forbearance is an act or forbearance made penal by some branch of the Law.

I am very ready to allow that the tribunal of a Jury would be a very unapt tribunal without the controlling power of Judges by profession. I am very ready even to allow that, except in constitutional causes, were we reduced to the necessity of taking the one alone, or the other alone, we might better dispense with the first than with the second. I am ready to go so far even as to allow that were the publicity of all legal operations to be kept perfect, and the liberty of discussing them entire and uncontrolled, on these terms but upon no other, I would allow that whether, even in constitutional causes, the power of deciding the fact were not as well in the hands of Judges as of Jurors, I mean for the purpose of obtaining such an opinion relative to the particular question in hand as shall be conformable to truth, *might* be matter of honest doubt.

All these concessions I am ready to make, and I think they are no inconsiderable ones, touching the question of abstract original utility. But with respect to the question of right as it depends upon actual usage, I cannot dissemble a plain matter of fact, which, viewing it in the light that I do, stares me in the face. I cannot help seeing that, in point of uniform and unvaried usage, Juries are, and ever have been, Judges of the Law; and that as fully and as necessarily as those Judges who are known commonly by that name. I cannot think, therefore, that in assuming openly and avowedly a right to determine the question of Law, they assume a new and extraordinary jurisdiction, or that those who lay claim to that right for them, claim such a Jurisdiction. I am very ready to allow that when they take upon them to determine the matter of Law, it touches their consciences, and they do it at their peril: but I cannot allow or conceive that it touches their consciences more than determining on the matter of fact touches their consciences, or that determining either touches their consciences more than a determination on the matter of Law by Judges touches the consciences of Judges.

I do conceive, and that with the fullest assurance, that there never was an instance of their giving a general verdict of guilty, where they did not determine the question of Law.

The word guilty of itself, it has been observed, asserts nothing. Something, however, it must mean; and till that something is specified, nothing is asserted; the proposition is incompleat. From this, it may be thought that much depends upon the manner of filling it up; and that as, in one way of filling it up, he that has pronounced the word guilty may be understood to have pronounced upon the question of Law, so, in some other way of filling it up, he cannot be understood to have so pronounced. But this is not the case. No matter what a man is guilty of, guilty of any thing, so he be guilty of something, he is pronounced to have done that which is contrary to some Law. Has he in fact not done that act which [he] is accused of having done? then is he not guilty. Is the [act],[1] which he actually has done, not contrary to any Law? yes, then also is he not guilty.

I am very ready to admit that, if a Jury pronounces concerning the question of Law without just grounds, it touches their consciences; but I am forced to see that if they, without just grounds, pronounce concerning the question of fact, in like manner does it touch their consciences. I am forced at the same time to see that if the Judge pronounces &c.

All this, it will be seen, nor do I wish to dissemble, is founded on the idea I annex to the word guilty. An idea, however, that, as I conceive, contains in it nothing novel, nothing peculiar to my self, nothing of my own putting in; but is the same as any man has ever given to it, from the time of him who first invented the word to the present hour.

I am very ready to admitt, and let our men of patriotism well consider it that if a Jury pronounces through affection or aversion to the man accused or to his party, it touches, and that grievously, their consciences. That it touches their consciences, as far as a violation of that sacred duty can touch their consciences, if, knowingly and willingly, they suffer such motives to have any influence on their decision; and that if, under the influence of the consideration that the man in question is the man they prefer, or that his party is the party they prefer, they give a verdict which, were the man in question a man they disliked, or his party a party they disliked, other circumstances remaining the same, they would not give, they *do* violate that sacred duty; whether ***knowingly and wittingly*** they be sway'd, when sway'd they are, is what I must leave them to settle with God and with their own hearts.

I am very ready to allow, that Juries do often, by their own act, committ to Judges the immediate and primary cognizance of the question of Law; and that where it is obscure to them, and very often in the present state of our Jurisprudence doth it behove to be obscure to them, much are they in the right to do so.[2] But I cannot but see, that these cases are but so many exceptions; and that these exceptions, as is the nature of all exceptions when acknowleged as such, serve but to confirm a general rule that is opposite.

[1] MS 'fact'.
[2] A jury was able to agree on the facts of a case, but refer the question of law on which the verdict would ultimately depend to the court by means of either a special verdict or a special case: see Blackstone, *Commentaries on the Laws of England*, iii. 377–8.

Yet more, I am very ready to see that Juries are in use thus to assign to Judges the question of Law: but I see not less plainly that they are in use also, perhaps even equally, thus to assign to them the question of Fact.

I see surprize and dissatisfaction in many an eye. 'Say you so? The Question of Fact determined by Judges after a verdict, the question of fact determined by Judges where there is a Jury? can this ever be?' Most certainly, unless the finding of the fact be reduced to the finding of the precise words spoken by the witnesses, or the precise contents of the written muniments produced, which any bystander might be left to find with equal safety, and concerning which, in point of fact, the Jury scarce ever are consulted. The drawing conclusions, I mean, from the facts as expressed by the *words spoken* (I will not say, and *looks exhibited*, for these *indicia* are lost when the words are stated upon paper for the confirmation of another Court), from the facts as expressed by the words spoken by the witnesses, and as apparent upon the face of the written muniments, concerning the having happen'd or not having happen'd of that which is alleged to have happen'd, or that situation of things which is alleged to have taken place, and which, the Law being supposed to bear a given aspect, is that immediate act or that immediate situation which renders the accused punishable or not punishable by Law.

This business too, this business when thus assigned, is abusively and improperly termed a business of Law. Not from the consideration of what it is in it's own nature, previous to it's being thus assigned, but merely on this sole account, that thus it is assigned. Whatever is business of Law appertaineth to the Judges, says the ancient and fallacious adage:[1] therefore *è converso,*

[1] See, for instance, *The Reports of Sir Edward Coke Kt. In English, Compleat in thirteen parts, With References to all the Antient and Modern Books of the Law*, London, 1727, 13 vols., viii. 155: 'Matter of fact is to be averr'd by the Party, and triable by the Jurors: The other, being Matter in Law, is to be discussed by the Judges of the Law, and *quemadmodum . . . ad quæstionem facti non respondent Judices; ita ad quæstionem juris non respondent Juratores*': i.e. 'in this way . . . the Judges do not deal with the question of fact; thus the Jurors do not deal with the question of Law.' Cf. Blackstone, *Commentaries on the Laws of England*, iii. 380: 'It is wisely therefore ordered, that the principles and axioms of law, which are general propositions, flowing from abstracted reason, and not accommodated to times or to men, should be deposited in the breasts of the judges, to be occasionally applied to such facts as come properly ascertained before them. For here partiality can have little scope: the law is well known, and is the same for all ranks and degrees; it follows as a regular conclusion from the premises of fact pre-established. But in settling and adjusting a question of fact, when intrusted to any single magistrate, partiality and injustice have an ample field to range in; either by boldly asserting that to be proved which is not so, or more artfully by suppressing some circumstances, stretching and warping others, and distinguishing away the remainder. Here therefore a competent number of sensible and upright jurymen, chosen by lot from among those of the middle rank, will be found the best investigators of truth, and the surest guardians of public justice.'

whatever appertaineth, that is whatever is made to appertain to the Judges is a business of Law. Now then, this being a business of Law, there is no business whatever that occurs upon a legal trial that is not business of Law: for even this mechanical business of declaring what are the words spoken, and what the contents of the written instruments produced, may be conceived to be assigned also to the Judges;[1] and then, by the supposition, it is a question of Law. In fact, it actually is assigned to the Judges, or, to speak what is more the exact truth, taken without ceremony and without asking out of their hands by the Judge and Counsel: the Jury for the most part being passive and unregarded spectators. Such is the practise when the Counsel think proper to have a special verdict taken, and neither the parties nor their attornies oppose it.[2] In this case, no ceremony is thought necessary to the Jury: but that assembly is usually dissolved much in the manner that the Rump Parliament was dissolved by Cromwell.[3]

Law) (Fact. Recapitulation—Introduction to.

1013. All legal jargon and all party chicane apart, a plain account of the usage that has subsisted, and does actually subsist, seems to be this. I venture boldly upon the matter of usage since it is matter of observation, and he that has eyes to see, may see. I venture with fear and trembling always upon the matter of right resulting from usage, since that is matter of opinion. And who shall say with confidence what is the opinion of another?

Law) (Fact.

1014. Will there ever be a time when men in general shall have master'd that prejudice, supposing it to be a prejudice? Possibly. But at that time, whenever it shall be, they will be as well able to discharge the function of Judges in any given instance as those that are so by profession, or else will be as able to see their inability to discharge it in that instance, and equally ready to surrender it accordingly.

---

[1] In the margin, Bentham has noted at this point: 'Special Verdicts, it is well known, are alter'd upon Motion by the Judges without consulting the Jury that was supposed to give them, and long after the Jury has been dissolved.'

[2] According to Blackstone, *Commentaries on the Laws of England*, iv. 354, a special verdict is given by the jury 'where they *doubt* the matter of law, and therefore *chuse* to leave it to the determination of the court'.

[3] During its dispute with Charles I, Parliament passed a Bill prohibiting its adjournment, prorogation, or dissolution without its own consent. The measure received the Royal Assent on 10 May 1641 (16 Car. I, c. 7). The Long Parliament, its members dwindling into the so-called Rump, was finally forcibly dissolved in April 1653 by Oliver Cromwell (1599–1658), who, in December 1653, took formal control of the executive as Lord Protector.

1015. Superfluous to introduce the motive into the definition of a State-Libel, when *vituperative* only and not *criminative*: Op. M. Libel vituperative ☓ criminative.

1016. 1st. Because the motive makes no difference in the effect of the act. Motive not to enter into the Definition.

2d. Because it is undiscoverable. There are no *indicia* of it. The agent knows it not even himself.

A State Libel of the simply vituperative kind is an assemblage of signs expressing a disapprobation entertained by the libeller against a person or persons in a political character, but without charging them with any individual offence.

Hale knew not of any such thing[1] as what we now mean by the Liberty of the Press, allow'd by Law.[2] The whole bent and current of the Law, from the origin of printing to this day, is hostile to it.

For these ten years, one might boldly venture to say, there has not been a single day which has not produced some publication or other which Hale would have deemed criminal.

1017. One Court in a state may be said to be subordinate to another, where the punishment which it belongs to the second to inflict on the common subject is greater than the punishment which it belongs to the first to inflict. Subordination, what between Powers.

1018. There are in the world two ways of carrying on the business of Government. The one is that of governing by Laws. The other is that of governing without Laws. Begin. Stat. Law = enuntiative ☓ Comm. = silent or mute.

When the business is carried on without Laws, it is either by particular transient commands or by punishment: by punishment alone; without any commands, general or particular, to announce it.

Of these three methods, the two first may be comprehended under the common denomination of *enuntiative*; for, under the one as well as the other, the mode of conduct which it is the will of the governing power to have observed is announced in terms before a man is punished for not observing it.

The last may be indicated by the term *silent*; for by this, nothing is, in *words*, *announced*: nothing is, by *words*, made known.

The process in the two first is, first a *word*, then a *blow*: in the last, it is pure blows without a word.

[1] The remainder of the sentence has been marked by Bentham for deletion.

[2] In the time of Sir Matthew Hale, the licensing of all publications, their compulsory registration at the Stationers' Hall, and the destruction of books and imprisonment of authors offensive to government, were authorized under 'An Ordinance for the regulation of Printing' of 16 June 1643: see *Acts and Ordinances of the Interregnum*, ed. C.H. Firth and R.S. Rait, 3 vols., London, 1911, i. 184–6. For Blackstone on libel and the liberty of the press see *Commentaries on the Laws of England*, iv. 150–3.

On the three objects thus distinguished, shall we now stamp their current appellations?

The two first are Statute; the last is Common Law—Lawyers, behold your idol.[1]

Conveyance)(a Promise.

1019. A Conveyance is not a Promise—for whatsoever was to be done is done at the instant. But of a Promise, the modal object is an act to be done in future. The promise is, to do something in future. It may be said it is a promise to abstain from exercising all acts of ownership on the thing convey'd—but this can not be the business of a conveyance. For the obligation of abstinence that results from the conveyance is no other than all other persons are under, by whom no promise has been made.

A Law, an object of Sense.

1020. A Law is the object of our senses—a Law spoken, of the sense of hearing—a Law written, of the sense of seeing, perhaps of touch.

Of what sense is the pretended Law of Nature an object?

Comm. Maxim)(Rule)(Custom.

1021. A Maxim is an extensive Rule. A Custom is among those things the existence of which it may be the purpose of a Rule of Law to announce.

Preface. Metaphysics. Words—importance of.

1022. It is the knowlege of the true signification of words, says Helvétius after Hobbes, that distinguishes one man in point of understanding from another.[a]

---

[a] Helvét. *de l'Homme.* Sect. ii. Ch. 11.[2]

[1] In the text Bentham has noted at this point: 'N.B. In a Note, make allowances for Mandamus, Injunctions, &c.' No such note has been identified.

[2] See Helvétius, *De l'homme, de ses facultés intellectuelles et de son éducation*, 2 vols., London, 1773, i. 126–7: 'Sur quoi j'observerai que si la supériorité de l'esprit, comme le remarque M. Hobbes, consiste principalement dans la connoissance de la vrai signification des mots'. The passage that Helvétius had in mind may have been Thomas Hobbes, *Leviathan* (first published in 1651), ed. N. Malcolm, 3 vols., Oxford, 2012 (*The Clarendon Edition of the Works of Thomas Hobbes*), Ch. IV, s.v. 'Necessity of Definitions', ii. 56: 'Seeing then that *truth* consisteth in the right ordering of names in our affirmations, a man that seeketh precise *truth*, had need to remember what every name he uses stands for; and to place it accordingly; or else he will find himselfe entangled in words, as a bird in lime-twiggs; the more he struggles, the more belimed. And therefore in Geometry, (which is the onely Science that it hath pleased God hitherto to bestow on mankind,) men begin at settling the significations of their words; which settling of significations, they call *Definitions*; and place them in the beginning of their reckoning.'

1023. Jurisprudence is the art of knowing what has actually been done in the way of internal Government. Jurisprudence.

1024. Jurisprudence, as far as it respects the Common Law, is the art of knowing what has been done in the way of Government according to the silent method. Jurisprudence of Com. Law.

1025. Jurisprudence, as far as it respects the Statute Law, is the art of knowing what has been done in the enuntiative method. Jurisprudence of Stat. Law.

1026. The end of knowing what has been done in the silent method by Government in past cases, is to conjecture what will probably be done in future ones supposed similar. This is what is certainly declared in the enuntiative. Jurisprudence of Comm. Law. It's end.

1027. A Science which might be conceived is, the art of knowing what *ought* to [be] done in the way of internal Government. Jurisprudence Critical.

Now the fact is, no such science as yet existeth. No wonder, therefore, there should be no name for it. No such science as yet exists: for no such book hath as yet appeared as professes to contain a body of any such science, or any regular branch of such a body. And such is the power of names, over the workmanship of the intellect, that scarcely can a science be said to exist, till it has a name. Bodies of Jurisprudence we have several: for our own State and for most others. Body of this art that I am speaking of, we have none. The science (the art, it matters not which) is not born.[a] Montesquieu and Beccaria have made large advances towards it's production—Our Author has done what he could to prevent it's birth. Dissuasive whispers are sown thick throughout his work. In fine, the disposition which prompts a

[a] **1028.** The same object which is called *an art*, viewed in another light is called *a science*. When we consider the mind as passive with respect to a set of ideas, we speak of them as constituting a science; when active, an art. The mind is conceived to be passive with respect to a set of ideas when they are lodged in the memory, and make their appearance without effort, and without fruit. The mind is conceived to be active with respect to a set of ideas, either when it is occupied about acquiring or about communicating them to others, or about directing them to the production [of] external action. Whether this will be found to be a satisfactory account of the distinction between these terms, I know not: at the worst, here is not much paper wasted. There *are* those who would have made a great book upon it. The distinction is of so little importance in practise, that whether it be accurately comprehended or no, is no great matter. What is here said, is said to calm the scruples that some might be apt to entertain concerning the use of these two terms. That a man may not lose much time in considering which of them he shall employ. That he had as good take the one or the other just as he happens to think it convenient: and that he may not feel much compunction, though he should even find himself prompted to do as I have done, and predicate the one of the other. Science X Art.

man to bring it to light, stands branded by him with the name of 'arrogance'.[1]

What name shall we find for it? Shall we call it the *Art of Legislation*? Shall we call it *Critical Jurisprudence*? Shall we call it the Science of Internal Politics? Shall we call it the science of Legal Politics? Shall we call it the science of Jurisprudential Politics?

All these names lie open to objections: to discuss all these objections would take no little time without much fruit. That of Critical Jurisprudence seemed to answer best upon the whole. If the language furnishes one that is more apposite, I should be much obliged to any one who would point it out.

Jurisprudence—what makes it a Science.

1029. If Common Law were transformed into Statute Law, the common end of both would be better answer'd, and Common Law Jurisprudence would of course have lost it's object. If Statute Law were what it ought to be and might be, the science of Jurisprudence would be at an end. The knowledge of what is contained in Statute Law would then not be a science.[2] It would no more be a science of itself than the knowlege of what is contained in newspapers is a science of itself. Art and science import difficulty. Difficulty of what is spoken concerning the familiar occurrences of life imports confusion in the ideas of him who speaks it.

Mind that man, says Epictetus, how big he looks, upon the strength of his commentary on Chrysippus.[3] And if Chrysippus had but understood what he meant, whereabouts would have been the commentary?

A remark of Epictetus, which has as much useful truth couched under it, as is contained in all the rest of his little book put together, and much more than is contained in many a much larger.

[1] See Blackstone, *Commentaries on the Laws of England*, iv. 4–5: 'It is true, that these outrageous penalties [such as the death penalty for cutting down a cherry tree in an orchard], being seldom or never inflicted, are hardly known to be law by the public: but that rather aggravates the mischief, by laying a snare for the unwary. Yet they cannot but occur to the observation of any one, who hath undertaken the task of examining the great outlines of the English law, and tracing them up to their principles: and it is the duty of such a one to hint them with decency to those, whose abilities and stations enable them to apply the remedy. Having therefore premised this apology for some of the ensuing remarks, which might otherwise seem to savour of arrogance, I proceed now to consider . . . the general nature of *crimes*.'

[2] In the margin, Bentham has added what he may have intended as an alternative opening to this paragraph: 'Transform Common Law into Statute-Law, the object of Common Law Jurisprudence vanishes. Make Statute Law speak plain and the whole science vanishes.'

[3] See Epictetus, *Enchiridion*, 49, mocking a person who 'gives himself airs because he can understand and interpret' the writings of Chrysippus (*c.* 280–*c.* 207 BC), Stoic philosopher, and observing, 'If Chrysippus had not written obscurely, this man would have nothing about which to give himself airs'.

The confusion in which our Statutable language is so thick envelopped is, in great degree, the effect of toil and study.

Why should it be a matter of Science to understand that which is nothing more [than] a description of the ordinary modes of action the parties respectively concerned in it are liable to be engaged in, with only this additional intimation, that of the idea of pain being liable to [be] annext to them?

The wrinkles of Science would soon be smoothed away, were there but half as much labour bestow'd on the object to make it clear, as is in constant use to be bestow'd on it to make it obscure. Would Legislators but lay aside the buskin (that buskin that sits on them so ungracefully), it would soon be no longer a matter of difficulty to discern their steps.

Law ⪤ Fact: Fact in question, what in Ejectment.

1030. N.B. In a cause concerning Title, the question frequently is, not concerning any act of the Defendant, but merely concerning some event or situation of things; and that an event or situation in the production of which he was not at all concerned. Thus, in an Action of Ejectment[1] brought against a person claiming Title to Lands by Heirship to the last undisputed proprietor, the question is, not whether the Defendant enter'd into the Lands in question (for that is confessed as a matter of course for the purpose of trying the action), nor concerning any other act of the Defendant, but concerning those events by which the Defendant, without any voluntary act of his own, became, if what he endeavours to prove be true, Heir to that last proprietor. So concerning Ejectment against a person claiming by any other Title. If he fails, he is pronounced Guilty. His guilt consists not in the act supposed to have been done by him, which perhaps in truth he never did, but in the circumstances: in the non-existence of any of those circumstances constitutive of title, one or other of which ought to have existed for him to have been a party not comprized in the general prohibition issued by the general Law of Appropriation.

So in other cases of Title.

So in the case of an Action brought against a Defendant whose Cattle have done mischief in the Ptf's grounds. The question is not concerning any act of the Defendant's, nor even any forbearance (since mischief of this kind may be done entirely without the owner's fault), but concerning that fact or situation, that conveyance or possession from birth, which made the Cattle in question

[1] According to Blackstone, *Commentaries on the Laws of England*, iii. 200, ejectment had 'become the common method of trying the title to lands or tenements'.

the Cattle of the Defendant: concerning the acts done by the Cattle; concerning the act or situation whereby the [Plaintiff][1] is possessor of the Lands damaged; with many others that may be supposed, none of them importing any act of his that is contrary to any Law.

Title to compensation from involuntary damage. Title by Calamity. Title from Negligence.

1031. A motion, an operation, of any thing that is one man's property, whereby another man is a sufferer, is an entitling circumstance giving to the party damaged title to so much *in value* (the individual articles undetermined) of the property of the first man as shall amount to a recompense.

Party involuntarily damaging or Damaging Proprietor. Title to compensation for involuntary damage supported by the Fiction of a Contract.

1032. Now, the same title might the party damaged have had if the party *involuntarily damaging*, we will call him, had promised that, upon such damage ensuing, he would make such recompense. The case of a title to valuables accruing from a Contract being more common and better known than the case of a title to recompense ensuing from such involuntary damage, the Roman Jurists, in order to bring the latter case within the description of one they were used to, had recourse to fiction: they feigned such a promise.[2]

The case was not so much that the case of a promise's being broken occurred before that of such a damage's being incurred (tho' even this might have contributed somthing, since contracts of many kinds would have been made and broken while land was as yet in common) as that the utility of compelling recompence for the breach of a promise came to be more early recognized than the utility of compelling recompence in the case of such a damage. Names of this sort afford an indication of the antiquity of the branches of Law they characterized as conclusive as any that can be imagined.

Rules of Law. Indications internal of their antiquity.

1033. A mode of Procedure feigned in similitude of any other subsisted, we may be certain, after the similitude whereof it was feigned.

---

[1] MS 'Def^{t}'.

[2] Bentham may have had in mind the *cautio damni infecti* discussed in Justinian, *Digest*, D. 39. 2, and in Johann Gottlieb Heineccius, *Elementa Ivris Civilis secvndvm Ordinem Institvtionvm*, Amsterdam, 1738, Lib. III, Tit. XIX, § 854, ii. 275, which dealt with anticipated damage, in particular to a person's property arising from a neighbour's property, such as overhanging parts of buildings. The person at risk was entitled to approach the praetor, who would order the owner of the property causing the risk to make a *stipulatio* (a unilateral formal contract) promising to pay money to the injured person should the injury occur. The promise was not so much 'feigned' as compelled.

1034. As the Law has appointed for entitling incidents and situations so many as constitute the several sorts of Titles which, from the frequent happening of individual circumstances of the classes marked out by them, have acquired known and settled names, so may it from time to time appoint, and so has it for particular purposes appointed, various other investing incidents and situations too rarely occurrent to have been thus distinguished.

Entitling and Dis-entitling occurrences particular.

Such an investing incident is the act of that man who has taken a Highwayman who, at the time he committed the robbery, was on Horseback; an act intitling him to the Horse. Such is the correspondent *divesting* situation of being the owner of a Horse on which a Highwayman was mounted when he committed a robbery.[1]

1035. *A Devesting fact* with respect to any specific article of property or portion of wealth may be either: 1st. An act or forbearance of his own. 2dly. A present situation of his own produced by former acts of his own. 3. A present situation of his own produced by acts of others. 4. An act or forbearance of another's. 5thly. A present situation of another's produced by former acts of that other. 6th. A present situation of another produced by former acts of a third person. 7. A mere physical event or situation. So *e contrà* of Investing facts.

Facts devesting—disentitling—Analysis of. Article of Property Ⅹ Portion of Wealth.

1036. .... That he was present when it was done.[2] A man is said to be present with respect to a thing, an event, a person, or an act; a thing, a person is said to have been, to have existed, an event to have happen'd, an act to have been done in his presence, when the thing or the person existed, the event happen'd, or the thing was done within the field of perception of such of his senses on which the object was qualified to make an impression.

Presence.

Presence, therefore, refers to any of the 5 senses; but principally to the sense of sight.

What is presence to a blind man?

A man is not present to the firing of a cannon which he hears at 40 miles distance.

---

[1] The Apprehension of Highwaymen Act of 1692 (4 Wil. and Mar., c. 8) entitled a person apprehending a highwayman to keep articles of personal property that were in the latter's possession at the time of arrest, including horses.

[2] In the text, Bentham has noted at the beginning of this sentence: 'v. 381.' See para. 939, p. 288 above.

Title to an *article of Property* to an object certain.

1037. A man may be said to have a right, a title, to an article of property when it is some certain individual portion of matter, known at the time his right commences, that he has a right to.

Title to a *mass of Wealth.*

1038. A man may be said to have a right to a portion of wealth, when it is not any certain individual portion of matter that he has a right to, but some uncertain portions of matter, of which nothing is known at the time his right commences but that it shall be to such a value. The individual article to which he has a right is in this case not known, not ascertainable: it depends upon the option of the party against whom he has a right.

Now, in this case, as money is the only species of property of the value of every individual article of which men are universally agreed, the Law goes thus far, as to declare that a portion of wealth which any man has a right to shall be deemed to be of the species money: but what individual articles, so the value of them be equal to that in question, is left always to the party *versus quem.*[1]

Laws and Decisions: Calculation they ought to be grounded on.

1039. When a Legislator or a Judge gives a thing to Titius in preference to Sempronius, a theorem that he ought to be able to prove is, that the happiness of the state, Titius and Sempronius both included, will be greater in the case of it's being given as he gives it, to Titius, than in the case of it's being given to Sempronius.

Now to do this he must sum up . . . accounts—

1st. The pleasure resulting to Titius in the case of it's being given to Titius.

2d. The pains, if there are any, resulting to Titius, upon it's being given to the same Titius.

3dly. The pleasure, if there be any, resulting to the rest of the Society in the case of it's being given to the same Titius, rather than Sempronius.

4. The pain or danger, if there be any, resulting to the rest of the society from it's being given to Titius in preference to Sempronius.

The clear quantity of pain or pleasure which remains after the sum of all these pleasures be subtracted from the sum of all these pains, or the sum of the pains from that of the pleasures, according

[1] i.e. the party 'against whom' judgment has been given. In the text, Bentham has noted at this point: 'Say rather Title to *money*: money being properly explained.'

as which sum turns out the greatest, will be the amount of the pleasure resulting to the society in the case of the thing's being given to Titius.

The same process being gone through with relation to Sempronius, the ratio of the number that represents the ballance of pleasure accruing to the society in the case of it's being given to Titius, to the number that represents the ballance of pleasure accruing in the case of it's being given to Sempronius, will represent the chance that the act of our Legislator or Judge has for being conformable to utility.

All this, it may be said, is but guess-work. Difficult it is to make these calculations: nor is there any certainty in them when made. Is it so? indeed it cannot be denied: but this may be boldly affirmed, that, bad as the chance may be which this method gives us of judging right, no other method is there that affords so good an one: and that any other mode of judging is right or wrong in proportion as it approaches to or deviates from this. This and this alone is that which is capable of giving to the mind the full satisfaction which the subject is capable of affording. The Judge or Legislator who has not proceeded at least upon some implicit and confused perception of this mode of calculation might better have decided by cross and pile. Suppose any mode of forming a judgment different from this, and the chance which that shall be liable to of deviating from expediency will be all the chance which this is liable to, superadded to the chance which results from the deviation.

Now to say, in any of these cases, whether any pleasure or pain exists, one must have found for it a name. Hence the necessity of the above-deliver'd Nomenclature.

Are these things so? hard then, it will be said, and novel is the task you have set to Judges. Nice and . . . the test you have set up of a well formed judgment. Where is the judge whose practise shall abide it?

Not to discompose the | | of the sages of the Law, and that I may set them down after this wild metaphysical excursion in the old beaten track they have been used to travel in, it will be proper to observe that to them in general the line of uniformity is the line of utility—that the road to utility lies in the beaten track of precedent; the which, the more steadily they adhere to the | |, do they discharge the business of their function.

Many a grave Magistrate, who judges causes as the Club-men before St. Dunstan's sound the hours,[1] and who, like Monsr

[1] An allusion to the mechanical figures who struck bells with their clubs in the clock installed in 1671 in the façade of St Dunstan-in-the-West, Fleet Street, London.

Jourdain in the play, has been talking prose all his lifetime without knowing a syllable of the matter,[1] may be surprized perhaps at this account of what he has been doing: but let him reflect a while, and then answer whether it is not a just one.

Prefat. New Words. Apolog.

1040. With the stock of nomenclature that is familiar to us, we go on discoursing and discoursing for evermore without understanding one another or ourselves. The subsisting stock of nomenclature, the stock we have in hand, it is plain, answers not the purpose. Solid instruction can not be convey'd through so imperfect and impure a medium. Shall we [go on discoursing] without obtaining any solid instruction, without gaining any true 'knowlege of those things that belong so intimately to our peace',[2] or shall we be at the pains of adding to and reforming our nomenclature?

Prefat. BEG. Metaph.

1041. How shall I ad[d]ress the reader? what stratagems, what soothings, what humiliations, shall I have recourse to, [to] dissipate that storm of contempt and aversion which must be treasured up for those who presume to obtrude with unfashionable offerings upon the public taste? or to persuade him to master his loathing to the nauseous mess I have to set before him?

I confess . . . with fear and trembling I confess . . . . . but as sooner or later it must appear against me, I will e'en out with it at once, that the subject of this book is in it's nature no other than metaphysical. That in short, as to a great part of it, it is neither more nor less than a treatise of metaphysics. I have spoken; and now, unless, by way of reward for my plain dealing, he thinks fit to indulge me with a few moments of his time, let him shut up the book for the last time.

To cry, as the vulgar proverb has it, stinking fish,[3] and, at the very outset set a name of disgrace upon the product of my labour was neither my business, nor would it have been my choice, had I known how to avoid it. Any other name that would have answer'd the purpose, could I have found any, I should unquestionably have preferred. Such, however, is my hard lot; no other, notwithstanding the most diligent researches, have I been able to find. If there be another in the language, it would be charity to give it me.

[1] An allusion to the comment made by the title character of *Le Bourgeois gentilhomme* by Molière (1622–73), first performed in 1670, and published in English as 'The Gentleman Cit. A Comedy', in *The Works of Mr. de Moliere*, 6 vols., London, 1714, iv. 223–88, at 241: 'Faith, then, I have talked Prose above this Forty years and never knew it.'

[2] An echo of Luke 19: 42.

[3] i.e. to disparage one's own efforts or products.

Ill-fated Science! Stigmatized in the Senate house, slighted from the judgment-seat, and ill-spoken of even in the closet of that philosophy with which, tho' driven from every other station, one should have expected there wouldst have found honourable refuge.[a] Nursing-mother, if not parent, of the whole train of Sciences, yet disowned and slighted by thy children!

Since thy name is in dishonour, and thy benefits unnoticed or forgotten by an ungrateful public, aid me with thy influence[1] . . . . me with the light of thy countenance[2] while with weak but well meant efforts I attempt to dissipate the prejudices that infest thee, to make known thy office, and to proclaim thy worth.

1042. Metaphysics is descended of creditable parents, Experience and Reflection. The precise date of her birth, she never could recollect. The first event she remembers is that at a very early age she found herself in the arms of one Aristotle, a man of an acute understanding and of an inventive genius, from whose conversation, had he lived long enough, she was in fair way of gaining improvement. Upon his decease, she fell into the hands of a whimsical crack-pated but smooth-tongued journeyman of his, one Plato, who begat on her a . . . . . race of Chimæra's called . . . . . &c. &c.[3] Metaphysics, Allegorical History of.

1043. How happy would it make me to be able to think otherwise! How happy would it make me could I hope to see his elegant drapery transferred to a body of doctrine that should be solid and instructive! That his book would have been a much better one than it is, had he *related* only, and had he never reasoned. Had he confined himself to the *that*, and never meddled with the *why* nor *wherefore*. Prefat. *Comm.*

To counteract the effects of those opiates which our Author ceases not to administer. To apply a stimulus to rouze them from that lethargy in which they have too long indulged, and in which our Author has shewn so much sollicitude to keep them. That such

[a] v. Diderot.[4]

---

[1] The phrase 'aid me with thy influence' has been marked by Bentham for deletion.

[2] An echo of Psalm 4: 6.

[3] Perhaps an allusion to Plato's doctrine of the forms.

[4] See *Encyclopédie, ou dictionnaire raisonné des sciences, des arts et des métiers*, 17 vols., Paris and Neuchâtel, 1751–65, s.v. 'Métaphysique' (written by Denis Diderot (1713–84), French philosopher and author), x. 440, referring to metaphysics as 'une science méprisable', but only when limited to 'considérations vuides & arbitraites sur le tems, l'espace, la matiere, l'esprit'.

at least whose fortunes will justify it to their private prudence may be brought to consider the study not merely as a source of lucre, nor yet as a subject of mere historical disquisition, but as a field of political and moral criticism: a field that will be fertile in the noblest kind of fame, to him who shall cultivate it with assiduity and penetration.[1]

Stare decisis—Mischief of Departure

1044. It adds to the pleasure of a part of the community: viz: those who are *favoured* by the obligation which it tends to establish or enforce; but adds to the pain of the whole of the community, those persons not excluded, by putting them in fear of seeing themselves, contrary to their expectation, deprived of expected rights and subjected to unexpected duties; not to mention their being subjected, without warning, to that punishment, which, in the way of Common Law, is necessary to the ademption of those rights and the imposition of those duties.

—is least in Procedure.

1045. The branch of the Law in which a propensity [to] the sacrifice of the general utility of certainty to particular original utility may be indulged with least mischief is that of *Procedure*.

A decision relative to this head takes away no old rights; imposes no new duties. The function of Rules of Procedure is to impose such and such duties on the Plff and Deft (party call'd in judgment), or their Substitutes, or the neutral Officers of the Court, such duties the accomplishment of which is made the condition to the application of that coercion which constitutes the right claimed by the Plff and contested by the Defendant. Every condition that is interposed of this kind is a new impediment thrown in the way of the execution of the Law, and of the enforcement of the right that is in question. Now, the only utility, in a manner, that can be aimed at by an eccentric decision on this head is the removal of such an impediment when thought superfluous for the purpose of protecting innocence.

[1] In the text, Bentham has noted at this point: 'Bl. and Dutens between them would lay asleep all Science—propose an Alliance as between Church and State.' Bentham perhaps had in mind Blackstone's statement at *Commentaries on the Laws of England*, i. 42: 'Upon these two foundations, the law of nature and the law of revelation, depend all human laws; that is to say, no human laws should be suffered to contradict these.' Louis Dutens (1730–1812), diplomatist, writer, and clergyman, was author of *Le tocsin*, Rome, 1769, in which he attacked the *philosophes*. For the *locus classicus* of the alliance see William Warburton, *The Alliance between Church and State or, the Necessity and Equity of an Established Religion and a Test-Law Demonstrated, From the Essence and End of Civil Society, upon the fundamental Principles of the Law of Nature and Nations. In Three Parts. The First, treating of a Civil and a Religious Society: The Second, of an Established Church: and The Third, of a Test-Law*, London, 1736.

The greatest part of these conditional regulations are made in favour of Def[ts]. They are so many barriers set up against the temerity of the Plff. Those which are established in favour of the [Plaintiff][1] are in general but so many exceptions to the former class. Those, indeed, that come under the title of Evidence are an exception. As both parties may have witnesses or muniments to produce, rigour in this article applies as much in disfavour of the one as of the other.

The utility, therefore, most likely to be sought in an anomalous decision under the head of Procedure is either: 1[st.] The dispensation of formalities deemed unnecessary: or 2[dly] a dispensation of those rules which restrain the power of obtaining evidence.

Now, in both these cases, what is done is done, not towards the establishment of any new right; but towards the support of one already acknowledged. No right, therefore, is looked upon as shaken by the decision. No alarm is raised in consequence. At least none among the people at large: none but among men of the profession who are in a condition to observe the tendency of such a proceeding, and to trace the consequences.

Improvement. Judges to make Ordinances of Procedure.

1046. I would have the Judges frame these regulations: but I would have the Parliament only to establish them: as things stand at present.

Or if they be such as usage will warrant the Judges in establishing, let them be established directly in their Legislative capacity, and not indirectly in their Judiciary.

By a Parliamentary Regulation—let it be established that Judges shall have power to make any ordinances touching the course of Procedure in causes of their respective competency, and touching Evidence.—That these ordinances shall be certified to the Parliament.—That they shall have force as soon as certified;[a] but that at any time in the course [of] two Sessions they may be vacated by a disagreement of the King or either House.

That upon observation of any particular inconvenience ensuing from the observance of the rules for the time being, the Counsel of either side be at liberty to propound it to the Court or to the Judge at Nisi Prius, and to propose an ordinance for the remedy of it; who, if he pleases, may propound it to the Court in which the cause

[a] Not so, for fear of general regulations being made to serve the purpose of a private party: let them wait a Session or two before they become in force. In the mean time, a party affected may have the opportunity to oppose them.

[1] MS 'Def:[t]' is a slip.

was instituted. That if the regulation be approved by the Court, the Counsel proposing receive the public thanks of the Court.

That each ordinance be signed by the Judges propounding; together with that of the Counsel, if suggested by a [Counsel].[1] That short reasons be given for each ordinance in number'd articles, after the manner of the Lord's Protest:[2] any dissenting Judge having power to give Counter-reasons.

That regulations touching the jurisdiction of the 4 superior Courts in Westminster Hall[3] be not propounded to Parliament unless signed by ⅔ of the whole number of Judges of all the Courts.

That regulations touching Evidence be in like manner propounded by all the Judges.

Ordinances of Procedure in Sessions of Justices of the Peace to be propounded by any Sessions to the King's Bench. The King's Bench to have power to propound them to Parliament, and to give them force either with respect to the whole Kingdom, or to the County of the propounding Sessions only. So in other Courts.

Judges to have like liberty to propound Substantive Regulations in matters of Contract—and Conveyancing: but these not to have force in the 1st instance—nor till the time of probation be expired.

If any particular cause suggested the inconvenience which it is the intent of the ordinance to remedy, that it be an instruction to the Judges to state the name of the cause and give a short history of it in as far as relates to the point in question. The reason being grounded on matter of actual experience will strike more forcibly than if grounded on suppositions of probability.

This will tend to the improvement of the Law manifestly: and not less to the certainty of it, by taking away all pretence for irregular decisions.

For making Laws, 3 qualifications are requisite—Interest, Knowlege, Power.

Judges have much more frequent opportunities of knowing the inconveniences that occur under the subsisting regulations for the adjustment of private rights than an Assembly of Legislators chosen among a class of men not Lawyers by Profession.

[1] MS 'Council'.

[2] According to Blackstone, *Commentaries on the Laws of England*, i. 162, peers had the right to have their dissent from the outcome of a parliamentary vote recorded in the *Journals* of the House of Lords, with a statement of their reasons. See, for instance, the protest, divided into three numbered articles, each corresponding to a separate reason, of eleven peers made on 15 January 1770 to a motion to adjourn the House at *Lords Journals* (1768–70) xxxii. 403.

[3] i.e. the Courts of Chancery, King's Bench, Common Pleas, and Exchequer.

A thousand inconveniences, and a thousand regulations as the obvious means of remedying these inconveniences, must present themselves to their observation every day: but these observations, and the inventions that are the fruits of them, are lost for want of a regular method of recording and communicating them. We have no Laws that are made *a priori*. They are all made from the observation of some particular incidents. The Judges are the only persons under whose observation the particular incidents that relate to Procedure fall; unless by accident. To judge is all their present business. To meddle with Legislation would be out of their sphere. It would be officiousness and a degree of usurpation. It would be touching the Sceptre with unhallow'd hands. N.B. the Legislative power of Judges has seldom, I believe, been extended to Allegations of Procedure—only to *Agenda*.

1047. Example under Evidence—Competency—Incompetency of an excommunicated person.[1] *Stare decisis.* Examples.

Under Procedure of the Plff. Allegation of *contra pacem* omitted in an Indictment.[2] For *steps* of Procedure find out some other.

Under Rights of Property—Half-blood.[3]

Under Public Duties | |.

Under Restraints | |.

1048. Unconstitutional is the only epithet of censure that can with propriety be applied to the proceedings of the Supreme Power. What it does may be, as it has been, unconstitutional. Nothing it can do can be *illegal*. Unconstitutional ※ Illegal.

1049. The supreme Legislative body, viz: the Parliament, it is usual to call simply without addition, the Legislature: and, on this Power Supreme ※ Power Legislative.

[1] According to Blackstone, *Commentaries on the Laws of England*, iii. 102, 'by the common law an excommunicated person is disabled to do any act, that is required to be done by one that is *probus et legalis homo*. He cannot serve upon juries, cannot be a witness in any court, and, which is the worst of all, cannot bring an action, either real or personal, to recover lands or money due to him'.

[2] Offences were said to be committed *contra pacem domini regis*, i.e. 'against the peace of the king' (see ibid., i. 113), with the phrase appearing in indictments, that is in the accusations of crimes presented by grand juries (see ibid., iv. Appendix, pp. ii–iii). Bentham may be suggesting that the omission of the words would cause the action to fail.

[3] According to ibid., ii. 224, it was one of the canons of inheritance under the Common Law 'that the collateral heir of the person last seised must be his next collateral kinsman, of the whole blood', and hence collateral relations of the 'half-blood', such as half-brothers and half-sisters, were unable to inherit.

account to say, it is the Parliament alone that has the right of making Laws. That power in a State to which belongs the Right of making Laws is the supreme Power. This language, tho' very common, is very inaccurate and productive of much confusion. There are persons accordingly that will tell you &c.

The generality or particularity of the several objects of a command is one thing: the supremacy or subordination of him who utters it is another and a perfectly distinct one.[1]

Historical development.

1050. When a *branch of the Government* is got into the habit of *punishing a party* of a certain description for *acts* or *forbearances* of a certain description, at the request of persons of a certain description, a person of the description of those that are thus *punished* may be stiled a *party coerced*: the *act* or *forbearance* for which he is *punished* may be stiled an *offence*: a person of the description of those at whose request a *party coerced* is liable to be punished may be stiled a *party favoured*. A proposition which any one should utter &c. may be stiled a *Rule of Law*. The *party favoured* may be said to have a *Right*.

Party co-erced. Party favoured. Rule of Law A Right.

A Duty. A Restraint.

1051. The *party coerced*, if it be *for a forbearance* that he is liable to be *punished*, to be *subjected* to a *duty*: if for an *act*, to a *restraint*.

Right and Duty and Restraint are *Simul Naturâ*

1052. The same habit of acting in the Government that *gives* one *party* a *right*, *imposes*, it is manifest, and that necessarily, *a restraint* or else *a duty* on another party.

—are Relatives.

1053. *Right* and *Duty*, as also *Right* and *Restraint*, are, therefore, *relatives*: the existence of the one supposes that of the other.

Relation alternative.

1054. What is remarkable is that the correlate to Right is not single, as is the case commonly between relatives, but alternative: *Restraint* in one case, *Duty* in another—*Restraint* where the *mode of conduct* punished is *action*: *Duty* where it is *Forbearance*.

—or bifurcate.[a]

1055. Where two terms of relation have the same term to express their correlative, such relation may be said to be alternative or bifurcate.

The word Right answers to two correlatives.

Dichotomous.

[a] **1056.** Any one who prefers a term of Greek original to one of Latin may call it *dichotomous*.

---

[1] In the text, Bentham has noted at this point: 'Power Legislative exercised by the H. of Lords over Heralds, by Order 1767. v. 3. *Comm.* on the subject of Pedigrees.' A Standing Order of the House of Lords of 11 May 1767 required the heralds of the Court of Chivalry to establish and maintain accurate pedigrees of the peerage: see Blackstone, *Commentaries on the Laws of England*, iii. 105–6.

1057. This is what is called Prudence, and Policy, and knowlege of affairs. Legislation temporizing.

It is so, upon supposition that the present time is every thing, and the future nothing.

To stave off a point from a time when the judgment is undisturbed, affections cool, particular persons not affected, no private interests concerned, no private partialities to master and set a bias on the judgment, to a time when the contrary is the case, and when the consideration of the general utility of the measure is in a manner drowned in that of the particular interests[1] of certain individuals;

To grudge a few dips of Ink for the settlement of that to settle which hereafter may otherwise take torrents of blood, | |.

'I, perhaps, shall not then be Minister.—I, perhaps, shall not be then in Parliament.—It may be the affair only of Posterity.—Let posterity take care of itself.—What has posterity ever done for me?', says . . .

But what is still more to the point.—What *will* it do for me?

This may be prudence; but if it be, it is prudence of the most selfish, the most sordid, kind. It is the prudence that is at enmity with public virtue. What will posterity do for thee, thou recreant? If these be thy deserts towards it, it will tear thy name out of the book of fame.—But to descend to the level of thy conceptions. What thou seeest of thyself, others may see too.—Thou seeest that it is sluggishness and cowardice that govern thee. I will tell thee what the present race will do to thee—they will tear off, if thou hast any, thy laurels—they will pour on thy head, the cup of their contempt. Thou wilt forfeit all that thou possessest of their admiration, their esteem, of thy reputation, thy influence, and with it of that power for which thou art ready to make any sacrifice. Thou wilt dissolve the spell which thy former merits had raised, and which encircled thee with all thy present dignity. The State-Hero[2] which figured in the eyes of the gazing multitude will shrink into the pigmy timeserver.[3]

I denounce thee to posterity as a betrayer of it's interests. And the present generation will anticipate it's judgments.

One single man, who has discernment and resolution, may bring to light thy secret, and by a single blast level to the ground that fabric of reputation which it has cost thee so many anxious years to rear.

---

[1] MS orig. 'utilities'.

[2] MS orig. 'Giant Statesman'.

[3] The folllowing paragraph has been marked by Bentham for deletion.

Consent presumptive.

1058. The consent presumptive a man may be said to have of another man, or more properly the presumption of his consent to an act's being done, when the circumstances of the case are such, in which the 2[d] man would, it is presumed, give an actual consent, either positive or tacit, to the act were he to know them.

A Party.

1059. A Party is a term I shall take leave for the sake of shortness to use indifferently to signify a single person of any class, or the whole assemblage of persons of that class.

Law of Property. Why it Shews nothing of *Offence*.

1060. It is not without repugnance that we can apply the term offender, delinquent, to a party who is punished when the act for which he is punished is such as carries no reflection with it on his moral character. For this reason, it may seem a stretch of language to apply these terms to an unsuccessful party *bonâ fide* defending himself against a claim of property.

It is no reflection on a man's moral character that he infringes a right of which he knew not the existence: that he disobey'd a Law to a given effect, when he knew not that a rule of Law to that effect existed. Accordingly, [for] all those offences that are characterized by the name of crimes, the Law which appoints extraordinary punishment supposes consciousness of the want of right to do them: consciousness of their being among the objects prohibited by the Law.

Duties absolute.

1061. Where the party *coerced* is the same as the party *favoured*, we hear nothing of the right: we hear only of the duty or the restraint.[1]

Where no individual has a *right*, and yet there is a *duty*: it is the public that has the *right*.

The Law gives no man pleasure, but by means of Pain.

1062. I looked upon our Author's work[2] as a grand obstacle to the improvement of the Science. It facilitated men's advancing thus far. It hinder'd their going further.

The task of censure is an extensive one. My Work contains my reason for undertaking it. It is the degree of celebrity of our Author, and not the degree only of his error, that [. . . ?] the utility

[1] In the text, Bentham has noted at this point: 'Explain this from pleasure and pain, and shew who is in this case the party *at whose request*.'

[2] i.e. Blackstone's *Commentaries on the Laws of England*.

of combating him. I have attacked him, not because I thought [. . . ?] full of errors, but because I thought those were mischievous ones.

1063. If he sees not in what respect the connection between punishment and action is concerned in the state of things intimated by the proposition before him, he may be assured he does not understand it. Comm. Law—a Proposition of—when understood.

Thus hapless is the lot of those who live under and have concerns with Common Law, to be perpetually obliged to talk of it, without ever knowing what it is they talk of.

1064. If it be any amusement to him to call me Atheist, or Deist, or Infidel upon this occasion, he has my free leave for it. The epithet Infidel, God be thanked, at this time of day carries with it no sting, any further than as it imports one who advances doctrines repugnant to the welfare of the state. If, then, the charge of infidelity be founded on this opinion of mine, that the welfare of the state is to be preferred by the ruling body of the state to every other consideration, I have no sort of objection to it's being urged against me. Infidel, my dear Brother in Christ, as long as you please: Cry aloud, and spare not: 'thump upon the bag of Anaxarchus.'[1] 'Strike but hear:'[2] or strike, if it amuses you, without hearing. On my side, I have one of the holiest, most renowned, most irrefragable Fathers of our Church.[3] Under his banner I plant myself. His hide I bear before me as a sevenfold shield, not unprovided with brass:[4] shoot on; your arrows will stick only in his carcase. Com. Law. Divine Law &c. *Defensoria.*

[1] Anaxarchus (mid to late fourth century BC), Greek philosopher, was put to death by Nicrocreon, Tyrant of Cyprus, by being beaten with iron pestles in a large mortar. According to Diogenes Laertius, 'Life of Anaxarchus' in *The Lives and Opinions of Eminent Philosophers*, IX. 59, he endured this torture heroically, exclaiming 'Pound, pound the pouch containing Anaxarchus; ye pound not Anaxarchus.'

[2] According to Plutarch, *Life of Themistocles*, XI. 3, when, in the course of a disagreement, Eurybiades, a Spartan naval commander, raised his staff to strike Themistocles, the latter said, 'Smite, but hear me', whereupon the former 'was struck with admiration at his calmness, and bade him speak'.

[3] Bentham may have had in mind William Warburton, who stated in *Alliance between Church and State*, p. 21, that the 'genuine precise determinate End of Civil-Society' was 'but the SECURITY OF THE TEMPORAL LIBERTY AND PROPERTY OF MAN', and that 'The great but spurious Rival of this End, THE SALVATION OF SOULS or the Security of Man's future Happiness, is therefore excluded from this Part of the Division'.

[4] In classical mythology, Ajax was said to lead his army while wielding a huge shield made of seven cow-hides with a layer of bronze.

I believe in very good Lexicographical words, and grammatical sentences without having any thing that can bear the name of an idea in my head that there are not 'not more Gods than one'.[1] All this I believe: penetrated to the marrow by that most logical, most perspicuous, most instructive, most cogent, most triumphant of all arguments, Incapacity for the first offence, Imprisonment for the second.[2]

He may be assured that he and I have on this point one voice: which to have, in the judgment of our holy mother Church, is perfect unity.

With joy and thanksgiving I lay hold with him on those firm bulwarks of truth, which [bury][3] under them that arch-enemy to it, free discussion. I *profess* with him (which is all that a man need do) that men cannot possibly have any reason to distrust of the merits of the cause, who arm it with such weapons.

I regret that all kinds of knowlege, natural as well as moral, is not injected by the same powerful engines. Nor know I any other account why all knowlege is not thus inculcated into all nations, than that men would mount the sky as if they had finished the tower of Babel,[4] or tasted for the second time of the Tree of good and evil.[5]

I do maintain, having heard it demonstrated in Lincoln's Inn Chapel for . . . guineas a lecture, that the Holy Roman Pontiff (whom God convert to Protestantism) is as Antichrist-like a person as ever was or will be.[6] Nay, as well am I convinced as if I had tickled him in the ribs, or | | that, speaking by the rule of contraries, he is verily and indeed the Christ.

The Church is on my side, whom need I fear? The Law is my protector: of whom need I be afraid?

---

[1] In the text, Bentham has noted at this point: 'Here quote the statute.' The Blasphemy Act of 1698 (9 & 10 Wil. III, c. 32) provided that 'any Person or Persons, having been educated in, or at any Time having made Profession of the Christian Religion within this Realm . . . [who] shall assert or maintain there are more Gods than one' were to be 'for the first Offence . . . adjudged incapable and disabled in Law', and if 'a second time lawfully convicted . . . shall also suffer Imprisonment for the Space of three Years'.

[2] In the text, Bentham has noted at this point: 'Here quote the words again.'

[3] MS 'buries'.

[4] For the story of the building and destruction of the Tower of Babel see Genesis 11: 1–9.

[5] For the story of the expulsion of Adam and Eve from the Garden of Eden, on account of their eating the fruit of the tree of the knowledge of good and evil, see Genesis 3.

[6] In his Warburtonian Lectures delivered at Lincoln's Inn in 1776, Samuel Hallifax (1733–90), Regius Professor of Civil Law at the University of Cambridge 1770–82, Bishop of Gloucester 1781–9 and St Asaph 1789–90, had argued that the Pope was the Antichrist foretold in the Bible: see *Twelve Sermons on the Prophecies Concerning the Christian Church; and, in particular, Concerning the Church of Papal Rome: preached in Lincoln's-Inn-Chapel, at the Lecture of The Right Reverend William Warburton Lord Bishop of Gloucester*, London, 1776.

1065. Charters *adopt* the By-Laws that are made in pursuance of them, *before-hand.*[1] Charters, are adoptive.

1066. There are two ways of referring from a present Law to a preceding. The one is by description of the words themselves of the Law referred to: the other is by description of the import. DIG. Quoting by *words* X by *import.*

The 1st is effectual, certain, and satisfactory.

The other is a miserable make-shift; the device of unfeeling laziness; a cruel device, which exposes thousands to punishment, to save one the trouble of telling them how to avoid it.

Was it, then, difficult for *him*? for him, a man of letters, a man practised in the study of the significance of words? For him, a man of Law professed? for him, a Legislator?[2] How much more difficult, then, must it be for the illiterate, unscrutinizing, incurious, inexperienced multitude?

So much of such an act as relates to such a matter, so much of it as does so and so. Here is a man sent to con over with fear and trembling the contents of a long-winded rigmarolle, of which perhaps not one twentieth part is that wherein he is concerned.

1067. Suppose a number of persons to be in the habit of being in the presence of one another, or at a given time actually in presence of one another, without being in the habit of acting for the most part according to the will of one person or body of persons of a certain description, the state such first-mentioned persons are in is what is called a state of nature, or a state of natural society. *Society natural. State of Nature.*

1068. | | Society *political.*

1069. Society consider'd as subsisting at a given moment is the situation a number of persons are in who are actually in the presence of one another. Society in general *actual.*

1070. Society consider'd as subsisting during a length of time is the state a number of persons are in who are in the habit of being in the presence of one another. *—habitual.*

1071. 'A Tacit promise is, where the Will is signified by other more diffuse signs than those of speech, but a will there must *Promise Tacit.* Hume.

[1] On the power of corporations to make by-laws see Blackstone, *Commentaries on the Laws of England*, i. 463–4.

[2] Blackstone was MP for Hindon 1761–8.

certainly be in the case, and that can never escape the person's notice, who exerted it, however silent or tacit.'[a]

King—his investitive power with regard to War and Peace.

1072. The King has the investitive power with respect to the classes of alien *enemy* and alien *amy*. Thus only does he modify the Laws of War and Peace. He cannot subject either to, or exempt either from, any new disabilities of his own creating.

Power Judicial)(Legislative. *Initiative.* Spontaneous. Self-moving.

1073. The commanding power of Judges is tied down by an extraneous *initiative*,[1] except on view of the offence. The power of the Legislature is *self-moving*.

The initiative right is the right of negativing before proposal.

Judges have not the initiative right except it be *super visum*.[2] In all other cases they are restrained by a foreign initiative. They are also restrained by conformity to Precedent.

Therefore, the Will of a Judge can not have effect without the concurrence of the Will of a Plff: and in some sort with the wills of his predecessors. And his will must be expressed with certain formalities: after debate, *adstante coronâ*,[3] and in certain forms of words. A Legislator is free from these restraints.

But in the Roman Commonwealth, the people in one respect, that of being subject to a foreign initiative, were in the condition of a Judge.[4]

---

[a] Hume, *of Hum. Nature*. B. 3. Part 2$^{d.}$ Sect. 8. Vol. 3$^{d.}$ p. 155.[5]

[1] In the text, Bentham has noted at this point: 'There is genius in the invention of that word initiative—it is M^{r} De L'olme's.' Jean Louis de Lolme (1740–1806), Genevan-born political writer, was the author of the celebrated *Constitution de l'Angleterre*, Amsterdam, 1771, which appeared in English as *The Constitution of England, or An Account of the English Government; In which it is compared with the Republican Form of Government, and occasionally with the other Monarchies in Europe*, trans. Gilbert Stuart, London, 1775. De Lolme may, as Bentham suggests, have been the first writer to use the word as a noun in English: see ibid., pp. 207–8 where De Lolme states that in 'most of the ancient free States', the executive power 'possessed that branch of the Legislative power which may be called the *initiative*', while the role of 'the People' was to 'approve, or reject, the propositions which were made to them, and to give the final sanction to the laws'.

[2] More fully *super visum corpore*, i.e. 'within sight of the body'.

[3] i.e. 'in the presence of the crown'.

[4] Bentham presumably had in mind the *indicium populi*, a criminal trial initiated by a magistrate, but with the verdict being given by an assembly of the people, either the *comitia centuriata* or the *comitia tributa*.

[5] See Hume, *Treatise of Human Nature*, Bk. III, Part II, § 8, i. 351. Bentham's citation is to the first edition, 3 vols., London, 1739–40, iii. 155–6. There are some minor inaccuracies in the rendering of the passage.

1074. *Primâ facie* Evidence is *Indicia* that are conclusive, if no opposite *indicia* be produced. Evidence *primâ facie.*

1075. *Indicia* may be distinguished into consentaneous and opposite or contrary. —consentaneous, opposite or contrary.

1076. When, among consentaneous *indicia*, one is supposed to be stronger, another weaker, the weaker is said to be corroborative of the stronger. —corroborative.

1077. An Event is rather a situation the consequence of an act, than the act itself. For event, we may use consequential situation. Event ✕ Act. Event = consequential Situation.

1078. Now, of a superior we may conceive thus much, viz: that he is superior, that is that he is able to cause pain to the inferior, without knowing by what particular means he is able: without considering from what situation of things, from what causes, such ability, such power, we will call it, is derived. Right &c. from Command or habit of Punishment, before the definition of a Law.

We may conceive yet further of such power, that it is *constant*; and this too without knowing, or without considering, from what causes such *constancy* is derived.

Indeed, from the superiority of a moment a certain right &c. may be derived; but then that right will be the right but of a moment.

1079. Jurisprudence expository or *conjectural*[1] enters into the province of critical Jurisprudence, as often as the consideration of direct utility is taken into the ground of the Rule of Law in question. Jurisprudence practical, where it enters into Censorial.

1080. Jurisprudence practical may be distinguished into expository and conjectural. Jurisprudence practical, 1st expository. 2d. Conjectural.

1081. I thank him—It shall go out—He has handled me pretty roughly: but that is as well as if it were otherwise. He himself, I suppose, is gratified: and the public is amused. *Defensoria.*

1082. An act is a motion or train of motions[2] in which a sentient being is the mover. An Act.

1083. For solemn falshood, into the lap [of] him that will say he believes what he does not believe, reward is poured in rich luxuriance. Snug benefices, comfortable retreats, rich sinecures, PREMIUMS. Preface.

[1] The words 'or *conjectural*' have been marked by Bentham for deletion.
[2] The words 'train of motions' have been marked by Bentham for deletion.

exalted stations: the tempting climax topped by one of the first salaries, added to the first dignity, in the state. For the bringing to light the deep-buried secrets in the art of governing, for labours of the first difficulty and the first importance, what premiums stand as yet annext? The title of projector, the enmity of knaves, the derision of fools.

Society natural.

1084.[1] Conceive a number of persons in the habit of seeing each other[a] without being in the habit of paying obedience to any person or any number of persons among them, and you have an idea of a number of persons in a *state of nature*: you have an idea of a state of nature; or what is the same thing, of a state of merely natural society as contradistinguished to political.

Society political.

1085. Conceive a number of persons in the habit of paying obedience, as above, and you have an idea of a number of persons in a state of government; you have an idea of a state of government, of a state of political society, as contradistinguished to society merely natural.

Society *political* not the necessary consequence of *natural.*

1086.[2] Now then, 'Society once formed, Government,' says our Author, 'results of course'.[b] What he means by 'of course', I know not. I should suppose, nothing: for '*of course*', if it means any thing, means, I take it, constantly and immediately, at least constantly. If this, then, be the meaning, what we are to understand from this passage is, that so sure as a number of men are in the habit of seeing one another, so sure are they, after a short time at least, in a habit of paying obedience to some certain person or number of persons among them: to some common governor or set of governors. Now, this is an assertion of a general matter of fact. Is it true? ask those who have visited the different assemblages of men that have been met with on the globe. Ask Travellers and Navigators. They will tell you that it is not: that it is not in the instance of the Hottentots, of the Patagonians, even of many North-American tribes, with whom we are so well acquainted, unless in time of war in short in a variety of other instances too notorious and too numerous to need specifying.

[a] 'Nay, but some of them may be blind.' Well, then, add, or of hearing or feeling one another.

[b] I. 48.[3]

[1] Above this paragraph, Bentham has noted: 'From p. 8. Formation of Government.' See 'A Fragment on Government', Ch. I, para. 11, in *Comment/Fragment* (*CW*), pp. 428–9.

[2] Cf. 'A Fragment on Government', Ch. I, para. 29, in ibid., p. 437.

[3] See Blackstone, *Commentaries on the Laws of England*, i. 48: 'For when society is once formed, government results of course, as necessary to preserve and to keep that society in order.'

After all, I would not engage for it that the phrase '*of course*', and the term '*necessary*' that follows it, mean any thing positive, whatever they might seem to do at first sight. At first, indeed, they do seem designed to assert a matter of fact, and to tell us how things *are*: but in the next sentence they may probably be deemed to have retracted that assertion, and to have given us to understand that all he meant to tell us was how it is expedient that things *should be*.[1]

1087. To have a clear idea of the effect of any act of public power, of any act of government, we must understand the alteration it produces on men's rights, duties and restraints. As the admitting of an Attorney, the creation of a Notary public.

Operation of Government—the effect of it to be explained by reference to men's rights, duties &c.

1088. The obedience paid to any *particular* Law rests ultimately on a circumstance extrinsic to all Laws, a *general habit* of obedience. A habit of executing, upon all occasions and in all points, commands of some one person at least, or body of persons, in the state. Such habit is at present firmly rooted in our own and every other civilized nation that we know of. Were it otherwise, indeed, in any nation, we should not denominate that nation civilized. This is a known indisputable matter of fact: and to trace the original of it would be at best but matter of barren speculation. As every habit consists of acts, and every act must have some motive, and every motive is the expectation of some pain or pleasure, for the origin of this habit we must find the expectation of some pain or pleasure: a capacity of producing most pain or pleasure, such a capacity subsisting in the superior who first began to command.

Law Stat. It's efficacy depends on a previous habit of obedience.

1089. As often, therefore, as I use a new-coined expression, it will be either my fault, or my misfortune: my fault, that is my want of skill, if there be already in the language a term in common use synonymous to such new-coined one; my misfortune, only, if there be none.

Prefat. New-Coined expressions.

---

[1] Bentham may not have had in mind the sentence immediately following, but a passage later in the paragraph stating that, 'In general, all mankind will agree that government should be reposed in such persons, in whom those qualities are most likely to be found, the perfection of which are among the attributes of him who is emphatically stiled the supreme being; the grand requisites, I mean, of wisdom, of goodness, and of power', and concluding that 'these are the requisites that ought to be found in every well constituted frame of government'.

Conditions of Procedure unnecessary, are mischievous.

1090. The Execution of the Law is more and more uncertain, the greater the number is of conditions of Procedure, and the more difficult any of them is to fulfill: every fresh condition that is annext to it creates an additional chance of failure; as the more duties are laid on a man, the greater is the chance of their not being all fulfilled. In one shape, therefore, there is no such condition but what tends to defeat the purposes of the Law: what can never, therefore, be dispensed with is, that in another shape it should have a tendency to promote them. No regulation, therefore, of procedure, any more than any other rule of Law, can be a matter of indifference. If it does no good, it cannot but do harm. All this is too plain to be denied: yet such is the system of procedure in this country, and perhaps in every other, that no one can give a moment's attention to it in this view, without discovering in it thousands of puerile, useless, burthensome regulations, which seem to have been dictated by nothing but the wantonness of caprice.

Rules should have Examples.

1091. A man should hardly trust himself to lay down general rules without particular examples before his eyes.

Reason, a.

1092. In the case of a practical measure, a mode of conduct in man, the making of a Law &c., what a man means by the *reason* of it is neither more nor less than any circumstance the mention of which, he supposes, will have the effect of making those to whom he is addressing himself pleased with it.[1]

Conduct of the Work. Method.

1093. After the chapter on Happiness, the end of Law—on the Law—i:e: the total assemblage of Laws—or what constitutes *one* Law.

Then go on and state by what commands it is that the Law creates the several sorts of fictitious legal entities—Powers over persons, over things; over persons—Rights to services—Protection &c. Then state the sorts of actions that are respectively Offences against these commands.

This will shew the difference and point out the relation between the natural and the technical methods of classification.

[1] In the text, Bentham has noted at this point: 'See I. *Comm.* 14.' Blackstone discusses the relationship between the Common Law and reason at *Commentaries on the Laws of England*, i. 70, rather than at i. 14, where he is in the midst of demonstrating 'the utility of some general acquaintance with the municipal law of the land, by pointing out its particular uses in all considerable situations of life' (ibid. 6).

The effect of this will be no more than to explain the meaning of the several expressions in which those terms are employ'd. The Chapter will be a collection of *Paraphrases* given of those terms.

It will not, however, be labour mis-employ'd. It will be of use in two ways. First, in making the meaning of those terms clearly understood wherever they occur in other writers. Secondly, in authorizing the employing of them in the present work. To banish them altogether would, perhaps, not even be practicable. If practicable, it could not fail to give an air of stiffness and singularity to the whole discourse that would stand very much in the way of it's being understood and relished.

These terms it will be sufficient to have explained. They will be made use of occasionally in discourse. But they will not be assumed as Titles of Divisions. They are leading terms in the science, though they are not heads in the arrangement that is here made of it. They will not govern the distribution that is to be made of the matter of the Law, that is of the several modes of conduct that are the objects of it. The Titles of Divisions will be the names of so many classes of the actions that are those objects. All that is deliver'd concerning these fictitious entities will, therefore, be a kind of Episode, a Parergon, that might or might not be inserted along with the rest. While it is going on, the thread of the analysis is suspended.

Title of the Chapter. Of several fictitious entities which it is common to speak of as being created by the Law, viz: Power, Right, Restraint, Duty, Protection &c.

Ch. | |. Of the several real entities that may be objects of a Law—Persons, Things, acts, and their circumstances—and of the End that a Law has in view.

Ch. | |. Of the Mischief of an act, the several ways in which it may affect a person who is the object of it, person—property—reputation, &c. Mischief direct and reflex. Primary and Derivative.

Ch. | |. Classification of Offences.

1094. The *specific property* of individuals consists chiefly in *instruments* of *sustenance* or *enjoyment*: the business of *securement* is committed for the most part to the public. Securement.

1095. The *specific property* of the public, on the other hand, consists chiefly in *instruments of security*; the sustenance and enjoyment reaped by individuals being but a collateral and accidental *use*. Property specific.

1096. The allotment of *representative* property, the stock of —representative.

Instruments of Sustenance.

money that is the property of the public, is allotted either to the purchase of those common *instruments* of *security* or to produce those allotments of the *instruments* of *sustenance* or *enjoyment* which are bestow'd on the several persons whose *office* it is to contribute, in their several departments, to the public *security*, to enable and to prompt them to exercise their respective functions.

Articles of wealth denominated from their most frequent use.

1097. The several objects of wealth are denominated Instruments of sustenance, of enjoyment, of offence, of defence, according to which of those uses they are principally adapted and most frequently applied [to]. The division is not to that degree compleat, that an object which comes under one of those denominations is incapable of coming under another. The stock of things in question admitts not of any such division. Bread no one would hesitate in classing under the head of instruments of sustenance, yet the same loaf which is to contribute to a man's sustenance, will contribute probably at the same time to his enjoyment, and may possibly have contributed to his security by warding off a blow or giving one.[a]

Prefat. Metaph. *Sylva terminorum.*[1] Old words reclaimed.

1098. The stock of materials, of implements, the stock in trade, in short, of a master of a science will consist of two sorts of articles. 1st of Words in common use, Words *fora naturae,* if one may be allowed the expression, reclaimed and fixed, reduced to a single sense, and that a certain one, by the requisite mode of exposition.[2] 2dly of words of his own original invention.

New words coined.

Implements of the first sort, where they are to be had, where the subject furnishes them, are, it is plain, by much the most eligible. It is necessity alone that can justify the resorting to those of the second.

When a word has more significations than one, those significations are either such as have other words to signify them beside that in question, or such as have no other. The way of reclaiming the word in question is different in these two different cases.

How coined.

1099 New-coined words are fabricated in [four][3] ways. 1st. By

[a] Sampson killed I forget how many thousand enemies with the jaw bone of an ass:[4] it would not, we may suppose, have been more difficult to him to have done the same execution with a leg of mutton.

---

[1] i.e. 'a collection of terms'.

[2] The phrase 'by the requisite mode of exposition' has been marked by Bentham for deletion.

[3] MS 'two'.

[4] According to Judges 15: 15, Samson killed 1,000 men.

Conjugation. 2$^{dly.}$ By Translation. 3. Conjugate extension: by giving to one conjugate the sense of another Conjugate, according to precedents established between Conjugates of other sorts. For example, saying 'a *Forbearance*' in emulation of 'an Action'. 4$^{thly.}$ Composition.

1100. Let there be three words, each of them in common usage, susceptible of the same three significations. In this case, give each it's signification in severalty, and all three of them are reclaimed. Reclaiming by partition = distinction.

1101. Let there be a given word, being susceptible, according to common usage, of three different significations: neither of those significations having any other word to denote them. In this case, the way of reclaiming the word is this. If it be already in the substantive form of speech, characterize it's 3 senses by 3 attributives subjoined to that substantive in the form of adjectives. If it be not in the substantive form of speech but in an attributive, viz. an adjective, take the abstractive conjugate of that attributive, and let that serve as the substantive to be determined by the three epithets or adjectives in question. —by epithetation.

1102. I enter into these intricate but useful speculations with the more good-will in that, while thus engaged, if any where I should be found to have taken two steps towards the advancement of Law, I shall thereby have taken at least one towards the advancement of science in general. Metaphysics being that common chamber of conference at which all sciences meet. 'Tis here that is to be found that ***quoddam quasi communi vinculum***, the ***quaedam connectio*** of which, in the way of a kind of confused anticipation, we hear such frequent mention made by Cicero.[2] Prefat. Metaphysics enter'd on *libenter quia Polychresta*.[1] Metaph. the Common Hall of the Sciences.

1103. The objects of Laws, as of any Commands whatever, are persons, things, acts. Law—3 objects of a.

These three very different articles of consideration have, however, this in common: that they are all liable to become objects of a Law. Let this appellation mark what belongs to them in common: that in which they differ.

Motions, even of the same body, are different from [other] motions: but rest is always uniform.

[1] i.e. 'freely because of public benefit'.

[2] See Cicero, *Pro archia poeta*, I. 2: ***Etenim omens artes, quae ad humanitatem pertinent, habent quoddam commune vinculum et quasi cognatione quadam inter se continentur***, i.e. 'Indeed, the subtle bond of a mutual relationship links together all arts which have any bearing upon the common life of mankind.'

Acts, therefore, may differ in themselves: but it is by circumstances only that forbearance can differ from forbearance.

Institution of Procedure.

1104. To understand the nature of a Regulation of Procedure, we must observe what is the effect of it's not being observed. This effect may be the absolution of the Defendant and nothing more. In this case, it is a Condition to the Command to punish.

The motive, in this case, given to the Plff to do his part to the observance of it is the loss of so much pleasure as he would reap from the punishment of the Defendant.

Institution of Procedure—whether a mandatory or only an exemptive provision.

1105. To understand the nature of a Regulation of Procedure, we must observe what are the effects of the non-observance of it, and, as far as they are penal, upon whom they fall.

1st. They may fall on the Plff only.[1] The least they can amount to in this case is so much pain as results to him from the acquittal of the Defendant.

When this is the case, the Sanction annext to them consists of that pain which the Plff is exposed to suffer from the acquittal of his adversary. This pain is a pain of disappointment, and the pleasure it takes it's rise from is a pleasure either of the irascible appetite alone or of that and the concupiscible together. A pleasure of the irascible appetite alone, when the burthen on the Defendant consisted either in a Pain of sufferance, or in a pain of Privation to the benefit of a third party. A pleasure of the concupiscible appetite, where the burthen on the Defendant consisted in a Pain of Privation to the profit of the Plff. But further. The carrying on of any suit is necessarily attended with costs on the one part and on the other: and of these costs, the party that happens to be unsuccessful, according to the common usages of Jurisprudence, not only bears his own share, of course, but in general a part or the whole of the share of the party who succeeds. Where this is the case, the Plff, in case of miscarriage, is exposed to the two pains following:

1st. A Pain of Privation, having for it's instrument so much of his own Costs as, in case of his being successful, would have been charged on the Defendant.

2d. A Pain of Privation, having for it's instrument so much of the Defendant's Costs as he the Plff is now charged with.

Now then, setting aside for a moment the Costs, the penalty on the Plff on non-compliance with the regulation consists wholly in what results from the acquittal of the Defendant: in this case, the

[1] Bentham does not go on to discuss any further instances.

regulation in question is purely a condition to the command, the non-observance of which constitutes the offence with which the Defendant has been charged.

Add now the Costs, and the regulation in question is not only a condition to the principal command, but also an express Command of itself: a Command having those costs for the matter of it's Sanction.

Let the Costs remain, and suppose the acquittal of the Defendant not to follow from the non-observance of it, it is then an independent Command, and not a condition to any other.

Let things be so that if the Plff pays the Costs in question, the Defendant will still be liable to conviction as if the regulation had not been broken: but if such costs be not paid, then the Defendant will be acquitted.[1] Then is the obligation to pay the costs the primary Sanction of the Regulation; the acquittal of the Defendant, a sanction succedaneous to the former. In this case, the regulation in question is a condition to the principal command; the regulation reversing the former upon the payment of the Costs, a condition upon such primary condition: a condition of the second order.

1106. Any regulation, therefore, the non-observance of which has the effect of acquitting the Defendant, whether that effect be defeasible in the first instance or indefeasible, operates as a Condition to the Command constituting the principal *extra-foraneous* offence and appertains to the Plff's Code; imposing a *duty* on the Plff, and belongs, therefore, to the Plff's Code. If it has not that effect, it is not a Condition to the *extraforaneous Command*.

Effect defeasible ⟗ indefeasible.

Offence Extraforaneous[2]—citra-litigational ⟗ inter-litigational.

1107. But the same regulation may have a double Sanction; one attaching on the Plff, another on a third person. The personal object of the Command it imports may be indistinctly the Plff and some other person; for instance his agent, or some Officer of the Court: or it may be purely the Officer: the Plff having no sort of influence on the point of conduct that is the modal object of the regulation: at the same time, the penal consequence that it denounces may bear either solely on the Plff, or partly upon the Plff and partly on such third person.

Command extraforaneous: ante-litigational ⟗ inter-litigational.

In this case, the regulation bears a double character: with respect to the Plff, it is but a condition to a Command: with respect to such third person, it is a Command of itself. It has, therefore,

[1] Bentham has interposed the following passage in the text at this point: 'A Regulation may be taken for a command having for it's personal object any such person as is exposed to suffer any pain whatever from the non-observance of it, supposing the conduct prescribed by it to be a mode of that person's own conduct, or any act or event subject to his influence.'

[2] For the sake of consistency with the main text, 'Extraforaneous' has been preferred to MS alt. 'ante-foraneous' in this and the following marginal heading.

two personal objects: nevertheless it is still but one regulation, since the modal object of it is but one: it is the conduct but of one.

Conditions infirmative ✕ restorative.

1108. A Condition annext immediately to a Command may be stiled, with respect to that Command, a Condition infirmative: since the effect of it is to weaken, to detract from the strength and efficacy of, the command. A second condition annext to this first may still, with reference to the Command itself, be stiled a condition restorative:[1] with respect to the first mentioned condition, namely that which we called infirmative, a condition infirmative.

Condition to a Command.

1109. After the same manner, we may conceive any number of conditions annext to a command: in alternate order, each of them either infirmative or corroborative of the command, and each infirmative of the condition preceding.

Let this chain be carried to any length, those links in it which are characterized by odd numbers will all of them be *infirmative* to the command those characterized by even numbers, *restorative*: any one which is *restorative* to the command being *infirmative* of any one that is [*infirmative*][2] to the same command; and *vice versâ*.

Regulations of Procedure. 1st infirmative of the ante-litigational command.

1110. In short, of those regulations of procedure whereof the acquittal of the defendant is among the effects of the non-observance, the whole system is *infirmative* of the *ante-litigational* command.

Of some of these, the purport is to prescribe the conduct to be observed in the course of the Prosecution by the Plff, or those under his direction: that is, they have for their modal object the modes of his conduct or of his agents.

Of others again, the purport is to prescribe certain points of the conduct to be observed by uninterested persons such as Judges, Registers, Ministerial Officers, Witnesses: that is, they have for their modal objects modes of conduct of such uninterested persons.

—2dly restorative.

1111. On the other hand, of those regulations of Procedure, whereof the execution of the Law upon conviction of the Defendant is among the effects of the non-observance, the whole system is *restorative* of the *ante-litigational* command.

In like manner, of some of them it is the *conduct* of the Defendant or his agents that is the *modal object*. Of others, that of such uninterested persons as before mentioned.

Let us now consider more particularly who are these un-

[1] MS orig. 'corroborative'. [2] MS '*restorative*'.

interested persons upon whose conduct may depend the acquittal of the Defendant on the one hand, or the conviction on the other.

1112. An infirmative Condition to a Command is a regulation appointing an infirmative circumstance to the mode of conduct which is the object of it:[1] that is intimating that the mode of conduct in question shall depend upon the circumstance assigned.

Condition to a Command.

1113. In treating of any branch of the subject, in the strict method, the best way is not to confine one['s] self to that part of the language which happens to have been already defined, much less to confine one's self to that part which bearest the nearest relation to that which is expressive of simple ideas, but to take what natural language occurrs, and so, by defining, fix that branch of the natural language which will thus be a fresh accession to the stock in hand.

Prefat. Metaphys. Conduct of the work *facilia necdum definita præferenda duris jam definitis.*[2]

1114. Marmontel, *Apologie du Théâtre*, p. 166. Ed. Haye. 1764.[3]

Pleasure—inconsistency of reprobating it as such. Rousseau—Marmontel.

Every amusement, says Mr Rousseau,[4] that is useless is an evil to a being to whom life is so short and time so pretious.[5]

For the word Amusement, I suppose, we may, without imputing any signification to his words different from what he intended they should have, render into pleasure. By the word unprofitable, or, as it is in the original, useless, we may render unproductive of other pleasures. According to this interpretation, then, what Mr Rousseau wished us to understand is that every pleasure that is not productive of other pleasures is an evil.

If this be the meaning of the proposition, one may venture, I think, boldly to deny the truth of it. We may venture to say, on the contrary, that every pleasure, although unproductive of other pleasures, so as it be not productive of any pains that are more than equivalent to it, is a good.

That a sophism like this, a sophism that carries on it the point of

[1] The remainder of the sentence has been marked by Bentham for deletion.

[2] i.e. 'easier things not yet defined are to be preferred to hard things already defined.'

[3] No edition of 1764 of *Apologie du Théâtre* by Jean François Marmontel (1723–99), French historian, author, and *encyclopédiste*, has been traced. The work was first published in *Contes moraux; par M. Mormontel; suvis d'une apologie du théâtre*, 2 vols., The Hague, 1761, ii. 211–89.

[4] Jean-Jacques Rousseau (1712–78), Genevan philosopher, author, and composer.

[5] See *J.J. Rousseau citoyen de Genève, a Mr. D'Alembert . . . sur son article Genève dans le* VIIme. *volume de l'Encyclopédie, et particulierement, sur le projet d'établir un théatre de comédie en cette ville*, Amsterdam, 1758, p. 14: 'tout amusement inutile est un mal, pour un Etre dont la vie est si courte & le tems si précieux', quoted in Marmontel, *Contes moraux*, ii. 217.

austere virtue, should have passed upon Mr Rousseau is not very extraordinary. What surprizes one is that a philosopher of such cool discernment as Mr Marmontel, a critic who has taken it into consideration for the express purpose of combating the conclusions drawn from it, should not have ventured to contest it. Such is sometimes the power of popular prejudice over the strongest minds.

Instead of denying the truth of the general proposition that an amusement that is useless is in itself an evil, he endeavours to elude the force of it. He alledges that, though the particular amusement in question, admitting it to be an evil, should be excluded from the place in question, another amusement equally an evil would fill it's place. 2dly. That the amusement in question is not useless. 3dly. That if it were, it would be difficult to bring men to give it up. 4^thly. That allowing it to be an evil, that is to the community yet if the community allows of it, there is no harm done.[1]

Effect) (Product) (Result.

1115. Effect) (Product) (Result. Effect to a substance when the form of it has been changed—otherwise not—therefore, not to Mercury in the Barometer. But to writing.—Though even here it may be said that it is not the substance itself that is spoken of as the effect, but only the new form that has been given to it: i:e: the new motions or situations given to it's insensible parts. Now, these motions or these situations are modes.

Injury) (Injustice. Ingratitude.

1116. Injury—Injustice—Definitions of these words to be given along with those of Offence, Misdeed, &c. The import of these words, consider'd as referring to the Law of the State, is narrower than that of Offence. It extends not to such misdeeds whereof the suffering objects are persons uncertain. Injustice is narrower still than injury: it is in general put only for such offences

[1] See Marmontel, *Contes moraux*, ii. 217–18: '1°. Il avouera que ce mal existe à Genève sans le spectacle, à-moins que boire, jouer et fumer ne lui semblent des occupations utiles. 2°. Un amusement qui délasse et console la vie laborieuse, qui occupe et détourne du mal la vie oisive et dissipée, n'est pas sans quelque utilité. 3°. Peut-être y a-t-il des devoirs pour tous les instans de la vie, peut-être une heure de dissipation est-elle un larcin fait à la société. Mais à qui le persuaderez-vous? [4°.] Et si la société se relâche elle-même de ses droits; si elle vous dit: J'exige moins, pour obtenir plus sûrement, plus librement ce que j'exige; si les hommes . . . se permettent par intervalles cet oubli mutuel et passager; s'ils vous répondent enfin qu'ils ne vivent ensemble que pour étre heureux, et que le délassement est un besoin de leur foiblesse; avez-vous à leur répliquer que vous êtes hommes comme eux, et que tous vos momens sont pleins? Je sçais qu'il n'y a que l'homme qui broute, dont la société n'ait rien à exiger; mais elle n'attend de personne une servitude assidue.'

as are invasions of the right of property, and produce a Pain of the class of those of Privation: it extends not to such as are invasions of the right of personal security; and produce Pain of the class of pains organical.

Considering them as referring to the fictitious Law of Morality, the import of injustice is wider than that of injury: along with that notion of injury, it includes that of witholding benefit.

The term injury is applied to signify a mode of conduct whereby some pain is inflicted which it is conceived ought [not] to have been inflicted. The term injustice is applied to signify such an article of conduct as has been mentioned, and besides that, any such other mode of conduct whereby a pleasure is forborn to be produced, or, as we say more commonly, a benefit is forborn to be conferred which it is conceived ought to have been conferred; especially if the like benefit has been conferred by the party in question to another person under like circumstances. Intentionally to make an innocent man suffer, whether friend or stranger, is an injury. Not to do good, where opportunity offers, to a friend to whom you are under obligations is ingratitude. Of two friends to whom you are under equal obligations, with equal opportunities of doing them good, to do good to the one and not to the other is injustice.

1117. Since some expression must be used to answer the purpose of that of the Law of Nature, let it be the Law of Morality. 'Law of Morality' to be substituted to Law of Nature.

The Law of Morality is an expression already in use; and in the sense which it is here proposed to give it.[1] It is, I think, more evidently figurative than the other: it is in less danger of being taken to denote an actually-existing object. It points to the source from whence the notion belonging to it is derived: it directs the attention to that one of the three Sanctions that may be termed the moral. It leaves the expression Law of Nature free to signify without ambiguity physical rules, rules indicative of matter of fact, expressing the result of observation: such Laws of Nature as those to which Sir Isaac Newton and other Natural Philosophers have given that name.[2]

---

[1] See, for instance, Montesquieu, *Spirit of Laws*, Bk. I, Ch. I, i. 4: 'Such a being [as Man] is liable every moment to forget himself; philosophy has provided against this by the laws of morality.'

[2] While Newton referred to the laws of motion and not to the laws of nature in his *Principia Mathematica* (see p. 175 n. above), the latter phrase has come into general use to designate the laws of physics.

Power Magisterial = Dictatorial.

1118. For Power *Magisterial* say *Dictatorial.*

DIG. Technical Language why worse looked upon[1] in Law than in any other Science.

1119. Why is it that men in general are so apt to feel a kind of uneasiness and even of indignation at what is called technical language in the Law, which they do not feel on the occasion of the technical language in any other science? Answer. In other sciences, the objects themselves are unfamiliar: people, therefore, do not wonder at finding the names of those ideas to be unfamiliar too. In Law, the objects themselves are to the last degree familiar: such of the objects as are modes, i:e: acts, are acts that the people themselves are practising every day: such of them as are substances are instruments they are acting with or acting upon with equal frequency. It is only the manner in which the ideas furnished by those objects are compounded into complex ideas, and the manner in which those complex ideas are denominated, that can be unfamiliar to men: perceiving that the elements themselves, and thence the names of those elements, are familiar, they expect that the different compositions made of those elements, and the names expressive of those compositions, should be familiar too. These denominations, being in many instances unskilfully devised, are very uncharacteristic and inapposite. They are not natural but huddled up by a convention of Lawyers among themselves: they are arbitrary: no analogy is discernible between the whole or any part of the bundle of ideas to which the name is taken and the primitive object from whence the name is borrow'd: or perhaps they are not borrow'd from any primitive object, in which case they are exactly upon a footing with the a and b of the Mathematicians: or perhaps from a primitive object which, however, is known by that name only in some foreign country, which comes to the same thing.

The rhombus parallellepida of Geometricians, the Square root of Arithmeticians, the Lens of Opticians, Barometer, Thermometer, Electrometer, &c. are not complained of:[2] while the Felony, Præmunire, Trover, Ejectment, &c. &c. of Lawyers are, and that in many instances not without foundation.

In other sciences, if the names are new, it is because the things are new: in Law, new names are given to common things. Hence mystery—this mystery—in many cases is unnecessary: in many where it is necessary, the reason why it is so does not appear.

It has the effect of shutting out men from the understanding of the things in question. Such is the effect: such appears, therefore, to

[1] MS alt. 'more complained of'.
[2] In the margin, Bentham has noted at this point: 'So names of uncommon substances.'

have been the intention. For when the bulk of mankind are ignorant of a thing equally necessary to be known by all; and those only are in possession of the knowledge of it whose business it is to sell their knowledge; what often is the result of weakness or inattention is imputed to interested contrivance. Nobody is surprized to find objects with which they are entirely unacquainted characterized by names with which they are entirely unacquainted.

1120. *Auxiliaries conscious* ϽC *unconscious*—to wit of the circumstances which render the *act* criminal.

Auxiliaries conscious ϽC unconscious.

1121. Even those who scruple not to plunder and to oppress are not backward in perceiving that it is their interest to be sole plunderers and sole oppressors. They know that it is the sum of it's uneasiness that causes a people to revolt: a sufficient inducement to them to banish all those grievances by which they do not profit.

Prefat.—Not unfit for absolute Governments.

Bating what belongs to the Law of Treasons and other points of Constitutional Law, I see nothing which an arbitrary sovereign, with the strictest attention to his separate interest in contradistinction to those of the people[1]

1122. Modes of exposition—*Ampliation* and *Restriction,* viz: of a word used in a particular technical sense in comparison of it's ordinary signification.—As Contingence applied to Remainders in Law.—The sense of it is there *Restricted*.[2]

Exposition—modes of. *Ampliation* and *Restriction*.

1123. Every Law or rule of Law respects some *act* or some *forbearance*. In every act or forbearance, some one person at least is concerned.

If one only, and the mode of conduct is an act, such act may be said to be intransitive.[3]

Act intransitive.

1124. Sanctions, Pains and Pleasures consider'd as being among the effects of an action, may be termed it's pathological effects.

Effects pathological.

---

[1] The passage has been abandoned at this point.

[2] For an account of contingent remainders see Blackstone, *Commentaries on the Laws of England*, ii. 168–72.

[3] In the text, Bentham has noted at this point: 'From thence go on through all the objects with their denominations.'

Power *dictatorial*)(*Despotic.*

1125. Power *dictatorial* has nothing but the circumstance of *time* to distinguish it from Despotic.

Apol. Metaphys. Du Marsais.

1126. Apology for Metaphysics in Du Marsais, p. 380.[1]

'Je n'ai pas été chercher de la Métaphysique, pour en amener dans une centrée étrangère; je n'ai fait que montrer à qui est dans l'esprit, relativement au discours et à la necessité de l'élocution. C'est ainsi que l'anatomiste montre les parties du corps humain sans en ajouter de nouvelles.'

Relation—what.

1127. When the mind is led to consider one object (be it mode or substance) by the consideration of another object, the two objects are said to be related: a relation is said to subsist between them. Relation is 1. real: viz: *in rebus ipsis*.[2] 2. ideal: *quoad nos*.[3] Real relation is 1. in causality: 2. in resemblance: 3. in *place*: 4. in *time*.

We see thus what relation is; it is nothing more than the condition any two objects are said to be in, in virtue of the mind's being determined to pass from the consideration of the one of them to that of the other.

Relation, what. Terms of Relation not to stand promiscuously as heads along with names of Modes and Substances.

1128. Relation, therefore, we see, is not any thing that exists. Substances are objects, modes are objects:[4] but the existence of relations is merely nominal. It is not that there is such a thing as a little being which, under the name of relation, gets into either or both of two objects that are related: but when we speak of a relation as subsisting between the two objects, it is no more than saying that the two objects are related: i:e: such as determine the mind, which considers one of them, to pass on to the consideration of the other. Relations, therefore, not being of the number of objects that exist, cannot properly be defined. They cannot, therefore, with propriety be made to stand as heads or entitling words: since these are but so many generical terms of wide extent. At least it is productive of confusion to rank these spurious *genera* promiscuously with such as are strict and genuine.

Words that can properly be defined are generical terms.

Act)(Circumstances.

1129. In every moral action there are two things to be consider'd: 1st the bare act itself that is done, or liable to be done. 2dly the circumstances in which it is done or liable to be done.

---

[1] See César Chesneau Du Marsais, *Logique et principes de grammaire*, Paris, 1769, p. 381 (not 380). There are some minor inaccuracies in the rendering of the passage.

[2] i.e. 'in the things themselves'.

[3] i.e. 'with respect to us'.

[4] MS orig. 'Substances exist, modes exist'.

1130. Circumjacent bodies *influencing* are either bodies *concurring, conspiring, assisting, promoting,* or *impeding, opposing, resisting.*

Causation—theory of. Circumstances influencing—Powers and Relations.

Among circumstances influencing the production of an effect at any given instant may be: 1st the exhibition of a relation: 2d the exertion of a *power*, whether active or passive.

A thought or motion is somthing instantaneous: a situation consider'd as simultaneous to a thought or motion is something instantaneous: in like manner must every object be that is conceived as simultaneous and assisting to or impeding the operation of a cause. It is not, therefore, a power or a relation that we can speak of in this view: because they are consider'd as things permanent: it must [be] a particular momentary instance of the exercise of the power in question, a particular momentary instance of the suggestion or manifestation of such a relation. Suppose what Locke supposes, and what, indeed, one cannot avoid supposing on this behalf: suppose what we call a power in a body to result from nothing but the motions and situations of it's insensible parts:[1] in this case, it is that set of motions and situations among those parts which, at the time in question, exerts the influence in question upon the body spoken of as the principal operating instrument in question, that constitutes that influencing circumstance that is meant by an instance of the exertion of that power of the body that is in question.

Suppose we had to enumerate the influencing circumstances attendant upon any given effect at the moment of it's production. This effect is instantaneous. Nor is the word effect that it is denoted by a word unfit to characterize that which is instantaneous. The names also that are given these influencing circumstances ought also to be such as are capable of expressing that which is instantaneous. But this, however, is not the case with the word *Power*, or the word *Relation*. What, then, is to be done? Either that which it is intended to be expressed can not be expressed, or some expression capable of denoting something that is instantaneous must be found to substitute in the room of them.

---

[1] See Locke, *Essay concerning Human Understanding*, Bk. IV, Ch. III, § 16, p. 547: 'But *as to the Powers of Substances* to change the sensible Qualities of other Bodies, which make a great part of our Enquiries about them, and is no inconsiderable branch of our Knowledge; I doubt, as to these, whether *our Knowledge reaches* much farther than our Experience; or whether we can come to the discovery of most of these Powers, and be certain that they are in any Subject by the connexion with any of those *Ideas*, which to us make its Essence. Because the Active and Passive Powers of Bodies, and their ways of operating, consisting in a Texture and Motion of Parts, which we cannot by any means come to discover: 'Tis but in very few Cases, we can be able to perceive their dependence on, or repugnance to any of those *Ideas*, which make our complex one of that sort of Things.'

Law restraining—Liberty and Property, how affected by it.

1131. To every Law belongs some person, or else some thing, which is it's passive object.

A thing that is the passive object of a Law is either the property of the agent or not.

There are but two ways in which a Law can respect an act that is the modal object of it: that is by commanding it to be done upon the thing which is the passive real object, or by forbidding it.

By a Law to either effect made with relation to a real passive object that is the property of the agent, his liberty is narrow'd: by a Law prohibiting the act with relation to that object, his property also is narrow'd.

A man's liberty, therefore, may be narrow'd without his property: but his property cannot be narrow'd without his liberty.

No Law, therefore, can be made with relation to a real passive object that is a man's property, without narrowing either his liberty, or his property and liberty both together.

By a Law that narrows one man's property, another man's may either be enlarged or not: the restriction which a Law imposes on a man's property may either be such as enlarges another man's, or it may not. A Law which gives Sempronius a right of way over the field of Titius,[a] such a Law, by the same operation whereby it narrows the property of Titius, enlarges that of another, viz: Sempronius. For by this, Titius is forbidden to hinder Sempronius from passing, while Titius is permitted to pass. But a Law which forbids Titius to plant, for instance, Tobacco;[b] such a Law, though it narrows the property of Titius, enlarges not, at least by it's direct operation, the property of any man. Titius himself is forbidden to plant Tobacco on the spot in question, but no man other [than] Titius is thereby permitted to plant on it, or do on it any thing else.

Directions.

1132. As the Law, when it issues simple *directions*, takes it's sanction from private individuals; so when it carries into effect dispositions of property, it takes it's *precept*.

Precept.

To *dispose.*

1133. A man may be said to make a disposition of an article of property when he either *transfers* or *charges* it.

To *charge.*

1134. An article of property may be said to be charged when

[a] As is done by Turnpike Acts.[1]

[b] As is done by . . . Car. 2.[2]

[1] The Turnpike Roads Act of 1773 (13 Geo. III, c. 84) facilitated the formation of Turnpike Trusts, which had hitherto required private Acts of Parliament.

[2] The growing of tobacco was prohibited by the Tobacco Planting and Sowing Act of 1660 (12 Car. II, c. 34) and thereafter by the Encouragement of Trade Act of 1663 (15 Car. II, c. 7) and the Tobacco Planting and Plantation Trade Act of 1670 (22 & 23 Car. II, c. 26).

either the entire article that is in question or the profits of it are made transferable upon a contingency: viz: to the incumbrancer in specie for a time: or in specie to the best bidder outright and to the incumbrancer in value outright.

1135. Any subordinate public or a private act of power may be said to be void, when it is such to which the superior Judicial Court will not lend the sanction of the supreme power. Void.

1136. It follows that, of the supreme governors themselves, no act whatever can be void: to speak of it as being so is a contradiction in terms. An instrument pretended to contain an expression of the will of the supreme governors may be spurious; and that either because that which is therein expressed was not in fact their will: or else because, though it were their will, the manner in which it is expressed is not in the number of those in which alone, when expressed, the people have been accustomed to observe it. A pretended act of the supreme body may, therefore, be spurious: but void it never can be. A Supreme Law may be Spurious but not void.

1137. Subordination is either simple or complex. Subordination.

1138. Subordination may be said to be simple when the parties among whom it subsists are no more than two: complex, where more than two. Simple ⲭ complex. Bipartite ⲭ tripartite.

The parties between whom subordination subsists when it is simple are 1st subjects, and 2dly governors. The parties among whom it subsists when it is complex, are 1st subjects; and 2d different ranks of governors.

1139. Subordination among governors subsists when the case is that, on any account, the will of the party who is superordinate has effect, that is, is obey'd by the subjects, in preference to him that is subordinate. Superordinate.

This may be brought about by the following different means.[1]

1140. In the immense quantity of literary productions of all sorts that issue from the press, it is a very small proportion, and those perhaps not always the most useful, that introduce their authors upon the roll of fame. Copy Right.

To suppose that a man, for having made a certain number of black marks upon a white ground, should become exempt from all the passions and all the wants of his fellow-creatures, that a man by writing of a book can learn to go without his victuals, is a notion which it is impossible to treat with any degree of seriousness: and

[1] The passage has been abandoned at this point.

yet I would not swear but that even this notion, when decked in the charms of eloquence, may have had some influence. Now it is a matter far enough as yet from having been proved that a man, by writing a book on cooking, will lose his appetite for plum-pudding: by writing love-elegies, all relish for the expensive caresses of the fair: by writing on the beauties of painting, his passion for virtue.

Punishment—the idea a fundamental one.

1141. The *anchor* by which the import of all these terms is fixed, the *link* by which it is connected, and the key by which it is laid open, the cement by which it is kept together, is Punishment. Take away from any of them the idea of Punishment, and you have mere sound without a meaning.

Placemen how to be taxed.

1142. Pensions paid out of the public purse may be taxed in two ways. 1st. By Deduction or witholding: i:e: by giving less than before. 2dly. By Assessment: viz: by first giving and then drawing back a part of what was given. These methods appear at first sight to be the same: but in effect they are really very different. In the first case, the real value of the places being lessen'd, the nominal value is lessen'd with it. In the 2d, the real value being lessen'd, the nominal value is left unchanged.

The latter mode is inconvenient in comparison to the other, both to the individuals affected and to the public.

1st. To the individuals. Because, their incomes sounding the same as ever, they are under the same moral obligation to spend as before, without the means. They, therefore, feel themselves more pinched by a tax imposed this way than they would by the same tax imposed the other. They remain exposed likewise to the odium of the whole salary, with the profit only of a part.

2dly. To the Public: because the individuals in question, being by this means more needy, are more rapacious. More of the public money is expended from time [to time] in satisfying their importunities.

A Tax on Placemen, when first issued, must of course (or at least does more naturally) assume the form of an Assessment: but in a course of time, to the next takers at furthest, it may assume the form of a deduction.

The point is so to manage that in the Court Calendars, &c. the real value may be annext to the offices instead of the nominal.[1]

Where the Profits consist in fees paid by individuals instead of a

[1] Lists of government office-holders, with their salaries annexed, appeared annually in such publications as the *Royal Kalendar, or, Correct Annual Register, for England, Scotland*

Salary paid by the public, it is obvious that the method of *Deduction* cannot be pursued. But then neither does the inconvenience subsist here, which the method of *Deduction* is calculated to obviate. There is no nominal value to catch the ear superior to the real. The difficulty still remains with regard to fees of office paid upon admission. These are, in many instances, very heavy: and, for the reason above given, very mischievous. These should be published: or what is much better, be abolished.

Placemen in general are the leeches of the public. These officers are the Leeches of these Leeches. The . . . . of these Leeches makes the 1st set still more ravenous. The Public pays for all.

1143. No department of science can receive any considerable improvement but the language must receive a new modification. New ideas struck off from the general mass must, like the old ones, have words of their own to dress them in. These words must be, in some sort, new.

Prefat. New Terms—necessity of.

1144. The unsupported command of an individual adressed to the community in general is idle and ineffective. But even this, when deriving a sanction [from] the Legislature, acquires the force of a Law. For it is in the sanction that the force of a Law consists. By this means it is, that the expression of the particular wills of individuals enter[s] into the general mass of Jurisprudence.

Conveyances—have the force of Laws.

1145. A Dictate[?] is ordinarily taken for concise, when the discourse is composed of short sentences. It is supposed that the number of the words used upon the whole is small when the sentences are short. In fact, it is the reverse. The shorter each sentence, the more sentences must go to express a given number of ideas.

Short sentences adverse to brevity. Example.

Peter walks; and John walks.[1] John for his health; Peter for recreation. Peter and John walk together through shooting woods overgrown with briars: part of the way over roads that in the day time are render'd dusty by travellers; and in the night time, dangerous by highwaymen.

---

and Ireland and the *London Calendar, or Court and City Register for England, Scotland, Ireland and America*.

[1] MS del. 'Peter walks; and John walks' has been editorially restored to the text.

1146. *Rights* { *Liberties = Immunities.* / *Powers.* }

Imperation not *manifested* in Conditionalizing institutions.

1147. In the one case, it is the Commands that are diversified; in the other, the conditions to them: in the one case, the acts that are the *direct* objects of the command: in the other, the circumstances that are the collateral objects.

Shut the window, I say to my servant. Here we have a command. If you see it rain—or if you see the dust rise, or if you see any carriage coming by. Here we have so many different conditions—the command continuing all the while one and the same. Were I, then, a Legislator, and this command were extended to all my windows, and all my servants, here we should have a Law. Here would be several conditions, but the command would be but one. It would, therefore, be but one Law. Here are but three conditions expressed: but ever so many more might be imagined: an assemblage large enough to fill a volume. This assemblage might be collected by the industry of Jurists, and made to occupy a large title of Law: a title that, in point of bulk, might match with two or three others which altogether might include the whole matter of the science. The matter of this title would of course be branched out into different divisions: these divisions would have different names to characterize them: in none of which names would the least trace of any such thing as the command, nor of the sort of act that was the object of it, be, perhaps, discernible.

Among the other Titles of the science, all this while, there might be none but what would include a great variety not of conditions only, but of commands. The divisions of these titles would of course, or might at least, be characterized by names indicating so many different classes of commands; or which comes to the same thing, of acts constituted offences: that is violations of so many commands.

This could not but make a striking difference between the aspect and appearance in these last-mentioned titles and that first-mentioned title which we supposed to consist wholly of conditions. A man who should hear Law spoken of as being universally a matter of command would at first sight doubt whether it were so. 'True,' he would say, 'the rest of it: but not that title: for not a syllable of the nature of command do I see here'—not considering that all these conditions are but so many appendages to a command: and that without a command they would neither have place nor meaning. In the same view, if he found your discourse turning always upon offences, he might be apt to observe to you that you never touched upon this title, which, perhaps, he might stile by some such name as civil Law: you confined yourself wholly to Penal Law: 'for you talk all along,' says he, 'of commands or of offences: and not a syllable of any thing like an offence, any more than a command, is here'.

Just so it is by that division of Law, which Jurists have been accustomed to distinguish by the Title of Rights of *Things*.[1]

1148. Rights and *Wrongs*, why they cannot properly stand as names of Titles.[2] DIG. Classification.

Why Offences may—and Why Offences rather than Laws.

'Rights' and 'Wrongs' chosen for this purpose because familiar and in every one's mouth.

The common notion concerning Rights is, that they subsist, at least many of them, some how or other of themselves: and that then human Laws come in and inforce them.[3] That they do not in themselves originate from human Laws; consequently that it is not from the notion of human Laws that the notion of these Rights is to be derived.

In order to see whether this notion be just, what we have to do is, in the first place, to suppose a state of things in which no institutions, no Statutes, nor rules of Common Law exist: and then see how the case would be with *Rights*. In the next place, to suppose rights to exist upon their present footing, and to shew that the case is that, upon the present footing, punishment follows the course that it would do upon the supposition of human laws being established, and of it's being human laws that created (which they could only do by means of punishment) those rights.

1149. Of Rights—some are synonymous to Powers, others to Liberties—limitations to Public Constitutional Powers—created by the absence of *coertion*.

Rights { Powers. Liberties. Rights in action, or *Jures prosequendi*.

Offences are universal in their description—Laws are not so.—They are liable to be confounded by Statutes. It is Statutes only, indeed, that have any real individual existence. It is not any single statute that is ever a perfect expression of the Will—a perfect command, with a compleat apparatus of those conditions by which it is limited and controuled.

---

[1] The second volume of Blackstone's *Commentaries on the Laws of England*, for instance, is entitled 'Of the Rights of Things'.

[2] The four Books of Blackstone's *Commentaries on the Laws of England* are respectively entitled 'Of the Rights of Persons', 'Of the Rights of Things', 'Of Private Wrongs', and 'Of Public Wrongs'. Blackstone explains the principles that led him to adopt this division at i. 118.

[3] See, for instance, Locke, *Two Treatises of Government*, Second Treatise, Ch. IX, §§123–31, pp. 350–3.

Conduct of the Work. *Preparatoria* to the Distribution.

1150. I take for an example some particular state—suppose our own.

A state is &c.

Here, then, I suppose a *fact*: the same that is actually verified in all those assemblages of men which we are accustomed to call states. A habit of obedience in one body, corresponding to a habit of commanding and punishing at pleasure in some other body or some single person. To save words, and for no other purpose, we will call this latter party, whether a body or a single person, by a single name; namely that of Sovereign. Under this name we will consider him and them with respect to every particular that concerns him or them, in as far as he or they are the party who governs. When we come to consider the circumstances by which the case of a *single* sovereign is distinguished from that of a *sovereign body*, it will then be time enough to make a distinction in the name.[1]

Trace out the generation of Quasi-Commands, and shew their equipollency to real Commands.

This done, for shortness sake, proceed all along in the distribution, upon the supposition of real *commands*.

Assume as a certain fact, that punishment will follow from the breach of a command—viz: at the long run. That is, that at the last, some persons will be found to give execution to the Law. Then shew how it is that Commands constitute Powers over persons, viz: in all governing bodies that are subordinate to the Sovereign. Powers over things. Restraints respecting things that are a man's own: and respecting persons that are within his power. Obligations respecting things that are his own, and persons that are within his power.[2]

State a fact, then from that fact draw a definition—thus—The state performs a certain operation, viz: issues a command to such an effect—this makes a power to such effect—or, constitutes such a kind of power.—After this give a formal definition, i:e: paraphrasis, of the sort of power in question.

N.B. the stating of the fact will be like the definition (in Mathematics) of a circle from it's generation: the definition in form will be like the definition of a circle from it's leading property.[3]

[1] In the text, Bentham has noted at this point: 'N.B. Previously to this, all objects of meditation and discourse must have been reduced to the two classes of Substances and Modes in order to characterize the several real, genuine, *objects* of the Law, and, by shewing the non-existence of the pretended objects called Rights and wrongs, distinguish the real from the spurious.'

[2] In the text, Bentham has noted at this point: 'See 452.' See para. 1050, p. 334 above.

[3] Euclid, *Elements*, i. 15 gives the definitive property of a circle as equal radii.

This will be necessary for the sake of the Vocabulary of definitions: that they may be referred to alphabetically and consulted separately.

Conduct of the Work. Titles.[1]

1151. Titles:
A Key to Universal Jurisprudence.
Elements of the Metaphysics of Jurisprudence.
Metaphysics of Jurisprudence.
Novum Organon Juris.[2]
A Key to the Nomenclature of Universal Jurisprudence.
N.B . . . . particularly adapted to that of our own Country.
Nomenclator of Universal Jurisprudence.

Conduct of the Work.

1152. *Themis illustrata.*
Illustrate the equipollency of Commands and Quasi-Commands by cases put from private life.
So of the dependency between Commands and Conditions.
Shew wherein the difference between the cases of private life and those of proper Jurisprudence lies.—N.B. This is to be done preparatory to the putting of any case from private life.
Quasi-Commands, not having their amplitude fixed, are enlarged and contracted at pleasure for the purpose of argumentation.
When this is done, it must be done by Quasi-Conditionalizing or Quasi-exceptive clauses, with their repealatives.
Give instances of these modifications, in parallelism to those of *proper* Commands. This is the only way in which the ideas belonging to them can be reduced to method.

Causes Phys. and Moral.

1153. A well known distribution of *causes* is that into physical and moral.

Productive instrument)(instrument modified.[3]

1154. By a moral cause, when explained, is meant nothing more than some motive which, by it's influence on the will, gives movement to some or other of those animal organs, those *instruments*, the action of which, as masses of matter, comes back again into the class of physical causes.

[1] For further details concerning 'the Work' and its titles see the Editorial Introduction, p. xxiii above.

[2] Cf. Francis Bacon, 'Novum Organum, sive Indicia Vera de Interpretatione Naturae' (first published in 1620), in *The Instauratio Magna Part II: Novum Organum and Associated Texts*, ed. G. Rees with M. Wakely, Oxford, 2004 (*The Oxford Francis Bacon: Vol. XI*), pp. 48–447.

[3] In the margin, Bentham has noted at this point: 'See 509.' See paras. 1158–9, p. 367 below.

These organs thus put in action are either the organs of the person himself in whose mind the motive in question is supposed to arise, or the organs of some other person, to whom the knowledge of the first person's will has been communicated by some or other of the established signs, and the tendency to conform to it excited by some different, perhaps, but competent motive.

Between the moral action of the motive in the mind of any man and the physical action of that man's bodily organs resulting from the former, there is no intermediate action: no intermediate cause. The moral cause is the immediate cause of the physical effect. But between the action of a motive, between in short the volition of one man and any physical action of another which can be said to [be] the effect of the former moral action, any number of intermediate causes may subsist. These will always stand in the following order: [1. motive acting in the mind of the first man.] 2. Volition in the first man: 3. physical action—i:e: such a single action or assemblage of actions as [have] the property of serving as a sign of the above volition—of the first man: [4.] motive acting in the mind of the second man: 5. volition in the second man: 6. physical action in the second man: 7. motive acting in the mind of the third man; and so on through a series of men to any number.

Government—how it's operation becomes a Cause of acts. An event, how it may depend on a conditionalizing clause.

1155. Now, then, as the *effectual operation* of this sort of cause that may be termed moral is in past instances a fact as well as that of physical, and the future effectual operation of them is a probability in many cases as *strong* as that of natural ones, hence it is that a clause in a Law, may be conditionalizing—may have the property, the effect, of a *conditionalizing* one: may annex a *condition* to a *command*: and, by consequence, to an *event*, to an act the consequence of a command.

Causes physical Ӿ moral.

1156. N.B. The actions significative of the volition of *Herus*[1] have not, it is to be observed, in their own nature any tendency to produce in the mind of *Servus* that motive which gives birth to the volition of Servus that is conformable to that of Herus: no more than they have, in truth, to produce in the mind of the latter the idea of the volition of the former: all depends upon the principle of association: all depends upon this fact, the idea of pain, and that in such sufficient degree, being associated in the mind of Servus with the idea of the sort of act that would be an act of disobedience to the will of Herus.

---

[1] i.e. master.

1157. Call these men Cæsar, Pater, Mater, Filius, Libertus, Servus, &c. Their names expressing in Latin the civil relations for the purpose of exemplifying which they are assumed. Nomenclature for fictitious persons.

1158. A productive instrument is that instrument of which the motion is (or is supposed to be) *a cause.* *Instrument productive.*

1159. A modified object is that instrument of which the motion (or change of appearance in consequence of motion) is or is supposed to be *an effect.* *Object modified.*

1160. An effective operation is that which, in the event, is followed by that action or appearance that was expected from it as it's effect. *Operation effective.*

1161. An ineffectual operation is that which, in the event, is not follow'd by that action or appearance that was expected to follow from it as it's effect. *—ineffective.*

1162. When the incipient links in such a chain are once laid, others may from time to time be added, as there shall be found occasion; and thus in progress of time, and by the industry of successive workmen, the whole language may be worked up and drawn together—may be woven, as it were—into one connected and consistent piece of work. Definitions in a Chain—may in time spread over the whole language.

1163. N.B. Consent is a modification of *will*—Volition passed in certain circumstances. Consent *individual*[1])(*corporate.*

A man's corporate will may be contrary to his *individual*: his specific contrary to his *general.*

Or, having had a corporate will, he may not have formed *any* solitary will: or having formed and expressed a *general* will, he may have neither expressed nor formed any specific one. Which, then, in any of these cases, shall be said to be his will: affirmative or negative?

Or 3$^{dly.}$ Qu. His personal will may be contrary to his will *ex delegatione*, by delegation. If this can with any degree of propriety be called his will.

But Qu. a specific will contrary to a generic one, is it not *pro tanto* a revocation? and therefore no otherwise contrary to a generic will than one generic will, or one specific will, may be to another?

[1] MS del. '*solitary*'.

Representatives ꓘ Delegates.

1164. N.B. Instead of the word Representatives should be used the word Delegates. This would save a deal of equivocation.

The King, Lords and Commons all together are sometimes said to *represent* the state. It could not be said that they were all *delegates* of the state.

The King alone in Absolute Governments is sometimes said to *represent* the state. It could not be said that he was the *delegate* of the State.

The word delegation expresses a plain fact. The word Representation expresses a figurative sophistical colouring given to a fact.

Consent ꓘ Assent.

1165. We say assent or consent indifferently to a mode of conduct proposed as the object of a *volition*: we say *assent* only to an assertion.

Represent, to: what.

1166. In a legal sense, a man is said to represent his principal, when, in virtue of the appointment of Law, the same consequences ensue to the principal from the acts which the representative does as representative, as would ensue were it the principal himself that did them.

Definitions—the most common words want them most.

1167. Duclos, *Considérations sur les moeurs*, Ch. 8.[1]

Plus un mot abstrait est en usage, moins l'idée en est fixe, parce que chacun l'étend, la restraint ou la change; et l'on ne s'apperçoit de la différence des principes que par celle des conséquences, ou par les différentes applications qu'on en fait.

☛ Si l'on vouloit définir les mots que l'on comprend le moins, il faudroit définir ceux dont on se sert le plus.

The words we least understand, are those that are most frequently in use.

Entities classed.[2]

1168. Give me matter and motion, said Descartes, and I will make a world.[3] By having, then, matter and motion, that philoso-

[1] See Charles Pinot Duclos, *Considérations sur les mœurs de ce siécle. Nouvelle édition*, Paris, 1751, pp. 186–7.

[2] MS del. 'What things exist.'

[3] This remark does not appear in the work of the philosopher and mathematician René Descartes (1596–1650), though Bentham's contemporaries repeatedly attributed it to him. Bentham's source may have been D'Alembert's 'De l'abus de la critique en matière de religion', in *Mélanges de littérature, d'histoire, et de philosophie*, iv. 330: '*Donnez-moi de la matière et du mouvement, et je ferai un monde*: ainsi parloit autrefois Descartes', which appeared in English translation as 'The Abuse of Criticism in Religion', in *Miscellaneous Pieces in Literature, History, and Philosophy*, London, 1764, p. 80: 'Give me matter and motion and I will make a world, said Descartes once'. It may be an echo of Voltaire, *La métaphysique de Neuton, ou parallèle des sentimens de Neuton et de Leibnitz*, Amsterdam, 1740, pp. 3–4 (reproduced in *Eléments de la philosophie de Newton*, ed. R.L. Waters and W.H. Barber, Oxford, 1992 (*Les Œuvres Complètes de Voltaire: Vol. 15*), p. 197): 'Dès qu'on s'est persuadé,

pher knew that he would have whatever is the object of our exterior senses. Not that even matter and motion are two distinct things. The motion is not any thing that exists separately from matter. Whether there be motion in any case or whether there be none, it is still matter and matter only that exists.

Of the same portion of matter, when it exhibits a certain sort of appearance, we say that it is in *motion*: when a certain other sort of appearance, we say that it is *at rest*. Motion is not a thing that is added to it in one case, any more than rest is a thing that is added to it in the other.

Condition.

1169. The will is that the event conditionalized, viz: act of punishment, shall be performed in the case of the several signals having been exhibited, viz: in the case of the several requisite formalities having been observed, and not otherwise.

This dependency is marked by some one or other of that class of particles which are called causal: by a class of conjunctions which, from this function of their's, may be stiled conditional or suppositious.

The punishment is to take place *if* so and so, and not otherwise.

Appointment—Etymology.

1170. By appointment it is that the *general* command of the Law in the behalf in question is brought to bear upon an individual point.

Possession—Property.

1171. He whose power over a thing is [an] indefinite and unlimited residuum in respect of the number of the acts it warrants, is said for the time being to have the possession of the thing.

Interested in.

He whose power is indefinite, with respect to the time during which the possession is to endure, is said to have the property.

Duration } of the Period
Earliness } of enjoyment.
Time.

1172. Various allotments of the acts which a person is empowered to exercise on the same *thing* constitute interests: various shares, portions and degrees of interest. Different interests may subsist in, may be carved out of, the same material subject, by the means of *time*: by the time or period, as it may be called, of enjoyment being of different duration, or of different degrees of remoteness from the present.

avec Descartes, qu'il est impossible que le Monde soit fini, que le Mouvement est toujours dans la même quantité: dès qu'on ose dire, donnez-moi du mouvement & de la matière, & je vais faire un Monde'.

Amplitude of the part enjoy'd. Space.

1173. If the material subject in question be capable of division, if the parts it consist of be capable of being enjoyed one of them at the same time that another is not enjoy'd, or rather of being enjoy'd one of them by one man, at the same time that another is enjoy'd by another man, here is a third principle of division by which different interests in the same thing may be carved out.

Quality of the use of any single part.

1174. Species of the act that may be exercised on the part.[1]

In respect to the power of continuing the succession of persons interested, the transfer may be absolute or conditional.

And the enjoyment of each successive taker may be diversified in like manner as that of the first: viz: by duration, earliness, and amplitude of the part enjoy'd, and by the species of the act that may be exercised on it.

Right—Possession—Power—Estate.

1175. The words right, possession, power, may be strung together in a three-linked chain: we may speak of a person as having a right to the possession of a Power over an Estate.

Definition—a paraphrasis of.

1176. A man is said to give a Definition of a word, when he names another word significative of an assemblage of different sorts of things of which that characterized by the word to be defined is one, and at the same time mentions some property or assemblage of properties in the sort of things characterized by the last-mentioned word, which belong to it and not to any other of the things that are of the sort indicated by the word first mentioned.[2]

Otherwise thus.

A man is said to give a Definition of a word, when he names the genus of things which that class of which it is the name belongs to, together with some distinctive property or properties that serve to distinguish that class from all other species of that genus.

Every definition, therefore, consists of two distinguishable parts.

The first is that which assigns the genus.

The other is that which mentions the distinctive property.

Suppose a Loadstone be the word to be defined, and the Definition given of it be, that it is a Mineral that attracts Iron. Here the saying that a Loadstone is a mineral is assigning the genus of things of which the class signified by the word Loadstone is a species. The saying that it attracts Iron is the mentioning it's

[1] In the text, Bentham has noted at this point: 'Enjoyment *vicissitudinous* of parts of the thing a question.'

[2] In the margin, Bentham has noted at this point: 'N.B. Explain the words Genus and Species first.'

having a property that is supposed to distinguish it from all other species of that genus.

The first part of a Definition is accomplished in a single word. The latter takes up a greater or a smaller number of words according as the characteristic of the species is constituted by a single property or takes a number of properties to constitute it; and according as the property or properties that constitute it belong to the species in all circumstances or only in certain particular circumstances.

1177. When that part which assigns the characteristic of the species occupies a considerable number of words, it is called, rather, a description. Description.

1178. Division is the converse of the first part of a Definition. A man is said to give a Division when, after mentioning a genus, he assigns it all it's species. Division.

1179. The more species are mentioned under one and the same genus, the more a Division approaches to an enumeration. Division ⪤ Enumeration.

Linnæus, in his Botanical System, has distributed the whole number of Plants into 24 classes. One of these classes he distinguishes by the name of Cryptogamia. Cryptogamia is a word of his invention, made to signify those in which the parts of fructification are concealed.[1]

He might, if he had pleased, have included the whole number of remaining plants under some such name as *Phanerogamia*. Phanerogamia, as applied to plants, is a word that would serve to signify all such plants in which the parts of fructification are *conspicuous*. Had he taken this method, his division, consisting but of two branches, would have been a strict one. Instead of that, it has seemed preferable to him to divide the vegetable kingdom, at the first step, into 24 classes. This makes a lax division, and one that, by the multitude of it's branches, partakes much of the character of an enumeration.

Each of these classes are again divided into Orders. Had he at one step, instead of stopping at those classes, divided the whole vegetable kingdom immediately into Orders, the division would have worn a still stronger appearance of an Enumeration.

These Orders, in fine, are divided again into Genera. These Genera are so numerous that the immediate recensition[2] of them, without any previous collection of them into Classes or Orders, would scarce by any body be spoken [of] under the name of a

[1] See Carl Linnaeus, *Systema Naturae*, Leiden, 1735, Table of 'Regnum Vegetabile', class 'z. CRYPTOGAMIA. *Flores absconditi*' [no pagination].

[2] i.e. recension.

Division. The recension of them would be stiled an Enumeration. To make that enumeration would be to give a list or Catalogue.

It is manifest from hence that there are no certain limits which bound Division and Enumeration.

Definition serves to distinguish things of one sort from things of another sort that, by some property or other, bear a resemblance to the former. It serves to distinguish it from things that are in danger of being confounded with it from resemblance.

Individuation. **1180.** Individuation serves to distinguish it from things that are in danger of being confounded with it from contiguity: or:

Individuation serves to mark out the boundaries of each individual.[1] It thereby serves to distinguish a whole thing of the sort in question: 1st. From parts of things of the sort in question. 2d. From a part or parts added to a whole. 3dly. From 2 wholes added together. 4th. From parts or wholes of things of another sort that lie contiguous.

Individuation circumscribes the limits of individuals of the sort in question.

It is of great use where the object is complex and it's parts distinctly valuable. As a House, an Estate in Land.

Distinction. **1181.** Distinction is where two sorts of things are distinguished, not each from all other things, as by Definition, but only each of them from the other.

Synonymation. **1182.** Synonymation is the assigning of another word expressive of the same sort of things with the word to be expounded, the former being a word of the same language with the latter.

Translation. **1183.** Translation is the assigning of another word expressive of the same sort of things with the word to be expounded, the former being a word of a different language from the latter.

Definition X Synonymation. **1184.** The difference between Definition and Synonymation is this. In Definition, the word made use of for the purpose of exposition is a word that signifies other sorts of things besides that which is signified by the word expounded: to confine it, therefore, to the sort of things in question, to which the business is to shew it to belong, it is necessary to go farther: it is necessary to mention some property that may serve to distinguish this from those others: viz: some property which this is found to possess and those others not. In Synonymation, on the other hand, the word assumed for the purpose of expounding signifies exactly the same sort of things as the word to be expounded does, and no others.

In the common books of Logic, two sorts of Definition, as they

[1] MS orig. 'Individuation serves to determine how much of the matter whereof a thing of any sort is composed goes to the making up of that thing.'

are both so called, are laid down. One called a Definition of the thing: the other, a Definition of the name.[1] That which is called a Definition of the thing is the same with that which I have termed simply a Definition. The other is what I have termed a Synonymation. I term it Synonymation, because in common speech words that are used to signify the same sort of things are called Synonymous. It may be worth while here to endeavour to shew why it is that the one sort of exposition comes to be called a definition of the thing, the other only a definition of the name: we shall thereby the more clearly understand wherein consists the difference between the one mode of exposition and the other.

Let us take an example. I am asked to give a definition of the word Magnet. A Magnet, then, I say, is a Mineral that has the property of attracting Iron. Now, what have I done in saying that it is a Mineral? I have intimated that the sort of thing known by the name of Magnet [is] possessed of all those properties that are understood to be possessed by the several sorts of things that are in use to be characterized by this word *mineral*. I go on, and say it has the property of attracting Iron. What have I done now? I have alledged that, over and above those properties that are common to the thing in question with all those other sorts of things that are equally known by the name of *mineral*, it has another property which none of them has.

Again, I am asked to give a synonymation of the word Magnet. In answer, a Magnet, I say, is a Loadstone. Now, in saying this, what knowlege is it I have convey'd? I have intimated that the properties possessed by the sort of thing called Magnet are precisely the properties, and no others, that are possessed by the sort of thing called Loadstone: that consequently, it is one and the same sort of thing called by those two different names.

Now then, what is it that the former mode of Exposition teaches more than the latter? In order to answer this, it will be proper to see what points of knowlege are respectively assumed by them, as being already possessed by the persons whom they are respectively calculated to inform.

When, for the purpose of explaining to you the word Magnet, I answer that a Magnet is a mineral, I assume and take it for granted that you are already acquainted [with] what it is that people mean by the word Mineral: what collection of properties it is used to signify. Otherwise, what I say is to no purpose. In like manner, when I go on and say that the mineral in question has the property

[1] For the distinction between *definitio rei* and *definitio nominis* see, for instance, Sanderson, *Logicæ Artis Compendium*, pp. 43–4.

of attracting Iron, I take for granted that you are already acquainted with what it is people mean when they talk of attracting, and of Iron.

Again, when I tell you that a Magnet is a Loadstone, I take it for granted that you have a notion of some properties which you suppose to be possessed by whatever thing men are accustomed to characterise by the name of Loadstone. The name Magnet, which before was unknown to you, I now give you to understand indicates that thing, whatever it be, whatsoever properties it possesses that you have been accustomed to hear characterized by that other name.

But telling you that the name Magnet signifies the same sort of thing that possesses the properties which are suggested by the name Loadstone does not tell you what those properties are. The property or properties you have been accustomed to look upon as belonging to any portion of substance to which men would give the name of Loadstone may not belong to it; or belonging to it, they may not be such as belong to it exclusively: so that although you suppose yourself to have been made acquainted with the characteristic properties of the thing known by the name of Magnet, by having been told that it is the same sort of thing as is known by the name of Loadstone, that may not be the case: whereas if I tell you expressly that it possesses the property of attracting Iron, and that be a property that really belongs to no other body, I am certain of having given you so much knowledge as consists in the knowing that every thing called a Loadstone possesses exclusively that property. Hence, if you were to chance to meet with a portion of substance which you were informed was a Loadstone, and which you found means to distinguish from the bodies it was contiguous to, not by this property of it's attracting Iron, a property which it might not be in circumstances to manifest, but by some other properties, such as the sensible properties of bulk, colour, hardness, texture, &c., you would, by means of my definition, have learnt a property of the thing, you would, by this means, have learnt in some sort the nature of the thing. In the other case, you would have learnt merely the signification of the word: viz: that it signified the sort of thing that was signified also by another word: but what are any of the properties possessed by the thing that both these words are in use to characterize is what, if you know at all, you know not the more for this exposition, but you must have known it already by some other means. By Definition that difficulty is solved, which Synonymation does but put off.

1185. Distribution supposes the subject in question to be in parts. Division supposes it to be a whole. When a Division of any subject is performed, you have it first given in form of a whole. You then have the same subject over again made into parts. When you perform the business of Division, you set out with a single article. Out of that one you make many; all of them together equal to that one. When you perform the business of Distribution, you set out with a number of articles: out of those many, by bringing together, you make fewer; and if you go on in the same way to the uttermost, in conclusion out of those fewer you make one. The few which are thus made out of the many take the name of ***heads***; and ***under*** those heads the many are said to be arranged.

Distribution ⅹ Division.

Heads, what.

N.B. This is the case in that method of Distribution which is the exact converse of Division: and the laying down a system of Logical subalternation in the order of ascent. In this case, as has been said, the articles mentioned as heads are wholes with respect to the articles arranged under them.

But there is another way in which an article may stand as a head to a number of other articles. And that is when the one article is mentioned not as a whole of which the others are parts, but as a somthing to which the number of articles bear some kind of relation. Thus it is, for example, with Offences against the Coin. Here the article Coin is assumed as a head under which the offences in question are distributed. But it is not that Coin is a genus of which the offences in question are so many species: it is not [that] Coin is a whole, of which the offences in question are so many parts. But the case is that Coin is an article to which the other articles in question, stiled offences, do in some manner or other ***relate***. A System of Natural History, or System of Botany, will furnish an example of the mode of distribution first-mentioned. The Genera are parts, the Genera are species, of the Orders: the orders, of the classes: the classes, of the universal name of the objects of the science, viz: Plants.

1186. A Definition may take up an extraordinary number of words on either of the accounts following. First, by it's specifying a number [of] properties as constitutive of the distinctive character. $2^{dly.}$ Although that character should be constituted by a single property, by it's specifying certain particular circumstances as being those or exceptions to those in which the thing in question possesses that property.

Definition ⅹ Description.

It may be necessary to specify a number of circumstances as constitutive of the distinctive character for this reason. The case may be, that these properties may be possessed each of them separately by some other sort of thing, but not by any sort of thing all of them together.

The truth is there is not perhaps any sort of thing that possesses any assignable property in all circumstances. A definition, then, that by saying nothing at all of any circumstances intimates that the thing possesses the property in question in all circumstances can never be exact. It can serve at best to give a loose general notion of the thing, such as may do wel[l] enough indeed for some purposes but must undergo many corrections and amplifications before it can be generally applied.

Exposition—modes of.

1187. Modes of Exposition.

Definition, Division, Individualization or Individuation or Circumscription, Enumeration, Distinction, Synonymation, Ampliation, Restriction, Paraphrasis, Archetypation or Derivation, Description, Distribution, Etymologization, Translation.

Under Definition (sc. *rei*) come Description, Distinction.

Under Definition (sc. *nominis*) come Synonymation, Translation, Ampliation, Restriction, Etymologization.

Under Division come Distribution (which is nearly Synonymous, the same operation consider'd under a different aspect), Enumeration.

Instead of Definition, for names of fictitious entities, is Paraphrasis.

Appendant to Paraphrasis is Archetypation.

Ampliation and Restriction.

1188. Ampliation and Restriction are supplements to Definition.

Definition marks out, in the first instance, the extent of the class. Ampliation widens that extent: Restriction narrows it.

Ampliation, therefore, and Restriction presuppose a Definition as being made, or what some might be apt to make, ranking not *so many* sorts of things under the name in question, as it is proposed to rank under it by the ampliation. Restriction, more.

Enumeration.

1189. The recension[1] of the narrowest, least extensive classes of those into which the writer in question has occasion to divide the assemblage of objects in question is what I would stile Enumeration. Enumeration, then, is the last step in a Division or system of Divisions.

Powers in a State, how created.

1190. He marked out sorts of actions as being to be avoided or pursued in certain cases.

[1] MS orig. 'specification'.

This he might do in either of two ways: the silent or the enuntiative.

I will suppose it to be one and the same person that does every thing: this one person I will call the Sovereign.[1] In this sovereign I will suppose all the powers in the government to be concenter'd. To this one person I will attribute the various operations I shall have occasion to display.

This supposition, it will be obvious, is not strictly true. It is not true, perhaps, in any state: certainly not in our's. I make it merely for shortness sake and to save words: that the reader may not be embarrassed with more things than is necessary at a time.

The powers of the government are in fact distributed among various sorts of persons. The operations that I shall have occasion to attribute to the Sovereign as a single person may accordingly be the operations of those various hands.

These operations I shall have to speak of in a certain order. They will of course be represented as if it were in that order they were performed. This perhaps may not be the case: they may in practise have been performed a number of them together, or, if separately, in order different from that in which they are spoken of.

Each will be represented as if performed and compleated at once, as it were *uno flatu*.[2] This also may not have [been] the case. In regard to such operations as have been performed in the way of what is called by Custom—in regard to powers that have been constituted by usage, it can not have been the case. The precise moment of establishment can never be assigned.

The business is to display every article of consideration separately in order to . . . and to avoid confusion.

The business is, therefore, to shew what are the respective characteristics of the several powers in themselves, making abstraction of three other points of consideration. $1^{st.}$ The *persons* by whom they have been constituted. $2^{d.}$ The *order*, or the relative periods, in which they have been constituted. $3^{dly.}$ The absolute period at which each has been constituted. In relation, then, to the first point: the number and qualities of the persons by whose agency the powers in question are constituted, I take as being the simplest number, one. In this case, it is impossible to speak in indeterminate manner: it becomes necessary to make a choice. Since the article of number cannot be touched upon without fixing either upon number one, or some other number equally precise and exclusive of all others: I mean, unless one were to have recourse to Algebra: which

[1] MS del. 'Legislator'.

[2] i.e. 'in one breath'.

would be involving the subject in further difficulties, in addition to the great number of those with which it is incumber'd of itself. Here, then, is one false supposition which is assumed at the outset, but which must afterwards be corrected.

In relation to the 2^d point, some certain order likewise must be assumed, to the exclusion of all those other [orders] which perhaps are equally possible. Here, then, is a 2^d false supposition which is afterwards to be corrected.

In relation to the third point, no definite time is at all alledged: all that is expressed in relation to time is, that it is past with respect to the time in which the author is [writing][1] or the reader reading. Here, then, is no supposition at all made but what is true.

* * * *

I suppose at first this obedience constant and inviolate: because I mean not to meddle with the circumstances of it's violation.

I then suppose it to be violated in the scatter'd instance of those persons who are the primary objects of the Law: but I still suppose it inviolate in the instance of some set at least of those particular classes of persons who, by ministering to the business of punishment, are to be the means of reducing to obedience the rest.

1191. There are two ways in which favour may be shewn to a party by the Law.

Power over Things.

One is by his being not restrained from exercising a certain class of acts upon a thing or certain class of things: while other persons *are* restrained. In this case, he is said to have a power over things: viz: over the thing[s] upon which the acts in question are exerted.

Power over Persons.

1192. Or if the passive object be a person, by his being not restrained from exercising a certain class of acts upon a person or certain class of persons. In this case, he is said to have a power over persons.

Right (without Power) as against Persons—to their being *con*strained.

1193. Another is, by *another* person's being constrained to exercise an act or certain class of acts, upon a thing or certain class of things: viz: such an act or class of acts the performance of which is of a nature to benefit the first party. In this case, he is said to have a right as against persons.

Protection (for his person) against Persons from corporal Pains. —restraints.

1194. |.

1195. The whole system of Jurisprudence displays itself in the coercing of one party for the benefit of another.

---

[1] MS 'writer'.

1196. The terms right and wrong are not fit to stand as the names of classes. Dig. Classification.

Classes are but superior genera. Names of classes, therefore, are but names of so many superior genera.

The individual things to be classed are either acts, viz: such acts as are made offences; or Laws; viz: the Laws that make them such.

Indeed, in speaking of them under the name of offences or of Laws, we have already assigned them their *common genus*. We could not, it is plain, do otherwise.

Acts, then (for to these we will at present confine ourselves), acts, I say, are the *summum genus* of the objects we are to consider. The several classes, then, into which we cast the objects in question must be species of acts.

What room, then, can there be for Rights or Wrongs? A *summum genus* neither of them is, it is plain. An act is not a species of right, nor a species of wrong.

1197. With as little truth can it be said, that they are either of them co-ordinate genera to acts. An act is not a species of any thing of which a right or a wrong is a species. No more than Sugar is a species of any thing of which sweetness is a species. With as little truth, lastly, can it be said that they are either of them subalternate genera to acts. A *right* is not, nor is a *wrong*, a species of act: no more than sweetness is a species of sugar. Rights and Wrongs unfit names. False *genera*.

1198. The terms *right* and *wrong* do not stand for any thing that *is*. They have no archetypes in nature. The objects they are put to stand for are objects which have no other than a figurative existence. Right and Wrong not *Subjicible*.

A proposition, therefore, in which either of them stands as a subject, in other words in which any thing is predicated of either of them, can not but be vague and inexact. It can never present any clear ideas. It turns the mind aside from that course in which it would be led to simple ideas: the only original elements of all knowledge.

1199. Rights and Wrongs mischievous in that they distract the attention from the contemplation or pursuit [of] the only natural method of Classification: which furnishes the plan, and the only perfect, universal and perpetual plan for a Digest. A Natural arrangement is the Plan of a Digest.

1200. Nothing can be predicated of them with truth, nor can they with truth be predicated of any thing. They are not species of Classification.

any thing that exists: neither is any thing that exists a species of them.

The sense of them is not to be made plainer by definition: if that only is to be deemed a definition, one part of which explains a word by assigning to it such a word as signifies a thing whereof the thing signified by the word to be defined is a species. For Right, as we have said, is not a species of any thing: no more is Wrong.

'Power' not definable, only expoundable.

1201. As to Powers, you have shewn how it is that the Law makes them. But what are they when made? What notion shall we form of them? How shall we define them?

What are they when made? I answer, nothing. They are not to be defined. They belong to no genus. Take them by themselves, no notion is to be formed of them at all. The words are Substantives: but they are not names of substances. Nor are they names of modes: they are not names of any thing[s] that exist.

To define the single word Power is impossible. Prefix to it the verb create, and you may make a phrase, as they say in Grammar. This phrase will be what in Grammar also is called a Sentence: and this Sentence is what in Logic is called a proposition.

This proposition may be translated into another proposition that is equivalent: and that is composed of words which, taken separately, shall either be capable of a definition, or what is still better, need none. To create a power in a person over a thing, or what is shorter and more familiar, to give a person a power over a thing, is to restrain another person from meddling with that thing, the first person being left unrestrained.

To say, then, that you have a power given you over your Coat is only another way of saying, that I am restrained from meddling with it, you being left unrestrained. I say another way. Q. and what way? not a proper one: for | | but a way that is figurative and improper.

The figure is this.

The Power in question is liken'd to a substance. The act signified by the word *give* is feigned to be a physical act exercised upon that substance &c. &c. &c.

Entities classed.[1] *Genera generalissima*, how many.

1202. There are | | *genera generalissima* of ideas.
Motion—from Substance in motion.
Rest—from Substances at rest.

[1] MS del. 'What things exist.'

Figure.
Substances—and Modes.
Situation.
Modes—Motion and Rest.
Space.
Time.
Motions peculiar to a thinking substance.
Volition.
Sensation: { Pain. / Pleasure. } { Bodily. / Mental. }
So Apprehension.
Memory.
Judgment.
Taste: Smells—Colours.
Internal feelings: Heat—Cold.
Touch: Extension—Number.

1203. These *Genera generalissima* are words expressive of simple ideas. They cannot be defined.

But words expressive of simple ideas that are species of these may.

They may any of them, by the assignment of some one of these as it's Genus, together with some circumstance establishing a specific difference.

As a Head-Ache is a species of pain felt in the head.

Non-definability of the term depends not, therefore, altogether upon the simplicity of the idea. It is not the idea of any individual pain, external motion &c. that gives us the whole idea we annex to those words in all the latitude in which they are applied.

But we are equally acquainted with a vast number of individual simple ideas that come equally under that general denomination.

From an idea's being termed a *simple* one, one should not expect it should contain any variety of individual particulars. Qu. to reconcile this.

1. Words that have no superior genus can not be defined.
2. *Genera generalissima* have no common genus.
3. *Genera generalissima*, how many.
4. How many mark real existences, single, distinct, objects of sense.
5. State—Power—Quality—Disposition.
6. State marks the aggregation of circumstances and circumjacent bodies round a given one in respect as well of Place as Time.

1204. It is not that an Infant, an ideot, &c. is incapable of giving his consent: for &c.

But the consent of an infant or ideot, though given, is deemed invalid: because neither an infant nor an ideot is deemed a competent judge of what is likely to profit or to hurt him. An Infant or an Ideot is as capable of feeling pleasure at the contemplation of an act or event as any other person: as capable of forming a volition in consequence: and as capable of expressing, of making known, that pleasure and that volition.

Consent of an Infant—Ideot, &c.

To deny that an Ideot or an Infant is capable of giving consent is only to make confusion.

Ideas.

1205. The several objects we are said to have in our mind when we are thinking, we call *ideas.*[1]

Ideas have been very usefully distinguished into ideas properly so called, and impressions.[2] It is an impression | |.

Of Ideas, some are exact, unvarying, literal copies of impressions, others not.

To take an example from the sense of sight. An impression of the object is that we have present to our mind when we see the object: a mere idea, when, without seeing it, we think of it, or remember to have seen it.

Ideas, how obtained. Extension—figure.

1206. On contemplating any one substance, we get the impression or Idea of extension, figure, void space, time.

Colour.

1207. If with the eye at a distance, we get besides, the idea of colour.

Tangible quality.

1208. If with the palate &c., we get the impression or idea of some tangible quality.[3]

Odorous quality.

1209. If with the nose, in contact or at a distance, we get the idea of some odorous quality.

Impenetrability. Figure.

1210. If with any part of the body indiscriminately in contact, we get the idea of impenetrability and figure.

Heat and Cold.

1211. If with any part of the body in contact, we may get the idea of heat and cold, if the foreign body vary in that respect from our own.

Space.

1212. The idea of space seems to be a negative idea: and to be furnished by notice taken of the absence of any one of those ideas.

Time.

1213. The idea of Time is obtainable from the observation of any two of the above-mentioned ideas, either of different sorts, or the same sort, one after another.

Time—what is meant by an event's depending upon such or such a time.

1214. When we say such an event &c. depends upon the Time, we mean that it depends upon such situations and motions of things as take place in a certain time: that is on such situations and motions of things nearly connected with the things in question as take place during such and such situations and motions of things remotely connected with them, i:e: of the whole mass of things that

[1] Cf. Locke, *Essay concerning Human Understanding*, Bk. I. Ch. I, §8, pp. 47–8.

[2] The distinction is made in Hume, *Treatise of Human Nature*, Bk. 1, Part 1, Sect. 1, i. 7.

[3] Bentham has appended the words 'void space' and 'time' to this and the following three paragraphs.

are: such universal situations and motions being ordinarily marked and signified by the motion of some one or in comparison few things, the motions [of] which are taken for what is called the standard of Time: i:e: whose motions and situations are spoken of in lieu of mentioning the rest. Such are those of the heavenly bodies, but particularly of the Sun and moon, with relation to the planet we inhabit.

It is not that the event depended upon the motion or situation of the Sun and Moon in particular, but more immediately upon the motion and situation perhaps of other bodies, whose motions and situations stand indicated by those of the two bodies chosen for standards of the rest.

It is motion that is the cause of all these ideas.

It is substance that is the *instrument* which produces them.

The idea itself of motion is suggested by some of them, but not by all.[1]

One may say that Relations do not exist: since they have not any separate existence from the things that are related: from the things *between* which the Relation is said to subsist.

1215. The term *way* is used where the purpose is to bring to mind in general the aggregate of the several circumstances that are spoken of as *means* by which the effect in question is produced. The complection of the metaphor, however, and by that means the turn of the phrase in the two cases is different. We say *by* the *means*: we say *in* the *way*: just as we say also *in* the *manner*. Way in it's *material* and *primitive* sense signifies a road. A road, then, is figured as leading from the first, in point of time or importance, of the means that are brought into consideration: and that road is supposed to pass, as it were, through, and so include, the several other means. And thus it is that speaking of the way *in* which a thing is done is made to answer the purpose of speaking of the means (to wit the characteristic means) *by* which a thing is done. *'Way'—'Manner'*. Paraphrasis and Investigation of the term.

Briefly thus:

Way is put for the aggregate of the means.

1216. See Personal Injuries Simple. 5.[2] Instrument.

1217. The word *Method*, at least as used in the business of Method.

[1] In the text, Bentham has noted at this point: 'Exemplify with the Apple or the Sword.'

[2] The cross reference is obscure, though 'Simple corporal injuries' are listed as one of 'nine *genera* or kinds of personal injuries' at *An Introduction to the Principles of Morals and Legislation* (*CW*), Ch. XVI, p. 224.

causality, means little if any thing else than the word *way*. We say '*in such a method*', as we say '*in such a way*'.

The word method is Greek in it's original. It is compounded of two words, μετα and οδος. The one οδος a substantive, such as *way* is, and which answers precisely to way in it's original signification. The other μετα a preposition, when coupled with the other adds little to it's signification. By itself it signifies *after*.

Prefat. Cromwell's times too early for Reformation.

1218. These were early days, perhaps too early, for Reformation. The exclusive interests of the profession found a strong rampart in the general ignorance of the age. The system of Procedure, indeed, would scarce have been otherwise than a gainer by an alteration that was likely to have been made in it. But the substantive part of the Law, and especially the Criminal Branch, would have taken a taint of fanaticism. It would have fared with us, as it has fared with some of the Colonies in America. The Mosaic Dispensation, in which, as a Right Reverend Politician lays down, perhaps in terms of greater latitude than was necessary, there is nothing that ought to be drawn for imitation,[1] would on most leading points have been taken as a model for our own.

1219. The Judgment is apt to be warped by the heat of the affections.

Proprietorship—how modified in respect of *proximity*.

1220. A Proprietary period, if neither past nor present, is future. If future, it is subsequent to some other period, or in other words, some other period is precedent to it.

The precedent period is either:

1st of certain duration, as of a certain number of years.

2d. Of uncertain duration—as of so many years as such a person shall live.

Whatever event or situation is not present but future is postponed to some period or portion of time.

Proprietary Period.

1221. Any period during which a party is to continue proprietor, may be called a proprietary period.

Period *forestalling*, *fore-running*, *præcursory*, *postponing*.

1222. A period thus standing in precedency to a proprietary period may, on account of such precedency, be termed, with reference to the proprietary period, the post-poning, or forestalling, or precursory, or fore-running period.

[1] Bentham may have had in mind William Warburton, *The Divine Legation of Moses Demonstrated, on the Principles of a Religious Deist, From the Omission of the Doctrine of a Future State of Reward and Punishment in the Jewish Dispensation*, 2 vols., London, 1738–41.

This forerunning period, then, may be either of limited and certain duration: or secondly of uncertain but limited duration; or 3dly of uncertain and unlimited duration.

Of limited and certain duration, as a certain number of years: 10, 20, or 50 years.

Of uncertain and limited duration, as of so many years as such a person shall live: i:e: a period equal to the life of such a person.

1223. The person whose life is the measure of the duration of a forerunning proprietary period is called in our Law a *Cestuy que vie*. *Cestuy que vie.*

Literally translated, the phrase *Cestuy que vie* signifies 'he whose life'.

This phrase is manifestly elliptical. Being compleated, it will stand thus. '*Cestuy durant la vie de qui le estate doit continuer*.' 'He during whose life the estate in question is to continue.'

For a proprietary period to be reputed equal in value to a life, take a number of years: let this number be large, for instance 100; and out of this let be deducted the number of years the *cestuy que vie* has to live at the time of the . . .

1224. In matters that come under the Law of Property and Contracts, the phrases employ'd are almost always such in which the word right is an ingredient. These phrases, ere they can be made to present clear ideas, must all of them be translated into other phrases that have in them such words as offence, command, prohibition, condition, &c. Conduct of the Work. 'Right' to be translated throughout.

This it will be very difficult, without practise, to effect. Therefore, after announcing in general the equipollency of the two kinds of phrases, it will be proper to show the method of rendering the first into the second, not by one or two only, but by a multitude of examples: such a multitude as shall exhibit all the varieties that can happen in the process.

1225. If half the pains had been taken to make them clear and consistent that has been taken to make them contradictory and confused, ... Digest Prefat. Consolidation, want of.

. . . Nothing is ever provided against: nothing is foreseen.

1226. An event or thing is said to be consider'd so and so, i:e: of such or such a quality, likely to be attended with such or such effects, in it's own nature, or simply in itself, or by itself, when it is supposed to be so consider'd in all or the greatest part of those circumstances in which it is likely to occurr. An Event in it's own nature, in itself, by itself.

—by accident, &c.

1227. It is said to be so by accident, or in particular circumstances, when it is so not in the greatest part of those circumstances, but in some few only in which it is least likely to occurr.

N.B. Strictly speaking, it is plain that no event ever does happen by itself.

Greater)(more than equivalent.

1228. In comparing pains to pains, in speaking of their difference we may speak of one pain as being greater than another: and the like of pleasures. In comparing pains to pleasures, it is better to speak of one as being *more than equivalent* to the other.

Archetypation.

1229. Archetypation to be used as the name of a mode of Exposition, in the room of Origination, Radication, Investigation. *Ostensio radicis.*[1]

'Tis by Paraphrasis and Paraphrasis alone that fictitious entities, entities expressed by improper substantives, can be *expounded.*

Paraphrasis, what.

1230. To expound an improper substantive by Paraphrasis is to compleat it into a sentence, and for that sentence to find an equivalent sentence consisting of words significative of real entities.

Sentence figured)(unfigured.

1231. In this case, the sentence expounded may be called the figured sentence: that other, by which it is expounded, the simple or unfigured sentence.

One simple sentence may serve for the exposition of many figurative ones: as the plain truth may be typified by many figures. One and the same thing, consider'd in different respects, may have several things like it, tho' no [one] of these things may be like another.

Necessary to give a compleat satisfaction to the mind with regard to the import of an improper substantive is another mode of exposition that may be termed Archetypation.

Archetypation, what.

1232. The word *archetypus*, a Latin word of Greek extraction, signifies a pattern. By Archetypation, then, I mean the finding of that real appearance of real entities that served as a pattern for the appearance suggested by any of those sentences of which an improper substantive makes a part.

Entities fictitious)(fabulous.

1233. By fabulous entities, I mean such beings as, in the fables of the Poets, for example, have been represented and spoken of as really existing. Such as the Heathen Gods, the Chimæra, the Dragon, the Cockatrice, &c.

[1] i.e. 'I show the root.'

1234. By fictitious entities, such as, without being represented seriously as existing, are feigned and endued with names that in strictness are proper only for real beings, viz: substantives, merely for the purposes of discourse. Such are Liberty, Right, Condition, Quality, disposition, &c. —fictitious.

1235. Names of fabulous entities are words which serve to exhibit to the mind assemblages of simple ideas which, though no where co-existing in any real subject, are manifest and determinate. —fabulous.

Names of fabulous entities are words which of themselves exhibit no idea at all, but which, by means of other terms they are combined with, are seen to be destined to represent an indefinite somthing as if it were in some of those situations which real beings are liable to be in, and by that contrivance, and that alone, to be raised to the class of beings.

1236.[1] n'exprime nullement le rapport qu'il peut y avoir: alors il faut congédier l'être fictif dont on s'est servi d'abord, et s'attacher à un autre.[2]

on perd ce qu'on a d'abord gagné.

exige le complément complet des parties d'oraison qu'il faut pour compléter la proposition, le nominatif de l'action, qu'on suppose, n'étant plus le même.

C'est comme s'ils étaient séparés par un immense gouffre entre [les] deux, qu'on ne saurait [pas] souder.[3] .

Autre désavantage. Ce qu'il faut marquer, ce sont les effets que puissent avoir les objets dont il s'agit sur le bien-être des hommes.

Tantôt ça et là—parfois— [4]

Avoir droit n'est pas action.

[1] The fragmentary French materials in paras. 1236, 1239–40, and 1242–5 may have been related to one or other of two projects. First, at the time of publication of *A Fragment on Government* in April 1776, Bentham was 'scribbling some French letters' to be sent to the French *philosophes* D'Alembert and André Morellet (1727–1819): see Bentham to Samuel Bentham, 17 April 1776, *The Correspondence of Jeremy Bentham*, vol. i, ed. T.L.S. Sprigge, London, 1968 (*CW*), p. 314. Second, in the Spring of 1778 Bentham sent to D'Alembert copies of *A Fragment on Government* and *A View of the Hard Labour Bill; being an abstract of a pamphlet, intituled, 'Draught of a Bill, to punish by Imprisonment and Hard-Labour, certain Offenders; and to establish proper Places for their Reception.' Interspersed with Observations relative to the subject of the above Draught in particular, and to Penal Jurisprudence in general*, London, 1778 (Bowring iv. 1–33), along with 'trois feuilles' containing a sketch of the larger work on punishment on which he was then engaged: see Bentham to D'Alembert, Spring 1778, *Correspondence* (*CW*), ii. 115–18.

[2] MS orig. 'y faire succéder un autre'.

[3] MS orig. 'franchir'.

[4] The passage has been abandoned at this point.

Faire ce qui est nécessaire pour s'acquitter d'une obligation, c'est agir ou bien s'en abstenir volontairement et [par se][1] propre cond[u]ite.

pour avoir droit, ce n'est pas agir. En effet, il n'y a rien à faire pour celui qui a droit, ce qu'il y a à faire c'est pour lui au dépens duquel le droit est établi.

Je vois beaucoup encore à faire, d'un côté pour [relier][2] les expressions communes à des notions exactes; de l'autre côté pour faire voir le rapport qu'ont des expressions fit à donner des notions exactes aux expressions communes.[3]

Les Titres des matières de la Loi doivent être les mêmes que les Titres des Loix mêmes. À présent on trouve la matière d'une seule Loi éparse sous mille titres différents.

Means. Bodies *auxiliary.* Circumstances *conspiring.*

1237. '*Means*' is a word the sense of which seems to include that of 1. Instruments. 2^d. Causes. 3dly. Auxiliary bodies. 4^thly. Conspiring circumstances.

Manner.

1238. The *Manner* seems to be used to discourse the state the several means by which an effect is produced are in at and previous to the instant of production.

1239. La mathématique n'est d'aucun usage, ni même d'aucune vérité, jusqu'à ce qu'on l'applique aux corps particuliers.

'Dire que | | dit Montesquieu, 'c'est dire qu'avant qu'on eut tracé de cercle, tous ses rayons n'étaient pas égaux.'[4] Paradoxe malheureux! comme s'il y avoit une chose appellée cercle qui eut des rayons égaux, avant qu'elle eut des rayons.

À D'A.[5] Loix non-écrites ne sont pas Loix.

1240. On a divisé les Loix en écrites et en non-écrites. Cette division est très malheureuse. Il est beaucoup d'inconvénient à arranger sous le même nom un être réel, et un être de raison. Une Loi écrite c'est un être réel. Une Loi non-écrite c'est un être de raison. La vérité est, que là où il n'y a point de loi écrite il n'y a point de Loi. Ce qu'il y a dans un tel cas, qu'est-ce que c'est? Ce sont des actes de punition de par le Juge. Il est vrai que ces actes se font comme s'il y avoit une loi qui les ordonnoit. Cependant un acte de punition n'est pas une Loi. Qu'on en ajoute autant qu'on voudra de ces actes, on n'en fera jamais une loi. Qu'il y ait une loi ordonnant

[1] MS 'de'. [2] MS 'rédiger'. [3] The sense is obscure.

[4] See Montesquieu, *De l'esprit des loix*, Livre I, Ch. I, p. 3: 'Dire qu'il n'y a rien de juste ni d'injuste que ce qu'ordonnent ou défendent les loix positives, c'est dire qu'avant qu'on eût tracé de Cercle tous les rayons n'étoient pas égaux.'

[5] i.e. D'Alembert: see p. 387 n. above.

de punir en tel cas, et qu'il se soit fait un acte de punition en conformité à cette loi. Il n'y a personne qui dira que la loi et l'acte de punition soient la même chose. À présent qu'on ôte la loi: l'acte de punition subsiste comme auparavant. Il est clair que si cet acte n'étoit pas loi auparavant, il ne l'est maintenant non plus.

C'est de l'habitude qu'on a pris d'étendre le nom de loi à cette espèce impropre qu'on appelle non-écrite, qu'on est venu apparemment à l'habitude de l'étendre plus en avant à cette autre espèce encore plus impropre, appellée loi de nature. Après le premier pas, le second n'étoit pas difficile. Les barrières de la vérité une fois franchies, on n'a guère sçu à quoi s'en tenir.

On ne voyoit pas que dire qu'un acte est une offense contre la loi de Nature, ce n'étoit qu'une façon de dire, que l'idée s'en trouvoit désagréable, sans qu'on pourroit dire pourquoi, ou bien une façon bien mauvaise de dire, qu'il est contraire au bien général: c'est à dire de produire plus de mal que de bien dans la société.

Je dis très mauvaise: car voici quelques inconvéniens qui en découlent.

D'abord à force de faire agir cette phrase, on s'est égaré du chemin de l'utilité;[1] seul guide qui mène à la vérité en faite de morale: seul dictateur légitime de nos jugemens de la bonté et de la méchanceté des actions. On a négligé l'expérience et le calcul; seuls instruments qui[2] | | tant pour la morale que pour la physique. On est parvenu à obscurcir la notion de la seule espèce de Loi qui est réelle et véritable. On a trouvé plus commode d'établir un Oracle dont on modifie les réponses à son gré: dont les décrets s'allient avec tous les préjugés qu'on veut leur épouser, et qu'on en peut s'épargner la peine[3] de la discussion.

C'est y dans cette phrase [qu']on a trouvé à la fois un appui pour l'obstination, une *weapon* pour l'intolérance, un *couch*[4] pour l'indolence, une parure pour la fausse éloquence, et un voile pour la sottise. Voici, comme il paroit, qu'on a dù raisonner. Puisque c'est une loi, il faudroit que ce soit la loi de quelqu'un. Or ce n'est pas loi d'homme: donc il faut que ce soit loi de Dieu. Or puisque c'est loi de Dieu, il y a de l'incrédulité à l'en nier l'existence, et de l'impiété à ne pas s'y soumettre. Non seulement le citoyen doit s'y soumettre, mais la Législature aussi: s'il ordonne ou même permette ce qu'elle défend, voilà sa loi qui est nulle, et lui voilà qu'il est rebelle à Dieu.

[1] MS orig. 'est parvenu à détourner les yeux du principe d'utilité'.
[2] In the margin, Bentham has noted at this point: 'Oracle.'
[3] MS orig. 'le travail'.
[4] MS orig. 'oreiller'. Bentham has employed the English words 'weapon' and 'couch'.

Quand une fois on est venu à se persuader qu'il y a de telles loix, et que ce sont loix de Dieu, on est aisément venu à n'en être pas fort difficile sur le choix. Le titre qu'elles ont toutes à cette qualité, n'est au fond que le déplaisir qu'on éprouve à considérer les espèces d'action qu'on veut en être défendu. Quant à ces actions, il paroit qu'on a dû commencer par celles contre lesquelles ce déplaisir devoit être le plus violent et le plus général: d'où on pouvoit dire tout ce qui tendroit à en augmenter l'horreur, sans craindre d'être contredit. C'est ainsi [qu'on] a fait sans façon et sans scrupule des loix de Nature, loix de Dieu, pour les défendre. Voilà donc des êtres imaginaires de raison érigés en loix de nature, loix de Dieu, *nemine contradicente*. Ces loix établies, n'importe quelles, ni en quel petit nombre, voilà un point d'appui, une espèce de noyau, autour duquel d'autres devroient venir continuellement s'arranger. Voilà des chimères qui se présentent en foule tous les jours pour obtenir, pour ainsi dire s'exprimer, de la sorte des lettres de naturalité, et qu'on admet pour les prétextes les plus légers, parce qu'on ne sçait pas à quel titre les exclure.

Il y a, se dit-on, des loix de nature:—Oui, sans doute, personne qui n'en soit d'accord. Or, voici donc une action qui est bien mauvaise, n'est-ce pas? Sans doute—je la trouve telle; et pour les autres hommes, ils doivent être de mon avis. Eh bien donc, puisqu'elle est si mauvaise, ne faut-il pas qu'elle doit être une offense contre la loi de nature? Ah, pourquoi ne serait-elle pas? Car quel titre, ces autres actes qui sont incontestablement offenses contre la loi de nature, ont-ils quelque qualité, que ceci n'a pas? aucun. La voici donc offense contre la loi de nature en général. Or puisque c'est une offense contre la loi de Nature en général, il faut qu'il y ait une loi de Nature qui la défende. Voilà donc une loi de nature tout[1] compte fait. Et c'est ainsi qu'on en peut faire autant qu'on voudra.

Si on pousse le scrupule au point de se questionner sur les motifs qu'on a pour le déplaisir qui est le fondement de toute cette opération, cela ne gêne pas.

On allégue[2] quelque raison tirée du principe d'utilité, ou au défaut d'une telle raison, quelque préjugé favori; il n'en faut pas davantage.

Si dire qu'un *acte* est une offense contre la Loi de Nature, n'est qu'une façon mauvaise de dire que cet acte est contraire au bien général: dire qu'une *Loi* est nulle parce qu'[elle] se trouve contra-

[1] MS orig. 'le'.

[2] 'On allégue' has been marked for deletion by Bentham but is required to maintain the sense.

ire à la Loi de Nature, c'est une façon toute aussi mauvaise, et encore plus dangereuse, de dire qu'une Loi est contraire au bien de la société au point qu'il vaut mieux ne pas s'y soumettre.

1241. It is not a quality that can form a part of a perception: it is not a quality that can come under the cognizance of our senses at any given time. It is only the operation of a quality. For by a quality we mean something that we look upon as being permanent: that is subsisting during a continued course of time. But a perception is a thing instantaneous; a thing that does not subsist through any continued course of time; but is consummated in an instant.

Qualities themselves not sensible.

1242. Comme ce qui fait l'essence d'une loi, ce en quoi consistent ses ressemblances, et ses différences, n'est que l'action qui en [est] l'objet, comme cette action même ne peut être characterisée que par le moyen de ces divers articles de considération qu'on vient d'exposer. Comme tous ces articles sont tous ce[ux] qui entre[nt] nécessairement dans la composition d'une action, et comme il n'y en a point d'autres, il s'ensuit, qu'entendre une loi, c'est pouvoir assigner ces diverses classes par rapport à l'action qui en est l'objet: et que, sans cela, on ne l'entend pas.

À D'A.
Ce que c'est qu'entendre une Loi.

1243. *Quis*? C'est *l'agent*. *Quid*? ce peut être le *sujet* quand ce sujet est une *chose*, ou ce peut être l'acte simplement considéré. *Ubi*? cela désigne le lieu. *Quibus Auxiliis*? on en parlera après les autres. *Car*? c'est ce qui désigne le *motif*. *Quomodo*? ce peut désigner la suite des actes simplement considérés, expliqués en détail avec leurs circonstances. *Quando*? c'est ce qui pointe vers le temps. *Quibus Auxiliis*? peut être considéré comme indiquant l'instrument irrationnel (quand il en a eu un) dont l'agent s'est servi pour faire l'acte simplement considéré. [Il] propose les mêmes questions touchant les actes de ceux dont les actes sont dans le nombre des circonstances nécessairement concurrens à l'action au tems même ou lieu où elle s'est faite, ou bien dans des lieux distans et des tems antiens.

Act *simply considered* or abstractedly.

1244. À l'égard [de] ce dernier *Quibus Auxiliis*, on voit que ce n'est pas par rapport à l'importance du même rang que les autres. C'est un article de considération qui n'entre pas essentiellement dans le nombre. L'action ne peut pas s'être faite, sans qu'il y ait eu [l]'agent, l'acte simplement considéré, le sujet, [les] circonstances nécessairement concurrens, [le] tems et [le] lieu. Mais elle peut s'être faite sans secours étranger. Elle peut s'être faite sans

Articles of *consideration* in an action.
À D'A.
Articles de considération appartenant à un action morale.

instrumens non-raisonnables.[1] Elle peut encore s'être faite sans que, dans le nombre des circonstances nécessairement concurrens, il y ait eu des actions d'aucuns autres hommes.

On peut avoir frappé un coup, par exemple, sans associé et sans instrument. On peut avoir mis le feu à une maison, si non sans instrument, au moins sans associé.

Quant à l'article du motif, il est peut-être vrai qu'il entre nécessairement dans la composition de chaque action volontaire: c'est pourquoi il entre toujours dans les vues de la morale. Mais ce n'est pas toujours qu'il entre dans les vues de la loi: parce que ce n'est pas toujours qu'il influe sur les effets sensitifs de la loi. Quand un écrit scandaleux,[2] par exemple, se publie, c'est à dire se vend, se lit, se distribue, le mal qui peut en résulter ne dépend guère du motif bon ou mauvais qui peut avoir déterminé l'auteur ou quelque autre à le publier. S'il [ne l'a][3] eu en vue, si ce motif a été la vue du bien de l'état, ou s'il a été le malheur de l'état, ou ce qui est tout aussi commun, si ce n'a été ni l'un ni l'autre, mais seulement son propre avantage, tout cela est égal: pour le mécon[ten]tement juste ou injuste que cet écrit peut exciter dans le peuple, ce motif ne fait aucune différence.

Tems. **1245.** L'idée de tems est tirée de tous les corps qui existent à la fois, soit qu'ils soient en état de repos, c'est à dire en état de position seulement par rapport les uns aux autres, soit qu'ils soient en état de mouvement. ⟨L'⟩idée donc de temps n'est pas l'idée [d'une][4] circonstance séparée, on peut dire, puisque le temps renferme celui de toutes ces autres circonstances. De tout ce qui se fait, il n'y a rien qui ne se passe en quelque *tems* et en quelque *lieu*. C'est pourquoi le tems et le lieu sont des circonstances qui entrent nécessairement, pour ainsi dire, dans la composition de chaque action.

Elle est tirée pareillement de toutes:[5] par ce que le corps, à n'en prendre qu'un seul par exemple, donc le mouvement est pris pour indiquer le tems, n'est pas ce qui constitue le temps, mais seulement ce qui le mesure: c'est à dire, qui sert pour noter l'existence des autres corps, chacun dans l'état soit de repos soit de mouvement, où ils sont pendant qu'il fait ou paroit faire l'espèce de mouvement dont on se sert pour mesurer, comme on dit, et pour exprimer ce temps: c'est à dire l'existence de tous ces corps dans un tel état.

[1] MS orig. 'irrationnels'.
[2] MS alt. 'libelle d'état'.
[3] MS 'n'a'.
[4] MS 'idée de'.
[5] MS orig. 'Il les renferme toutes.'

L'idée donc de tems, on pourrait dire, ne doit pas être mentionnée comme idée de circonstance séparée, puisque l'idée de temps renferme l'idée de tous ces autres que vous avez nominé circonstances.

À cela, il faut répondre: l$^{me.}$ Que, quoique cela étoit, on pourroit rapporter la somme ent⟨ière d⟩e tous les êtres[1] existants co⟨mme un a⟩rticle de considération distincte de ⟨celui⟩ de ce très petit nombre des êtres ⟨parti⟩culiers dont l'existence influe sensiblement sur la production du fait particulier dont il s'agit.

2^{d}: Que ce n'est pas l'idée de ces mêmes êtres, qui est l'idée que nous avons du temps: par exemple, l'idée de temps n'est pas idée de position ni idée de mouvement: ni idée de position [et] de mouvement tout ensemble; mais que c'est une idée qui bien que tirée de[2]

Les corps circonvoisins étant tels qu'ils sont, pendant que le corps dont il s'agit est | | nous disons qu'il est dans un tel lieu.

La multitude universelle des corps ayant été, comme il nous paroit, une fois tels par rapport à la position ou au mouvement qu'ils ont été pendant que ce corps particulier dont il s'agit a été dans tel état, et ensuite autres, nous disons qu'il s'est fait en tel ⟨temp⟩s. Qu.[3] Si un seulement d'entre eux ⟨eut⟩ subi un autre mouvement, c'eut été un autre temps. Si pas un d'eux n'eut subi aucun mouvement, il n'y eut pas eu de temps.

1246. If a man whose authority was thought to give weight to party opinions were to say with respect to a system of proceeding in Government: 'The Sun does not shine at noon-day: *ergo*: the system of proceeding is a bad one:' those who were dissatisfied at the system of proceeding would be ready to say with him, 'The sun shines not at noon-day.' Dr Price—Party.[4]

1247. As a Butcher or a Surgeon becomes callous to that mode of unhappiness in a sensitive being that consist[s] in the sufferings of the body, so does a Lawyer become callous to the sense of those miseries that a man suffers by the impairement of his fortunes. Lawyers, why callous.

---

[1] MS orig. 'phénomènes'.

[2] The passage has been abandoned at this point.

[3] 'Qu.' was Bentham's customary abbreviation for the English word 'Query', but in this case he may have had in mind the French word 'Question'.

[4] The allusion may be to the success of the work of the philosopher, demographer, and political radical Richard Price (1723–91), *Observations on the Nature of Civil Liberty, the Principles of Government, and the Justice and Policy of the War with America*, London, 1776, which quickly ran to its eleventh London edition.

Interpretation.

1248. 'Tis also in the above analysis that we have given of the several classes of the objects of a Law[1] that we are to look for the only precise and explicit rules that can be given on the head of interpretation.

Difficulty of settling these Rules.

To interpret a Law when applied to a Court of Judicature has been understood to mean something else than executing the genuine sense of the words of it. To interpret has been understood to mean to modify: in short, to alter. For it is no uncommon thing to observe men to deny the right of interpreting a Law, understand a Law of the *adjective* kind, to Judges, of whom it is at the same time expected that they should obey it, that is should, as far as upon them depends, carry the substantive Law to which it is subservient into execution.

The most obvious and the most general rule that can be laid down in this behalf for Judges, is that they follow what they suppose to have been the actual sense of the Legislators. That they 〈. . 〉 consider the words indicative of the several acts (understand acts abstractedly consider'd) that 〈it〉 is the will of the Law should be performed.

Historiographical omissions excepted in Adjective Laws.

But not in Substantive. Qu? why? A. because the annexing the punishment to one single act in a train of obnoxious ones may serve in a certain degree to stop the obnoxious practise, and hence no necessity of extension. And as, among these, some may lead also to non-obnoxious acts, hence the danger.

Exposition—modes of. Origination or[2] *Investigation* or *Radication*.

1249. An item to be added to the account of the different modes of exposition—Origination. Shewing the material image from whence an expression denoting an intellectual idea is derived. This process, of course, obtains only in regard to such phrases as are expressive of intellectual ideas.

It comes naturally as an appendage to *Paraphrasis*.

It might also be called Investigation.

Example—Relation—undefinable.

Phrases to be investigated and paraphrased—To stand in a relation to—To bear relation to.

Circumstances constitutive of the act.

1250. . . . may be called *Ingredients in the description* of the action. They are necessary features of the picture which it exhibits.

---

[1] The phrase 'that we have given . . . Law' has been marked by Bentham for deletion.
[2] MS del. 'Origination or' has been retained to reflect its employment in the text.

1251. Remplissage—Vers de Remplissage. D'Alembert. Mel. v. 458.[1]

1252. The aggregate assemblage of as many actions as are performed in subserviency to one and the same *end*, such an assemblage, consider'd as a whole, may be termed a *course of action*. A *course of action*.

1253. Matter, according to the language of the Schools, is divisable *ad infinitum*. The truth is, it is very difficult to assign any bounds to the division some species of it in particular [are] actually capable of undergoing, and still less so to that which it may be conceived as capable of undergoing. Here instance light of the candle, effluvia of some odorous bodies, salts in the fluids of a microscopic animal, gold in gilt ware, &c. *An Act*—Individuation of.

Motion ⟨. . .⟩ of some portion of matter. An organical act is motion. Even in an act of the mental kind, some distinguishable, assignable portion of matter is necessarily concerned. What, therefore, shall be deemed one act only and what several, is no more determined, than what shall be deemed one body and what several. There is no body that can for any purposes be spoken of as a whole, but what may to other purposes, with equal propriety, be spoken of as distinguished into parts. There is no quantity of motion, therefore, that can be spoken of as one act, but may with equal propriety be spoken of as several acts.

1254. What determines a portion of matter to be spoken of as one is unity of name. What determines a quantity of motion to be spoken of as one is, in like manner, unity of name. That may be spoken of as one act which is the act of one body. Definition describes the bounds of the species. Individuation marks out the bounds of the Individual.

1255. Motion further divisible by space.

It may fail of being the same kind of motion either 1st by the body's applying itself to a portion of space of a different configuration in the same time: 2dly by applying itself to a space of the same configuration in different portions of time. One motion of body may be different from another motion of the same body.

One individual apple, for instance, that which has the properties that determine it to come under that name—[2]

---

[1] See 'Suite des Réflexions sur la Poësie, et sur L'Ode en particulier', in *Mélanges de littérature, d'histoire, et de philosophie*, v. 458: 'Combien de fautes légeres & comme imperceptibles, d'expressions qui ne sont pas tout-à-fait justes, de tours un peu contraints, de mots & quelquefois de vers de remplissage, qu'on est forcé de pardonner au Poëte?'

[2] The sentence has been abandoned at this point.

1256. What the Law does not constrain a man to do, it restrains all other persons from constraining him to do. Whatever it does not restrain a man from doing, it restrains all ⟨. . .⟩ persons from restraining him from doing. 'Tis thus that it gives him all the security he possesses: and all the liberty for which he is indebted to the Law. If it gave him not this, it would give him none.

By-Laws are Laws.

1257. The effect of a Corporation By-Law, if any, is, like that of every Law, either to constrain or to restrain. The effect of a Corporation By-Law is, therefore, to repeal *pro tanto* the General Law of the Land.

Title of the Book.

1258. Principles of Universal Law—applied chiefly to the[1] Law of England.

Simple Ideas concerned in Law, or which fall under the consideration of the Law, enumerated.

1259. The simple ideas which are the elements of those about which the Law is conversant are as follows: viz:

Entities Classed: *Genera generalissima.* Pain and Pleasure.

1260. 1st. Those various species, or modes as they are called, of Sensation: that is of Pain and Pleasure.

Volition.

1261. 2dly. The idea of Volition; which, being a thing entirely simple and undiversified, admitts of no modes or species.

Space and Time.

1262. 3dly. Ideas that are furnished by the various bodies or, as they are otherwise called, substances or portions of matter that fall within the cognizance of our senses: by such bodies, all or any of them, I mean those of Space and Time, with their several modes or species.

Particular Bodies.

1263. 4thly. Such as are suggested by particular bodies, and constitute, by their different combinations, the several species of those bodies.

Motion.

1264. 5thly. The idea of motion: with it's several modes or species that lie within the reach of our conception.

What things exist.

1265. These are such as are suggested by the operations of the several powers, as they are called, of bodies.

These are: 1st. Figure or Configuration, and it's several species or modes, as they are called.

[2nd.] Hardness and it's several species or, [as] they are called, degrees.

[3rd.] Colour, the several species of it or, as they are called, shades: and, what are of a nature nearly approaching to that of colour, resplendency, it's different species, or, as they are called, degrees.

[1] In the margin, Bentham has added, 'estimating the merits', but then marked the phrase for deletion.

Powers of bodies are distinguished (by Locke) into active and passive.[1]

Active powers again may be distinguished into such as are so with respect to sensitive bodies only, such as is our own, and such as are so with respect to bodies in general, sensitive or not sensitive.

The objects we have reason to survey are all such objects as are liable to fall within the consideration of the Law; in other words, which are liable to become objects of the Law's concern.

It happens that these objects are all sorts of things almost that fall within the cognizance of our senses, and all sorts of persons, with their respective actions: in a word, almost every class of existences that offers itself to our perception. All things in their present state at least, if not in their original formation. '*Res omnes*', if not '*cunctarum primordia rerum*'.[a]

On this account it becomes necessary to include in our survey the whole circle of existence as far as it is made known to us. To collect the several particular existences into classes—to enumerate and mark down the several sorts of simple ideas with which they furnish us. The names of these simple ideas are what we shall have perpetual occasion to make use of, even when occupied about the lowest and most familiar details of Jurisprudence.

The existences that fall within the cognizance of our senses are comprizable in a single appellative, Bodies.

What is common to all these Bodies is that they are either in a state of rest, or in a state of Motion.

By Rest merely, no Body is distinguishable from any other body: nor is the state of the same body at one time distinguishable from the state of the same body at another time. Rest is uniform.

A circumstance by which one body may be distinguished from another body, or even the same body at one time from the same body at another time, and at ever so many other times, is Motion. Motion is infinitely diversified.

Since, therefore, any given body may be distinguished from itself by virtue of it's motion singly, and as bodies that are different

[a] Barrow's encomium prefixed to Milton's *Paradise lost.*[2]

---

[1] See Locke, *Essay concerning Human Understanding*, Bk. II. Ch. XXI, §2, p. 234.

[2] Samuel Barrow (1625?–83), physician and lawyer of the army, was author of the laudatory poem 'In Paradisum Amissam Summi Poetæ Johannis Miltoni', prefixed to John Milton, *Paradise Lost. A Poem in Twelve Books* (first published in 1667), 2nd edn., London, 1674, and which contained the lines '*Res cunctas, & cunctarum primordia rerum, Et fata, & fines continet iste liber*', i.e. 'This book takes in all things, and the beginnings of all things, and their fates and ultimate ends.'

in themselves may, in respect of their motion, be the same, in a word, as there may be occasion to consider the motion of any body, when there is no occasion to consider any thing else respecting the same body, hence men have learnt to find in motion a distinct article of consideration: to speak of it as a thing distinct from the body to which it belongs. To speak of motion by itself, without considering of what body it is the motion; although, in fact, there never existed or can exist such a thing as motion separate from body: there never is nor can be such a thing as a motion that is not the motion of some body.

Entities Classed. **1266.** After this explanation, however, we may find, perhaps, in the above consideration, sufficient to warrant us to establish for the purposes of discourse two general classes of existences, to wit Bodies and Motions. The former class existing of themselves: the latter not without the former: the latter no otherwise than *in* the *former*.

Bodies may exist without motion: since bodies may exist at rest; which is nothing but the absence of all motion. Motion can not exist without Bodies, since, let it shew itself where it will, it is but the motion of some body.

Over and above Motion, all that is considerable in Bodies may come under the idea of operations of powers: of the several sorts of powers which body is found, as the phrase is, to possess.

The idea of the operation of any power on any body ⟨. . .⟩ instant of time corresponds to the idea [of] any individual motion ⟨. . .⟩ body at the same instant of time. The idea of that power itself corresponds to the idea of Motivity in general.

It will hardly be said that in any strict and proper sense of the word existence, the word Motivity marks any thing that exists. Motion, any individual motion, when you add to it any body whatsoever that is (as the phrase is) in that motion is what exists: it makes an impression on the sense: it paints, as it were, a separate picture in the imagination. The absence or presence of it is cognizable to the senses. It will hardly be said that *motivity* exists in the same sense that *motion* does.

The word, indeed, wears the same grammatical form as those do by which real existences, even independent existences, substances, are characterized: the part of speech in use to denote it is that which is called a substantive: the part of speech by which, and by no other, substances are expressed. But this part of speech, this sort of word, a substantive, is no ways necessary to express the idea we have when we employ it, at least so far as that idea is conformable to experience and to the truth of things. We say, indeed, that a body, a stone for instance, is endued with motivity, or with a power of motivity: but all that there is of truth in that proposition, with respect to the past, is that we have found the stone (or bodies which appear to us of the same nature in this respect as the stone) in motion at some times; and that thence, with respect to the future, we are led to expect to find it, in the same circumstances, in motion at other times.

Qu. It appears not that the operation of any power is itself a motion; since it manifests itself without any change of place. But it seems reasonable to suppose that either motion or position is the cause of it: that is the motions or the position of the insensible parts of the body possessed of the power in question: since such motions or such position is all that we can conceive as capable of constituting such cause. See Locke.[1] The truth is, however, that all the time these motions, if such they be, are performing, the chain of causes is concealed to us: we recover it again only when some perceptible motion, or some new appearance, offers itself to the sense.

Whether the case be or no that qualities can be said properly to exist, we are still led on to substance as their necessary support. If a power exists, it is as the power of some body that [it] exists. Without body, no power. Where there exists no body, there exists no power.

We can imagine motion without body better than we can imagine power without body—because we can imagine a portion of space travelled over, and we can imagine the time during which it was travelled over, without imagining any particular body as travelling over that portion of space in that portion of time. The reason is, I take it, that *any* body is sufficient for the purpose—but, however, *some* body is necessary.

When [the] business, then, is to get an idea of motion, any body will serve the turn: on account of the resemblance there is between all motions. But what we call by the name powers are so various and so different from each other, there is so little that is common between the ideas that respectively belong to them that the word can scarcely be said to afford any determinate idea at all, till the idea of some one sort of power in particular be called in to exemplify it's meaning.

1267. The imperative part, or the part descriptive of the act, of the Law of Property is very short. It is either mandatory or Law of Property.

[1] Bentham perhaps had in mind Locke, *Essay concerning Human Understanding*, Bk. II, Ch. XXIII, §7, pp. 299–300, discussing powers as qualities of subjects.

prohibitory, according to the circumstances the party favoured and the party coerced by it are in. It may be conceived to run thus: Meddle not with | |.

Do not any thing that may disturb any man in the possession (meaning physical possession) of that to which he has title.

If he has possession already, *forbear* to disturb that possession.

If he has not that possession, but stands in need of an act of thine to have possession, *do* that act.

Circumstantializing part of a Law.

1268. It is the circumstantializing part[a] of the Law, that makes the bulk of it.

These are:

1st. Circumstances descriptive of the person who is the party favoured.

The statement of these circumstances is performed by the exposition of the word *Title.*[1]

Consent ⟷ *Good-liking* = Approbation.

1269. King William ascended the throne with the free corporate consent of the Lords and Commons, that is with &c.

Consent corporate ⟷ *individual.*

1270. He ascended the throne with the individual consent of a majority of that assembly.[2]

He ascended the throne with the good-liking of a great part of | |.

He continued on the throne with the forced consent of all such as took the Oaths to exempt themselves from punishment.

He continued in the throne with the express dissent of all those by whom these oaths, being tender'd, were refused. Qu. viz: Quakers, &c.[3]

Personification. Substantification.

1271. When these fictitious entities are represented as of that class of beings that are called persons, that is when they are represented as being in such situations as only persons are in in reality, or as undergoing such motions as only persons are subject

[a] Circumstantiating, or the part descriptive of the circumstances.

[1] Bentham does not go on to list any further circumstances.

[2] The title of William III (1650–1702), King of England, Scotland, and Ireland from 1689, and Mary II (1662–94), Queen of England, Scotland, and Ireland from 1689, to the Crown rested on the Parliament Act of 1688 (1 Will. & Mar., c. 1), duly passed by majorities in both Houses of Parliament.

[3] The Oaths of Allegiance and Supremacy Act of 1688 (1 Will. & Mar., c. 8) required all office-holders, Members of Parliament, and clergy to swear allegiance to William and Mary. The Archbishop of Canterbury, five bishops, and approximately four hundred lower clergy refused to take the oaths. Quakers also refused to take the oath, being opposed to the swearing of oaths of any kind.

to in reality, the mode or figure, as it is called, of speech by which this is done has already got a name and is called Personification. By the same rule, a more general mode of speech might be laid down by which sounds are made to represent beings by those motions or situations being attributed to them which in reality are to be met with only in the things signified by the names of real substances: and one might call it *Substantification*.

> Existence saw him spurn her bounded reign
> And panting Time toiled after him in vain.[1]

Here Existence and Time are fictitious entities made by personification. They are represented as persons because it is persons only that are subject to exercise the actions respectively attributed to them. It is a feigned somthing that is represented as seeing: and as seeing is an action that belongs only to a *person*, that is to an animated substance (for thus ample is the import of personification), the word existence is thereby represented as being the name of such a person.

1272. Improper substantives, names of fictitious entities, are unfit to serve as titles of Divisions. A proper substantive, the name of a real entity, is understood immediately and of itself it offers a certain image to the conception. An improper substantive offers no such image. Of itself it has no meaning. It means nothing till, with other words, it be compounded into some sentence. It then is seen to have a meaning, which is the clearer, the more clearly it is seen to be equivalent to some sentence the terms of which are names of real entities.

DIG. Improper Substantives not fit for Titles.

Again, in marking out a subject into Divisions, another thing that is requisite is that it should be capable of being divided further as often as there may be occasion: and that, if possible, upon the same plan as it was begun upon. For the above reason, the genera expressed by the names that stand as Titles of Divisions should be indefinitely divisible:[2] they should be such as are capable of being divided into inferior genera so as to compose a train of descending subalternates, or ranked under superior genera so as to be attached to a train of ascending subalternates to an indefinite extent, as occasion may arise. Such is the case with those real

[1] Samuel Johnson, *Prologue and Epilogue, Spoken at the Opening of the Theatre in Drury-Lane 1747*, London, 1747, p. 2. There are minor inaccuracies in the rendering of the passage.

[2] In the margin, Bentham has noted at this point: 'Every name that is not a proper one expresses a genus of entities of some sort or other, real or imaginary.'

genera that are indicated by the names of real entities. The number of possible genera that might be made out of them is absolutely indefinite. It is much larger than, for any purpose, there can ever be occasion to make use of. It is not limited even by the number of individuals. If, in any instance, we learn to distinguish one individual from another, it is by virtue of some one property at least which the one of them is seen to have, and the other is not seen to have. This one property is enough to serve for the character of a genus: and when a name is invented and agreed to be the sign of all such individuals, actual or possible, in which such property is or shall be found, the genus is made up. Let there be two such properties found in the two individuals, and more genera than there are individuals are already made. So well adapted, so much better adapted, is plain expression than any other to the purposes of method.

With regard to fictitious entities, the case is very different. The genera they indicate[1]

Act, Nature of a.

1273. The Nature of an act, consider'd in a moral view, consists in it's pathological effects.

Effects pathological.

1274. By Pathological effects, I mean such of it's effects as come under the class of sensations: sensations painful or pleasurable: pains or pleasures.

Case.

1275. By the word case is meant much the same as would be signified by the phrases a set, system or assemblage of circumstances.

Otherwise thus:

A case is an assemblage of circumstances. We say in such a case, instead of saying on, in or under, such a set of circumstances.

Prefat. Princ. of Utility. 'Right Reason dictates' &c.

1276. These phrases I have never in any single instance permitted myself to use. I saw and was thoroughly satisfied that in speaking thus, I should be saying nothing. This phraseology, but too often resorted to even by our most admired writers, is for the writer indeed one of the most happy, but for the science, for the public the most unhappy, expedients that ever was devised for reconciling ignorance with self-sufficiency. It is my earnest wish, and in some measure my hope, that what is said in the course of this work will have the effect of banishing this pernicious phraseo-

[1] The passage has been abandoned at this point.

logy, this fruitless and insipid babbling, from books written on the science. Henceforward, I hope that nothing will be accepted, and therefore that nothing will be offer'd, under the name of a reason for a Law, but the indication of some utility, that is a tendency to procure some pleasure or avert some pain, as the result of it. If in this single endeavour I am successful, I shall rejoice myself with the thoughts of having done good service.

To have restrained myself simply and silently from this | | would not by any means [have][1] answer'd my purpose. It would have saved this work from the reproach of giving this sort of nonsense, but I could not have had any hopes of it's doing any thing [towards][2] banishing it from the works of other men.

By this alone, a new face will be given to the science: the old rubbish, under which whatever of life and spirit it had in it lay smother'd, will be cleared away. Grotius and Puffendorf, rich in history, but almost altogether destitute of all reasoning but what is of the kind just-mentioned, will be consulted only as historical common-place books. Burlamaqui, who has no facts, and whose work is made up altogether of this mock-reasoning, will sleep altogether undisturbed. Men will either sit silent or say somthing. Utility will reign sole and sovereign arbitress of all disputes. The only evidences admitted will be matters of fact: facts conjectured from facts experienced: against opinion, under every other guise than that of mere opinion, the door will be shut inexorably.

There will be much less written probably than there would otherwise, but what little is written will be written to much more purpose.

1277. Among fictitious entities, some are characterized by names original, as Power, Liberty: others are characterized by names borrow'd from real entities—as a Head used as synonymous to a Title in discourse. Entities, fictitious. Names whence taken.

1278. A Tarif is a table shewing the species of one thing corresponding to the degrees of another; or the species of one thing corresponding to the species of another; or the degrees of one thing corresponding to the degrees of another. Tarif.

1279. Phrases expressive of contingent causation. Contingence—Phrases expressive of.

To be apt to produce—to be in a way to produce. To have a

[1] MS 'of'. [2] MS 'from'.

tendency to produce. To be of a nature to produce—to be liable to produce—to be possible to produce—to be likely to produce: contingent particles may, might, can, could, would, should: contingent conjunctions if | | could, would, and should, put before the noun or pronoun followed with '*but*' and the verb in the infinitive mood: was, (or rather) were, put before the noun or pronoun followed by a verb in the infinitive mood, with or without '*but*' before it.

Description X Limitation.

1280. I. Of the difference between the effect of words of description, as applied to Heirs, and words of limitation—in that the one are understood to be significative of single takers, the other of lines of takers. When the word Heir or Heirs is supposed to be significative of a single taker, or an assemblage of takers, who, it is designed, should enjoy the estate at once, there the phrase in use upon the occasion is that the word[s] Heir or Heirs in the instrument of conveyance was a word of *description*: and that the person or persons characterized by the word Heir or Heirs take by purchase: where it is supposed to be significative of a line of takers, or an assemblage of persons who are to enjoy in succession, there the phrase is that the word[s] Heir or Heirs are words of *limitation*; and that the person or persons characterized by the words Heir or Heirs take by *descent*.[1]

As to the word Heir in the singular number, it is plain that, in the natural import of it, it can not indicate a line of takers: neither accordingly has it ever that signification given it by the Law. On the other hand, Heirs in the plural, although naturally and usually, in common usage as well as in legal import, it serves to indicate a line of takers, yet in certain cases it may serve [to] indicate a single taker; that is two or more single takers, each standing single after some one person to whom each is respectively the Heir. Thus, if one Estate were to go to A. and afterwards to his heir, and another to B. and afterwards to his (viz. B.'s) heir, it would not be inconsistent with common speech to say, speaking of the two Estates together, that they were to go to A. and B. and their heirs.

The words Description and Limitation seem but indifferently suited to express those differences they are made by Lawyers to

[1] For the distinction between title by descent and title by purchase see Blackstone, *Commentaries on the Laws of England*, ii. 241: 'Purchase . . . is . . . the possession of lands and tenements, which a man hath by his own act or agreement; and not by descent from any of his ancestors or kindred. In this sense it is contradistinguished from acquisition by right of blood, and includes every other method of coming to an estate, but merely that by inheritance; wherein the title is vested in a person, not by his own act or agreement, but by the single operation of law.'

indicate. The word *Description* is the word which happens to be applied to the case where the supposal is that it is a single person who is to take. The word Heir in that case is said to be a word of description; that is, with reference to a single person meant by the word Heir, a word descriptive of a single person. But is there less propriety in calling a word that is descriptive of a line of takers, a word of description? Is not a word equally a word of description whether it be so with reference to one single person, or to a succession of single persons?

On the other hand, the word Limitation is the word which is applied to the case where the supposal is that it is a line of persons that are to take. The word Heirs in this case is said to be a word of limitation; that is a word of limitation with reference to a line of takers: a word limitative of a line of takers. But would there be less propriety in calling a word that is limitative of a single person, as a person who is to take, a word of limitation? Is not a word equally a word of limitation, whether it be so with respect to a succession of single persons or to one single person?

The word Heir is used to describe the person or line of persons to whom the estate is to go. The word Heir is used to limit the estate to such a person or line of persons. Do not the two modes of expression seem equipollent and interconvertible?

To Lawyers, however, it has seemed otherwise. Without any warrant from common use, they have taken upon them to narrow the import of the two modes of expression in such manner as to confine one to indicate one of the above cases alone, and the other, the other. The word description they use only with reference to a single taker—the word limitation, in this case where they oppose it to description, with reference only to a line of takers.

I say in this case, for in other cases, where the word description does not come in question, and where no doubt is made whether the disposition in question is meant to be made in favour of a single person (or what comes to the same thing, of an assemblage of persons all taking at once) or of a line of persons, the word limitation is applied as freely to single persons as to lines of persons. Thus, if an Estate be given to A. for life, remainder to B. for life, remainder to C. for life. No scruple is made to say that the Estate is *limited* to A. for life, remainder to B. for life, remainder to C. for life. Upon the same plan, all these three different dispositions are severally called limitations. To A. for life is said to be the first limitation: to B. the second: to C. the third, and so on. Just in the same manner as to A. and the Heirs of his body, Remainder to B. and the heirs of his body, Remainder to C.

and the heirs of his body—expressions appointing so many lines of takers, would be severally stiled limitations.

II. Of the difference that it makes whether the word Heirs is to be understood as indicative of single takers or of lines of takers with regard to the *power of alienation*.

Good positive X negative.

1281. I use good as a general term to express indifferently either pleasure or the avoidance of pain. In the first of these cases, I call it positive good: in the other, negative.

Evil positive X negative.

1282. In like manner, I use evil as a general term to express indifferently either pain or the loss of pleasure. In like manner, in the first of these cases, I call it positive evil; in the other, negative.

Succession to Property.

1283. Rule excluding ascendants from succession, and the half-blood[1]—a source of inexhaustible injustice—I say injustice. For what is injustice but acting counter to expectation?

Felony, the punishment analysed.

1284. The punishment for the offences stiled Felonies without benefit of Clergy consists of the following particulars.[2]

Punishment *propriâ personâ*.

I. Punishment affecting person. Death by hanging.[3]

II. Punishment affecting property. [1st.] Forfeiture of all his Lands—and rights of entry to Lands, *upon* Judgment passed—*from* the time of the [act][4] committed.[5]

2dly. Forfeiture of all his goods and chattels, *upon* conviction, *from* the time of conviction.[6]

3dly. Incapacity of bringing an action.[7] Qu.

[1] For the Common Law rule that inherited property 'shall never lineally ascend' and the rule excluding the half-blood from inheritance see Blackstone, *Commentaries on the Laws of England*, ii. 208–12, 224–34, respectively.

[2] The following passage appears to be based in the main on ibid., Bk. IV, Ch. 29. Of Judgment and it's Consequences, iv. 368–82.

[3] For the punishment of death by hanging see ibid. 370.

[4] MS 'fact'.

[5] According to Blackstone, *Commentaries on the Laws of England*, iv. 374–5, where judgment of death for treason or felony or judgment of outlawry had been given against a man, he was 'said to be attainted', whereupon he forfeited all his lands and tenements from the time at which the crime was committed.

[6] In ibid. 380–1, Blackstone notes that while lands were forfeited upon attainder, goods and chattels were forfeited on conviction.

[7] Blackstone does not explicitly mention this and the following two points in Bk. IV, Ch. 29 (though the question concerning the inability to make a will is explicitly dealt with elsewhere), but Bentham may have inferred them from the passage noted below concerning the 'credit or reputation' of an attainted person.

4thly. Inability to make a will.[1] Qu.
5thly. Incapacity to bear an office. Qu.
III. Punishment affecting reputation.
Incapacity of being heard in evidence.[2]

Punishment *alienâ personâ*
or
Tralatitious punishment.

1st. His Wife forfeits her Dower.[3]
2dly. His Real Representative[4] forfeits his real property—his Lands, Houses, etc.[5]
3dly. The Personal Representatives forfeit his personal property—his Money, Moveables, interest for years in real property.[6]
4thly. All his Heirs forfeit their right not only to the real property that had been his, but to all real property to which he, though he never came into possession of it, stood before them in succession. As if there be Grandfather, Father and Son. The Father committs a Felony. The Son can not by descent take any Land that was the Grandfather's. There is nothing, however, to hinder the Grandfather's leaving it to him by Will. This is what is called corrupting his blood.[7] This, of all others, the King can not pardon. The King, who is permitted to save the guilty from punishment, is not permitted to save the innocent. Guilt, the Law looks on with an indulgent eye: to innocence alone it gives no quarter. If you want a reason, Lawyers have one ready. Blood that once stinks, cannot be made sweet again.[a]

[a] 4 *Comm.* 395.[8]

[1] See ibid., ii. 499: 'Persons incapable of making testaments, on account of their criminal conduct, are in the first place all traitors and felons, from the time of conviction; for then their goods and chattels are no longer at their own disposal, but forfeited to the king.'

[2] According to ibid., iv. 373–4, an attainted person 'is no longer of any credit or reputation; he cannot be a witness in any court; neither is he capable of performing the functions of another man: for, by an anticipation of his punishment, he is already dead in law.'

[3] According to ibid. 375, the dower of the wife of an attainted person 'is forfeited, by the express provision of statute', namely by the Treason Act of 1551 (5 & 6 Edw. VI, c. 11).

[4] MS orig. 'Heir'.

[5] On the forfeiture to the Crown of real property as a consequence of attainder in high treason see Blackstone, *Commentaries on the Laws of England*, iv. 374–8. In petit treason and felony, the forfeiture was for a year and a day: see ibid. 378–9.

[6] On the forfeiture of goods and chattels 'in every one of the higher kinds of offence' see ibid. 379–81.

[7] On the corruption of blood see ibid. 381–2.

[8] Blackstone explains that the effect of a pardon by the King was 'to make the offender a new man; to acquit him of all corporal penalties and forfeitures annexed to that offence for which he obtains his pardon', but if the pardon was not obtained until after attainder, then 'nothing can restore or purify the blood when once corrupted . . . but the high and transcendent power of parliament'.

5thly. A man who has bought real Estate of him at any time between the commission of the crime of which he [is] attainted and the time of the attainder, although he knew nothing of the crime, loses the estate without recompense.[1] In the case of Eugene Aram, a murder was discover'd 14 or 15 years after it was committed.[2] In the case of Horne, 30 or 40 years.[3] If Aram or Horne had sold Land to any body, the purchaser must have lost it.

6thly. A man who has any property in dispute, and whose title to it depends upon the testimony of the felon, loses it. If a man, without intending Death, kills another upon a sudden quarrel, or in a duel, or gives an idle stroke to another's horse which happens to run over a child and kill him, this person's testimony is to go for nothing.[4]

In Felony within Clergy, every thing else is the same except the corporal punishment.

This, instead of being death, is either | |[5]

Punishment *propriâ personâ* incident to Felony within Clergy, in case of a second offence punished with the same punishment.

If, after having been convicted of one clergyable Felony, no matter what the offence, a man is attainted of another, he is to suffer death.[6] A man sends a Sheep abroad: it is only felony within

[1] According to Blackstone, *Commentaries on the Laws of England*, iv. 375, 379, the forfeiture of real property, following attainder in treason, petit treason, and felony, related back to the time of the offence committed.

[2] Eugene Aram (bap. 1704, d. 1759), philologist and schoolmaster, was convicted and hanged in 1759 for the murder of Daniel Clark, shoemaker, who had disappeared in 1745.

[3] William Andrew Horne (1685–1759) was tried at Nottingham Assizes and subsequently hanged in 1759 for the murder of an infant in 1724: see *A Genuine Account of the Life and Trial of William Andrew Horne, Esq; Of Butterley-Hall, in the County of Derby; Who was convicted at Nottingham Assizes, August 10, 1759, for the Murder of a Child in the Year 1724, and executed there on the 11th of December 1759. To which is prefixed, A particular Detail of all the Circumstances tending to the Discovery of this long-conceal'd Murder*, 3rd edn., Nottingham, 1759.

[4] Blackstone, *Commentaries on the Laws of England*, iv. 183–94, mentions these and similar offences in his discussion of excusable homicide and manslaughter, the latter being a felony without benefit of clergy.

[5] See ibid. 365: 'all the commons [as opposed to peers] of the realm, not in orders, whether male or female, shall for the first offence be discharged of the punishment of felonies, within the benefit of clergy; upon being burnt in the hand, imprisoned for a year, or less; or, in case of larciny, being transported for seven years, if the court shall think proper'. As Blackstone explains more fully at ibid. 363–4, a person convicted of larciny and entitled to benefit of clergy, instead of the traditional punishment of burning in the hand or whipping, was liable to be transported to America for seven years, at the discretion of the court. Otherwise, according to ibid. 367, a felon receiving benefit of clergy forfeited his goods to the King, but, after being branded on the hand, was 'restored to all capacities and credits, and the possession of his lands, as if he had never been convicted'.

[6] According to ibid. 360, unless the offender was an 'actual' clergyman, he or she was 'not allowed to claim the clerical privilege more than once'.

Clergy.[1] But if the same man who once exported a sheep afterwards whips a horse, and the horse happens to run over a child and kill it, or happens by an unlucky blow to kill a man who struck him first, though it were 20 years after, he is to be hanged.

As to whatever comes under the denomination of tralititious punishment, all this S[r] W[m] Blackstone is perfectly well satisfied with. He says, if the Law punishes one man for another's crime, it is not the Law's fault; it is the criminal's.[2]

1285. Catalogue to be made of Trades or money-getting occupations that are absolutely forbidden. This catalogue must be inserted in the General Code. Such are those of Fire-work-making, Tobacco-planting, Lottery-making, etc.[3] DIG. Trades prohibited.

1286. Another Catalogue of occupations prohibited *sub modo*: that require either a license or an apprenticeship or some other condition to be complied with. Trades appropriated.

1287. Ch . . . Of the entities that are the objects of discourse: which are real and which fictitious. Entities real and fictitious.

Upon a careful and long continued review, I cannot find that we have any direct and unfigurative way of bringing into view by words any objects of conception besides substances, and them only in a state of rest.

1288. Entities I call fabulous are fictitious entities personalized.[4] Entities fabulous.

---

[1] On the offence of 'owling', that is 'transporting wool or sheep out of this kingdom, to the detriment of it's staple manufacture', see ibid. 154–5. Under the Act against carrying over Sea, Rams, Lambs or Sheep alive of 1566 (8 Eliz. I, c. 3), only a second offence of this kind was considered felony, while first offenders suffered the forfeiture of their goods and one year's imprisonment, at the end of which their left hand was to be cut off and displayed in public.

[2] In the margin, Bentham has noted at this point: 'Run a muck—cast lots—punish blindfold.' See Blackstone, *Commentaries on the Laws of England*, iv. 379: 'This [i.e. forfeiture of real property on attainder relating back to the time of the offence] may be hard upon such as have unwarily engaged with the offender: but the cruelty and reproach must lie on the part, not of the law, but of the criminal; who has thus knowingly and dishonestly involved others in his own calamities.'

[3] On the prohibition of lotteries and the making and selling of fireworks as common nuisances see Blackstone, *Commentaries on the Laws of England*, iv. 168–9. For the laws forbidding tobacco cultivation in England and Ireland see p. 358 n. above.

[4] In the text, Bentham has noted at this point: 'Force and velocity fictitious entities. 4 D'Alemb. 205.' See D'Alembert, 'Essai sur les Élemens de philosophie', in *Mélanges de littérature, de l'histoire et de philosophie*, iv. 197–205, where 'force' and 'vitesse' form part of the analysis of 'mouvement' and 'inertie'.

Law of Nature.

1289. Were this privilege of giving a man's own opinion abolished, a great part of those who are in use or who propose to entertain the public with their sentiments on this subject would be reduced to silence, and the science would not be the worse for it.

I can not expect that what I have said against the abuse of this phrase should be acceptable to those who have written great books and whose whole books have consisted of nothing else.

Improvement.[1]

1290. Judges to propound alterations.

Judges to propound alterations. Ex.

1291. Instance of Judges of different courts conferring together to alter a mode of Procedure—the proposition coming from L[d] Mansfield.[a]

Prefat. Law of Nature &c.

1292. He may make himself pretty sure of the enmity of the multitude of those Writers and those discoursers whose reputation or chance of reputation is founded on the abuse of words and phrases that have a meaning, or the use of those that are without meaning. And of these, unhappily the bulk of writers and discoursers on subjects of a moral nature is composed.

It is easily practised: it is a way of slurring over every difficulty. A man talks in this stile when he can say nothing else. Comme l'Algébriste: c'est ainsi qu'il se procure des moments de repos.[2]

Off. ag. Justice. Declining to assist through fear or disaffection.

1293. In the offence of declining to assist a Minister of Justice, a great difference ought to be made in the punishment, according as the refusal appears to be through *fear*, viz: of the delinquent, or through *disaffection*. When it is through disaffection, the party might be punished as an accessary after the fact. It is analogous to *Rescue*.[3]

---

[a] [4][4] Burr. 2118.[5]

[1] MS del. 'advancement'.

[2] Perhaps an allusion to Voltaire, 'Epître à un ministre d'Etat sur l'encouragement des arts' (written in 1740 and first published at Geneva in 1743), ed. R. Goulbourne, in *Œuvres de 1738–40 (II)*, Oxford, 2007 (*Les Œuvres Complètes de Voltaire: Vol. 18b*), pp. 431–61 at 454–8, where the 'algébriste' is satirised for his useless learning and his contempt for culture.

[3] See Blackstone, *Commentaries on the Laws of England*, iv. 131: 'Rescue is the forcibly freeing another from an arrest or imprisonment; and is always the same offence in the stranger so rescuing, as it would have been in the party himself to have broken prison. A rescue therefore of one apprehended for felony, is felony; for treason, treason; and for a misdemesnor a misdemesnor also.'

[4] MS '3'.

[5] The case of *Belither v. Gibbs* (1767) prompted Chief Justice Mansfield to arrange a conference between the Justices of the Courts of King's Bench and Common Pleas, with the aim of establishing a consistent rule regarding the eligibility of defendants in actions of debt

1294. Ask them what sort of an act it is, relative to which the Law makes such or such a disposition. They heap words upon words, and at last, the answer they make you comes to this: that it is that sort of act which the Law makes punishable. They explain in a circle; they give a word at one time one meaning, and at another, without warning, a quite opposite one: they talk backwards and forwards: they say and unsay:[1] and this hard-straining and noisy ignorance they put off upon the gaping multitude for deep learning and recondite science.[a]

Lawyers—their language nugatory.

1295. What the Law wants as much as any thing is that *simplicity* which is the result of uniformity. From it's own intrinsic store, patterns might be taken of almost every thing that is excellent in a system of Jurisprudence.

DIG. Pref. Engl. Law.

1296. A Law is compleat when it contains a compleat specification of the sort of act prohibited or commanded by it, as also of the circumstances in which it is meant respectively to be prohibited or commanded, as also a signification of the punishment, where there is one, by the apprehension of which the observance of it is enforced. To have a precise idea of a *compleat* Law, in contradistinction to one that is *not* compleat, it is necessary to have precise ideas to annex respectively to the terms *act* and *circumstances*: *act which* is prohibited or commanded, and circumstances *in* which it is prohibited or commanded.

Law when compleat—thence consider Circumst.[s] &c.

If it be asked where there is to be found an example of a compleat Law, I answer, in the imagination: and hitherto perhaps, no where else. I much doubt whether there exists or ever has existed in the world an instance of a Law, a written Law, thoroughly compleat, the matter whereof is all drawn together.

1297. The Sanction of the Law is either a threat or a promise: it is most commonly a threat. Why it is so is a question that will meet us in it's place.

Sanction not a part of a Law—but an appendage to it.

The sanction is not properly speaking a part of a Law. It is not a

[a] See Buller *ad verbum* 'Assault'.[2]

---

for either common or special bail: see Burrow, *Reports of Cases adjudged in the Court of King's Bench*, iv. 2118.

[1] In the margin, Bentham has noted at this point: 'They give a supposed institution in other words as a reason for itself.'

[2] i.e. 'Of Assault and Battery' in [Francis Buller], *An Introduction to the Law relative to Trials at Nisi Prius*, London, 1767, pp. 14–21, which begins as follows: 'In treating of the Action of Assault and Battery, it will be necessary to see what the Law looks upon as such.'

necessary part of a Law. Though a usual, it is not even a necessary, appendage.

A Law is a command: now, neither threat nor promise is any necessary part of a command. A command is an expression of will. Now, I may express my will, without denouncing any evil of my appointment as about to ensue to the non-observer, or good upon the observer of my will.

A Command is one thing: and one entire thing. A threat or a promise is another.

A command is an expression of a volition, the modal object of which is some act of the party to whom the command is addressed. A threat or promise is an expression of a volition, the modal object of which is an act not of the party addressed, but either the party addressing or some other supposed to be about to act in pursuance of some other command of such addresser. A Law is a command: but a threat or a promise is a *prediction*.

Example. You command me and say, 'shut the door.' Here you are the party addressing, I the party adressed: the act is the modal object of this command: and this is the act of me, the party adressed. You add, 'if you do not, you shall receive a blow on the face.' This is a prediction: and the prediction, being a prediction of an event evil in it's nature, is a threat. The act whereby it is *foretold* me I am to receive the blow (in the case of my not obeying the command in question) may be either my act[1] or the act of any person besides, other than your's to whom I am adressing myself. If my act, no command for the purpose of producing it, no further expression of volition, is necessary: for of my own volition, I am conscious without expressing it. In this case, the prediction is the prediction of an act at large of one whose prediction it is. If not my act, then a further command is necessary. I must express my will to him whose act I design it should [be],[2] in order to [secure] his performance of the act by which the threat is to be executed.

Thus it is that a command and a threat differ not in that the one is an expression of volition, the other an assertion. For in truth, an expression of volition is but one species of assertion: as indeed every expression of any act of the mind is an assertion, asserting to wit that that act of the mind takes place.

---

[1] Bentham appears to have inadvertently altered the narrator's perspective from the party addressed to the party addressing.

[2] MS 'me'.

1298. To know what acts are to be deemed offences, it is necessary to know who are the persons who have the appointment of the acts that are to be deemed offences.[1]

Constitutional Law, how connected with Criminal.

1299. Powers Legislative—Judicial—Powers Dispensatorial—Powers Military—Powers Investitive and Divestitive with respect to persons—Powers Investitive and Divestitive with respect to persons invested with powers Legislative, Judicial, Dispensatorial, Military, Investitive and Divestitive.

1300. Constitutional Law is not made up so much of commands; i:e: portions of discourse designative of offences—marking out what shall be deemed offences, as of descriptions of those by whom Commands shall be issued, and of the cases in which commands may and may not be issued by those persons. These descriptions are so many portions of discourse serving to indicate the circumstances that must concur to the placing of any act in that case in which it is to be deemed an offence—in short so many sets of incriminative circumstances. The want of any article in the requisite assemblage of these incriminative circumstances is an exemptive circumstance; takes the act out of that case in which, according to the course of the Law, it is an offence. To speak in the usual language, a Law made by persons not duly authorised to make Laws in that behalf is void.

Constitutional Law.

It is one offence, and in a manner but one, that is concerned throughout the whole of the Law of Property.

The power of appointing what acts shall be deemed offences divide into Legislative and Judicial. Judicial, the dictatorial tied down to *conditions*.

One branch, then, of Constitutional Law will consist in the indicating to what sorts of persons, as distinguished by such and such names, belongs, in such and such cases, Legislative or Judicial power.

Another will consist in indicating what circumstances a man must be in, in order to his being consider'd as being of any of the sorts of persons respectively indicated by those names.

The sorts of commands which it belongs to persons invested with any portion of Dispensatorial power to give are confined to such acts of which the things the disposal of which belongs to such power are the objects.

[1] In the margin, Bentham has noted at this point: '*Sic postea* Law of Property.' The reference has not been identified.

To the same persons to whom belong Powers of the Legislative [or] Judicial kinds may also belong powers of the Dispensatorial, Military or Investitive or Divestitive kind. In this case, under titles taken from the names of those sorts of persons, along with the specification of the one sort of power, must be contained a specification of the other.

Law Maxims. **1301.** Tort dies with the person.[1]—Where ever the Law gives a right, it gives a remedy.—Under the Law there is no right without a remedy.[2] This magnificent aphorism, expressed according to it's real import comes precisely to neither more nor less than this, viz: that the Law punishes in every case in which it punishes. Of this stamp is the wisdom so much in honour among Lawyers.

The propositions one meets with in the books of Law under the name of maxims may be distinguished into maxims of fact, and maxims of policy. By maxims of fact, I mean such propositions as are designed to convey notions concerning what is Law. By maxims of policy, I mean such propositions the design of which is to convey some notion or other concerning what, in the judgment of him who first advanced them, ought to be Law.

Of these maxims, such of them as are maxims of policy are as generally erroneous as such of them as are maxims of Law are false. There is extant a collection that has been made of them by some industrious compiler. The collection occupies a moderate duodecimo volume. I have turned over that volume, and from the beginning to the end I have not been able to find one which would bear examination.[3]

The form in which they make their appearance is that of an universal proposition: and that proposition, so far as it is intelligible, so far as it may be seen to mean any thing, may be seen to mean somthing which is not true.

[1] According to Blackstone, *Commentaries on the Laws of England*, iii. 302, 'in actions merely personal, arising *ex delicto*, for wrongs actually done or committed by the defendant, as trespass, battery, and slander, the rule is that *actio personalis moritur cum persona* [i.e. a personal action dies with the person]; and it never shall be revived either by or against the executors or other representatives'.

[2] *Ubi jus ibi remedium est*, i.e. 'Where there is a right there is a remedy'. See Coke, *First Part of the Institutes of the Lawes of England*, fo. 56r: 'whensoever the Law giveth any thing, it giveth also a remedy for the same'; and Blackstone, *Commentaries on the Laws of England*, iii. 23: 'In all other cases [i.e. except where there is a remedy 'by the mere operation of law'], it is a general and indisputable rule, that where there is a legal right, there is also a legal remedy, by suit or action at law, whenever that right is invaded.'

[3] See *Principia Legis & Æquitatis: Being an Alphabetical Collection of Maxims, Principles or Rules, Definitions and memorable Sayings in Law and Equity*, London, 1753, a duodecimo volume of 129 pages.

Take them, then, altogether, maxims of policy and maxims of fact, one may say of them in general that they are either unintelligible or false: if a maxim has no meaning at all, [it] can not have a false meaning: but if it has any, it is sure to be a false one. One or other of these properties, then, belongs to every maxim in the collection: but besides these, there is yet another which is possessed by some of them: I mean that of being ambiguous. Many there are of which there is no knowing whether it was designed as a maxim of policy or a maxim of Law, or whether, what perhaps is oftenest the case, it were not meant to serve for both: as indicating at once what the Law is and what it ought to be.

One character more we must add to the above, and we shall have as many characters as will serve to mark the four classes of maxims into which the whole collection may be divided. This is that of nugatoriness.

The whole assemblage of them may stand distributed into 4 classes: the unintelligible, the nugatory and the false; and of such of them as are either nugatory or false, many are besides ambiguous. I shall enumerate some instances of each class. Of the unintelligible sort, but too many are to be found collected, and many of them invented, by Lord Bacon.[1] They are as so many sparks, coruscations struck out by the efforts of a lofty genius fighting it's way through a chaos of darkness and confusion.

Persona conjuncta æquiparatur interesse proprio.[2]

1302. By investitive power, I mean the power of appointing what individual persons or things shall be reputed to be of such and such sorts of persons and of things. Power investitive—what.

1303. This power, like any other, may be possessed either in severalty or in association. —integral X partial.

In the first case, the power may be said to be integral: in the second, partial.

A person may be said to be possessed of an entire portion of investitive power, or of a portion of the investitive power in severalty, when the minds of men, whether by Law or custom, are [so] disposed, that upon his declaring it to be his will that any person shall be treated as being of the sort of persons, or a thing of the sort of things, over which his power extends, such person or such thing is accordingly reputed to be of such sort. The

[1] See Francis Bacon, 'Maxims of the Law' (first published in 1630 in *The Elements of the Common Law*), in *The Works of Francis Bacon*, ed. J. Spedding, R.L. Ellis, and D.D. Heath, 14 vols., London, 1857–74, vii. 307–87.

[2] i.e. 'a person united equal one's own interest', discussed in ibid., vii. 368–9.

business is to shew how this species of power connects with the Legislative.

It is plain it is not the same with the Legislative power itself. The acts of the Legislative power are commands: but an act of this investitive power is not a command. To every command belongs a modal object: the act or the forbearance of the person who is the personal object of the same command. But of an exertion of the investitive power, there is no such modal object. To appoint a person to be an officer is one thing: to command that person to do or to forbear doing any act is another. You bid me open the window. This is an expression of Will. You thereby issue a command which calls for an act of mine who am the personal object of that command; viz: the act of opening the window. You appoint me your servant: this appointment too is an expression of will. But this appointment does not call for any act of mine who am the material, and being a person am accordingly the personal, object of the appointment. Let no command be issued to me either by you or by any other person, I should no more be called upon to do or forbear any act in consequence of such appointment of your will, than if no expression of your will at all had been ever utter'd. In what manner, then, is it that an exertion of the investitive power, an appointment of the sort in question, can influence the acts, the *conduct*, of any persons who are the objects of it?—thus. It subjects them (being so many individuals) to whatever commands are adressed to sorts of persons distinguished by that specific name which those individuals are, by that appointment, made to bear.

You have already appointed me your servant. You now say, 'let my servant' (we will suppose you have no other besides myself), 'let my servant open the window.' That volition which you have last expressed now calls for an action on my part: viz: the act of opening the window. If you had contented yourself with appointing me your servant, and had stopt there, no action wou'd have been called for in consequence. Had you begun at first with saying, 'let my servant open the window,' without having appointed me or any one else your servant, it would have been the same.

Servant is a name of a sort of persons; a specific name. The command is compleat and effectual when the individual appointment is brought in union with a command addressed to the generic name. When I have been appointed your servant, and understand that your servant has been commanded to open the window, then it is, and not before, that I understand that I am the individual person by whom the act of opening the window is to be performed.

If you had said to me at once, 'Such an one' (naming me) 'open the window,' the same effect would have been produced.

1304. The several objects of a command may all of them be either individual or generic (specific).

Command, objects of a—individual ⅹ generic.

A Command is never compleat and effective, till by virtue of the terms of the command itself, or by help of a competent exertion of the investitive power, all the several objects of it are render'd individual; in other words, till it is brought home to individuals.

It must be brought home in every instance to individual objects, before it can be shewn to have been disobey'd in that instance.

It must be understood to what individual objects of each of the three classes it relates before any person can set himself to obey it.

1305. Call the Investitive power the nominating—the Divestitive power the disnominating.

Power nominating ⅹ disnominating.

1306. To exercise the investitive power with respect to an office of trust is to appoint the person who shall be the party favoured by the fictitious command of other persons in that behalf: i:e: by the general Law of Property: with respect to such objects of property of which, by virtue of his office, he has the custody and use.

1307. Mem. Consider and explain the power of creating Offices.

Power of creating Offices.

1308. Public Stations may be distinguished into active and inactive. The inactive are Dignities. The active are Offices.

Dignities—Offices.

1309. Offices are either merely operative, alias curative, or merely lucrative, or mixt. Lucrative are such as neither oblige nor entitle the possessors to do any thing more than to receive money or other valuables: viz: to do acts that are beneficial to the officer himself and him alone. These are often called Sinecures.

Offices operative or curative ⅹ lucrative.

Sinecures.

Operative or curative are such as oblige or entitle the possessor to exert himself in some way or other in acts which it is designed should be beneficial in some way or other to the community at large: they are such as invest the possessor with public powers.

1310. Operative offices are either: 1$^{st.}$ Legislative. 2$^{d.}$ Judicial. 3$^{dly.}$ Dispensatorial. 4$^{thly.}$ Investitive with respect to either of the

Offices of Power, *quot.*

above three sorts of offices, as also with respect to those which are themselves investitive. [5]thly. Divestitive with respect to the same offices, as also with respect to them that are themselves Divestitive. To these may be added the Power of creating the offices themselves.

Power investitive absolute ✕ limited.

1311. The power of investment may be either absolute or limited.

When limited, it may be limited with respect either 1st to the choice of the *persons* themselves who are made objects of the appointment: [or] 2dly with respect to the ceremonies and the circumstances that must accompany the exertion of the power.

Offices of Trust.

1312. Offices of Trust is a name more usually given to such offices as confer power over public things, than to such as confer power over persons.

Force ✕ Perspicuity.

1313. *Force* and *Perspicuity* are two very different qualities in a discourse. An expression may serve to render a sentiment *emphatical*, without rendering it *clear*. It is one thing to *enliven*: it is another to explain.

To expound = to explain = to make clear.

1314. To explain, to expound, a phrase, is to refer the object indicated by it to some one of the universal classes of objects to which all objects belong, and to distinguish it from other objects of the same class.

PROP. Contracts—*do ut des* &c.

1315. The Distribution made by the Civilians of the different sorts of Contracts, *do ut des, do ut facias, facio ut des, facio ut facias,*[1] is remarkably emphatical, but it is not yet quite clear. What yet remains to make it clear is to expound the several words that are concerned in it.

Law of Nature. Mischief of the expression.

1316. This, then, being assumed and taken for granted, that there is such a Law as the Law of Nature. What remains is to lay down in every behalf what it ordains.

Now, that this Law ordains so or so in any behalf being a proposition in it's own nature utterly incapable of proof (since a real Law is a command, a command an expression of will, an expression of will the expression of the will of some person, and there is no person of whose will the Law of Nature can be said to be

[1] i.e. 'I give so that you give', 'I give so that you do', 'I do so that you give', 'I do so that you do'.

the expression), when a man wants to make it be believed, that the pretended Law has ordained so and so, that it has commanded or has forbidden such an action, all that he has to do, and all indeed that he can do, is simply and without ceremony to say so. To attempt to prove as much, to attempt to alledge any facts as proof of such a proposition, would be to quit this ground and proceed upon another. Supposing, then, the persons he is adressing himself to accustomed like himself to pay themselves with this phrase, whether he satisfies them or not depends upon this, whether the action pretended to be commanded by this Law of Nature, if it be the forbearance of it that is supposed to be contrary to this Law, be an action which the party in question approves of as one that he thinks a man ought, no matter for what reason or whether for any reason in particular, to think himself bound to perform: or whether the action pretended to be forbidden by this Law, if it be an action which the party in question disapproves of as one that he is of opinion, no matter for what reason or whether for any reason in particular, a man ought to abstain from. In the first case, his observation, his argument, is thought to be a just one: he is thought to have proved his point. In the other case, his argument is thought a deficient one: he is thought not to have proved his point.

The great convenience of this mode of expression is that it makes a man a moralist, and in some sort a politician, at a cheap rate. He has but to take this phrase into his mouth, and the business is done.

Those who [are] altogether ignorant in the science may, by keeping altogether in this . . . . . . keep up a shew of knowledge. And those whose knowledge is any where at a fault, or who, when arguing against knowledge, find themselves hard-pressed, find a convenience in flying to it occasionally, as a Hare to cover.

1317. In the Personal Codes make two heads: 1st of the Person's Rights or Privileges. 2[dly] of his Duties. DIG. Personal code—Rights and Duties.

1318. The conduct of Justice, in deciding the right to an article of property in dispute between two parties, is governed by two considerations. The one respecting the parties themselves. The other respecting the public: that is such persons of the public as are in a way to hear of the decision. Property—principle of decision.

1. To consider the parties themselves, it ought to bestow the article in question upon that one of them in whom the *expectation* of having it is the strongest.

2. To consider the public, it ought to bestow it upon that one of the parties on whom the public expectation expects most strongly to see it bestow'd.

It would seem at first sight that these considerations would be apt in many cases to dictate opposite decisions. This, however, is not the case. To know, by any direct means, in which of two parties the expectation of having a thing is the strongest is seldom possible. In some instances, perhaps, such a fact might be known with tolerable certainty by an individual who should have opportunity of conversing with the parties on the subject, without reserve, and for a length of time—who should set himself to fish it out of them without their having any suspicion of his design, or of their being interested in the opinion he might form upon the matter. To a man acting in character of a Judge, such knowlege may be pronounced to such a degree impossible, that he could have no reasonable ground for expecting to obtain it. The instant the Judge was perceived to set about making the enquiry, it would be impossible the real strength of either party's expectation should appear. Each of them, understanding that he whose expectation should be deemed the strongest was to gain his point, each, I say, however weak his expectation might be in reality, would use every means to make it appear as strong as possible.

If it be impossible for a Judge, by any direct means, to measure the comparative strength of expectation in two known and given individuals, so *a fortiori* must it be to measure it in those unknown and uncertain individuals who in this behalf compose the Public.

What, then, has the Judge to do? One thing, and one only: and that is to put himself in the place of both: of the parties, and also of the public. He supposes himself first in the situation of one of the parties; then in that of the other. He observes in which of the two situations his own expectation would be strongest: and that party in whose situation he finds his expectation to be the strongest is the party in whose favour he determines.

This situation, it is easy to understand, must be the situation relative to the object of property in dispute: a situation composed of those *circumstances* which constitute the *title* he has to make to it. The peculiar temper of the man whereby the expectation of an article of property, if an instrument of pleasure, might be more strong in him *cæteris paribus* than the other, this temper, I say, being a circumstance of which the Judge could not be in a way to form any more than a very inadequate æstimate, is a circumstance which, on the account even of the parties themselves perhaps, there could be no great use in his attending to. On account of the public, there would be great mischief in his professing to ground his decision upon any attention paid to it—to make it in any degree the measure of his decision.

The reasons which a man could find for deeming one man's temperament more sanguine than another's must be founded on ocular inspection, or at least in presence, and that in a variety of situations and for a length of time. Such reasons are in their nature incommunicable by words. They consist in the most minute and indescribable differences in the sensible qualities exhibited by the persons in question: in point of colour, in point of countenance, that is of the figure of the minute parts of his face, in point of gesture, that is of the figure of other parts of his person, in point of voice, that is of the sounds utter'd by such of his organs as are peculiarly adapted to that purpose.

These appearances, then, being indescribable, the Judge could have no means of satisfying the public of the existence of such of them, on the supposal of which he might propose to ground his decision. So that it would not be in his power to give the public any stronger reason for supposing him to have grounded his decision on these considerations, than they would have for supposing it grounded on considerations of his own private interest, or any other circumstances alike independent of all such on which this or any title in the parties could depend.

The stronger a man's expectation is of having a thing, the stronger his disappointment proves if he fails to have it: in other words, the greater is the pain of disappointment he feels in consequence of such failure.

On this account, therefore, more good will ensue upon the whole from giving it to him whose expectation is the strongest.

But it may be urged on the other hand, that the less a man expects to have a thing, the greater is his pleasure in case of his getting it. On this account, therefore, more good should ensue from giving the thing to him in whom expectation is the weakest.

Here, then, seem two contrary reasons; one which pleads for the giving of the thing in question to him in whom expectation is the strongest: another for giving it to him in whom expectation is the weakest.

In order to see which reason is strongest, it will be necessary to sum up and divide the quantities of pleasure and pain that are the pathological effects of the two different modes of disposition.

The pleasures and pains that are concerned in the matter are 4: depending upon two events.

Those pleasures and pains are: 1st. The Pleasure of A., depending upon the event of his getting the thing in question, and B.'s losing it.

2dly. The pain of A., depending upon the event of his losing it, and B.'s getting it.

3dly. The pleasure of B., depending upon the event of his getting the thing in question, and A.'s losing it.

4thly. The pain of B., depending upon the event of his losing the thing in question, and A.'s getting it.

By the same event by which A. enjoys a pleasure, B. suffers a pain, and *vice versâ*.

The question is, then, which is the greater: the difference between A.'s pleasure and B.'s pain in the case of A.'s getting it, or the difference between B.'s pleasure and A.'s pain in the case of B.'s getting it: and on which side the difference is in each case, whether on that of pain or pleasure.

Let A.'s expectation be the strongest, and let A. get it. I say there will be less clear pain upon the whole if the difference be on the side of pain, and more clear pleasure if the difference be on the side of pleasure, than were B. to get it.

The total ballance as between A. and B. will, if on the side of pleasure, be greatest, if on the side of pain, least, in the case of his getting the thing in question, whose expectation is the strongest.

1. If two men's expectations are of an equal strength, it is probable that the pain produced in the one by disappointment is more than equivalent to the pleasure produced in the other by success.

2dly. It is not true without exception that a pleasure is greater, the less the instrument of pleasure is expected.

It *is* true, indeed, when the idea of the pleasure to be reaped from the instrument in question is alike in both cases: but in general the idea of a pleasure is apt to be more lively, the more the instrument is expected: at least when the instrument in question is the general instrument of pleasure, viz: money: and consequently the pleasure in question is pleasure in general, pleasure of any kind that is to be had for money. The longer a man has been expecting the possession of an instrument of pleasure, the more likely is he to have found a use for it.[1]

If I &c.

N.B. But the true reason seems to be that, in a case of this sort, the weaker one man's expectation is, the stronger is the other's. The same cause that makes the expectation of the one weak,

[1] In the text, Bentham has noted at this point: '*Sed* Qu. The consequence.'

makes that of the other strong. The weaker the one man's title is, the stronger is the other's; at least, as against the former.

1319. Ways are of 4 sorts:

Ways, 4 Sorts.

1st. Upon solid land—Roads.
2d. Upon Water over land—Rivers—Canals.
3dly. Upon Land, to wit an immoveable portion of matter artificially thrown over water—Bridges.
4th. Upon a moveable portion of matter floating upon water—Ferries.

1320. To *have, having,* is a fictitious *operation*—as *power* is a fictitious entity.

Operations fictitious as well as Substances.

1321. Laws Substantive)(Adjective. Peere Williams. Vol. III. p. 471, speaks of the felony of a principal as a *substantive* felony in contradistinction to the Felony of an Accessary.[1]

Laws Substantive)(Adj. Peere Will:s.

1322. In the Law of Inheritance.

Rules of Descent.

1. The first object is to avoid *defeating natural expectation*: to cause the succession to property to flow throughout in the channel of expectation.
2. Where the channel of natural expectation may be deemed to end, that system of descent is the best which can be exhibited in the fewest words.
3. If any considerations of a public nature intervene, which dictate an exception to the provisions made in conformity to the above rules, and are of sufficient importance to pay for the inconvenience of the irregularity, let such exceptions be made accordingly.
4. On the above principle it may be of use, when there are no relations but what are beyond the line of ordinary expectation, to give the inheritance to the public.
5. The Poor Laws afford a popular argument for this, an argument *ad homines*, a superficial colour of Equity.

---

[1] See William Peere Williams, *Reports of Cases Argued and Determined in the High Court of Chancery, and Of Two Special Cases Adjudged in the Courts of Common Law*, 3 vols., London, 1746–9, iii. 439–82 at 471, reporting the author's own argument in *R. v. Burridge* (1735): 'I take it, that *Burridge's* assisting *Palmer*, then in Custody for Felony, to escape out of Prison, was Felony in *Burridge*, who thereby became a Principal Felon, and not an Accessary only; and that this Assisting of a Felon to escape out of Prison when in the Hands of Justice, and in Custody of the Law, is (as I may call it) a *Substantive* Felony.'

Substances the only real entities.

1323. The only objects that really exist are *substances*: they are the only real entities. To convey any notion by words which are the names of any objects [other] than substances, we are obliged to attribute to such objects what in truth is attributable only to substances: in a word, we are obliged to feign them to be substances. Those others, in short, are only fictitious entities.

PREPARATORY PRINCIPLES: INTRODUCTION

MARGINAL CONTENTS

[1] Bentham has given two paragraphs the number 27.

INTRODUCTION

1. We all know what VOLITION is: 'tis what we are all practising incessantly. Volition.

2. The object of VOLITION is always some EVENT. We understand tolerably well what an EVENT means. It is the result of either some motion or stoppage of motion, or the aspect of certain things in consequence, that we perceive. Event.

3. An event may be said to be an *object* of our Will; our Will, to be *directed* to that event, when we *will* (or, in other words, our will is) that that event should happen.[a]

4. An *event* in the production of which a being capable of volition is instrumental, we stile an ACTION. Action.

[a] The Will is a faculty. *Volition* is the exercise of that faculty. The Will performs acts of volition. Such has been the language. Not that there is any such thing as a little being that, under the name of Will, gets into men's heads and performs acts of volition or any other acts: as some appear to have imagined:[1] but it is Man that wills, that performs acts of volition; that perceives, that exercises perception; that imagines, that exercises imagination; that judges, that exercises judgment: that remembers, that exercises memory: howsoever, it may be found convenient for many purposes to say that the Will does so and so, instead of saying that man wills in this or that manner. It varies the discourse and oftentimes saves words.

This conceit, if seriously entertained, would not be absolutely without parallel. The ancient Physicians were, as sure as if they had seen it, universally ready to swear that the Womb was an animal within an animal, having its own peculiar affections.[2]

---

[1] Cf. Locke, *Essay concerning Human Understanding*, Bk. II, Ch. XXI, §6, pp. 236–7: 'These Powers of the Mind, *viz.* of *Perceiving*, and of *Preferring*, are usually call'd by another Name: And the ordinary way of Speaking is, That the *Understanding* and *Will* are two *Faculties* of the mind; a word proper enough, if it be used as all Words should be, so as not to breed any confusion in Mens Thoughts, by being supposed (as I suspect it has been) to stand for some real Beings in the Soul, that performed those Actions of Understanding and Volition.'

[2] In the margin, Bentham has noted at this point: 'Law has never been established but men have already been in the habit of observing that secondary will.'

The notion that the womb wandered around the body and was like an animal within an animal appears to have been a common view in ancient Greece: see, for instance, John Astruc, *A Treatise On all the Diseases Incident to Women. Containing An Account of their Causes, Differences, Symptoms, Diagnostics, Prognostics, and Cure*, London, 1743, p. 8: '*Plato* and *Aristotle*, said, *The Womb was an Animal within an Animal*'; and Plato, *Timaeus*, 91: 'whenever the matrix or womb, as it is called,—which is an indwelling creature desirous of child-bearing,—remains without fruit long beyond the due season, it is vexed and takes it ill; and by straying all ways through the body and blocking up the passages of the breath and preventing respiration it casts the body into the uttermost distress, and causes, moreover, all kinds of maladies'.

Motive. Restrictive.

5. The intellectual instrument of an action, or, as some would say, the cause of it, is stiled a *motive*.

Action. Point of Conduct. Forbearance.

6. A motive is an idea: it is the idea of some pleasure or some pain: the pleasure conceived as about to exist, or the pain as about not to exist, in consequence of our action.

Cessation of Pain may be spoken of as Pleasure.

End. Object. Object material.

7.1. The Pleasure, of which the idea becomes a motive, is stiled an *End*: it is also stiled an Object. It may be stiled in either manner: *thither* the mind's prospect is directed: there it *terminates*.[a]

We must, in great measure, take language as we find it. It is common to apply the word action to include forbearance: and there is no help for it: we must submit to usage. It may, however, be of use to have established the distinction in order to refer to should there ever be occasion.

Forbearance.

7.2. A *forbearance* is the privation of action; being to an action what rest in general is to motion in general.

Restrictive.

7.3. A restrictive is a term that might be employ'd to signify such an instrument of forbearance, as motive is of action.

Article of Conduct.

7.4. An Article of Conduct is a neutral expression which might be employ'd to signify indifferently action or forbearance. A *mode* of conduct may signify indifferently one article of conduct or many.

Determinative.

7.5. A determinative is a neutral expression, that might be employ'd to signify indifferently a motive or restrictive.[b]

☛ Maxim 1st or Axiom.

8. The End of an action or forbearance may be distant; and ill-defined: but no man acts or forbears without an end: no man acts without a motive.

Resolution.

9. A Volition that for it's object has an act of that person himself who *wills* if an act conceived to be in his power, is stiled *a Resolution*.

Wish.

A Volition, whereof the object is an event at large, or an act of a person other than he himself who wills, is stiled a wish.

A Wish is said to have attained it's object when the event wished for has taken place.

[a] However, for this purpose, the term {end} is more commodious: the term {object}, besides the sense here given in which it is synonymous to the term {end} as here employ'd, has too many other senses, which might be apt to suggest themselves instead of this.

[b] **7.6.** We must submit to usage: the term forbearance is not very common: the terms restrictive and determinative still less so: ⟨an⟩ action is commonly used in the sense of a forbearance: a motive in that of a restrictive. To that usage, therefore, it may be often better to submitt, rather than, by departing from it, give an air of uncouthness to the discourse. But it may still be convenient to have established these words with an import belonging to them that may be appealed to upon occasion, to clear away any ambiguity that may arise.

A Wish, to attain it's object, must be made perceptible to the party whose act it is meant to cause. It must be *expressed*, or, what means nearly the same, must be *communicated*, *declared*. Axiom 2^d.

10. For a wish to be communicated to any person, two ideas must, in the mind of that person, be excited, 1st the idea of the event wished for: 2dly the idea of the act of volition in the wisher. Wish, a, how communicated.

11. The means whereby a *wish* can be expressed are certain actions: these actions are said to be the *signs* of the wish they serve to express. Signs of a Wish.

12. The signs most frequently employ'd for this purpose are such actions as produce certain sounds: these sounds are stiled words spoken, or, in a collective expression, speech; and, when put together after a certain mode of assemblage, become themselves signs, among other things, of correspondent wishes. Words spoken.

13. Sounds act upon the sense but for an instant: that instant over, they are gone: Visible marks remain: on this account it is found convenient to employ visible marks as the signs of sounds. These marks are stiled words written. I mean, in the most extensive sense of the word written. Words written.

14. A wish communicated takes a different name according to the relation which the party whose action is the object of it is, for the purpose, conceived to bear: whether that of a superior to the party uttering it, of an equal, or of an inferior: if of a superior, an *intreaty*, a *petition*: if of an equal, a *desire*, a *request*, a *requisition*, a *demand*: if of an inferior, an *injunction*, a *command*. Petition. Request. Command.

15. Inferiority, Equality, Superiority are attributed to one man with reference to another in various respects. The import of these terms in all cases seems not to be precisely settled: but for the present purpose it may be said, a superior is one who is supposed able to occasion more pain and pleasure to another, than that other is to him: an equal, about as much, and no more: an inferior, not so much. Inferiority—Equality—Superiority.

16.[1.] A Command not to do an act, is stiled a forbiddal, a prohibition. Forbiddal.

16.2. A forbearance is to a forbiddal, as an action is to a positive command. Forbearance. Command.

A permission is the revocation of a Command.

17. A Command, framed by a certain person or persons, issued on certain occasions, expressed in a certain way, having a certain assemblage of actions for its objects, is stiled a Law. Law.

18. The idea of a Law has never yet been precisely settled: the conditions requisite to reduce the idea of a command so as to render it commensurate to that of a Law have never been ascertained. This task it is my purpose to attempt: what, then, is it I have to do? My business is, therefore, not to remind the reader what *is* meant by a Law: for no one certain thing is as yet meant by a Law: but to declare what *shall* be meant by a Law. If the meaning which I, or any one else, limits it to is deemed a commodious one, what follows? Not that any one is censurable for deviating from it, till sanctified, if it ever be sanctified, by common usage. But any one is censurable if, without warning, he contradicts the common usage of mankind: much more is he, if he contradicts his own.

A Law. **19.** A Law is of that sort of command that is directed to a person or persons inasmuch as he or they is or are a member or members of a State.

A State. **20.** A State is a number of persons accustomed or agreed to act, in all points whatsoever, as one or more persons of a certain description shall have commanded.

Purpose of a Definition. **21.** The purpose for which any word in general is defined is to distinguish the idea belonging to it from others, that is from such others as are so far different from it as to be distinguishable from it, but so far resembling [it] as to be in danger of being confounded with it: that is of rising up in place of it, or along with it, upon the mention of the word: as if any of them, and not the proper one, or any of them as well as the proper one, were belonging to that word.

Prefat. **22.**[1] Great is the multitude of different ideas to which the word Law has been indiscriminately applied: all distinguishable, all highly necessary to be distinguished. 'Tis for want of their being distinguished that a great part of the political disputes that distract the world have arisen. 'Tis by pointing out the difference between these ideas, and tying each of them down to it's proper name, that those disputes, if at all, are to be appeased.[2]

Shall I do this thing? 'No,' says my neighbour, 'the Law forbids it.' Let me be satisfied that the Law does forbid it, that is what I mean by Law, and I am satisfied not to do it. But it is about 12 to one that, by the word Law, I do not mean what my neighbour means by it. That is, if we are equally cool and equally sincere. But if we are of opposite parties, if we are angry, if we are disingenuous, as most are when they are angry, 'tis infinity to one we never shall agree.

This Law concerning —— is not a good Law: it ought to be repealed. 'I think so,' says my neighbour, 'it ought to be recast.' We

[1] This paragraph is a later addition to the text, and duplicates the number of the following paragraph.

[2] The following passage in an adjacent margin may belong here: 'To do this, it is necessary to ascend to ideas the most general and simple we are conversant with. Ideas expressed by words about the signification of which we are all agreed.'

seem to be agreed; but when it comes to trial, it is infinity to one we do not mean the same quantity [by] that which we both agree in calling Law.

22. The ideas with which the word Law is most in danger to be confounded are as follows: viz: PREFAT.

1st.[1] A *command* of any sort whatsoever[2] given by any person whomsoever: as well by such whose commands do not make Law, as of such whose commands do make Law.

2. A *Resolution* of opinion.
3. A Resolution of Volition is not a Command: for &c.
4. A Promise is not a Command: for &c.
5. A Compact.
6. An Order.
7. A dictate of Utility.
8. A Custom.
9. An Official order.
10. A Judicial Opinion or Decision.
11. A Judicial Order or Writ of Execution.
12. A Maxim of Jurisprudence.
13. A Statute.
14. Regulation of a Voluntary Society.
15. A Maxim in Jurisprudence.
16. A Proscription, with respect to the person *proscribed.*
17. An imaginary cause of perfect uniformity in the motions of unsentient beings.
18. An imaginary cause of uniformity in the actions of sentient beings.

[items 2–18:] No command.

23. A Law is a command: it is a species of command. The sort of command that is a Law stands distinguished from any sort of command that is not a Law no otherwise than as a *species* does from a *genus*. This distinguishes it from the . . .[x] first of the articles abovementioned. Every Law must be a command: but it is not every command that is a Law.[3] Law a command.

24. It agrees with commands at large in it's substance. The same instrument that is now the expression of the will of him who has power to make his will be Law, once probably was the expression of the will of one who had no such power. How it agrees with others.

[1] The enumeration of the following list has been editorially supplied. Bentham drew up an initial list that he numbered consecutively, but, on adding more items, failed to amend the numbering. Item 12 is repeated as item 15.

[2] The phrase 'of any sort whatsoever' has been marked by Bentham for deletion.

[3] In the margin, Bentham has noted at this point: 'Every thing, therefore, that is not a command, is not a Law.'

How it differs. It stands distinguished from commands at large: first in it's source:[1] 2^ly in the formalities that accompany the expression of it.

By it's origin. **25.** By it's source, I mean the person or persons whose command it is.

These persons are persons of a particular description in a state: in different states, the description of them is different.

State.[2] **26.** A State is a number of persons agreed or accustomed to conduct themselves in all things according as a person or persons of a certain description have commanded.[a]

Government. **27.** The person or persons thus related to a state are stiled by one collective appellation, *Government*: that person in Government, or that number of persons acting in a body, which commands all the rest, and is commanded by none, The *Supreme power*.

1. A Resolution of Opinion not a Law. **27.**[3] A Resolution of Opinion or Judgment is not a Law. It may be the ground of a Law: as an act of the Judgment may be the ground of an act of the will. For a resolution of Judgment is an act of the understanding. But a Command is an act of the Will: it is an expression of the Will: and a Law is a Command.

2. Nor a Resolution of Volition. **28.** A Resolution of Volition is not a Law: for a Resolution of Volition is such an act of the Will whereof an act of the party whose will it [is] is an object. But a Command is such an act of the Will as has for it's object the act, not of the party willing, but of some other; and a Law is a Command.

I now[?] can define Power. A Power *is a* Faculty: may be so: but what's a Faculty? A Faculty is a—No—neither a Power nor a Faculty is an—any thing. If a Power was a Faculty, it would be a species of Faculty, and there would be other faculties that were not Powers. If a Faculty were related to any thing else, it would be a

[a] This Definition will not easily go down at first with men whose affections are warm on the side of liberty. To such it will be apt to give at least a momentary shock. To these, all I can say is to request them to suspend their censure till they have proceeded a little further. They will be apt to tell me that this is a definition of a slavish state, and of no other. But my notion is that what is called Liberty in a state, does not depend upon any circumstance that will take it out of this definition. For the present, let them be assured, that Slavery will find no advocate in me. But this definition is the most extensive I could devise: and is framed to include one state as well [as] another: well-governed or ill-governed, and whether by Laws or without them. It is my care throughout to keep distinct, by every attention possible, those two ideas so apt to be confounded, the idea of what *is*, from the idea of what *ought to be*.

[1] In the margin, Bentham has noted at this point: 'efficient cause—Author.'

[2] In the margin, Bentham has noted at this point: 'v. Ins. p. 1.' See 'PP: Inserenda', para. 3, p. 61 above.

[3] Bentham has given two paragraphs the number 27.

species of that somthing else: and so on for everlasting. But a Power is not a species of any thing. A Faculty is not a species of any thing. The term power, the term faculty, have neither of them any superior genus. To define them, therefore, after the common method *per genus et differentiam* is a thing impracticable. The more of such definitions bestow'd upon a term, the less is it intelligible. The attempt originates in error, and terminates in confusion.

29. A *Promise* is not a Law: for a promise is but the sign of a resolution of the party willing, manifested to some other person. But a Law is a command. 3. Nor a Promise.

30. A Compact is not a Law: for a Compact is but a pair of promises given reciprocally. But a Law is a Command. 4. Nor a Compact.

31. A *Custom* is not a Law: for a Custom is nothing but a successive assemblage of acts, exterior and in number many, suggesting the idea of uniformity to any one that considers them: an assemblage of acts produced by as many resolutions of volition without command.[1] But a Command is one act: an interior act of the mind, tho' with signs exterior to express it; an act of volition, having the act of some party other than the party willing for its object. And a Law is a Command. 5. Nor a Custom.

32. An imaginary and unspecified cause of a Custom, that is of imperfect uniformity among the actions of voluntary agents, is not a Law. Such are those which compose one sort of the pretended Laws of Nature. For a Command is not a thing imaginary, ⟨bu⟩t real. Before communication, it is internally perceived by him whose Will it is. After communication, it manifests itself by real signs, which may be heard at least, if not seen and handled. 6. Nor an imaginary cause of Uniformity among Actions.

33. An imaginary and unspecified cause of uniformity in the motions of involuntary agents is not a Law: such as are the Laws, more properly stiled Rules,[2] of Motion, of Attraction, of Optics, of Mechanics, of Vegetation, &c. &c.—branches of another sort of the pretended Laws of Nature. For, as one motion among exterior objects is not an interior act of the mind, so neither are ten thousand such motions. No more yet is the resemblance among such motions: no more is the cause of those motions, so long as that cause is not an Interior act of some mind, a wish of a superior, communicated to the things moving, exciting ideas in them—ideas of those motions. 7. Nor an imaginary cause of Uniformity among phænomena.

[1] In the margin, Bentham has noted at this point: 'There is no confining a word to a single sense. The word Custom accordingly has two. A Custom is either the assemblage of the acts themselves that are conformable: or the conformity there is between them.'

[2] The phrase 'more properly stiled Rules' has been marked by Bentham for deletion.

If a word which we use in order to make as if we knew the cause of an uniformity amongst phænomena, phisical or moral, be a Command, the Letters x and y in Algebra are Commands. It is inconvenient to rank a non-entity and a thing existing under the same ⟨genus⟩ and the same name. Whatever is said of the non-entity ⟨as⟩ a thing existing is not true. Any fabric that is grounded on such a supposition is grounded on a quick sand.

8. Nor a Dictate of Utility.[1]

34. A *Dictate of Utility* is not a Law: for a dictate of utility is nothing but some one's *opinion* that such a mode of conduct tends to augment or to diminish the mass of happiness shared among [the] ranks of the persons it concerns.[2] Admitt it for a reality, and all is Chaos. An opinion is an act of the understanding. But a Command is an act of the Will: and a Law is a Command.

35. A Law, then, is a Command. But it is not every Command that is a Law. Now, there are several sorts of Commands, distinguishable from a Law, and from each other, in [the] description that may be given of them, but not yet sufficiently distinguished, all of them, by any description that has been given.

Nor a Domestic Order.

One sort may be said to be that which is issued to an inferior by a superior, who is so not accidentally and occasionally, but in virtue of some established and permanent relation: yet that not a public, but domestic one.[3]

Commands may differ in their | |.

36. A Law may differ from other sort[s] of Command in one or another of four particulars: either 1st in it's *matter*;[4] 2. in it's *source*; 3dly in it's expression; 4. in the *circumstances* attending it's *expression*. These circumstances are what, in the instance of that sort of Command which every one recognizes as containing the matter of a Law, are spoken of under the name of its *formalities*.[5]

Substance or Matter.

37. Two Laws may be said to differ in Matter when the conduct commanded by them is different.

Source.

38. They may be said to be different in their *source*, when the person or persons whose commands they are, are different.

Circumstances.

39. They are different in the circumstances attending their expression when they differ in respect of any such other events or phænomena on which, on whatever account, it depends whether

[1] In the margin, Bentham has noted at this point: 'for a Note v. p. 50, 51.' See 'PP: Inserenda', paras. 184–5, p. 88 above.

[2] In the margin, Bentham has noted at this point: 'As a metaphorical expression, it might be tolerated: tho' even there it were better not to use it: from the continual danger there is of it's being taken for a reality.'

[3] In the text, Bentham has noted at this point: '☛ Continued at Inserenda p. 34, 35.' See 'PP: Inserenda', paras. 143–4, p. 81 above.

[4] MS orig. '*substance*'.

[5] In the margin, Bentham has provided the following alternative to this paragraph: '**36.** The particulars in which a Law may differ from other sorts of Commands, or from another Law, are reducible to four: it's Source; it's Substance; it's expression; and it's formalities.'

they shall be taken to be the commands of those whose commands they purport to be.

'Tis in it's formalities that a regular Law differs from a Law which, tho' it may have all the other properties of a Law, is, on account of it's wanting these formalities, irregular and, therefore, void. Formalities.

40. They may be said to differ in their expression when they differ in respect of the words or other signs employ'd to communicate them to those from whom obedience is expected. N.B. The same Law may differ from itself in the expression. Expression.

'Tis in it's Matter, however, that a Law differs from &c.

Before we can proceed any further to point out the several sorts of Commands from which a Law is to be distinguished,[1] it will be necessary to fix the import of several terms and expressions that bear a reference to the term Law. They will be of use to us in the explaining of that term itself: nor is this proceeding in a circle, as at first might be suspected, since the import of them is equally conceivable by means of their reference to the word Command. The word Law will be employ'd along with them: but in order to understand it sufficiently for the purpose of explaining them, nothing more need be understood than that it signifies a Command. These terms and expressions are in constant use with every body; and, for any thing that appears in print, clearly understood by nobody. If we can succeed in disengaging them from the cloud of complexity that has hitherto involved them, they will be seen to dispell with wonderful facility more than half the difficulties that there are round the field of Law.

41. Obedience is the embracing that mode of conduct which is commanded; that is, which [is] the object of the Command. A Command may be simple or on conditions. Obedience.

42. Phænomena that are made Conditions of, are either such as are [1st] *naturally* connected with the act: or 2dly *artificially*. Conditions, *Circumstances*. Not Circumstance.

Phænomena naturally, i:e: without the instrumentality of man, connected with the act are called it's circumstances.

[1] The phrase 'to point out . . . to be distinguished' has been marked by Bentham for deletion.

PREPARATORY PRINCIPLES: WHAT A LAW IS

MARGINAL CONTENTS

[1] Bentham has given two paragraphs the number 25.

[1] Bentham has not written any text for this paragraph.

WHAT A LAW IS

1. We all know what VOLITION is: 'tis what we are all practising almost continually. The idea we have of it is a simple one: the term is not to be defined. Volition.

2. The object of VOLITION is always some EVENT. We understand tolerably well what an EVENT means. Such a motion, or assemblage of motions, as we take notice of, among things that we take notice of, or the stoppage of such motion or motions, we stile an EVENT. The idea we have of motion is a simple one. The idea we have of the stoppage of it is so too. The terms are not to be defined. An Event. Motion.

3. An *event* may be said to be an *object* of our will: our will to be *directed to* that event, when *we will*, or, in other words, *when our will is*, that that event should happen.[a] An Event, an object of the Will.

4. An EVENT, in the production of which a being capable of volition is instrumental, we stile an ACTION. An Action.

5. The *intellectual instrument* of an action, that *instrument*, or, as some would say, *cause* of it, that is in the mind, is stiled a MOTIVE. A Motive.

6. A MOTIVE is an idea: it is the idea of some pleasure or some pain: the pleasure conceived as about to exist, or the pain as about not to exist, in consequence of our action. A Motive.

7. Cessation of Pain may be spoken of as Pleasure. The Pleasure, then, whereof the idea becomes a MOTIVE, is stiled an END. It is also stiled an *Object*. It may be stiled either way: thither the mind's prospect is DIRECTED, there it TERMINATES. An End—An Object.

[a] 'The Will is a *faculty*.' 'Volition is the exercise of that faculty:' 'The Will exercises acts of volition.' Such has been the language.[1] Not that there is really any such thing as a little being that, under the name of *Will*, gets into men's heads, and exercises acts of volition, or any other acts: as some appear almost to have imagined.[*a*] But it is man that exercises these various acts, that perceives these various emotions: it is man that wills, that exercises acts of volition: that perceives, that exercises perception: that remembers, that exercises memory: that imagines, that exercises imagination: that judges, that exercises judgment: howsoever it may be found convenient for many purposes to say that the will does so and so, rather than that man wills in this or in that manner. It varies the discourse, saves words, and marks out the different operations more distinctly.

[*a*] This conceit, if seriously entertained, would not be absolutely without a parallel. The ancient Physicians, at least, could have made no difficulties about it. The Womb, ac[c]ording to them, was of itself an animal: insomuch that every female consisted of two animals, one within another.[2]

---

[1] See p. 429 n. above.

[2] See p. 429 n. above.

An End.

8.[1] 'Tis then to Pleasure only that the term {End} can, in strictness, be applied. There is another thing, however, to which it frequently *is* applied; but which, tho' intimately connected with, is perfectly distinguishable from, the former. This is, the event, *an* event, in short, whatever it be, from which a pleasure is derived. And it is in this sense, that some Ends are said to be ultimate: others to be subordinate. But if we look for the prime and ultimate end of any action (prime in contemplation, ultimate in practise) it is always pleasure. Now the event, the action from whence arises a pleasure, and the pleasure arising from that action, are perfectly distinguishable. The action may be a mode of the body. But the Pleasure is a mode always of the mind.

Two things dissimilar but intimately connected signified by the word {End} (i:e: of an action).

Finding there was this ambiguity in the application of the term {end}, I thought it proper to give warning of it. The inconvenience of it, however, is not very considerable. One has seldom any thing to say of an end in the one sense of the word, but what might as well be understood to be said of it in the other. Over the pleasure you have no power, but through the power you have over the event that gives it.

The term {end} is at any rate more precise; it is at any rate better calculated to express that whereof the idea becomes a motive, than the term object is. By end, we mean at any rate a mode: for we mean pleasure, and pleasure is a *mode*: or at least we mean an act; which is motion; and motion is a mode. The word {object} we have perpetual occasion to apply to *substances*: and there is not a more frequent source of darkness and confusion, than the applying of the same word to signify a mode and a substance indiscriminately. If any one, after what has been said here, is at a loss for the difference between Mode and Substance, I must refer him to Locke's *Essay*.[2]

[1] This paragraph is an alternative draft taken from UC lxix. 76, inserted as per Bentham's instructions. The original draft, which has been cancelled by Bentham, is as follows: '**8.** There is nothing less fixed than the signification of abstract terms; accordingly the term END is as often employ'd to denote also the EVENT that serves to produce the pleasure.'

A further alternative draft, with the marginal heading 'End (of an action)—it's two senses', is also at UC lxix. 76: 'The word end is liable to be taken to mean either of two things: two things that are perfectly dissimilar, though intimately connected as cause and effect, viz: 1st an event tending to produce pain or pleasure, 2dly the pain or pleasure itself which such event has a tendency to produce. In general it is no matter, I believe, in which of them it be taken. If it were necessary on occasion to distinguish, the 1st might be termed the *internal* end (namely with reference to the party whose volition is in question), the other the *external*. This distinction, indeed, does not hold good with respect to such acts as are themselves merely internal.'

[2] See Locke, *Essay concerning Human Understanding*, Bk. II, Ch. XII, §§3–6, pp. 164–6. A note on '*mode* and *substance*', mainly deleted by Bentham, but concluding with the undeleted words '*mode* and a *substance*: For the difference between *mode* and substance see Locke's *Essay*', is at UC lxix. 70.

9. Acts are either of the Body, or of the Mind. An act of the Body is stiled an exterior or external act: an act of the Mind is stiled an interior or internal one. Acts exterior ⵋ interior.

10. Forbearance is the privation of ACTION: it is to *action*, what rest in general is to MOTION in general. We may say A FORBEARANCE, where rest is the OBJECT of VOLITION, as we say AN ACTION, where motion is the OBJECT of VOLITION. A Forbearance.

11. AN ARTICLE OF CONDUCT is a *middle*[a] expression, that may be employ'd to signify indifferently an action or a forbearance. An Article of Conduct.

12. A MODE OF CONDUCT is, to an article of conduct, what the species is to the individual. A Mode of Conduct.

12.* A course of conduct may be used for an assemblage of articles of conduct in succession. A Course of Conduct.

13. A RESTRICTIVE is to FORBEARANCE, what a MOTIVE is to ACTION. A Restrictive.

14. A DETERMINATIVE is a *middle* expression, capable of signifying indifferently A MOTIVE or A RESTRICTIVE.[b] A Determinative.

15. The END of an ACTION may be distant and ill-defined: but no man acts without an END: no man acts without a MOTIVE. Every action has it's END; it's MOTIVE. ☛ Maxim.

16. A VOLITION, whereof the OBJECT is an ARTICLE OF CONDUCT of that person himself who WILLS, is stiled, when the ARTICLE OF CONDUCT is conceived to be in his POWER, A RESOLUTION. Such an [ARTICLE OF CONDUCT][1] may, in reference to the resolution, be stiled, the ARTICLE OF CONDUCT RESOLVED ON. A Resolution.

17. A VOLITION whereof the OBJECT is an ACT of the person himself who WILLS, but not conceived to be absolutely in his power; or an EVENT at large, or an ACT of a person other than he himself who *wills*, is stiled, A WISH. Such an EVENT, may, in reference to the WISH, be stiled the event WISHED FOR. A Wish.

[a] I use the word {middle} here in the sense in which it is used by Grammarians, when applied to that voice in verbs which, in the Greek, is capable of occupying the place sometimes of the active, sometimes of the passive.

[b] The term *forbearance*, with the article *a* before it, is not very common. The terms restrictive and determinative are not more so. *Action* is used in it's own proper sense and that of *forbearance*: the same term to denote two contraries. Motive, in like manner, is used in it's own sense and that of restrictive; as command is, in that of prohibition. And so it is in many other instances. So then it must be. There is no help for it. We must submitt to usage, and in great measure be content to take language as we find it: nor attempt throughout to make a new one; least we find none willing to be at the pains to understand it but ourselves. It may be of use, however, to have register'd these distinctions, in order to refer to them in case of need.

[1] MS 'ACT' has been replaced elsewhere in the paragraph by 'ARTICLE OF CONDUCT'.

A Wish communicated.

18. A *wish*, when the OBJECT of it is an ARTICLE OF CONDUCT of another person, must, in order to produce it's OBJECT, be *communicated* to that other person. For it to be communicated to him, two ideas must be excited in his mind: 1st the idea of the *article of conduct wished for*: 2dly the idea of the ACT of VOLITION in him who WISHES it. It is this latter that is to furnish him with the motive.[1]

Signs of a WISH or other ACT OF THE MIND.

19. The means, and only means, whereby a wish, or any other act of the mind, can be communicated must be some EXTERNAL ACTIONS. These actions are said to be signs of the wish, or other act of the mind, they serve to communicate.

Speech: Words Spoken.

20. The signs most frequently employ'd for this purpose are such actions as produce certain particular sounds. These sounds are stiled WORDS SPOKEN, or by a *collective* appellation, SPEECH: and, from their connection with the SIGNS just mentioned, do, when put together after a certain mode of assemblage, become SIGNS themselves.

Writing: Words written.

21. Sounds address the sense but for an instant: that instant over, they are gone.[2] Visible marks remain: they are substances: masses of matter, or interruptions of masses of matter, disposed in a certain order. On this account, among others, it is found convenient to employ visible marks as the signs of sounds. These marks, put together after a certain mode of assemblage, are stiled WORDS WRITTEN: or, by a collective appellation, WRITING.[3]

Writing, it's generic sense. —specific.

The word writing has two senses: the one generic and more extensive the other specific and more confined. In the first it signifies the making of any kind of marks to serve as signs for certain spoken words or parts of them, and that with any instrument, upon any substratum. In the latter it signifies the making of such marks with a particular kind of instrument (as a pen and ink or pencil, upon a particular kind of substratum (as paper or parchment).

Prayer, Entreaty, Petition, Request: Requisition, Demand: Injunction, Order, Command.

22. A WISH COMMUNICATED takes a different name according to the relation which the party whose WISH it is, is conceived as standing in to the party whose ACTION is the OBJECT of it; that of an INFERIOR, that of an EQUAL, or that of a SUPERIOR: if that of an inferior, a prayer, an entreaty, a petition, a request: if that of an equal, a

[1] In the margin, Bentham has noted at this point: 'I may obtain the Object of my wish without communicating such wish to the Person who is to be instrumental to such event.'

[2] In the margin, Bentham has noted at this point: 'Sounds are but modes: modes of motion in the air. Like other modes, they are evanescent.'

[3] The following paragraph is taken from UC lxix. 70, inserted as per Bentham's instructions.

requisition, a demand: if that of a superior, an injunction, an order, a command. But of many of these the import is apt to fluctuate.[1] Be that as it may, such an act as has been mentioned may, with *reference* to any of these sorts of WISHES, be termed respectively the ACT PRAY'D, ENTREATED, REQUESTED, REQUIRED, DEMANDED, ENJOINED, ORDER'D, or COMMANDED.

Act pray'd, entreated, requested, required, demanded, enjoined, order'd, commanded.

23. INFERIORITY, EQUALITY, SUPERIORITY are attributed to one with reference to another in various respects. The import of these terms in all cases is not easy perhaps to settle: but for the present purpose it may be said—An INFERIOR is one who is supposed not able to occasion so much pain or pleasure to another as that other is to him: an EQUAL, as much but not more: a SUPERIOR, more.

Inferiority, Equality, Superiority.

24. A COMMAND, of which the OBJECT is A FORBEARANCE, that is a command *not* to do an ACT, is stiled a PROHIBITION, a FORBIDDAL.[a] Such act may, with reference to the PROHIBITION, the FORBIDDAL, be stiled the ACT PROHIBITED, the ACT FORBIDDEN.

A Prohibition. A Forbiddal.

25. We are come now then to A LAW. A Law is a Command. It is a species of Command. Thus much we must conceive of it on all occasions, to conceive clearly. Every thing that is not a Command, therefore, is not a Law.

A Law is a Command.

25.[2] A MOTION of an inanimate being is not a Law: no more are ten thousand MOTIONS of ten thousand such beings: no more is any *uniformity* we see or fancy among such MOTIONS, no more is the unknown and unostensible cause of such motions and of their uniformity. For an unanimate being is a being *not* endued with mind. But a Command is an ACT of a being that *is* endued with mind. It is an ACT *of* the mind. And a Law is a COMMAND.

Things that are not Laws, because not Commands. 1st. Laws, as they have been called, of unanimated Nature.

26. This stone, placed in certain circumstances, moves towards the earth. This motion is not a Law. Ten thousand stones, placed in similar circumstances, move also towards the earth. Neither is here a Law. There is a certain *uniformity* observable in the motions of all these stones. But neither is this *uniformity* a Law. Finding that other motions have their cause, and concluding that these must have one too, we give a name before-hand to that cause, not professing to know any thing of it's nature. We call it attraction: 'tis in virtue of attraction, we say, that stones move towards the earth. But it is not in virtue of any Law, that stones move towards the earth. Attraction is not a Law. For what a Law is, we know. But of

Example.

[a] v. note {c}.[3]

[1] The following sentence is taken from UC lxix. 70, inserted as per Bentham's instructions.

[2] Bentham has given two paragraphs the number 25.

[3] See p. 445 n. above.

Attraction we know nothing, beyond the name. And thus we are cleared of one branch of the pretended Laws of Nature.[a]

2. Customs. **27.** An EXTERIOR ACT of an *animated* being, an exterior act of a *man*, is not a Law. No more are ten thousand such acts: no more is any uniformity we observe among such acts. For a Command is an ACT INTERIOR. No more is any INTERIOR ACT that is not A COMMAND; nor any assemblage of such acts; nor any uniformity among such an assemblage. A Custom, therefore, is not a Law. For a custom is an assemblage of acts in some respect or other uniform: or else it is the uniformity there is between those acts. But a Law is a COMMAND.

Example. **28.** All men within the Manor of Dale carry their corn to be ground at John Trott's Mill: they have done so this year: they did so last year: they have done so every year. It has been their CUSTOM. The successive assemblage of resembling acts here spoken of is not a LAW. For to be one of many who for a length of time have, without COMMANDING, carried their corn to John Trott's Mill is one thing: to COMMAND them there to carry it, or to COMMAND any one to punish them for not carrying it, is another.[b]

[a] Of this stamp are the *Laws of Motion*, as they are called; Laws concerning the motions of bodies in general: The Laws of Mechanics; Laws concerning the motions of bodies solid: The Laws of Hydrostatics; Laws concerning the motions of bodies fluid: The Laws of Pneumatics; Laws concerning the motions of bodies in the state of vapour: The Laws of Optics; Laws concerning the motions of the particles of light: The Laws of Vegetation; Laws concerning the motions of particles solid, fluid and vapourous in such bodies as we call Plants. By the word Law, in all these instances, is meant either some point of uniformity among the individual motions or things moving that are in question: or else some proposition asserting it. In all these instances, the meaning of the word Law is plainly figurative; and as such may in this case be tolerated with little or no inconvenience. Why it may in this case, and not in another, we shall see presently.[1]

[b] Of this stamp, or somthing like it, are Montesquieu's four Laws of Nature. Placed, he says, in a state of nature, men would do four things. 1st they would run away from one another: 2dly they would eat: 3dly they would propagate their kind: 4thly they would seek society.[2] These are Montesquieu's Laws of Nature. All this he sees men do: and this, therefore, is what, in a state which he imagines, he imagines they *would be disposed* to do. A *disposition*, a propensity, is Montesquieu's Law of Nature: or he leaves you to imagine a cause for it; and it is this cause that is to be the Law of Nature.

I am sorry for a great man to whom the science is under many signal obligations: who has polished the garb of it; enriched it with many useful truths; and taught it to address itself to the heart. I am sorry for him: but his method and his general principles, as witness this specimen, are such as no man

[1] Bentham does not, in fact, take up this point in the present essay.

[2] See Montesquieu, *Spirit of Laws*, Bk. I, Ch. II, i. 5–6.

29. Utility is not a Law. For utility is but a quality, a property: a property an act has of encreasing happiness; that is of averting pains or encreasing pleasures. Utility is a quality of many kinds of acts. But a Command is one particular kind of act itself. And a Law is a Command. 3. Utility.

30. A dictate of utility is not a Law.[a] For a dictate of utility is but some one's opinion that there is utility in a certain mode of 4. A dictate of Utility.

alive can profit from. He has met lately with two formidable antagonists in his friends Helvétius and Voltaire.[1] These two philosophers have display'd in a spirited manner the falshood, or to speak more properly the inanity, of many of his notions.

[a] **Notes.** A dictate of utility *is not* a Law: but it *is* a reason, however, for a Law, as it is for any other ARTICLE OF CONDUCT, and the only sort of reason that deserves the name: all else is but empty declamation.

When a man takes upon him to *blame* or *approve* a mode of conduct, and can give a reason for it, his reason is always of this sort. His reason, then, is an assertion of a general matter of fact, the truth of which rests upon experience. When I say, the custom in Parents of providing sustenance for their children is an useful custom, when I blame the not observing it, and give the utility of it as a reason for observing it, or, what comes to the same thing, when I give the mischief of not observing it as a reason for blaming the non-observance of it, I assert a matter of fact. I put in issue a set of facts, and call in experience to witness. I allege the existence of certain pains and pleasures in the case I speak of: pleasures, the customary consequences of the mode of conduct I approve of: pains, the consequences of it's opposite: pains and pleasures such as men have felt in themselves, or recognized in others: pains and pleasures felt not by any new-discover'd moral sense, sole property of the discoverers: but by the old stock of senses, such as all men have, and all men know of. Of this sort, then, are a man's *reasons*, if he has any. When a man chooses the pleasure of deciding, but does not choose the trouble of finding reasons, there are various contrivances for avoiding it. One says he has an understanding, and his understanding, without the trouble of hearing *pro* and *con*, pronounces an action to be right or to be wrong: and so there is a Law of Nature for it or against it. This is the way Dr Price makes Laws of Nature.[2] Another says he has a sense on purpose: and it is this sense that pronounces what is right and what is wrong. This is the way that Lord Shaftesbury,[3] Dr Hutchinson,[4] and the triumvirate of Doctors lately slaughter'd,

[1] See Helvétius, *De l'esprit*, which was a response to *De l'esprit des loix*, and Voltaire's critical comments under the heading 'Lois' in *Questions sur l'Encyclopédie, par des amateurs: VII. Langues–Prières*' (first published in 1770–2), ed. N. Cronk and C. Mervaud, Oxford, 2012 (*Les Œuvres Complètes de Voltaire: Vol. 42b*), pp. 73–121 at 92–119.

[2] See, for instance, Richard Price, *A Review of the Principal Questions and Difficulties in Morals; Particularly Those relating to the Original of our Ideas of Virtue, its Nature, Foundation, Reference to the Deity, Obligation, Subject-Matter, and Sanctions*, London, 1758, Ch. I, §3, pp. 59–89.

[3] See, for instance, [Anthony Ashley Cooper, third Earl of Shaftesbury], *An Inquiry Concerning Virtue, In Two Discourses; I. Of Virtue, and the belief of a Deity. II. Of the Obligations to Virtue*, London, 1699, Bk. I. §III, pp. 40–81.

[4] See, for instance, [Francis Hutcheson], *An Inquiry into the Original of our Ideas of Beauty and Virtue; In Two Treatises. I. Concerning Beauty, Order, Harmony, Design. II. Concerning Moral Good and Evil*, London, 1725, Treatise II, §1, pp. 107–24.

conduct; that is that the mode of conduct in question is likely upon the whole to be productive of more good[1] than it is of evil.[2] An opinion is an act of the understanding. But a COMMAND is an ACT of the WILL. And a Law is a command. And thus we are cleared of another branch of the pretended Law of Nature.

Example. **31.** Parents provide sustenance for their young. It is their CUSTOM. In this CUSTOM, I say, there is UTILITY: it is an *useful* one. The several acts of which it consists are acts which, taken together, make the mass of happiness that is in the world greater

not to say butcher'd, by Dr Priestly make Laws of Nature.[3] For though, as Euclid told King Ptolemy, there is no short cut, no *royal road* to Geometry;[4] there are these two, it seems, to Morals. I know not whether even these philosophers do not consider themselves sometimes as giving reasons, and whether you are not expected to take the following as a reason, for instance, against your doing an act: viz: that your *understanding*, or your *moral sense* (which ever is the word), tells you that you ought not. If so, the distinguishing property of these reasons is to be of sovereign efficacy wheresoever they are not wanted. If your understanding does not happen to tell you precisely the same things as Dr Price's, or your sense as Dr Hutchinson's, you have not got the reason. If it does, you have it without their giving it. The wonder is, that men should have said so much to prove that nothing is to be said about the matter. What reason a man in any of these ways of thinking can find to give himself for saying any thing about the matter to any other [man][5] is more than I can find. The reasons he might find for saying nothing seem obvious and unanswerable. 'Those who are with me', he might [say], 'are wise without study: to them all I could say would be unnecessary. Those who are against me are foolish without remedy: to them, all I could say would be unavailing.' It is but putting an *action* instead of a *person*, and one short epigram of Martial's will better express the system of these philosophers than all the volumes they have given or can ever give us:

Non amo te, Sabidi: nec possum dicere quare:
Hoc tantum possum dicere, non amo te.[6]

It may be the ground of a Law: it may be that consideration which DETERMINES those, whose concern it is, to make a Law: as any act of the judgment may be that which serves to DETERMINE any act of the Will. It may be the ground of a Law. But it is not itself a Law, or any part of one.

---

[1] MS orig. 'pleasure'. [2] MS orig. 'pain'.

[3] The works criticized in Joseph Priestley, *An Examination of Dr. Reid's Inquiry into the Human Mind on the Principles of Common Sense, Dr. Beattie's Essay on the Nature and Immutability of Truth, and Dr. Oswald's Appeal to Common Sense in Behalf of Religion*, London, 1774 were Thomas Reid, *An Inquiry into the Human Mind, On the Principles of Common Sense*, Edinburgh, 1764; James Beattie, *An Essay on the Nature and Immutability of Truth; in opposition to Sophistry and Scepticism*, Edinburgh, 1770; and [James Oswald], *An Appeal to Common Sense in Behalf of Religion*, 2 vols., Edinburgh, 1766.

[4] The answer of Euclid when asked by Ptolemy I Soter whether there was not a shorter road to geometry than through the *Elements*: see *Proclus's Summary* (i.e. *A Commentary on the first book of Euclid's Elements*).

[5] MS 'manner'.

[6] See Martial, *Epigrammata*, I. 32: 'I do not like you, Sabidius, though I can't tell why. All I can tell is this: I like you not.'

than it would be without them. This is what I say: this is my opinion: and my opinion further is, that most other men, if asked, would be of the same. But it is not my saying so, nor their saying so, that is a Law: no, tho' I were Puffendorf: no, tho' I were a Legislator. For to say, that it is useful for men to do thus and thus, is one thing: to command them to do so, is another.

5. A Resolution of Opinion.

32. Two very different things, two very different ACTS of the mind, are current under the common name of RESOLUTION: one, which may be termed a RESOLUTION OF JUDGMENT or OPINION: and another, which may be termed a RESOLUTION OF VOLITION:[a] but it is not either of them that is a LAW. A RESOLUTION of OPINION is not a Law: For a Resolution of Opinion is an act of the Understanding: But a Command is an act of the Will: And a Law is a Command.

Example.

33. 'Resolved that General Warrants are illegal.' This Resolution was not a Law: tho' it was an ACT of one of the three branches of the body which makes Laws.[1] It would not have been a Law, though it had been the ACT of all the three. For an opinion that an ACT is already among ACTS forbidden, is one thing: a COMMAND forbidding it is another.

A Resolution of Volition.

34. A RESOLUTION OF VOLITION is not a Law. For a RESOLUTION OF VOLITION is such an ACT of the WILL as has an ACT of the party himself whose WILL it is for it's OBJECT. But a COMMAND is such an ACT of the WILL as has for it's object the act, not of the person whose WILL it is, but of some other person. And a LAW is a COMMAND.

Example.

35. 'RESOLVED, that this House will, on Friday next, resolve itself into a Committee to consider of the legality of General Warrants.' This RESOLUTION was not a LAW: tho' it was an ACT of one of the three branches of the BODY which makes LAWS. It would not have been, tho' it had been the ACT of all the three. For a discourse serving to

Resolution of Opinion—peculiar to assemblies. How the word Resolution came to be applied in this Sense.

[a] Of these two very different senses of the word Resolution, that in which it is put for an act of the Will is much the more common: in the other it is applied chiefly, if not entirely, to bodies of men. It is scarce ever, if at all, applied to individuals. Perhaps it is only by means [of] an Ellipsis that it is applied where it is. 'Resolved that General Warrants are illegal.'[2] The meaning of this sentence, when explained at large, I take to be no other than this. Resolved that it be declared or published as the *opinion* of this assembly that General Warrants are illegal. If this be a true interpretation of it, it is a Resolution of Volition: an expression of a Volition, the object of which is the act of declaring the opinion in question to be the opinion of the assembly in question.

---

[1] i.e. monarch, House of Lords, and House of Commons.

[2] On 22 April 1766 the House of Commons resolved, 'That a General Warrant for apprehending the Author, Printer, or Publisher, of a Libel, is illegal; and, if executed on the Person of a Member of this House, is also a Breach of the Privilege of this House': see *Commons Journals* (1766) xxx. 753.

communicate an intention of doing an ACT *one's self*, is one thing: a discourse serving to communicate such a WISH as shall cause *other persons* to do it, is another.

A Promise. **36.** A Promise is not a Law. For a Promise is but the expression of a Resolution of Volition.[a] But a Law is a Command.

Example. **37.** 'Lewis my people shall be at peace with thine.' This is not a Law. For the expression of a Resolution to do those acts, to issue those commands, which shall make the people of him who speaks at peace with those of Lewis, who is spoken to, the expression, I say, of such a Resolution, is one thing. But the act itself that is resolved on, is another.

A Compact. **38.** A Compact is not a Law. For a Compact is but a pair of Promises reciprocal.[b] But a Law is a Command.

Example. **39.** 'Lewis, my people shall be at peace with thine, upon condition that thy people be at peace with mine.' 'George, my people shall be at peace with thine, upon condition that thy people be at peace with mine.' All this together is not a Law. For it is but a pair of PROMISES: and it is not a thousand pair of PROMISES that can constitute a COMMAND.

40. | |[1]

Three Particulars in which a Law may differ from other Commands. **41.** A Law, then, is a Command. Nor yet is every thing that is a Command a Law. Commands there are that, in common speech, do not go by the name of Laws. If, then, a Command is not a Law, it is on account of one or other of three particulars, in which the sort of Command that is a Law is understood to differ from those that are not. These are it's Source, it's Substance, or it's formalities.

1. Source. **42.** By the Source of a Law, I mean the person or BODY OF PERSONS whose command it is.

[a] A PROMISE may be thus defined at length. In every PROMISE, there are two persons at least concerned: one *by* whom it is communicated; the PROMISER: another, *to* whom it is communicated; the PROMISEE. A PROMISE, then, is a sign or assemblage of signs utter'd to the END that a certain belief may be produced in the mind of a PROMISEE: viz: a belief that a certain RESOLUTION subsists in the mind of the PROMISER. The ACT which it is designed should be believed by the promisee to be the ACT RESOLVED ON, is the act promised.

[b] A COMPACT may be thus defined at length. A Compact is a pair of Promises by two parties reciprocally given, the one of them in CONSIDERATION of the other.

One PROMISE is said to be THE CONSIDERATION of another, or, in other words, given IN CONSIDERATION of another, when the one party's having been made, or resolved to make, the one promise is the condition of the resolution expressed by the other party in *his* promise.[2]

[1] Bentham has not written any text for this paragraph.

[2] In the margin, Bentham has noted at this point: 'See Ins.[a] p. 154.' See 'PP: Inserenda', paras. 418, 418*, pp. 139–40 above.

43. A body of persons, stiled commonly, for shortness sake, a body, is an assemblage of persons acting in a body. An assemblage of persons are said to act in a body, when every act they do is first willed by, made the object of the volition of, the greater number of them, the wills of the lesser number being ineffective. A Body of Persons, what. To act in a Body.

44. By the Substance of a Law, I mean the sign, or assemblage of signs, viz: the words expressing the command, and the act, or assemblage of acts, that is the object of it. 2. Substance.

45. By the Formalities of a Law, I mean, those transactions or other circumstances extrinsic to the Law, on which depends whether it shall be taken to have issued from that source, from which in itself it purports to have issued. 3. Formalities.

46. But here we must make a pause. In order to do what yet remains to distinguish a Law from the several sorts of things that are liable to be confounded with it, in order to shew by which of the three particulars just mentioned it stands distinguished from Commands at large, there are a set of terms and expressions standing in relation to it that will require to be explained. Nor is this discoursing in a circle, as at first might be suspected. To explain them, the import they have will indeed be referred to the import of the term Law: but, for this purpose, nothing more need be understood of it, than that it signifies a Command issuing from the requisite source, and accompanied by the requisite formalities, to constitute it a Law. What is that source, of what nature are those formalities, will be more commodiously explained afterwards.

47. A Law, in the first place, may be distinguished into 1st a Primary Law, 2dly a Secondary Law. Laws Primary)(Secondary.

48. By a Primary Law, I mean any Law that may be understood of itself, without reference to another. 'Steal not,' may be taken for the example of such a Law. Law Primary.

49. By a Secondary Law, I mean a Law that is not of itself to be understood, nor without reference to some such Law as that just mentioned. Law Secondary.

By a Penal Command,[1] I mean a Law commanding Punishment to be applied *for* an offence; that is to be applied on him who shall have committed an offence; against a Primary one. '*Whosoever shall have stolen, hang him*;' may serve for an example of a secondary Law: a Law subservient to the primary Law before instanced, '*Steal not.*'[2]

[1] MS orig. 'Secondary Law'.

[2] In the margin, Bentham has noted at this point: 'A Command, tho' the objects of it be individual, taking an object out of a Law, we call a Law, at the same time that we do not give that name to a Command issued in execution of a Law. A Warrant of Execution is not a Law. A Pardon by the King is not a Law. Is a Statute Pardon a Law? A Naturalization act for an individual is a Law.'

Offence. **50.** I have mentioned Offence: I have mentioned Punishment. An Offence is a mode of conduct contrary to the MODE OF CONDUCT COMMANDED by a Law: A FORBEARANCE, when the mode of conduct commanded by the Law is ACTION: AN ACTION, when the MODE OF CONDUCT COMMANDED by the LAW, as in the example, is *forbearance.*

Punishment. **51.** Punishment is nothing but Pain inflicted by, or by command of, a superior for, or in other words on account of, an act done.[a]

Act of Disobedience. **52.** An act of disobedience is synonymous to an offence.

Act of obedience. **53.** An act of obedience is the opposite to an offence. It is a mode of conduct conformable to the mode of conduct commanded by the Law. An Action, where the mode of conduct commanded by the Law is Action: a forbearance, where the mode of conduct commanded is forbearance.

[a] I stop here. I do not go on and say 'by that inferior:' because that would exclude the sort of punishment that is called Vicarious.

INDEX OF SUBJECTS

Note. The following is a unified index that refers to the texts of all the essays included in the present volume, without identifying the particular work in question. The passages in French have been indexed in English translation.

References to notes are given by means of the page numbers followed by the letter 'n.'

The symbol 'v.' is used to indicate 'as distinct from' or 'as opposed to'.

INDEX OF NAMES

Note. The following is an index of names of persons and places appearing in the editorial introduction, text, and notes; the last (whether Bentham's or the editors') are indicated by 'n.' Under Bentham's name, only references to his other works are indicated.